W9-CBC-615

POPULATION PROBLEMS

Population Problems

WARREN S. THOMPSON, Ph.D.

Director Emeritus of the Scripps Foundation
for Research in Population Problems,
Miami University

DAVID T. LEWIS, Ph.D.

Professor of Sociology,
Miami University

FIFTH EDITION

McGraw-Hill Book Company
New York • St. Louis • San Francisco
Toronto • London • Sydney

PREFACE TO THE FIFTH EDITION

Although this book has been almost entirely rewritten for this edition, there has been no change in its basic purpose. It aims to present the most important facts relating to population in a form that is readily understandable by both the nonspecialized college student, to whom it is primarily addressed, and the lay reader interested in learning the significance of population growth and changes as factors influencing many aspects of our daily life in today's world. However, some change has been made in the amount of space devoted to the various aspects of population changes. Composition of the population has received considerably more attention. There is also a somewhat expanded discussion of population policies, which are rapidly becoming of concern to all people.

The greatly increased amount of information regarding population presented in our popular media of communication since World War II has made it less necessary to include materials intended to convince most people who try to keep up with the *news* that it is important to know something about population growth and changes as well as the relationships of these changes to the cultural, social, political, and economic happenings of our day. Certain information intended primarily to arouse interest in the study of population problems has therefore been curtailed or omitted.

Since this edition, as were its predecessors, is primarily intended to help the nonspecialized reader understand the significance of the basic facts relating to population growth and changes, only a few of the simpler methods of handling population statistics are used. The authors believe that this simple statistical treatment of the basic facts and processes of population change is sufficient to enable the reader to see the specific relationships between these facts and the other aspects of life with which he is concerned as he considers ways and means of improving man's condition in the world.

Although this treatment of population data, based almost entirely on the fundamental processes of arithmetic, is the same as in previous editions, considerable effort has been expended in organizing this material to make it easier for the teacher to present and easier for the student to apply arithmetic to the essential calculations. In a word, the authors concentrate attention on the broad social significance of population facts and make use of the fewest and simplest statistical methods that seem consistent with their primary purpose.

ACKNOWLEDGMENTS

The senior author wishes to express his great indebtedness to P. K. Whelpton and Arthur A. Campbell for making certain facilities of the Scripps Foundation available to him as well as for permission to refer to certain results of the second study on the Growth of American Families, not yet published. He also wishes to express his sincere appreciation of the help of Mrs. Ruth W. Smith and Mrs. Evangeline D. Minnis in bringing up to date many of the tables used and in rendering other types of assistance too numerous to mention.

The junior author wishes to express his deep appreciation for the privilege of working so closely with Dr. Warren S. Thompson on this edition, and he wishes to thank Dr. William Fred Cottrell, chairman of his department, and Dr. John D. Millett, president of Miami University, for all they have done to make it easier for him to work with Dr. Thompson. The influence of many generations of students on his part of this undertaking has been great, but is too complex and diffuse to recognize adequately here. However, there are a few people who, as students, played an important and direct part in this work, and to whom thanks are due: Robert Atchley, William H. Gregory, Jr., John Edward Lotz, James Skeel, Suzanne E. Taylor, and Thomas T. Tolg. Most of all, the junior author wants to express his thanks to his wife, Jeannette T. Lewis, for her continuous moral support, general secretarial help, and particularly for her painstaking and skilled editorial work at every stage in the writing of the manuscript.

WARREN S. THOMPSON
DAVID T. LEWIS

GENERAL REFERENCES

Some general reference works on population and the chief periodicals in which demographic materials appear are listed below.

Reference Works

Bogue, Donald J.: *The Population of the United States*, The Free Press of Glencoe, New York, 1959.

Davis, Kingsley (ed.): "A Crowding Hemisphere: Population Change in the Americas," *Annals of the American Academy of Political and Social Science*, vol. 316, March, 1958.

Hatt, Paul K. (ed.): *World Population and Future Resources*, American Book Company, New York, 1952.

Spengler, Joseph J., and Otis Dudley Duncan (eds.): *Population Theory and Policy*, The Free Press of Glencoe, New York, 1956.

————: *Demographic Analysis*, The Free Press of Glencoe, New York, 1956.

Taeuber, Conrad, and Irene B. Taeuber: *The Changing Population of the United States*, John Wiley & Sons, Inc., New York, 1958.

Periodicals

Demography, an annual journal devoted to reporting population research, Population Association of America, Chicago. The first issue appeared in 1964.

Milbank Memorial Fund Quarterly, New York.

Population, the quarterly review of the National Institute of Demographic Studies, France. (In French)

Population Index (formerly *Population Literature*) is a periodical chiefly devoted to an annotated bibliography. Hundreds of items are cited each year. There is excellent coverage of governmental publications of foreign countries.

Population Studies, a quarterly of the Population Investigating Committee, England.

Statistical Bulletin, issued monthly by the Metropolitan Life Insurance Company.

United Nations *Demographic Yearbook* continues the *International Statistical Yearbook* published under the auspices of the League of Nations from 1927 to 1945. The United Nations has also assumed publication of the *Monthly Bulletin of Statistics*, formerly put out by the League.

CONTENTS

PART ONE

THE STUDY OF POPULATION

PART TWO

THE COMPOSITION OF POPULATION

PART THREE

MAJOR DEMOGRAPHIC PROCESSES

CHAPTER TWENTY   527

Population Policies

CHAPTER TWENTY-ONE   549

Population Policies (Continued)

The Study
of Population

CHAPTER ONE

Introduction to the Study of Population

WHY STUDY POPULATION?

Today, most of the people likely to read this book know that the world's population is supposed to be increasing rapidly. Some even know that the population was estimated to be approximately 3 billion in 1960, that it was growing by about 50 million per year, and that, if this rate of growth continued, it would double in approximately 35 years. For a number of years the junior author has been asking students in introductory sociology classes to write what they think are the answers to such questions as: "How many people are there in the world today?", "What is the current population of the United States?", "What was the population of the United States in 1900, in 1800?", etc. Although no longer surprised at occasional fantastic answers to these soundings of student knowledge, the junior author is still a bit taken aback at seeing the 1960 world population placed at anywhere from 10 million to a million billion—a one with fifteen zeros after it. The other questions have produced comparably wild replies. The most recent distribution, 1963, of 65 replies to the question "How many people are there in the world today?" went as follows: less than 800 million—9; 1 billion to 10 billion—36 (15 students said 3 billion); 10 billion to 200 billion—10; 200 billion to 900 billion—9; one student said 1 million billion and another wrote "Good Heavens!" Even among those who answer most of the above questions correctly, very few realize the extent to which current growth patterns differ from past ones or understand the regional and national variations in population growth, the relationship between population growth and agricultural and industrial development, and the connection between a nation's population growth and its status in international politics and trade.

Some Americans know that the population of the United States was nearly 180 million in 1960, but fewer know that it was only 75 million in 1900 and less than 4 million in 1790. How many Americans realize that between 1950 and

1960 the population of the United States increased by 28 million, a figure nearly equal to the combined 1960 populations of Norway, Denmark, Sweden, Australia, and New Zealand? Very few Americans are aware of the factors responsible for the high rate of growth their country has experienced or the relationship between this growth and the political, economic, and cultural life of the United States. It is obvious, for instance, that the aged (people 65 years of age and over) are playing an increasingly significant part in our society, but few people know what is meant by the expression "an aging population," or understand how a population becomes "older." It is even more important to know the complicated effects of this "aging" on the economy, the government, and the social values of our society.

The student and the responsible citizen will find the study of population to be of more than academic interest as they discover how intimately their own lives are affected even by distant population events. Population phenomena in India, China, and Japan are inextricably involved with international tensions, threats of war, and ultimately with the world's very chances of survival. In short, a knowledge *about* population is becoming increasingly essential to the individual's education and indispensable to his exercise of intelligent citizenship.

Since this book will probably be used primarily by undergraduate students in colleges and universities, no definite academic prerequisites are deemed necessary. The student is assumed to have a knowledge of the basic arithmetic procedures, and a willingness to learn the meanings and uses (in population study) of such concepts as ratio, rate, absolute increase, relative increase, etc. Although this book is intended primarily for a college audience, the authors have made a definite effort to render it understandable to the interested layman.

WHAT MAY THE STUDENT EXPECT TO LEARN?

We hope that when the student finishes this book he will have learned four things. (1) He will have found out how social scientists approach the study of human behavior. If it is his first course in the social sciences, his discovery of this point of view will be a stimulating, perhaps even a disturbing, experience. He will have developed an appreciation of the methods by which social scientists study man, for population phenomena lend themselves more easily than any other kind of human behavior to objective recording and mathematical expression. Unlike many other social facts, most population data do not have to be transformed into numerical terms, being numerical in nature to begin with. The reader will have learned that the application of the scientific method to population phenomena means collecting the data with scrupulous care, processing the material as objectively as possible, and drawing only those conclusions warranted by the data. The authors have intended to keep their personal values and prejudices out of the analysis as far as possible and to present the facts clearly so that the reader can use them in arriving at his own conclusions regarding their significance. They consider it their duty to point out to the reader what they conceive to be the significance of these facts. Whenever they have injected opinions which may differ from those of other students, they have tried to make clear that these *are* opinions and not inevitable conclusions from the facts.

(2) The student will have acquired a good idea of the material that population students use, as well as a store of useful facts about world population. In the process of gaining this information he also will have developed an increased understanding of the interconnections among the population variables, such as the way that changes in a country's fertility, mortality, and migration can cause changes in the proportions of males and females and in the proportions of the various age groups. He will have also developed an appreciation of the relationship between changes in these variables and changes in social, economic, and political phenomena. Although he will not have come out with any one overall theory of population, he should have assimilated a great many facts and have reached some rather broad conclusions based on these facts.

(3) The student will have acquired a working technical vocabulary. Some terms with which he is already familiar will necessarily have been more sharply and specifically defined; for example, "life span" and " life expectancy" are both commonly misused. Other terms will be new, such as "age-specific birth rate" and "parity" (which has no connection with "farm parity"). Throughout the book, however, the authors will use technical language only when necessary. Technical concepts will be defined when they first appear, although the definition may not be complete when a concept is used ahead of its full treatment in the text. Such concepts will be defined in the body of the text rather than in footnotes or appendixes.

(4) The student, we expect, will have become familiar with the simpler techniques used to collect, process, and analyze population data. At the same time, he should have developed a healthy skepticism concerning the "goodness" of much population data, but as a guard against a too critical attitude he should have come to realize that many millions of hours of careful work are needed each year for the collecting, processing, and analyzing of the up-to-date population facts which are regularly made available to the public by government agencies. The student will not have become a professional population researcher by virtue of reading this book, but he should have acquired some insight into the frustrations and rewards of research. And he should never again be caught off his intellectual base by the "statistics" of a sensational Sunday-supplement writer.

NATURE OF POPULATION STUDY

So much for the general purposes of this book. What follows is a more specific statement about the scope and nature of population study as it is treated in the text. The authors have tried to cover the major elements of population study, at the core of which are three main questions:

1. How many people live in a given population group, what changes are taking place in the *size* of the group, and how are these changes in size effected?

2. What kind of people live in the population group, and how do they differ from the people in another group? This study of the characteristics of a population is usually discussed under the general heading of "the *composition* of the population."

3. How are people distributed in the area under study, and what changes are taking place in their *distribution?*

These three major elements of study can be remembered easily in terms of the three words emphasized above: size, composition, and distribution. The population student is interested in a population's size, composition, and distribution; and in *changes* in these aspects through time, and the causes of these changes. Ultimately he is interested in these changes because they are related to human welfare.

Size. The question of how many people live in a given place at a given time must seem at first rather simple, a mere matter of counting noses. Conceptually, it is a simple question, but the process of getting an accurate answer involves careful definitions of "place," "person," and "time" and the use of carefully worked-out methods for securing the most accurate information.

Most of us are not content with knowing how many people are in a given place at a given time; we usually want to know whether this number is larger or smaller than it was at some previous time and what the number is likely to be at some time in the future. Facts like these, concerned with changes in population, are eagerly sought by industrial concerns, hospital boards, school superintendents, college presidents, and legislators, as well as by demographers and other social scientists. In addition to the question of how much numerical increase has taken place is the more complex one of finding the rates of change and the trends shown by these rates. For example, the population of the United States was approximately 150 million in 1950 and approximately 180 million in 1960. The numerical (absolute) increase was nearly 28 million; the percent change, or relative change, was 18.5 percent. If this rate of growth were to continue, the population of the United States would double in about 44 years.

In trying to account for population changes, the demographer seeks the causes of these changes. The immediate causes are found in the operation of the major demographic processes: "natality" (births), "mortality" (deaths), and "migration." Anything which affects the numbers of people in a given place manifests itself in changes of one or more of these three processes. In one sense, then, these processes and these alone can account for any changes in numbers in any given population. Our attempt to understand what causes population change via these demographic processes (natality, mortality, and migration) involves our consideration of biological, social, and cultural variables. It is at this juncture that we must move beyond simple biological statistics, and become social scientists.

Composition. The second of the major elements in population study, as stated above, is composition. This term covers all the measurable characteristics of the people who form a given population. The composition of one group is said to differ from that of another when one of the groups has a larger or a smaller proportion of persons with a given characteristic. Generally, the composition of one population differs in a number of ways from that of another. The student of population is guided in selecting the characteristics he studies by two major considerations: These characteristics must be effectively related to the demographic processes, and they must be relevant to his attempt to understand certain specific aspects of community or national life. The most widely used characteristics are age and sex. If a person knows that people within certain age groups have most of the babies and that the proportions of people dying also vary from one age group to another, then he will come to expect that communities which differ from each other in the proportions of their populations that are male and female and which also differ from each other in the proportions of their populations in the various age groups will, in consequence, differ from each other in their birth rates and death rates. All other things being equal, the population with the larger proportion of men and women in the early reproductive years (18 to 35 years of age) would have a higher crude birth rate (the number of births per 1,000 of the total population). Likewise, the population with a much larger proportion of old people would have a higher crude death rate. Again, the community that has a large proportion of its total population between the ages of 15 and 65 holds an unquestioned advantage, as far as productive manpower is concerned, over communities which have smaller proportions of their total population in these potentially active years. Some other important population characteristics are urban and rural residence, marital status, occupation, education, and religion. Each of these characteristics is related to the number of births and deaths occurring in a given area and also to the number of people who migrate into and out of the area. The student of population is interested not only in the composition of a population at a given moment of time but also in the changes taking place in the composition, the causes of these changes, and their effect on community life.

The relationship between the composition of a population and its mortality, fertility, and net migration is a reciprocal one; i.e., composition affects the demographic processes, and these processes in turn affect the composition by determining the age and sex structure of a population.

Distribution. The third major question mentioned above was: How are people distributed, and what changes are taking place in their distribution? Depending on the demographer's purpose, the "where" may be a large inclusive area such as a continent, or a small area such as a census-enumeration district or a city block. Between these extremes are world regions, countries, intracountry regions, states, provinces, metropolitan cities, small cities, towns, villages, and rural-farm areas. For example, the population of the world can be divided into three categories on the basis of degree of urbanization and industrialization. In this case, the demographer would ask: How much of the world's population lives in countries belonging in the categories labeled "advanced urban-industrial," "newly urban-industrial," and "pre-urban-industrial"? The answer to such a question is certainly important in today's world. The changes taking place in the numbers and proportions of the world's population living in these three categories are important, and so are the causes of these different rates of change.

When we focus our attention on the internal distribution of a population like that of the United States, such questions arise as: How many Americans live in rural-farm and rural-nonfarm communities, and how many live in different types of urban communities? The answers to such questions are significant politically, economically, and socially. The nature of the changes taking place in this internal distribution is also important. Examples of such changes are the tremendous increase in the population of the Far West at the expense of other areas; the increasing growth of already large urban places and the development of new large urban places; the spread of urban populations into the surrounding countryside (suburbanization); and the increasing proportions of Negroes in the North and West and the decreasing proportions of Negroes in the South.

What causes the changes in numbers and proportions of people living in the various areas of the world? Basically, these changes are caused by the cumulative effect of differences in mortality, natality, and net migration rates. The student of population wants to know why these rates differ in various parts of the world and from one region to another within a country. He asks how the world's people are distributed among and within continents, world regions, and countries and how their numbers and proportions change, and he wants to know the political, economic, and social causes and results of these changes. To answer these questions, he must learn what the demographer means by size, composition, and distribution; he must understand natality, mortality, and migration; and, finally, he must search for the social significance of the statistics he has studied under these headings. Emphasis on this last aspect—the significance of population facts and events with respect to man's life—has been a distinguishing feature of the earlier editions of this book. The present edition continues to emphasize the social, economic, and political significance of population facts and changes in these facts.

BASIC DEMOGRAPHIC CONCEPTS

Relative numbers. Ratios and rates help us to understand the facts we have gathered; they summarize data and the relationship between sets of data. Before we can use them, however, we must learn how they are calculated. Ratios and rates are always relative figures; they express a relation between two or more numbers. When they appear to be standing alone, the student should ask himself: What is the context in which they are used? Relative numbers are not always "better" or more useful than the absolute numbers they are derived from; sometimes the absolute number is the one we want to use. A few examples will help to explain how ratios and rates are calculated and used.

Absolute numbers are the raw data of demography: the number of children under 5 years of age in a given population, the number of babies born in a given community in a given year. For many purposes, such as running a school district or a hospital, only absolute numbers are needed. But if you want to know whether Oxford, Ohio, is more or less heavily burdened with dependent children under 15 years of age than is New York City or Oskaloosa, Iowa, a comparison of absolute numbers will not help much. You want to know how many children each community has *relative* to its total population; this relative number is a ratio—a number whose significance depends not on the magnitude of the two numbers (the number of children in the community and the number of its total population) but rather on the relationship between these two numbers. If you want to compare, even in a very rough way, the reproductive behavior of the populations of New York State and Iowa, finding the absolute number of births in a given year will not be enough; you will have to find the relationship between the number of births and the population in each state. The same kind of relationship must be found when your aim is to compare the fertility of a population at a given time with the same population's fertility at another time.

Ratio. A "ratio" is a single term which expresses the size of one number in relation to the size of another. The sex ratio in the United States is an example. In the population of the United States in 1960 there were 89,008,000 males and 90,996,000 females. Dividing the number of males by the number of females shows that there was 0.978 male per female. Multiplying 0.978 by 100 (to make the ratio easier to read) gives us 97.8. This operation makes it possible to express in a single figure—a ratio—the fact that there are 97.8 males per 100 females. A ratio of 100 would mean that the number of males is equal to the number of females, whereas a ratio over 100 would mean that there are more men than women, and a ratio less than 100 would mean there are fewer men than women.

Proportions. A "proportion" is a particular kind of ratio. It does not express the size of one part of a whole in relation to the size of another part of the same whole, as does the above example; a proportion shows the ratio of one part to the whole, or base number. It is found by dividing the "whole" number into the "part" number. Its value is always between 0 and 1. Dividing the total population of the United States in 1960 (180 million) into the number of males in 1960 (89,008,000) gives us 0.494—the proportion of males in the total population. When there are only two components, as in this case, the proportion of females in the total population can be calculated by subtracting the proportion of males from 1. The sum of all the component proportions of a population must add up to 1.

Percents. A "percent" is a proportion multipled by 100. A percent is a ratio calculated on the assumption that the base number equals 100. For example, if the proportion of males in the United States in 1960, 0.494, is multiplied by 100, it gives us 49.4, the percent of the population that is male, i.e., the number of males per 100 population. For popular consumption, demographers turn their proportions into percents, because the percent is more commonly used and more generally understood.

Rates. A "rate" is computed as are the other ratios, but it has the additional feature of expressing what has happened in terms of a certain unit of *time*. Usually, in demographic work, the unit of time is a year if no other time unit is specified.

The two most commonly used rates are crude birth rates and crude death rates. To calculate the crude birth rate, we divide the total number of births in a given year by the total midyear population of the area, a process which gives us the number of births "per person" for the year in question. The midyear population is used because it is probably the figure which is both nearest to the average population for the year and readily obtainable. To make this ratio easier to read it is usually multiplied by 1,000. Since the resulting figure relates to a unit of time—one year—it is called a rate. The procedure for calculating the crude birth rate can be expressed as follows:

$$\text{Crude birth rate} = \frac{\text{total number of births in a given area during a given year}}{\text{total number of people living in the area at the midpoint of that year}} \times 1{,}000$$

The crude death rate is calculated in the same way. These rates are called "crude" because they use the total population as a base number, rather than parts of the population (for further clarification see Chapter 9). The crude birth rate for the United States in 1960 is calculated, according to the above formula, as follows:

$$\text{Crude birth rate} = \frac{4{,}307{,}000 \text{ (total births in the U.S. in 1960)}}{180{,}676{,}000 \text{ (total population of the U.S., July 1, 1960)}} \times 1{,}000$$

or

Crude birth rate = 23.8

The crude death rate for the United States in 1960 is calculated as follows:

$$\text{Crude death rate} = \frac{1{,}702{,}000 \text{ (total deaths in the U.S. in 1960)}}{180{,}676{,}000 \text{ (total population of the U.S., July 1, 1960)}} \times 1{,}000$$

or

Crude death rate = 9.4

Natural Increase and Rate of Natural Increase. The "natural increase" of a population is an absolute number obtained by algebraically subtracting the total number of deaths from the total number of births which occur in a year. If more deaths than births happen to occur, the number is usually preceded by a minus sign and is then called a negative natural increase or natural decrease. Migration is not considered in the calculation of a natural increase. In 1960, the United States had a natural increase (which excludes migration) of 2,545,000 because there were 4,247,000 births and 1,702,000 deaths. The *rate* of natural increase for a population is expressed as so many per thousand per year, a number which can be obtained by simply subtracting the crude death rate from the crude birth rate. Using the above figures, we should subtract 9.4 from 23.8, thus obtaining 14.4, the rate of natural increase for the United States in 1960. This means that the population of the United States increased (with respect to births over deaths) by 14.4 per 1,000 per year. To express this increase as a percent increase, we must convert the above "per 1,000" rate to a "per 100" rate, which we do by moving the decimal point one place to the left. This process converts the above rate of 14.4 to a percent of 1.44.

Calculating a country's rate of natural increase helps us, for example, to find out how long it will take the country to reach any given size if the rates continue at the same level. If a population has a rate of natural increase of 10.0, it is, of course, growing at the rate of 1 percent per year. (A country's *rate of increase* may be somewhat larger or smaller than its *rate of natural increase* because it may have either net immigration or net emigration.) But with this annual rate (1 percent per year) the population will double in only 70 years because populations grow according to the principle of "compound interest" rather than of "simple interest." The base is increased each year by the amount of the increase during the preceding year. For example, if a population numbers 1,000 at year 0 and is growing at the rate of 1 percent per year, it would number 1,010 at the end of the first year. At the end of the second year, the number would be 1,020.10, and at the end of three years, it would be 1,030.301.

It is very important to keep in mind this principle of compounding, since it shortens the period within which population doubles, and shortens it much more than most people would think probable when they are told that population is growing by 1 percent or by any other specified percent per year. Thus the natural increase of the population of the United States in 1960 was 1.44 percent, or 14.4 persons per 1,000. If this fixed number of persons (14.4) were added to each 1,000 in the 1960 population each year, it would take approximately 70 years for the population to double, but because of compounding doubling would actually require only about 50 years. The following table gives the approximate number of years required for a population to double at different annual rates of increase, assuming that the rate will remain constant and that there is no net in- or out-migration.

Annual percent increase	Years necessary for a population to double
3.0	24
2.5	29
2.0	35
1.5	47
1.0	70
0.5	140

Fecundity. As defined by demographers, "fecundity" is a biological potential—the physiological capacity to participate in reproduction. The absence of this potential is known as "infecundity" or sterility (see Chapter 9 for further discussion).

Fertility. Among students of population, the term "fertility" is generally used to indicate the actual reproductive performance of a woman or group of women. The crude birth rate (number of births per 1,000 population per year) is only one measure of fertility (see Chapter 9).

KINDS AND SOURCES OF DATA

The data used by demographers are primarily of two kinds: (1) information about *persons*, i.e., such characteristics as age, sex, residence, and education, or (2) information about *events*. Births and deaths are universally considered *vital events,* and their rates are called "vital rates." Three other events also affect the composition of and the changes in a population, and are often treated under the heading of vital events: migration, marriage, and divorce.

These two kinds of information are usually obtained by different methods. The most common way for a country to get data about the characteristics of its population is to conduct an *enumeration* of the total population as *of a given moment in time.* This is called a "census." On the other hand, the collection of data on vital events usually involves some sort of *registration* procedure, which records the events (births, deaths, etc.) *as they occur* and keeps the record by calendar years. In the registration of such events, certain pertinent characteristics about the people involved are also generally obtained. For example, in the registration of births, data on the sex of the baby, its race, generally the age of the mother, and in some countries the birth order of the baby, occupation of the father, religious preference of parents, and so forth are also recorded. In the case of death registration, age and sex of the deceased are always recorded and also a number of additional items, which vary considerably in number from country to country. There are, however, no hard and fast rules governing the use of these procedures. During a census, information can be obtained about vital events, and a "complete registry," such as is kept by Sweden and the Netherlands, contains information concerning the total number of people and their characteristics. Both these kinds of information are usually collected, processed, and published by governmental bodies. Today, the United Nations makes available a great many international demographic data in its publications.

In the United States, the census material relating to the entire nation has always been collected, processed, and published by the Federal government as one of its duties under the Constitution. The registration of vital rates (births, deaths, marriages, etc.) has always been the responsibility of the states. About 1920, the Federal Bureau of the Census took over the task of bringing together the vital statistics collected by the various states, organizing and publishing the data on a countrywide basis. Later, this function was transferred to another Federal agency which is now a part of the Department of Health, Education, and Welfare. Today, another technique for getting demographic data is being developed—the sample survey. This method produces the same kinds of information as the other two techniques, but the information is often much more detailed, since it is based on a small sample rather than on the total population. Since we want to generalize from the sample to the total population from which the sample is drawn, we must exercise great care in drawing the sample. Most demographic data contain some errors, and the demographer must learn to recognize the sources of the error and to understand the limitations of the data he uses. If the demographer recognizes these errors he can often make adjustments to compensate for them. Examples of these adjustments will appear from time to time in the following chapters.

SOME BASIC FACTS

A number by itself is without meaning; it must be related to other numbers. For instance, the population figure for the United States in 1960 (180 million) takes on meaning as soon as it is compared with the population of the United States in 1950 (150 million) or in 1790 (slightly less than 4 million), or with the population of the Soviet Union in 1960 (214 million). Therefore, certain *key* figures should be committed to memory, because they give meaning to other numbers. Some examples of such key figures are: the population of the United States in 1790, 1800, 1850, 1900, 1950, and 1960; the proportion of the population that was urban and rural in 1960 and the proportion in these categories in 1900; and the crude birth and death rates for the United States, currently and at certain dates in the past. Such key numbers provide a statistical framework within which comparable data for other countries and other times are meaningful. The student of population should become familiar with a few principal sources where he can readily find those population facts that he needs but has not committed to memory. In addition to learning these numbers, the student should familiarize himself with certain demographic trends.

Tables, figures, graphs, and charts are designed to help the student see more vividly the relationships and trends he is reading about. The student should not shy away from these representations; he should learn to use them. When he sees a table or chart, he must first ask himself what it is about. (Many students have trouble with tables simply because they jump into them without first reading the heading.) Then he should try to draw some generalizations from the table before he reads the accompanying text.

It may be of some help to the student who is undertaking the study of population if he can get a glimpse of the conditions out of which the serious study of population arose. It will also benefit him to know something about the man who may truly be called the father of modern population study—Thomas Robert Malthus.

CHAPTER TWO

Malthus's Place in the Study of Population

To the authors it seems eminently just that an outline for the study of population problems should contain almost at the beginning a statement of Malthus's views on population. This judgment is held not because he was the first person to enunciate a number of the views expressed in his *First Essay* (1798) but rather because he soon showed (1803) that he clearly appreciated the close relation between population growth and changes, on the one hand, and other socio-economic changes, on the other, and thus aided materially in hastening the investigations of population changes as an integral and dynamic factor in the development of the larger organic whole which we commonly call "society." It is quite true, as many of his critics claimed, that some of his ideas were not original. In fact, as we shall note shortly, Malthus himself soon found out that more had been accomplished in this field of study than he knew about when he wrote his first essay.

We should point out here that most people who have heard of Malthus associate his name with the doctrine that man's propensity to reproduce is so strong that great poverty and misery will always exist because he cannot produce the necessites of life fast enough to keep up with his reproduction. Although there was some reason to consider this view as the essence of Malthus's views in the *First Essay*, this judgment is not just, as we shall soon see from the second and later editions of his Essay.

MALTHUS AND HIS TIME

In order to appreciate fully the writings of Malthus, we must have a general idea of the intellectual, political, and economic conditions in which he lived. Thomas Robert Malthus was born in England in 1766 and died in 1834. He had a distinguished undergraduate career at Cambridge University and entered the

Church of England as a minister in 1797. He was a professor of history and economics from 1806 until his death in 1834.

During his lifetime important changes were taking place in the social and economic organization of Western Europe that were fairly favorable to a slow rise in the rate of population increase. The most important of these changes was the slow improvement in man's productivity in agriculture and industry, which made possible some betterment in the living conditions of some segments of the population. It will help us to understand Malthus's theory if we recall that mercantilism was the prevailing economic system of Western Europe. Although the mercantilists regarded a favorable balance of trade as a desirable condition for a nation, they also taught that a nation's strength depended upon the extent to which it was economically self-sufficient and upon the numbers of its people. Indeed, a large and growing population was coming to be looked upon as a sure sign of national health and vigor, regardless of the conditions under which the people had to live. *Numbers* were believed to ensure both economic and military strength.

Malthus saw clearly that an increase in numbers depended chiefly on an increase in the means of subsistence, since the great majority of people lived very close to the subsistence level. This led him to conclude that any permanent improvement in the lot of mankind was going to be extremely difficult to attain so long as increased production was accompanied by a like increase in numbers.

During Malthus's time the conception of a purely static social order, in which man played a passive role and was a plaything of destiny, was slowly changing. The French Revolution had done much to set thoughtful men to pondering on man's future and what he could make of it. The idea of *human progress* was becoming a meaningful concept.

Furthermore, the development of science was leading to the discovery of "natural laws," i.e., uniformities in the occurrence of physical phenomena, which some men believed would soon lead to a great increase in man's productivity and therefore in his welfare. At the same time, some men were also coming to believe that if natural laws operated in the physical world, they might also operate to determine human behavior. On the other hand, some philosophers held that no natural law limited man's ability to improve his conditions of life. They believed that man could use scientific natural laws to improve his production, his health, and his general welfare, but that he himself was not subject to any natural law of growth that could seriously interfere with a rapid and indefinite increase in his welfare. Because Malthus did not agree with some of the ideas expressed by these social philosophers, who believed in the rapid "perfectibility" of human life, he wrote his first Essay to show that man's ability to reproduce was greater than his ability to produce the necessities of life. This was his "principle of population."

One aspect of Malthus's writing on population should be explained before we begin to describe his doctrines, because unfair attacks have been made against him by many, both in his day and ours. The motive in all his work was humanitarian. He was always thinking about the welfare of men, and he arrived at his theories on population in the process of trying to understand how population growth was likely to affect human welfare. No one would have combated more vigorously than Malthus himself the attitude of the conservatives who, accepting his doctrine in its crudest form, held that the poverty and misery of the workers were due to the tendency of population to increase faster than subsistence and that employers, whether agricultural or industrial, could do little to alleviate these wretched conditions. Malthus certainly did not believe that the tendency of population to increase too rapidly for its own good absolved the employer from a moral obligation to treat his employees as human beings rather than as chattels to be used for his own enrichment.

The immediate inspiration for the writing of the first Essay in 1798 grew out of conversations between Malthus and his father regarding the feasibility of certain reforms advocated by Godwin and Condorcet for the attainment of happiness by man. Approximately two-thirds of the first edition of the Essay is devoted to a philosophical discussion of these utopian ideas and is only indirectly related to Malthus's principle of population. In general, the Utopians regarded man's suffering as due primarily, if not solely, to bad laws, corrupt government, evil rulers, greedy employers, and so forth. They believed that these evils not only produced suffering directly but also caused those traits of human nature which are commonly styled "selfish," "base," and "evil." Thus, if some of man's institutions were reformed and some abolished, not only would the suffering disappear, but *man's very nature would undergo a radical organic change so that he would no longer be his own worst enemy*. His passions would be subdued; his vices would disappear; his thoughts would become exalted; and he would be well on the way to establishing an earthly paradise. It is not difficult to see why the advocates of such views were called Utopians.

Malthus did not believe that man was likely to undergo any significant biological change. Because he could see no evidence that the nature of man had changed or was changing, he believed that man's sexual passion and his other basic impulses were likely to remain what they had always been. The structure erected by the Utopians on their belief in the possibility of such changes seemed to Malthus extremely flimsy.

MALTHUS'S THESIS

Malthus's principle of population as developed in the first edition of the Essay is as follows:[1]

[1] The full title of the first Essay was *An Essay on the Principle of Population As It Affects the Future*

I think I may fairly make two postulata; First, That food is necessary to the existence of man. Second, That the passion between the sexes is necessary, and will remain nearly in its present state.[2]

Assuming then, my postulata as granted, I say, that the power of population is indefinitely greater than the power in the earth to produce subsistence for man.

Population, when unchecked, increases in a geometrical ratio. Subsistence increases only in an arithmetical ratio. A slight acquaintance with numbers will shew the immensity of the first power in comparison of the second.[3]

The ratios Malthus had in mind were:

Population: 1-2-4-8-16-32-64
Subsistence: 1-2-3-4- 5- 6- 7

Malthus considered the units of time (represented by the hyphens) in which population *could* double, *if* it were not impeded by lack of subsistence, to be about 25 years. *If* these ratios endured, population would increase to 64 times its original size in 150 years, while subsistence would increase to only 7 times its original amount. Clearly, this situation would be impossible. Malthus intended the ratios to represent differences in potentials—the difference between the "power of population" to increase and the "power in the earth to produce subsistence for man." He expressed the consequences of the difference between these two "powers" in the following short paragraphs:

By that law of our nature which makes food necessary to the life of man, the effects of these two unequal powers must be kept equal.

This implies a strong and constantly operating check on population from the difficulty of subsistence. This difficulty must fall somewhere; and must necessarily be severely felt by a large portion of mankind.[4]

Malthus could not accept the views of the Utopians. He believed that two of man's characteristics essential to the maintenance of life were *immutable*, were natural laws, and were *antagonistic:* (1) the "need for food," and (2) the "passion

---

Improvement of Society, with Remarks on the Speculations of Mr. Godwin, M. Condorcet, and Other Writers. London. Printed for J. Johnson in St. Paul's Church-Yard, 1798. All references given here to this first Essay are taken from the facsimile reprinting of the original, sponsored by the Royal Economic Society and issued by Macmillan & Co., Ltd., London, 1926. Some notes by James Bonar were added as was also the preface to the second edition, bearing the date June 8, 1803.

[2] *Ibid.*, p. 11.
[3] *Ibid.*, pp. 13–14.
[4] *Ibid.*, p. 14.

between the sexes." Malthus assumed that the latter would always lead most people to marry at a relatively early age and hence would result in such a large number of births that population would double every few years if "unchecked" by "misery" and "vice." Since population had seldom doubled in a few years, and then only under very unusual conditions, Malthus devoted about one-third of his first Essay to examining the operation of the positive and preventive "checks" that had kept population from growing at a geometrical ratio in every generation.

The Positive Checks. Malthus considered positive checks all factors that operated chiefly as determiners of the *death rate*, i.e., as destroyers of life "already begun." He believed that the positive checks on population growth arose basically from the pressure of population on subsistence. According to Malthus, some of these positive checks were "vicious customs with respect to women, great cities, unwholesome manufactures, luxury, pestilence, and war. . . . All these checks may be fairly resolved into misery and vice." It is quite obvious that Malthus used "misery" as a general term for the suffering which was caused by lack of the necessities of life and which therefore led frequently to premature death.

The Preventive Checks. The second kind of check to the growth of population Malthus called the preventive or "prudential" check, because it operated to *reduce the birth rate;* in his opinion, the postponement of marriage was and would remain the chief preventive check.

Malthus believed then that these two checks, the preventive and the positive, "are the true causes of the slow increase of population in all the states of modern Europe . . ." and that a "comparatively rapid increase has invariably taken place, whenever these causes have been in any considerable degree removed."[5] In support of this view he cites the relatively rapid growth of some of the Greek colonies in ancient times, but places most emphasis upon the growth of the European colonies in North America, which even then were known to be increasing at a very rapid rate. (The first census of the United States was taken in 1790.) He also found some evidence that even the long-settled countries of Europe had generally recovered quite rapidly from the ravages of war, pestilence, and famine. After a war was over, after a pestilence had subsided, or after a famine had been succeeded by a return to normal crop production, population would grow relatively fast until it again began to suffer severely from the hardships arising out of the growing pressure on the means of subsistence.

Malthus did not believe that the preventive check would so reduce man's rate of reproduction that the positive checks would not operate more or less continuously. Consequently, he was not convinced that the schemes being pro-

[5] *Ibid.*, p. 100.

posed for improving human welfare by reforming man's institutions were ever likely to do much to increase man's happiness. It seemed to him that however good human institutions became, they would serve only to mitigate the positive checks for a short time—until man's numbers would again grow up to his productive capacity under his new institutions—and that man would then suffer from hunger, disease, war, and a host of other ills (positive checks) as he always had in the past. He did not think that the preventive checks, which he believed to be operative in varying degrees through "all the ranks of society in England" and in most of the countries of Western Europe, would ever be sufficiently strong to eliminate the operation of the positive checks arising chiefly from the pressure of population on subsistence.

All his life he believed firmly that man's "sex passions" and his material needs were in essential conflict. There was a minimum below which subsistence could not be reduced without causing great hardship, and there was not the least indication that "man's sex passion" was undergoing any change. Thus man was doomed to the suffering inevitably caused by trying to maintain a population greater than the available means of subsistence would support in comfort. In other words, the positive checks—hunger, disease, vice, war, cold, and so forth—were bound to be in the future, as in the past, the chief destroyers of man, the chief forces which could keep his numbers from becoming what his nature strove to make them.

He concluded from this examination that:

> It is, undoubtedly, a most disheartening reflection, that the great obstacle in the way to any extraordinary improvement in society, is of a nature that we can never hope to overcome. The perpetual tendency in the race of man to increase beyond the means of subsistence, is one of the general laws of animated nature, which we can have no reason to expect will change. Yet, discouraging as the contemplation of this difficulty must be, . . . no possible good can arise from any endeavours to slur it over . . . the most baleful mischiefs may be expected from the unmanly conduct of not daring to face the truth, because it is unpleasing.[6]

It is not surprising that because of this pessimistic conclusion, Malthus was regarded by the "perfectionists" as a prophet of gloom, or that they frequently regarded him as a hard-hearted conservative attempting to hide his callousness to the pitiful lot of the great mass of the people by calling to his aid a natural law over which man had no control. His opposition to the Poor Laws and to the changes in them which, in his judgment, could only lead to greater hardships within a short time because they did not recognize any responsibility on the part of the individual to practice prudential preventive checks, only confirmed his Utopian opponents in their belief that he was the tool of the wealthy

[6] *Ibid.*, p. 346.

conservative landowners and the rising industrial entrepreneurs who were anxious to avoid their social responsibilities.

EVALUATION OF THE FIRST EDITION OF THE ESSAY ON POPULATION

No one seriously questions Malthus's two *postulata* that formed the starting point for his argument: (1) the absolute necessity of food, and (2) the unchanging nature of the passion between the sexes. However, many questions have been raised regarding his ratios—a geometric ratio for population increase and an arithmetical ratio for the increase of food (subsistence) in any specified period of time. The assertion that population "when unchecked" can double in a fixed period of time—Malthus thought the period to be about a generation of 25 years or less—and can continue to do so indefinitely, can be accepted as a sound statement of physiological *potential*.

On the other hand, there is no clear evidence that food (subsistence) always and everywhere can increase only in an arithmetical ratio. Malthus, of course, clearly recognized the inconclusiveness of the data when he pointed out that in the United States in his day food (subsistence) grew as fast or even faster than population. However, he considered that this situation was due to the abundance of good land, not yet tilled, a condition which could endure for only a relatively short period in most lands and in the world as a whole. "The power in the earth to produce subsistence for man" might continue to increase indefinitely, but it could not continue indefinitely to double during every generation, as could man's numbers. It is unfortunate that in his first Essay, to illustrate the inevitable consequences of a lower rhythm of growth for subsistence than for population, he picked a specific mathematical rhythm for growth of subsistence, viz., the arithmetical ratio. Some of his opponents quickly seized upon this weakness in the first Essay, and because they could show that this arithmetical rhythm of increase in subsistence did not hold at all times and in all places they were inclined to consider Malthus's entire argument without significance.

In judging this first Essay of Malthus, we should recognize that any statement of a general principle of population based on the study of population changes in the past would be bound to be both incomplete and rather dogmatic, chiefly for the following reasons: (1) The first Essay was intended as a contribution to a controversy then being vigorously pursued between the "perfectionists" and the "conservatives," and such contributions are quite likely to *overstate* the position of the contributors to both sides; (2) at that time few facts were available to show population changes; (3) information regarding the social and economic changes associated with population changes was even more meager and imprecise–e.g., the relation between good and poor crops and the growth of population in Norway and Sweden during the latter half of the eighteenth century was not widely known in 1798; (4) finally, the great social and economic changes which were to flow from the agricultural and the industrial revolutions, and the changes in rate of population growth associated with them, were not yet clearly discernible. However, the authors believe that in spite of its shortcomings, Malthus's first Essay (1798) deserves study even today. It is highly readable, and it is a thoughtful and stimulating effort to use knowledge relating to population changes to enhance the understanding of the social and economic development of society. The later and more scholarly editions of the Essay would never have attracted attention to the importance of studying population changes, as the first Essay did. But the authors believe that no useful evaluation of Malthus's work on population can neglect to place chief emphasis on the development of his ideas in the second and later editions of his Essay. It seems reasonable to suppose that Malthus himself held this view, considering the way he revised and rewrote the first edition. He clearly regarded the first Essay as an unsatisfactory statement of the *principle of population*. It seems strange, therefore, that so many of his critics (both the dead and the living) have written as though they were unaware that the first edition of the Essay had ever been revised, expanded, and improved.

LATER EDITIONS OF THE ESSAY[7]

The first Essay almost immediately aroused a great deal of interest in the relationship of population growth to the improvement of human welfare. However, Malthus's *conclusion* was used so widely by the conservatives in the current political controversy over the Poor Laws (the laws which provided public assistance to the indigent) that the Essay might very well have been lost sight of as an evanescent political pamphlet. Moreover, Malthus himself might almost as easily have been forgotten, and quite certainly would have received little attention from scholars, if he had not soon written a treatise on population, to replace his first Essay.

In 1803, five years after the first Essay, a second edition appeared. During this interval Malthus had not only read widely, searching for material bearing on the historical changes in population, but he had also visited most of the countries of Western and Central Europe and had spent some time in Russia. His writings show that on these visits he not only observed the living conditions of the people closely but that he also gathered a considerable amount of statisti-

[7] The reference to Malthus's later work (after 1798), unless otherwise indicated, will be taken from the Everyman's Library edition in two volumes, nos. 692 and 693, issued by J. M. Dent & Sons, Ltd., Publishers, London, and E. P. Dutton & Co., Inc., New York, 1914.

cal material and constantly inquired about customs and practices (cultural factors) that might have significance as checks to population in different countries.

Although this 1803 treatise was called a second edition, it was in fact a new book. Malthus said, "In its present shape it may be considered as a new work, and I should probably have published it as such, omitting the few parts of the former which I have retained, but that I wished it to form a whole of itself, and not to need a continual reference to the other. On this account I trust that no apology is necessary to the purchasers of the first edition."[8] The authors think that the readers of this text will enjoy seeing the full title of this second edition.

An Essay on the Principle of Population
or
A view of its past and present effects
on Human Happiness
with an inquiry into our prospects respecting the
future removal or mitigation of the evils
which it occasions.
A new edition very much enlarged
By T. R. Malthus, A.M.
Fellow of Jesus College, Cambridge
London, printed for J. Johnson in St. Paul's
Church-Yard, by T. Bensley, Bolt Court, Fleet St.

The second edition of the Essay was several times longer than the first and reflected the extensive reading and traveling Malthus had done in the interim. In writing the first edition he supposed that his ideas about the conditions determining population growth were more original than they really were, and he makes this fact explicit early in the second edition:

> In the course of this inquiry I found that much more had been done than I had been aware of, when I first published the Essay. The poverty and misery arising from a too rapid increase of population had been distinctly seen, and the most violent remedies proposed so long ago as the times of Plato and Aristotle. And of late years the subject has been treated in such a manner by some of the French Economists, occasionally Montesquieu, and, among our own writers, by Dr. Franklin, Sir James Stewart, Mr. Arthur Young, and Mr. Townsend, as to create a natural surprise that it had not excited more of the public attention. . . .
>
> Though it had been stated distinctly, that population must always be kept down to the level of subsistence; yet few inquiries had been made into the various modes by which this level is effected; and the principle had never been sufficiently pursued

[8] *Ibid.*, vol. 1, p. 12.

to its consequences, nor had those practical inferences [been] drawn from it, which a strict examination of its effects on society appears to suggest.[9]

Ultimately, seven editions were published at rather short intervals, the last one shortly after Malthus's death in 1834. In the authors' judgment, it is primarily this continued and *highly objective* interest in the factors affecting population growth and in the relation between this growth and human welfare that entitles Malthus to be called the father of modern population study. Since it is impossible to go into detail regarding the development of Malthus's thought in the different editions of the Essay, the discussion only of his matured views will be given here; they will be based on the Everyman's Library reprint of the seventh and last edition.

The change in his general position on population growth between the first and seventh editions can be shown by placing his later statement beside his earlier statement of the case.

First edition:

1. That population cannot increase without the means of subsistence, is a proposition so evident, that it needs no illustration.

2. That population does invariably increase, where there are the means of subsistence, the history of every people that have ever existed will abundantly prove.

3. And, that the superior power of population cannot be checked, without producing misery or vice, the ample portion of these too bitter ingredients in the cup of human life, and the continuance of the physical causes that seem to have produced them, bear too convincing a testimony.[10]

Seventh (last) edition:

1. Population is necessarily limited by the means of subsistence.

2. Population invariably increases where the means of subsistence increase, unless prevented by some very powerful and obvious checks.

3. These checks, and the checks which repress the superior power of population, and keep it on a level with the means of subsistence, are all resolvable into moral restraint, vice, and misery.[11]

The above quotations show that in the final (seventh) edition, Malthus still held that population had "a constant tendency to increase beyond the means of subsistence," although his later studies had led him to believe that the preventive checks were much more effective in certain populations than he had

[9] *Ibid.*, vol. 1, pp. 1–2.
[10] Facsimile ed., pp. 37–38.
[11] Everyman's Library ed., vol. 1, pp. 18–19.

at first supposed. He did not, however, abandon his belief that "when un-checked," man's numbers would double in about 25 years or less, although he recognized that in no human society had population growth ever been com-pletely "unchecked." He also came to recognize that from the beginning of *society* there had been social checks in operation which were more or less pre-ventive in character. Even so, the positive checks which destroyed life "already begun" remained by far the most important. In a footnote to the second state-ment (2) in the Everyman's Library edition as just quoted, Malthus himself comments on his changed viewpoint when he says, "I have expressed myself in this cautious manner, because I believe there are some instances where population does not keep up to the level of the means of subsistence."[12]

In the later editions Malthus did not change his definition of the positive checks, but he did modify slightly his evaluation of their significance. The following quotations from the Everyman's Library edition will give his most mature thinking on the positive checks:

> The positive checks to [the increase of] population are extremely various, and include every cause, whether arising from vice or misery, which in any degree con-tributes to shorten the natural duration of human life. Under this head, therefore, may be enumerated all unwholesome occupations, severe labour and exposure to the seasons, extreme poverty, bad nursing of children, great towns, excesses of all kinds, the whole train of common diseases and epidemics, wars, plague, and famine. . . . The ultimate check to population appears then to be a want of food. . . . But this ultimate check is never the immediate check, except in cases of actual famine.[13]

> I think it appears that in modern Europe the positive checks to population pre-vail less and the preventive checks more than in past times, and in the more uncivilized parts of the world.
>
> War, the predominant check to the population of savage nations, has certainly abated, even including the late unhappy revolutionary contests; and since the prevalence of a greater degree of personal cleanliness, of better modes of clearing and building towns, and of a more equable distribution of the products of the soil, from improving knowledge in political economy, plagues, violent diseases, and famines have been certainly mitigated and have become less frequent. [The comma after "soil" is ours.][14]

The following quotations, though short, seem to the authors to be a fairly clear statement of Malthus's most mature views regarding the influence of the preventive checks on the growth of population:

[12] *Ibid.*, vol. 1, pp. 18–19.
[13] *Ibid.*, vol. 1, pp. 12–14.
[14] *Ibid.*, vol. 1, p. 315.

The germs of existence contained in this earth, if they could freely develop themselves, would fill millions of worlds in the course of a few thousand years. . . .

In plants and irrational animals, the view of the subject is simple. They are impelled by a powerful instinct to the increase of their species; and this instinct is interrupted by no doubts about providing for their offspring. Wherever therefore there is liberty, the power of increase is exerted; and the superabundant effects are repressed afterwards by want of room and nourishment.

The effects of this check on man are more complicated. Impelled to the increase of this species by an equally powerful instinct, reason interrupts his career, and asks him whether he may not bring beings into the world for whom he cannot provide the means of support. If he attend to this natural suggestion, the restriction too frequently produces vice. If he hear it not, the human race will be constantly endeavoring to increase beyond the means of subsistence.[15]

Of the preventive checks, the restraint from marriage which is not followed by irregular gratifications may properly be termed moral restraint.[16]

The following quotation is but a small part of an interesting and illuminating discussion by Malthus of the motivations behind the exercise of the preventive checks:

The preventive check, as far as it is voluntary, is peculiar to man, and arises from that distinctive superiority in his reasoning faculties which enables him to calculate distant consequences. The checks to the indefinite increase of plants and irrational animals are all either positive, or, if preventive, involuntary. But man cannot look around him and see the distress which frequently presses upon those who have large families . . . without feeling a doubt whether, if he follow the bent of his inclinations, he may be able to support the offspring which he will probably bring into the world. . . . Will he not be unable to transmit to his children some advantages of education and improvement that he himself possessed? Does he even feel secure that, should he have a large family, his utmost exertions can save them from rags and squalid poverty, and their consequent degradation in the community? And may he not be reduced to the grating necessity of forfeiting his independence, and of being obliged to the sparing hand of Charity for support?

These considerations are calculated to prevent, and certainly do prevent a great number of persons in all civilized nations from pursuing the dictate of nature in an early attachment to one woman.[17]

The preventive check, according to Malthus, is brought into play through late marriage and abstinence within marriage. The following quotation shows

[15] *Ibid.*, vol. 1, pp. 5–6.
[16] *Ibid.*, vol. 1, p. 14.
[17] *Ibid.*, vol. 1, pp. 12–13.

that Malthus was afraid that the "double standard" threatens the success of "moral restraint" as a means of keeping population from growing too fast.

> With regard to the preventive check to populations, though it must be acknowledged that that branch of it which comes under the head of moral restraint, does not at present prevail much among the male part of society, yet I am strongly disposed to believe that it prevails more than in those states which were first considered; and it can scarcely be doubted that in modern Europe a much larger proportion of women pass a considerable part of their lives in the exercise of this virtue than in past times and among uncivilized nations. But however this may be, if we consider only the general term which implies principally a delay of the marriage union from prudential considerations, without reference to consequences, it may be considered in this light as the most powerful of the checks which in modern Europe keep down the population to the level of the means of subsistence.[18]

Malthus recognized that during the expansion into new lands such as those of the United States, subsistence could increase at a very rapid rate and, like population, could double in about 25 years. The fact that man's numbers did not generally show such a rapid increase as in the United States was proof that vice and misery, the positive checks, were chiefly responsible for his relatively slow growth over long periods of time. But to the end, Malthus believed that to assume an indefinite period of time during which man's subsistence could continue to double every few years " . . . would be contrary to all our knowledge of the properties of land. The improvement of the barren parts would be a work of time and labour; and it must be evident to those who have the slightest acquaintance with agricultural subjects that, in proportion as cultivation extended, the additions that could yearly be made to the former average produce must be gradually and regularly diminishing."[19] In this quotation Malthus comes close to a statement of the *law of diminishing returns* in agriculture.

SOME OF THE POPULATION DATA INFLUENCING MALTHUS

Malthus found that the positive checks operated strongly in all the societies he surveyed but especially in past societies as compared with Europe in his day. To his surprise, he also found travelers often referring to practices of preventive character among "savage" peoples. Likewise, he found abundant evidence that many of the almost continuous tribal wars between neighboring groups of savages killed such a large proportion of their people that these groups did not increase in numbers or increased but slowly. Moreover, it appeared that these wars were often caused by the need of more land to ensure a larger sub-

[18] *Ibid.*, vol. 1, p. 315.
[19] *Ibid.*, vol. 1, p. 9.

sistence base for the aggressive tribe. The practices of abortion and infanticide among primitive peoples were also thought to be largely a consequence of the scarcity of subsistence. Today, our cultural anthropologists would point out that among such peoples many other cultural factors exercise varying amounts of control over the birth rate and population growth, many of them of a positive character.

Most present-day observers would probably emphasize even more than Malthus did the extremely high death rate from contagious and infectious diseases as a depressant of population growth. But in his day all the world had such high death rates from these diseases that they were regarded as normal and unavoidable. In fact, for only one of the more deadly of these diseases—smallpox—was a specific preventive known during Malthus's life, and the discovery of this specific is generally dated in 1798—the year in which the first Essay was published. It was not until about 1820 that even the persons better informed in such matters saw the possibility of eradicating smallpox, and considerably later that vaccination came into wide use.

Malthus found that a number of practices were operating more or less effectively in European countries to postpone marriage for several years beyond puberty and thus to reduce the number of children born to the average married couple. In Norway, compulsory military service and the way in which agriculture was organized encouraged (and at times forced) postponement of marriage for many couples for several years. Since Norway had a very low death rate for that time (about 20.5 from 1795 to 1799, which was probably well below the usual rate) and since it also had a low birth rate (about 28.6, according to Malthus's findings), he concluded that the preventive checks operated quite effectively in Norway. In some other countries, particularly Russia and Prussia, he found birth rates as high as 40 and above. But he saw that even Norway's growth rate, about 8 per 1,000 per year, could not have prevailed for long, or Norway's population would have been much larger than it was in 1800 (about 800,000).

In Sweden the preventive checks did not appear to be so effective as in Norway, and both birth rates and death rates were substantially higher, although lower than in most of Europe. Malthus interpreted this to mean that the pressure on subsistence was greater in Sweden than in Norway. This view was also supported by data showing the numbers of marriages, births, and deaths in the four years 1757 to 1760. During the first two of these years there were poor harvests; during the latter two years there were good harvests. In 1757 and 1758 the number of marriages and births was substantially smaller and the number of deaths much higher than in the years 1759 and 1760, when the harvests were good.

The available evidence indicated that in Russia the preventive checks were almost absent, while the positive checks were slightly milder than in most of Central Europe. Hence, population in Russia was growing fairly rapidly, at a rate that would double it in about 44 years. There was still an abundance of good untilled land in Russia, and subsistence was relatively easy to obtain.

In some countries, Malthus found both birth rates and death rates averaging 40 to 45 over a period of years. Because the positive checks were very severe, there was little or no increase in population. But he also found clear evidence that where substantial improvements in agriculture were made and/or where manufacturers and trade flourished, population was also increasing because the death rate was declining. Also, rather to his surprise, he came across evidence showing that by about 1825 France had a declining birth rate, presumably due to the increasing effectiveness of the preventive checks, but that the rate of population growth was rising because of the still more rapid decline in the death rate. Data available in 1825 led Malthus to write as follows:

> This increased rate [i.e., of population growth] appears to be owing to a diminished mortality, occasioned by the improved situation of the labouring classes since the revolution. It shows that an acceleration in the rate of increase is quite consistent with diminution in the proportion of births, and that such a diminution is likely to take place under a diminished mortality from whatever cause or causes arising.[20]

As regards the growth of population in Great Britain after regular censuses were inaugurated (1801), Malthus found that the rate of increase prevailing between 1801 and 1821 would double the population in about 50 years. He regarded such a rate of increase as one "which in the nature of things cannot be permanent. It has been occasioned by the stimulus of a greatly-increased demand for labour, combined with a greatly-increased power of production, both in agriculture and manufactures."[21]

SOME OF MALTHUS'S ERRORS OR SHORTCOMINGS

The Ratios. Malthus's continued use of the arithmetical and geometric ratios was unfortunate. To the end he used the contrast between a geometrical ratio for population and an arithmetical ratio for subsistence *to illustrate* his point that the rhythm of potential ("unchecked") population growth was, as a rule, faster than the rhythm of the growth of subsistence—even though he no longer regarded this arithmetical ratio as a precise statement of the potential quantitative growth of subsistence. He said: "The rate [rhythm] according to which the productions of the earth may be supposed to increase . . . will not be so easy to determine [i.e., as the potential rate of population growth]. Of this, however, we may be perfectly certain, the ratio of their increase in a limited

[20] *Ibid.*, vol. 1, pp. 234–235.
[21] *Ibid.*, vol. 1, p. 261.

territory [the entire world is, of course, a limited territory] must be of a totally different nature from the ratio of the increase of population."[22] Malthus came to recognize that the possible growth rate of subsistence in a given area at a given time depended on a number of social and economic conditions as well as on natural conditions, and that it might vary considerably from time to time. However, he remained convinced that, as a rule, the rhythm of potential growth of subsistence, though less calculable, was of a slower order than that of population growth.

Definition of Subsistence. Malthus never made completely clear whether he really meant that population was limited by food or by subsistence, nor did he express exactly what he considered the difference between them. He frequently spoke of food as the limiting factor, and at times he spoke of the means of subsistence as the limiting factor. Food is a fairly definite entity, while subsistence tends to become synonymous with standard of life, and is anything but definite. The position Malthus really held in later years is probably best expressed by "means of subsistence," which he was coming to think of as a standard or level at which a group or class customarily lived.

Voluntary Control of Family Size. It is interesting that in Malthus's discussion of the preventive checks in the Scandinavian countries and in France, he did not mention *contraceptive* practices. We now know that such preventive practices were used, although to only a limited extent, in France as early as 1750, and also that their use was increasing slowly in Malthus's day. There is also good reason to believe that the relatively low birth rates in Norway and Sweden about 1800 were due in part to contraceptive practices. If Malthus knew of these practices, he made no mention of them. In 1800 it would have been very easy, even for an observant traveler interested in the factors affecting the growth of population, to overlook such practices.

Even in the latest edition he makes no unequivocal reference to the *voluntary control of conception*, i.e., contraception, as a preventive check. This is an important and surprising omission. Since Malthus did not die until 1834, he must have known that contraception was being vigorously advocated in England by Francis Place and a number of other people as early as 1820. However, *only one highly ambiguous passage*, interpreted by some readers as referring to contraception, is found in the first Essay, and it is repeated in exactly the same words in the seventh edition. The passage occurs in Malthus's discussion of the arguments of Condorcet relating to the "perfectibility of man." Malthus interprets Condorcet as saying that man need not fear that at some time in the future his numbers might so increase as to endanger his welfare. He then goes on to say:

[22] *Ibid.*, vol. 1, p. 8.

He [Condorcet] proceeds to remove the difficulty in a manner which I profess not to understand. Having observed that the ridiculous prejudices of superstition would by that time have ceased to throw over morals a corrupt and degrading austerity, he alludes either to promiscuous concubinage, which would prevent breeding, *or to something else as unnatural.* [Italics are ours.][23]

Having examined Condorcet's statement both in the French and in the English translation, the authors believe that although Condorcet may have referred to contraception, his actual statement remains ambiguous.

Since Malthus does not specify what his "something else as unnatural" means, and since Condorcet's statement is vague, we can never be sure whether Malthus was referring to contraception. But since Malthus certainly must have known, at least ten years before his death, that the practice of contraception was spreading in England, we must conclude either that (1) he considered any form of contraception he knew about as "unnatural" and "immoral," and hence classified as vice, and/or that (2) he regarded it as so unlikely to have any significant effect on the number of children born per couple that it did not merit discussion. The former alternative appears somewhat more probable to the authors because Malthus was highly orthodox in his religious views. It is quite likely that he regarded what his Church labeled "unnatural" as also "immoral." He was, it should be remembered, an ordained minister of the Church of England. In any event, it is reasonably certain that he never considered contraception as a permissible preventive check and hence overlooked the possibility that it might, under certain conditions, make subsistence relatively more available by adjusting the rhythm of man's growth in numbers to the rhythm of growth of his subsistence.

FINAL COMMENTS ON MALTHUS'S PRINCIPLE OF POPULATION

In the opinion of the authors, Malthus was essentially correct in his view that in the absence of *effective preventive checks*, man, with only occasional and short-lived exceptions, had long suffered and would continue to suffer from the *positive* checks. He believed that the meagerness of subsistence was one of the most important causes of high death rates, i.e., that more children would continue to be born than could be reared in decency, and that the balance between numbers and subsistence would be maintained by the excessive deaths arising from hardship. Today, students of population have much more reason than Malthus to believe that the preventive checks can and will supersede the positive checks, although the larger part of mankind still lives under the conditions

[23] *Ibid.,* vol. 2, p. 5.

described by Malthus, in which only the severity of the positive checks prevents a far more rapid rise in numbers. Malthus deserves great credit for bringing this problem to the attention of people as well as for the calm and objective manner in which he analyzed the facts available to him and thus increased our understanding of one extremely important element affecting human welfare. Even today, too many people dwell on Malthus's mistakes and overlook his contribution to our understanding of population changes.

MALTHUS ON OTHER ASPECTS OF POPULATION PROBLEMS

We find that, in addition to the ideas discussed above, Malthus expressed himself quite fully on many other aspects of population growth which interest us greatly today. It would be doing him an injustice not to state his position on some of the more important problems, because the omission would leave the impression that his thinking was less comprehensive than it actually was.

Emigration. Malthus saw clearly that emigration was an important factor in population growth, and he discussed the effects both upon the mother country and upon the country of destination. From the standpoint of the country sending out emigrants he believed that such a policy would be useless as a permanent means of relieving poverty, since it would result almost immediately in earlier marriages and a greater number of births per marriage. Moreover, if emigration did temporarily reduce poverty by lessening pressure on subsistence, it would also reduce the death rate; hence, the pressure would soon be as great as it had ever been. The following passage states his position plainly:

> It is clear, therefore, that with any view of making room for an unrestricted increase of population, emigration is perfectly inadequate; but as a partial and temporary expedient, and with a view to the more general cultivation of the earth, and the wider extension of civilization, it seems to be both useful and proper; and if it cannot be proved that governments are bound actively to encourage it, it is not only strikingly unjust, but in the highest degree impolitic in them to prevent it. There are no fears so totally ill-grounded as the fears of depopulation from emigration.[24]

Specialization. Malthus also recognized that any country could develop a high degree of specialization in agriculture and in manufacturing industries, provided that it could trade its products for those of other countries specializing along different lines. The following quotation will show his ideas:

> A country which excels in commerce and manufactures may purchase corn [cereals] from a great variety of others; and it may be supposed, perhaps, that, proceed-

[24] *Ibid.*, vol. 2, p. 36.

ing upon this system, it may continue to purchase an increasing quantity, and to maintain a rapidly increasing population, till the lands of all the nations with which it trades are fully cultivated. As this is an event necessarily at a great distance, it may appear that the population of such a country will not be checked from the difficulty of procuring subsistence till after the lapse of a great number of ages.

There are, however, causes constantly in operation which will occasion the pressure of this difficulty long before the event here contemplated has taken place, and while the means of raising food in the surrounding countries may still be comparatively abundant.[25]

Malthus believed that the country which depended on such factors as skill and capital could not long hope to maintain its economic security because of the many forces at work to undermine its power. Other countries can also accumulate capital as time goes on, and work skills are easily acquired when there is a demand for them. Consequently, commercial and manufacturing countries would always be in a more or less precarious position because of potential competition from other countries having abundant land as well as other natural resources.

In reading Malthus's discussion of the relative advantages and disadvantages of countries largely given over to industry and commerce and of countries having large reserves of land, one can almost imagine that he is reading a description of present-day conditions confronting Great Britain, on the one hand, and Australia or Argentina, on the other. He clearly depicts the limitations of a nation which acts as a manufacturer, middleman, and carrier and has small agricultural resources, and the advantages of a nation which has a combined agricultural and commercial system. One cannot but feel that he was very clear-sighted when he anticipated the effects of commercial and agricultural systems, in various combinations, upon population growth.

From Malthus's view on the advantages and disadvantages of the industrial specialization of nations, one may deduce what he considered to be a desirable distribution of population between agriculture and other industries. He believed that a nation should be largely self-supporting if it wished to be reasonably independent of the vicissitudes in the fortunes of other nations. According to his view, any country which supported a considerable part of its population by imported food was bound, sooner or later, to suffer from such a deficiency.

Social Welfare. It was probably even more true in Malthus's time than it is today that the death rate was much higher among the "improvident" than among the "prudent"; hence, among the children of the improvident, the number reaching maturity was not so much greater than among the children of the prudent as Malthus might have been led to suppose by the difference in

[25] *Ibid.*, vol. 2, p. 79. See also the quotation from Malthus on page 116 of this text relating to agriculture as the basis of nonagricultural social development.

birth rates between the groups. He was opposed to poor-law charity not because it allowed an inferior class to increase at the expense of a superior class (as is so often argued today), but because it increased the improvidence of the paupers and defeated its own ends by increasing the numbers dependent upon charity for support. He believed the direct relief of poverty was like the labor of Sisyphus—it was unending—and the better it succeeded at one time the greater was the disaster later on.

Malthus says that "the mode of essentially and permanently bettering the condition of the poor involves explaining to them the true nature of their situation. . . ."[26] Later he returns to this idea and advocates a great extension of national education as the only way to make the mass of the people realize the necessity of keeping the size of their own families within the limit they can reasonably hope to support. He had no illusions regarding the difficulties of thus educating the public to understand what must be done and strengthening their will to do it. But he saw no other way out, since all the plans advocated by the perfectionists and those supported by the conservatives for bettering the conditions of the poor were calculated to encourage the more rapid growth of population by mitigating the immediate hardships of those families having more children than they could support in decency.

PESSIMISTIC OUTLOOK

In the first edition of the Essay, Malthus's pessimism was unmitigated and profound, because he did not believe that the preventive check could be made sufficiently effective. But as he continued to observe population changes, many circumstances led him to believe that man could more or less control his numbers if he would and that in many societies he was actually doing so to a limited extent. If he could exercise this control, then there was no reason why his miserable condition should not steadily improve, even though there would always remain a certain amount of pressure on the means of subsistence. The following quotation from the close of the seventh edition of the Essay gives Malthus's final judgment regarding the "future improvement of society":

> From a review of the state of society in former periods compared with the present, I should certainly say that the evils resulting from the principle of population have rather diminished than increased, even under the disadvantage of an almost total ignorance of the real cause. And if we can indulge the hope that this ignorance will be gradually dissipated, it does not seem unreasonable to expect that they will be still further diminished. The increase of absolute population, which will of course take place, will evidently tend but little to weaken this expectation, as everything

[26] *Ibid.*, vol. 2, p. 172.

depends upon the relative proportion between population and food, and not on the absolute number of people. In the former part of this work, it appeared that the countries which possessed the fewest people often suffered the most from the effects of the principle of population; and it can scarcely be doubted that, taking Europe throughout, fewer famines and fewer diseases arising from want have prevailed in the last century than in those which preceded it.

On the whole, therefore, though our future prospects respecting the mitigation of the evils arising from the principle of population may not be so bright as we could wish, yet they are far from being entirely disheartening, and by no means preclude that gradual and progressive improvement in human society which, before the late wild speculations on this subject, was the object of rational expectation. . . .

It would indeed be a melancholy reflection that, while the views of physical science are daily enlarging, so as scarcely to be bounded by the most distant horizon, the science of moral and political philosophy should be confined within such narrow limits, or at best be so feeble in its influence, as to be unable to counteract the obstacles to human happiness arising from a single cause. But however formidable these obstacles may have appeared in some parts of this work, it is hoped that the general result of the inquiry is such as not to make us give up the improvement of human society in despair. The partial good which seems to be attainable is worthy of all our exertions; it is sufficient to direct our efforts, and animate our prospects. And although we cannot expect that the virtue and happiness of mankind will keep pace with the brilliant career of physical discovery; yet, if we are not wanting to ourselves, we may confidently indulge the hope that, to no unimportant extent, they will be influenced by its progress and will partake in its success.[27]

CONCLUSION

If the preceding quotations and comments have succeeded even moderately well in presenting the more salient features of Malthus's thinking, evidently he has been greatly misrepresented by many people. Probably the chief sinners in this respect have been those who never read him carefully. Others have been unable to see any truth whatever in his position because they believed that the ratios would not hold. Furthermore, there are those today who seem to hold Malthus responsible for all the practices now called "neo-Malthusian," practices which these critics believe are harmful to the race, both physically and morally. They hold, therefore, that his doctrines embody something inherently reprehensible. The critics fail to realize that only because there is a large measure of truth in Malthus's doctrines do men feel the need of resorting to contraception to keep their families within reasonable limits. Those who do not believe in contraception should not cavil at Malthus, since he was only the

[27] *Ibid.*, vol. 2, pp. 261–262.

expositor of what he believed to be facts; they should rather condemn nature, which has made man more fertile than he should be if he is to reproduce without hindrance and yet live in decency and modest comfort. Malthus was as interested in increasing human welfare as were the Utopians, but he thought their enthusiasm should be tempered with reason based on fact—that it served no good purpose to encourage visions of an improved level of living which was unattainable. Thus, while he was strongly humanitarian in his sympathies, he tried to be scientific in evaluating the probabilities of attaining the ease of living pictured by the Utopians. He wanted the facts to speak for themselves, and in the authors' opinion, Malthus made good use of the facts which were available to him.

Malthus's primary contribution to the study of population, and the one which in our opinion makes him the real father of modern population study, was his use of facts for the support of his general doctrine regarding the dynamics of population growth and change in their relation to man's welfare. He is more responsible than anyone else for bringing population study within the field of social science. It had been largely philosophical and speculative before his time, but thenceforward, with only a few exceptions, men discussed the changes in population as a question of direct public concern, a problem on which action might be taken for the purpose of increasing human welfare. No longer could man's growth in numbers be looked upon as something which did not concern him because he could do nothing about it. The study of population was to become a proper field of investigation, with the aim of gaining knowledge with which to better man's living conditions. Of course, Malthus's Essay could not have had this effect if the time had not been ripe. A general expansion of scientific study of society was under way. Social science was beginning to supersede social speculation, and man was beginning to undertake more actively the guidance of his own destiny. Malthus was a social scientist rather than a social philosopher. For this reason we still find much value in his work.

SUGGESTIONS FOR SUPPLEMENTARY READING

Bonar, James: *Malthus and His Work*, The Macmillan Company, New York, 1924.

Field, James A.: *Essays on Population and Other Papers*, The University of Chicago Press, Chicago, 1931.

Glass, D. V. (ed.): *Introduction to Malthus*, John Wiley & Sons, Inc., New York, 1950.

Godwin, William: *Of Population: An Enquiry Concerning the Power of Increase in the Numbers of Mankind. Being an Answer to Mr. Malthus's Essay on That Subject*, Longman, Hurst, Rees, Orme, and Brown, London, 1820.

Griffith, Grosvenor Talbot: *Population Problems of the Age of Malthus*, Cambridge University Press, London, 1926.

Keynes, John Maynard: *Essays in Biography*, Harcourt, Brace and Company, Inc., New York, 1933.

Levin, S. M.: "Malthus, Conception of the Checks to Population," *Human Biology*, vol. 10, no. 2, pp. 214–234, 1938.

Malthus, Thomas Robert: *An Essay on Population*, 2 vols., J. M. Dent & Sons, Ltd., Publishers, London; E. P. Dutton & Co., Inc., New York, n.d. (Everyman's Library, nos. 692–693).

————: *First Essay on Population, 1798*, with notes by James Bonar. Printed for the Royal Economic Society, Macmillan & Co., Ltd., London, 1926. A facsimile reprint.

Petersen, William: "John Maynard Keynes's Theories of Population and the Concept of 'Optimum'," *Population Studies*, vol. 8, no. 3, pp. 228–246, 1955.

Place, Francis: *Illustrations and Proofs of the Principle of Population, Including an Examination of the Proposed Remedies of Mr. Malthus, and a Reply to the Objections of Mr. Godwin and Others*, ed. by Norman E. Himes, Houghton Mifflin Company, Boston, 1930.

Spiegel, Henry W.: *The Development of Economic Thought: Great Economists in Perspective*, John Wiley & Sons, Inc., New York, 1952.

(See especially the works of Bonar, Fay, and Keynes on Malthus, pp. 144–157.)

Stangeland, Charles Emil: *Pre-Malthusian Doctrines of Population: A Study in the History of Economic Theory*, Columbia University Press, The Macmillan Company (agents), New York, 1904.

CHAPTER THREE

Some Population Theories Since Malthus

The Industrial Revolution, with its increasing efficiencies in production, was well under way in England when Malthus wrote his first Essay (1798), and it continued to develop quite rapidly in Western Europe. It also spread, with varying degrees of rapidity, into Central and Northern Europe and into the colonies settled by Western Europeans. An agricultural revolution, likewise increasing the efficiency of labor, either preceded or accompanied the Industrial Revolution in most of these countries. The development of more efficient transportation made increasingly available to Europe the agricultural products and many other natural resources of the less-developed areas, and thus greatly stimulated international trade. Everywhere in Western Europe and North America careful observers were finding small but significant improvements in the living conditions of large numbers of people, even though the rates of population growth were often substantially higher than those of the past, especially in the new countries. It is not surprising, therefore, that interest in Malthus's principle of population weakened as the nineteenth century progressed. A very comfortable feeling that "scientific progress" had proved Malthus wrong once and for all prevailed quite widely among the fortunate classes in the more developed countries of the West.

SOME NATURAL-LAW THEORIES OF POPULATION GROWTH

In view of the great benefits to man that would certainly ensue from the operation of a "natural law" of population growth automatically limiting man's numbers and preventing any significant pressure on subsistence, we shall note briefly some of the chief natural-law theories propounded during the nineteenth century.

Malthus's natural law was, in general terms, that man's numbers tended to increase faster than his subsistence because of the passion between the sexes. Because this was "natural," vice and misery would be man's inevitable lot unless *preventive* measures were widely adopted. Malthus did not expect such measures to be taken quickly. In spite of later modifications which made him less pessimistic, he still believed that man's instinctive tendency to reproduce at too rapid a rate would continue to cause much hardship and suffering. Clearly, if Malthus were entirely wrong about his "law"—if the true natural law of population made for the most desirable possible balance between man's numbers and his subsistence—there would be no need for worry about a too rapid growth of population. Moreover, there would be no reason for man to take any positive measures to control his numbers. *Nature* would do this for him, and man's lot would improve automatically with his increased per capita ability to produce useful goods and services.

Sadler. Michael Thomas Sadler (1780–1835) was an English social reformer and economist, a contemporary of Malthus. He believed that the natural law of population growth was exactly contrary to that expounded by Malthus. He held that man's tendency to increase in numbers would diminish naturally as the density of settlement increased, and that his numbers would cease to grow at the exact point where the number of people would enjoy the greatest happiness, *all other things being equal.* His most succinct statement of this natural law of population was as follows:

> The principle of human increase thus obtained may be very briefly enunciated and is simply this: The fecundity of human beings is, *caeteris paribus* [all other things being equal], in the inverse ratio of the condensation of their numbers; and, still in direct contradiction to the theory now maintained [Malthus's], the variation in that fecundity is effectuated not by the wretchedness and misery but by the happiness and prosperity of the species. . . .
>
> Excluding, of course, cases of extreme distress, a state of labour and privation is that most favorable to human fecundity. A dispersed and scanty population invariably implies that state; but as mankind advance to the agricultural states of existence, and ultimately rise to the highest condition of civilization, labour becomes divided and consequently diminished in its duration and intensity, and many are liberated from its drudgeries, so as to devote themselves to other and more intellectual pursuits, or are rendered independent of it altogether; while the means of subsistence become progressively augmented, and ease and luxury more generally diffused. At every step the principle of increase contracts, and, as I contend, would pause at that precise point where it had secured the utmost possible degree of happiness to the greatest possible number of human beings.[1]

[1] Michael Thomas Sadler, *Ireland: Its Evils and Their Remedies. Being a Refutation of the Errors of the Emigration Committee and Others, Touching That Country. To Which Is Prefixed a Synopsis of*

Just as Malthus believed that he had stated a natural principle or law of population growth which precluded faith in the *rapid* improvement of man's lot in this world, so Sadler believed that he had discovered a natural principle or law of population growth that furnished a rational basis for faith in the *rapid* perfectibility of man's lot. He says: "The law of population, by which the increase of mankind has been and still is, in all cases, regulated, is simply this: *The fecundity of human beings under similar circumstances* varies inversely as their numbers increase on a given space."[2]

The reader will have been somewhat confused by the use of the terms "fecundity" and "principle of increase" in the above quotations. In the second paragraph quoted Sadler seems to have used fecundity as the term is generally defined today, viz., the physiological capacity to conceive and bear living children. However, when he used fecundity in the statement of Malthus's views (in the first paragraph quoted), to the effect that variation in fecundity is "effectuated" not by wretchedness and misery but by happiness and prosperity, either he was using fecundity to mean actual reproduction, i.e., "fertility" (see Chapter 9), or he saw no difference between fertility and fecundity.

A population cannot have high fertility without also being highly fecund, but it can be highly fecund without having either a high fertility (because of the practice of contraception, or abortion, or other practices), or a high rate of increase (because of the mildness of the positive checks). Sadler should have recognized this, but because he did not distinguish clearly between fecundity and fertility he believed that there was no antagonism between man's natural capacity to reproduce, which he never defined, and his capacity to produce adequate subsistence for all who would be born. He could not have had any clear evidence of a significant decline in fertility in the English cities of his day that could reasonably be interpreted as a decline in the natural capacity to reproduce.

Doubleday. Thomas Doubleday (1790–1870), like Sadler, was an English economist and social philosopher. Writing about twenty years later than Sadler, he thought he had found a different principle or natural law governing the growth of population. Whereas Sadler believed that the density of population caused a decrease in fecundity and, hence, largely eliminated the influence of the positive checks to population increase, Doubleday held that man's increase in numbers was inversely related to his food supply. The better the food

---

the Original Treatise About to Be Published on the Law of Population; Developing the Real Principle on Which It Is Universally Regulated, 2d ed., John Murray (Publishers), Ltd., London, 1829, pp. xviii–xix.

[2] *Ibid.*, p. xxviii.

supply, the slower the increase in his numbers. He stated his "general [natural] law" as follows:

> *The great general law* then, which, as it seems, really regulates the increase or decrease both of vegetable and of animal life, is this, that whenever a *species* or *genus* is *endangered*, a corresponding effort is invariably made by nature for its preservation and continuance, by an increase of fecundity or fertility; and that this especially takes place whenever such danger arises from a diminution of proper nourishment or food, so that consequently the state of depletion, or the deplethoric state, is favorable to fertility, and that on the other hand, the plethoric state, or state of repletion, is unfavorable to fertility, in the ratio of the intensity of each state, and this probably throughout nature universally, in the vegetable as well as in the animal world; further, that as applied to mankind this law produces the following consequences, and acts thus:
>
> There is in all societies a constant increase going on amongst that portion of it which is the worst supplied with food; in short, amongst the poorest.
>
> Amongst those in the state of affluence, and well supplied with food and luxuries, a constant decrease goes on. Amongst those who form the mean or medium between these two opposite states, that is to say, amongst those who are tolerably well supplied with good food, and not over-worked, nor yet idle, population is stationary. Hence it follows that it is upon the *numerical proportion* which these three states bear to each other in any society that increase or decrease upon the whole depends.[3]

Recently a variant of this theory has been supported by Josué de Castro, to the effect that a high protein content in the diet reduces fecundity, while a low protein content raises it.[4] Hence all that is needed to reduce fecundity among the poorer peoples of the world is to increase substantially the protein content of their diet.

The only comment needed on these theories is to say that there is no scientific basis for the belief that the density of population, the proportion of protein in the diet, or the relative abundance of calorie intake have any noticeable effect upon fecundity. On the other hand, although Sadler and Doubleday could have had very little factual evidence for their theories, we now know that in the countries more developed economically, the urban populations have for some time had a lower fertility than the rural populations, and that certain other differential birth rates have developed. However, this is an altogether different phenomenon from that discussed by Sadler, Doubleday, and de Castro. We now know that the fertility of any population, i.e., the actual bearing of living children, may be affected substantially by preventive checks of various kinds, while fecundity remains unchanged.

[3] Thomas Doubleday, *The True Law of Population Shewn to be Connected with Food of the People*, 2d ed., George Pierce, London, 1847, pp. 5–7.

[4] Josué de Castro, *The Geography of Hunger*, Little, Brown and Company, Boston, 1952, pp. 71–72, revives Doubleday's theory and apparently gives it a scientific foundation.

Spencer. Herbert Spencer (1820–1903) was a famous English philosopher concerned principally with explaining social and biological development by natural forces. He wrote many treatises in these fields. It is not in the least surprising that he proposed a natural law of population growth in his biological writings which constituted an important portion of his *Synthetic Philosophy*.[5] In some respects Spencer's theory of population was similar to those of Sadler and Doubleday, in that he believed there was a natural law that would absolve man from any responsibility for the control of his increase in numbers, nature achieving this end by weakening man's interest in reproduction while leading him to devote more time and effort to personal, scientific, and economic development. He held that there is in nature an antagonism between *individuation* and *genesis*. Hence, the more strenuous the effort the individual must make to ensure his personal advancement in any field of endeavor, the weaker will be his interest in reproduction. Thus Spencer believed there was a *natural* decrease in reproductive capacity, i.e., in fecundity, especially in women, as *individuation* or personal development claimed more time and energy. This decrease in fecundity ensured a slower increase in population, because social evolution was inevitably accompanied by increasing individuation.

> That absolute or relative infertility is generally produced in women by mental labour carried to excess, is more clearly shown. Though the regimen of upper-class girls is not what it should be, yet, considering that their feeding is better than that of girls belonging to the poorer classes, while in most other respects, their physical treatment is not worse, the deficiency of reproductive power among them may be reasonably attributed to the overtaxing of their brains—an overtaxing which produces a serious reaction on the physique. This diminution of reproductive power is not shown only by the greater frequency of absolute sterility; nor is it shown only in the earlier cessation of child bearing; but it is also shown in the very frequent inability of such women to suckle their infants. In its full sense, the reproductive power means the power to bear a well-developed infant, and to supply that infant with the natural food for the natural period. Most of the flat-chested girls who survive their high-pressure education are incompetent to do this. Were their fertility measured by the number of children they could rear without artificial aid, they would prove relatively very infertile.[6]

It should be said that while there is much reliable information showing a decline in fertility in most Western countries during the past century, especially in the better-educated classes, there was little or no information regarding this matter in Spencer's day. There is no *conclusive* evidence even now showing that declining fertility was or is a consequence of a decline in fecundity. In addition,

[5] Herbert Spencer, *The Principles of Biology*, vol. 2, D. Appleton & Company, Inc., New York, 1867–1868, pp. 485–486.
[6] *Ibid.*, p. 506.

even if more individuals in the nineteenth century than in the century before began to suffer from physiological disturbances that affected in varying degrees their ability to reproduce, there is no proof that these personal physiological defects were a result of a natural evolutionary process of "individuation." Nor is there proof that these defects were transmitted to children who, in turn would have reduced fecundity, which would be transmitted to their children.

The search for a natural law of population growth, of which the theories noted above are examples, seems to have been pursued largely by two types of people: (1) The more scientifically minded persons were primarily interested in discovering "laws" of nature which applied to man as a living being as well as to inanimate objects. Even if they had never heard of Malthus's theory, they would have been interested in a natural law governing population growth. The search for natural laws was a vital element in the intellectual atmosphere in which such people lived. (2) Another group was interested primarily in the improvement of man's lot. These people felt that they must refute Malthus's theory. Some of them, however, realized that it was not sufficient merely to deny it. They should find the *true* natural law which would show the falsity and/or the irrelevance of Malthus's theory and thus dispose of the Malthusian dilemma, which was that man must make more use of preventive checks than he has ever done in the past, or he must continue to suffer greatly from the operation of the positive checks.

Again it should be said that no evidence has yet been produced showing that man's fecundity is diminished according to a natural law over which he has no control that is adequate to ensure the adjustment of his numbers to his means of subsistence. On the other hand, there is steadily mounting evidence that in many populations fertility is decreasing and that man himself is developing the powerful preventive checks which in some populations are already resolving the dilemma posed by Malthus. However, it should be said that the preventive checks now being used consist only in small part of those which Malthus envisioned.

Gini. Corrado Gini (1884–   ) is an Italian student of social science who became interested in population changes as they affected the evolution of society and, in particular, the evolution of nations. He thought that the evolution of a nation or of any society was closely linked to the changes in their rates of population growth and to the varying proportions of this growth coming from the different social classes. Gini's theory is treated here as a natural-law theory because he believed that the basic factor in population growth is biological change rather than social and economic change. Gini held that the different rates of increase in different classes or sections of a national population led very rapidly to changes in the biological traits of the entire population. He based this belief on his study of the statistics of several countries (e.g., see Chapter 10), which showed that a comparatively small proportion of one generation produces the majority of the people in the succeeding generation.[7] The process of the growth of nations he described as "the cyclical rise and fall of population."[8] This cycle of growth in a population is likened to the life cycle of the individual. There is first a period of extremely rapid growth, followed by a period of slower growth and mature achievement; then comes a period of senescence, during which numbers decline and the quality of a civilization deteriorates. Every nation in its youth is simple and undifferentiated in structure and has a high rate of fertility, because each generation springs from the people who are hereditarily most prolific, i.e., highly fecund. As a consequence, such a nation grows rapidly in numbers; this growth in numbers is accompanied by a growing complexity of organization, as is manifested by the development of social classes and the growth of industrial and commercial activities. With increasing numbers, the pressure of population begins to be felt, and expansion takes place through war or colonization, or both.

In the next stage, there is still an increasing complexity of social and economic organization, accompanied by a decrease in rate of population growth; this decrease is due in part to a loss of the most energetic people through war and colonization, and in part to an increase in the proportion of the population in the upper classes, which are always less prolific than are the lower classes. The chief cause of slower population growth, however, is biological.[9] Gini believed that the biological factor in declining fertility was the fundamental factor, that it really underlay the influence of economic and social factors, which only *apparently* determined the decline in fertility. In other words, the decline in fertility (the actual number of children born) is due to a decline in fecundity (the ability to bear children). This decline in fertility is first manifest in the upper classes; once it begins there, however, in a comparatively short time it becomes apparent in all classes. Indeed, as the more energetic and prolific members of the lower classes are absorbed into the upper classes, they too become relatively sterile, like the older portion of these classes, not merely infertile, and do not revive the fertility of the class as a whole. According to Professor Gini, even the sterility of these climbers is not a consequence of the social conditions surrounding their climbing; it is, rather, a result of the weakening of the reproductive instinct and is an inevitable phase of the cycle of population growth.

Professor Gini also holds that when reproduction begins to decline, there is an accompanying decline in the qualities of the individual and that, so far as

---

[7] Harris Foundation, *Population. Lectures on the Harris Foundation, 1929*, by Corrado Gini, . . . Shiroshi Nasu, . . . Robert R. Kuczynski, . . . Oliver Edwin Baker, . . . , pp. 17–18, The University of Chicago Press, 1930.

[8] *Ibid.*, p. 4.

[9] *Ibid.*, p. 21.

one may judge, both of these declines follow upon some biological change in the hereditary qualities of the individual. To quote:

> The ideas set forth above may throw new light on the phenomenon of the different rate of growth of the social classes, which has led many students in the past to fear progressive decline in the quality of nations. On the contrary, we now see it is a providential mechanism for the elimination of those family stocks which have fulfilled the cycle of their evolution.[10]

Allowing that the word "providential" is not happily chosen, it still appears that Gini believed in some inevitable natural force which determines the rise and fall of populations and, hence, of societies. This he finds in the mixture of races and in the proportional survival of the new types arising from this mixture. Thus he invokes some mystical biological changes, quite beyond man's control, as the basic factors determining not only man's quantitative growth, i.e., his fecundity, fertility, and survival, but also his qualitative development, i.e., the distinctive characteristics of man's different civilizations.

SOME SOCIAL THEORIES OF POPULATION GROWTH

Malthus's first Essay was written to call attention to the underlying weakness of the schemes of the perfectionists for the rapid and permanent improvement of man's welfare. He believed that this weakness was due to their failure to consider the constant natural tendency of man's numbers, *when unchecked,* to increase at a higher rate than the means of subsistence could be increased. Since Malthus's day, all the advocates of such schemes for the improvement of man's lot have felt impelled to deny any validity to Malthus's thesis. As we have already shown, some of them believed they had discovered natural laws of population growth which would automatically keep men's numbers at the most desirable level. Other types of population theory also rejecting or ignoring Malthus's principle are referred to here as "social theories." Since Malthus, social theories of population growth have been numerous and varied. Only a few of the principal theories can be noted here, and these very briefly.

George. Henry George (1839–1897) was an American economist and social reformer best known for his advocacy of the "single tax." He believed that if what the economists call "rent" of land (not including improvements), consisting of what people are willing to pay for the privilege of using the land, were

[10] *Ibid.*, pp. 24–25.

taken as a tax by the public, there would be no need for any other tax. In addition, he believed that if landlords were not given the right to collect rent for land, its use would come into the hands of those best fitted to make it more and more productive. Hence, the land would yield much more than it had been yielding under the prevailing system of private ownership and there would be no need to worry about overpopulation or scarcity of subsistence. Thus Henry George had a social panacea (cure-all) to offer; like all such reformers in Western countries since Malthus's day, he felt he must deny any validity to the principle that there was a basic antagonism between man's natural tendency to increase in numbers and his ability to provide subsistence for them. Indeed, George goes so far as to claim: ". . . unlike that of any other living thing the increase of man involves the increase of his food. . . ."[11] But he believes that this condition will prevail only if men have equal access to the resources of the earth and a few are thus prevented from monopolizing them. George's own statement of the law of population is as follows:

> If the real law of population is thus indicated, as I think it must be, then the tendency to increase, instead of being always uniform, is strong where a great population would give increased comfort, and where the perpetuity of the race is threatened by the mortality induced by adverse conditions; but weakens just as the higher development of the individual becomes possible and the perpetuity of race is assured. In other words, the law of population accords with and is subordinate to the law of intellectual developments, and any danger that human beings may be brought into a world where they cannot be provided for arises not from the ordinances of nature, but from the social maladjustments that in the midst of wealth condemn men to want. . . .[12]

We have placed George's theory with the social theories, although he seems to assume like Spencer (see above) that fecundity and/or fertility will decrease as individual intellectual development becomes more widespread. However, like all perfectionists, he placed primary emphasis on his reform (single tax) as releasing man from any hardships that might have been incurred in the past by reason of too great fertility. He also seems to have counted on some weakening of fertility to aid his reform. Whether he believed this weakening of fertility would result from a natural weakening of fecundity or from a voluntary control of family size is not clearly apparent from George's own works; but he may very well have thought of contraception as an important means of reducing fertility. George's *Progress and Poverty* was first published in 1879, when voluntary control

[11] Henry George, *Progress and Poverty: An Inquiry into the Cause of Industrial Depressions and of Increase of Want with Increase of Wealth. The Remedy*, Doubleday, Doran & Company, Inc., New York, 1905, p. 131. (The authors believe the word "involves" is used here in the sense of "inevitably leads to.")

[12] *Ibid.*, pp. 138–139.

of the size of the family was already making appreciable headway in many Western countries.

Dumont. Arsène Dumont (1849–1902) was a professor in the University of Strasbourg. His theory of population growth seems to be based largely on his study of the growth of population in France during the latter part of the nineteenth century. He called it the "theory of social capillarity." Briefly stated, his belief was that the individual tends to mount to higher levels in his social environment by a process similar to physical capillarity. In this process of climbing upward, he becomes less and less likely to reproduce himself; he is drawn out of his natural milieu and away from the family. As a consequence, he loses interest in the family and in the welfare of the race. He becomes interested chiefly in moving upward in a way that will benefit him personally, regardless of whether such movement will benefit the community or the race. Dumont believed that in a society where upward movement from class to class is rather easy, social capillarity is as inevitable as gravity. He says: "What gravity is to the physical world, capillarity is to the social order." He also regards this movement from class to class as a direct cause of the decline in the birth rate, for he says: "The development of numbers in a nation is in inverse ratio to the development of the individual."[13] But he does not imply that change in numbers is due to biological changes, as did Spencer.

Naturally, social capillarity is more effective in a country where obstacles to the movement from class to class are few and weak; hence in France, where democracy was well established, the movement was rapid, and the birth rate suffered greatly in consequence. Furthermore, in a democratic society, large cities exert a powerful attraction upon those living near them, thus increasing the capillary pull on the people and hastening the decline in the birth rate of the society. People at a distance from centers of attraction and in occupations where individual ambition has little opportunity to develop are not drawn into this capillary movement so rapidly and hence are not likely to reduce their birth rate to the same degree. They will continue to increase and thereby to supply new candidates for capillary action; these, in turn, will become ambitious social climbers and will soon die out.

In countries like India, where social capillarity is relatively inactive because of a rigid caste system, there is no tendency for the birth rate to decline and for population to die out. A rigid social structure may prevent upward movement in society, and thus help to keep individual development from becoming so engrossing that the individual has no time for rearing a family.

One is reminded again of Spencer's theory of the antagonism between individuation and genesis. These two theories certainly have some points in common, although Dumont's theory allows for a much larger personal choice in deter-

[13] Arsène Dumont, *La Morale basée sur la démographie*, Schleicher Frères, Paris, 1901, p. 33.

mining reproductive behavior than does Spencer's. On this point Dumont says: "From the moment when the imagination and the attraction of the ideal enter the scene, we find ourselves in the presence of a new principle of population."[14]

On the whole, this statement of the relation between individuation and genesis seems a decided improvement over Spencer's. It has the merit of directing more attention to the actual conditions under which people live as important factors in developing preventive checks to population growth, checks which could render the subsistence check less operative. Malthus hoped for this result, although he did not approve of contraception as Dumont clearly did.

Carr-Saunders. Alexander Morris Carr-Saunders (1886–   ) is an English economist and student of population. He taught in the University of Liverpool and was later Director of the London School of Economics. His theory is that man has always striven to attain an *optimum* number. "This is the number which—taking into consideration the nature of the environment, the degree of skill employed, the habits and customs of the people concerned, and all other relevant facts—gives the highest average return per head." Man has, then, always more or less controlled his numbers, with a view to attaining the optimum; this optimum, of course, varies from time to time. The optimum ". . . is not fixed once and for all. On the contrary, it is constantly varying as the conditions referred to vary, and as skill has tended to increase throughout history, so has the number economically desirable tended to increase."[15]

In brief, Carr-Saunders may be said to sponsor the theory that man's growth in numbers has been largely determined by his notions of the economically desirable numbers under his conditions of life. He says that man has had to develop such practices as abortion, infanticide, segregation of women, etc., to help control his growth. Carr-Saunders thus places more emphasis on man's actual control over his growth in numbers than did Malthus, and less on the positive checks.

Carr-Saunder's theory is also interesting because it started some discussion of the optimum population in purely economic terms. This discussion soon died out, probably because the discussants could never agree even on what constituted an *economic* optimum, to say nothing of agreeing that such an optimum was attainable. But since Carr-Saunders regards man's growth as wholly within his control and as conditioned by the attitudes of mind that he has developed under his institutions and the particular physical conditions of his life, his theory stands in sharp contrast to those which were based on natural law. Even so, the authors cannot agree with Carr-Saunders that man generally attained the optimum number as he defined it. Moreover, even if many popula-

[14] *Ibid.*, p. 35.
[15] Alexander Morris Carr-Saunders, *The Population Problem: A Study in Human Evolution,* Clarendon Press, Oxford, 1922, p. 476.

tions did attain such an optimum ("highest average return per head") this by no means proves that the positive checks—hunger, disease, and war—have not played a large part in determining man's actual growth.

Marx. Karl Heinrich Marx (1818–1883) was a German social philosopher who, with Friedrich Engels, became a founder of modern Communist theory. His theory of population was only incidental to his general theory that communism was the only cure for all man's economic hardships. The theory of population growth held by Marx has been placed last among the social theories noted here because it is at present of great practical importance. In a very real sense the appeal of communism as an economic cure-all rests on the doctrine that when this system is in operation there can be no poverty and hardship, regardless of the growth rate of the population. Marx *believed* that his view in this matter was exactly the opposite of that of Malthus. The word "believed" is used here because a study of Marx's views on population leads to the conclusion that Marx never took the trouble to examine Malthus's doctrines carefully. Indeed, it seems highly doubtful that he ever read more than a few passages from Malthus's first Essay and, probably, the preface to the second edition. As an extremist himself, with a panacea for all the world's ills, he attributed to Malthus the equally extreme view that all poverty and hardship were due solely to man's inherent tendency to grow in numbers faster than his production of subsistence would permit. He apparently never knew, and he certainly never acknowledged, that Malthus had considerably modified his views in the second and later editions of his Essay. In these editions, Malthus clearly recognized that the rate of man's growth in numbers was not determined solely by the growth of subsistence (see Chapter 2), although he insisted to the end that the passion between the sexes tended to make the rhythm of actual reproduction faster than the rhythm of increase in subsistence.

Marx, on the other hand, claimed that man's tendency to press on the means of subsistence was due solely to the evils of capitalism, which would disappear if his system—communism—were to be adopted. His most concise statement regarding a law of population follows:

> It is the working population which, while effecting the accumulation of capital, also produces the means whereby it is itself rendered relatively superfluous, is turned into a relatively surplus population; and it does so to an ever increasing extent. This is a law of population peculiar to the capitalist method of production; and, in fact, every method of production that arises in the course of history has its own peculiar, historically valid, law of population. It is only for plants and animals that there is a law of population in the abstract; and that only in so far as man does not interfere with them.[16]

[16] Karl Marx, *Capital. A Critique of Political Economy. The Process of Capitalist Production*, trans-

As this statement indicates, Marx held that poverty was entirely a consequence of unemployment or underemployment conditions due to the inability of the capitalistic system to provide jobs for all regardless of how fast new jobs were needed—that is to say, regardless of the speed with which population increased.

There can be no question of the sincerity of Marx's belief in the evils of capitalism as the sole basis of poverty, but it is hard to understand why he should have confined his efforts to discredit Malthus's views to personal ridicule and vilification.[17] Apparently, Marx must have had deep-seated doubts that Malthus's views could be sufficiently disposed of by an appeal to facts and reason. However, since the logic of his (Marx's) position demanded that he dispose of them, he chose the easiest way and attacked Malthus personally (arguments ad hominem).

An example or two of Marx's refutation of Malthus may interest the reader:

> The admirers of Malthus do not know that the first edition of the author's *Principle of Population* was—apart from its purely declamatory contents, mainly a transcription from Steuart (though Wallace and Townsend were additional sources).[18]

This charge of plagiarism is repeated in a note on diminishing returns in agriculture:

> . . . a theory which Malthus, a master of plagiarism (his whole theory of population is a shameless plagiarism) annexed in 1815.[19]

Again:

> If the reader should remind me of Malthus, whose Essay on Population was published in the year 1798, I should like to remind him that this work, in its first form, was nothing more than a school-boyish, superficial, and parsonic declamatory plagiarism from DeFoe, Sir James Steuart, Townsend, Franklin, Wallace and others; and did not contain a single sentence thought out by Malthus himself. It was nothing but partisan interest which directed so much attention to this pamphlet. The French revolution had found ardent defenders in the kingdom of Britain. The "principle of population," slowly elaborated during the eighteenth century, and then, during an extensive social crisis, proclaimed with drums and trumpets as the infallible antidote to Condorcet, etc., was greeted with acclamation by the English oligarchy as the great eradicator of all hankerings after human progress.

---

lated from the 4th German edition by Eden and Cedar Paul, International Publishers Company, Inc., New York, 1929, pp. 697–698.

[17] *Ibid.*, p. 679.

[18] *Ibid.*, p. 371, note. See also Malthus's statement regarding his predecessors quoted in the preceding chapter.

[19] *Ibid.*, p. 548.

Malthus, hugely astonished at his own success, now set himself to work once more, stuffing into the old framework of his book a lot of half-digested material gathered from various sources, with new matter not discovered by him but simply annexed. It should be further noted that . . . Malthus was a parson in the Church of England. . . . [20]

From this point on, this note of Marx very literally "rants" for a thousand words or more against parsons, apparently considering such an exhibition of his spleen against Malthus and parsons in general sufficient refutation of the *principle of population.* Clearly Marx, in an attempt to demolish Malthus's views on population, deemed personal abuse and invective quite sufficient for this purpose, as it no doubt was and is to his devout followers.

Thus, while there is not a clear statement of a Communist law of population in Marx's *Capital,* one must assume from the first quotation from Marx above that there is such a law and also that it is of a character diametrically opposed to Malthus's statement that population has a consistent tendency to increase faster than subsistence unless powerful preventive checks are operating. Marx must have believed either in some law of population growth peculiar to the Communist method of production, a law that automatically kept man's numbers from becoming excessive, or in the ability of the Communist method of production to give full employment and a good living to all able-bodied workers no matter how greatly or how fast their original number increased. This latter alternative appears the more likely.

Communist Population Doctrine Today. It appears that *doctrinaire* communism today maintains much the same general position regarding the relation of population growth and the economic system as did Marx, viz., that poverty is inevitable under capitalism, and that communism is the only remedy because it alone can guarantee to produce employment as fast as, or faster than, man can reproduce. This view, therefore, admits no need to worry about the increase of population under communism. Although one cannot be certain that the following quotations represent exactly the views of the highest authorities in the U.S.S.R., it seems highly probable that they do, and they seem to agree fully with Marx's position.

In 1947, at the United Nations Population Commission, the Soviet delegate, Mr. Rabichko, spoke unequivocally. "We consider any proposition formulated by this commission in favour of limiting marriages or births in wedlock as barbarous. Overpopulation is only a fruit of capitalism; an adequate social regime (socialism being understood), can meet any increase of population. It is the economy which should be adapted to the population, and not vice versa.

[20] *Ibid.,* pp. 679–680, note 3.

This view was often repeated, in almost identical terms (Malishev, Riabouchkin, (etc.) at other sessions of the same commission, at the Economic and Social Council and at the World Congress of Population in Rome in 1954.

"There cannot be any surplus population under a socialist regime, in spite of rapid demographic growth," says the Great Soviet Encyclopaedia. (Article on *Over-population*, vol. XXXII, 1955.)[21]

The continuously reiterated denunciation by the Communists of the poverty of the people in underdeveloped countries as arising out of their exploitation by capitalists and imperialists also follows the Marxian pattern, viz., that the growth of population will never become an economic problem in a communist state. The U.S.S.R. has at times seen fit to bestow handsome largesses on mothers of very large families, while at the same time permitting relatively easy abortion and the open sale of contraceptive materials. These actions suggest an official attitude of *laissez faire* as regards any public effort to control the birth rate. At present the birth rate in the U.S.S.R., as given by the United Nations (for the accuracy of which the United Nations assumes no responsibility), is about 25 per 1,000 and has hovered around this level since 1950. Hence, it has recently (1950–1960) been only about 1 to 1.5 per 1,000 higher than that of the United States. This too suggests that the government is following a hands-off policy. However, some uncertainty must remain as to the actual level of the birth rate in the U.S.S.R. as long as the government is so chary of publishing more detailed demographic data. Accepting the birth rate of the U.S.S.R. as 25 per 1,000, any experienced student of population would feel reasonably certain that contraception was now widely practiced in the U.S.S.R. At the time of the Revolution (1917), the birth rate in Russia was 40 per 1,000 or higher. As this book goes to press, there are rumors to the effect that the birth rate in the U.S.S.R. has fallen further—to perhaps 22 to 23 per 1,000. If this is so, it merely confirms the view just expressed.

It seems to the writers that communism, like all other utopian schemes, does not dare to admit the possible existence of any antagonism between the increase of subsistence and the actual growth of population. If communism admits this possibility, it can no longer claim that its particular utopian scheme for the elimination of poverty is the only and ultimate panacea. It would appear that a laissez-faire (hands-off) policy as regards population growth suits the U.S.S.R. today and is not considered inconsistent with the belief that the support of population will never become a problem in a communist state.

The attitude of the Chinese Communists toward Malthus's views will be discussed rather briefly in Chapter 21 (Population Policies).

[21] Alfred Sauvy, *Fertility and Survival, Population Problems from Malthus to Mao Tse-Tung*, Criterion Books, Inc., New York, 1961, pp. 201–202. Quoted by permission.

IS THERE A LAW OF POPULATION GROWTH?

The foregoing statement of population theories is, of course, incomplete and too brief to be very satisfactory, but the selection has been made with a definite purpose in mind: to show the two general types of theories that have predominated in the discussion of population growth since Malthus's day—*natural* theories and *social* theories. The former are based essentially on the belief that something inherent in the nature of man and/or the world in which he lives determines his growth at a rate and in a direction, largely or wholly, beyond his control. Many of the natural-law theorists except Malthus have said that the "naturally determined" rate of growth would lead to the most satisfactory balance between population and subsistence. This is apparently a seductive type of quest; social reformers and biologists, in particular, have appeared eager to find *the* law of population growth. Their belief seems to be that once this is discovered and is given definite expression, the search for causes that might be useful in the control of population growth may be abandoned because the deliberate control of the size of the family by each couple is not needed.

In the social theories of population growth, on the other hand, the underlying assumption is that population growth is not subject to some immutable natural law but is rather determined by man's inherited characteristics as developed in the total milieu (both physical and cultural) in which he lives. To one who accepts this view it would be folly to search for a simple natural law of population growth; what should receive attention is rather the factors which determine its growth at a particular time. The authors believe that the social theories are working in the right direction. This does not mean that Marx and George are any nearer right, except in their approach to the problem, than are Spencer and Doubleday. The man who has a particular panacea for all man's ills is quite as likely to misinterpret facts so that they fit into his scheme of redemption as is the man who believes he has discovered a law of nature. But it does seem reasonable to hold that the way to discover the dynamics of population growth at any given time and place and in any given group is to study the total environment of this population group in order to find the factors, if discoverable, which affect its birth and death rates as well as its fecundity. When these are found, then we can tell with considerable accuracy whether or not man in this particular group can exercise any effective control over his fertility, and we shall also probably gain light as to the methods by which control can be exercised. After all, social science can find its raison d'être only in the practical application of all its findings to the welfare of man.

No attempt will be made in this book to develop a complete theory of population. The chief factors in population growth in the modern world will be studied in some detail on the assumption that there is no *natural* biological law of population growth, but that the physical and social conditions of life determine this growth and that it varies from group to group as these conditions vary.

The points just noted can, perhaps, be made somewhat clearer by a brief statement of the most salient features of the theories described.

1. Initially, Malthus regarded man's nature, or that aspect of it he described as the passion between the sexes, as inevitably leading to such a high fertility that there would always be a severe conflict between his fertility and his ability to produce subsistence from his physical environment. Because of this conflict man had little chance of escape from the perpetual poverty and suffering resulting from the positive checks. Later he modified his theory by recognizing that man might be able to use preventive checks which would so reduce his fertility (not fecundity) that his hardships might be greatly reduced—largely by postponement of marriage and secondarily by continence within marriage. He never assumed, as many "natural" theorists did, that man's fecundity would diminish.

2. Sadler and Doubleday held that without any interference or control on man's part, certain changes in his physical environment would cause a diminution in his fecundity, and hence, in his fertility. Sadler believed that the growing density of population would work this change in fecundity, while Doubleday thought that an increasing abundance of food would have the same effect.

3. Spencer and Gini believed that the evolutionary changes in society were based on biological adaptations in man, and that such natural changes were decisive in their effects on cultural development. One of these decisive biological changes was a reduction in man's fecundity. Thus man had little or no control over his reproduction. An element of mysticism here absolves man from any need to concern himself with his rate of reproduction; the forces of evolution are quite beyond his control.

4. The social theorists, Henry George and Karl Marx, were utopians. They believed the social reforms they advocated would yield such marvelous economic returns that there was no need to give any attention to the growth of population, however rapid or large it might be. They may have believed that man, as his economic position improved, would exercise some voluntary control over his growth in numbers, but they certainly did not consider this essential under their proposed systems of social reform.

5. Dumont and Carr-Saunders focused their attention on man's voluntary control of his growth, which they believed he would exercise as prudential considerations more and more impressed upon him the need for smaller families if he would improve his economic status and at the same time attain a more satisfying personal development.

These different theories of population growth seem to be closely related to very strong currents of thought prevailing at the times they were promulgated. This is not in the least surprising, but it should warn us to go slow in claiming that the pattern(s) of population growth we see about us provide a "law" of growth. What seems to be sound doctrine today may not appear so sound even a few decades from now, to say nothing of a century hence.

SUGGESTIONS FOR SUPPLEMENTARY READING

Doubleday, Thomas: *The True Law of Population Shewn to Be Connected with the Food of the People*, 2d ed., George Pierce, London, 1847.

Dumont, Arsène: *La Morale basée sur la démographie*, Schleicher Frères, Paris, 1901.

George, Henry: *Progress and Poverty: An Inquiry into the Cause of Industrial Depressions and of Increase of Want with Increase of Wealth. The Remedy*, Doubleday, Doran & Company, Inc., New York, 1905.

Harris Foundation: *Population. Lectures on the Harris Foundation, 1929*, by Corrado Gini, . . . Shiroshi Nasu, . . . Robert R. Kuczynshi, . . . Oliver Edwin Baker, . . . , The University of Chicago Press, Chicago, 1930.

Levin, S. M.: "Marx vs. Malthus," *Papers of the Michigan Academy of Science, Arts, and Letters*, vol. 22, pp. 243–258, 1936.

Marx, Karl: *Capital. A Critique of Political Economy. The Process of Capitalist Production*, translated from the 4th German edition by Eden and Cedar Paul, International Publishers Company, Inc., New York, 1929.

Sadler, Michael Thomas: *Ireland: Its Evils and Their Remedies. Being a Refutation of the Errors of the Emigration Committee and Others, Touching That Country. To Which Is Prefixed a Synopsis of an Original Treatise About to Be Published on the Law of Population: Developing the Real Principle on Which It Is Universally Regulated*, 2d ed., John Murray (Publishers), Ltd., London, 1829.

Spencer, Herbert: *The Principles of Biology*, 2 vols., D. Appleton & Company, Inc., New York, 1867–1868.

PART TWO

The Composition of Population

CHAPTER FOUR

Introduction to the Composition of Population

Since we shall be talking about a good many different kinds of populations, we should make clear at the outset what we mean when we use the term "population" as a label for a human aggregate. In most instances we shall apply the term population to the total number of persons (usually residents) in a given area at a given time. Most of the populations named, described, and analyzed will be aggregates subject to the influences of the demographic processes of fertility, mortality, and migration. We shall look at such populations *in relation* to these processes, i.e., we shall see how a population is a *living* and *changing* organism—a product of demographic processes—and how, in turn, these processes are affected by the character and culture of the population.

POPULATION

What we mean by a population may become clearer if we explain that such aggregates of people as the audience at a drive-in theater or the members of the General Assembly of the United Nations are not populations in the sense that this text will use the term. They are not populations because their size and character are more immediately a result of economic, cultural, and political influences rather than of demographic influences. It is more meaningful to think of the size and character of the United States Senate, for example, as the product of political factors and processes than as the product of fertility, mortality, and migration. Population specialists rarely study this kind of purposeful grouping, which is organized to perform a particular social function.

Both students of population and laymen are familiar with the areas according with which populations are generally identified, such as cities, counties, states, provinces, regions, countries, and continents. Since some of these politically and geographically defined areas, such as cities and regions, are not defined in the same way by everyone who uses them, the student of population must exercise care when he makes comparisons, using these concepts. While it is true that politically defined areas are by far the most universally familiar, they are often unrelated to the natural groupings of population. Political boundary lines often cut through socioeconomic boundaries. Some political units, therefore, particularly within countries, are inadequate as categories for collecting and analyzing population data. As demography has developed, so has the need for more adequately defined areas, i.e., areas defined in ways that comprise the natural socioeconomic clusterings or groupings. To meet its needs in this respect, the United States Bureau of the Census has developed such categories as "enumeration district," "census tract," "urbanized area," and "standard metropolitan statistical area." These concepts will all be defined later in the text. None of these areas is a political or administrative unit. They were designed to provide the student of population with areas containing populations that "belong" together on the basis of various social, economic, or cultural characteristics or interrelationships. But for all this, the most frequently used populations will be those of countries such as the United States, Great Britain, and other political entities.

The reader who is familiar with the language of sociology knows that most of the aggregates studied by demographers cannot properly be called groups in the sociological sense. "Group" is applied by most sociologists only to those human collectivities within which there is observable communication, which are socially structured, and which have some sense of separate identity. Human collectivities which are treated as a unit but do not meet these criteria might more accurately be called categories, classes, or aggregates. Most of the populations we shall discuss, however, do not meet any of the qualifications which would characterize them sociologically as groups. In a recent census publication, for instance, the following are called groups: The United States, South, Urban, White, Negro, Other Nonwhite, Under 18 Years of Age, Single, and Married. Obviously, the census uses the term in its *statistical* rather than its sociological sense. The authors will also use "group" in this statistical sense; it would be awkward not to do so.

Sometimes a *part* of all the people in a city, state, or country is treated as a population. Examples of these "subpopulations" are the Negro population of the United States in 1960, the Catholic population of Cleveland, and the suburban population of Pennsylvania. Each of these categories can be treated as a population, because they have births and deaths, and some of their people migrate into or out of the area—that is, their characteristics as populations are directly influenced by the processes of fertility, mortality, and migration.

On occasion we shall refer to certain hypothetical populations. In Chapters 5 and 12, for example, we shall talk about life-table populations. Formal demographers, and others interested in problems related to population growth and change, use hypothetical populations to see what changes in age and sex distribution would result from different combinations of fertility and mortality rates. A recent book entitled *Population Growth and Economic Development in Low Income Countries* makes extensive use of this approach.[1] The various age and sex distributions that can result from different birth and death rates can then be related to such things as possible changes in the proportion of total population in the different age groups.

POPULATION CHARACTERISTICS

The characteristics that demographers could use to classify and describe the populations they study today are almost infinite in number. The development of modern industry and commerce is producing societies, and communities within larger societies, that are characterized by an increasingly complex division of labor. "Labor" is used here in the very broadest sense, to include all the social and economic activities that exist in any society. This kind of complexity and activity produces a great many attributes or characteristics. The number of these attributes and the proportion of people to whom they apply can be meaningfully used to describe these complex urban industrial populations. A relatively small, isolated, and slowly changing society is much less complex, and therefore the individuals in it have relatively few demographically significant characteristics. This developing socioeconomic complexity has served to increase greatly the differences between the communities within industrialized countries, as well as to increase the differences between the populations of different societies at various stages of economic and industrial development. Although the demographer deals with aggregates rather than with individuals or small groups, the items he uses to describe these aggregates (populations) are characteristics or traits which individual human beings possess. These characteristics have a connection with the demographic processes or are considered important by the society he is studying. Whether or not a characteristic is used in population studies depends also on whether it is capable of being identified and recorded accurately by those who collect the data used by demographers.

Since most of the population data presented in this book will come from United Nations publications or United States census publications, let us see what population characteristics they use. The following list was used in the census for 1960 in the United States.

---

[1] Ansley J. Coale and Edgar M. Hoover, *Population Growth and Economic Development in Low Income Countries*, Princeton University Press, Princeton, N.J., 1958.

Social characteristics
1. Sex
2. Age
3. Race
4. Color
5. Place of residence: rural, urban, etc.
6. Nativity
7. Place of birth
8. Parentage
9. Mother tongue of foreign born
10. School enrollment
11. Years of school completed
12. Veteran status
13. Marital status
14. Relationship to head of household
15. Children ever born

Economic characteristics
1. Employment status (employed, unemployed, armed forces)
2. Weeks worked in 1959
3. Occupation of worker
4. Industry worked in
5. Class of worker (private wage, government, self-employed, and unpaid family worker)
6. Place of work
7. Means of transportation to work
8. Income

The United Nations uses most of these characteristics and, in addition, others such as citizenship, religion, and literacy. The United Nations does not include veteran status, relationship to head of household, weeks worked in 1959, place of work, means of transportation to work, and income, some of which are obviously of concern only to the United States.

According to Amos Hawley (professor of sociology at the University of Michigan), the demographer is concerned with the composition of populations for the following four basic reasons.[2]

1. Data on composition make possible an elaboration of the description of a population and therefore permit detailed interpopulation comparisons.

2. Such data also constitute an inventory of the human resources of a society.

3. These data describe the variables [age, sex, marital status, etc.] essential for analyzing demographic processes, e.g., birth, death, migration, and growth. In the absence of direct information on demographic processes, composition data, particularly age and sex data, provide a means for estimating the incidence of birth and death.

4. Demographic variables, together with population size, are important conditions affecting the formation and change of social structure.

[2] Amos H. Hawley, "Population Composition," *The Study of Population*, ed. by Philip M. Hauser and Otis Dudley Duncan, The University of Chicago Press, Chicago, 1959, p. 361.

The characteristics of age, sex, race, and religion are familiar to all of us. Furthermore, we all know that communities differ with respect to some of these characteristics. But unless our attention is directed to the *significance* of these demographic differences, we are unlikely to recognize it. The authors hope to focus attention on certain demographic differences between communities, to show how social, economic, and political differences are related to the demographic ones, and to give the reader a basis for judging the relative significance or weight that should be assigned to given demographic facts when they are used to explain differences in social conditions between communities or within a given community.

The history of the United States offers some interesting demographic differences between communities. In its early years of settlement, the United States had a large preponderance of males in every part of the country. Only gradually, as the danger of Indian attack diminished, as the gold rush subsided, and as the land passed from the hands of speculators into those of cultivators, did the proportion of females increase until there was a near equality of numbers between the sexes. It is generally known that certain types of communities continue to attract a large proportion of males long after other types cease to do so. Communities in which mining is predominant, especially the mining of precious and semiprecious metals, and communities in which cattle ranching has been developed on a large scale, continue to maintain a high proportion of males after farming areas have been reduced to only a small preponderance of males, and long after cities have achieved a preponderance of females.

A moment's thought will lead to the further realization that most of these predominantly male communities are peculiar in another way: The people living in them are heavily concentrated in certain age and sex groups. Migrants to predominantly male areas are, as a rule, young adults ranging in age from the late teens to 35 or 40 years of age. Since there are relatively few women in these communities, there are also comparatively few children. There are also relatively few people over 45 years of age until settlement has been established for some years.

Moving from the past to the present, we come upon a relatively new type of community, with which most of you are familiar. It is quite interesting in its demographic makeup. It contains very few people over 40 years of age, a great number of people between the ages of 25 and 40 almost evenly divided between the sexes, practically no teenagers, and a great number of babies and children. You may have guessed that this community is a new residential suburb of modestly priced, relatively small, single-family homes, each with a small yard of its own. The age composition of these communities will change rapidly during the next two decades.

Communities vary in innumerable other ways, in addition to differing in the proportions of people who are male and female and who are in the different age groups as described in the above examples. There are larger proportions of first- and second-generation Central European peoples in New York and Cleveland than in Phoenix, Arizona; there is a greater proportion of Negroes in Washington, D.C., than in Detroit, Michigan; there is a larger proportion of Roman Catholics in Boston than in Minneapolis; a much larger proportion of Connecticut's population than of Iowa's is employed in industry.

The term "age and sex composition" applied to a community or a country refers to the manner in which the numbers and/or proportions of the population are distributed among the various age and sex categories. This arrangement is sometimes called the population structure. In the following chapter we shall see some graphic representations of different population structures. The mining community and the suburb described above obviously have very different structures. Such differences in age and sex distribution imply further differences—in birth rates, death rates, migration, and also in such phenomena as school attendance, prostitution, juvenile delinquency, and garden clubs.

Demographers traditionally have regarded age, sex, and race as biologically produced traits. Sex, age, and race (with reservations and qualifications which will be discussed at some length beginning on page 64) are three characteristics of individuals which are hereditary and unchangeable, i.e., neither the individual nor society can alter these qualities. However, most of the socially acquired traits or characteristics of individuals which are socially significant can be altered by the will and effort of the individual and the community in which he lives. If any population as a whole wishes to make a significant change in these physical characteristics, e.g., have a higher proportion of males or more young people, this can only be accomplished by changing the death rates of males relative to those of females, or those of young people as compared with those of older people, or by forbidding or encouraging certain types of persons to migrate. A change in demographic processes would have to take place. On the other hand, changes in the proportion of the population having certain social characteristics, such as a college education, can be effected by strengthening the educational inducements and opportunities.

SOCIAL ORGANIZATION AND CULTURE

Sociologists and anthropologists who study the way a society works view it as a complex organization of "statuses" or positions, all of which must be occupied by enough individuals who are adequately trained for the "roles" (or jobs) that the statuses require and sufficiently motivated to do the required work. Perhaps the concept of status will be more significant if we give the names of a few positions. The first that come to your mind may be occupations such as doctor, lawyer, teacher, machinist, secretary, etc. But when we speak of the way a society "works," we mean nearly everything that is done by the members of a society. In addition to occupational statuses, there are others such as man, woman, boy, girl, mother, father, senior citizen, political party member, high school student, scoutmaster, etc. Statuses vary as to what they encompass, the nature of their duties and privileges, the importance society attaches to them, the method of recruiting occupants, and the significance they have for membership in other statuses.

Ralph Linton, one of the most outstanding anthropologists in the United States, was the first to point out one of the major *kinds* of differences among statuses. He divided statuses into two categories, ascribed and achieved. Ascribed statuses are those which an individual occupies by virtue of certain characteristics over which he has no control—e.g., the statuses of male, female, adult, Negro, ascribed to individuals on the basis of their sex, age, family, "race," etc. Achieved statuses are those which are open to individual choice, and into which an individual may move as a result of some effort on his part. Societies vary a great deal in the degree to which they rely on one or the other method for filling their social statuses. In the United States, great emphasis is placed on the achieved statuses; in India, while the caste system was in full force, the social structure was made up largely of ascribed statuses based on age, sex, and caste. In no society are all statuses filled exclusively by one or the other of these methods; there is bound to be some achieving in a caste system and some ascription in an open-class system. There are advantages and disadvantages in each method. The ascribed method largely ignores the range of individual differences in potential and assumes that most "jobs" will be done well enough if left in the hands of certain classes. It works best in stable, slowly changing, pre-industrial societies. The achieved method makes possible the development and utilization of individual talents, permits adjustment to rapid social change, but runs the risk of leaving some statuses unfilled and of having others filled by individuals who are not adequately prepared psychologically or otherwise to do what is required of them.

Moreover, in an open-class society such as the United States, a person's ascribed status may limit the number and kind of statuses he can achieve. In the United States, the physician's status is an achieved one, but females, Negroes, and the foreign born have a much harder time achieving it (all other things being equal) than do the native-born white males in the society.

In trying to understand a human society, then, we need to know both what its physical composition is, i.e., the number and proportion of its population in the various age, sex, and race groups, *and* we need to know also what the society believes to be true about age, sex, and race. No society views these various categories solely from the point of view of what is known to be scientifically true about them. Physical facts establish the *limits* of human behavior, but physical facts themselves do not *determine* the behavior. For example, while no country can have a labor force larger than the total number of able-bodied people in its population, it might employ only a fraction of that total if its social norms more or less disqualify females, all males under 15 and over 65, and certain other categories based on family, rank, etc., from various types of labor.

AGE AND SEX

The authors view age and sex as physiological variables, and also as variables which have great social and cultural significance. Consequently, we are interested in the effects of the age and sex composition upon the social organization and life of a people, as well as their effect on fertility and mortality rates. These effects are partly a consequence of the biological facts of age and sex and partly of the way a society regards age and sex. Anthropologists have taught us that *every society uses* the attributes of age and sex in one way or another for sorting its population into the various groups considered essential to its orderly operation. Every society believes that what it expects of each age and sex category is "natural," and hence develops cultural patterns—systems of beliefs and attitudes—that rationalize, as biologically necessary and inevitable, its requirements of each age and sex group. But a great many, perhaps most, behavioral and attitudinal differences in functions assigned to the sexes are customary rather than biologically necessary. How else should we explain the fact that most of the physicians in the U.S.S.R. are females, whereas in the United States they are predominantly males, and that Hopi Indian men spin cotton and do the weaving while among their neighbors, the Navahos, women do these tasks?

Societies vary greatly in the extent to which they elaborate their behavior requirements of age and sex groups beyond what is biologically necessary. However, the fact that some age and sex differences in behavior cannot be accounted for in biological terms does not mean that they do not have tremendous biological and demographic significance. What we believe about biological facts may be more important than the facts themselves.

If a society believes that women are not ready for marriage and procreation until the age of 20, very few babies will be born to women under 20. Every society has prescribed age and sex categories that are to some degree functional—that is, some of the behavior requirements fit the biological differences associated with age and sex. While age and sex themselves are largely beyond the individual's or his society's determination, the *attention* paid to them, and the *meaning* given to them vary considerably from society to society and among the various parts of a society. But in spite of all these cultural differences in the functions assigned to sex and age groups, such groups are basic to all demographic study.

Nevertheless, the physical characteristics of age and sex are the central demographic variables. Formal demographers still deal almost exclusively with observed or calculated variations in these two variables, relating age and sex composition to variations in fertility, mortality, and migration. It is easy to see why some demographers prefer to use only the atrributes of age and sex, since the reciprocal relationships between the age and sex structure of a given population on the one hand, and rates of fertility and mortality on the other, can be worked out mathematically, using very few assumptions. In this way important advances have been made toward understanding the nature of the interdependence of these variables. Using advanced statistical techniques, demographers can investigate questions that have both theoretical and practical importance. One such question could be the following: What changes would take place in the age and sex composition of Ceylon during the next 10 years if the death rate for each age remained constant at its present level but the birth rate at each age of women, 15 to 19, 20 to 24, etc., dropped at a given rate per year during the next 10 years? Another such question might be: What would happen to the age composition if Ceylon's age-specific birth rates remained the same but the death rates at certain ages dropped at specified rates per year during the next 10 years? Coale and Hoover consider questions like these in their book referred to earlier. In dealing with such hypothetical situations, however, it is important to beware of mistaking our assumptions for facts and our models for pictures of reality.

RACE

"Race" is a most ambiguous, controversial, and explosive concept the world over. The authors believe, therefore, that the use of race as a major demographic variable needs some explanation. From a biological point of view, race is similar to age and sex in that one's racial identity is a physical fact that neither the individual nor society can alter; it is a matter of biological inheritance. Furthermore, indications of an individual's racial identity are, as are differences in age and sex, assumed to be revealed in visible differences. But before going any further we must distinguish between race as a biological concept and race as a social concept. There is bound to be confusion when the same word—race—means different things to different people. Most of the groups called races by the public are not races at all in the sense of being true biological categories.

Race As a Biological Concept. Anthropologists and biologists, using biologically inherited traits as their criteria for classifying the human species into smaller units, generally accept three major divisions of mankind which are more or less arbitrary: (1) Caucasoid, people who until modern times lived in Europe, Southwest Asia, and in Africa north of the Sahara, (2) Mongoloid, found mainly in Asia, the Pacific islands, and in the Western Hemisphere (American Indians), (3) Negroid, originally confined to Africa but now found in considerable numbers in the Western Hemisphere. These three categories, variously called subspecies, stocks, or races, represent geographic populations, described in terms of the biological traits of skin color and hair type. The Caucasoid or "white" are described as having light skin ranging from very fair to brown, abundant body hair, and wavy hair on the head. The Mongoloid or "yellow" are described as being from light brown to brown, with a slight amount of body hair, and the hair of the head black and straight. The Negroid or "black" are described as being from yellowish to dark brown, with a slight amount of body hair, and the hair of the head black and tightly curled. There are some populations whose classification is doubtful, such as the Polynesians and the Australian aborigines. In recent years geneticists have developed more refined classifications. Both anthropologists and biologists would insist that race is based on *biologically inherited traits* and that the three broad racial categories just noted are based on gross averages, there being greater range of biological variation *within* these races than there is *between* the races. For example, the Negroid population includes both the tallest and the shortest people in the world as well as many who are lighter in skin color than some Caucasians. Our main purpose in noting the biological approach to race is to point out the kinds of categories which are *not* our concern. Few demographic studies have been done on races as defined biologically, because biological "boundary lines" do not coincide with actual social groupings. Some of the populations which we shall discuss will fall within racial categories, but many of them cut across the biological lines of the racial categories. While scientists can classify people into "stocks," and further subdivide these into races on the basis of biologically transmitted characteristics, these characteristics do not biologically determine other kinds of traits. We now know that a man's biological race has nothing to do with the language he speaks, the nationality or culture he honors and lives by, nor the religion he follows. The biological groupings devised by the scientist to help him solve problems of human evolution and migration have no connection with the political, social, economic, and residential groupings that men form, identify themselves with, and have recently come to regard as races. The anthropological position is made clear in the following quotation:

The concept of race is unanimously regarded by anthropologists as a classificatory device providing a zoological frame within which the various groups of mankind may be arranged and by means of which studies of evolutionary processes can be facilitated. . . . National, religious, geographical, linguistic, and cultural groups do not necessarily coincide with racial groups; and the cultural traits of such groups have no demonstrated connexion with racial traits.[3]

Social Concept of Race. In his recent book, *Race, Class, and Power*, Professor Mack says,

> Race in the biologist's sense has no biologically caused consequences, but what men *believe* about race has social consequences. In other words, most of men's discussions about race are discussions of their beliefs, not biological facts. Most of men's actions about race are based on what they have been taught to believe about it, not on what scientists know about it.[4]

To make this point clear, Professor Mack goes on to say,

> Many Negroes in the United States have more Caucasoid ancestry than Negroid, but they are still considered Negro if they are known to have had a Negro ancestor. This is pure social definition and pure biological nonsense. In no other area of biology would we reason similarly. Imagine a dog breeder saying, "Most of this pup's forebears were cocker spaniels, but he's really a Doberman pinscher"— meaning that one of his great-grandparents was.[5]

The criteria by which men identify racial groups vary from time to time, within a given society and from society to society. Physical characteristics such as skin color and hair color are used, but many nonbiological characteristics such as nationality, language, religion, and dress are also used. For example, many people erroneously consider the following to be the names of racial groups: English, Latin, Sikh, Jew, Japanese, German, Arab, Creole. None of these are biological races. They are a mixture of classifications: language (English and Latin), religion (Sikh and, to some extent, Jew), citizenship or nationality (Japanese and German), common geographic location (Arab), common culture and tradition (Creole). At no time have societies used the racial categories defined by biologists—and for a good reason: The biological concept of race is a statistical category having no social reality whatsoever. The authors do not intend to imply that there is no connection between physical characteristics and human groupings. If you were to travel from one geographic area to another (from Italy to Norway, or from Vladivostok to London), you would find differences in physical appearance, dress, language, religion, food habits, architectural styles, and music. If the human species had been less migratory, a given geographic area would probably be occupied by a population that would be rela-

[3] Juan Comas, "'Scientific' Racism Again?" *Current Anthropology*, vol. 2, no. 4, p. 304, October, 1961. This quotation is from a text prepared by physical anthropologists and geneticists at UNESCO House, Paris, June 8, 1951.
[4] Raymond W. Mack, *Race, Class, and Power*, American Book Company, New York, 1963, p. 91.
[5] *Ibid.*, p. 92.

tively homogeneous racially, sharing a common culture, speaking the same language, and participating in the same religious observances. But because people have moved around so much (especially in Europe) there is no clear-cut, consistent connection between racial, geographic, linguistic, religious, and cultural characteristics.

The American Negro provides an excellent example of this lack of congruence among the various sociological boundary lines: his ancestry is largely Negroid; he speaks English; he is a native-born American; his culture is American; and he is found in all the major religious denominations. The American Negro, then, can be classified according to several overlapping but biologically unconnected points of view. Scientifically, the concept of race is clearly distinguished from other geographic and cultural concepts. To further confound an already thoroughly confusing situation, the social definitions of what a Negro is may differ not only from country to country but also *within* a country. For example, many people considered "white" in Brazil would be "Negro" in the United States. One great-grandparent Negro and seven great-grandparents white defines a person as a Negro in some states of the United States.

The United States Census Definition of Race. The United States Bureau of the Census follows the social rather than the scientific definition of race.[6]

> The concept of race, as used by the Bureau of the Census, is derived from that which is commonly accepted by the general public. It does not, therefore, reflect clear-cut definitions of biological stock, and several categories obviously refer to national origin. Three major racial groups—white, Negro, and "other races"—are shown separately in several of the census reports. . . .
>
> *Color.*—the term "color" refers to the division of the population into two groups, white and nonwhite. Persons of Mexican birth or ancestry who are not definitely of Indian or other nonwhite race are classified as white. . . .
>
> *Negro.*—In addition to the persons of Negro and of mixed Negro and white descent, this classification, according to instructions to enumerators, includes persons of mixed American Indian and Negro descent, unless the Indian ancestry very definitely predominates or unless the individual is regarded as an Indian in the community. . . .
>
> *Mixed parentage.*—Persons of mixed racial parentage are classified according to the race of the nonwhite parent, and mixtures of nonwhite races are classified according to the race of the father, with the special exceptions noted above.

Although the definitions used by the census are not zoologically valid, they reflect *social* reality. They recognize lines of *social* cleavage; the census recognizes

[6] U.S. Bureau of the Census, *U.S. Census of Population: 1960, General Population Characteristics*, United States Summary, Final Report PC(1)-1B, 1961, pp. x and xi.

that a "color line" is drawn in the United States. The categories used by the census are white and nonwhite. The nonwhite category is subdivided into Negro and other races. Other races include Indian, Japanese, Chinese, Filipino, and a residual category called all other.

Why Is the Student of Population Interested in "Race"? Nearly every racially mixed society uses "racial differences" (along with age and sex) as criteria for the ascription of status, i.e., for establishing the degree of an individual's eligibility to occupy various social, economic, and political statuses. In many societies a person's racial status determines where he can live, what occupations he can enter, and how much political power he can exercise. As a member of a discriminated-against racial group, he may not only be denied certain statuses but he may even be denied the opportunity to struggle for them. Although the situation is changing rapidly in the United States, it is still true that Negroes are denied the right to vote in many areas of the South, are not allowed to buy or rent homes in the open market in most cities, and are not employed as teachers in predominantly white schools even when they are otherwise qualified. Societies which use race as a basis for such judgments generally believe that racially delimited opportunities are made necessary by biological differences and are not a matter of unreasonable prejudice. Some racially mixed societies, however, largely ignore racial differences in deciding who may occupy the statuses which comprise their social organizations. They do not consider the racial differences to be socially relevant. Brazil and Hawaii, for instance, pay much less attention to a person's racial characteristics than to his occupation, educational level, and general style of life.

NATIONAL AND ETHNIC POPULATIONS

Many populations that are called races would be more accurately described if they were labeled nationalities or ethnic groups. The term "ethnic" refers to such people as the Irish and the Gypsies, who are identified on the basis of a common culture and who therefore have a sense of collective identity. These groups may also share a common language and religion, and occupy a given piece of territory (at least at some time in their history). An ethnic population may or may not be a nationality in the sense of having a political as well as a cultural identity. Some national and ethnic groups *think* of themselves as having a common biological ancestry. The term ethnic correctly applies to such populations as Poles, Hungarians, Gypsies, Jews, Amish, French Canadians, Mexicans, Italians, Slovaks, and Afrikaners. To the casual observer, French Canadians appear to be physically different from Mexicans, and Poles seem to differ physically from Italians; these populations, however, are cultural communities rather than racial units. An ethnic or national population may be made up only of members of a particular race, or it may cut across several racial categories. An individual's membership in an ethnic category is nearly always a matter of birth rather than of choice or achievement; in this respect ethnicity is similar to age, sex, and race. The characteristics used to identify ethnic or national groups are cultural characteristics such as language, manner of dress, food habits, and religious observances. These traits are learned; they are socially, not biologically, transmitted from generation to generation. In this text "ethnic" and "national" will often be used interchangeably.

In some countries the proportions of the total population belonging in different racial and ethnic categories are very important—socially, economically, and politically. Countries (as well as communities within countries) vary considerably in the degree to which they are racially or culturally homogeneous. In almost every country today there are subpopulations that differ from the politically dominant population racially or culturally. These subpopulations are often very important to the student of population, because societies attach significance to the racial and cultural differences involved, and because there are often demographic differences among the racial and cultural groups.

Racial and Ethnic Minorities. If the politically and economically dominant segment of a society regards those who are racially or culturally different as inferior, and discriminates against them on this basis, the living conditions imposed on these "different" groups will affect their composition and their demographic processes. If such minorities are discriminated against in education and in the labor market, the discrimination will have an effect on their fertility and mortality. As the proportions of these populations change, we also expect certain changes in other aspects of the country's composition. And as a minority's economic and social position in the total society improves, the demographic differences between the minority and the larger society are likely to decrease. Variations in the proportions of minorities are often related to many other important population differences among communities. Furthermore, if racial, national, or ethnic minorities have cultures that differ from the society's dominant culture, and if these minority cultures require behavior that affects birth rates, death rates, migration, or occupation, the demographer is obliged to take these minorities into account.

Minorities which are *only* ethnically different from the dominant group in a society can disappear in a generation or two, but populations which are racially different cannot lose their physical distinctiveness. In the United States, many ethnic groups have already lost their culturally distinctive characteristics. On the other hand, the descendants of Negroes who came to the United States many generations ago are ethnically American but are still regarded as a distinct population segment because they cannot change their physical characteristics.

Second- and third-generation Japanese in the United States may be largely American culturally and still be set apart because of their biologically inherited traits.

Most ethnic populations in the United States strive to become culturally indistinguishable from native Americans and resent any hindrances placed in their way. In Europe, however, the situation is different; many of the ethnic and nationality populations take pride in maintaining their separate cultural identities and resist attempts at eliminating cultural differences. In spite of the forced migrations that occurred during and after World War II, some countries in Central Europe still contain quite a few people who speak languages different from the language of the politically dominant population. Many of these ethnic minorities feel more loyalty to the nations whose language they speak than to the nation in whose territory they reside. Under these circumstances, the numbers and proportions of ethnic and nationality populations living within different countries become matters of prime importance.

United Nations demographic publications and United States census publications both contain data on nationality and ethnic composition, although the data are not directly comparable. In addition to data on "country of citizenship," which are quite similar to the United States' "nativity" data, the United Nations presents data on "country of birth," "language," "ethnic group (race)," and "religion."[7] The *Demographic Yearbook* explicitly recognizes a terminological confusion when it says,

> Although grouped for convenience under a single title [population by ethnic composition and sex], the data shown in this table are actually classified into single or combined categories of race, religion, color, stock, ethnic origin, or ethnic nationality (as distinct from legal nationality). . . . Statistics on ethnic groups, which as will be seen below may represent a variety of concepts, are useful as one facet of the "ethnic composition" picture. Although it is impossible to define these concepts precisely, the terms remain in use in national statistics and find application in analysing national data. . . . The data have their greatest utility . . . at the national level where the concepts and connotations are clearly understood.[8]

The United States census publications do not have any information on the country of citizenship of the population of the United States, but their "place of birth" data make possible the following classifications: "native-born," "foreign-born" (by country), "native-born of foreign or mixed parentage." In the 1960 census, the last two categories were combined into "foreign stock," comprising all first- and second-generation Americans. The foreign-born population was

---

[7] *Demographic Yearbook 1956*, Statistical Office of the United Nations, New York, 1956, pp. 32 and 33.
[8] *Ibid.*, p. 32.

also classified on the basis of answers to the following question: What language was spoken in your home before you came to the United States? In the United States census the native-born and foreign-born populations are subdivided on the basis of "race" and "color."

Census data show significant demographic differences among racial and ethnic categories. When demographers classify a population on the basis of race (that is, race socially defined), the question arises as to whether any of the demographic differences among the racial groups are biological in origin. Most members of the dominant group are willing to believe that the differences in mortality, education, etc., between themselves and other racial and ethnic groups have some kind of biological basis. Scientists cannot say unequivocally whether such differences reflect innate variations, but many people still regard them as evidence of *innate* physical and intellectual differences among the groups involved. The authors believe that racial and ethnic differences are socially relevant to the division of labor today, and that many demographic differences between racial and cultural minorities and dominant groups are the result of an unequal distribution of opportunities, based upon race and ethnicity. Racial and cultural minorities do not fully share the environment of the dominant population. The authors believe that differences in occupation and intelligence test scores are *associated* with racial differences, but are not *caused* by race differences.

The demographic significance of racial and ethnic differences will be discussed primarily in relation to the United States. The United States probably has more racial and cultural strains than any other country in the world, although it does not have a monopoly on racial and ethnic problems. If racial or cultural criteria divide a population into categories, these divisions are social facts and must be recognized. When the authors use racial categories, it will be with the understanding that these categories do not represent clear-cut biological divisions of mankind.

In this chapter we have emphasized age, sex, race, color, nativity, nationality, and ethnicity because these variables involve a combination of biological and cultural elements, and because they are ambiguous terms which arouse strong emotional reactions. We shall now proceed to present data regarding the composition of populations.

SUGGESTIONS FOR SUPPLEMENTARY READING

Aird, John S.: *The Size, Composition and Growth of the Population of Mainland China,* U.S. Bureau of the Census, International Population Statistics Reports, ser. P-90, no. 15, 1961.

Bennett, John W., and Melvin M. Tumin: *Social Life: Structure and Function,* Alfred A. Knopf, Inc., New York, 1948. (Particularly the following chapters: "The Condition of Man," "Functional Prerequisites of Continuous Social Life," "Status and Role: I," and "Status and Role: II." The last two are an expansion of Linton's original formulation.)

Bogue, Donald J., and Wilson H. Grabill: *The Population of the United States*, The Free Press of Glencoe, New York, 1959.

Hawley, Amos H.: "Population Composition," in Philip M. Hauser and Otis Dudley Duncan (eds.), *The Study of Population*, The University of Chicago Press, Chicago, 1959.

Linton, Ralph: *The Study of Man: An Introduction*, D. Appleton-Century Company, Inc., New York, 1936. (Particularly the following chapters: "Society," "Status and Role," and "The Raw Materials for Society.")

Taeuber, Conrad, and Irene B. Taeuber: *The Changing Population of the United States*, John Wiley & Sons, Inc., New York, 1958.

CHAPTER FIVE

Age and Sex Composition of Populations

Countries differ greatly in the way their populations are distributed in the various age and sex categories. Because the age and sex groups of a population aggregate are the building blocks that go into the construction of a society, the age and sex composition of a society is important both biologically and socially. The relative proportions of males and females and the proportions of the various age groups in a country at a given time are the result of the preceding 100 years of births, deaths, and migration. First we shall compare the sex distribution of selected populations without regard to age; then we shall compare the age distributions of these populations without regard to sex; finally, we shall see how these populations differ with respect to the proportions of each sex in the various age categories.

SEX COMPOSITION

Calculation of the Sex Ratio. The most common measure used to show the balance of the sexes in a population is the "sex ratio." The sex ratio is the number of males per hundred females; it is obtained by dividing the total number of males by the total number of females and multiplying the result by 100. (Some countries calculate their sex ratios so as to arrive at the number of women per hundred men.) It can be calculated for a total population, or for any given part of a population. In a population with an equal number of males and females, the sex ratio is 100; with more males than females, it is over 100; and with fewer males than females it is less than 100. A relative number like the sex ratio is valuable, because it permits us to make a direct comparison of the sex compositions of all distinguishable population groups regardless of size, of place of residence, of racial composition, and of time. Although proportions or percents would be just as useful and could be calculated just as easily, it has become conventional to use the sex ratio for this purpose.

In all the countries for which we have data there are more male than female births. In the urban-industrial countries where prenatal losses are low, the sex ratio at birth is generally around 105, but in those countries where prenatal losses are high, the sex ratio varies around 102 in spite of the fact that females are more likely to be underregistered than males. It is generally true that males have a higher death rate than females. In urban-industrial countries where the birth rate is moderate to low, where the maternal death rate is low, and where girl babies are as well cared for as boy babies, the male death rates are higher than the female death rates at *every age*. The initial numerical excess of the males is progressively cut down until in the older ages females outnumber males; thus the sex ratio for most populations when not affected by migration is near 100— or, more likely, slightly below 100. This general pattern does not hold true for some populations, because of certain "distorting" events. For example, the sex ratio for a population may be higher than we have said because of (1) net out-migration of females, (2) net in-migration of males, (3) anything that produces relatively high *female* mortality, and (4) errors in the data, e.g., underreporting of females or overreporting of males. The sex ratio may be lower because of (1) net in-migration of females, (2) net out-migration of males, (3) excessive male deaths, as in the case of war, and (4) errors in the data.

International Comparisons. Let us compare the sex ratios for some of the countries for which data are available. Table 5-1 shows how sex ratios can vary from one country to another, from a high in excess of 110 in a few countries such as Ceylon and Pakistan to a low of approximately 80 in East Germany and the U.S.S.R. The sex ratio of the United States (97.1) is higher than most of the European countries and lower than most of the Asian. Demographers (for reasons discussed in the above paragraph) consider that the usual sex ratios for national aggregates are between 95 and 100, and that any ratio outside this range calls for an explanation. The abnormally low sex ratios of East Germany and the U.S.S.R. have resulted from war deaths and, in the case of East Germany, also from a net out-migration of males. The high sex ratios of Ceylon (111.5) and Pakistan (111.0) cannot be so satisfactorily explained. These high ratios may be a result of a combination of excessive female mortality during early childhood and at the beginning of childbearing, and also of faulty data; in the case of Pakistan, more Muslim males than females probably survived the ordeal of the partition of Pakistan from India. Most of the European countries have sex ratios below 95; most of the Asian countries are over 100; Africa's ratios are variable, and are based largely on unreliable data.

United States: Geographic Divisions. Table 5-2 presents the sex ratios of the United States and its geographic regions and divisions for 1850, and for each decade from 1900 to 1960. Figure 5-1 shows how the census divides the United

TABLE 5-1.   SEX RATIO OF THE POPULATION AND SEX RATIO AT BIRTH. SELECTED COUNTRIES AND TERRITORIES: LATEST DATE AVAILABLE

Regions and country or territory	Total population		At birth	
	Date	Sex ratio	Date	Sex ratio
Africa:				
Algeria (Muslim)...........	1954	102.9	1956*	109.0
Mozambique..............	1950	91.7	1957*	105.3
America, North:				
Canada..................	1956	102.8	1958	105.8
United States.............	1960	97.1	1957	105.1
Mexico..................	1960	99.5	1957	106.4
America, South:				
Argentina................	1960†	100.6	1958†	103.8
Chile...................	1960†	96.2	1956	102.8
Asia:				
Ceylon..................	1953	111.5	1957*	103.2
Formosa.................	1956	103.8	1958	105.9
India...................	1961†	106.3	1957*	110.6
Japan...................	1960†	96.5	1958†	105.5
Pakistan.................	1961	111.0	1953*	115.5
China (Mainland)..........	1953	107.6	———	———
Europe:				
Bulgaria.................	1956	99.6	1958	105.7
France..................	1954	92.2	1958	104.5
Germany				
East..................	1950	80.2	1958*	106.9
Federal Republic.........	1956	88.3	1958†	106.7
Italy...................	1961†	96.1	1957	105.5
Netherlands..............	1947	99.1	1958†	105.6
Poland..................	1960†	93.6	1958†	106.8
Sweden.................	1960	99.5	1958†	106.8
Switzerland..............	1960†	94.1	1958	105.5
United Kingdom..........	1961†	93.7	1958	105.9
U.S.S.R.................	1959	81.9	———	———

* Data are unreliable or of unknown completeness.
† Provisional.
Source: United Nations, *Demographic Yearbook, 1959, 1960,* and *1961.*

States into the four geographic *regions* and the nine geographic *divisions*. (If you do not know into which divisions the 50 states fall, and if you do not learn it from this map, you will need to refer to it many times as you progress through this text.) The country is becoming much more homogeneous with respect to the balance of the sexes. If we compare the sex ratios of the four geographic regions for 1850 to 1960, the reductions in the differences among them show up very clearly. The differences among the nine divisions have become much smaller over the years, and the Mountain and Pacific divisions have had consistently the highest ratios. Areas of more recent settlement are those with the higher sex ratios. In 1850, almost three out of four people in the West were male. As the

TABLE 5-2.   SEX RATIO OF THE POPULATION OF THE UNITED STATES, BY REGION AND DIVISION: 1900–1960 AND 1850

Geographic region and division	Year							
	1960*	1950	1940	1930	1920	1910	1900	1850
Northeast:...............	94.7	96.1	98.6	100.0	100.6	102.3	100.0	101.2
New England............	95.0	95.7	97.0	97.2	98.5	99.3	97.7	99.1
Middle Atlantic..........	94.5	96.2	99.1	100.9	101.4	103.3	100.9	102.2
North Central:............	97.4	99.5	102.0	104.2	105.9	107.5	106.6	108.7
East North Central......	97.3	99.3	101.9	104.1	105.7	106.0	104.7	108.3
West North Central......	97.7	100.1	102.1	104.2	106.1	109.9	109.7	110.7
South:....................	97.0	98.5	99.6	100.9	102.6	103.2	102.4	102.8
South Atlantic..........	97.1	98.2	99.1	99.6	101.2	101.2	100.0	100.3
East South Central.......	96.2	97.9	99.1	100.2	101.1	101.9	101.9	103.5
West South Central......	97.4	99.5	100.8	103.3	105.8	107.2	106.7	112.7
West:....................	100.6	102.1	105.7	109.5	114.6	128.9	128.1	278.9
Mountain..............	101.2	104.4	107.4	111.3	115.7	127.9	128.0	107.5
Pacific.................	100.4	101.4	105.0	108.7	113.9	129.5	128.2	778.5
United States.............	97.1	98.6	100.7	102.5	104.0	106.0	104.4	104.3

* Includes Alaska and Hawaii.
    Source: U.S. Bureau of the Census, *U.S. Census of Population: 1960, General Population Characteristics, United States Summary*, p. 1-165; other years from earlier censuses.

sex ratio went down, so did the swinging saloon doors, the gun toting, the lynching, the wide-open gambling, and the prostitution. The areas that have been settled the longest had relatively low sex ratios even in 1850.

United States: Trends in Sex Ratios. During the 90-year period from 1810 to 1900, the sex ratio ranged from a low of 102.2 in 1870 to a high of 104.4 in 1900.[1] In 1910 it reached its highest point, 106. It has declined steadily ever since,

[1] Donald J. Bogue, *Population of the United States*, The Free Press of Glencoe, New York, 1959, p. 153.

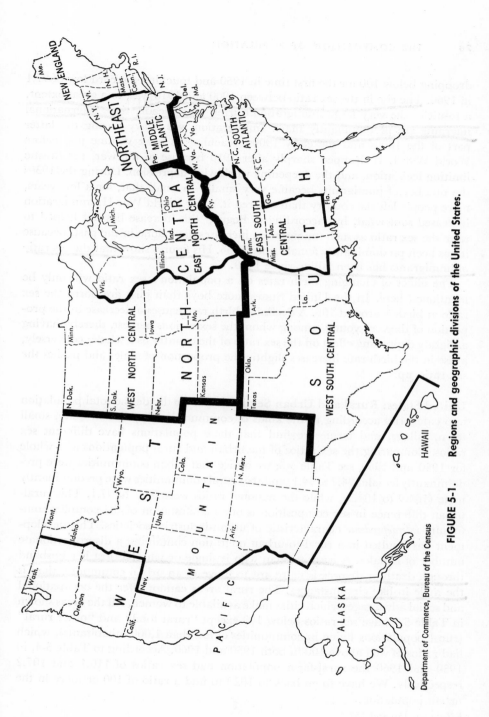

FIGURE 5-1. Regions and geographic divisions of the United States.

Department of Commerce, Bureau of the Census

dropping below 100 for the first time in 1950 and touching a record low of 97.1 in 1960. The rise in the sex ratio between 1900 and 1910 was, to a great extent, a result of the very large immigration during that decade, since international migrants are predominantly male. Immigration was heavy during the latter part of the 1800s and the early 1900s, reaching its peak volume just before World War I. It dropped sharply after 1910 because of the war, the drastic limiting legislation, and the deepening worldwide depression. During the 1930s the number of immigrants became very small—so small that, for a few years, more people left the country than entered it. After World War II, immigration increased somewhat, but according to Bogue,[2] this increase has not helped to raise the sex ratio as such immigration increases have done in the past, because it has been predominantly female since 1936. His figures show that the sex ratio of immigrants has been falling since 1910.

The effect of changing birth rates on a population's sex ratio will only be mentioned here. In the United States more boys than girls are born; the sex ratio at birth is around 105. A declining birth rate causes a decrease in the proportion of the very young, among whom the sex ratio is highest, thereby having a slightly depressing effect on the sex ratio of the country as a whole; conversely, a rise in the birth rate increases slightly the proportion of males and pushes the sex ratio up.

United States: Rural and Urban Sex Ratios. If we divide the total population into categories according to the kinds of communities they live in—city, small town, village, and farm—we find that these populations have different sex ratios. Comparing the sex ratios of the urban and rural populations as a whole for 1950 and 1960, see Table 5-3, we notice that urban communities were predominantly female (94.7 to 94.1) and that rural communities were predominantly male (104.9 to 104.3), while the national ratios were 98.7 to 97.1. This rural-urban difference in sex composition is one manifestation of the complex community *interdependence* characteristic of urban-industrial societies. This development has resulted in a rural-to-urban migration containing a disproportionate number of females. A rural woman who is single or who has lost her husband through death or divorce is more apt to move to an urban community than is the male in like circumstances. The rural areas cannot offer the occupational and social advantages which cities make available to women. All the areas shown in Table 5-3 have sex ratios below 100 except "rural total" and "other rural" (rural populations living in communities of less than 1,000 inhabitants), which had ratios of well above 100 in both 1950 and 1960. According to Table 5-4, in 1950 and 1960 the rural-farm population had sex ratios of 110.1 and 107.2 respectively. We have to go back to 1920 to find a ratio of 100 or more in the urban population.

[2] *Ibid.*, pp. 156 and 157.

TABLE 5-3.   SEX RATIO OF THE POPULATION OF THE UNITED STATES, BY SIZE OF PLACE: 1960 AND 1950

Year	United States	Urban						Rural		
		Total	Urbanized areas		Other urban		Total	Places 1,000 to 2,500	Other rural
			Central cities	Urban fringe	Places 10,000 and over	Places 2,500 to 10,000			
1960*	97.1	94.1	92.9	96.2	94.1	93.5	104.3	94.1	105.8
1950	98.7	94.7	93.5	95.1	93.3	93.1	104.9	94.3	106.4

* Includes Alaska and Hawaii.
Source: U.S. Bureau of the Census, *U.S. Census of Population: 1960, General Population Characteristics, United States Summary,* p. 1-143; U.S. Bureau of the Census, *U.S. Census of Population: 1950, Characteristics by Size of Place,* PE No. 5A, pp. 5A-16–19.

TABLE 5-4.   SEX RATIO OF THE POPULATION OF THE UNITED STATES, BY URBAN-RURAL RESIDENCE: 1910–1960

Year	Urban	Rural	
		Nonfarm	Farm
1960*	94.0	103.3	107.2
1950	94.6	103.6	110.1
1940	95.5	103.7	111.7
1930	98.1	105.0	111.0
1920	100.4	106.5	109.1
1910	101.7	109.8	

* Excludes Alaska and Hawaii.
Source: U.S. Bureau of the Census, *U.S. Census of Population: 1960, General Social and Economic Characteristics, United States Summary,* p. 1-200; other years from earlier censuses.

United States: Race, Color, and Nativity. Each of the race, color, and nativity groups that make up the population of the United States has its own sex-ratio history; no two are alike today, nor have they ever been. Table 5-5 shows sex ratios of the race and color populations from 1860 to 1960. You will be able to interpret this table more easily if you know that during the time-span of the table, 1860 to 1960: "all classes" (column 2) was between 85 and 90 percent "white"; "nonwhite" total (column 4) was between 94 and 98 percent

TABLE 5-5. SEX RATIO OF THE POPULATION OF THE UNITED STATES, BY COLOR AND RACE: 1860–1960

Year	All classes	White	Nonwhite				Other races			
			Total	Negro	Total	Indian	Japanese	Chinese	Filipino	All other
(1)	(2)	(3)	(4)	(5)	(6)	(7)	(8)	(9)	(10)	(11)
1960	97.0	97.3	94.3	93.3	111.5	101.1	91.6	139.4	172.4	131.1
1950	98.6	99.0	95.7	94.3	131.7	108.7	117.7	189.6	296.8	122.3
1940	100.7	101.2	96.7	95.0	140.5	105.5	130.9	285.3	680.2	249.3
1930	102.5	102.9	99.1	97.0	150.6	105.1	143.3	394.7	1,437.7	435.3
1920	104.0	104.4	100.9	99.2	156.6	104.8	189.8	695.5	1,410.2	777.0
1910	106.0	106.6	101.3	98.9	185.7	103.5	694.1	1,430.1	——	——
1900	104.4	104.9	101.0	98.6	185.2	101.5	2,369.6	1,887.2	——	——
1890	105.0	105.4	102.2	99.5	182.5	102.6	687.3	2,678.9	——	——
1880	103.6	104.0	100.7	97.8	362.2	104.8	——	2,106.8	——	——
1870	102.2	102.8	98.4	96.2	400.7	95.0	——	1,284.1	——	——
1860	104.7	105.3	101.2	99.6	260.8	119.0	——	1,858.1	——	——

Source: U.S. Bureau of the Census, U.S. Census of Population: 1960, General Population Characteristics, United States Summary, p. 1–145.

Negro; and "other races" (column 6) was approximately between 50 and 70 percent Indian for the years 1890 to 1960 (data gathered on Indians before 1890 are suspect). Consequently, the all-classes ratio is close to the white, the nonwhite total ratio (column 4) is close to the Negro, but the other-races total ratio, while closer to the Indian than to the ratios of the nonwhite other races, is still badly distorted by the large excess of males in the nonwhite other races, not including Negroes.

A number of trends and relationships can be seen in Table 5-5. The white population has always had a higher ratio than the nonwhite, hence the white sex ratio has always been slightly higher than the sex ratio for the country as a whole. After early fluctuations, these sex ratios decreased steadily from 1910 to 1960, the nonwhite ratio falling below 100 by 1930 and the white and all classes ratios falling below 100 by 1950.

The Negro sex ratio has never been above 100 and was extremely stable until about 1930. Since then it has fallen steadily. We do not know why the Negro sex ratio has been so low, but we suspect it may be due in part to an underenumeration of Negro males and in part to a high male death rate both before and after birth. The underenumeration and high prenatal death rate would also account for the lower-than-average Negro sex ratio at birth. During the years from 1935 to 1955 the sex ratio at birth for the white population ranged between 105.5 and 106.3, averaging 105.8, while the Negro sex ratio at birth varied between 101.1 and 103.3, averaging 102.4. The Indian sex ratio fluctuated slightly between 1880 and 1900 and is now very near 100. The very low Indian ratio of 95 in 1870 is undoubtedly due to underenumeration of the male Indian population at that time.

The other races (Japanese, Chinese, Filipino, and all other) have been overwhelmingly male in composition at all censuses, except for the Japanese in 1960. In 1890, there were approximately 2,700 Chinese males for every 100 Chinese females; in 1900, there were approximately 2,400 Japanese males for every 100 Japanese females; and in 1920, there were approximately 1,400 Filipino males for every 100 Filipino females. These exceptionally high sex ratios are partly a result of the general fact that males predominate in international migration specifically when distances are great and the migrating peasants are very poor and are partly a result of legislation aimed at stopping immigration from China and Japan. These laws were passed after many men had arrived and had become established, but before many females from their countries of origin had joined them. These high ratios began to fall in the early decades of the 1900s because some wives were being admitted, because the older immigrant group (who were mostly males) were dying off, and because there was an increasing number of births among the young families. While the Chinese sex ratio is still high (139.4), the Japanese ratio for 1960 shows a marked predominance of females (91.6). The extreme change in the Japanese sex ratio is only partly accounted for by the facts that a number of Japanese men were killed while members of the U.S. Armed Forces during World War II and that many went back to Japan after the war. Further explanation will have to await more information on the age distribution of our Japanese population and the immigration to this country by Japanese between 1945 and 1960.

In 1910 only 160 Filipinos were recorded as living in the United States; subsequent immigration had raised this figure to 106,426 by 1960. In 1920, when the Filipino population was 5,603, the sex ratio was 1,410.2 males per 100 females. The sex ratio has since fallen sharply but is still high at 172.4.

All the racial populations in this country have larger proportions of females today than ever before; in fact, the white, Negro, and Japanese populations have more females than males. The Chinese, Filipino, and all-other races categories also have lower sex ratios than formerly, but they continue to be predominantly male.

United States: Foreign-born White Sex Ratios. We have said that the extremely high sex ratios that characterized the nineteenth century Japanese and Chinese populations in this country were a result of their almost exclusively male immigrations. The heavy white migration from Europe to the United States which took place about the same time also had a high sex ratio, but not nearly so extreme as that of the migration from the Far East; probably extreme poverty, great distance, and greater uncertainty of remaining abroad will account for much of this difference between the sex ratios of European and Oriental immigration.

Table 5-6 allows us to compare the sex ratios of the native-born white and the foreign-born white populations for the years 1850 to 1960. (The sex ratios for the total white and the native-born white have always been close; they have been getting even closer in recent years, for the simple reason that in 1890 the total white was 83 percent native born, and in 1950 the total white was 92 percent native born.) Until 1960, the foreign-born population was predominantly male. The sex ratio for the foreign-born white population reached its height in 1910, when it was 129.2. The foreign-born white population increased from 10.2 million in 1900 to 13.3 million in 1910, a 31 percent increase in just 10 years. The sex ratio of the immigrants in 1900 was 212, and in 1907 it was 257. Then, not only did the volume of immigrants (white and nonwhite) fall sharply, but the sex ratio also dropped until it reached a low point of 82 for the period 1936 to 1940.

The Importance of Sex Composition. The sex ratios of the Japanese, Chinese, Filipino, all other races, and foreign-born populations have been so far from the normal range (for national aggregates, normal is between 95 and 100) as to leave little doubt of their social and demographic significance. It should be obvious

TABLE 5-6. SEX RATIO OF THE WHITE POPULATION OF THE UNITED STATES, BY NATIVITY: 1850–1960

Nativity of population	1960	1950	1940	1930	1920	1910	1900	1890	1880	1870	1860	1850
Total white:	97.3	99.0	101.2	102.9	104.4	106.6	104.9	105.4	104.0	102.8	105.3	105.2
Native	97.5	98.6	100.1	101.1	101.7	102.7	102.8	102.9	102.1	100.6	103.7	103.1
Foreign born	94.2	103.8	111.1	115.8	121.7	129.2	117.4	118.7	115.9	115.3	115.1	123.8

Source: U.S. Bureau of the Census, U.S. Census of Population: 1960. Detailed Characteristics. United States Summary, p. 1-359; other years from earlier censuses.

that we *must* take into account the extreme imbalance between the number of males and females revealed by these ratios when comparing these populations with others having different ratios, such as the United States as a whole. Unless sex composition is taken into account, rates which are affected by variations in the proportions of males and females cannot be used for significant comparisons between populations that have differing sex ratios. This point will be enlarged upon when sex differences by age are assessed. An unrecognized imbalance between the sexes produces misleading statistics on such events as birth, death, and delinquency, and even on the consumption of whisky, tobacco, and lipstick. For instance, communities that differ in their sex ratios can be expected to differ in their marriage rates, in age composition, and birth rates. Sometimes a failure (conscious or unconscious) to take these differences into account has produced quite misleading statistics.

The other populations we have been discussing, native-born white, Negro, etc., have national sex ratios that fall within the normal range, but we must be very careful not to assume that all of these populations have "normal" sex ratios in the various communities within the country. We should certainly expect local variations among subpopulations, considering the regional and urban-rural differences we have discussed with respect to the population as a whole. An example of an abnormal local sex ratio is that of the 1960 Negro population of New Rochelle, New York: 72.7. This abnormality is even more marked for the age group 20 to 24, which in 1960 had a ratio of 55.7 nonwhite males per 100 nonwhite females. In many cases, of course, other factors may be more important than the sex ratio in explaining such socioeconomic differences between communities as marriage rates, birth rates, school attendance, extent of employment of women outside the home, amount of prostitution, and status of women in the community. Variations in sex ratios must be kept in mind, however, whenever populations are compared with respect to those other characteristics that vary as do the proportions of males and females.

AGE COMPOSITION

Although we have been concerned, up to this point, largely with the discussion of sex composition alone, we have nevertheless found it necessary on occasion to mention age. The age composition of a population is much more complicated than its sex composition, because the ages in a population can be classified in a great number of ways. There is usually comparatively little confusion regarding the definition, reporting, and recording of an individual's sex, but problems can arise concerning the definition, reporting, and recording of his age. One sex may be missed more often than the other during a census; but the problems of finding out how many people are in which age groups involves not only errors of underenumeration (individuals missed in the census), but additional errors connected with ignorance and with the deliberate misreporting of age for political, economic, or personal reasons.

Two types of questions are used in getting age data. Some countries ask: "How old were you at your last birthday?" This question produces "completed-years" data. Other countries ask: "When were you born?" The answer to this question provides "date-of-birth" data. Some countries use a combination of both questions. By subtracting the date of birth from the date of the census when the question was asked, completed years of age are easily calculated. When the United States census asked, "How old are you?", the data showed a tendency to "heap" at the ages ending in 0 and 5. This "age heaping" is less likely to happen when people are asked, "When were you born?" Policemen, tavern operators, and others who need to know the ages of people they are dealing with have learned that it is much easier for a person to falsify his age when asked "How old are you?" than when he is asked "When were you born?" In 1960 the census used the date-of-birth question for the first time since 1900, believing it would provide more accurate data on age than the completed-years question. A casual inspection of the 1960 age data for single years, however, also reveals an important error. In the 1960 census there is a *marked* heaping at age 59. This undoubtedly means that many people who were born around the turn of the century but not in the precise year 1900, still gave that year as the date of their birth (see Figure 5-5).

The possibility of errors in age data is of greatest concern to the research demographer. The errors are most serious when age classifications are based on single years, less serious when five-year categories are used, and least serious when age distributions are grouped into even larger categories such as "less than 15 years old," "15 to 59 years of age," and "60 years of age and over." Fortunately, we shall have little occasion in this book to discuss the single-year categories, where the errors are the greatest.

Median Age. The age distribution of a population is very simply and most commonly described by its median age, i.e., the age which divides a population into two equal parts, half above the median age and half below it.[3] The trend of the median age from 1820 to 1960 is presented in Table 5-7 and in Figure 5-2. In 1820 half of the population was under 17 years of age. From that time until 1950 the median age rose without an interruption. From 17 in 1820 it moved

---

[3] The other two measures of central tendency, mean and mode, are less often used in population studies. The mean (the average, in everyday speech) is the average value of a distribution, and is found by summing all the values and dividing by the number of cases in the distribution. The mean is more difficult to calculate, is influenced by extreme values, and can be manipulated mathematically, while the median cannot. The mode is that value which occurs most frequently in a distribution.

slowly upward in an almost straight line to 26.6 in 1930; then sharply up to 29 in 1940; and slowly up to 30.2 in 1950. In 1960, for the first time in our history, the median age went down, dipping to 29.5.

Aging. How does a population get older? What are the demographic processes that cause an increasing proportion of a population to appear in the older age groups? No precise answer to this question will be attempted here because it would require some rather elaborate statistical calculations which would be of

TABLE 5-7.   MEDIAN AGE OF THE POPULATION OF THE UNITED STATES, BY REGIONS: 1820–1960

Year	United States total	Northeast	North Central	South	West
1960	29.5	32.4	29.7	27.3	28.8
1950	30.2	32.7	31.2	27.2	30.7
1940	29.0	31.2	30.3	25.5	31.0
1930	26.6	28.3	27.9	23.1	29.3
1920	25.3	27.1	26.5	21.7	28.1
1910	24.3	26.4	25.1	20.7	26.9
1890	22.1	25.3	22.2	18.8	25.2
1870	20.2	23.1	19.3	18.7	24.2
1850	19.0	21.2	17.9	17.8	25.1
1840	18.1	19.5	16.9	17.0	——
1820	17.0	17.7	15.6	16.4	——

Source: U.S. Bureau of the Census, *U.S. Census of Population: 1960, General Population Characteristics, United States Summary,* p. 1-173; other years from earlier censuses; 1820–1930, W. S. Thompson and P. K. Whelpton, *Population Trends in the United States,* pp. 110, 120, and 121.

no interest to the reader. In general terms, however, it may be said that, *other things remaining equal,* a declining crude death rate and birth rate would be likely to lead to a rise in the median age of a population. Conversely, a rising crude death rate and birth rate would be likely to issue in a decline in the median age of a population. But since many possible specific changes in birth rates and death rates may occur, and since other things seldom remain equal in any society, no more specific statement regarding the demographic effects of death rates and birth rates on the median age of a population will be undertaken here. The effect of migration on the median age of a population depends on whether a country is primarily sending or receiving migrants, on the size of the net migration, and on the age of the migrants.

United States: Median Age. The steady rise in the median age of the United States population from 1820 to 1950 was due largely to the combined effects of a declining mortality (after about 1850) and a declining fertility. The rapid fall in fertility during the 1930s was an important cause of the rapid rise in median age between 1930 and 1940. The high fertility in the 1950s helped to reduce the median age a little in 1960. This country was once a "young" country, but

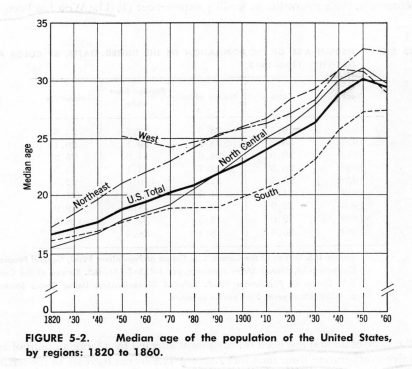

FIGURE 5-2.   **Median age of the population of the United States, by regions: 1820 to 1860.**

our population has been aging steadily for more than 100 years and is now relatively "middle-aged." However, the various subpopulations that make up the total population have median-age histories that differ significantly both from the total and from one another.

United States: Median Ages of Regions. The general impression gained from Figure 5-2 is of rather similar trend lines moving upward from low ages to relatively high median ages, then rounding off in the 1940s and turning slightly downward in the 1950s. There has never been a difference of more than seven years between any regions, and the lowest median age for any region in 1960 (South, 27.3) is higher than the highest for any region before 1920. There are some differences in the median ages and in their trends among the regions, due to their varied experience with respect to fertility, migration, and, to a much smaller extent, mortality. The North central region's median-age trend line has always been quite close to that of the country as a whole. The median ages of the other three regions differ from the national average because of certain differences in their migration or fertility experience: (1) The West has been the

TABLE 5-8.   MEDIAN AGE OF THE POPULATION OF THE UNITED STATES, BY COLOR AND NATIVITY: 1880–1960

Year	Total	Native white	Foreign-born white	Nonwhite
1960	29.5	28.5	57.7	23.5
1950	30.2	28.6	56.1	26.1
1940	29.0	26.9	51.0	25.2
1930	26.5	23.7	44.1	23.5
1920	25.3	22.4	40.0	22.5
1910	24.1	21.5	37.2	21.1
1900	22.9	20.3	38.5	19.9
1890	22.0	19.5	37.1	18.5
1880	20.9	18.4	38.3	18.0

Source: U.S. Bureau of the Census, *U.S. Census of Population: 1960, General Population Characteristics, United States Summary,* pp. 1-153–1-154; U.S. Bureau of the Census, *U.S. Census of Population: 1960. Detailed Characteristics, United States Summary,* p. 1-359; other years from earlier censuses.

most erratic of all and has been the area most affected by a large amount of age-selective in-migration from the other regions. The recent increase in the fertility of the resident population has added its effect. (2) The South has had the youngest median age, largely because of its high birth rate and its high rate of out-migration. (3) The Northeast differs from the national average because of its low fertility and its moderately high out-migration. It contains the "oldest" population, and has consistently followed the general trend but always at a higher median-age level.

United States: Median Ages by Nativity and Color. Comparing the median-age histories of the native-born white and the nonwhite as they are presented in Table 5-8 and in Figure 5-3, we see that the median ages and the trends of these groups have been quite similar until the 1930s, when they began to diverge rather sharply. Because the nonwhite population is predominantly native born (97.5 percent in 1900 and 97.8 percent in 1960), these trends have been more affected by fertility and mortality than by migration. The foreign-born white median age has always been high and has gone up sharply since 1910. The trend

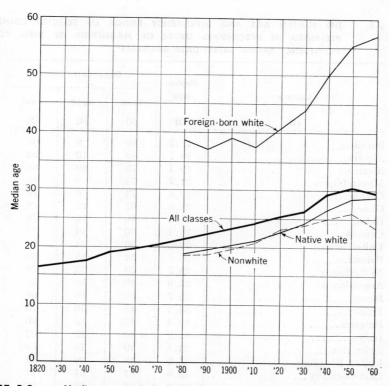

FIGURE 5-3. Median age of the population of the United States, by color and nativity: 1820 to 1960. Median age of the Negro is given for 1960. Median of "other races" in 1960 was 24.3 years. The difference is negligible. (Tables 5-7 and 5-8.)

of the foreign-born white median is a result of migration and mortality—fertility can play no part in the change. The rapid rise in the median age of this group is due to the near cessation of migration into the country, caused first by World War I and then by the restrictive Immigration Act of 1924. By 1960, one-half of all the foreign-born white population was over 57.7 years of age.

International Comparisons of Median Age. Table 5-9 shows that the median ages of the different countries vary considerably, ranging from a low of 17.7 years in Formosa to a high of 36.2 in Sweden. (The dependency ratios in this table will be discussed below.) The significance of this difference may be made

TABLE 5-9.   **THE MEDIAN AGE AND DEPENDENCY RATIOS OF SELECTED COUNTRIES PRESENTED IN DESCENDING ORDER OF MAGNITUDE OF THEIR YOUTH-DEPENDENCY RATIOS: LATEST DATA AVAILABLE**

Country	Median age	Dependency ratio		
		Youth	Aged	Total
(1)	(2)	(3)	(4)	(5)
Formosa	17.7	89	8	97
Algeria	18.7	82	10	92
Mexico	19.1	79	10	89
Mozambique	21.7	74	9	83
Ceylon	19.8	73	6	79
Chile	21.6	67	12	79
India	21.4	66	10	76
Canada	26.4	60	19	79
United States	29.5	56	24	80
Poland	26.2	54	15	69
Netherlands	28.7	53	23	76
Argentina	25.0	49	10	59
Japan	25.7	49	15	64
France	33.3	45	30	75
Bulgaria	30.4	42	18	60
Italy	31.2	40	22	62
Switzerland	33.1	39	25	64
United Kingdom	35.9	38	29	67
East Germany	35.6	37	34	71
Sweden	36.2	36	28	64
Federal Republic of Germany	34.0	35	26	61

Source: United Nations, *Demographic Yearbook, 1960 and 1961.*

clearer by a few additional data not presented in the table: Only 26 percent of the Swedish population is under the median age for Formosa, and only 23 percent of the Formosa population is over the median age for Sweden. Generally speaking, the youngest populations are found in Africa, Asia, and South America, while the oldest populations are found in Europe and in countries of predominantly European settlement, such as Canada and the United States.

The complete listing of all countries of over 5 million population for which data are available in the *Demographic Yearbook* (from which the selection in the table was taken) show Argentina and Japan to be "older" than the other countries in South America and Asia, respectively, by about 3.5 to 4 years. There are no countries in Africa, Asia, or South America (according to the data available) with median ages higher than the very lowest median ages in Europe.

When populations are compared with respect to median age on the one hand, and birth and death rates on the other, there is a strong negative (or inverse) correlation between these statistics: the higher the birth and death rates are, the younger the population is; the lower these rates are, the older the population is. The United States in the early part of the nineteenth century had a median age lower than any of those found in Table 5-9.

The "dependency ratio" of a population is a more complex but more useful way of describing the age distribution of a population than is the median age. The dependency ratio is based on the fact that every member of a society is a consumer but that only some members are producers. A country with a larger proportion of its population producing goods and services is economically better off than a country with a smaller proportion of producers—other things being equal. Unfortunately, other things are not equal. There is no internationally uniform basis on which the various countries decide who may be economically productive and who may not. Societies differ with respect to the parts of their populations which are expected to be economically active. In some societies, small children are expected to be members of the labor force; in others, school attendance is required of young men and women until they are in their late teens. In some societies, the aged are required to work; in others, they are permitted to work, and in still others, they are denied the opportunity to be economically productive.

When is one old enough to work, and when is one too old? Biology may set the extreme limits, but the actual decisions vary greatly from one society to another; the variation is an evidence of the role culture plays. While recognizing this variation among societies, we shall assume that age 15 is the approximate lower limit of productive power and that age 60 is near the top limit. In some countries, life is so hard, disease so widespread, and mortality so high that very few people are able to do a day's work as they approach the age of 60. In other countries, control of debilitating and crippling diseases, shorter work hours, good working conditions, and low death rates make it possible for a sizable proportion of men and women to carry on a good day's work well beyond the age of 60. For purposes of international comparison we shall call those under 15 the dependent youth and those over 60 the dependent aged. The age group 15–59 will be considered the economically active part of the population, and will be the base for calculating the dependency ratios (see Table 5-9).

The youth-dependency ratio is calculated by dividing the number of people

$$\frac{uncle\ 45}{15-49} \times 100$$

aged 15–59 into the number of people under 15, and multiplying the resulting quotient by 100. A country with a youth-dependency ratio of 45 has 45 people under 15 to every 100 people aged 15–59 (column 3). Similarly, the aged-dependency ratio is calculated by dividing the number of those aged 15–59 into those 60 years of age and over, and multiplying the quotient by 100 (column 4). A population with an aged-dependency ratio of 10 has 10 people 60 years of age and over to every 100 people aged 15–59. A total-dependency ratio is simply the sum of the youth-dependency ratio and the aged-dependency ratio. A country with the above youth- and aged-dependency ratios would have a total-dependency ratio of 55, i.e., a total of 55 people under 15 and over 60 years of age for every 100 people in the productive ages of 15–59. Table 5-9 presents dependency ratios for selected countries and territories that have more than 5 million population and fairly reliable population data.

The youth-dependency ratios vary from a high in Formosa of 89 people under 15 years of age for every 100 people aged 15–59, to a low of 35 in the Federal Republic of Germany; this is a range of 54 points. Table 5-9 shows that the countries with high youth-dependency ratios have twice as many people under 15 years of age (relative to the number of people aged 15–59) as do the countries with the low youth-dependency ratios. The arrangement of the table reveals that the youth-dependency ratios and the median ages of the countries listed are, as we should expect, negatively associated with one another, i.e., they run in opposite directions. Countries with high youth-dependency ratios (55 or above) are found in all the regions of the world *except Europe.* In fact, when all the 45 countries with 5 million inhabitants (the countries for which usable data are available in the *Demographic Yearbook*) are examined, we find that the 15 lowest youth-dependency ratios are *all* in Europe, and that of the 20 countries with median ages over 25, 18 are in Europe, the other 2 being the United States and Canada.

The aged-dependency ratios vary from a low of 6 people over 60 years of age for each 100 people aged 15–59 in Ceylon to a high of 34 people aged 60 and over for each 100 people aged 15–59 in East Germany. While this 28-point difference in aged-dependency ratios is not as great as the 54-point difference between the high and the low youth dependencies, the highest aged-dependency ratio is still five times as great as the lowest one. The correlation of median age with aged dependency is a direct (positive) one, just the reverse of the relation between median age and youth dependency. The correlation of median age with aged dependency is not as close as with youth dependency, but it is still easy to see the pattern by inspecting the table. All countries in Europe have very high median ages, low youth-dependency loads, and high aged-dependency loads; while the opposite is true for the countries which are not yet highly urban and industrial. In countries with high aged-dependency ratios, an increasing number of people are working to age 65 or 70.

Total-dependency Ratios. The two dependency categories—the young and the old—are not the same in their relationship to total dependency. In every country listed in Table 5-9, the part of the population which is under 15 years of age is larger than the part which is 60 or over, and therefore the youth-dependency ratio in these countries is the larger of the two components which make up the total-dependency ratio. In some countries the youth ratio comprises nearly all of the total-dependency ratio; for example, Ceylon in 1955 had a total-dependency ratio of 79, made up of a youth-dependency ratio of 73 and aged-dependency ratio of only 6.

A high total-dependency ratio always means that a large proportion of the population is under 15 years of age. Table 5-9 allows us to compare the distributions of youth and aged dependency (columns 3 and 4) with that of total dependency (column 5). The total-dependency ratios are very closely and positively associated with youth-dependency ratios, and are inversely, but less closely, associated with aged-dependency ratios.

Dependency and Economic Development. The problem of the economic development of underdeveloped countries is related in several ways to the age composition of a country. There is real irony in Table 5-9: the countries which are trying desperately to increase their production and their level of living are those burdened with the highest total-dependency ratios. The countries with the lowest total-dependency ratios are already highly urban and industrial and have high levels of living. The poor countries have high fertility; high fertility creates a heavy dependency load, which makes it difficult, if not impossible, for such countries to improve their living conditions. Those countries that can afford dependents the *least* have the *most* dependents, and those countries that can afford to support a good many dependents have the fewest. A sudden drop in fertility would quickly reduce the total dependency ratios in underdeveloped countries, because the number of dependent young would decrease, while the number of people over 15 years of age would be unaffected for 15 years, i.e., until the time when those born in the year when the birth rate went down began moving into the 15-year-old age group.

On the other hand, if a country with a high birth rate were to lower its death rate sharply, it would experience an immediate and sizable increase in its total-dependency ratio, because the lives saved would be primarily those in the youngest age groups. The effect would be nearly the same as a large increase in the birth rate. Unhappily, from a demographic and economic point of view, many underdeveloped countries have seen their death rates drop very fast in a relatively short time, while their birth rates have remained high. This process has increased the dependency load in the very countries which can least afford an increase in the parts of their populations that consume but do not produce or produce very little.

Table 5-10 gives the percent of the population that is economically active at ages 15–19, 60–64, and 65 and over, with respect to the countries listed in Table 5-9 for which usable data are available. Again the authors would call attention to the fact that the term "economically active" has different meanings among the various countries listed in the table.

TABLE 5-10.   MEDIAN AGE AND PERCENT OF POPULATION ECONOMICALLY ACTIVE AT VARIOUS AGES IN SELECTED COUNTRIES PRESENTED IN ASCENDING ORDER OF MEDIAN AGE: LATEST DATA AVAILABLE

Country	Median age	Economically active			
		15–19	20–59	60–64	65 and over
Mexico..................	19	44.8	53.3	——	50.7
Algeria..................	19	68.3	73.3	71.0	54.5
Ceylon..................	20	43.0	64.2	——	55.1[a]
Chile....................	22	47.0	61.0	50.6	38.7
Mozambique.............	22	53.4	49.1	34.8	31.8
Japan...................	26	49.9[b]	73.0	——	44.1[a]
Canada.................	26	48.3	60.5	48.5	22.1
Netherlands.............	29	67.7[c]	59.6[d]	——	20.2
United States...........	29	35.5	61.8	49.7	23.6
Switzerland.............	33	68.9	64.6	52.7	28.5
France..................	33	67.0	71.8	55.4	35.3
East Germany...........	36	75.9[b]	68.2[e]	56.7[f]	22.2
United Kingdom.........	36	81.1	66.8	46.7	16.3
Sweden.................	36	64.5	64.3	47.7	20.9

[a] Age category of 60 and over.
[b] Age category of 14–19.
[c] Age category of 16–19.
[d] Age category of 20–64.
[e] Age category of 20–54.
[f] Age category of 55–64.
Source: United Nations, *Demographic Yearbook, 1956.*

On the basis of the data presented in Table 5-10, for most of the countries, "under 15 years of age" seems better than "under 20 years of age" as a dividing line between the dependent youth and the economically active population. In all the countries except the United States, over 40 percent of those aged 15–19 are economically active, and in half of these countries the figure is over 60 percent.

According to Table 5-10, the upper age limit defining the economically active part of the population for most countries should be 65. A goodly proportion of people continue to work between ages 60 and 64, but for most of them the proportion drops off abruptly in the 65-and-over age groups. Among the 29 countries from which the selection in Table 5-10 was drawn, most had a larger percent of those aged 15–19 economically active than of those aged 60–64. The average percents economically active in the age groups 15–19, 60–64, and 65 and over, for 12 *European* countries, were: 65 percent of those 15–19, 47 percent of those 60–64, and 25 percent of the 65-and-over age group.

These tables and other such information based upon internationally supplied population statistics are very useful, but they are not to be accepted uncritically. Most generalizations based on them must be considered tentative and viewed with skepticism. The United Nations demographers do an excellent job of alerting users of their tables to the variations in definition employed in the same tables by different countries, the tremendous range in the completeness and accuracy of census counts that are reported, and so forth.

United States: Dependency Ratios. The dependency ratios for the United States from 1860 to 1960, and those projected for 1970, are presented in Figure 5-4. This graph is based on a table by Bogue[4] in which he uses the categories of under 20 and over 65 years of age as the upper and lower limits of his youth- and aged-dependency groups. (The United States in 1950, according to Table 5-10, classified as economically active only 35.5 percent of those aged 15–19, and only 50 percent of those aged 60–64.) The curves in Figure 5-4 make possible the following generalizations:

1. Youth dependency has always been the major component of total dependency and it still is, but its portion is becoming smaller as the proportion of the population 65 and over increases.

2. Total- and youth-dependency ratios declined steeply from 1860[5] to 1940, at which time they leveled off for a short period and then, reversing an almost century-old trend, began to shoot up in the 1950s.

3. The aged-dependency ratio increased slowly until 1930, then climbed sharply until 1960, rising higher in those 30 years than it had in the previous 70.

4. The slight increase in total dependency during the 1940s was due to the increase in the proportion of the population over 65, because during that decade the youth dependency remained nearly level.

5. According to the assumptions used by the census in making its projection for 1970, the 1960s will see the dependency ratios continue their climb but at a slower rate than during the 1950s.

The projected increase in the aged-dependency ratio will probably turn out to be fairly accurate in 1970 (barring major catastrophes), since the mortality and migration assumptions are less subject to error than the fertility assumptions,

[4] Bogue, *op. cit.*, p. 102.
[5] *Ibid.* According to Bogue, the decline began at least as early as 1820.

and fertility variations cannot affect the projection of the aged-dependency ratio until 1975.

The relationship between the numbers of young and old people in a population and the number of people in the productive years of their lives changes in response to the population's changing fertility, mortality, and, to a lesser

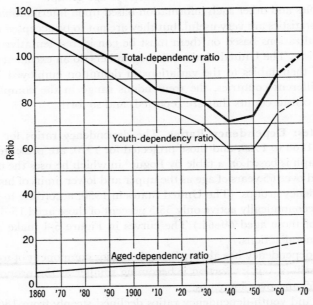

FIGURE 5-4.   Total-dependency ratio, youth- (0–19) dependency ratio, and aged- (65 and over) dependency ratio of the population of the United States: 1860 to 1960 and estimated for 1970, assuming continued fertility to 1970 at the 1955 to 1957 level.

extent, its migration. In Figure 5-4, the patterns for the period prior to World War II are largely a result of continuously falling birth and death rates, while the patterns after World War II are a consequence of higher fertility combined with low death rates still falling slowly.

Comparing the trend of the United States median age in Figure 5-2 with the trend of the total-dependency ratio in Figure 5-4, we find that these lines have nearly identical patterns but opposite trends. While the median-age line is rising, the total-dependency line is sloping down; and during the last decade, when the median age dropped slightly, up went the total dependency.

TABLE 5-11. MEDIAN AGE AND DEPENDENCY RATIO OF THE POPULATION OF THE UNITED STATES, BY REGIONS, URBAN-RURAL RESIDENCE, NATIVITY, AND COLOR: 1960

Median age and dependency ratios	All classes	Regions				Residence group				Nativity and color			
		North-east	North Central	South	West	SMSA*	Urban	Rural-nonfarm	Rural-farm	White Total	White Native	White Foreign-born	Non-white†
Median age.........	29.5	32.4	29.7	27.3	28.8	30.1	30.3	26.8	29.6	30.3	28.5	57.7	23.5
Dependency ratio:													
Total...........	*90.7	83.1	93.8	96.5	90.3	85.4	85.7	102.5	105.4	88.9	90.3	68.3	106.3
Youth (0–19).....	73.5	64.7	74.7	80.1	74.0	69.3	68.9	84.5	86.2	71.1	75.2	11.9	93.7
Aged (65 and over)	17.2	18.4	19.1	16.4	16.3	16.1	16.8	18.0	19.2	17.8	15.1	56.4	12.6

* SMSA stands for Standard Metropolitan Statistical Area. See page 143 for a complete definition.

† Negroes are 92.1 percent of the nonwhite population.

Source: U.S. Bureau of the Census, U.S. Census of Population: 1960, General Population Characteristics, United States Summary, pp. 1-159, 1-173, 1-186; U.S. Bureau of the Census, U.S. Census of Population: 1960, General Social and Economic Characteristics, United States Summary, p. 1-199; U.S. Bureau of the Census, U.S. Census of Population: 1960, Detailed Characteristics, United States Summary, p. 1-359.

In Table 5-11, we see that in the United States, regions differ less among themselves than do the urban-rural groupings with respect to all three dependency ratios—total, youth, and aged. Differences among color categories are substantial, but it is among nativity groups that the variations are the most extreme. Among the four regions, the South has the lowest median age and the highest total- and youth-dependency ratios. Among the residence groups, the rural-farm population has the highest total-, youth-, and aged-dependency ratios. The ratios of the rural-farm and the rural-nonfarm are very similar, and are markedly higher than the urban and SMSA ratios.[6]

United States: Foreign-born White and Nonwhite. The foreign-born white population is extremely different demographically in every respect from every other population group in Table 5-11. In 1960, one-half of the foreign-born white population was over 57.7 years of age. This median age is nearly twice that of the one nearest to it, which is 32.4 for the Northeast population. The youth-dependency ratio of 11.9 and the aged-dependency ratio of 56.4 for the foreign-born white are both so different from the ratios of the other groups that one cannot help being suspicious of them at first. Any population with this kind of an age distribution should never be compared with other populations on matters which include age as a relevant variable, unless the age compositions of the populations are taken into account in some way. Another population which differs somewhat from all the others is the nonwhite; it is younger, and has higher youth-dependency and lower age-dependency ratios.

The irony in the fact that the poor nations, which can least afford dependents, have the largest dependency ratios was pointed out earlier; now we find that certain *intra*national comparisons show similar ironies. The South, the rural-farm, and the nonwhite populations in the United States, which are the least able to support dependents, have more than their share of the nation's dependents.

AGE AND SEX COMPOSITION

Population Pyramid. We have discussed sex composition and age composition separately; now it is time to treat them together. An experienced student of population can quickly detect important differences in age and sex composition among various populations by scanning tables containing age data for each sex, whether classified by single years of age or by five-year groups. The uninitiated often find it hard to see the patterns of age and sex composition unless the data

[6] SMSA stands for Standard Metropolitan Statistical Area (a concept developed by the census), and includes the population living in metropolitan cities and in the densely settled fringe area around them. For a detailed definition and discussion of these areas, see Chap. 8.

are presented in graphic form. The most readily understood kind of graphic representation is called the "population pyramid." When the age and sex compositions of most populations are plotted graphically, the result is a pyramid; the broad base represents the youngest ages, and the sides gradually slope toward a point, representing the decrease brought about by deaths in each successive age group. The construction of population pyramids is not, in itself, demographic analysis; the purpose of these pyramids is to help people "see" age and sex composition so that they can make meaningful comparisons among populations which vary in these respects.

The population pyramid may be based either on absolute numbers or on proportions. The creator of the pyramid must decide what point he wants to convey, and what kinds of comparisons he wants to make possible. Pyramids based on numbers can be used for comparing both the sizes and the shapes of populations. The limitation of such a pyramid is that when there are great differences in size between two populations, such as those of Mainland China and Switzerland, the use of a common scale means that the smaller population looks *too* small and the larger one looks *too* large. Even if they could be drawn on the same sheet of paper, the great difference in size would obscure the meaning of the two population "shapes" and would make comparison difficult. Pyramids based on numbers are most useful for comparing populations of nearly the same size. For example, pyramids representing a given population at two different times (e.g., 10 years apart) illustrate very clearly the amount and the distribution of absolute change among the various age and sex groups during the intervening years (see Figure 5-5).

If a demographer wants to show how a number of populations differ in age and sex composition without regard to the size of the total populations, he can make this comparison most clearly by constructing pyramids based on proportions. When proportions are used, the areas of all the pyramids are the same. The pyramids *differ in shape*, but their *areas are identical*. These differences in shape are apparent to the eye when the pyramids are placed side by side, but they are much more striking when one pyramid is superimposed on another. Although single-year groups are sometimes used, five-year groups are generally adequate and involve much less work.

Whether absolute numbers or percents are used in a pyramid, it is conventional to record age on the vertical axis and to measure the numbers or percents of the population at each age along the horizontal axis, with males to the left of the vertical line and females to the right. The pyramid is nothing more than two bar graphs placed on their sides and put back to back. The vertical center line represents zero, and when the pyramid is based on percents, the sum of the length of *all* the bars (including both the male and the female sides) is always the same: 100. In Figure 5-6 the bottom bar on the left tells us that males aged 0–4 make up a little more than 5.5 percent of the total population. The pyramids

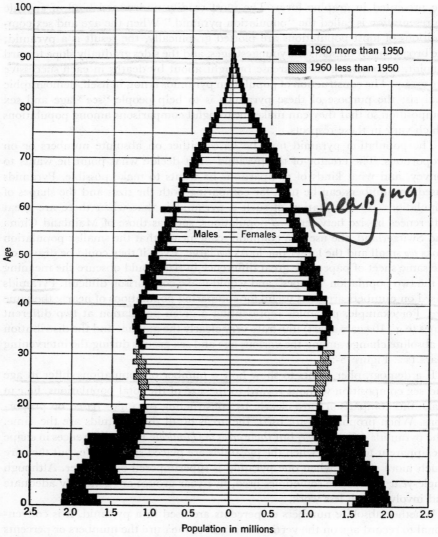

Department of Commerce, Bureau of the Census

FIGURE 5-5.   Population of the United States, by single years of age and sex: 1960 and 1950.

in Figures 5-6 and 5-7 are identical in area, and differ only in shape, thus drawing attention to the differences in relative distribution of the various age and sex groups. The relative size of each age and sex group in the United States's pyramid can be compared directly with the same age and sex groups in the

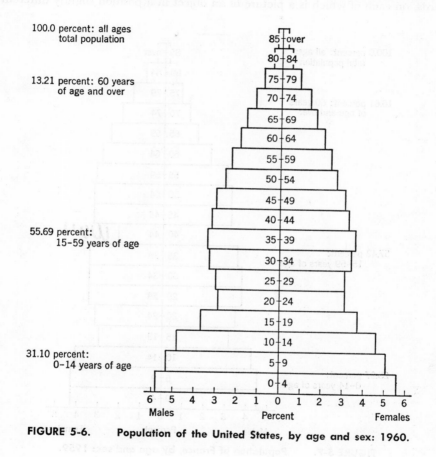

FIGURE 5-6.   Population of the United States, by age and sex: 1960.

French pyramid. For example, the United States has proportionately more people under age 20 than has France, and has nearly the same proportion aged 20–39; the United States has many more in the age category 40–44, and many fewer, particularly females, in the age category 45-and-over.

A population is always changing, whereas a pyramid is a static picture. The proportions of people in the various age and sex categories change because of the continuous action of mortality, fertility, and migration. The population pyramid freezes this motion at a particular moment in time. From a slightly different perspective, the pyramid can be viewed as a picture of the biological history of a population—the result of 100 years of births, deaths, and migration.

We have all seen the animated-cartoon effect produced by riffling a stack of cards, on each of which is a picture of an object in a position slightly different

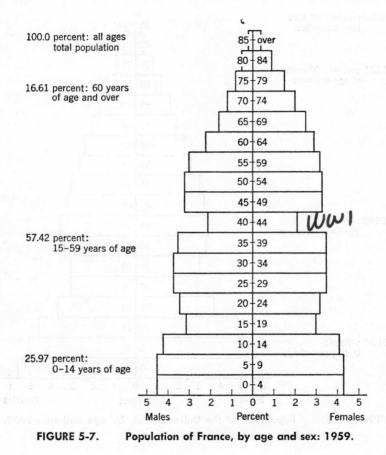

FIGURE 5-7.   **Population of France, by age and sex: 1959.**

from its position on the card preceding. If population pyramids were made which represented the population of the United States at intervals of five years, covering, in all, a period of 170 years; and if these pyramids were put on cards and arranged so that the pyramid for 1790 (first United States census) was followed by the pyramids of 1795, 1800, and so on; the illusion of motion created when these cards were riffled would show crests and troughs of waves rippling up through the pyramid and out of the top. This example assumes that the country has experienced some changes in its birth rates or its death rates and/or in the proportions of migration by age during the period in which the original pyramid (1790) was built up. If these rates had remained unchanged (and if there had been no migration) in the preceding 30 to 40 years and no change in them after 1790, the proportion in each category would remain so nearly stable that the eye would not detect any significant ripple.

If a country's birth rate drops and then goes up, the resulting trough and crest of the wave travel up through the age categories of the pyramid until all the people represented by the bars (age groups) are dead (assuming there has been no migration). In Figure 5-7 (France) there is a deep trough in the pyramid, caused by the relatively small size of the 40–44 age group. By counting back, we discover that this age group (which we will call a cohort) represents the persons born during World War I. The birth rate was lower in France during those years than it was in the years before and after World War I, and thus the age group 0–4 was relatively small in 1920. Since the birth rate returned to its prewar level after the war, the cohort born during the war years became a permanent trough in the population structure; as the years passed, it moved up through the successive age groups until, by 1959, it had become the 40–44-year age group. The other trough in France's 1959 pyramid is at the ages 15–24, representing the cohort that was born during the low-fertility years of the Depression and World War II, i.e., 1934 to 1944. Part of the drop in fertility from 1934 to 1944 was also due to the fact that the small cohort born during World War I was then passing through its early reproductive years, being 15 to 19 years old in 1934 and 25 to 29 years old in 1944. Thus, the low birth rate of 1914 to 1918 helped to lower the birth rate during the period from 1934 to 1944. The secondary effect of an event like World War I (the low birth rate in 1934 to 1944) is rarely as sharply defined, or as easily recognized, as the direct effect (the low birth rate in 1914 to 1918).

In contrast to the French pyramid, the United States's population structure of 1960 has no marked irregularities. The United States pyramid does have a slightly pushed-in place at the 20–29 age group, representing the survivors of the cohort born during the 1930s, the decade of economic depression and of the lowest birth rate in United States history. Toward the end of the 1930s, the birth rate started to climb slowly and then jumped abruptly after World War II. This sudden rise produced the bulge in the pyramid beginning with the age group 10–14.

By now, the reader probably realizes that the various bulges and dents in a population pyramid cannot be explained by the pyramid itself; they must be accounted for by the analyst, on the basis of his knowledge of the country's historic events and their effect on the major demographic processes. For example, the pinched-in place in the 1959 French pyramid at age 40–44 could have been caused either by a sudden temporary drop in fertility 40 to 44 years before, or by a sizable emigration of this age group, or by the fact that at some time this cohort experienced a higher death rate than the age groups near it, or by some combination of these three possibilities. But some guides can be used to explain dents and bulges in a pyramid when the actual causes are not known. A very sharp indentation involving equally both males and females usually indicates a drop in fertility at the time the cohort was born. If there are significantly fewer males than females at any given age level (early adulthood and above), the difference may be due either to war deaths or to a large male emigration. The pyramid for France in 1959 shows that males were relatively much fewer in number than females in the age group 60–64, compared with the age group 55–59. We can be fairly sure that such a dent was not a result of any changes in fertility, but without a knowledge of historical events we cannot tell whether it was due to war or to male emigration. We cannot decide on any one cause just by looking at the pyramid, but by counting back we find that the 60–64 age group was aged 20–24 during World War I (1914–1918); the correct answer, therefore, is probably that the difference between the ratios of the two groups is a result of unusually high male mortality during the war years.

At this point it might be helpful to look at a population pyramid which has no irregularities at all—a pyramid based upon a population which has a constant number of births each year, an equal number of deaths, and no migration whatsoever. Where can one find such a population? No populations like this exist, but a hypothetical one can be constructed. Figure 5-8 is a pyramid based on such a hypothetical population, one which would result from a constant number of births added each year and an equal number of deaths subtracted each year. The deaths are distributed among the age and sex groups according to the actual death rates for those groups as they occurred in the United States in 1901. A population created in this way is called a "life-table population." (We shall discuss life tables and their construction in Chapter 12.) The age and sex composition of such a population never changes. The total number never changes; it is a *stationary population*. The crude birth and death rates of such a population are always the same. In this instance, both rates are 20.2 per 1,000 per year. Figure 5-8, then, represents the shape which the age and sex composition of a *closed* (no migration) population would assume as a result of nearly 100 years of a constant annual birth and death rate of 20.2. Notice that the base is the broadest part of the structure and that the sides taper in very gradually after 0–4 years to 30–34 years, then more sharply in succeeding age groups until finally all have died.

If we construct another pyramid, using the death rates for each age and sex group as they occurred in the United States in 1960, we shall secure a population pyramid for the life table of 1960 (Figure 5-9). The difference in age and sex composition between these two hypothetical populations is the result of a change in one variable—a mortality rate that was lower in 1960 than it had been in 1901 but one that had declined more at some ages than at others and more for females than for males. The annual number of births remains constant, and there is no migration. Since the greatest reduction in mortality took place

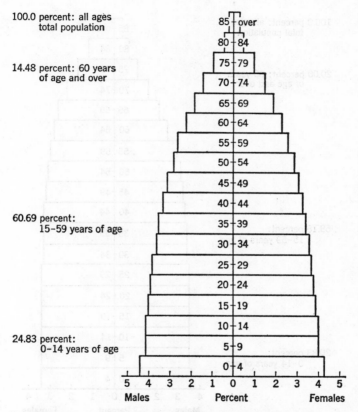

100.0 percent: all ages
total population

14.48 percent: 60 years
of age and over

60.69 percent:
15–59 years of age

24.83 percent:
0–14 years of age

FIGURE 5-8. Life-table population of the United States, by age and sex, based on the mortality rates of the white population in the registration area of the United States: 1901. (*U.S. Life Tables—1890, 1901, 1910, 1901 to 1910*, pages 64 and 70.)

among the youngest age groups, the sides go almost straight up until the 25–29 bar is reached, and then they bend in only slightly. Near the 50-year-old mark, the sides move toward the center at a somewhat slower rate than they did in the 1901 pyramid (Figure 5-8).

Because the number of births annually (100,000) is the same in the 1901 and the 1960 life-table populations, and because mortality rates are lower, especially in the earlier ages in the 1960 population, the total number of people is larger in the 1960 life-table population than in the 1901 population (in the ratio of

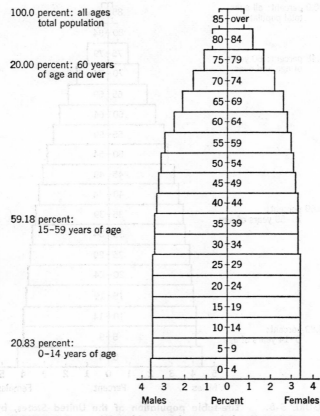

FIGURE 5-9.   Life-table population of the United States, by age and sex: 1960.

approximately 3 to 2). The life-table death rate and birth rate for the 1960 population are the same: 14.3 per 1,000 per year. So Figure 5-9 has the shape of a closed population which has experienced a constant birth rate and a constant death rate for nearly 100 years.

If we construct a population with birth and death rates even higher than those of the 1901 United States life-table population, we get a shape which looks much more like a pyramid than the life-table populations of 1901 and 1960. The base is broad because of the high birth rate, and the sides slope in sharply, particularly in the early years, because of the high mortality. The total number of people in this hypothetical population is, naturally, much smaller than the total 1901 population.

Figures 5-8 and 5-9 point up some other interesting demographic differences, differences related to the composition of the two populations:

Life-table population	1901	1960
Median age	31.5	36.3
Sex ratio	99.6	96.0
Birth and death rates	20.2	14.3
Dependency ratio:		
Total	64.77	68.99
Youth (0–14)	40.91	35.21
Aged (65 and over)	23.86	33.78

We have said that a population with high birth and death rates is represented by a pyramid which has a broad base reflecting its high fertility, and relatively large steps between successively older age groups reflecting its high mortality. If such a population has not experienced any fluctuations in its birth and death rates for a long time, the steps are rather large all the way up to 60 years of age. A good example of this type of pyramid is India's, shown in Figure 5-10. This broad-based pyramid is typical of countries whose birth rates and death rates are both high. And generally speaking, irregularities that are not due to faulty data or to migration are almost always due to changes in mortality rather than to changes in fertility. Before about 1650, *all* the countries in the world probably had population structures similar to the one in Figure 5-10.

A number of countries today have pyramids similar to India's, but because of recent and spectacular successes in the reduction of infant and child mortality rates, the bases of some pyramids are even broader than India's. These countries are growing more rapidly than India, have high total-dependency ratios, and have younger median ages. Mexico, the Philippines, Brazil, and Ceylon are examples of rapidly growing countries with increasingly large numbers and proportions in the young age groups and consequently with very broad-based population pyramids. Notice, for example, in Figure 5-11, how far the bar representing Ceylon's 5–9 age group for 1955 extends beyond the bar representing the 10–14 age group, and how far the 0–4 age-group bar extends beyond that of the 5–9 age group.

Japan's population pyramid for 1960 (Figure 5-12) is very different from those we have discussed so far. It shows the effect of a rapid reduction in fertility on the age structure of an urban-industrial society. Before World War II, the Western European countries and the United States had pyramids similar in

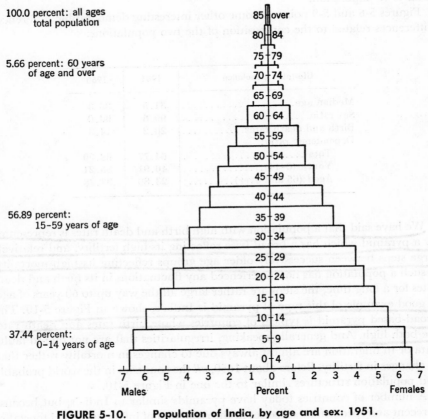

FIGURE 5-10.   Population of India, by age and sex: 1951.

shape to Japan's 1960 pyramid. If we were to compare Japan in 1960 with the United States in 1940 (Figure 5-6, age 20 and above), however, we would see that while both pyramids have narrowing bases, the United States pyramid is wider at the older ages; this difference indicates a longer history of low mortality in the United States, and a less sharp reduction in fertility. Japan's fertility has been reduced through a strong national effort; birth-control clinics have been set up, and abortion has been made legal, safe, and inexpensive. The effect of war on Japan's population composition can be seen in the age group 35–49, which contains a great many fewer males than females—fewer than we should expect as a result of the usual death-rate differences between the two sexes. If we count back, it is obvious that the age group 35–49 was between the ages

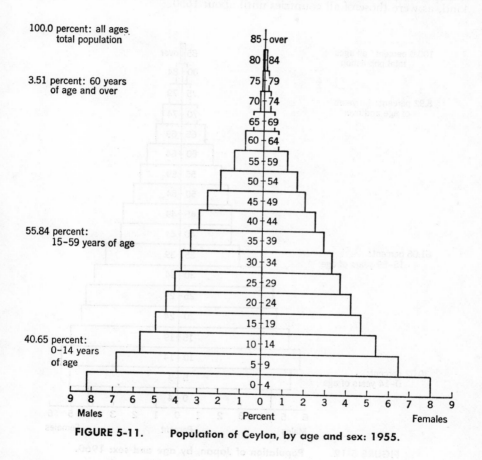

100.0 percent: all ages total population

3.51 percent: 60 years of age and over

55.84 percent: 15–59 years of age

40.65 percent: 0–14 years of age

FIGURE 5-11.   **Population of Ceylon, by age and sex: 1955.**

of 18 and 32 in 1942. Turning back to the United States in 1960 (Figure 5-6), we see what happens to age-sex composition when a country reverses a long-term trend of fertility reduction: the base of the structure begins to push out.

Classification of National Population Structures. The pyramids we have been discussing can be classified according to the five stylized examples in Figure 5-13.

1. This pyramid has a broad base and gently sloping sides. It is typical of all high birth- and death-rate countries before they have exercised control over either births or deaths. The median age is low, and the youth- and total-dependency ratios are high. India's pyramid for 1951 (Figure 5-10) is of this kind, as were those of all countries until about 1650.

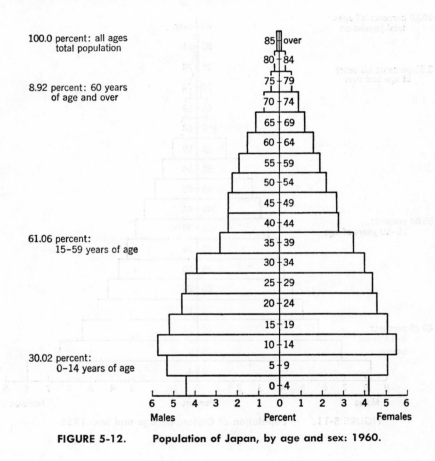

100.0 percent: all ages
total population

8.92 percent: 60 years
of age and over

61.06 percent:
15–59 years of age

30.02 percent:
0–14 years of age

6   5   4   3   2   1   0   1   2   3   4   5   6
Males   Percent   Females

FIGURE 5-12.   Population of Japan, by age and sex: 1960.

2. This pyramid has a broader base than no. 1, and the sides bow in much more sharply as they slant from the 0–4 age group to the top. Pyramid no. 2 is typical of countries that are beginning to grow rapidly as a result of marked reductions in infant and child deaths, and are not yet reducing their fertility. In such countries populations are increasing rapidly, median ages are falling (in fact, they are now the lowest in the world because of decreasing death rates

of infants and young children), and youth- and total-dependency ratios are the highest in the world. Ceylon, and other countries such as the Philippines, Brazil, and Mexico belong in this category.

3. This pyramid resembles an old-fashioned beehive. It represents countries with low birth rates (a narrow base) and low death rates (an almost impercep-

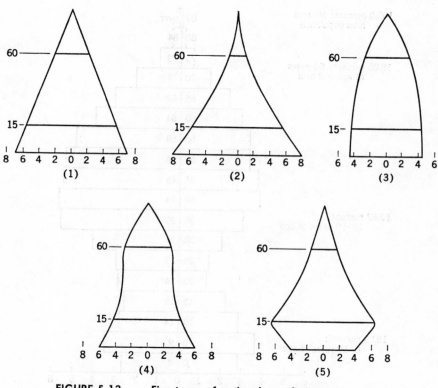

FIGURE 5-13. Five types of national population structures.

tible indentation for each age group after the first, until near the top). Its shape could represent most of the populations of Western Europe. The population of the United States was forming this kind of a pyramid until the downward trend in its fertility was reversed during and after World War II. The population represented by pyramid no. 3 has the following characteristics: Its median age is the highest, its total dependency is the lowest of all the populations, and its largest component of dependency is in the older ages.

4. The bell-shaped pyramid is a type recently produced by such countries as

the United States and Canada. This shape represents a population which, after more than 100 years of declining birth and death rates, has reversed the trend in fertility while keeping the death rate low. A population with a pyramid shaped like this is growing, has a declining median age, and has increasingly high youth- and total-dependency ratios. It is a transitional type.

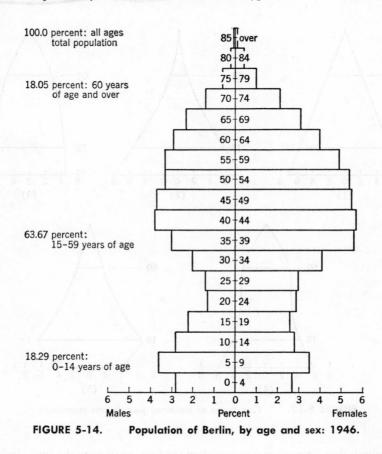

100.0 percent: all ages
total population

18.05 percent: 60 years
of age and over

63.67 percent:
15–59 years of age

18.29 percent:
0–14 years of age

85 over
80 84
75 79
70 74
65 69
60 64
55 59
50 54
45 49
40 44
35 39
30 34
25 29
20 24
15 19
10 14
5 9
0 4

6 5 4 3 2 1 0 1 2 3 4 5 6
Males   Percent   Females

FIGURE 5-14.   Population of Berlin, by age and sex: 1946.

5. This last pyramid represents a population which is experiencing a marked and rapid decline in fertility and which, if the decline continues, will soon show an absolute loss in numbers. This type of population has a low death rate and has reduced its birth rate very rapidly. At present, Japan is the only country in this situation, but many Western European countries were similar to this in the 1930s (see Figure 5-6 and Figure 5-7), beginning with the 15–19-year-old age group. Number 5 is also a transitional type.

We have seen how countries can vary in the age and sex proportions which their population structures assume. Similar variations also exist *within* countries. In fact, some of the greatest structural differences in population occur among the subpopulations of nations. One of the most oddly shaped community population structures appeared just after World War II. Figure 5-14 is the pyramid for the city of Berlin in 1946, a city of over 3 million people. Not only is it extremely top-heavy, but it is also markedly lopsided. The extreme imbalance of the sexes, particularly at the ages 20–35, is rare for a community of such size. Such a structure could not be simply the result of the usual occurrence of births and deaths and migration; extremely disturbing influences obviously had been at work on this population. Imagine only *68* males for every *100* females in the city as a whole, and even relatively fewer males in the early adult categories.

Additional specific examples of varying population structures among national subpopulations will be given in subsequent chapters. Age and sex composition will be an inevitable part of the discussion of nearly every population topic covered in this book. In the future, even if tables are presented without their corresponding pyramids, we hope that the foregoing discussion will make it easier to *see* population structures, to have some idea of the principal conditions which helped produce them, and to suggest some of the deeper implications.

SUGGESTIONS FOR SUPPLEMENTARY READING

Burgess, Ernest W. (ed.): *Aging in Western Societies*, The University of Chicago Press, Chicago, 1960.

Coale, Ansley J., and Edgar M. Hoover: *Population Growth and Economic Development in Low-income Countries*, Princeton University Press, Princeton, N.J., 1958.

Eason, Warren W.: "The Soviet Population Today: An Analysis of the First Results of the 1959 Census," *Foreign Affairs*, vol. 37, no. 10, pp. 598–606, 1959. (Notes on population size and structure indicated by the statistics released May 10, 1959, special reference to imputed war losses and recent vital trends.)

Sheldon, Henry D., and Clark Tibbits: *The Older Population in the United States*, John Wiley & Sons, Inc., New York, 1958.

United Nations: "Demographic Aspects of Manpower, Report 1, Sex and Age Patterns of Participation in Economic Activities," *Population Studies*, no. 33, Department of Economic and Social Affairs, New York, 1962.

CHAPTER SIX

Rural, Urban, and Metropolitan Composition

EVOLUTION OF THE CITY

The First Cities. One of the most important things to know about any society today is what proportion of its population is urban. Considering how long man has been on earth, we can realize that the city is a fairly recent human invention. Because scholars use different criteria in defining cities, they disagree on precise dates, but they agree that the first "true" cities appeared between 3000 and 5000 B.C. There is evidence that large human groupings existed in Neolithic Europe; today there are various large groupings in Africa and among the Pueblo Indians of the United States. Few of these are considered truly urban groupings, because size and density are not the only considerations involved in defining an urban residential grouping. According to Sjoberg, these large villages should not be classified as urban populations, because they do not have "a significant number of full-time specialists including a literate group, engaged in a relatively wide range of non-agricultural activities."[1]

Gordon V. Childe considers the city the nucleus of civilization, and defines civilization as

> . . . the aggregation of large populations in cities; the differentiation within these of primary producers, . . . full-time specialist artisans, merchants, officials, priests, and rulers; an effective concentration of economic and political power; the use of conventional symbols for recording and transmitting information (written language), and equally conventional standards of weights and of measures of time and space leading to some mathematical and calendrical science.[2]

The first cities were not simply large villages, but were a new *kind* of social organization.

[1] Gideon Sjoberg, *The Pre-industrial City*, The Free Press of Glencoe, New York, 1960, p. 32.
[2] Gordon V. Childe, *Social Evolution*, Abelard-Schuman, Limited, New York, 1951, p. 161.

Since the existence of an urban population depends on a rural population able to produce more than it needs for its own sustenance, the first cities were in areas whose soil and climate were so favorable that even the limited technology of that time could produce a surplus of foodstuffs: the rich river valleys of the Nile in Egypt, the Yellow River in China, and the Indus River in India. Each of these areas also had a water supply adequate for the needs of a large urban population. While these physical resources are necessary, they do not by themselves account for the appearance and development of preindustrial cities. The fact that a society is able to produce more food than is needed for subsistence by the people who raise the food does not mean that the society will automatically begin supporting a nonagricultural class of urban specialists. The culture of the society must also make city life desirable, and the social organization of the society must make it possible to siphon off and centralize the small surpluses produced by the many otherwise unconnected agricultural producing units. These units are usually kinship groupings. The attitudes and values of the people must allow the surplus food to be used to support a non-food-producing segment of the society. Cities could not exist if a culture required that all surplus food be displayed and allowed to rot as part of a religious ceremony. The early cities, in their social organization and cultural complexity, were a revolutionary departure from all the human communities that had preceded them. In the perspective of time, then, cities appear to have been a change from one kind of social organization and community to another kind, and not simply a change in degree.[3]

Industrial Cities. Beginning about 1750, however, man learned to exploit effectively the high-energy fuels, first coal and then petroleum products, releasing energy far in excess of that expended in producing it. Professor Cottrell has shown clearly how demographic as well as social, economic, and political phenomena inevitably change, though not everywhere in the same way, with every change in the amount of surplus energy available to communities and societies.[4] There is no doubt that the residence in urban areas of a large percent of a country's population is a situation peculiar to the industrial age. The technology and the economic systems of past civilizations were unable to produce enough agricultural surplus to support any considerable part of their populations in cities. Only within the last two centuries has agriculture become productive enough to spare more than *20 to 25 percent* of a people from agricultural labor. In the absence of some kind of international arrangement, therefore, the efficiency of a country's agricultural production sets limits on the proportion

[3] Gordon V. Childe, *What Happened in History*, Penguin Books, Inc., Baltimore, 1946. In his chapter, "The Urban Revolution in Mesopotamia," Childe develops his thesis concerning how and why written language, mathematical notation, objective time systems, class structure, and political systems were both causes and results of urban development.

[4] W. Frederick Cottrell, *Energy and Society*, McGraw-Hill Book Company, New York, 1955.

of its people who can live in its towns and cities. Malthus had this to say about the relative numbers of agricultural and urban populations:

> It must ever be true that the surplus produce of the cultivators taken in its most enlarged sense, measures and limits the growth of that part of the society which is not employed upon the land. Throughout the whole world the number of manufacturers, of merchants, of proprietors, and of persons engaged in the various civil and military professions must be exactly proportioned to this surplus produce and cannot in the nature of things increase beyond it.[5]

Some countries have a larger proportion of their population living in cities than can be supported by the agriculture of the country itself through surpluses which are made available to the urban country either through trade (usually the exchange of manufactured products for food and fiber) or through the political domination of the agricultural country by the urban country. The most notable example of a country with a disproportionate part of its population living in cities is Great Britain. This internal imbalance made Great Britain's survival through World Wars I and II more precarious than it otherwise would have been, because the trade routes between Great Britain and many other countries were extremely vulnerable to enemy attack. The necessary flow of goods into Great Britain was maintained only at a tremendous cost in men and ships. Even in peacetime, Great Britain's dependence upon international trade makes her position precarious in the face of changing world conditions. Other examples of national urban-rural imbalance are the Netherlands and Japan; both of these countries found themselves overpopulated when they lost the colonial possessions which had supplied them with natural resources.

When the tremendous power of the steam engine was exploited for industry and transportation, major changes took place in urban organization. Prior to 1750, cities differed in some particulars, but they were all similar enough to be meaningfully classified as pre-steam or preindustrial cities. This does not mean that the use of coal (or any other energy source) was responsible for all the changes we shall discuss. There is no doubt, however, that the vast agglomerations of human beings living in our early industrial cities could not possibly have come together and survived without the development of power-driven machines, both for manufacturing and transportation, which was made possible by the use of steam. Efficient transportation not only ensured a more dependable supply service for large cities by increasing the number, the variety, and the size of the areas supplying food and raw materials, but it also allowed these cities to sell their goods and services to people scattered throughout the world.

Advances in scientific knowledge and technology during the past 200 years

[5] Thomas Robert Malthus, *An Essay on Population*, vol. 1, J. M. Dent & Sons, Ltd., Publishers, London; E. P. Dutton & Co., Inc., New York, n.d. (Everyman's Library, nos. 692–693), p. 76.

not only have enabled many countries to support a larger proportion of their populations in cities than ever before, but they have also made it possible to create "super" cities—cities of well over 1 million inhabitants. Although we do not know exactly how big the preindustrial cities were, we can be certain that even the largest cities in the old civilizations did not approach in size the largest cities of today. Those civilizations simply did not have the necessary sanitary facilities or the mechanical means of supplying the necessities of life to the huge urban populations that now live in such metropolitan centers as New York, London, Los Angeles, Tokyo, Paris, and Moscow. The greatest cities of antiquity probably did not have more than 500,000 or 600,000 inhabitants, although Rome under Augustus or Babylon at its zenith might have approached 1 million. It was not possible to supply an appreciably larger number of people, living in a constricted space, with food, fuel, and the materials of manufacture, so long as transport depended only upon manpower, domestic animals, and boats navigated without steam. Thus, while agricultural productivity and systems of distribution set upper limits to the *proportion* of a country's population which could live in cities (assuming no significant international trade in agricultural goods), the transportation (used in the broadest sense to mean the movement of people, goods, and messages) was a major limit on the *size* of the individual city.

The tremendous size of some of today's cities is not the only thing that differentiates them from the urban places of other eras. Before the use of steam power, factories were small (manufacturing was usually done in the workers' homes) and very little office work was needed to carry on the business of a firm; hence, there was no economic reason for the concentration of any large number of people in a given place. In those days the large city was necessarily organized so that most people could work either at home or in their immediate neighborhood. When the senior author wandered about some of these Asian cities in the 1920s and the 1930s, he could not help but be impressed by the absence of a central business area, by the large amount of home manufacture, and by the resultant uniformity of most parts of the city. In many respects, each part of the city was a nearly self-sufficient community. The city was not divided into highly specialized sections or districts, such as the financial, retail-trade, wholesale-trade, heavy-industry, and residence sections to which we are accustomed in modern cities. The author had the impression of going through a series of small cities rather than one large city.

If steam power was to be used effectively in transportation and manufacturing, major adjustments had to be made in the social, political, and economic systems of the communities and countries where steam power was coming into use.[6]

---

[6] For an excellent account of the major social, political, and economic changes associated with developing industrialization in Great Britain see: Karl Polanyi, *The Great Transformation,* Holt, Rinehart and Winston, Inc., New York, 1944; and W. Frederick Cottrell, *Energy and Society,* McGraw-Hill Book Company, New York, 1955.

Since steam power could not be readily adapted to home industry, its use generally required a separation between where a man lived and where he worked. Steam power is most efficient when it is produced by large steam engines and then used by machines which are concentrated nearby. Steam power used directly, as it was until about 50 years ago, lost power rapidly with distance; this meant that for reasons of efficiency, large factories were built around a central steam plant. (More recently steam power has been used to produce electric power, resulting in an altogether different power gradient; electric power can be transported by wire over considerable distances with relatively little loss.)

Not only did the early use of steam power separate a man's place of work from his home; it also necessitated the concentration of great numbers of workers in small areas during their working hours. Before the automobile, bus, or electric streetcar were in general use, these factory workers had to walk to work, and because of their common requirements, factories were close together rather than scattered throughout the area. These conditions encouraged large concentrations of residential population within a comparatively small radius of the factories. Tenements, lack of open space, and terrible room crowding were some of the hideous by-products of the congestion of that time. These conditions, which seem unbelievable when we read the fictional accounts of them in the books of Charles Dickens, are not very different from the conditions existing today in many of the large cities of the Far East, such as Calcutta. When industrial cities were first taking form, there were probably no alternatives to the centralization of manufacturing and business and the resultant crowded living conditions. These cities were definitely mononucleated and had concentrations of population unique in human experience. But in cities which were well established before industrialization, such as Paris and London, the new technology based on steam power had to act through existing urban forms; therefore, these cities never became as clearly mononucleated as cities which developed after industrialization.

The Emergence of the Contemporary City. Technological changes which began in the late nineteenth century have provided a base for the radical redistribution of population and the reorganization of all kinds of economic activities. From our point of view the most important of these developments was the use of electricity to provide communication, as well as power for motors, heat, and the internal-combustion engine.

Electricity has freed industry from the space and distance strictures imposed by direct steam power. Plants no longer need to be clustered near coal-supply points, because electricity does not have to be used near the place where it is produced. It can be distributed over considerable distances comparatively cheaply, without regard to fixed transportation routes, and with little power loss. Because it is easy to transmit, electric power can be sent in many directions from a single source, and industries using electricity can be scattered over a much wider area. Furthermore, since electricity can be efficiently used to run motors of all sizes, the size of a factory can now be decided on other grounds than the nature of the power plant itself. Not every factory is forced to be large or to employ large numbers of workers to assemble its products. Since cheap power can be bought from a central station, the little producer who wants to establish a small factory is saved the capital expense of installing his own power plant, and the large producer can now divide his factory into smaller units and place them at strategic points determined by considerations other than power costs. With the recent advances in electronics, we are also beginning to see a *new type* of factory, electrically controlled and far more efficient than even the most completely electrified but man-controlled factories. This new automated factory uses only a fraction of the manpower needed in older factories of similar size.

The effect of power made available by the internal-combustion engine, particularly the portable engine, has been different from, but nearly as dramatic as, that of electricity on the meaning and significance of *distance* for men. The automobile and truck can carry relatively small loads and make frequent stops with very little loss in efficiency and can travel in any direction, provided some sort of roadway exists. For example, workers no longer need to live within walking distance of their place of employment. Their ability and willingness to commute 10, 20, or more miles to work has the double consequence of enlarging their opportunities for employment and providing the employer with a larger area from which to draw employees.[7]

Families and industries which have responded to these new opportunities have helped to create still a third kind of urban community. Most large urban areas are no longer the compact communities which were called cities until early in this century. The suburban movement, greatly accelerated by the appearance of the automobile and truck, has also been speeded by the public construction of highways and by the extension of such characteristically urban utilities as sewage disposal, water, gas, electricity, and telephones. Families have been further encouraged to live outside the city by the development of the shopping center, a social invention offering local facilities for retail trade, service, and banking. These centers, located in the newly populated areas around cities, are designed for the car-driving shopper. Increasingly, shopping centers are appearing ahead of the movement of population, although their location is based on careful studies of where future population growth is most likely to take place. Sometimes the developer-builder puts up the center and also the houses.

In the last 50 to 100 years, technological factors have made possible the creation of a third and truly new kind of urban community, one that is still in

---

[7] The 1960 census included questions on "journey to work," and the U.S. Bureau of the Census has published a volume (1963) devoted to a detailed analysis of this phenomenon: *U.S. Census of Population: 1960, Subject Report, Journey to Work*, Final Report PC(2)-6B.

the process of change and will be more accurately described later as a transitional type. Pre-steam cities were clusters of nearly identical villages surrounding a center which had religious or political significance but not much industrial importance. The early post-steam cities, which were large, densely populated, and mononucleated, were organized around industry and trade. Now a third type is emerging, a new urban complex similar to the large pre-steam cities in its clusterlike arrangement, but extending over an enormous area and capable of containing vast numbers of people. The largest pre-steam city would be

TABLE 6-1.   PERCENT OF WORLD'S POPULATION LIVING IN CITIES OF 20,000 OR MORE
AND 100,000 OR MORE: 1800–1960

Year	Cities of 20,000 or more	Cities of 100,000 or more	World population* (in millions)
1960	22.4	15.6	2,995
1950	20.9	13.1	2,510
1900	9.2	5.5	1,571
1850	4.3	2.3	1,091
1800	2.4	1.7	919

* 1900, 1850, and 1800 World Population, Wilcox's Estimate, table 13-1.
   Source: Kingsley Davis, "The Origin and Growth of Urbanization in the World,"
   American Journal of Sociology, vol. 9, p. 433, March, 1955; United Nations, Demographic
   Yearbook, 1960, p. 349; Demographic Yearbook, 1961, p. 120.

dwarfed if it were compared with some of today's large urban areas, but this new kind of urban agglomeration is not simply an expansion of the older post-steam city; it is different in *kind*, not just larger in area and population.

Tables 6-1 and 6-2 show that the last 150 years have brought a significant increase in the *number* of the world's large cities, and an increase in the *proportion* of the world's population living in big cities. It is estimated that in 1800, fewer than 3 of every 100 people in the world lived in cities of 20,000 or more; in 1960, approximately 22 people of every 100 lived in cities of this size. For bigger cities the trend is almost identical: Fewer than 2 people of every 100 lived in cities of 100,000 or more in 1800, and in 1960, approximately 16 of 100 people lived in such cities.

Table 6-2 shows that only one city (London, England) came close to having 1 million inhabitants in 1800. In 1900, ten of the world's cities had populations of 1 million or more. The 1960 figures in Table 6-2 show how much the large concentrations of populations would be understated if only the city proper totals were given, because they exclude a large part of the total agglomeration center-

TABLE 6-2.   POPULATION OF THE WORLD'S LARGEST CITIES: 1800–1960 (IN THOUSANDS)

City and country	1960* City proper	1960* Urban agglomeration	1950	1900	1850	1800
Tokyo, Japan	8,303	9,505	5,385	1,819	—	—
New York, U.S.A	7,782	10,695	7,892	3,437	696	79
Shanghai, China	6,900	—	6,204	457	—	—
Moscow, U.S.S.R.	5,032	—	4,137	1,175	323	189
Bombay, India	4,941	—	2,839	776	—	—
Peking, China	4,010	—	2,768	1,000	—	—
Buenos Aires, Argentina	3,768	—	2,981	821	76	140
São Paulo, Brazil	3,674	—	2,017	240	—	—
Chicago, U.S.A	3,550	6,221	3,621	1,699	30	—
Berlin, Germany†	3,296	—	3,336	2,712	429	173
London, United Kingdom	3,225	8,222	3,348	4,536	2,363	959
Tientsin, China	3,220	—	2,694	750	—	—
Rio de Janeiro, Brazil	3,124	—	2,303	688	166	43
Calcutta, India	3,040	5,909	2,549	—	—	—
Leningrad, U.S.S.R	2,888	3,300	3,191	1,440	487	220
Osaka, Japan	2,887	—	1,956	996	—	—
Cairo, U.A.R. (Egypt)	2,852	2,993	2,091	570	—	—
Paris, France	2,850	4,824	2,725	2,661	1,053	548
Djakarta, Indonesia	2,814	—	1,865	116	97	—
Mexico City, Mexico	2,698	—	2,335	345	—	—
Los Angeles, U.S.A	2,479	6,743	1,970	102	2	—
Shenyang, China	2,411	—	2,300	418	—	—
Madras, India	2,208	—	1,416	509	406	—
Wuhan, China	2,146	—	1,427	137	—	—
Chungking, China	2,121	—	1,772	620	—	—
Philadelphia, U.S.A	2,003	4,343	2,072	1,294	121	41
Madrid, Spain	—	1,966	1,618	540	281	160
Rome, Italy	—	1,947	1,556	463	184	153
Karachi, Pakistan	1,916	—	1,009	—	—	—

* Actual city populations as far as it is possible to judge from the data and for the date nearest that given for the column. In the 1960 column, both city and agglomeration are given. Agglomeration is defined as "including the suburban fringe or thickly settled territory lying outside of, but adjacent to, the city boundaries."

† Combined East and West Berlin.

Source: United Nations, *Demographic Yearbook, 1960,* table 7; and for 1800 to 1950, Warren S. Thompson, *Population Problems,* 4th ed., McGraw-Hill Book Company, New York, 1953, p. 389.

ing on most of these cities—that is, people living under urban conditions but beyond the political limits of the city. The figures for the agglomerations are given in the second column under 1960. In some cases the agglomeration or metropolitan population is nearly two or more times the size of the "city proper"—London 8.2 and 3.2 million, Calcutta 5.9 and 3 million, and Philadelphia 4.3 and 2 million, respectively.

PROBLEMS OF INTERNATIONAL COMPARABILITY

We must always be careful when we make international comparisons, because there is considerable variation among the criteria used by various countries in delimiting the territory considered to include an urban population. In some cases the population in the built-up areas beyond a city's political limits is included, and in other cases this population is excluded. The *Demographic Yearbook* uses the word *agglomeration* to name the population living in a condition of urban density, regardless of whether the inhabitants live inside or outside the official political boundaries. Unfortunately, the problem of making significant international comparisons involves something more basic than the lack of agreement on where to draw the boundary lines around urban populations. There is no international consensus on the basic concepts "urban" and "rural" themselves. With respect to the meanings of these terms, the *Demographic Yearbook, 1952*, says:

> . . . The urban-rural classification is usually a dichotomy which divides the population into two parts, one urban, the other rural. Since there is no point in the continuum from small clusters to large agglomerations at which "rural" ends and "urban" begins, the line drawn between urban and rural is necessarily an arbitrary one. [p. 9.]

The various countries of the world have selected widely differing points along this continuum. In the *Demographic Yearbook, 1960*, we find this comment:

> Urban status may be granted to places with as few as 250 inhabitants in Denmark, while in Korea the lower limit is 40,000 persons. In Northern Ireland and Bulgaria, urban means places with urban status regardless of size; in Israel, it implies predominantly non-agricultural centers; in Malta, it is defined as built-up areas devoid of agricultural land. The lack of strict comparability as evidenced by the vague and diverse definitions will be immediately apparent. [p. 34.]

United Nations demographers have made a great effort to establish and gain acceptance for a universally applicable set of definitions for rural and urban populations. At the present time, however, the rural-urban distributions presented in the *Demographic Yearbook*, some of which are presented in Table 6-3, are based on each country's own definition of what constitutes urban and rural populations. The qualifications we have made, however, do not mean that the data in the above tables are of no value. They are very useful for broad comparisons but too variable in their precision to permit detailed comparisons.

URBANIZATION AND URBANISM

The term "urbanization" refers to the process whereby an increasing *proportion* of a country's population come to live in cities. "Urbanism" refers to the way of life usually found in large urban centers.

Urbanization. W. S. Thompson calls urbanization the "movement of people from communities concerned chiefly with agriculture to other communities, generally larger, whose activities are primarily centered in government, trade, manufacture, or allied interests."[8] The speed, or rate, of urbanization varies from time to time and from country to country. During the approximately 5,000 years since the appearance of the first cities, urbanization on a worldwide scale took place very slowly. About 100 years ago, urbanization began to take place at an increasing rate all over the world, and it has continued to do so, although it has not taken place evenly over the face of the earth. (For a further discussion of the factors associated with this uneven development, see Chapter 15.)

Urbanism. To most sociologists, the concept of urbanism refers to the style of life that characteristically develops under urban conditions. Louis Wirth, in his article "Urbanism as a Way of Life," used the term in this sense.[9] He regarded transiency, superficiality, and anonymity as the distinctive features of interpersonal relations in the urban milieu. Wirth argued that living in *large, dense, and heterogeneous populations* (his definition of the urban milieu) produced these characteristics and that they were inevitable and adaptive. Although some commentators argue against Wirth's position, the virtue of his article was that it drew attention to the fact that cities are more than large numbers of people engaged in a variety of specialized tasks and living in a limited area; he pointed out that city life also involves special ways of thinking and behaving. In the past, cities have always produced and perpetuated a style of life different from that of the surrounding rural areas and consequently would be expected to have significantly different demographic characteristics. Since the urban dweller has to adjust continuously to a wide variety of new and strange things, events, and

[8] W. S. Thompson, "Urbanization," *Encyclopedia of the Social Sciences*, vol, 15, p. 189.
[9] *American Journal of Sociology*, vol. 44, July, 1938, pp. 1–24.

TABLE 6-3.   PERCENT OF POPULATION LIVING IN LOCALITIES OF 20,000 OR MORE IN SELECTED COUNTRIES: LATEST DATA AVAILABLE

Country	Year census—C estimate—E	Type of locality*	Total population (in thousands)	Percent in localities of 20,000 or more
England and Wales..............	1951—C	a	43,758	70.8
Japan.........................	1955—C	c	89,276	65.7
Australia......................	1954—C	a	8,987	62.4†
Philippines....................	1948—C	b	19,234	55.6
Scotland......................	1951—C	b	5,096	54.4
New Zealand..................	1956—C	a	2,174	51.9
Netherlands...................	1947—C	a	9,625	49.7
Argentina.....................	1947—C	b	15,894	48.3
Chile.........................	1959—E	b	7,465	46.3
Colombia.....................	1951—C	b	11,548	45.8
United States.................	1960—C	b	179,323	44.5†
Denmark......................	1955—C	a	4,448	43.5†
Federal Republic of Germany.....	1950—C	c	47,696	41.5
Italy.........................	1951—C	c	47,516	41.2
Austria.......................	1951—C	c	6,934	39.8
Spain.........................	1950—C	c	27,977	39.8
Hungary......................	1960—C‡	b	9,977	37.0
Egypt.........................	1957—E	b	22,997	36.9†
East Germany..................	1959—E	c	16,204	36.2
U.S.S.R......................	1959—C	b	208,827	35.5
North Ireland.................	1958—E	b	1,402	34.8
Cuba.........................	1953—C	b	5,829	34.7†
Canada.......................	1956—C	b	16,081	33.3†
France.......................	1954—C	c	42,774	33.3
Sweden.......................	1950—C	a	7,042	33.0
Union of South Africa...........	1960—C‡	a	15,841	32.9
Norway.......................	1950—C	a	3,279	32.8
Belgium......................	1947—C	c	8,512	32.0
Finland.......................	1958—E	b	4,395	31.2
Venezuela.....................	1950—C	b	5,035	31.0
Switzerland...................	1960—C‡	c	5,411	29.9
Republic of Korea..............	1955—C	b	21,526	29.2†
Greece.......................	1951—C	b	7,633	28.1
Poland.......................	1950—C	b	25,008	25.6
Mexico.......................	1950—C	b	25,791	24.1
Czechoslovakia.................	1950—C	b	12,338	21.6†
Federation of Malaya...........	1957—C	b	6,279	20.8‡
Brazil........................	1950—C	b	51,944	20.2
Turkey.......................	1955—C	b	24,065	18.2
Romania......................	1948—C	b	15,873	17.1
Portugal......................	1950—C	b	8,441	16.5

TABLE 6-3.   PERCENT OF POPULATION LIVING IN LOCALITIES OF 20,000 OR MORE IN SELECTED COUNTRIES: LATEST DATA AVAILABLE (*Continued*)

Country	Year census—C estimate—E	Type of locality*	Total population (in thousands)	Percent in localities of 20,000 or more
Bulgaria	1946—C	b	7,029	15.2
Algeria	1948—C	b	7,787	14.1
India	1951—C	b	356,879	12.0
Yugoslavia	1953—C	b	16,937	11.3
Ceylon	1953—C	b	8,098	11.1†
Congo (Leopoldville)	1959—E	b	13,984	9.1
Burma	1953—E	b	19,272	8.2†
Pakistan	1951—C	b	75,842	8.0
Madagascar	1959—E	b	5,287	8.0
Tanganyika	1957—C	b	8,788	3.3
Nepal	1954—C	b	8,473	2.1
Mozambique	1956—E	b	6,105	1.6

* Type of locality: a—Agglomerations without regard to fixed boundaries; b—localities with fixed boundaries, commonly under the jurisdiction of local or "urban" forms of government; c—relatively small or smallest administrative subdivision having fixed boundaries and, in sum, comprising the entire country.

† 25,000 or more.

‡ Provisional.

Source: United Nations, *Demographic Yearbook, 1960*, table 8.

ideas, his reaction to newness and change is likely to be very different from that of the rural person. He is much more mobile and must learn to adjust not only to his own mobility but also to other urban dwellers who are physically and socially mobile. Nels Anderson sums up this situation very well when he says, "Urbanism as a way of life is both complex and fluid, and tends to become more so."[10] The typical urban person, then, is inclined to be more sophisticated, less bound by tradition—in fact, more "urbane"—than the rural person.

The Diffusion of Urbanism. The phenomenon of urbanization is easier to define geographically than is urbanism, its sociocultural by-product. Every reader knows rural people whose tastes and reactions are as urbane as those of any urban dweller. The attitudes, values, and behavior which originate in urban milieus are not necessarily restricted to urban areas. When the ability of a society to move its people and goods is limited, the exposure of its rural people

[10] Nels Anderson, *The Urban Community: A World Perspective*, Holt, Rinehart and Winston, Inc., New York, 1959, p. 3.

to urban life is also limited. As a society's ability to move its goods and people increases, however, so will the urban way of life found in its cities increasingly diffuse from them to the rural areas.

Until recently, ideas, attitudes, values, and ways of doing things were *carried* from one place to another by people and required the same transportation methods and the same length of time as human travel. At one time, then, the conditions that governed the speed of communication between men were the very same conditions that governed man's ability to travel. But these conditions have been virtually eliminated as variables affecting the speed with which we can move messages today. The invention of the radio, telephone, and television has made it possible to use electromagnetic waves as *carriers* of messages, and messages can now travel almost instantaneously in nearly every direction. Extensive exposure of rural people to urban ways is not only possible but is one of the most pervasive realities of modern industrial society. Today, a rural people can be exposed not only to the urban life of their own country, but to the urban life of any country in the world. The consequences of this expansion of horizons are not easy to foresee, nor are they all necessarily desirable. The influence of the city has always extended beyond those who live within its boundaries, but at no previous time has its influence been felt by so many people and communities far beyond its physical boundaries.

The Metropolis and Urbanism. Along with man's increased ability to move things and ideas through space has come the weaving of larger and larger areas, made up of an increasing assortment of communities of varying sizes and specializations, into an increasingly complex economic fabric. A very succinct but still complete statement concerning this development was made by Bogue.[11]

> The metropolis is usually the largest and most complex (the farthest removed from the "average" city) of all of the cities in the territory. Because it is able to assemble cheaply a varied array of raw materials and products from all parts of the world; because a large number of specialized components and skills are required in the production of the goods required to sustain human beings at their present level of living; because up to a certain point machine production increases in efficiency with an increased scale of operations; and because certain mutual benefits appear to accrue to business enterprises from their location in proximity to each other, the large city is able to produce and distribute more varied goods and services than is a smaller city. The more specialized the goods, and the more the goods are amenable to mass production, the greater these industrial and commercial advantages of large cities seem to become. From these facts it has been concluded that the metropolis, or modern large and complex city, exercises an organizing and integrative influence on the social and economic life of a broad expanse of territory

[11] Donald J. Bogue, *The Structure of the Metropolitan Community*, The University of Michigan Press, Ann Arbor, Mich., 1949, pp. 5, 6.

far beyond the civil boundaries, and thereby dominates all other communities within this area. The hypothesis of metropolitan dominance assumes that there is a system of interdependency among cities, and that there are considerable differences between the activities of individual cities. It maintains that the organizing agent, and one of the forces making for intercity differentiation, is the metropolis.

Urban and Rural Societies. The effect of the city on small-town and rural life is a combination of many converging forces. For one thing, nonurban people have had to adjust to new economic relationships resulting in part from the development of modern rapid transportation. The city has also affected the country through new methods of communication such as radio and television. The increased *accessibility* of city to country in advanced societies has eliminated or blurred some of the sharp differences once represented by the terms "city slicker" and "country hick" and has made the rural person more urban in outlook and behavior. The way of life that once characterized only city people is becoming common to all the people in industrial societies. To be sure, important social differences between urban and rural people are still reflected in persisting demographic differences, as we shall soon see; in general, however, rural and small-town people in the United States today reflect the fact that they live in an *urban* society. Both the urban and the rural person in the United States today probably resemble the city dweller of 100 years ago more closely than today's rural person resembles the rural person of 100 years ago. Because of the urban nature of industrial societies, therefore, we cannot significantly equate rural America with, for instance, rural India.

When comparing the populations of different countries, or comparing populations of the same country at different times, we find it important to distinguish between (1) how many cities there are and what proportion of the country's population lives in them, and (2) the degree of influence which these cities exert over the surrounding countryside; i.e., we must understand the nature of the relationship between the urban and rural communities. For example, although India has seven cities of 1 million or more, she is more accurately described as an agrarian-village-rural society than as an urban society. The low level of literacy and the fact that mass media cannot reach the bulk of the 550,000 villages mean that the rural person in India is still markedly different from the Indian city dweller.

URBANIZATION IN THE UNITED STATES

When the first United States census was taken in August, 1790, only 5.1 percent of the total population of 3,929,000 was urban. In fact, there were only 24 urban places in the whole country. New York (Manhattan borough) was the largest, with a population of 33,131. The city of New York was New York City only, before an act of consolidation in 1898 combined the five boroughs into Greater New York. In 1790, the population of the area that later became the boroughs of the the Bronx, Brooklyn, Manhattan, Queens, and Richmond totaled 49,401.

Philadelphia (28,522), Boston (18,320), Baltimore (13,503), and Charleston, South Carolina (16,359) were the four next largest cities. The remaining 19 cities all contained between 2,500 and 10,000 inhabitants each. As of April 1, 1960, nearly 70 percent (125,268,750) of the people in the United States were classified as urban. Approximately 92 percent of these urban people were living in 5,445 urban places (see Table 6-7).[12] New York City's population was 7,781,984 in 1960, nearly twice the size of the total United States population in 1790.

Table 6-4 and the corresponding Figure 6-1 show that the process of urbanization in the United States has been continuous from 1790 to 1960, with the exception of the decade from 1810 to 1820. Even during this decade, there was urban growth, but the rural population increased a little more than the urban; the proportion of the population classified as urban in 1820 was less than it had been in 1810, slipping from 7.3 percent to 7.2 percent. During the decade from 1910 to 1920, the United States became predominantly urban for the first time: The 1920 census placed the urban population at 51.2 percent of the total. During the decade of the Great Depression, 1930 to 1940, there was almost no increase (0.3 percent) in the proportion of the population that was urban. In fact, the United States as a whole (and the urban population) had a lower growth rate in this decade than in any other decade from 1790 to 1960 (see Table 6-5). Between 1940 and 1960 the rate of urbanization picked up, and by 1960 the United States was almost 70 percent urban.

Table 6-5 compares the urban and rural rates of growth with each other, and with the rates of growth of the country as a whole, for each decade from 1790 to 1960. The largest percentage increases in the urban population and in the population as a whole took place before 1870, with the exception noted above. The rate of increase in the rural population has declined during every decade between 1810 and 1920, except 1870 to 1880. In the decade from 1950 to 1960, the rural population in the 48 states showed *an absolute as well as a relative decline* (see Table 6-5, note *). The last column shows the ratio of urban to rural growth for each decade during the period 1790 to 1960. The greatest differences in growth rates were during the decades 1910 to 1920 and 1920 to 1930, when the ratios of urban to rural growth were 9.1 and 6.2 respectively.

Between 1790 and 1960, the urban-rural ratio in the United States changed dramatically: In 1790 only 1 person in 20 lived in an urban area; in 1960, 14 out

---

[12] The total number of urban places included 4,699 incorporated places of 2,500 or more, 620 unincorporated places of 2,500 or more, 126 urban towns and townships, and 1 urban county (Arlington, Va.) of 2,500 or more inhabitants.

TABLE 6-4.   PERCENT DISTRIBUTION OF THE POPULATION OF THE UNITED STATES IN URBAN AND RURAL AREAS: 1790–1960

Year	Total, all classes	Urban	Rural		
			Total	Nonfarm	Farm
1960	100.0	69.9	30.1	22.6	7.5
1950—new definition	100.0	64.0	36.0	20.7	15.3
1950—old definition	100.0	59.0	41.0	25.7	15.3
1940	100.0	56.5	43.5	20.5	22.9
1930	100.0	56.2	43.8	19.3	24.6
1920	100.0	51.2	48.8		
1910	100.0	45.7	54.3		
1900	100.0	39.7	60.3		
1890	100.0	35.1	64.9		
1880	100.0	28.2	71.8		
1870	100.0	25.7	74.3		
1860	100.0	19.8	80.2		
1850	100.0	15.3	84.7		
1840	100.0	10.8	89.2		
1830	100.0	8.8	91.2		
1820	100.0	7.2	92.8		
1810	100.0	7.3	92.7		
1800	100.0	6.1	93.9		
1790	100.0	5.1	94.9		

Source: U.S. Bureau of the Census, *U.S. Census of Population: 1960, General Population Characteristics, United States Summary,* PC(1)-1B, p. 1-148; *General Social and Economic Characteristics, United States Summary,* PC(1)-1C, p. 1-199; other years from earlier censuses.

of 20 people lived in urban areas. During this period, however, the *nature* of urban settlement changed, requiring changes in definition.

Census Definitions of Urban and Rural Population. The census defined urban population for the first time in 1910, saying simply that all people living in *incorporated places of 2,500* or more at the time of a decennial census were to be classified as urban. The rural population was a residual category, containing the people who remained after the urban population had been identified. In 1910 this definition had two virtues: (1) It fitted the facts of settlement; because 2,500 was the lower limit for urban places, urban communities were clearly separated from the more scattered farm and village communities; and (2) the definition was simple and could be easily applied to the first census, thereby pro-

TABLE 6-5.   DECENNIAL RATES OF INCREASE FOR THE URBAN AND RURAL POPULATIONS
OF THE UNITED STATES: 1790–1960

Year	Decennial rates of increase			Ratio of urban to rural growth
	Total	Urban	Rural	
1960*	18.5	29.3	− 0.8	——
1950†	14.5	20.6	6.5	3.2
1940	7.2	7.9	6.4	1.2
1930	16.1	27.3	4.4	6.2
1920	14.9	29.0	3.2	9.1
1910	21.0	39.3	9.0	4.4
1900	20.7	36.4	12.2	3.0
1890	25.5	56.5	13.4	4.2
1880	30.1	42.7	25.7	1.7
1870	22.6	59.3	13.6	4.4
1860	35.6	75.4	28.4	2.7
1850	35.9	92.1	29.1	3.2
1840	32.7	63.7	29.7	2.1
1830	33.5	62.6	31.2	2.0
1820	33.1	31.9	33.2	0.96
1810	36.4	63.0	34.7	1.8
1800	35.1	59.9	33.8	1.8
1790	——	——	——	——

* The change from 1950 to 1960 is based on current definition of urban. Alaska and
Hawaii are included. (If only conterminous United States is used, the increase for the
United States, urban, and rural, would be 18.4, 29.3, and −0.9.)
† The change from 1940 to 1950 is based on the earlier definition of urban.

viding data which have made possible comparisons of the urban-rural composition of the population from 1790 to 1950.

In 1950 a new definition of urban was developed, the old concept having
become less and less coincident with reality. The concept developed in 1910
assumed that politically defined city limits would embrace practically all the
people who were living under truly urban conditions. This assumption became
increasingly untenable as urban populations spilled over the political limits of
the city in ever-increasing numbers, a process which we now call the suburban
movement. Bogue states that some "sub-urban settlements" existed prior to the
Civil War (the early train commuters and their families), but that

For the most part, city growth in the nineteenth century took the form of fairly
compact and dense settlement at the periphery, which was rather promptly

annexed. Since 1910, new settlement has become more diffuse at the outer periphery, and annexation has failed to absorb the new urban-like subdivisions and housing developments which have spread over extensive areas.[13]

Many of the people living in these urban agglomerations were not classified as urban dwellers under the old definition, either because their communities were not annexed as part of the city they were peripheral to, or because they were too small (less than 2,500), or because they were not politically incorporated. The 1940 census showed that the suburban trend not only continued during the Depression of the 1930s, but that it did so at an accelerated rate even while the cities themselves barely grew at all. The suburban building boom that began in 1946, right after World War II, demonstrated that a new definition of urban would have to be made in time for the 1950 census. Without this new definition, a large share of the truly urban population would be categorized as rural, a classification which would underestimate the true rate of urban growth and would reduce the actual rural-urban differences by including urban people in the rural category. No longer could the political city be considered coterminous with the physical city. No longer could a city's political boundaries be regarded as the limits of the total urban settlement which is economically and socially (if not politically) a unit, involved in daily interaction which transcends the traditional political lines of city demarcation.

The New Definition of Urban. Taking into account the new pattern of urban settlement, the U.S. Bureau of the Census developed a new concept, the "urbanized" area. "The urbanized area can be characterized as the physical city as distinguished from both the legal city and the metropolitan community. In general, urbanized areas represent the thickly-settled urban core of the (larger) standard metropolitan areas."[14] Census geographers have done their best to make the outer limits of the urbanized area coincide with the limits of *urban settlement* by including territory (beyond the central city) having urban residential density or devoted to commercial, industrial, transportational, recreational and other purposes functionally related to the central city. "The major objective of the Bureau of the Census in delineating urbanized areas was to provide a better separation of urban and rural population in the vicinity of the larger cities. . . . [Urbanized areas] correspond to what are called 'conurbations' in some other countries. . . . An urbanized area may be thought of as divided into the central city [of 50,000 or more], or cities, and the remainder of the area, or the *urban fringe*."[15] The urban fringe includes popula-

[13] Donald J. Bogue, *The Population of the United States*, The Free Press of Glencoe, New York, 1959, p. 21.
[14] U.S. Bureau of the Census, *U.S. Census of Population: 1950, General Characteristics*, P-B, p. vi.
[15] U.S. Bureau of the Census, *U.S. Census of Population: 1960, General Social and Economic Characteristics, United States Summary*, Final Report PC(1)-1C, p. ix. [Emphasis ours.]

tions which would not have been classified as urban under the old definition. *All* the fringe population is classified as urban, not just the population in incorporated (or even unincorporated) places of 2,500 or more.

Many cities of less than 50,000 inhabitants have fringe populations which, realistically, should be classified as urban rather than rural; however, census officials found that limitations of time and money made it impossible to delineate the densely settled fringes of cities with less than 50,000 inhabitants. In 1953, one of the authors found that the small town of Oxford, Ohio, with a population of about 4,000, had a "fringe" population of approximately 1,100. Almost 1,000 of these fringe inhabitants were living neither on farms nor in incorporated communities of 2,500 or more. They were a real part of the urban community of Oxford, but they would be classified as rural even under the new definition. Bogue writes on this matter as follows:

> Although the rural-nonfarm population produced by the new definition is more homogeneous than the old population, it still fails to satisfy the ambition of some demographers, who would like it to be synonymous with rural village population. At present, incorporated places of all sizes, from 50,000 down to a few hundred, have suburban fringes that were classed as rural-nonfarm in 1950. In addition, around the larger cities there are many hundreds or thousands of nonfarm dwellings that house workers who live along main highways and commute to work in the city. Although these residences are not sufficiently clustered and close to each other to be a part of an urban fringe, many of the people who occupy them are undoubtedly more urban than rural in their characteristics.[16]

We must bear in mind that the term "urbanized area" refers to a statistical category; it is a useful device for the assembling and analyzing of population data, but it is not a political or administrative unit.

The U.S. Bureau of the Census also added another group of people to the urban category in 1950 by including in it not only incorporated places of 2,500 or more but *unincorporated* places of 2,500 or more as well. The definition of "urban population" remained substantially the same between 1950 and 1960. The 1960 definition is as follows:

> *Urban-Rural Residence.* In general, the urban population comprises all persons living in urbanized areas and in places of 2,500 inhabitants or more outside urbanized areas. More specifically, according to the definition adopted for use in the 1960 Census, the urban population comprises all persons living in (*a*) places of 2,500 inhabitants or more incorporated as cities, boroughs, villages, and towns (except towns in New England, New York, and Wisconsin); (*b*) the densely settled urban fringe, whether incorporated or unincorporated, of urbanized areas. . . (*c*) towns in New England and townships in New Jersey and Pennsylvania which

[16] Bogue, *The Population of the United States*, p. 25.

contain no incorporated municipalities as subdivisions and have either 25,000 inhabitants or more or a population of 2,500 to 25,000 and a density of 1,500 persons or more per square mile; (*d*) counties in States other than the New England States, New Jersey, and Pennsylvania that have no incorporated municipalities within their boundaries and have a density of 1,500 persons or more per square mile; and (*e*) unincorporated places of 2,500 inhabitants or more. . . .

This definition of urban is substantially the same as that used in 1950; the major difference between 1950 and 1960 is the designation in 1960 of urban towns in New England and of urban townships in New Jersey and Pennsylvania. The effect on population classification arising from this change was actually small because, in 1950, most of the population living in such places was classified as urban by virtue of residence in an urbanized area or in an unincorporated urban place. . . . In all definitions, the population not classified as urban constitutes the rural population.

The most important component of the urban territory . . . is the group of incorporated places having 2,500 inhabitants or more. A definition of urban territory restricted to such places, however, excludes a number of equally large and densely settled places merely because they are not incorporated places.[17]

The effect of these changes in the census definition on the number and proportion of the urban population is shown in Table 6-6 and in Figure 6-1. The population classified as urban in 1950 was larger by 7.5 million, or 8.5 percent, than it would have been under the 1940 definition, and in 1960 the urban population was larger by 12.2 million, or 10.8 percent, than the old definition would have permitted it to be. The biggest part (approximately 6.2 million in 1950 and

TABLE 6-6.   COMPOSITION OF THE INCREASE IN THE URBAN POPULATION OF THE UNITED STATES RESULTING FROM THE CHANGE IN DEFINITION OF URBAN: 1950 AND 1960

Composition	1950	1960
Total urban under 1950 and 1960 definition........	96,467,686	125,268,750
Total urban under 1940 definition................	88,927,464	113,056,353
Net increase in number urban..................	7,540,222	12,212,397
Net increase in percent urban.................	8.5	10.8
Increase to urban under new definition............	7,877,819	12,720,334
Within urbanized areas......................	6,203,596	10,733,350
Outside urbanized areas......................	1,674,223	1,986,984
Loss from urban under new definition of urban under 1940 rules...............................	−337,597	−507,937

Source: U.S. Bureau of the Census, *U.S. Census of Population: 1960, Number of Inhabitants, United States Summary*, p. xiv; U.S. Bureau of the Census, *U.S. Census of Population: 1950, Characteristics of the Population*, p. 12.

[17] U.S. Bureau of the Census, *U.S. Census of Population: 1960, General Social and Economic Characteristics, United States Summary*, PC(1)-1C, p. vii.

10.7 million in 1960) of this gain in each decade is a result of the new concept "urbanized area," which made *all* people in the fringe urban whether or not they lived in incorporated places of 2,500 or more. The further inclusion of unincorporated urban places of 2,500 or more (as well as urban towns and townships in New England) outside of urbanized areas added to the urban category approximately 1.7 million in 1950 and 2 million in 1960. These additions to the urban population are not quite a net gain, because a few people (300,000 in 1950 and 500,000 in 1960) who would have been urban under special rules in 1940 are now classified as rural.

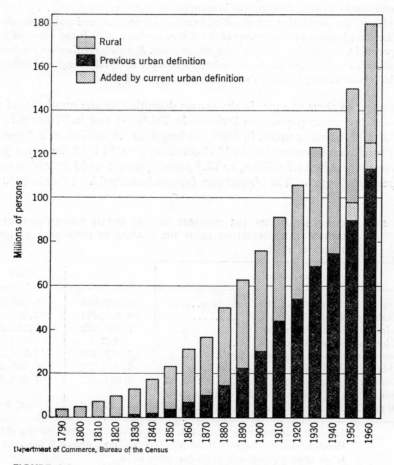

Department of Commerce, Bureau of the Census

FIGURE 6-1.   Urban and rural populations, United States: 1790 to 1960. (Table 6-4.)

While it is true that the new urban definition more accurately distinguishes between urban and rural communities than did the old one, it is also true, unfortunately, that such a change breaks the continuity of comparable urban and rural statistics. The 1940 definition can be applied to data for 1950 and 1960, but the new definition cannot be applied to 1940 data. Almost all the urban data in the 1950 census publications (and some data in the 1960 publications) are presented according to the old as well as the new definition of urban. By 1970, a single series will probably be presented, the new definition being applied to the 1950 and 1960 data, and the old one to the data for 1940 and earlier. The table will have a footnote for the year 1950, saying that the big jump in the percent urban between 1940 and 1950 was partly a result of the change in definition that took place between those dates. Some day a young sociologist may look at such tables and, if he skips the footnotes, may try to explain the apparent jump entirely in terms of socioeconomic variables. The student can easily appreciate how demographers are torn between wanting to modify their definitions to reflect changes in social reality and, at the same time, wanting to avoid changes that will hamper statistical comparability. Since a decision to change such definitions is never easy, the census circularizes the people who use its data in order to get their opinions on proposed revisions. In spite of the seeming confusion involved in these changes, however, more than 85 percent of the population classified as urban in 1950 and 1960 would have been classified as urban in 1940, because they lived in incorporated communities of 2,500 or more.

Table 6-7 shows the proportionate distribution of the total urban population according to the various categories that make up the 1960 definition. Most of the

TABLE 6-7.   COMPOSITION OF THE URBAN POPULATION OF THE UNITED STATES ACCORDING TO THE CURRENT DEFINITION: 1960

Area	Population	Percent
Total urban	125,268,750	100.0
Within urbanized areas	95,848,487	76.5
Central cities	57,975,132	46.3
Other incorporated urban places	25,342,758	20.2
Unincorporated urban places	2,679,492	2.1
Outside urban places	9,851,105	7.9
Outside urbanized areas	29,420,263	23.5
Incorporated urban places*	26,993,672	21.5
Unincorporated urban places	2,426,591	1.9

* Includes urban towns and townships with a total population of 173,022.
Source: U.S. Bureau of the Census, U.S. Census of Population: 1960, Number of Inhabitants, United States Summary, p. xiv.

urban population lives in or on the outskirts of cities of 50,000 or more. These *urbanized areas* (see also Figure 6-2) account for slightly more than three-fourths of the total urban population, while only one-fourth of the urban population lives outside the urbanized areas. The central cities of these urbanized areas contain nearly one-half of the urban population, while their densely settled fringes hold almost one-third of the urban population.

Rural-nonfarm and Rural-farm. Beginning in 1920, the census divided the rural population into rural-farm and rural-nonfarm populations. Just as the distinction between urban and rural was based upon the definition of urban, the population not thus defined being regarded as rural, so also the distinction between farm and nonfarm depends upon the definition of farm, the population not thus defined being regarded as nonfarm. "In the 1960 Census, the farm population consists of persons living in rural territory on places of 10 or more acres from which sales of farm products amounted to $50 or more in 1959 or on places of less than 10 acres from which sales of farm products amounted to $250 or more in 1959."[18] The rural-nonfarm population, therefore, is the remaining population living in what is regarded as rural (any nonurban) territory. This definition of the farm population is not comparable with the 1950 definition, which was based on the answer to the question, "Is this house on a farm (or ranch)?" Regardless of the answer given to this question, however, people who "paid cash rent for the house and yard only" were classified as nonfarm in 1950. According to a census study, the change in definition between 1950 and 1960 meant that 4.2 million persons were classified as nonfarm population in 1960 who would have been in the farm-residence category according to the 1950 definition. This figure represents about 21 percent of the population that would have been classified as living on farms in 1960 if the 1950 definition had been used. The census goes on to say,

> In view of the magnitude of the change, and of the fact that its impact has probably been very uneven from one area to another, no statistics on farm-nonfarm residence from earlier censuses are shown in this report. One reason for the change was to make the definition of farm residence essentially consistent with the definition of a farm used in the agricultural census, beginning with the 1959 Census of Agriculture.[19]

In Table 6-4 we see that the farm population fell from approximately 25 percent of the total population in 1930 to an extremely low 7.5 percent of the total population in 1960. (The percents are based on the definitions used in the

[18] U.S. Bureau of the Census, *U.S. Census of Population: 1960, General Social and Economic Characteristics (State Reports)*, p. VIII.
[19] *Ibid.* p. VIII.

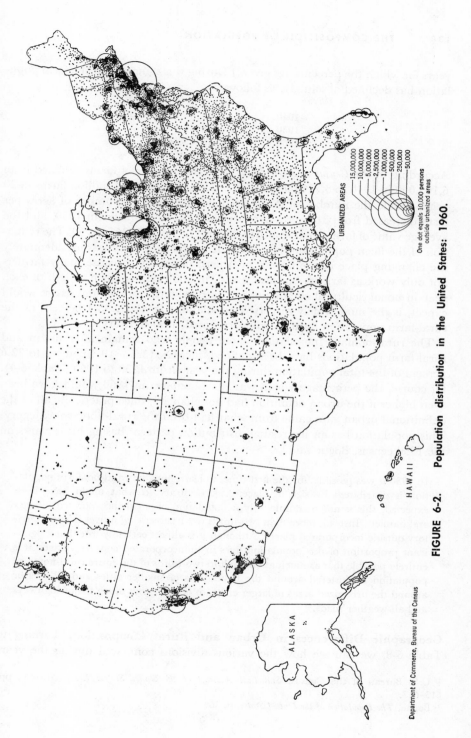

One dot equals 10,000 persons
outside urbanized areas

URBANIZED AREAS

15,000,000
10,000,000
5,000,000
2,500,000
1,000,000
500,000
250,000
50,000

FIGURE 6-2.   Population distribution in the United States: 1960.

Department of Commerce, Bureau of the Census

years for which the percents are given.) During this same period the farm population has declined absolutely, as follows:[20]

1940	30,547,000
1950	23,048,000
1960	15,635,000

According to the *Census of Agriculture, 1959*, the number of farms declined from 6,103,000 in 1940 to 3,711,000 in 1959—a loss of almost 2.4 million farms in 20 years. While the number of farms declined, the average number of acres per farm increased from 216 acres per farm in 1950 to 303 acres in 1959, and the average value of farms went from $13,983 in 1950 to $34,826 in 1959. The reduction of the farm population, marked as it is, still does not measure adequately the changing place of the farmer in American society, because many farmers not only work as farmers but also spend, in addition, as much as half of each year in nonagricultural occupations. The rural-farm population, as we would expect, is the most widely dispersed population: In 1959, 98.4 percent of the rural-farm population lived in unincorporated rural territory.

The rural-nonfarm population, those people who remain after urban and rural-farm populations have been defined, increased from 19.3 percent to 22.6 percent of the total population during the years from 1930 to 1960 (Table 6-4). Of course, the percentage which was rural-nonfarm in 1960 would have been even higher if the urban definition had not changed, since practically all of the definitional urban gain came from what had been the rural-nonfarm category. This population has an interesting distribution pattern. Basing his remarks on the 1950 census, Bogue said,

> In 1950 it was possible, for the first time, to learn how the rural-nonfarm population is distributed by size of place. . . . Contrary to what might have been expected, this is not predominantly a population of small incorporated villages and hamlets. Instead, more than two-thirds (69.1 percent) of it lives in rural territory outside incorporated places. Although it is almost certainly true that a significant proportion of this population lives in unincorporated country villages, it is entirely possible that as much as one-half to two-thirds of the entire rural-nonfarm population is clustered around the boundaries of smaller cities and villages or around the urbanized areas of larger cities, or is strung out along major highways and all-weather roads.[21]

Geographic Differences in Urban and Rural Composition. Turning to Table 6-8, we can see how the various divisions compared during the years

[20] U S. Bureau of the Census, *Statistical Abstract of the United States: 1963*, 84th ed., pp. 613–617.

[21] Bogue, *The Population of the United States*, p. 36.

TABLE 6-8. PERCENT DISTRIBUTION OF THE URBAN AND RURAL POPULATION OF THE UNITED STATES, BY DIVISIONS: 1940–1960

| Year and area | U.S. | Northeast | | North Central | | South | | | West | |
		New England	Middle Atlantic	East North Central	West North Central	South Atlantic	East South Central	West South Central	Mountain	Pacific*
1960—total.........	100.0	100.0	100.0	100.0	100.0	100.0	100.0	100.0	100.0	100.0
Urban............	69.9	76.4	81.4	73.0	58.8	57.2	48.4	67.7	67.1	81.1
Rural-nonfarm....	22.6	21.9	16.5	19.9	22.9	33.8	34.3	23.3	24.6	15.9
Rural-farm.......	7.5	1.7	2.1	7.1	18.4	8.9	17.3	9.0	8.3	3.1
1950—total†........	100.0	100.0	100.0	100.0	100.0	100.0	100.0	100.0	100.0	100.0
Urban............	64.0	76.2	80.5	69.7	52.0	49.1	39.1	55.6	54.9	75.0
Rural-nonfarm....	20.7	19.4	14.9	18.1	21.5	29.1	25.7	22.3	28.2	17.6
Rural-farm.......	15.3	4.3	4.6	12.2	26.5	21.9	35.3	22.1	16.9	7.4
1940—total‡........	100.0	100.0	100.0	100.0	100.0	100.0	100.0	100.0	100.0	100.0
Urban............	56.5	76.1	76.8	65.5	44.3	38.8	29.4	39.8	42.7	65.3
Rural-nonfarm....	20.5	17.6	16.8	17.3	21.1	27.3	21.8	21.6	30.8	22.1
Rural-farm.......	22.9	6.3	6.4	17.2	34.6	33.9	48.9	38.6	26.5	12.6

* Excluding Alaska and Hawaii in 1940 and 1950.
† New urban definition.
‡ Old urban definition.

Source: U.S. Bureau of the Census, U.S. Census of Population: 1960, General Social and Economic Characteristics, U.S. Summary, PC (1)-1C, p. 1-250; Donald J. Bogue, The Population of the United States, The Free Press of Glencoe, New York, 1959, p. 69; U.S. Bureau of the Census, U.S. Census of Population, 1940, vol. 2, part 1, U.S. Summary, p. 51.

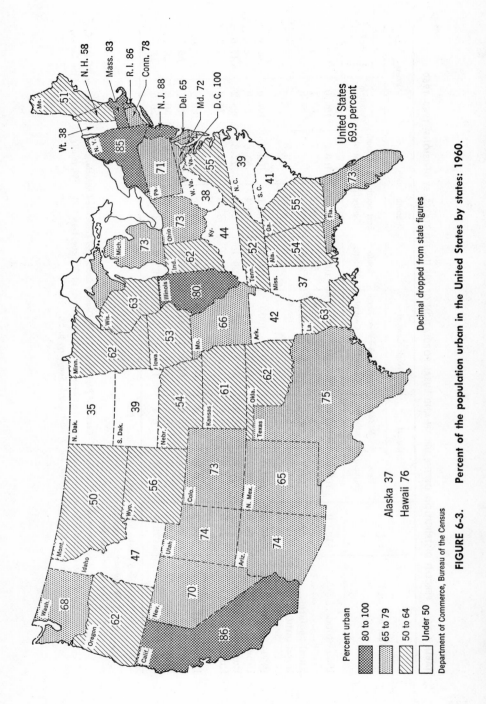

FIGURE 6-3.   Percent of the population urban in the United States by states: 1960.

Department of Commerce, Bureau of the Census

Decimal dropped from state figures

Percent urban

80 to 100
65 to 79
50 to 64
Under 50

United States
69.9 percent

Alaska 37
Hawaii 76

N. H. 58
Mass. 83
R. I. 86
Conn. 78
N. J. 88
Del. 65
Md. 72
D. C. 100

1940–1960 with respect to the distribution of their population among urban, rural-nonfarm, and rural-farm categories. (See Figure 6-3.) In 1960, there was still considerable variation among the divisions in the percentages of their populations that were urban (48.4 to 81.4), although they are more alike in this respect than they were in 1940 (29.4 to 76.8). This convergence is another of many instances of diminishing differences through time among our geographic regions and divisions. The New England and Middle Atlantic divisions are very much alike in their rural-urban composition, and they were the most urban and the least farm of all the divisions in 1940 and 1950. In 1960, these two divisions were joined by the Pacific division with respect to percent urban and percent rural. The East South Central division was the least urban between 1940 and 1960 (29.4 percent in 1940 and 48.4 percent in 1960); in fact, in 1960 it was the only division still more rural than urban. In 1940 it also had the largest percentage of rural-farm population; in 1960 its farm population was 17.3 percent, very little short of the division with the *most* farm population—the West North Central, which was 18.4 percent rural-farm in 1960. Although in 1940 five of the nine divisions had between 25 and 50 percent of their populations living on farms, by 1960 only two divisions were as high as 15 to 20 percent rural-farm. In 1960, the three divisions with the smallest farm populations (New England, Middle Atlantic, and Pacific) had 3 or fewer persons per 100 living on farms.

METROPOLITANIZATION IN THE UNITED STATES

Definition of Metropolitan. Ever since 1910, the U.S. Bureau of the Census has recognized the existence of what may be called a metropolitan population: a central city and its surrounding territory. Such outer territory contains a population which is rather closely integrated with the metropolis economically and socially. This area extends beyond the closely built up urban fringe discussed above under the category of urbanized areas. Even though this kind of metropolitan category is not a political or administrative entity as yet, there are many practical and theoretical reasons for considering it as a separate population unit. The first metropolitan population was defined in 1910 by the U.S. Bureau of the Census as follows:

> The "metropolitan district" . . . has, as its nucleus, a city of at least 200,000 inhabitants, includes the population and area of the central city itself and of all minor civil subdivisions lying within the "adjacent territory" except, as a rule, those which had a density of population of less than 150 a square mile.[22]

[22] U.S. Bureau of the Census, *Thirteenth Census of the United States: 1910*, vol. I, p. 73. For a much more extensive treatment of this subject see: Warren S. Thompson, *Population: The Growth of Metropolitan Districts in the United States: 1900–1940*, U.S. Government Printing Office, Washington, D.C., 1947.

The minor civil divisions in such a district include other cities, towns, villages, or townships surrounding the central city. There were 25 metropolitan districts in 1910. At that time the census also recognized another metropolitan category: cities between 100,000 and 200,000 population with their "adjacent territory," which included all civil divisions within 10 miles of the central city. There were 19 such units in 1910; combined with the 25 "metropolitan districts," they made up a total of 44 metropolitan units. Some changes were made in the definitions of these metropolitan units between 1910 and 1940, but the major change took place in 1950, when counties rather than minor civil divisions were used as the areal units for arriving at the total metropolitan population. In 1950 the name of this metropolitan population was changed from "metropolitan district" to "standard metropolitan area" (SMA). As is the case with almost all changes in definitions, a problem of comparability arose between the new SMA and the old metropolitan district. It is relatively easier, using the new definition based upon county units, to go back to 1910 than it is to use the old definition and apply it to 1960 data. Bogue, who has perhaps done more work in the past 20 years on the nature of the metropolitan population than anyone else, has this to say about the change in definition:

> These areas [SMA's] differ from the metropolitan districts in two important respects. (a) Whereas the metropolitan districts consisted of whole townships or towns, the SMA's consist of whole counties. (b) Whereas population density was the principal criterion for including additional units of area in metropolitan districts, possession of metropolitan characteristics and close social and economic integration with the metropolis is the basis for determining whether contiguous counties are to be included as a part of SMA's. The joint effect of these changes is to increase the size of the metropolitan area. Such a broader delimitation acknowledges that nearby rural-farm and rural-nonfarm as well as urban populations are integrated into the economy of the central city. . . . The labor market area of metropolitan centers is known to be much more extensive than the built-up area. . . . Economically, socially, and demographically such groups are most realistically thought of as belonging to the metropolitan area rather than to the category of open country, villages, and farm shopping centers. . . .
>
> The validity of this broader delimitation is supported by a voluminous body of research, extending over several decades. In fact, the establishment of SMA's represents recognition in official government statistics of repeated assertions that the area of "daily contact" or the "zone of direct participation" with the metropolis is a social and economic unit worthy of widespread attention.[23]

In 1960, the standard metropolitan area (SMA) became the standard metropolitan statistical area (SMSA). The change in name was made in order to

[23] Donald J. Bogue, *Population Growth in Standard Metropolitan Areas 1900–1950, with an Explanatory Analysis of Urbanized Areas*, Housing and Home Finance Agency, Washington, D.C., 1953, p. 5.

emphasize the "statistical" (nonpolitical) nature of the category. Some slight changes in definition, made between 1950 and 1960, need not concern us here. The following is the definition of the SMSA as it is found in the 1960 census:

> Except in New England, an SMSA is a county or group of contiguous counties which contains at least one city of 50,000 inhabitants or more, or "twin cities" with a combined population of at least 50,000. In addition to the county, or counties, containing such a city, or cities, contiguous counties are included in an SMSA if, according to certain criteria, they are essentially metropolitan in character and are socially and economically integrated with the central city. The criteria followed in the delineation of SMSA's relate to a city, or cities, of sufficient population size to constitute a central city and to the economic and social relationships with contiguous counties that are metropolitan in character.[24]

> The criteria of metropolitan character relate primarily to the attributes of the contiguous county as a place of work or as a home for a concentration of non-agricultural workers. In New England, the city and town are administratively more important than the county, and data are compiled locally for such minor civil divisions. Here, towns and cities are the units used in defining standard metropolitan statistical areas. In New England, because smaller units are used and more restricted areas result, a population density criterion of at least 100 persons per square mile is used as the measure of metropolitan character.

> The criteria of integration relate primarily to the extent of economic and social communication between the outlying counties and central county.

> A county is regarded as integrated with the county or counties containing the central cities of the area if either of the following criteria is met:

> *a.* 15 percent of the workers living in the county work in the county or counties containing central cities of the area, or

> *b.* 25 percent of those working in the county live in the county or counties containing central cities of the area.[25]

In cases lacking conclusive evidence of the kind mentioned above for determining whether there is integration between the outlying counties and the central county, other criteria are used, such as telephone calls and newspaper circulation between counties, the extent of retail-store trade, the extent of public transportation facilities, and finally, whether "local planning groups and other civic organizations operate jointly." The reader is urged to study the complete discussion of criteria used to select the "contiguous counties," which is found in the introductory pages of the U.S. Census of Population publications. See Figure 6-4 for a schematic representation of these areas.

[24] U.S. Bureau of the Census, *U.S. Census of Population: 1960, Number of Inhabitants, United States Summary*, PC(1)-1A, p. xxiv.
[25] U.S. Bureau of the Census, *U.S. Census of Population: 1960, General Social and Economic Characteristics, United States Summary*, PC(1)-1C, p. x.

In 1960 another metropolitan category was invented: the "standard consolidated area" (SCA). The census had this to say about the new concept:

> In view of the special importance of the metropolitan complexes around New York and Chicago, the Nation's largest cities, several contiguous SMSA's and additional counties that do not appear to meet the formal integration criteria but do have strong interrelationships of other kinds, have been combined into the New York–Northeastern New Jersey and the Chicago–Northwestern Indiana standard consolidated areas, respectively.[26]

It should be noted here that some of the SMSAs and both of the SCAs cut across state lines.

[26] *Ibid.*

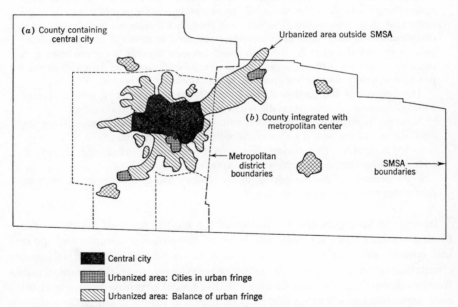

FIGURE 6-4.   Schematic diagram of relative sizes and arrangement of standard metropolitan statistical areas, urbanized areas, and metropolitan districts. [*Population Growth in Standard Metropolitan Areas 1900–1950, op. cit.*, **p. 8. (The only modification is the substitution of SMSA for SMA.)]**

Metropolitan Growth and Metropolitanization. In the monograph on metropolitan growth mentioned earlier, Bogue provides us with SMSA data for years prior to 1950, by assembling county statistics. Table 6-9 is largely based on this work. Only the SMSAs which had a total population of 100,000 are presented for the period prior to 1950. It is apparent that the decennial rates of increase have been much higher for the SMSAs than for the country as a whole

TABLE 6-9. DECENNIAL RATES OF INCREASE IN THE POPULATION OF THE STANDARD METROPOLITAN STATISTICAL AREAS OF THE UNITED STATES: 1900–1960

Year	Total SMSAs	Decennial rate of increase			Percent of total U.S. increase claimed during preceding decade		
		Total	Central cities	Rings	SMSA total	Central cities	Rings
All SMSAs—1960	212	26.4	10.7	48.6	84.2	20.1	64.1
All SMAs—1950	162	21.8	13.9	34.7	80.6	31.6	49.0
Principal SMAs*							
1950	147	21.8	13.7	34.8	79.3	30.7	48.6
1940	125	8.3	5.1	13.8	57.7	22.8	34.9
1930	115	27.0	23.3	34.2	76.2	43.3	32.9
1920	94	25.2	26.7	22.4	67.6	46.8	20.8
1910	71	32.6	35.3	27.6	53.1	37.4	15.7
1900	52	——	——	——	——	——	——

* SMAs of 100,000 or more population at the time of the census.
Source: Donald J. Bogue, *The Population of the United States,* The Free Press of Glencoe, New York, 1959, p. 49. U.S. Bureau of the Census, *U.S. Census of Population: 1960, Number of Inhabitants, United States Summary,* PC(1)-1A, p. 106.

except for the Depression decade, when neither the SMSAs nor the country grew very much (8.3 percent and 7.2 percent respectively). Since 1920, the territory in the SMSAs outside of the central cities, which is generally called the "ring," has grown at an increasingly more rapid rate than have the central cities themselves. Another way of viewing the growth of these metropolitan populations during this 60-year period is to see what percent of the national population increase took place within the SMSAs. During the period covered by the table, the SMSAs have always accounted for at least half of the total growth. In 1960 the SMSAs claimed approximately 84 percent of the total United States increase —of every 100 people by which the United States increased between 1950 and 1960, nearly 85 were living in SMSAs by 1960. The rings increased their share of the total national gain from 15.7 percent in the decade 1900 to 1910 to 64.1 percent in 1960.

Table 6-10 shows what percentages of the United States population have
lived in these metropolitan areas between 1900 and 1960. By 1960, 63 percent
of our population (112.9 million) was living in 212 SMSAs; these people were
about equally divided between the central cities and the rings. Each decade has
seen an increasing number and proportion of people living in our metropolitan
areas. (See Figure 6-5.)

TABLE 6-10.   PERCENT OF THE UNITED STATES POPULATION IN STANDARD METRO-
POLITAN STATISTICAL AREAS, CENTRAL CITIES, AND RINGS: 1900–1960

Year	Number of SMSAs*	Population (in millions)	Percent of U.S. population		
			SMSA total	Central cities	Rings
All SMSAs—1960	212	112.9	63.0	32.3	30.6
All SMSAs—1950†	212	89.3	59.0	34.6	24.4
All SMAs 1950	162	85.6	56.8	32.8	24.0
Principal SMAs‡					
1950	147	84.3	56.0	32.3	23.8
1940	125	67.1	51.1	31.6	19.5
1930	115	61.0	49.8	31.8	18.0
1920	94	46.1	43.7	28.9	14.8
1910	71	34.5	37.6	25.0	12.7
1900	52	24.1	31.9	31.2	10.7

* SMA before 1960.
† Based on the SMSA as defined in 1960.
‡ SMAs of 100,000 or more.
Source: Donald J. Bogue, *The Population of the United States*, The Free Press of
Glencoe, New York, 1959, pp. 47 and 48; U.S. Bureau of the Census, *U.S. Census
of Population: 1960, Number of Inhabitants, United States Summary*, PC(1)-1A,
p. xxvi.

Metropolitan Planning. The transformation of this sprawling, unplanned,
urban complex into a metropolitan community which is economically, socially,
and politically integrated has been retarded by the unrealistic and obsolete
political boundaries which were drawn many decades ago, when the United
States was a rural society based on an agrarian economy. Political, economic,
and social adaptations which could improve the organization and the community life of the metropolitan complex have come slowly and in piecemeal
fashion. Planning groups, however, are beginning to realize that thinking in
terms of metropolitan and regional areas is the most practical way to provide
for the needs of the city itself. An example of such an approach is the newly pro-

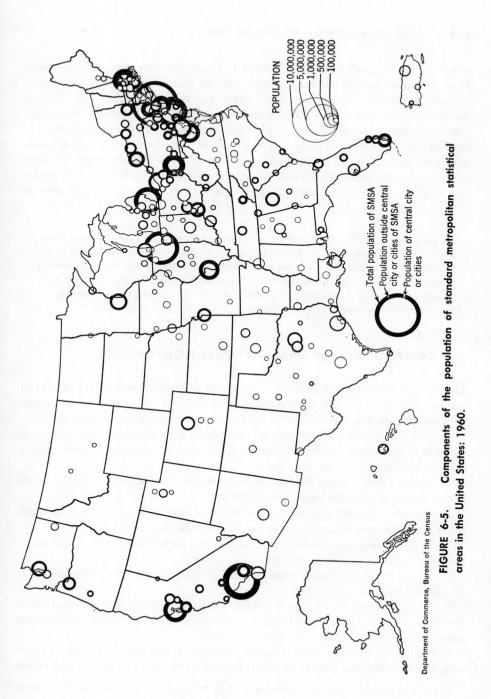

POPULATION

10,000,000
5,000,000
1,000,000
500,000
100,000

Total population of SMSA

Population outside central
city or cities of SMSA

Population of central city
or cities

FIGURE 6-5. Components of the population of standard metropolitan statistical areas in the United States: 1960.

Department of Commerce, Bureau of the Census

posed Ohio-Kentucky-Indiana Regional Transportation and Development Plan. It embraces eight counties and centers on Hamilton County, which contains the largest city in the area, Cincinnati. The completed plan, with 1990 as the design year, will be based on extensive research in the following nine separate but interrelated divisions: (1) physical features, (2) economic features, (3) land-use arrangements, (4) population, (5) utility systems, (6) development controls such as zoning laws and building codes, (7) financial structures of local governments, (8) community facilities such as schools and parks, and (9) correlation of travel, population, and housing characteristics.[27] The prospectus goes on to say,

> In recognition of this clear need to meet the problems of the O-K-I [Ohio, Kentucky, and Indiana] area in a coordinated and comprehensive fashion, it is the objective of this proposal that the local authorities work jointly with the several states to produce a comprehensive development plan for the eight-county area which will serve as a development policy guide for the various official agencies or instrumentalities herein, and for private groups in the planning region.[28]

COMPONENTS OF URBAN POPULATION CHANGE

The facts of urban growth in the United States raise the question: What are the components of the change, from one census to the next, in the number of people who are classified as urban? There are five possible components; they are relatively independent of each other, and their individual and collective influence changes from decade to decade, both with regard to individual urban places and the urban population as a whole.

1. *Natural increase:* the difference between the number of births and the number of deaths among the urban population.

2. *Migration:* the net migration between rural and urban areas, and between other countries and urban areas in the United States.

3. *Political annexation or detachment:* the political inclusion or exclusion of rural territory with respect to an existing urban place.

4. *Change in the definition of urban populations:* This particular change has been discussed above in some detail.

5. *Change from one classification to another:* the gain or loss of enough population from one census to another to cause a community to change from a rural to an urban, or from an urban to a rural, classification.

It is difficult to make even a rough estimate of the role that each of these sources of change has played in urban growth in the past, so scanty and crude

[27] Taken from a prospectus for the study drawn up by Wilbur Smith and Associates, July, 1963.
[28] *Ibid.*, p. 7.

are the historical data. It is safe to say, however, that the relative influence of each on the net urban growth has varied from country to country and from time to time. To simplify our discussion of the relative influence of each of these sources we shall talk about the changing size of individual cities and of the total urban population of a given country. First we shall sketch in a general way the part played by natural increase and net migration in city growth in Western Europe and the United States.

Natural Increase, Migration, and Urban Growth. Historically, rural areas have "produced" populations, and urban areas have "consumed" them. The growth of larger cities prior to the Industrial Revolution was probably due solely to in-migration. A record of baptisms and deaths in Paris covering a period of approximately 12½ years in the latter part of the 1600s shows an excess of 22,790 deaths over births. For the 81-year period from 1707 to 1789, Landry states that in Paris there were 5,078 more deaths than births.[29] There is also evidence that in London the death rate was as high as 50 per 1,000 in 1750, and that it was still over 30 per 1,000 in 1800.[30] It is estimated that in the period from 1700 to 1750 there were 500,000 *more deaths than births* in London—an excess of deaths over births of about 10,000 per year, a figure equivalent to about 20 per 1,000 of the total population. Until about the middle of the 1700s it was practically impossible to supply any city, even a small one, with wholesome food, good water, a small measure of sanitary sewage disposal, moderately decent housing, or the limited medical care that then existed. At what time the larger European and British cities began to show an excess of births over deaths, we do not know.

In the United States, after the first settlements were well established, living conditions were generally favorable, and there was a large excess of births over deaths. We do not know whether a period existed when our cities had death rates which were higher than their birth rates, but in the days before 1860 very high death rates did prevail in the cities. The increasing rate of urban growth in the United States after the middle of the 1800s was primarily a consequence of net migration from rural areas and from other countries. After our urban death rates began to fall and while birth rates were still high, there probably was a period when our urban growth was sizable because of natural increase; even then, however, because of the high rate of natural increase in rural areas, urbanization (urban growth outstripping rural growth) would not have taken place without a net rural-to-urban migration. Until quite recently, in fact, migration was the reason usually advanced not only for urbanization but for nearly all

[29] Adolphe Landry, "La Démographie de l'ancien Paris," *Journal de la société de statistique de Paris*, vol. 76, no. 2, p. 37, 1935.
[30] M. C. Buer, *Health, Wealth, and Population in the Early Days of the Industrial Revolution (1760–1815)*, chap. 3, George Routledge & Sons, Ltd., London, 1926.

urban growth. Even as late as the mid-1940s some students of population believed that cities of 50,000, with the area immediately around them (metropolitan districts), would not be able to maintain their numbers if they were deprived of in-migrants for a few years and if there were no increase in their birth rates. But by the 1950s it had become apparent that the urban populations in the United States were growing mainly as a result of their own natural increase. Bogue has estimated that "About 70 percent of the increase in city dwellers comes from reproductive change (natural increase) and about 30 percent from rural-urban migration."[31]

Urban growth in the United States is no longer due primarily to migration from the farms to the cities, not only because the natural increase of the farm population is declining, but because the farm population is becoming such a small part of the total population of the country. Every year, more of the total urban growth is due to an excess of births over deaths in the urban populations and to the reclassification of rural territory as urban. Increasingly, also, the different rates of growth that exist among urban places are due less to differences in the rates of natural increase in these places and more to differences in net migration. This migration is now largely interurban in nature. Although the following generalization is based on an extensive analysis of migration, using 1940 census data, Bogue believed it was still valid in 1959: "The largest single type of migration among rural and urban areas was not the flow of migrants from rural to urban areas, as might be supposed. It was the flow of migrants between cities."[32]

Some of our cities have always had migrants from other countries as well as from rural areas. Since about 1880, the rapidly developing industrial and commercial cities of the northern Atlantic coast and the Great Lakes received large numbers of foreign migrants, most of whom were from Southern and Eastern Europe. The stream of migrants from this part of the world almost dried up during World War I, and remained very light after the war because of the restrictive legislation enacted by our Congress. During this period these same cities began to experience a large influx of another sort: native-born Americans, both white and Negro, who came almost exclusively from the South. Hard times in the South and a rapidly expanding need for labor in the North because of the severe and sudden curtailment of European migration were the main reasons for this first large exodus from rural areas in the South to the metropolitan centers of the North. The migration of Southern, and predominantly rural, Negroes to Northern cities began just after the Civil War (although it was a small-scale movement until World War I) and has continued without a falter up to the present. Even through the Depression years of the 1930s this migration to the urban North continued, and as industry expanded explosively

[31] Bogue, *The Population of the United States*, p. 39.
[32] *Ibid.*, p. 409.

after the approach of World War II, the volume of migrants became record-breaking. Although Negroes began migrating from the South to the Far West about 1900, the industrial expansion of the West Coast metropolitan centers just before World War II attracted an increasing volume of Negro migrants.

The migration of white Southerners to the cities of the North almost ceased after World War I but picked up again during and after World War II and became very heavy in the 1950s. Most of these white migrants came from the East South Central states to industrial cities in the East North Central states of Ohio, Indiana, Illinois, Michigan, and Wisconsin.

Our Northern and Western urban populations, then, have grown very rapidly in the last 80 years as a result of natural increase, foreign immigration (to the Northern cities from Southern and Eastern Europe and to the West Coast cities from Asia), and internal migration. Until the twentieth century, Southern cities grew more slowly than those in the North. Their growth had to come through their own natural increase and through migration from Southern rural areas, since Southern cities attracted few migrants from abroad or from other regions in the United States. Now that many Southern cities are becoming increasingly industrial, they are growing rapidly because of a significant rise in the amount of in-migration.

Natural Increase and Migration As Components of Population Change in Metropolitan and Nonmetropolitan Areas. Table 6-11 makes clear the relative parts played by natural increase and net migration in the growth of metropolitan and nonmetropolitan areas within the United States between 1950 and 1960.[33] (The pattern is similar to that which obtained in the period from 1940 to 1950. The difference is that the net in-migration to metropolitan areas was slightly lower and the net out-migration from nonmetropolitan areas was slightly larger in the forties.) By inspection, we can estimate that about 90 percent of the nation's growth was the result of natural increase and 10 percent the result of immigration from abroad. The metropolitan areas increased through the combined effect of their own natural increase (65 percent) and of net migration into them (35 percent). Although the nonmetropolitan areas grew between 1950 and 1960, they did so because their natural increase of slightly over 10 million was large enough to offset their loss of nearly 5.5 million through net out-migration. The metropolitan areas' gain through migration (8,143,000) was equal to the sum of the foreign immigration (2,660,000) plus the net out-migration (5,483,000) from nonmetropolitan areas.

The roles played by migration and natural increase in population change between 1950 and 1960 varied from region to region (and from division to

[33] U.S. Bureau of the Census, *Current Population Reports*, ser. P-23, no. 7, *Components of Population Change, 1950 to 1960, for Counties, Standard Metropolitan Statistical Areas, State Economic Areas, and Economic Subregions.* This section is based largely on this report.

TABLE 6-11.   ESTIMATES OF THE COMPONENTS OF CHANGE IN THE RESIDENTIAL POPULATION, 1950–1960, BY METROPOLITAN STATUS AND BY REGIONS

| | Net change, 1950–1960 | | Components of change, 1950–1960 | | | |
| | | | Natural increase | | Net total migration | |
	Amount (1,000s)	Rate* (per 100)	Amount (1,000s)	Rate* (per 1,000)	Amount (1,000s)	Rate* (per 100)
Total metropolitan and non-metropolitan state economic areas:†						
United States.............	27,997	18.5	25,337	15.3	+2,660	+ 1.8
Northeast..............	5,200	13.2	4,864	11.6	+ 336	+ 0.9
North Central..........	7,158	16.1	7,280	15.2	− 121	− 0.3
South.................	7,776	16.5	9,180	18.0	−1,404	− 3.0
West..................	7,863	38.9	4,013	16.6	+3,850	+19.1
Metropolitan state economic areas:						
United States.............	23,249	26.4	15,107	15.1	+8,143	+ 9.2
Northeast..............	4,203	13.2	3,895	11.5	+ 309	+ 1.0
North Central..........	5,766	23.7	4,486	16.5	+1,281	+ 5.3
South.................	6,809	36.6	4,090	18.6	+2,719	+14.6
West..................	6,471	48.6	2,637	15.9	+3,834	+28.8
Nonmetropolitan state economic areas:						
United States.............	4,748	7.5	10,231	15.6	−5,483	− 8.7
Northeast..............	996	13.1	969	11.9	+ 27	+ 0.4
North Central..........	1,392	6.9	2,794	13.4	−1,402	− 7.0
South.................	967	3.4	5,091	17.5	−4,124	−14.4
West..................	1,392	20.3	1,377	18.2	+ 16	+ 0.2

* The rates of population change and migration are based upon the 1950 population and are decade rates. The rate of natural increase is based upon estimated mid-decade population and is an average annual rate for the decade.

† There were 509 state economic areas in 1960. According to the census they are relatively homogeneous subdivisions of states, consisting of single counties or groups of counties which have similar economic and social characteristics. The larger standard metropolitan statistical areas (those in 1960 with a central city of 50,000 or more and a total population of 100,000 or more) have been recognized as "metropolitan state economic areas."

Source: U.S. Bureau of the Census, *Current Population Reports*, ser. P-23, no. 7, *Components of Population Change, 1950 to 1960, for Counties, Standard Metropolitan Statistical Areas, State Economic Areas, and Economic Subregions*, pp. 2, 3, and 83.

division within the regions), and they also differed with respect to the metropolitan and nonmetropolitan areas in each region. For the United States as a whole, the nonmetropolitan areas have a slightly higher rate of natural increase than the metropolitan areas: 15.6 per 1,000. This is not true for all of the regions, however; the metropolitan areas in the North Central and South regions, for instance, have higher rates of natural increase than their respective

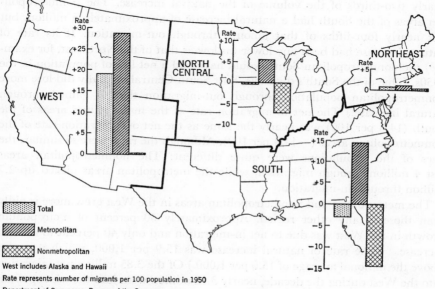

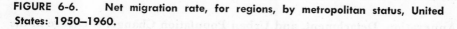

Total
Metropolitan
Nonmetropolitan

West includes Alaska and Hawaii

Rate represents number of migrants per 100 population in 1950

Department of Commerce, Bureau of the Census

FIGURE 6-6.   Net migration rate, for regions, by metropolitan status, United States: 1950-1960.

nonmetropolitan areas. (Metropolitan areas have an age composition, however, which is slightly more favorable for a higher rate of natural increase than have the nonmetropolitan areas.)

In every comparison, migration rates (per 100 of the 1950 population) were more variable by far than rates of natural increase. The maximum difference between the highest and the lowest average *annual* rate of natural increase in Table 6-11 is 7.1 persons per 1,000, while the migration rates (for the 10-year period) ranged from a loss of 14.4 persons per 100 of the 1950 population in the nonmetropolitan areas of the South to a gain of 28.8 persons per 100 in the metropolitan areas of the West. (See Figure 6-6.)

In the Northeast, both the metropolitan and nonmetropolitan areas grew slightly, and in each case the growth was due almost entirely to natural increase. In the North Central region, approximately 80 percent of the metropolitan areas' growth was due to natural increase, while the nonmetropolitan areas lost just over one-half of their natural increase (2,794,000) through out-migration (−1,402,000) and therefore grew very slowly.

The increase in the South's metropolitan areas came from a relatively high natural increase (4,090,000) and a net in-migration (2,719,000), which was nearly two-thirds of the volume of the natural increase. The nonmetropolitan areas of the South had a natural increase of approximately 5 million, but lost nearly four-fifths of that amount through out-migration. If its rate of natural increase had been any lower (as low as that of the Northeast, for example) the nonmetropolitan South would have had a net loss of population in the 1950s. (One of the South's divisions, East South Central, actually did lose more nonmetropolitan population through out-migration than it gained through natural increase.) The net in-migration rate of the metropolitan areas of the South (14.6 per 100) was nearly the same as the net out-migration rate of the nonmetropolitan areas (−14.4 per 100). Although the rates were so similar, the sizes of the populations were quite different: The nonmetropolitan areas lost 4 million through migration, while the metropolitan areas picked up 2.7 million through in-migration.

The metropolitan and nonmetropolitan areas in the West grew more rapidly than those of any other region. Approximately 60 percent of metropolitan growth in the West was due to net in-migration and only 40 percent to natural increase.   (The rate of natural increase was 15.9 per 1,000, which was also above the national average of 15.0 per 1,000.) Of the 3.85 million net migration into the West during the decade, nearly 3.12 million went into the metropolitan areas of the Pacific division of the West.

Annexation, Detachment, and Urban Population Change. A change in the population of an urban place between two censuses will sometimes reflect the effect of the annexation or detachment of any area containing population. If an annexed area would not otherwise have qualified as urban, its annexation increases the population of the place which annexes it and also increases the United States urban total by the amount of people involved in the annexation. If the detached area had enough population to classify it as urban even after detachment, then the total United States figure is not diminished, but the city from which it was detached experiences a loss of urban population. According to the 1960 census, detachments occur far less frequently than annexations and generally involve smaller areas and fewer people. In 1960, the census made its first separate count of population in annexed areas, thus enabling us to analyze the part played by annexation in the growth of particular cities or classes of cities,[34] but because the census did not distinguish between urban and rural with respect to annexed areas, we cannot say how much the *total* urban population was increased by annexation between 1950 and 1960. During this decade, 103 cities which had populations of 25,000 or more in 1950 annexed areas containing 10,000 or more residents. Phoenix, Arizona, annexed the largest population—332,398, or 75.7 percent of its 1960 population; Appleton, Wisconsin, annexed 10,040. An additional 57 cities which had populations of 25,000 or more in 1950 annexed areas containing between 5,000 and 10,000 residents. When the 103 cities are arranged according to the percent which the annexed population is of the 1960 population of the city, we get the following frequency distribution:

Annexed-population percentage of 1960 population	Number of cities
70–79	2
60–69	3
50–59	2
40–49	8
30–39	20
20–29	33
10–19	29
0–9	6

In 1960, a total of 8.8 million people lived in territory annexed during the preceding decade by places containing 2,500 or more population; but there is no way of knowing how many of these 8.8 million would have been classified as urban even if they had not been annexed. The 1960 census gives information on detachment for only three cities. The largest number of persons involved was in Tuskegee, Alabama, when an area containing 5,490 persons was detached from the city.

Annexation and Metropolitan Growth. The 1960 census enabled us to see for the first time the effect of annexation on the relative growth of the central cities and rings of our SMSAs. Of the total of 212 SMSAs, 160 were affected to some degree by the central city's annexation of territory during the decade. (Since the basic unit of the total SMSA is the county, and since constant areas for 1950 and 1960 are easy to establish on a county basis, annexation as such had no effect whatsoever on the total growth of SMSAs either individually or collectively.) Table 6-9 showed that in the decade 1950 to 1960, SMSAs as a

[34] Most of this discussion is based on U.S. Bureau of the Census, *U.S. Census of Population: 1960, Number of Inhabitants, United States Summary*, PC(1)-1A, pp. xxiii–xxvii.

TABLE 6-12.   POPULATION AND CHANGES IN THE POPULATION OF STANDARD METROPOLITAN STATISTICAL AREAS, BY SIZE OF AREA: 1950 AND 1960

Size and component parts of SMSA	Change, 1950 to 1960			
	Total		Based on 1950 limits of central cities	
	Number	Percent	Number	Percent
All sizes:				
In SMSAs.....................	23,568,275	26.4	23,568,275	26.4
Central cities...............	5,618,692	10.7	767,209	1.5
Outside central cities.........	17,949,583	48.6	22,801,066	61.7
3,000,000 or more:				
In SMSAs.....................	5,974,532	23.2	5,974,532	23.2
Central cities...............	173,010	1.0	99,318	0.6
Outside central cities.........	5,801,522	71.3	5,875,214	72.2
1,000,000 to 3,000,000:				
In SMSAs.....................	5,960,458	25.0	5,960,458	25.0
Central cities...............	670,378	5.6	−270,275	−2.2
Outside central cities.........	5,290,080	44.8	6,230,733	52.7
500,000 to 1,000,000:				
In SMSAs.....................	5,089,189	36.0	5,089,189	36.0
Central cities...............	1,786,099	21.4	396,636	4.8
Outside central cities.........	3,303,090	57.1	4,692,553	81.1
250,000 to 500,000:				
In SMSAs.....................	3,225,930	25.6	3,225,930	25.6
Central cities...............	1,079,216	16.2	146,234	2.2
Outside central cities.........	2,146,714	36.2	3,079,696	51.9
100,000 to 250,000:				
In SMSAs.....................	2,972,132	25.8	2,972,132	25.8
Central cities...............	1,603,666	24.2	305,082	4.6
Outside central cities.........	1,368,466	28.0	2,667,050	54.5
Under 100,000:				
In SMSAs.....................	346,034	24.4	346,034	24.4
Central cities...............	306,323	29.2	90,214	8.6
Outside central cities.........	39,711	10.9	255,820	69.9

Source: U.S. Bureau of the Census, *U.S. Census of Population: 1960, Number of Inhabitants, United States Summary,* PC (1)-1A, table Q, p. xxvi.

whole increased by 26.4 percent; their central cities increased by 10.7 percent; and their rings increased by 48.6 percent—*when annexation is not taken into account.* But when annexation *is* taken into account as in Table 6-12, the central cities are seen to have increased by only 1.5 percent, while their rings increased by 61.7 percent. During the 1950s the central cities annexed territory which included 4,851,000 people at the time of the 1960 census. The apparent gain of 5,619,000 between 1950 and 1960 shrinks to an increase of only 767,000 when the 1950 boundaries are used in connection with 1960 data. The growth of the ring in relation to the central city shows up even more dramatically when allowance is made for the territory the ring lost to the central city through annexation. The rings grew approximately five times faster than the central cities according to the 1960 political boundaries of the central cities, while the rings increased approximately 40 times faster than the central cities according to the 1950 boundaries. If no annexation had taken place, the rings would have absorbed 97 percent of the total growth of the SMSAs during the 1950s.

Unadjusted for annexation, the central cities accounted for 20 percent of the nation's total growth, and the rings for 64 percent. After adjustment is made for annexation, the central cities picked up less than 3 percent, while their rings accounted for more than 81 percent of the total United States growth.

Table 6-12 indicates that the larger the SMSA was, the less effect annexation had on the relative growth of the central cities and their rings. In general (on the basis of 1960 city limits), the larger SMSAs experienced more growth in their rings and much less growth in their central cities than did the smaller SMSAs. It is clearly apparent that the rate of suburbanization in the last decade (for the SMSAs as a whole and particularly for the smaller ones) would be grossly understated if no allowance were made for the territorial expansion of the central cities during that period. As Professor Schnore says in a recent article,

> One must always be aware, however, of the fact that cities grow horizontally, extending their areas at the periphery of settlement. . . . Kingsley Davis pointed out that the growth by political annexation represents an approxima- tion of the actual spread of the physical city and that the demographers' pro- clivity for holding area constant tends to ignore this fact. Cities grow outward (in area) as well as upward (in density), but there is still no satisfactory model that accommodates both types of increase. . . .[35]

Urban Growth As a Result of Change in Classification. The most straight- forward statement about how change in classification affects the relative growth of rural and urban areas was made recently by Donald J. Bogue:

> Emergence of new urban places is an important source of urban growth. To the urban population it adds the entire population of the place whose classification is being changed from rural to urban. In most instances, several decades were required to accumulate this population, yet it is credited as a lump addition to the decade

[35] Leo F. Schnore, "Municipal Annexations and the Growth of Metropolitan Suburbs, 1950– 1960," *American Journal of Sociology*, vol. 67, p. 417, 1962.

in which the place becomes urban. Thus, rapid urbanization and a rapid rate of growth in the urban population do not necessarily require a rapid average rate of growth for cities already in existence.

This process of reclassification has the effect of continuously depleting the rural population. The more rapidly a rural place grows, the greater are the probabilities that it will be classed as urban at the next census. When reclassification does occur, the entire population of the place as recorded at the preceding census is treated as a loss to the rural population. By the rules of the game, the rural population can grow only by limited amounts and in a dispersed pattern. Rapid growth of a rural village or a suburb leads quickly to its reclassification as urban. This reclassification will be even more frequent under the new urban definition.[36]

The first urban place listed in the 1960 census happens to be Abbeville, Alabama, which was a *rural* community of 2,162 in 1950 and an *urban* community of 2,524 in 1960. Thus the total rural population of the United States lost 2,162 and the urban population gained 2,524 in the decade, although the community of Abbeville increased by only 362.

RURAL, URBAN, AND METROPOLITAN DIFFERENCES

Age and Sex Composition. Earlier in this chapter we said that rural-urban differences are diminishing in our society, and in other urban-industrial societies, because the city's influences are felt far beyond its physical boundaries. We also noted that, even though a sizable population still lives in rural settlements (both farm and nonfarm), our society is best described as an urban society. Figure 6-7 and Table 6-13 show, however, that significant differences still exist among the various residence groupings. The difference between the age and sex composition of the urban population and the farm population is dramatically portrayed when we place one population pyramid on top of the other as in Figure 6-7. Compared to the urban population (percents and proportions are being compared), farm communities in 1960 had many more people in the age group 5–19 (particularly males 15–19), many fewer in the productive years of 20–44, and more males in the age group 45 and over. There are some additional obvious differences in the relative numbers of each sex at certain ages.

The rural-nonfarm age and sex composition differs from the urban in several respects, but not nearly so much as does the farm population. Compared with the urban population, the rural-nonfarm population has more males and fewer females in the age group 20–24. Above the age of 25, for the most part, there are slightly smaller proportions of both sexes in the rural-nonfarm population.

[36] Bogue, *The Population of the United States*, p. 38.

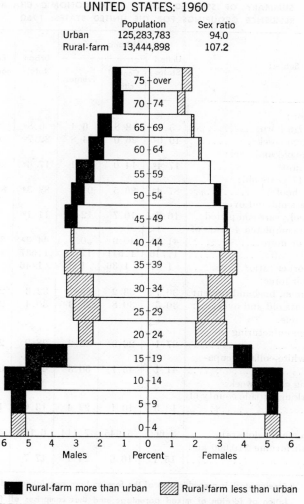

UNITED STATES: 1960

	Population	Sex ratio
Urban	125,283,783	94.0
Rural-farm	13,444,898	107.2

■ Rural-farm more than urban ▨ Rural-farm less than urban

FIGURE 6-7.   Distribution of the rural-farm and urban populations by age and sex, United States: 1960.

The importance of taking these different age and sex distributions into account when comparing the fertility and mortality rates of urban and rural populations will be pointed out in some detail in the chapters on fertility and mortality. All manner of areal comparisons obviously require a knowledge of the urban and rural composition.

TABLE 6-13.   SUMMARY OF SELECTED SOCIAL AND ECONOMIC CHARACTERISTICS BY RESIDENCE GROUPINGS FOR THE UNITED STATES: 1960

Subject	United States	Urbanized areas		Urban total	Rural- nonfarm	Rural- farm
		Central cities	Fringes			
Total population:						
Percent foreign born.............	5.4[g]	8.8	6.4	6.8[g]	2.5[g]	1.6[g]
Percent foreign stock[a]..........	19.0[g]	26.0	24.8	22.7[g]	10.6[g]	9.4[g]
Persons 5 years old and over:						
Percent migrant[b]...............	17.4[g]	14.0	21.1	17.6[g]	20.0[g]	8.8[g]
Persons 14 to 17 years old:						
Percent in school...............	87.4[g]	86.5	91.0	88.3[g]	85.1[g]	87.4[g]
Persons 25 years old and over:						
Median school years completed...	10.6[g]	10.7	12.0	11.1[g]	9.5[g]	8.8[g]
Percent who completed 4 years of high school or more.............	41.1[g]	40.9	50.9	44.3[g]	34.4[g]	29.5[g]
General fertility rate[c]..............	1,746	1,541	1,715	1,637	1,999	2,133
Nonworker–worker ratio[d]..........	1.57	1.36	1.55	1.46	1.87	1.79
Percent in labor force:						
Married women, husband present.	30.7	33.2	29.7	32.3	28.4	21.9
Males 65 years old and over......	30.5	30.8	29.9	30.4	23.5	49.7
Employed persons:						
Percent in manufacturing industries........................	27.1	26.9	32.2	28.2	28.7	12.0
Percent in white-collar occupations[e]........................	41.1	45.1	50.3	46.1	32.8	13.4
Workers during census week:[f]						
Percent working outside county of residence......................	13.9	10.1	22.4	13.6	16.7	9.2
Families:						
Median income (in dollars).......	5,660	5,945	7,114	6,166	4,750	3,228
Percent with income $10,000 and over..........................	15.1	16.6	24.1	17.7	9.0	6.8

[a] Foreign stock is a combination of the foreign-born population and the native population of foreign or mixed parentage and thus comprises all first- and second-generation Americans.

[b] Persons who lived in different counties in the United States in 1955 and 1960.

[c] Children ever born per 1,000 women 15 to 44 years old of all marital classes.

[d] Ratio of persons not in labor force (including children under 14) to labor force.

[e] Includes the major occupation groups of professional, managerial (except farm), clerical, and sales.

[f] Includes members of the Armed Forces.

[g] Conterminous United States, excluding Alaska and Hawaii.

Source: U.S. Bureau of the Census, *U.S. Census of Population: 1960, General Social and Economic Characteristics, United States Summary,* Final Report PC (1)-1C.

Urban, Rural-nonfarm, and Rural-farm Differences in Social and Economic Characteristics. Table 6-13 shows the farm population to be markedly different from the urban population with respect to most of the characteristics listed. Compared with the urban populations, the farm communities included many fewer persons who were foreign born or of foreign stock (see explanation accompanying Table 6-13), only one-half as many migrants, more nonworkers, fewer married women, and more older men in the labor force. The farm population also had less schooling, much higher fertility, a median family income one-half as high as that of the urban population, and less than one-half as large a proportion of families with incomes of $10,000 or more. These data, and others not given here, indicate clearly that significant urban and rural-farm differences persist in spite of the spread of urbanism as a way of life.

The rural-nonfarm population usually holds an intermediate position between the urban and farm populations in such characteristics as nativity, schooling, fertility, working wives, and income. The rural-nonfarm population is higher than the other two in some things (percent of migrants) and lower in others (percent of older men in the labor force). Even though the rural-nonfarm category is a rather heterogeneous one, the new definition of urban has helped to distinguish more sharply between rural-nonfarm and urban populations.

Urbanized Areas, Central Cities, and Fringe. The central cities are similar to the total urban population in many respects.[37] Relatively speaking (using percents), they have more people of foreign stock, fewer migrants, and fewer families earning $10,000 or more. There are sharper differences between the central cities and their fringe communities than between the central cities and the total urban population. The fringe differs from all the other categories in many ways: Its population is by far the most educated and the most wealthy, and it has more migrants, more white-collar workers, more people employed in manufacturing industries, and more workers employed in counties other than the one they live in. The fertility rate of the fringe is higher than that of the central city; it is also higher than the total urban rate, but lower than the rates of the two rural categories.

Central Cities of Urbanized Areas. Just as differences sometimes exist among residence groupings, variations also exist within them. The rural-farm populations in Mississippi, Wisconsin, and Texas, for example, do not have similar proportions of foreign-born population, or the same median family income. Because space does not permit us to show the range of variation within each residence category for each of the characteristics, we shall show how much the individual central cities of some urbanized areas differ from each other and

[37] The total urban population is made up of 46 percent central city population, 30 percent ring population, and 24 percent other urban population.

from the average of all central cites (CCs) combined with respect to certain characteristics.

1. Percent foreign born: CCs—8.8, New York—20, Gadsden, Alabama—0.3
2. Percent migrants: CCs—14, Orlando, Florida—36.4, Scranton, Pennsylvania—3.4
3. Median school years completed: CCs—10.7, Ann Arbor, Michigan—13.7,[38] Laredo, Texas—6.4
4. Percent employed in manufacturing industries: CCs—26.9, Weirton, West Virginia—58.8, Las Vegas, Nevada—4.5
5. Percent employed in white-collar occupations: CCs—45.1, Ann Arbor, Michigan—66.2, East Chicago—24.4
6. Percent working outside the county of residence: CCs—10.1, New York—39.6, Honolulu—0.6
7. Median family income: CCs—$5,945, Las Vegas, Nevada—$7,662, Laredo, Texas—$2,935

METROPOLITAN GROWTH AND RACE

Central cities and their rings differ in proportions of white and nonwhite populations, and the differences are increasing. In fact, this growing difference in racial composition between the central cities and their rings, combined as it is with differences in education and housing, is one of the major social problems facing the United States. Table 6-9 showed how rapidly the rings have grown and how slowly the central cities have grown in the last decade. (No adjustment for annexation will be made in the discussion of this topic. The adjustment would, if anything, strengthen the position developed in this section.) When these figures are divided into white and nonwhite populations, startling differences between them appear with respect to the proportions of whites and nonwhites in the central cities and rings.[39]

Table 6-14 presents the basic information which enables us to see fundamental differences in the patterns of population change according to race. There are many ways of bringing out these differences (ways of contrasting and comparing absolute numbers and percents), but space limitation forces us to choose the method which will enable the reader to comprehend most fully the

---

[38] In 1950 and 1960, college students were considered by the census as residents of the communities in which they were living while attending college. Since Ann Arbor is the home of the University of Michigan, the college population helps to raise the median years of school completed.

[39] In Table 6-14, "Negro" is used and in Table 6-15 "nonwhite"; but since the nonwhite category is over 90 percent Negro, and since the populations we shall be discussing are large, this variation in classification is of little consequence.

TABLE 6-14. CHANGE IN THE POPULATION OF CENTRAL CITIES AND RINGS OF STANDARD METROPOLITAN STATISTICAL AREAS, BY RACE, NUMBER (IN THOUSANDS), AND PERCENT: 1950 AND 1960*

Race	1950			1960			Amount and percent change of 1950–1960			Percent distribution of change in each residence category by race			Percent distribution of change in each racial category by residence		
	SMSA total	Central cities	Rings	SMSA total	Central cities	Rings	SMSA total	Central cities	Rings	SMSA total	Central cities	Rings	SMSA total	Central cities	Rings
All classes	88,964	52,138	36,826	112,385	57,710	54,675	23,421	5,573	17,848	23,421	5,573	17,848	23,421	5,573	17,848
	100.0%	100.0	100.0	100.0	100.0	100.0	26.3	10.7	48.5	100.0	100.0	100.0	100.0	23.8	76.2
White	80,249	45,441	34,808	99,509	47,575	51,934	19,260	2,134	17,126	19,260	2,134	17,126	19,260	2,134	17,126
	90.2%	87.2	94.5	88.5	82.4	95.0	24.0	4.7	49.2	82.2	38.3	96.0	100.0	11.1	88.9
Negro	8,360	6,456	1,904	12,194	9,704	2,490	3,834	3,248	586	3,834	3,248	586	3,834	3,248	586
	9.4%	12.4	5.2	10.8	16.8	4.6	45.9	50.3	30.7	16.4	58.3	3.3	100.0	84.7	15.3

* Conterminous United States, excluding Alaska and Hawaii. The difference between the sum of the "white" and "Negro" figures and those for "all classes" represents nonwhite population other than Negro. In all cases the differences are extremely small.

Source: U.S. Bureau of the Census, *U.S. Census of Population: 1960, Selected Area Reports; Standard Metropolitan Statistical Areas,* PC(3)-1D, p. 1.

meaning and significance of what is taking place. We believe this can best be accomplished if we list in short paragraphs the most important generalizations.

1. *a.* Eighty-nine percent of the total SMSA increase in white population occurred in the rings.

   b. Eighty-five percent of the total SMSA increase in Negro population took place in the central cities.

2. *a.* The white population in the central cities increased by less than 5 percent—by 2.1 million.

   b. The Negro population in the central cities increased by 50 percent, approximately 10 times the white rate of growth. The Negro increase was 3.2 million, or 1.1 million greater than the white increase.

3. *a.* In the rings, the white population increased *relatively* only 1.6 times as fast as the Negro population, while its *absolute* increase was 29 times that of the Negro population.

   b. The 49 percent increase in the white population living in the rings resulted from an absolute increase of 17 million.

   c. The 31 percent increase in the Negro population living in the rings was based on an absolute increase of only 0.6 million.

4. *a.* The white population accounted for only 38 percent of the central city's increase, while comprising 96 percent of the ring's increase.

   b. The Negro population was responsible for 58 percent of the central city's increase, while comprising only 4 percent of the increase in the ring's population.

5. *a.* Negroes increased from 12.4 percent to 16.8 percent of the population in the central cities.

   b. Negroes decreased from 5.2 percent to 4.6 percent of the population in the rings.

The figures in Table 6-14 are for all the 212 SMSAs combined, and therefore give us no information on differences *among* the SMSAs. Table 6-15 gives data for individual SMSAs, but only for the very largest—those which were 1 million or more in 1960. Each of these largest 24 SMSAs experienced an increase in the percent of nonwhites in its central city population. For all central cities of the 24 SMSAs combined, the percent which was nonwhite rose from 13.2 percent in 1950 to 20.3 percent in 1960. The combined twin central cities of the Minneapolis–St. Paul SMSA had the smallest proportion of Negroes both in 1950 and in 1960—1.8 percent and 3.1 percent. The central cities with the largest proportions of nonwhite population were Atlanta, Georgia, in 1950, with 36.6 percent and Washington, D.C., in 1960, with more than one-half (54.8 percent) of its population nonwhite.

The proportion of nonwhite population in the rings around these largest

TABLE 6-15.   PERCENT DISTRIBUTION OF THE TOTAL POPULATION AND OF THE NON-
WHITE POPULATION IN CENTRAL CITIES AND RINGS AND THE PERCENT OF
THE POPULATION IN CENTRAL CITIES AND IN RINGS WHICH IS NONWHITE,
STANDARD METROPOLITAN STATISTICAL AREAS OF 1 MILLION OR MORE
IN 1960; IN 1950 AND 1960*

SMSA	Total population		Nonwhite population		Percent of central city nonwhite	Percent of ring nonwhite
	Central city	Ring	Central city	Ring		
Atlanta:						
1960	47 9	52 1	80 5	19 5	38 3	8 6
1950	45 6	54 4	70 3	29 7	36 6	13 0
Baltimore:						
1960	54 4	45 6	85.8	14 2	35 0	6 9
1950	67 6	32 4	82.9	17.1	23 8	10 2
Boston:						
1960	26.9	73 1	78 6	21 4	9 8	1 0
1950	33.2	66.8	75.8	24.2	5 3	0.8
Buffalo:						
1960	40.8	59.2	82 2	17 8	13 8	2 0
1950	53 3	46 7	78 9	21 1	6 5	2 0
Chicago:						
1960	57.1	42.9	91.0	9 0	23 6	3 1
1950	69 9	30.1	91 9	8 1	14 1	2 9
Cincinnati:						
1960	46.9	53.1	84.8	15 2	21 8	3 5
1950	55 7	44.3	82.3	17.7	15.6	4 2
Cleveland:						
1960	48.8	51.2	97 1	2.9	28.9	0.8
1950	62 4	37 6	97 0	3 0	16.3	0.8
Dallas:						
1960	62 7	37 3	83 1	16 9	19 3	6 6
1950	58 4	41 6	57 1	42 9	13 2	13 9
Detroit:						
1960	44 4	55 6	85.9	14 1	29.2	3 8
1950	61 3	38 7	83 9	16.1	16.4	5 0
Houston:						
1960	75.5	24.5	87.3	12.7	23.2	10 4
1950	73 9	26.1	83.5	16.5	21.1	11.8
Kansas City:						
1960	45.7	54.3	71.1	28 9	17 7	6 1
1950	56 1	43 9	63 6	36 4	12 3	8 9
Los Angeles–Long Beach:						
1960	41 9	58 1	72 7	27 3	15 3	4 1
1950	50 9	49 1	79 0	21 0	9 8	2.7
Milwaukee:						
1960	62 1	37 9	98 0	2.0	8 9	0.3
1950	66.6	33 4	96 7	3 3	3 6	0.2

TABLE 6-15.   PERCENT DISTRIBUTION OF THE TOTAL POPULATION AND OF THE NON-
WHITE POPULATION IN CENTRAL CITIES AND RINGS AND THE PERCENT OF
THE POPULATION IN CENTRAL CITIES AND IN RINGS WHICH IS NONWHITE,
STANDARD METROPOLITAN STATISTICAL AREAS OF 1 MILLION OR MORE
IN 1960; IN 1950 AND 1960 (*Continued*)

SMSA	Total population		Nonwhite population		Percent central city nonwhite	Percent of ring nonwhite
	Central city	Ring	Central city	Ring		
Minneapolis–St. Paul:						
1960	53.7	46.3	90.9	9.1	3.1	0.4
1950	72.4	27.6	95.4	4.6	1.8	0.2
Newark:						
1960	24.0	76.0	61.3	38.7	34.4	6.8
1950†	29.9	70.1	56.0	44.0	17.2	5.8
New York:						
1960	72.8	27.2	88.6	11.4	14.7	5.0
1950	82.6	17.4	91.2	8.8	9.8	4.5
Patterson-Clifton-Passaic:						
1960	23.6	76.4	59.5	40.5	9.4	2.0
1950†	29.8	70.2	49.5	50.5	4.4	1.9
Philadelphia:						
1960	46.1	53.9	78.5	21.5	26.7	6.3
1950	56.4	43.6	78.3	21.7	18.3	6.6
Pittsburgh:						
1960	25.1	74.9	62.2	37.8	16.8	3.4
1950	30.6	69.4	60.5	39.5	12.3	3.5
St. Louis:						
1960	36.4	63.6	72.5	27.5	28.8	6.2
1950	49.8	50.2	71.1	28.9	18.0	7.3
San Diego:						
1960	55.5	44.5	78.5	21.5	7.8	2.7
1950	60.1	39.9	77.0	23.0	5.5	2.5
San Francisco-Oakland:						
1960	39.8	60.2	67.2	32.8	21.0	6.8
1950	51.8	48.2	65.2	34.8	11.8	6.8
Seattle:						
1960	50.3	49.7	87.9	12.1	8.4	1.2
1950	55.4	44.6	86.7	13.3	5.8	1.1
Washington, D.C.:						
1960	38.2	61.8	83.8	16.2	54.8	6.5
1950	54.8	45.2	83.1	16.9	35.4	8.7

* 1950 areas made comparable with 1960 areas.
† Not an SMSA in 1950.
Source: U.S. Bureau of the Census, *U.S. Census of Population: 1960, General Popu-
lation Characteristics* (State Reports), table 20; U.S. Bureau of the Census, *U.S.
Census of Population: 1950, Characteristics of the Population* (State Reports), chap. B,
table 33.

SMSAs changed very little between 1950 and 1960; the changes varied from a drop of 7.3 percentage points to an increase of 1.4 percentage points.

The totals for the 24 largest SMSAs were generally similar to those for all of the 212 SMSAs but differed from them in a few interesting ways. The largest 24 accounted for only 50 percent of the population increase in the combined 212, but these 24 had 70 percent of the nonwhite increase. Furthermore, the central cities of the 24 SMSAs showed a total decrease of 1,449,625 in white population. Their total population increased by 843,378 only because of a 2,293,003 nonwhite increase. Perhaps two examples will serve to show how basic shifts in metropolitan populations can be obscured if the data are not classified according to race. New York City lost 109,000 population between 1950 and 1960. This was a result of a white decrease of 474,000 and a nonwhite increase of 365,000. Chicago decreased in the same period by 71,000 as a result of a 400,000 white decrease and a 329,000 nonwhite increase. The movement to the suburbs is not general; it is almost exclusively white. The differences which exist between central cities and their fringes with respect to such social and economic characteristics as income, education, and employment (see Table 6-13) take on added significance when racial differences in metropolitan growth are brought into sharper focus. Unfortunately, many Americans have little idea of the nature of recent metropolitan changes or of the complex causes which are bringing these changes about.

SUMMARY

We were a rural-agricultural society until the twentieth century. In the middle of the 1800s our rate of urbanization began to accelerate, and when World War I came, we were an urban-industrial society. By that time, however, we were already on our way to becoming a metropolitan-industrial society; urbanization was giving way to metropolitanization. Before we could acquire the skills and the political structures necessary for the development of a more humanly satisfying urban life, we found ourselves facing urban problems on an ever-increasing scale in our rapidly developing metropolitan communities. In trying to cope successfully with these problems we have been severely hampered by some of the attitudes and values which survive from our agrarian days: our outmoded political structures; the prevalent view that public planning is somehow undemocratic; the ability of the affluent members of our society to escape the more vicious urban problems; false ideas concerning urban and metropolitan growth; and prejudice against the low-income and minority populations who inhabit the inner city. But ours *is* an urban society, and its successful continuance will depend largely upon our ability to solve the more pressing problems which our urban communities are facing.

SUGGESTIONS FOR SUPPLEMENTARY READING

Beale, Calvin L., and Donald J. Bogue: *Recent Population Trends in the United States with Emphasis on Rural Areas*, Agricultural Report, 23, U.S. Department of Agriculture, Washington, D.C., 1963.

Chapin, Jr., F. Stuart, and Shirley F. Weiss (eds.): *Urban Growth Dynamics in a Regional Cluster of Cities*, John Wiley & Sons, Inc., New York, 1962.

Cook, Robert C. (ed.): "The World's Great Cities: Evolution or Devolution?" *Population Bulletin*, vol. 16, no. 6, pp. 109–130, 1960.

Cottrell, William Frederick: *Energy and Society*, McGraw Hill Book Company, New York, 1955.

Dobriner, William (ed.): *The Suburban Community*, G. P. Putnam's Sons, New York, 1958.

Duncan, Beverley, and Philip M. Hauser: *Housing a Metropolis–Chicago*, The Free Press of Glencoe, New York, 1960.

Duncan, Otis Dudley, et al.: *Metropolis and Regions*, The Johns Hopkins Press, Baltimore, 1960.

Duncan, Otis Dudley, and Albert J. Reiss, Jr.: *Social Characteristics of Urban and Rural Communities, 1950*, John Wiley & Sons, Inc., New York, 1956.

Gibbs, Jack P., and Leo F. Schnore: "Metropolitan Growth: An International Study," *American Journal of Sociology*, vol. 66, no. 2, pp. 160–170, 1960.

Gist, Noel P., and L. A. Halbert: *Urban Society*, 4th ed., Thomas Y. Crowell Company, New York, 1956.

Gottman, Jean: *Megalopolis: The Urbanized Northeastern Seaboard of the United States*, The Twentieth Century Fund, New York, 1961.

Hauser, Philip M. (ed.): *Urbanization in Asia and the Far East*, UNESCO, Research Centre on the Social Implications of Industrialization in Southern Asia, Calcutta, 1957.

Hauser, Philip M. (ed.): *Urbanization in Latin America: Proceedings of the Seminar on Urbanization Problems in Latin America*, UNESCO, Technology and Society Series, New York, 1961.

Hawley, Amos H.: *The Changing Shape of Metropolitan America: Deconcentration Since 1920*. The Free Press of Glencoe, New York, 1956.

Hoyt, Homer: *World Urbanization: Expanding Population in a Shrinking World*, Urban Land Institute, Technical Bulletin 43, Washington, D.C., 1962.

McEntire, Davis: *Residence and Race: Final and Comprehensive Report to the Commission on Race and Housing*, University of California Press, Berkeley, Calif., 1960.

Mumford, Lewis: *The Culture of Cities*, Harcourt, Brace and Company, New York, 1938.

Ogburn, William F.: "Technology and Cities: The Dilemma of the Modern Metropolis," *Sociological Quarterly*, vol. 1, no. 3, pp. 139–154, 1960.

Polanyi, Karl: *The Great Transformation*, Farrar & Rinehart, Inc., New York, 1944.

Schnore, Leo F.: "Municipal Annexations and the Growth of Metropolitan Suburbs, 1950–60," *American Journal of Sociology*, vol. 62, pp. 406–417, January, 1962.

Sharp, Harry, and Leo F. Schnore: "The Changing Color Composition of Metropolitan Areas," *Land Economics*, vol. 38, no. 2, pp. 179–185, 1962.

Sjoberg, Gideon; *The Pre-industrial City, Past and Present*, The Free Press of Glencoe, New York, 1960.

Slotkin, James S.: *From Field to Factory: New Industrial Employees* (Publication of the Research Center in Economic Development and Cultural Change), The Free Press of Glencoe, New York, 1960.

Turner, Roy (ed.): *India's Urban Future*, University of California Press, Berkeley, Calif., 1962.

Vernon, Raymond: *Metropolis 1985, An Interpretation of the findings of the New York Metropolitan Region Study*, Harvard University Press, Cambridge, Mass., 1960.

Wingo, Jr., Lowdon: *Transportation and Urban Land*, Resources for the Future, Inc., Washington, D.C., 1961.

CHAPTER SEVEN

Economic and Educational Composition

In the first parts of this chapter we shall discuss economic composition—the economic characteristics of a population. We shall try to answer some of the following questions: At any given moment, how many people in our society are engaged in producing our goods and services? How many are not so engaged? How many people are nonproducers by choice and how many through circumstance? Does the ratio of producers to nonproducers change through time? What is the composition of the labor force with respect to age, sex, educational attainment, marital status, and residence? Is this composition changing? How is the labor force distributed among the various occupations? How is the labor force distributed among the various industries? In what ways are these distributions changing? What are the effects of technological change upon the composition of the labor force, upon the industrial composition, and upon the level of unemployment? In the latter part of this chapter we shall be concerned with the educational level of the United States population, with the different levels according to sex, color, and residence, and with the changes in these levels. We shall also be trying to answer such questions as: What proportions of each school-age group are actually attending school? Do these proportions vary with region, size of community, sex, and race? What have been the changes in the proportions of the various age groups enrolled in elementary school, high school, and college? And, perhaps most important of all, what are the future enrollments likely to be?

LABOR FORCE

The United States census considers that the labor force is made up of all the people 14 years of age and over who, at a particular moment, are either employed or unemployed but looking for work. The labor force includes farm laborers, physicians, people who work for themselves as well as those who work for others, people who work for wages, for salaries, and for fees. The labor force includes members of the Armed Forces, except when the term civilian labor force is used. Not considered in the labor force are all people under 14 years of age and all those 14 years of age and over who are doing only incidental unpaid family work (less than 15 hours during the particular week to which the data relate), the latter group being mostly

. . . students, housewives, retired workers, seasonal workers enumerated in an "off" season who were not looking for work, inmates of institutions, or persons who cannot work because of long-term physical or mental illness or disability. Of these groups not in the labor force, only inmates of institutions are shown separately.[1]

The United Nations uses the same type of classification, but instead of "labor force" it uses the terms "economically active" and "economically inactive."[2]

The ratio of that part of the population which is in the labor force to that part which is not (or the ratio of the economically active to the economically inactive part of the population) reflects some of the cultural values of a society, such as the significance it attaches to differences in age, sex, and color. As we noted in Chapter 4, no society exploits the full economic potential of its human resources. As we shall see later, not only is the ratio of economically active to inactive population in part a function of cultural values, but the employment-unemployment ratio in the labor force is also a reflection of certain cultural values.

Some International Labor Force Comparisons. In Chapter 5 we discussed various countries with respect to the proportion of population in the productive

Country	Nonworker to worker ratio	Percent of labor force that is female
India*	1.53	16
United States	1.51	27
Italy	1.41	25
Japan	1.34	39
Yugoslavia	1.16	34
United Kingdom	0.94	31

* Data are only for self-supporting persons; thus they exclude earning-dependents and persons whose activities were unclassifiable.

[1] U.S. Bureau of the Census, *U.S. Census of Population: 1960, General Social and Economic Characteristics, United States Summary,* PC(1)-1C, pp. xxvii and xxviii.

[2] See United Nations, *Demographic Yearbook,* 1956, p. 43. See also pp. 91–96 in Chap. 5.

years as compared with the proportion of population in the dependency years of under 15 and over 65. Now we shall use a slightly different statistic—the ratio of nonworkers to workers, or the ratio of the non-labor-force population to the labor-force population.[3]

These figures vary from approximately 1 nonworker for every worker in the United Kingdom to approximately 1½ nonworkers for every worker in India and the United States. This variation is largely a result of three factors: (1) differences in age distribution among the populations (see Chapter 5), (2) differences among the societies with respect to their willingness to use women, the young and the old, in the labor force, and (3) variations in defining the term "economically active." Other factors can affect this ratio, such as the existence of a large leisure class or, as in the United States, a relatively prolonged period

TABLE 7-1.   LABOR-FORCE-PARTICIPATION RATE BY SEX, UNITED STATES: 1940–1960
(Numbers in thousands)

Sex	1960		1950		1940	
	Number	Percent	Number	Percent	Number	Percent
Total...............	69,877	55.3	60,329	53.5	53,011	52.2
Male...............	47,668	77.4	43.766	78.8	40,123	79.0
Female.............	22,410	34.5	16,564	28.9	12,887	25.4

Source: U.S. Bureau of the Census, *U.S. Census of Population: 1960, General Social and Economic Characteristics, United States Summary*, PC(1)-1C, p. 1-214, table 83.

of education. The second column of the table shows the degree to which each country employs women; the variation extends from Japan, where women compose approximately 40 percent of the labor force, to India, where only 16 percent of the labor force is made up of women (see footnote with the table).

The Labor Force in the United States. Table 7-1 shows how the two sexes compare with respect to their proportions in the labor force at 14 years of age and over. Three things are important to note in this table. First and most obviously, males have a much higher participation rate than females. Second, women have significantly increased their participation rate from approximately 25 percent of all women 14 years of age and over in 1940 to nearly 35 percent in 1960. Third, although the shift is slight, it is important to note that the participation rate of males has declined, particularly between 1950 and 1960.

In Table 7-2 we can see how the increase in the labor force compares with

[3] United Nations, *Demographic Yearbook, 1956*, table 12.

TABLE 7-2. INTERCENSAL RATES OF INCREASE OF POPULATION 14 YEARS OF AGE AND OVER AND LABOR FORCE, BY SEX, FOR THE UNITED STATES: 1940–1960 (Numbers in thousands)

Sex	1940–1950				1950–1960				1940–1960			
	Increase 14 years old and over		Increase in labor force—14 years old and over		Increase 14 years old and over		Increase in labor force—14 years old and over		Increase 14 years old and over		Increase in labor force—14 years old and over	
	Number	Percent	Number	Percent	Number	Percent	Number	Percent	Number	Percent	Number	Percent
Total.........	11,344	11.2	7,319	13.8	13,475	11.9	9,548	15.8	24,819	24.5	16,867	31.8
Male.........	4,802	9.5	3,642	9.1	5,743	10.3	3,702	8.5	10,545	20.8	7,344	18.3
Female......	6,542	12.9	3,676	28.5	7,732	13.5	5,846	35.3	14,274	28.2	9,523	73.9

Source: U.S. Bureau of the Census, U.S. Census of Population: 1960, General Social and Economic Characteristics, United States Summary, PC(1)-1C, p. 1-214, table 83.

the increase in the total population aged 14 years and over for the United States and for each sex. The labor force for the country as a whole has been increasing faster than has the number of people 14 years of age and over. The number of females who are in the labor force has been increasing two to three times as fast as has the number of females who are 14 years of age and over. The increase in the labor-force-participation rate for the total population is obviously due to the change in the proportion of women in the labor force, because the proportion of men 14 years of age and over has been increasing faster than has their proportion in the labor force. Even though females were only 25 percent of the labor force in 1940, their increase in the labor force (9.5 million) between 1940

TABLE 7-3.   PERCENT OF THE POPULATION IN THE LABOR FORCE, BY AGE, MALE AND FEMALE, UNITED STATES 1940–1960

Age	Male			Female		
	1960	1950	1940	1960	1950	1940
14–17......................	26.5	25.5	18.6	14.0	11.4	7.7
18–24......................	80.1	77.8	81.2	45.3	43.3	43.6
25–34......................	94.9	92.1	95.2	35.3	31.8	32.9
35–44......................	95.6	94.5	94.7	42.7	35.0	26.9
45–64......................	89.0	88.2	88.7	41.6	28.8	19.8
65 and over...............	30.5	41.5	41.5	10.3	7.8	5.9
14 and over...............	77.4	78.9	79.0	34.5	29.0	25.4
35–64......................	91.7	90.8	91.2	42.0	31.4	22.8

Source: U.S. Bureau of the Census, *U.S. Census of Population: 1960, General Social and Economic Characteristics, United States Summary,* PC(1)-1C, p. 1-214, table 84.

and 1960 represented 56.5 percent of the total increase in the labor force. In 1940 one-fourth of all women over 14 were in the labor force, and one-fourth of the labor force was female; in 1960 one-third of all women over 14 were in the labor force, and one-third of the labor force was female.

Turning to Table 7-3 and to Figure 7-1, we can see the changes in the proportions of males and females in the several age classes composing the labor force. The numbers of women in all age groups, except in the group aged 18–24, increased between 1940 and 1950 and between 1950 and 1960; the greatest change occurred in the 45–64-year age group, which increased from 20 percent in 1940 to 42 percent in 1960. The next largest increase in proportions of women in the labor force was in the age group 35–44, which climbed from 27 percent in 1940 to 43 percent in 1960. Between 1950 and 1960, women in *each* age group showed a gain in participation rate. Among males, the labor-force-participation rate remained rather stable between 1940 and 1960 for the ages 18 to 64. Between 1950 and 1960, the participation rate of males aged 65 and over dropped from 42 percent to 31 percent, reflecting a lowering of the age when males retire (both voluntarily and involuntarily) from the labor force.

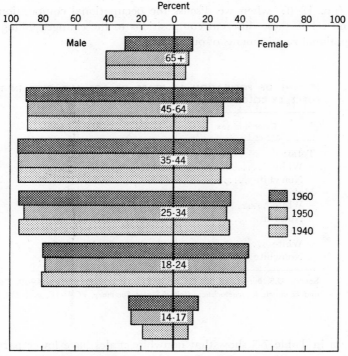

Department of Commerce, Bureau of the Census

FIGURE 7-1.   Percentage of population in the labor force, by age and sex, United States: 1940 to 1960. (Table 7-3.)

Labor-force Participation According to Color, Residence, and Marital Status. Table 7-4 shows how labor-force participation varies significantly by color. The nonwhite male has experienced a continuous and sizable decline in his participation rate over the 20-year period, while the rate for white males has been rather stable. Both white and nonwhite females had higher participation rates in 1960 than in 1940. White female rates experienced a large and steady increase. Although nonwhite females had a much larger proportion in the labor force than white females had in 1940, the nonwhite rate experienced a smaller increase up to 1960, although their proportion remained well above that of the white female. The nonwhite male had a slightly higher participation rate (80 percent) than the white male in 1940 (78.9 percent), but the nonwhite male rate declined sharply, to 72.1 percent in 1960, while the white male rate declined slightly to 78 percent in 1960. A large part of the explanation of these sex and color differences in labor-force participation will be uncovered a little later on (pp. 184ff.) when we discuss the occupational composition of these groups and relate these different compositions to the changes taking place in the occupational requirements of our society.

TABLE 7-4.   PERCENT OF POPULATION 14 YEARS OF AGE AND OVER IN THE LABOR FORCE, BY COLOR AND SEX, UNITED STATES 1940–1960

Color and sex	1960	1950	1940
Total:			
White................	55.2	53.2	51.6
Nonwhite............	56.3	55.8	58.2
Male:			
White................	78.0	79.0	78.9
Nonwhite............	72.1	76.2	80.0
Female:			
White................	33.6	28.1	24.1
Nonwhite............	41.8	36.7	37.2

Source: U.S. Bureau of the Census, U.S. Census of Population: 1960, General Social and Economic Characteristics, United States Summary, PC(1)-1C, p. 1-214, table 83.

The data in Table 7-5 show that nonwhite males have lower participation rates and nonwhite females have higher participation rates than white males and white females, respectively, in every residence group. Both white and nonwhite married women who were living with their husbands at the time of the census had lower labor-force-participation rates if they had children under 6 years of age than if they had no young children. The difference was greater, however, among white women.

Unemployment. The data in Table 7-5 show that nonwhites have higher unemployment rates than whites for both sexes and in every residence group. In a rapidly changing industrial economy, a certain amount of unemployment is inevitable, and no group is invulnerable. Some categories, however, continue to experience unemployment out of all proportion to their numbers in the labor

TABLE 7-5.   EMPLOYMENT STATUS AND SELECTED LABOR-FORCE CHARACTERISTICS, BY COLOR AND SEX, FOR THE UNITED STATES, URBAN AND RURAL: 1960

Status	White				Nonwhite			
	United States	Urban	Rural-nonfarm	Rural-farm	United States	Urban	Rural-nonfarm	Rural-farm
Male:								
Percent of total males 14 years and over in labor force..........	78.0	79.2	74.3	78.8	72.1	75.0	62.4	70.3
Percent of civilian labor force unemployed....	4.6	4.5	5.9	2.4	8.8	9.3	8.6	3.4
Female:								
Percent of total females 14 years and over in labor force..........	33.6	36.2	28.5	22.7	41.8	45.8	31.5	24.4
Percent of civilian labor force unemployed....	4.9	4.8	5.8	4.4	8.5	8.5	8.7	7.8
Percent of married women, husband present:								
In labor force..........	29.7	31.2	28.0	21.6	40.7	44.1	33.3	25.3
With own children under 6 years old, in labor force..........	18.0	18.1	18.2	15.6	31.0	33.1	26.5	21.6
Without own children under 6 years old, in labor force..........	35.5	37.5	33.4	23.9	46.7	50.6	38.0	27.6

Source: U.S. Bureau of the Census, *U.S. Census of Population: 1960, General Social and Economic Characteristics, United States Summary*, PC(1)-1C, p. 1-213, table 82.

force. A recent publication, *Manpower Report of the President*, had this to say about the situation:

> The most serious, persistent, and intractable employment problems are those of (1) young people, (2) older workers, (3) nonwhite workers, (4) the relatively unskilled, and (5) workers attached to declining industries or to those characterized by highly seasonal or otherwise unstable employment. For those unfortunate workers who fall in more than one of these groups, the problems are, of course, intensified.[4]

Both employment and unemployment rates are affected to some degree by the same conditions. Although it seems obvious that an increase in employment

[4] U.S. Department of Labor, *Manpower Report of the President* and a *Report on Manpower Requirements, Resources, Utilization, and Training*, 1963, p. 40.

will produce a commensurate drop in unemployment, at times this does not "automatically" happen; for instance, as unemployment increases, some of the unemployed may withdraw from the labor force and therefore not contribute to the increase in the unemployment rate. Many things may cause employment to vary. Some of the changes occurring at a given moment may have a cumulative effect, while others may, to some extent, cancel each other out. In our complex society, demographic, industrial, economic, and cultural changes can alter the employment-unemployment picture. Among the demographic changes, the most important are the rate at which the population between 14 and 65 years of age is growing (or shrinking), and the compositional changes in such characteristics as age, sex, race, and education. Changes in industrial composition, usually brought about by variations in technology, industrial organization, and the amount and distribution of resources, require changes in the size and composition of the labor force. In a society whose economy is expanding, labor-force requirements differ greatly from those in a society whose economic conditions are relatively static or are deteriorating. The employment problem, in its simplest terms, is a function of the relationship between the changing size, composition, and geographic distribution of the labor force on one hand, and the changing number, nature, and geographic distribution of work opportunities on the other.

INDUSTRIAL COMPOSITION

A society's industrial organization includes its total range of productive enterprise and is not restricted to manufacturing alone, although in common usage the term often has the more limited meaning. The United States census has classified industries according to 155 fairly detailed categories, but it also presents data according to more condensed lists. The countries in Table 7-6 were chosen to show a range of industrial composition, but they are not a representative sample of all the countries reporting to the United Nations. There are a number of extremes. In the United Kingdom only 5 percent of the population is engaged in agriculture; in India 71 percent is so engaged; in the United Kingdom 37 percent is employed in the manufacturing industries, in India, only 9 percent. In the United Kingdom and the United States most of the people are employed in manufacturing, commerce, and service industries. Most of Sweden's people are employed in manufacturing and agriculture, with commerce and the service industries next in line. In Italy 42 percent of the labor force is employed in agriculture, followed by manufacturing (24 percent) and service industries (22 percent). In all the more developed countries except Japan and Italy, the service industries are the main source of employment for women. In Japan relatively more women than men are employed in agriculture and manufacturing, and relatively more men than women are employed in service industries.

TABLE 7-6.   PERCENT OF ECONOMICALLY ACTIVE MALES AND FEMALES EMPLOYED IN
SELECTED INDUSTRIES, PERCENT DISTRIBUTION OF TOTAL ECONOMICALLY AC-
TIVE BY SEX, AND NONWORKER-TO-WORKER RATIO FOR SELECTED COUNTRIES,
AROUND 1950

Industry group	United States, 1950	United Kingdom, 1951	Sweden, 1950	Italy, 1951	Japan, 1950	Yugo-slavia, 1953	India, 1951
0 Agriculture, fishing, hunting, and forestry:							
Total	12.2	4.9	20.3	42.2	48.3	66.8	70.6
Male	15.4	6.4	25.3	42.5	40.2	59.8	69.4
Female	3.7	1.7	6.4	41.4	61.2	80.1	76.6
1 Mining and quarrying:							
Total	1.6	3.8	0.5	*	1.7	1.6	0.6
Male	2.2	5.4	0.7	*	2.4	2.4	0.5
Female	0.1	0.2	0.0	*	0.5	0.3	0.6
2-3 Manufacturing industries:							
Total	26.8	37.4	31.5	24.1	17.3	11.3	9.0
Male	28.0	37.1	33.9	22.9	20.0	13.4	9.4
Female	23.6	38.0	24.8	27.7	12.9	7.3	6.7
4 Construction:							
Total	6.2	6.2	7.9	7.5	4.3	2.5	1.1
Male	8.4	8.7	10.5	10.0	6.5	3.6	1.1
Female	0.6	0.7	0.4	0.2	0.8	0.6	0.9
5 Electricity, gas, water, and sanitary services:							
Total	1.3	1.6	1.0	0.5	0.6	——	0.5
Male	1.6	2.2	1.2	0.6	0.9	——	0.4
Female	0.6	0.4	0.2	0.1	0.2	——	0.8
6 Commerce:							
Total	18.5	14.1	13.0	——	12.1	3.1	5.8
Male	17.2	11.7	10.2	——	12.1	3.1	6.2
Female	21.6	19.1	20.8	——	12.2	3.0	3.4
7 Transport, storage, and communication:							
Total	7.0	7.7	8.1	4.0	4.4	2.1	1.9
Male	8.1	9.8	9.1	5.0	6.4	2.8	2.2
Female	4.0	3.2	5.2	1.1	1.3	0.7	0.4
8 Services:							
Total	23.7	23.7	17.0	21.7	11.2	0.9	10.6
Male	16.6	18.2	8.4	19.0	11.4	0.8	10.7
Female	42.4	36.2	41.2	29.5	10.9	1.1	10.6

TABLE 7-6.   PERCENT OF ECONOMICALLY ACTIVE MALES AND FEMALES EMPLOYED IN SELECTED INDUSTRIES, PERCENT DISTRIBUTION OF TOTAL ECONOMICALLY ACTIVE BY SEX, AND NONWORKER-TO-WORKER RATIO FOR SELECTED COUNTRIES, AROUND 1950 (Continued)

Industry group	United States, 1950	United Kingdom, 1951	Sweden, 1950	Italy, 1951	Japan, 1950	Yugo-slavia, 1953	India, 1951
9 Not classifiable elsewhere:							
Total.................	2.7	0.4	0.8	——	0.1	11.7	——
Male.................	2.4	0.4	0.7	——	0.1	14.1	——
Female..............	3.3	0.4	0.8	——	0.1	7.1	——
Totals.................	100.0	100.0	100.0	100.0	100.0	100.0	100.0
Percent of total economically active							
Male.................	72.5	69.2	73.6	74.9	61.5	65.9	70.8
Female..............	27.5	30.8	26.4	25.1	38.5	34.1	29.2
Nonworker-to-worker ratio	1.5	1.2	1.3	1.4	1.3	1.2	1.5

* Combined with Group 2–3.
Source: United Nations, Demographic Yearbook, 1956, tables 10 and 12.

Industrial Composition in the United States. Table 7-7 shows how the percent distribution of employed persons changed among the different industrial categories between 1940 and 1960. Even when such gross categories are used, significant shifts are apparent over the 20-year period; most notable are the reductions in agriculture, forestry, fisheries, mining, and personal services, and the increase in professional and related services. One of the major industrial changes in the postwar period shows up very clearly when we distinguish between employment in goods-producing industries and service-producing industries.[5] A surprising fact is brought out by this table: By 1957 the United States had changed from a predominantly goods-producing society to a predominantly service-producing society.

Industries	1962	1957	1947
Goods-producing...........	41.8%	45.9%	51.3%
Service-producing...........	58.2	54.1	48.7

Service-producing industries changed most dramatically in the area of government employment; between 1947 and 1962, this category increased

[5] Manpower Report of the President, pp. 17 and 21.

from 10.5 percent to 15.2 percent of all persons employed in nonfarm industries. Total government civilian employment—Federal, state, and local—rose from 5.5 million in 1947 to 9.2 million in 1962, or increased by over 65 percent—more than 2½ times the rate of growth for all nonfarm employment.[6] Contrary to the view that the Federal government is responsible for this increase in governmental employment, it is due largely to the growing payrolls of state

TABLE 7-7.   INDUSTRY GROUP OF EMPLOYED PERSONS, UNITED STATES: 1940–1960

Industry group	Percent of employed persons		
	1960	1950	1940
Total..	100.0	100.0	100.0
Agriculture, forestry, fisheries........................	6.7	12.5	18.8
Mining..	1.0	1.7	2.0
Construction......................................	5.9	6.1	4.6
Manufacturing....................................	27.1	25.9	23.4
Transportation, communication, and other public utilities.	7.0	7.8	6.9
Wholesale and retail trade..........................	18.2	18.8	16.7
Finance, insurance, real estate......................	4.2	3.4	3.2
Business and repair services........................	2.5	2.5	1.9
Personal services.................................	6.0	6.2	8.9
Entertainment, recreation services...................	0.8	1.0	0.9
Professional and related services....................	11.6	8.3	7.3
Public administration..............................	5.0	4.4	3.9
Industry not reported..............................	4.0	1.5	1.5

Source: U.S. Bureau of the Census, *U.S. Census of Population: 1940*, vol. II, *Characteristics of the Population*, part 1, p. 49.

U.S. Bureau of the Census, *U.S. Census of Population: 1950*, vol. II, *Characteristics of the Population*, part 1, p. 1-103.

U.S. Bureau of the Census, *U.S. Census of Population: 1960*, *General Social and Economic Characteristics*, *United States Summary*, PC(1)-1C, p. 1-223.

and local governments. The percentage of all employed civilian persons working for the Federal government rose only from 3.6 percent to 3.9 percent between 1947 and 1962, while the state and local governments' share of total civilian employment rose from 6.9 percent to 11.3 percent. While state and local government employment increased during this period by nearly 90 percent, Federal government employment increased by only about 25 percent. State and local governments now employ three-fourths of all government

[6] *Ibid.*, p. 21.

workers. The greatest single percent increase among persons in non-Federal employment has been in the category of educational services, which accounted for over one-half of the proportionate increase between 1947 and 1962. By 1962, nearly one-half of all state and local government employees were connected with education—a response to the rapid increase in public school enrollments.

TABLE 7-8.   INDUSTRY GROUP OF EMPLOYED PERSONS, FOR SELECTED PLACES: 1960

Industry group	United States	Iowa	Con-necticut	Urban	Fall River, Mass.	Austin, Texas
Total..........................	100.0	100.0	100.0	100.0	100.0	100.0
Agriculture, forestry, and fisheries....	6.7	20.7	1.8	1.1	{0.5*	{1.3*
Mining.........................	1.0	0.2	0.1	0.6		
Construction....................	5.9	5.2	5.6	5.5	3.9	8.7
Manufacturing...................	27.1	18.6	40.2	28.2	52.3	7.5
Transportation, communication, and other public utilities.............	7.0	6.3	4.7	7.5	4.0	4.9
Wholesale and retail trade..........	18.2	19.5	15.4	19.6	15.1	19.7
Finance, insurance, and real estate..	4.2	3.6	5.4	4.9	2.1	5.2
Business and repair services........	2.5	2.0	2.3	2.7	1.5	2.6
Personal services.................	6.0	4.8	4.3	6.3	2.9	10.1
Entertainment and recreation services.......................	0.8	0.6	0.5	0.9	0.4	0.8
Professional and related services....	11.6	12.7	12.0	12.7	9.1	23.2
Public administration..............	5.0	3.2	3.4	5.5	5.4	10.8
Industry not reported.............	4.0	2.5	4.2	4.5	2.8	5.1

* Agriculture, forestry, and fisheries combined with mining.
Source: U.S. Bureau of the Census, *U.S. Census of the Population: 1960, General Social and Economic Characteristics, United States Summary,* PC(1)-1C, pp. 1-221 and 1-281; U.S. Bureau of the Census, *U.S. Census of the Population: 1960, Detailed Characteristics, Texas,* PC(1)-45D, p. 45-1046; U.S. Bureau of the Census, *U.S. Census of the Population: 1960, Detailed Characteristics, Massachusetts,* PC(1)-23D, p. 23-483.

Internal Differences in Industrial Composition. There are wide differences in industrial composition among the areas within the United States (see Figure 7-2). The proportion of a given area's population engaged in manufacturing, in trade, and in the various services appears to depend upon the particular function served by that area. Table 7-8 indicates that Iowa and Connecticut have widely different industrial compositions. One major contrast is that Iowa has almost the same number of people engaged in manufacturing as in farming, while Connecticut has about 20 times as many.

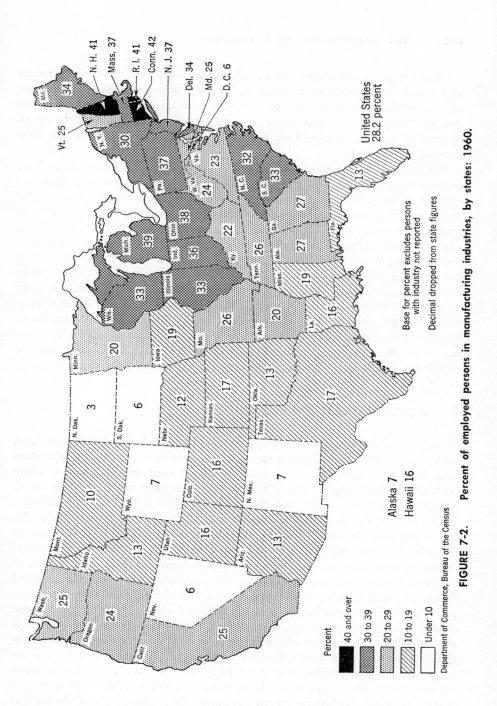

FIGURE 7-2. Percent of employed persons in manufacturing industries, by states: 1960.

Department of Commerce, Bureau of the Census

Percent

- 40 and over
- 30 to 39
- 20 to 29
- 10 to 19
- Under 10

United States
28.2 percent

Base for percent excludes persons
with industry not reported

Decimal dropped from state figures

N. H. 41
Mass. 37
R. I. 41
Conn. 42
N. J. 37

Del. 34
Md. 25
D. C. 6

Me. 34

Vt. 25

N. Y. 30

Pa. 37

W. Va. 24
Va. 23
N. C. 32
S. C. 33

Mich. 39

Ohio 38

Ind. 36

Ky. 26
Tenn. 26

Ala. 27
Ga. 27

Miss. 19
Fla. 13

Ill. 33

Wis. 33

Minn. 20

Iowa 19

Mo. 26

Ark. 20

La. 16

N. Dak. 3

S. Dak. 6

Nebr. 12

Kansas 17

Okla. 13

Texas 17

Mont. 10

Wyo. 7

Colo. 16

N. Mex. 7

Idaho 13

Utah 16

Ariz. 13

Wash. 25

Oregon 24

Nev. 6

Calif. 25

Alaska 7

Hawaii 16

Over the years, the differences in industrial composition among the regions and among the states have diminished. This is another instance of decreasing regional differences. A number of industries have moved to the South and to the West, and new industrial areas have emerged in association with the development of atomic energy—Oak Ridge, Tennessee, and Albuquerque, New Mexico, for example.

Cities also show significant variations in their industrial composition. Two extreme cases are found in the last two columns of Table 7-8. Occupational differences are often greater between industrial communities within one state than they are between states as different as Iowa and Connecticut. There are many one-industry communities, such as mining towns, textile cities, steel cities, and automobile cities. The predominance of one particular industry in a community often makes it different from other communities with respect to various demographic characteristics. Mining communities, for instance, differ rather markedly from others. Generally the women have little opportunity to work outside of the home, unless there has been a special effort to develop light industries. In some of the mining regions in the Appalachian Mountains of Pennsylvania and, more recently, in West Virginia, the reduction of mine labor has resulted in a rather severe exploitation of female labor under poor working conditions, a situation which may depress birth rates and raise death rates.

OCCUPATIONAL COMPOSITION

Changes in occupational composition naturally follow industrial changes, and both of these affect the life of the community in various ways. A relative decline in agricultural employment opportunities is often accompanied by an absolute decrease in rural population, thus changing the rural-urban distribution of population both regionally and nationally (see Table 6-5). In the Western world, at least, the changes in the industrial make-up of a society are the major causes of change in occupational composition; a changing occupational composition does not cause an industrial reorganization. (Of course, in underdeveloped countries and to some extent in urban industrial ones, a lack of people with certain occupational skills hinders and often prevents certain needed industrial changes.) One would expect, then, that since the industrial composition of the United States has changed, the occupational composition has changed also. The occupational composition of the United States from 1900 to 1960 is shown in Table 7-9. As we might expect, the most notable change is the continual and steep drop in the farming occupations. "Farmers and farm managers" and "farm laborers and farm foremen" combined, which composed approximately 40 percent of the labor force in 1900, were reduced to only 6 percent by 1960. "Laborers, except farm and mine," also decreased during this period, dropping from 12.5 percent to 4.8 percent of the total labor force. Progressive and sizable increases were made by "professional, technical, and kindred workers," "clerical and kindred workers," and "sales workers."

Table 7-10 gives the decennial rates of change for each of the occupational groups. The rate of decline in farm occupations has steadily increased for each

TABLE 7-9.   OCCUPATIONAL COMPOSITION OF THE EXPERIENCED LABOR FORCE, UNITED STATES: 1900–1960

Occupation group	Percent of total employed						
	1960	1950	1940	1930	1920	1910	1900
Total.........................	100.0	100.0	100.0	100.0	100.0	100.0	100.0
Professional, technical, and kindred workers......................	11.2	8.6	7.5	6.8	5.4	4.7	4.3
Farmers and farm managers.......	3.9	7.4	10.4	12.4	15.3	16.5	19.9
Managers, officials, and proprietors, except farm....................	8.4	8.7	7.3	7.4	6.6	6.6	5.8
Clerical and kindred workers.......	14.4	12.3	9.6	8.9	8.0	5.3	3.0
Sales workers..................	7.2	7.0	6.7	6.3	4.9	4.7	4.5
Craftsmen, foremen, and kindred workers......................	13.5	14.2	12.0	12.8	13.0	11.6	10.5
Operatives and kindred workers....	18.4	20.4	18.4	15.8	15.6	14.6	12.8
Private household workers.........	2.7	2.6	4.8	4.1	3.3	5.0	5.4
Service workers, except private household.....................	8.4	7.9	7.0	5.7	4.5	4.6	3.6
Farm laborers and foremen........	2.2	4.4	7.0	8.8	11.7	14.4	17.7
Laborers, except farm and mine....	4.8	6.6	9.4	11.0	11.6	12.0	12.5
Occupation not reported...........	4.9						

Source: U.S. Bureau of the Census, *U.S. Census of Population: 1960, General Social and Economic Characteristics, United States Summary,* PC(1)-1C, p. 1-216.
1900–1950: Donald J. Bogue, *Population of the United States,* The Free Press of Glencoe, New York, 1959, p. 475.

decade since 1920. No other occupational category has shown such a consistent drop. The slow rate of population growth and economic growth during the depression decade of the 1930s showed up most significantly in the white-collar occupations of "professional, technical, and kindred workers," "managers, officials, and proprietors, except farm," "clerical and kindred workers," and "sales workers." Table 7-11 gives the occupational distribution of the labor force according to color for the three census years of 1940, 1950, and 1960. It is obvious that the nonwhite populations are disproportionately concentrated in the occupations in the bottom half of the distribution, and are underrepresented in the upper half—"craftsmen, foremen, and kindred workers" and above. In 1940, with the exception of "farmers and farm managers," 6.1 percent of the nonwhite labor force was in the white-collar occupations, as compared with 35.7 percent of the white population. By 1960 the proportion of the nonwhite labor force in white-collar occupations had increased by $2\frac{1}{2}$ times, reaching 15.1

TABLE 7-10.   PERCENT CHANGE IN OCCUPATION GROUPS OF EMPLOYED PERSONS BY DECADE, UNITED STATES: 1900–1960

Occupation group	Percent change over preceding decade						
	1960	1950	1940	1930	1920	1910	1900
Total............................	14.9	14.0	6.3	15.4	13.2	28.5	——
Professional, technical, and kindred workers........................	47.3	31.0	17.2	45.0	29.9	42.4	——
Farmers and farm managers.......	−41.8	−18.4	−11.1	−6.4	4.5	7.0	——
Managers, officials, and proprietors, except farm....................	7.8	36.7	4.3	28.9	13.8	45.1	——
Clerical and kindred workers.......	35.0	45.2	14.9	28.1	70.3	126.6	——
Sales workers....................	18.1	19.8	12.8	48.6	17.3	34.3	——
Craftsmen, foremen, and kindred workers........................	12.3	34.6	−0.7	13.9	27.0	41.0	——
Operatives and kindred workers...	6.8	26.4	23.8	16.8	21.1	46.3	——
Private household workers........	22.6	−36.2	20.7	41.6	−23.8	17.2	——
Service workers, except private household......................	27.0	26.9	31.8	45.9	11.1	63.4	——
Farm laborers and foremen........	−39.8	−29.0	−15.3	−13.3	−7.9	4.8	——
Laborers, except farm and mine....	−9.4	−20.3	−8.6	8.7	9.6	23.7	——

Source: U.S. Bureau of the Census, U.S. Census of Population: 1960, General Social and Economic Characteristics, United States Summary, PC(1)-1C, p. 1-216.
1900–1950: Donald J. Bogue, Population of the United States, The Free Press of Glencoe, New York, 1959, p. 475.

percent. During the same period, the white labor force increased its proportion in the white-collar occupations from 35.7 percent in 1940 to 44.1 percent in 1960. We can express this change in another way: In 1940 there were relatively six times as many white as nonwhite persons in white-collar occupations, and in 1960 there were relatively three times as many white as nonwhite persons in white-collar occupations. According to Table 7-11, the percent of the nonwhite labor force in laboring categories has decreased somewhat, but even in 1960, nearly 18 percent of the nonwhite labor force was in one of these categories as compared with 6 percent of the white labor force. The two "service" categories together claimed the largest proportion of nonwhite workers. Approximately 30 percent of the nonwhite labor force was in these occupations in 1960, as compared with 9 percent of the white labor force.

TABLE 7-11.   OCCUPATIONAL COMPOSITION OF THE EMPLOYED LABOR FORCE, BY COLOR, UNITED STATES: 1940–1960

| Occupation group | Percent distribution | | | | | |
| | 1960 | | 1950 | | 1940 | |
	White	Nonwhite	White	Nonwhite	White	Nonwhite
Total........................	100.0	100.0	100.0	100.0	100.0	100.0
Professional, technical, and kindred workers......................	11.9	5.3	9.4	3.5	8.0	2.7
Farmers and farm managers.......	4.0	2.9	7.6	9.5	11.1	15.1
Managers, officials, and proprietors, except farm............	9.1	1.8	9.8	2.0	9.2	1.4
Clerical and kindred workers.......	15.3	6.4	13.4	3.6	{18.5	{2.0
Sales workers...................	7.8	1.6	7.7	1.3		
Craftsmen, foreman, and kindred workers.......................	14.3	6.4	15.0	5.3	12.3	3.0
Operatives and kindred workers.....	18.3	19.3	20.2	18.9	19.4	10.5
Private household workers.........	1.4	14.0	1.2	14.8	2.7	21.9
Service workers, except private household....................	7.5	16.5	6.9	15.4	7.3	11.8
Farm laborers and foremen.........	1.9	5.5	3.7	9.8	5.7	17.7
Laborers, except farm and mine.....	4.0	12.1	5.1	15.9	6.0	14.0
Not reported...................	4.5	8.2	—	—	—	—

Source: U.S. Bureau of the Census, *U.S. Census of Population: 1960, General Social and Economic Characteristics, United States Summary,* PC(1)-1C, p. 216.
1940–1950: Donald J. Bogue, *Population of the United States,* The Free Press of Glencoe, New York, 1959, p. 506.

Until now we have been discussing the occupational composition only according to color. Table 7-12 shows the occupational distribution both by color and by sex for 1960. Since the many differences in this table preclude our mentioning each one, we shall note only some of the major differences between white and nonwhite for each sex. If farmers and farm managers are excluded from the table, 37 percent of the white males would be in the sales-workers category and above, whereas only about 13 percent of nonwhite males are in these white-collar classifications. We also notice that white males are found twice as often as non-white males in the "craftsmen, foremen, and kindred workers" category. Perhaps the most disturbing statistic in Table 7-12 is the 57 percent of all nonwhite males who are in the following three occupational categories: "operatives and kindred workers," "laborers, except farm and mine," and "service workers, except private household." Among white females, 59.2 percent are in the white-collar categories, whereas only about 20 percent of the nonwhite females are in

TABLE 7-12.   OCCUPATION GROUPS OF EMPLOYED PERSONS, BY COLOR AND SEX, UNITED STATES: 1960

Occupation group	Male		Female	
	White	Nonwhite	White	Nonwhite
Total	100.0	100.0	100.0	100.0
Professional, technical, and kindred workers.....	11.0	3.9	13.8	7.5
Farmers and farm managers..................	5.6	4.4	0.5	0.7
Managers, officials, and proprietors, except farm.	11.5	2.3	4.0	1.2
Clerical and kindred workers.................	7.1	5.0	32.7	8.5
Sales workers..............................	7.4	1.5	8.7	1.7
Craftsmen, foremen, and kindred workers.......	20.5	10.2	1.3	0.7
Operatives and kindred workers...............	19.5	23.5	15.7	12.8
Private household workers....................	0.1	0.7	4.1	34.3
Service workers, except private household.......	5.2	13.7*	12.4	20.7
Farm laborers and foremen...................	2.3	7.1	0.9	2.9
Laborers, except farm and mine...............	5.6	19.4	0.5	1.0
Occupation not reported.....................	4.2	8.4	5.3	8.1

* This 13.7 percent was made up of 0.7 percent "protective service workers," 2.5 percent "waiters, bartenders, cooks, and counter workers," and 10.5 "other service workers."
Source: U.S. Bureau of the Census, U.S. Census of Population: 1960, General Social and Economic Characteristics, United States Summary, PC(1)-1C, p. 1-218.

white-collar occupations. The salient features in the female occupational distribution are the high percent of white females in "clerical and kindred workers" (nearly 33 percent) and the high percent of nonwhite females (55 percent) in the two service occupational categories.

The import of the changes in the occupational composition of our labor force and the significance of the differences between white and nonwhite occupational composition become more apparent when we discuss some of the basic causes of these changes—the relationship between occupation and education and between occupation and income—and when we study projections concerning the occupational composition of the United States up to 1970.

Industrial Changes and Occupational Shifts. In his *Manpower Report* to the Congress in March, 1963, President Kennedy said:

> From 1953 to 1962 investment in scientific research and development tripled. The rapid flow of technological innovation promises a future in which material want is all but unknown. But this future can only be reached by change, often with dislocation. In the process, the manpower requirements of the Nation will be profoundly altered.
>
> Occupationally, the new technology has been altering manpower requirements in favor of occupations requiring more education and training. In the earlier decades of this century, technological change developed mass-production, mass-assembly techniques, with great expansion in opportunities for semiskilled workers with relatively little education. In the fifties, the new technology was increasingly devoted to automating production and materials-handling processes, with concomitant increased demand for more highly trained and skilled manpower and lessened demand for workers in semiskilled occupations. The signs in the early sixties are that extension of automatic data processing is also limiting manpower needs in some office and clerical occupations, further compounding problems of adjustment.[7]

Figure 7-3, which is based on the first column of Table 7-10, gives us a graphic view of the occupational shifts between 1950 and 1960. The increasing substitution of machines for men, known as automation, has resulted in a sharp restriction in the employment of operatives and kindred workers and an absolute decline in the need for laborers, in every industrial sector from farming to manufacturing.

Technological change has had an uneven impact on our society and its economy; some types of jobs for which we have had a more than ample supply of labor have been sharply reduced, while other job opportunities have increased much faster than they can be filled. These job-reducing and job-increasing changes have not been such that the persons whose jobs were eliminated by technological change could easily move into the jobs which the change itself had created. In fact, rarely has this movement been possible. Job opportunities have been increased for the educated and the skilled but reduced for the uneducated and the unskilled.

The fact that employment gains have been concentrated in occupations at the top of the ladder in terms of education and skill is apparent from the trends discussed above. Requirements for personnel have increased fastest of all in professional and technical fields but rapidly also in many occupations in the managerial, clerical, sales, service, and skilled categories. And within each of these broad occupational groups, the trend has been toward increased utilization of workers

[7] *Ibid.*, p. XIII.

at the top of the skill range for the group and toward narrowing opportunities for those with minimum qualifications.[8]

Technological change has had an uneven effect territorially as well; for example, the mining areas of Pennsylvania and West Virginia have been hit very

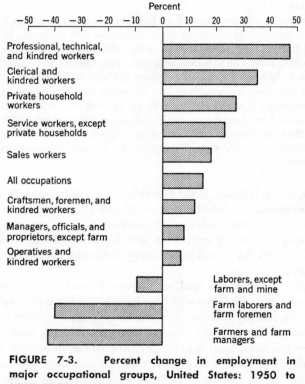

FIGURE 7-3.   Percent change in employment in major occupational groups, United States: 1950 to 1960. (Table 7-10.)

hard by technological change. In fact, the estimate is that in the decade 1950 to 1960 the number of mining operatives in these places dropped by as much as 50 percent. This Appalachian area has become the focus for President Johnson's attack on poverty. In other areas, such as those around Boston on the East Coast and around Los Angeles and San Francisco on the West Coast, a tremendous expansion in job opportunities for skilled technicians and scientists (par-

[8] *Ibid.*, p. 30.

ticularly mathematicians and physicists) has been provided by the developing electronics industries. One of the paradoxes facing today's labor force is the fact that in the same city a shortage of highly educated and skilled personnel can exist side by side with a very large number of unemployable workers who have been made jobless by technological change.

Table 7-13 shows the median years of schooling and the median income for each occupational category. In 1960, "private household workers," "laborers, except farm and mine," "farmers and farm managers," and "farm laborers and

TABLE 7-13.   MEDIAN YEARS OF SCHOOLING (1962), MEDIAN INCOME (MALES, 1959) BY OCCUPATION GROUP, UNITED STATES

Occupation group	Median years of schooling	Median income
Professional, technical, and kindred workers.............	16.2	$6,619
Managers, officials, and proprietors, except farm..........	12.5	6,664
Clerical and kindred workers...........................	12.5	4,785
Sales workers...	12.5	4,987
Craftsmen, foremen, and kindred workers...............	11.2	5,240
Operatives and kindred workers........................	10.1	4,299
Private household workers.............................	8.7	1,078
Other service workers.................................	10.8	3,310
Laborers, except farm and mine........................	8.9	2,948
Farmers and farm managers............................	8.8	2,169
Farm laborers and foremen............................	8.5	1,066

Source: U.S. Department of Labor, Manpower Report of the President and A Report on Manpower Requirements, Resources, Utilization, and Training, transmitted to the Congress, March, 1963, p. 13.

U.S. Bureau of the Census, U.S. Census of Population: 1960, Detailed Characteristics, United States Summary, PC(1)-1D, pp. 1-553 and 1-554.

foremen" were the only occupational categories in which an eighth-grade education was the median, and these categories are shrinking in size. Some schooling beyond high school is the median for the four occupational categories at the top of the list. The *Manpower Report* says,

In 1956, for the first time in our history, professional, managerial, clerical, and sales employees outnumbered employees in manual occupations. By 1962 there were close to 30 million workers in these white-color jobs—9.7 million more than in 1947. This increase accounted for ninety-seven percent of the total employment increase in all fields of work over the 15-year period. . . . The occupations with expanding employment opportunities generally demand prolonged education and training. And displaced workers without these qualifications have a hard time finding jobs—accounting for the high unemployment rates in the lower skilled groups."[9]

Future Changes in Occupational Composition in the United States. Table 7-14 shows a continuation and acceleration of the shifts in occupational composition which we have already observed in the above tables. Professional,

TABLE 7-14.   EMPLOYMENT BY OCCUPATION GROUP, UNITED STATES: 1960 AND PROJECTED 1970

Occupation group	Actual, 1960		Projected, 1970		Percent change
	Number (in millions)	Percent	Number (in millions)	Percent	1960–1970
Total..........................	66.7	100.0	80.5	100.0	21
Professional, technical, and kindred workers..................	7.5	11.2	10.7	13.3	43
Managers, officials, and proprietors, except farm..............	7.1	10.6	8.6	10.7	21
Clerical and kindred workers......	9.8	14.7	12.8	15.9	31
Sales workers...................	4.4	6.6	5.4	6.7	23
Craftsmen, foremen, and kindred workers.......................	8.6	12.8	10.3	12.8	20
Operatives and kindred workers...	12.0	18.0	13.6	16.9	13
Service workers.................	8.3	12.5	11.1	13.8	34
Laborers, except farm and mine...	3.7	5.5	3.7	4.6	——
Farmers, farm managers, laborers, and foremen..................	5.4	8.1	4.2	5.3	−22

Source: U.S. Department of Labor, *Manpower Report of the President and A Report on Manpower Requirements, Resources, Utilization, and Training,* transmitted to the Congress, March, 1963, p. 100.

technical, and kindred workers are expected to increase by 43 percent, or more than twice the national average for all occupations, in the decade 1960 to 1970. Since the growth will not be uniform among the occupations within this category, we shall note the changes which are expected to occur during this period for some of the most rapidly growing occupations: Engineers will increase by 550,000, to 1.4 million; scientists will rise from 335,000 to 580,000, with

[9] *Ibid.,* p. 5.

mathematicians and physicists increasing faster than others; technicians working with scientists and engineers will increase from their present figure of approximately 775,000 to 1.5 million; and full-time teachers, the largest profession, will increase from 2 million to 2.5 million (the most rapidly increasing need will be for college and university teachers—an expected 80 percent increase, from 175,000 to 315,000). Some of these increases will be due to the changing size of the population, but others will be the result of the increasing complexity of our technology.

During the same decade, 1960 to 1970, in which we expect the professional categories to increase by 3.2 million (or by 43 percent), the number of people in farming occupations will decrease by 22 percent. It is expected that the number of laborers will be about the same at the end of the decade and that this category will thus become a smaller part of the total labor force. The need for workers in the category of operatives and kindred workers (semiskilled workers) will grow by approximately 1.6 million, or 13 percent, but this increase will not be large enough to maintain its present proportion in the total labor force. The operatives category would have to increase during the decade by 2.5 million instead of by the 1.6 million projected, in order to maintain the same proportion in the labor force in 1970 that it had in 1960; this means that unskilled persons or those with little education will find shrinking employment opportunities and almost no chance for occupational advancement.

INCOME COMPOSITION

In our society most of us do not *make* a living—rather, we earn the money with which to *buy* a living. We have already seen the employment pattern in the United States and discussed the occupational composition; now we shall see how income is distributed with respect to employment and occupation.

The first column of Table 7-15 shows how the median annual income in 1959 for individual males (without regard to color) varied from one residence group to another. The ranking from highest to lowest is as follows: "urban fringe" ($5,444), "central cities of urbanized areas" ($4,318), "other urban" (outside of urbanized areas) in places of 10,000 or more ($3,901), "other urban" in places of 2,500 to 10,000 ($3,780), "rural-nonfarm" ($3,297), and the very lowest in "rural-farm" communities ($2,098). (See Figure 7-4). The income of nonwhite males follows the same pattern but at a much lower annual median-income level than that of white males in each of the residence groups. The median income of the nonwhite male for 1959 is closest to that of the total male population in the central cities of urbanized areas, where the ratio of nonwhite male to total male income is 0.71. In the urban fringe, the ratio of nonwhite male to total male income falls to 0.58; in each successive residence group this ratio drops lower and lower, until in the rural-farm communities, nonwhite male income is only 37 percent as high as the income for all males.

The median annual income of white and nonwhite females varies by residence in the same way as it did with the males, except that for the females, central cities and urban fringe are reversed. There is more correspondence between the annual median incomes of nonwhite females and those of the total female population than between the incomes of nonwhite males and those of the total male population.

TABLE 7-15.   MEDIAN INCOME IN THE UNITED STATES BY SEX, COLOR, AND SIZE OF PLACE OF RESIDENCE: 1959

Place	Total		Nonwhite	
	Male	Female	Male	Female
United States...............	$4,103	$1,357	$2,273	$ 909
Urban:				
Total....................	4,532	1,532	2,794	1,105
Urbanized areas:				
Total....................	4,757	1,700	3,080	1,284
Central cities.............	4,318	1,711	3,069	1,300
Urban fringe.............	5,444	1,677	3,152	1,173
Other urban:				
Total....................	3,846	1,159	1,782	709
Places of 10,000 or more....	3,901	1,215	1,925	749
2,500 to 10,000...........	3,780	1,091	1,595	654
Rural:				
Total....................	2,972	902	1,081	456
Rural nonfarm............	3,297	942	1,270	493
Rural farm...............	2,098	731	778	367

Source: U.S. Bureau of the Census, *U.S. Census of Population: 1960, General Social and Economic Characteristics, United States Summary*, PC(1)-1C, p. 1-236.

The nonwhite median income varies more widely among the residence groups than does the median income of the total population. It is interesting to note that the median annual income for all males is much higher in the suburban fringe than it is in the central city, whereas for nonwhites only a very slight income difference is recorded between fringe and central city.

Since Table 7-15 includes part-time workers, persons living in all kinds and sizes of households, and persons of all ages who have reportable income according to the census definition, it is of limited value in assessing the general economic well-being of family units. To overcome this limitation we shall present income data for an urban family of four, a meaningful unit, which is rather easily pictured by the reader. The 1960 census provides data for a family of four which contains a husband and wife living together with two children under 18, and in which the head of the family is an earner. From such data the reader may gain a clearer picture of the distribution of family income, of the differences

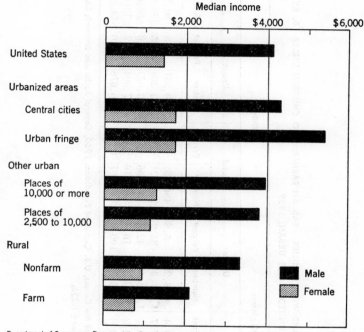

Department of Commerce, Bureau of the Census

FIGURE 7-4.   Median income in 1959 of persons, by sex, for the United States, by size of place: 1960. (Table 7-15.)

of income with respect to color, and also some idea of how urban families compare with all families.

Table 7-16 presents statistics for this type of relatively homogeneous family unit. The table becomes even more significant in the light of a budget produced by the Bureau of Labor Statistics a few years ago; based on 1959 buying power, it concludes that for an urban family of four, an income of approximately $6,000 a year would provide maintenance above minimum standards but well below

TABLE 7-16. INCOME OF HUSBAND-WIFE, FAMILIES, HEAD AN EARNER, TWO CHILDREN UNDER 18, BY COLOR, UNITED STATES TOTAL POPULATION AND UNITED STATES URBAN: 1959

Family income	All classes				White				Nonwhite			
	Total		Urban		Total		Urban		Total		Urban	
	Number	Percent	Number	Percent	Number	Percent	Number	Percent	Number	Percent	Number	Percent
Less than $3,000.	577,377	9.4	258,225	5.8	486,252	8.2	200,981	4.8	91,125	31.4	57,244	24.2
$3,000–5,999....	2,342,532	37.7	1,577,615	35.2	2,213,521	37.4	1,463,258	34.5	129,011	44.4	114,357	48.3
$6,000–9,999....	2,400,473	38.7	1,896,173	42.3	2,343,856	39.7	1,843,629	43.6	56,617	19.5	52,544	22.2
$10,000 and over	890,084	14.3	740,384	16.5	876,716	14.8	727,904	17.2	13,368	4.6	12,480	5.2
Median income..	$6,206	100.0	$6,580	100.0	$6,297	100.0	$6,678	100.0	$4,096	100.0	$4,469	100.0

Source: U.S. Bureau of the Census, U.S. Census of Population: 1960, General Social and Economic Characteristics, United States Summary, PC(1)-1C, pp. 1-225 and 1-226.

the luxury level.[10] Using this income of $6,000 as a dividing line, we find that 41 percent of all *urban* families of four earned less than $6,000 in 1959, 39.3 percent of the *white urban* families earned less than $6,000, and 72.5 percent of the *nonwhite urban* families earned less than $6,000 a year. In fact, approximately one out of four nonwhite urban families has an income amounting to only one-half or less of the budget figure of $6,000, i.e., an income of less than $3,000 a

TABLE 7-17.   **MEDIAN INCOME OF FAMILIES, BY COLOR, FOR THE UNITED STATES: 1947 TO 1962 (In current dollars)**

Year	Total	White	Nonwhite	Ratio of nonwhite to white
1962	$5,956	$6,237	$3,330	0.53
1961	5,737	5,981	3,191	0.53
1960	5,620	5,835	3,233	0.55
1959	5,417	5,643	2,917	0.52
1958	5,087	5,300	2,711	0.51
1957	4,971	5,166	2,764	0.54
1956	4,783	4,993	2,628	0.53
1955	4,421	4,605	2,549	0.55
1954	4,173	4,339	2,410	0.56
1953	4,233	4,392	2,461	0.56
1952	3,890	4,114	2,338	0.57
1951	3,709	3,859	2,032	0.53
1950	3,319	3,445	1,869	0.54
1949	3,107	3,232	1,650	0.51
1948	3,187	3,310	1,768	0.53
1947	3,031	3,157	1,614	0.51

Source: U.S. Bureau of the Census, *Current Population Reports: Consumer Income,* ser. P-60, no. 41, p. 11.

year for a family of four in which the head is an earner. Approximately twice as many nonwhite urban families as white urban families have incomes of less than $6,000. Approximately twice as high a proportion of white urban families as nonwhite have incomes between $6,000 and $10,000, and approximately three times as many white as nonwhite urban families have incomes of $10,000 and over.

Table 7-17 gives the median incomes of families (in current dollars), by color,

[10] See further, Michael Harrington, *The Other America: Poverty in the United States,* Penguin Books, Inc., Baltimore, 1962.

for the United States for each year from 1947 to 1962. The median income of white families increased continuously from 1947 to 1962, but the nonwhite median income actually dropped during several of those years. In the last column we can see that the ratio of nonwhite median income to white median income has not steadily increased, but has rather fluctuated from a low of 0.51 to a high of 0.57, and that in 1962 it was 0.53. During this time, the white family income increased by slightly more than $3,000, while the nonwhite family income increased by approximately $1,700.

> The relatively low nonwhite median income in 1962 reflects in part the fact that about one-half of nonwhite families still live in the South, where average family income is relatively low for both the white and nonwhite populations, and where, moreover, the ratio of nonwhite to white family average income is below the corresponding national figure. For regions outside the South, this ratio was about two-thirds in 1962, whereas for the South it was less than one-half. Another major reason for the lower incomes of the nonwhite group is the relatively heavy concentration of workers in nonwhite families in lower paid service and laborer occupations, which generally have comparatively fewer persons employed full-time the year round than other occupation groups.[11]

(See Figure 7-5, which shows how median income of families varies by state.)

Working Wives and Family Income. One of the most significant changes in family-income patterns has been the increasing number of working wives, particularly at the upper income levels. To quote from a recent census publication:

> One of the factors contributing to the relatively large gain in income made by husband-wife families, as compared with other types of families, has been the increasing proportion of working wives in recent years. In April, 1952, only 2 out of 10 of the married women were in the paid labor force. This proportion increased to 3 out of 10 by March, 1963 [see Figure 7-6]. The increase in the wife's labor force participation since 1951 has been most pronounced at the upper income levels, suggesting that the wife's contribution has been a major factor in moving families up the income scale. For the year 1962, wives in the paid labor force as a percent of husband-wife families was 17 percent at the lowest income level (under $3,000) as compared with 44 percent for families in the $10,000-and-over bracket.[12]

[11] U.S. Bureau of the Census, *Current Population Reports, Consumer Income*, ser. P-60, no. 41, *Income of Persons and Families in the United States: 1962*, pp. 10 and 11.
[12] *Ibid.*, p. 10.

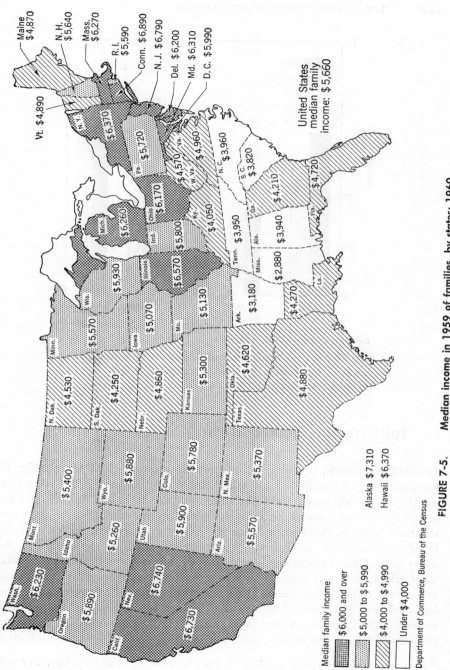

Maine $4,870
N.H. $5,640
Mass. $6,270
R.I. $5,590
Conn. $6,890
N.J. $6,790
Del. $6,200
Md. $6,310
D.C. $5,990

Vt. $4,890
N.Y. $6,370
Pa. $5,720
Ohio $6,170
Ind. $5,800
Illinois $6,570
Mich. $6,260
Wis. $5,930
Minn. $5,570
N. Dak. $4,530
S. Dak. $4,250
Nebr. $4,860
Iowa $5,070
Mo. $5,130
Kansas $5,300
Okla. $4,620
Ark. $3,180
Texas $4,880
La. $4,270
Miss. $2,880
Ala. $3,940
Ga. $3,820
Fla. $4,720
S.C. $3,960
N.C. $4,210
Tenn. $3,950
Ky. $4,050
W. Va. $4,570
Va. $4,960

Colo. $5,780
N. Mex. $5,370
Wyo. $5,880
Mont. $5,400
Idaho $5,260
Utah $5,900
Ariz. $5,570
Nev. $6,740
Calif. $6,730
Oregon $5,890
Wash. $6,230

United States
median family
income: $5,660

Alaska $7,310
Hawaii $6,370

Median family income

$6,000 and over

$5,000 to $5,990

$4,000 to $4,990

Under $4,000

Department of Commerce, Bureau of the Census

FIGURE 7-5. Median income in 1959 of families, by states: 1960.

199

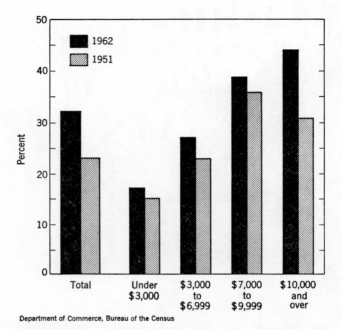

Department of Commerce, Bureau of the Census

FIGURE 7-6.   Working wives as percent of husband-wife families, by family income in constant (1962) dollars, United States: 1962 and 1951.

EDUCATIONAL COMPOSITION

In relatively simple, unchanging societies the growing child can acquire the knowledge and the skills that will allow him to take his place as a mature adult simply by participating in and observing the "family drama" going on about him.[13] By observing the behavior of the adults around him day after day, even the rural child in the United States not many years ago could learn at first hand the knowledge, skills, and attitudes needed by a successful farmer. But today in the United States and in any society which is becoming more industrial, more urban, and more complex, such informal experience is woefully inadequate as a means of preparing the child for adulthood. Formal education carried on by specialists (teachers) is an essential feature of complex urban industrial societies. The increasing volume of knowledge to be transmitted, the growing complexity of the intellectual skills needed—in reading, writing, and arith-

[13] From an unpublished paper by Aesel T. Hansen, professor of anthropology, University of Alabama.

metic—and the rapidly changing occupational requirements make it impossible for any home to provide the training essential for adult participation in urban societies. When we turn to Table 7-18 we see that in only 20 years—from 1940 to 1960—the educational level of adults in the United States went up markedly. The median schooling of all persons 25 years of age and over increased by two full years, from 8.6 to 10.6 years of school completed. Over one-half of our total adult population now has more than a tenth-grade education.

TABLE 7-18.   **PERCENT OF PERSONS 25 YEARS OF AGE AND OVER COMPLETING SPECIFIED YEARS OF SCHOOL, UNITED STATES: 1940, 1950, AND 1960**

Years of school completed	1960	1950	1940
Total..............................	100.0	100.0	100.0
College:			
4 years or more....................	7.7	6.0	4.6
1 to 3 years.......................	8.8	7.2	5.4
High school:			
4 years...........................	24.6	20.2	14.1
1 to 3 years.......................	19.2	17.0	15.0
Elementary school:			
8 years...........................	17.5	20.3	27.8
5 to 7 years.......................	13.8	15.9	18.3
1 to 4 years.......................	6.1	8.3	9.8
No school years completed.............	2.3	2.5	3.7
School years not reported..............	—	2.7	1.4
Median school years completed.........	10.6	9.3	8.6

Source: U.S. Bureau of the Census, *U.S. Census of Population: General Social and Economic Characteristics, United States Summary,* PC(1)-1C, pp. 1-208 and 1-209.

Years of School Completed. The proportions of adults with more than eight years of school completed and those with less exactly reversed themselves during 1940 to 1960—from 40 percent having more than eight years of schooling in 1940, to 40 percent having eight years of schooling or less by 1960. The proportion of adults who had completed high school increased from 24 percent in 1940 to 41 percent in 1960. These figures (for the total population 25 years of age and over) do not tell the whole story, however, because educational experiences vary with respect to such characteristics as sex, color, and residence.

Table 7-19 shows that in the adult white population a slightly smaller percentage of females than males complete no more than eight years of schooling; a larger percentage of white females complete one to three years of high school, and a significantly larger percentage complete four years of high school than

TABLE 7-19. YEARS OF SCHOOL COMPLETED BY PERSONS 25 YEARS OLD AND OVER, BY COLOR AND SEX, UNITED STATES: 1960

Color and sex	Total 25 years old and over	Years of school completed								Median school years completed
		Elementary school				High school		College		
		None	1 to 4	5 to 7	8	1 to 3	4	1 to 3	4 or more	
Male										
White	100.0	2.0	5.5	13.7	18.4	18.9	22.2	9.1	10.3	10.7
Nonwhite	100.0	6.8	20.9	23.0	12.3	17.0	12.1	4.4	3.5	7.9
Female										
White	100.0	1.9	4.1	11.9	17.8	19.6	29.2	9.5	6.0	11.2
Nonwhite	100.0	4.6	15.1	23.7	13.3	20.2	15.2	4.4	3.6	8.5

Source: U.S. Bureau of the Census, U.S. Census of Population: 1960, General Social and Economic Characteristics, United States Summary, PC(1)-1C, p. 1-207.

is the case for white males. Slightly larger proportions of white women than white men complete one to three years of college, but a significantly larger proportion of white men than white women complete four years or more of college (10.3 percent as compared with 6 percent). Among the nonwhite population, the relationship between the educational level of the sexes is approximately the same. There are significantly fewer nonwhite women with less than five years of schooling (20 percent as compared with 28 percent for the men); practically equal numbers of nonwhite males and females with five to eight years of schooling; significantly more nonwhite females than nonwhite males with one to four years of high school (35 percent as compared to 29 percent for

TABLE 7-20. MEDIAN SCHOOL YEARS COMPLETED, BY SEX, COLOR, AND RESIDENCE, UNITED STATES: 1940–1960

Sex, race, and residence	1960[c]	1950[b]	1940
Male.....................	10.3	9.0	8.6[b]
Female..................	10.9	9.6	8.7[b]
White...................	10.9	9.7	8.7[b]
Nonwhite................	8.2	6.9	5.8[b]
Urban..................	11.1	10.2	8.7[a]
Rural-nonfarm..........	9.5	8.8	8.4[a]
Rural-farm.............	8.8	8.4	7.7[a]

Sources: [a] U.S. Bureau of the Census, *U.S. Census of Population: 1940, vol. II, Characteristics of the Population, Part 1, United States Summary*, p. 40.

[b] U.S. Bureau of the Census, *U.S. Census of Population: 1950, vol. II, Characteristics of the Population, Part 1, United States Summary*, p. 1-96.

[c] U.S. Bureau of the Census, *U.S. Census of Population: 1960, General Social and Economic Characteristics, United States Summary*, PC(1)-1C, p. 1-207.

the males); and, unlike the white population, approximately the same proportions of male and female nonwhites complete one to four years or more of college.

In 1960 the median number of school years completed by white adults, both male and female, was higher by two to three years than the median number completed by nonwhites. The nonwhite medians are close to the median of the total population in 1940—8.6 years of school completed. The differences in educational level between the white and the nonwhite populations is diminishing and is doing so at an increasing rate because nonwhite school enrollment is increasing more rapidly than white school enrollment.

Table 7-20 shows a steady improvement in educational status for each of the populations represented. Since the most favored have been female, white, and urban, it is not surprising that white urban females have had the highest median years of school completed—11.6 years. As we should also expect, nonwhite rural farm males had the lowest median years of school completed—4.8 years. Obviously, educational achievement is not evenly divided with respect to sex, color, or community size. There are also large regional differences in educational level and differences among the states. In 1960, for example, Utah and Alaska ranked highest in the percentage of their adult population who were high school graduates (56 percent and 55 percent respectively); and Mississippi and Arkansas had the smallest proportion of high school graduates among their adults (30 percent and 29 percent).

TABLE 7-21.   PERCENT OF PERSONS OF SPECIFIED AGES ENROLLED IN SCHOOL IN CENSUS YEARS, UNITED STATES: 1910–1960

Year	Age				
	5 and 6	7–13	14–17	18 and 19	20–24
	Percent enrolled				
1960	63.8	97.5	87.4	42.1	14.6
1950	55.8	95.7	83.9	32.3	12.9
1940	43.0	95.0	79.3	28.9	6.6
1930	43.2	95.3	73.1	25.4	7.4
1920	41.0	90.6	61.6	17.8	——
1910	34.6	86.1	58.9	18.7	——

Source: U.S. Bureau of the Census, *U.S. Census of Population: 1950*, vol. II, *Characteristics of the Population*, part 1, p. 1-95.
U.S. Bureau of the Census, *U.S. Census of Population: 1960, General Social and Economic Characteristics, United States Summary*, PC(1)-1C, p. 1-205.

School Enrollment. The rising level of education among adults is, of course, a result of a previous increase in enrollment figures among these adults when they were of school age. Table 7-21 shows the proportion of each age group which was enrolled in school at each census from 1910 to 1960. The smallest change has been in the 7–13 age group, which had a high enrollment rate (86 percent) as early as 1910; it reached 98 percent by 1960. The proportion of the various age groups which were enrolled in school changed most in the 5- and 6-year-old group (29 percentage points) and changed least in the 20–24 age group (7 percentage points). The *relative* changes, however, were largest in the 18–19 age group, where the proportion enrolled more than doubled (125 percent) and in the 20–24 age group, which almost doubled its enrollment rate (97 percent).

In Table 7-22 we can see that by and large, these three age groups (7–13, 14–17, and 18–24) correspond to elementary, high school, and college attendance. The correspondence is closest for the elementary school age groups. There are more males than females enrolled in school at every year of age; this difference is greatest beyond 22 years of age, when students are finishing college and are doing graduate work toward advanced degrees. The larger number of males enrolled in the early years (17 years of age and under) is largely a result of the demographic fact that there are more males than females in these ages (see Chapter 5), whereas the larger male enrollment in the older age groups is related to the different roles males and females are expected to play in our

TABLE 7-22.   SCHOOL ENROLLMENT FOR THE CIVILIAN NONINSTITUTIONAL POPULATION 7 TO 34 YEARS OLD; TOTAL NUMBER ENROLLED AND PROPORTION IN DIFFERENT LEVELS OF SCHOOLS, BY AGE AND SEX, UNITED STATES: 1960 (Numbers in thousands. As of October 1)

Age	Male				Female			
	Total enrolled	Elementary school	High school	College	Total enrolled	Elementary school	High school	College
7–13	13,074	97.8	2.2	——	12,547	97.4	2.6	——
14–17	5,248	12.1	86.0	1.9	4,994	7.3	90.2	2.5
18–24	1,999	0.2	17.4	82.4	1,168	0.2	18.5	81.3
18–21	1,580	0.3	21.5	78.3	1,054	0.2	19.0	80.8
22–24	419	——	1.9	98.1	114	——	14.0	86.0
25–34	621	——	4.7	95.3	171	1.2	6.4	92.4

Source: U.S. Bureau of the Census, *Current Population Reports*, ser. P-25, no. 232, p. 8.

society. (In Table 7-17, compare the proportions of white males and white females who have completed one to three years of college, and then compare the proportions of white males and white females who have completed four or more years of college.)

School Enrollment in the United States from 1950 to 1980. The following discussion will be based almost entirely on a recent census publication concerning enrollment projections; Table 7-23 comes from that publication (see the source). The differences in the two projections of elementary and kindergarten enrollment given in the table are due almost entirely to the different fertility assumptions, because enrollment rates are not expected to vary much at these ages. Enrollment in the elementary grades increased by 52 percent in the 1950s, but it is not expected to increase at nearly so fast a rate in the 1960s or in the 1970s. (An increase of from 12 to 20 percent is estimated for the 1960s and an increase of from 13 to 27 percent for the 1970s.) The absolute increase

TABLE 7-23. SCHOOL ENROLLMENT BY LEVEL OF SCHOOL, UNITED STATES, ESTIMATED 1950–1960, AND PROJECTED TO 1980 (Numbers in thousands—for fall of year)

Level of school and enrollment series*	Estimated		Projected	
	1950	1960	1970	1980
All school levels....................	30,276	46,259		
II-A............................	——	——	60,344	75,102
III-C............................	——	——	55,731	62,245
Elementary school or kindergarten....	21,406	32,441		
II-A............................	——	——	38,430	48,696
III-C............................	——	——	36,360	41,151
High school......................	6,656	10,249		
II-A............................	——	——	14,894	17,388
III-C............................	——	——	14,110	14,752
College or professional school.........	2,214	3,570		
II-A............................	——	——	7,020	9,018
II-C............................	——	——	5,261	6,342

* II-A assumes a continuation to the end of the projection period of the fertility levels experienced in the 1955–1957 period and a continued increase in enrollment rates by age with some leveling off by future dates. III-C assumes a decline from the 1955–1957 fertility level to the 1949–1951 level by the middle of the projection period, with fertility then remaining constant to 1980 and enrollment rates remaining constant at the 1957–1959 level to 1980.

Source: U.S. Bureau of the Census, Current Population Reports, ser. P-25, no. 232, p. 2.

which is expected will be sizable, however, even though the rate of increase will decline. (The absolute increases projected range from 4 million to 6 million in the 1960s and from 5 million to 10 million in the 1970s. For further discussion of population projections, see Chapter 17.)

Since all the people who will be of high school age in 1970 were already born in 1960, the difference (784,000) between the projected 1970 figures (14,894,000 and 14,110,000) is due to different assumptions regarding enrollment rate rather than regarding fertility, as was true of the elementary school enrollment projections. High school enrollment projections for 1980, however, involve both fertility and enrollment rates as variables and are therefore more difficult to project. High school enrollment jumped 54 percent during the 1950s and is expected to increase by another 38 percent to 45 percent in the 1960s, reaching a figure between 14 million and 15 million; it is expected that in the 1970s, enrollment will increase much more slowly, by 4 to 17 percent.

Enrollment increased faster in colleges and professional schools during the 1950s than in elementary and high schools, rising by 61 percent in the former, from 2.2 million to 3.6 million students. The biggest jump shown by Table 7-23 is that expected in college and university enrollments between 1960 and 1970. The increases projected range from 1.7 million to 3.4 million, or increases of between 47 and 97 percent. The only variable which must be taken into account in these projections is the enrollment rate. The rise in college enrollment is due largely to the great increase in the number of births which began within a year after World War II, increasing the number of people who became of college age by 1963 and 1964. No wonder the existing college facilities are already feeling the strain. The difficulty of projecting college enrollment is explained by the census as follows:

> The trend in college enrollment is particularly difficult to project with confidence because—unlike enrollment at the lower levels, which results from generally stable enrollment rates—prospects for higher education are dependent to a great extent on such factors as attitudes toward college attendance, the growth of the community college system, the availability of dormitories and other college facilities, the financial support for both institutions and potential students, admission practices in institutions of higher education, and legal requirements for teachers to acquire additional college credits.[14]

SUMMARY

Since the late 1950s the United States has been plagued with a persistent increase in the level of unemployment, in spite of a period of unprecedented general prosperity. Since 1957 the unemployment level has been slightly higher at the end of each business recession than it was before the recession began. Long-term unemployment is also on the increase. More women are working; an increasing number of married women have incomes which, combined with their husbands' incomes, place the family at a higher economic level.

[14] U.S. Bureau of the Census, *Current Population Reports*, ser. P-25, no. 232, p. 3.

One of the most significant shifts in our industrial composition has been the change from employment in productive industries to employment in service industries. Our changing technology and our changing industrial composition have caused major changes in the occupational composition of our labor force. Opportunities are expanding at the upper end of the occupational scale and are diminishing at the lower end. The day has nearly arrived when a man can no longer exchange his muscles for dollars. This contraction of opportunities in semiskilled and unskilled labor makes the failure of many young people to complete high school a matter of serious concern. An eighth-grade education may have been adequate in 1910 or even 1920, but it is not enough today.

We found significant differences between males and females in occupational composition, and we also found significant differences in occupational composition between whites and nonwhites. The nonwhite population has raised its general occupational level during the last 40 years, but nonwhites are still overrepresented at the lower end of the occupational scale and underrepresented in the upper levels. Nonwhite income has increased over the years, but it has not increased relative to white income in the last 15 years.

In this chapter we have seen how rapidly the educational level of the society has risen over the last few decades. Educational attainment has varied significantly according to sex, color, and residence—particularly with respect to the last two characteristics. In 1960 more than one-half of the United States population had at least a tenth-grade education. Finally, looking into the future to see what school enrollments might be at various levels, we have discovered that elementary and high school enrollments will continue to grow, largely because of an increase in the number of people at those ages. The increase in college and university enrollment during the last decade, however, has been due largely to an increase in enrollment rates rather than to an increase in the college-age population. In the 1960s and 1970s college enrollment is expected to climb rapidly, because an increasing number of people will be arriving at college age and an increasing proportion of them will try to enroll in college.

As a final comment, we quote once again from the President's report on manpower:

> Growth and change in manpower requirements vary by industry, occupation, and area, as do changes wrought by technology and by other powerful forces. Our manpower resources also grow irregularly: Skills, age distribution, and other characteristics are in constant flux. Public policies must encourage and facilitate the adjustments made necessary by the ever-changing pattern of job requirements. Private industry and trade unions must also exercise initiative and responsibility to adapt jobs and employment practices to make the fullest use of manpower resources, and to do so in a humane and efficient manner.[15]

[15] U.S. Department of Labor, *Manpower Report of the President*, 1963, pp. XI and XII.

SUGGESTIONS FOR SUPPLEMENTARY READING

Chapin, Jr., F. Stuart: *Urban Land Use Planning*, Harper & Brothers, New York, 1957.

Galbraith, John K.: *The Affluent Society*, Houghton Mifflin Company, Boston, 1958.

Moore, Wilbert E., and Arnold S. Feldman (eds.): *Labor Commitment and Social Change in Developing Areas*, Social Science Research Council, New York, 1960.

Sharp, Harry, and Leo F. Schnore: See ref. in Chap. 6.

Slotkin, James S.: See ref. in Chap. 6.

Smuts, Robert W.: *Women and Work in America* (comparison between 1890 and 1950), Columbia University Press, New York, 1959.

United Nations: "Demographic Aspects of Manpower, Report 1, Sex and Age Patterns of Participation in Economic Activities," *Population Studies*, no. 33, Department of Economic and Social Affairs, New York, 1962.

U.S. Bureau of the Census: *Current Population Reports, Illustrative Projections to 1980 of School and College Enrollment in the United States*, ser. P-25, no. 232, 1961.

U.S. Bureau of the Census: *Current Population Reports, Income of Families and Persons in the United States: 1959*, ser. P-60, Consumer Income, Washington, D.C., 1961.

U.S. Bureau of Labor Statistics: *Population and Labor Force Projections for the United States, 1960 to 1975*. Prepared by Sophia Cooper and Stuart Garfinkle. Bulletin no. 1242, Washington, D.C., 1959.

U.S. Department of Labor: *Manpower Report of the President* and *A Report on Manpower Requirements, Resources, Utilization, and Training*, 1964.

U.S. Women's Bureau: *1960 Handbook on Women Workers*, Washington, D.C., 1960.

U.S. Women's Bureau: *Women Workers in 1960: Geographical Differences*, Women's Bureau Bulletin 284, Washington, D.C., 1962.

Wolfbein, Seymour L.: *Employment and Unemployment in the United States*, Science Research Associates, Inc., Chicago, 1964.

CHAPTER EIGHT

Racial, Ethnic, Religious, and Marital Composition

This chapter is divided into six parts. In addition to the four aspects of composition which appear in the title, we shall discuss miscellaneous elements in the composition of a population; the sixth part will be a final statement on population composition generally. The first two characteristics, race and ethnicity, have already been discussed in Chapter 4, but the presentation of their chief demographic aspects has been left for this chapter. Religious affiliation has not been touched on as yet. A good deal of what was said in Chapter 4 about racial and ethnic identity is also relevant to religious identity, if religious identification is the basis for determining an individual's eligibility to occupy certain social, economic, and political statuses, or if it is the basis for political divisions within a society. Even when "minority status" is not associated with a particular religious affiliation, religious composition is still important to the degree that different religious bodies have distinctive beliefs which produce different demographic effects. When either of the above conditions exist, it becomes important for every country to know the religious composition of its population.

RACE AND COLOR

Growth of the Negro Population in the United States. Since most of our discussion will concern the United States, we shall use the census definition given in Chapter 4. Table 8-1 shows the number of white, nonwhite, Negro, and other races for each census year from 1790 to 1960, wherever available, and the percent each group constituted of the total population for every census year.

Although the Negro was first brought to this country shortly after the Pilgrims settled at Plymouth, not until about 1700 was the value of the Negro as a laborer in the tobacco fields fully realized. Then importation of slaves began on a grand scale. By 1790 there were over 757,000 Negroes in the United States,

TABLE 8-1. POPULATION, BY RACE, IN NUMBER AND PERCENT FOR THE UNITED STATES: 1790–1960 (Number in thousands)

Year	All classes		White		Nonwhite					
					Total		Negro		Other	
	Number	Percent	Number	Percent	Number	Percent	Number	Percent	Number	Percent
1960*	178,464	100.0	158,455	88.8	20,009	11.2	18,860	10.6	1,149	0.6
1950	150,697	100.0	134,942	89.5	15,755	10.5	15,042	10.0	713	0.5
1940	131,670	100.0	118,215	89.8	13,455	10.2	12,866	9.8	589	0.4
1930	122,775	100.0	110,287	89.8	12,488	10.2	11,891	9.7	597	0.5
1920	105,711	100.0	94,821	89.7	10,890	10.3	10,463	9.9	427	0.4
1910	91,973	100.0	81,732	88.9	10,241	11.1	9,828	10.7	413	0.4
1900	75,994	100.0	66,809	87.9	9,185	12.1	8,834	11.6	351	0.5
1890	62,948	100.0	55,101	87.5	7,847	12.5	7,489	11.9	358	0.6
1880	50,156	100.0	43,403	86.5	6,753	13.5	6,581	13.1	172	0.3
1870	38,558	100.0	33,589	87.1	4,969	12.9	4,880	12.7	89	0.2
1860	31,444	100.0	26,923	85.6	4,521	14.4	4,442	14.1	79	0.3
1850	23,192	100.0	19,553	84.3	3,639	15.7	3,639	15.7	—	—
1840	17,070	100.0	14,196	83.2	2,874	16.8	2,874	16.8	—	—
1830	12,866	100.0	10,537	81.9	2,329	18.1	2,329	18.1	—	—
1820	9,639	100.0	7,867	81.6	1,772	18.4	1,772	18.4	—	—
1810	7,240	100.0	5,862	81.0	1,378	19.0	1,378	19.0	—	—
1800	5,308	100.0	4,306	81.1	1,002	18.9	1,002	18.9	—	—
1790	3,929	100.0	3,172	80.7	757	19.3	757	19.3	—	—

* Excluding Alaska and Hawaii.

Source: U.S. Bureau of the Census, *Statistical Abstract of the United States*, 1963, p. 24.

and they constituted 19.3 percent of our total population. Very rapid increase in the Negro population during the eighteenth century must be attributed not only to the direct importation of slaves but also to their rapid rate of natural increase. By 1790 probably about three-fourths of the Negroes in the United States were native born. After 1808 the importation of slaves was illegal, but this did not prevent a large number being smuggled in. Indeed, after the invention of the cotton gin in 1793, the cultivation of cotton became increasingly profitable, and up to the time of the Civil War there was a very brisk demand for slaves on the Southern cotton plantations. After studying the available evidence, Dublin[1] concludes, however, that the unlawful trade in slaves could have increased the Negro population by no more than one-half of 1 percent a year from 1808 to 1860. Hence, the remaining increase of about 2 percent a year came from the excess of births over deaths (natural increase). A natural increase of 20 per 1,000 per year is a relatively high rate, but the fact is that the Negro rate was not so high as the white rate at that time. The white birth rate is known to have been very high in the first half of the nineteenth century, and it may have equaled or even surpassed that of the Negro up to the time of the Civil War, whereas the death rate of the white population has always been substantially lower than that of the Negro. Furthermore, the natural increase of the white population was augmented by immigration to an even greater extent than that of the Negro, even before 1860.

Except during the decade 1800 to 1810, the proportion of Negroes in our population declined steadily from 1790 to 1930. Since 1930, when it constituted 9.7 percent of our total population, the proportion has increased—to 9.8 percent in 1940, 10 percent in 1950, and 10.6 percent in 1960. Negro immigration stopped almost completely after 1860, whereas white immigration continued high until World War I; naturally, the result was a decline in the proportion of Negroes in our population. But the authors are disposed to think that the relatively high death rate among Negroes was a very important factor in keeping their natural increase below that of the white population during most of this time.

A number of factors help to explain the change in Negro and white growth rates since 1920. The contribution which European immigration made to white population growth, through the immigrants themselves and through their high birth rates, fell to a low level as immigration was sharply reduced after 1924. Moreover, the Negro birth rate has been considerably higher than the white birth rate, quite possibly since the Civil War, and the Negro death rate has been falling rapidly in the past 30 or 40 years. Hence it is not surprising that the *natural increase* of the Negroes has been greater than the *total increase* of the whites since the 1920s. The date when this difference first appeared cannot be specified exactly, but it was probably in the late 1920s or early 1930s.

[1] Louis I. Dublin, *Health and Wealth*, Harper & Brothers, New York, 1928, p. 256.

TABLE 8-2. NUMBER AND PERCENTAGE DISTRIBUTION BY RACE AND COLOR FOR THE UNITED STATES, 1930 TO 1960

Race	1960* Number	1960 Percent	1950 Number	1950 Percent	1940 Number	1940 Percent	1930 Number	1930 Percent
Total	178,464,236	100.0	150,697,361	100.0	131,669,275	100.0	122,775,046	100.0
White	158,454,956	88.8	134,942,028	89.5	118,214,870	89.8	110,286,740	89.8
Negro	18,860,117	10.6	15,042,286	10.0	12,865,518	9.8	11,891,143	9.7
Other	1,149,163	0.6	713,047	0.5	588,887	0.4	597,163	0.5
Indian	508,675	0.3	343,410	0.2	333,969	0.3	332,397	0.3
Japanese	260,059	0.1	141,768	0.1	126,947	0.1	138,834	0.1
Chinese	198,958	0.1	117,629	0.1	77,504	0.1	74,954	0.1
Filipino	106,426	0.1	61,636	0.0	45,563	0.0	45,208	0.0
All other	75,045	0.0	48,604	0.0	4,904	0.0	5,770	0.0

*Excluding Alaska and Hawaii.

Source: U.S. Bureau of the Census, U.S. Census of Population: 1960, General Population Characteristics, United States Summary, PC(1)-1B, p. 1-145.

TABLE 8-3. NUMBER AND PERCENT DISTRIBUTION OF "OTHER RACES" FOR UNITED STATES: 1860 TO 1960 (Numbers in thousands)

Year	Total		Indian		Chinese		Japanese		Filipino		All other	
	Number	Percent	Number	Percent	Number	Percent	Number	Percent	Number	Percent	Number	Percent
1960*	1,149	100.0	509	44.3	199	17.3	260	22.6	106	9.3	75	6.5
1930	597	100.0	332	55.7	75	12.6	139	23.2	45	7.6	6	1.0
1890	358	100.0	248	69.4	107	30.0	2	0.6	—	—	—	—
1860	79	100.0	44	55.8	35	44.2	—	—	—	—	—	—

* Excluding Alaska and Hawaii.

Source: U.S. Bureau of the Census, U.S. Census of Population: 1960, General Population Characteristics, United States Summary, PC(1)-1B, p. 1-145.

Population Changes of Other Races. Table 8-1 reveals that nonwhite races other than the Negro have not increased steadily in every decade; during two decades there was a drop in numbers as well as a drop in percents (the 1890s and the 1930s). The number of races in the other-races category has increased since 1860 (see Table 8-3), and the proportion of each race in the total population has also changed. In 1860 the other races included only the Indians and Chinese. Moreover, only the Indians living outside of the Indian Territory and outside of Indian reservations were reported in the census at that time. Almost all of Oklahoma was known as Indian Territory at that time. The

TABLE 8-4.   INTERCENSAL INCREASE BY RACE AND COLOR, FOR THE UNITED STATES,* 1930–1960

Race	1930–1940		1940–1950		1950–1960	
	Number	Percent	Number	Percent	Number	Percent
Total..........	8,894,229	7.2	19,028,086	14.5	27,766,875	18.4
White.........	7,928,130	7.2	16,727,158	14.1	23,512,928	17.4
Negro.........	974,375	8.2	2,176,768	16.9	3,817,831	25.4
Other..........	−8,276	−1.4	124,160	21.1	436,116	61.2
Indian.......	1,572	0.5	9,441	2.8	165,265	48.1
Japanese.....	−11,887	−8.6	14,821	11.7	118,291	83.4
Chinese......	2,550	3.4	40,125	51.8	81,329	69.1
Filipino......	355	0.8	16,073	35.3	44,790	72.7
All other.....	−866	−15.0	43,700	891.1	26,441	54.4

* Excluding Alaska and Hawaii.
Source: U.S. Bureau of the Census, *U.S. Census of Population: 1960, General Population Characteristics, United States Summary,* PC(1)-1B, p. 1-145.

abrupt jump in the number of Indians reported between 1860 and 1890 in Table 8-3 is due to the inclusion of Indians living on reservations or in Indian Territory in the census year of 1890. The figures certainly contradict the notion that the Indian was vanishing and doomed to early disappearance. Concerning the changes in the Indian population from the time of Columbus to the present, Professor Brewton Berry has this to say:

There were probably 800,000 Indians in what is now the United States at the time of discovery. By 1800 their numbers were down to 600,000. Smallpox, tuberculosis, massacres, and general dissipation took heavy tolls until the Indian population reached a low point of about 250,000 in 1850, and there it remained for some fifty years. Shortly after the turn of the century, however, it began to rise.

The 1910 census reported 266,000 Indians, the 1940 census 334,000, and in 1950 there were 342,226. The Indian, on the basis of these figures, was indeed on his way to oblivion, but is currently staging a comeback, though he still has far to go to regain the numerical position he formerly held.[2]

In the same article, Professor Berry makes some interesting points when discussing the vagueness of the definition of "Indian."

. . . the term "Indian" nowadays has very little relation to racial purity. Under the effects of different laws the same individual may be counted as Indian for some purposes and non-Indian for others. . . . Accordingly, population figures leave much to be desired. Even so, there is no evidence that the Indians are fewer in number than they were in 1492. This would be true (in Latin America, but not in the United States) even if we counted as Indians only the full-bloods. If, on the other hand, we follow the same practice with respect to the Indian that we do with the Negro (namely, "one drop of Negro blood makes one a Negro"), the number of Indians today would run into the tens of millions. But whatever the criteria, be they broad or narrow, it can safely be maintained that the Indian is by no means a vanishing race.[3]

In 1860 the only other race besides Indians enumerated in the United States was the Chinese; their number reached a high point with 107,000 in 1890, declined to 61,000 by 1920; it then rose to 199,000 in the census of 1960. In 1870, 55,000 Japanese were enumerated; the number has grown in each decade except 1930 to 1940, until now the Japanese number 260,000. (Table 8-3 gives the numbers for only a few years.) Only 160 Filipinos were recorded in the census of 1910; by 1960 they numbered 106,000, or 9 percent of the other non-white races. "All other" races first appeared in census statistics in 1910, when the category numbered only 3,000. The 1960 total of 75,000 includes "Hawaiians, Eskimos, Aleuts, Koreans, Asian Indians, Malayans, etc."

Although in the 100 years between 1860 and 1960 the other races increased by nearly 15 times (79,000 to 1,149,000) while the Negro increased approximately four times and the white increased about six times, the other-races category now comprises only 0.6 percent of the total population of the continental United States.

The admissions of Alaska and Hawaii to the Union have had a much greater demographic effect on the other-races category than on the total population of the United States. These new states have increased the total population of the United States only by 859,000, or 0.5 percent, while they increased the other-races category by 471,000, or 41 percent. The Negro population was increased by only 12,000 on the admission of Alaska and Hawaii. In 1960 Alaska's popula-

[2] Brewton Berry, "The Myth of the Vanishing Indian," *Phylon*, vol. 21, no. 1, p. 54, 1960.
[3] *Ibid.*, p. 55.

tion of 226,000 was 23 percent nonwhite, and Hawaii's population of 633,000 was 68 percent nonwhite.

Regional Distribution of the Negro Population. Until recently, Negroes in the United States were heavily concentrated in the South. As late as 1900 almost nine-tenths (89.7) of all American Negroes lived in the South, but by 1960 this figure had fallen to 60 percent. The proportion of the Negro population living in the North during the same period increased from 10 to 34.4 percent, and the proportion living in the West increased from 0.3 to 5.7 percent.

TABLE 8-5.   NUMBER AND PERCENT DISTRIBUTION AND DIFFERENCE OF WHITE, NEGRO, AND OTHER RACES FOR THE UNITED STATES (50 STATES), AND CONTERMINOUS UNITED STATES (48 STATES): 1960 (Numbers in thousands)

Race	Conterminous United States (48 states)		United States (50 states)		Difference (effect of adding Alaska and Hawaii)	
	Number	Percent	Number	Percent	Number	Percent
Total..............	178,464	100.0	179,323	100.0	859	0.5
White..............	158,455	88.8	158,832	88.6	377	0.2
Negro..............	18,860	10.6	18,872	10.5	12	0.1
Other..............	1,149	0.6	1,620	0.9	471	41.0
Indian............	509	0.3	524	0.3	15	3.0
Japanese..........	260	0.1	464	0.3	204	78.5
Chinese...........	199	0.1	237	0.1	38	19.1
Filipino..........	106	0.1	176	0.1	70	66.0
All other.........	75	0.0	218	0.1	143	190.7

Source: U.S. Bureau of the Census, *U.S. Census of Population: 1960, General Population Characteristics, United States Summary,* PC(1)-1B, p. 1-145; U.S. Bureau of the Census, *Statistical Abstract of the United States: 1963,* table 22, p. 29.

The rapid movement of Negroes out of the South began during World War I with the urgent need for labor in the North, but in 1920 the proportion of all Negroes living in the South was still 85.2 percent. During the next decade it declined rapidly, to 78.7 percent in 1930. The northward movement of Negroes slackened during the Depression of the 1930s; 77 percent of all Negroes were still in the South in 1940, but the proportion again fell rapidly during the 1940s and 1950s, to 60 percent in 1960. Even these data do not give an adequate picture of the high concentration of Negro population existing before 1910 in

TABLE 8-6. NUMBER AND PERCENTAGE DISTRIBUTION OF THE NEGRO POPULATION, UNITED STATES BY REGIONS: 1860–1960
(Numbers in thousands)

Region	1960*		1950		1940		1900		1860	
	Number	Percent	Number	Percent	Number	Percent	Number	Percent	Number	Percent
United States........	18,860	100.0	15,042	100.0	12,866	100.0	8,834	100.0	4,442	100.0
Northeast........	3,028	16.1	2,018	13.4	1,370	10.6	385	4.4	156	3.5
North Central........	3,446	18.3	2,228	14.8	1,420	11.0	496	5.6	184	4.1
South........	11,312	60.0	10,225	68.0	9,905	77.0	7,923	89.7	4,097	92.2
West........	1,074	5.7	571	3.8	171	1.3	30	0.3	4	0.1

* Excluding Alaska and Hawaii.

Source: U.S. Bureau of the Census, U.S. Census of Population: 1960, General Population Characteristics, United States Summary, PC(1)-1B, p. 1-164.

the relatively small area known as the "black belt." (This region was so named originally because of the color of its soil, not because of its large Negro population.) In 1890 there were 529 counties, most of them in the black-earth region of the Southern states, whose populations were more than 30 percent Negro. These counties then contained 81.3 percent of the total Negro population of the United States. By 1960 the number of counties with 30 percent or more of their population Negro had declined to 401, and the proportion of the total Negro population found in these counties had declined to 31.7 percent.

Another way of looking at the geographic distribution of the Negro population is to see what proportion it now is of the total population in a given area and how the distribution has changed over the last 100 years. The proportion of the population which was Negro in each region in 1960 is as follows: Northeast, 6.8 percent; North Central, 6.7 percent; South, 20.6 percent; and West, 3.9 percent. In 1860 the proportions were: Northeast, 1.4 percent; North Central, 2 percent; South, 36.8 percent; and West, 0.7 percent.

Rural-Urban Distribution of the Negro Population. Before the Civil War, the Negro population was overwhelmingly rural, probably by at least 90 percent, but after 1860 the Southern Negro began to move to the cities in increasingly large numbers. By 1940 the proportion of the Negro population which was urban had grown to 48.6 percent; by 1950 it had become 62.4 percent; and by 1960 it was 73.2 percent. Negroes who migrated northward and westward went almost exclusively to the cities. In the South, on the other hand, Negro urbanization has proceeded at a slower rate. In 1950 only 47.8 percent of Southern Negroes lived in urban communities, and by 1960 the figure was only 58.4 percent. In the Northeast, North Central, and West, over 90 percent of the Negroes now live in urban communities. In summary, the distribution of Negroes in the United States is very different from that of whites, both regionally and with respect to rural-urban communities within the several regions (see Chapter 6). Such community and regional differences in racial composition compel us to be very careful when comparing the South with the North, or the Southern Negro with the Northern Negro, or whites with nonwhites on such characteristics as occupation, education, and income.

Geographic Distribution of Other Races. The "other races" are not evenly distributed among the various states. In 1960 eight states contained 67 percent of all the Indian population: Arizona, 16 percent; Oklahoma, 12 percent; New Mexico, 11 percent; California, 8 percent; North Carolina, 7 percent; South Dakota, 5 percent; Montana, 4 percent; and Washington, 4 percent. The Indian population is distributed among more states than are the other members of the category "other races." The Chinese, Japanese, Filipino, and all other (than Negro) nonwhite races are, for the most part, concentrated in California and Hawaii (see source for Table 8.6).

State	Chinese, percent	Japanese, percent	Filipino, percent	All other, percent
California...........	40	34	37	10
Hawaii..............	16	44	39	52
Total...............	56	78	76	62

Other states having large percentages of some of these "other races" are: New York, 16 percent of the Chinese and 3 percent of the Filipinos; Washington, 4 percent of the Japanese and Filipinos; Illinois, 3 percent of the Japanese and 2 percent of the Filipinos; and Alaska, 13 percent of the category all other races. Except for the Indian group, which was 72 percent rural in 1960, the other nonwhite races were predominantly urban: Japanese, 82 percent; Chinese, 96 percent; Filipino, 74 percent; and all other, 69 percent.

ETHNIC COMPOSITION

Language Composition. Many countries contain considerable numbers of people who speak languages different from that of the politically dominant group. If the language of a minority group is spoken by the politically dominant population in some neighboring nation, the minority language group may come to feel more loyalty to the nation whose dominant language it speaks than to the nation in whose territory it resides. It then becomes a matter of pride, as well as of custom, for these minority groups to keep their language and their social customs distinct from those of the dominant political group.

Under these circumstances, the nationality and the language affiliations of the peoples living within the different nations become of great importance. Not only does the presence of different language groups create many political problems; it also creates social and economic problems, many of which have a strongly divisive influence in the life of the nation. The mere inability of different groups to communicate readily with one another makes for suspicion and reluctance to cooperate fully in matters of national interest. Thus the presence of different language groups may make it more difficult to develop national policies in health matters, in the organization of education, in the use of natural resources, in the organization of the national economy, and in many other respects. Moreover, where distinct language groups persist, they are almost certain also to be distinguished from one another by certain other cultural characteristics, such as religious beliefs, marriage customs, agricultural practices, and dietary habits, which make it difficult to weld all the groups living within a given national territory into a unified nation.

The *Demographic Yearbook, 1956*, describes the three types of data on language found in its tables as follows:

1. Mother tongue, meaning the language spoken in the home in early childhood
2. Language currently or usually spoken in the home
3. Knowledge of a specified language or languages

In discussing the relative value of these kinds of language data for exploring the *ethnic composition* of a population, the *Yearbook* says,

Language is perhaps a more sensitive index than birthplace, because linguistic differences tend to persist until complete cultural assimilation has taken place. Common ancestral customs may be reflected in the mother tongues [number 1 above] of individuals long after these persons have changed their citizenship—perhaps several times. Thus important ethnic groups, not only among foreign-born alone but also among native-born or second-generation populations, may be distinguished by language differentials.[4]

The United Nations publication quoted above discusses data on "language currently or usually spoken in the home" as follows:

[They] are less appropriate for the identification of ethnic groups in the population, but they are adaptable to other uses, such as the investigation of linguistic assimilation of immigrant groups. . . . Of the three types of data, statistics based on knowledge of a specified language or languages are perhaps the least useful for identifying ethnic groups, but they do have utility in connexion [sic] with problems of educating and communicating with linguistic minorities, and they serve as a means of pointing out the heterogeneity of languages within a country and of measuring their individual strength. Such data are especially important nationally in multi-lingual countries, where more than one official language is recognized.[5]

Table 8-7 is language data for selected countries; the type of data presented is indicated by the table's footnotes. India is shown to be a country of many "mother tongues," not one of which is the "official" language. India's official language is English. When India gained independence, the party which first came to power promised the people a national language; no such language has yet evolved, nor is it likely to appear in the near future.

[4] United Nations, *Demographic Yearbook, 1956*, p. 34.
[5] *Ibid.*

Although language and nationality are not so politically and socially important in the United States as they are in some other countries, we have long had a larger and more diverse foreign-born population than any other country. For

TABLE 8-7.   PERCENTAGE DISTRIBUTION OF THE POPULATION BY LANGUAGE, SELECTED COUNTRIES, LATEST YEAR AVAILABLE

Country and language	Percent	Country and language	Percent
Belgium* (1947)	100.0	India (1951) (*Con't*)	
Flemish	41.8	Gujarati	4.6
French	34.2	Kannada	4.1
French and Flemish	15.6	Malayalam	3.8
Other	8.4	Oriya	3.7
		Other	10.5
Canada† (1951)	100.0		
English	59.1	Romania† (1948)	100.0
French	29.0	Romanian	85.7
Ukrainian	2.5	Hungarian	9.4
German	2.4	German	2.2
Indian and Eskimo	1.0	Yiddish	0.9
Polish	0.9	Other	1.8
Yiddish	0.7		
Italian	0.7	Switzerland‡ (1950)	100.0
Netherlands	0.6	German	72.1
Other	3.1	French	20.3
		Italian	5.9
India† (1951)	100.0	Other	1.7
Hindi			
Urdu	42.0	Yugoslavia† (1953)	100.0
Hindustani		Serbian and Croatian	73.2
Punjabi		Slovenian	8.8
Telugu	9.3	Macedonian	5.5
Marathi	7.6	Squiptarian	4.6
Tamil	7.4	Hungarian	3.0
Bengali	7.0	Other	4.9

* "Ability to speak the language."
† "Mother tongue."
‡ "Language currently spoken."
Source: United Nations, *Demographic Yearbook, 1956,* table 9.

many decades foreign-born whites have constituted a substantial proportion of our total population (see Table 8-8).

In the 1920s legislation was passed which severely reduced the number of entering immigrants (except from other countries in the Western Hemisphere), and each subsequent year has seen a decline in the number of foreign-born persons living in the continental United States. The largest number of foreign-born white population was recorded in 1930, when it numbered approximately 14 million, but foreign-born white composed the largest proportion of the total white population 20 years earlier in 1910, when it was 16.3 percent of the total white population. In 1930 the foreign-born white population was 13 percent of the total white population, and by 1960 it had fallen to 9.3 million, or just 5.9 percent of the total white population living in the continental United States.[6]

Country of Origin of the United States's Foreign-born Population. Each foreign-born group entering the United States brought with it certain customs and traditions which created a temporary barrier between it and the people

TABLE 8-8.   NUMBER AND PERCENT OF WHITE FOREIGN BORN IN THE WHITE POPULATION IN THE UNITED STATES: 1900–1960* (Numbers in thousands)

Year	Number	Percent
1960†	9,279	5.9
1950	10,095	7.5
1940	11,419	9.6
1930	13,983	12.7
1920	13,713	14.5
1910	13,346	16.3
1900	10,214	15.3

* For the total United States in 1960 the nonwhite foreign born numbered 444,110 out of a total foreign-born population of 9,738,143, or 4.6 percent.
Source: U.S. Bureau of the Census, *U.S. Census of Population: 1960, General Social and Economic Characteristics, United States Summary,* PC(1)-1C, p. 1-201.
† Excluding Alaska and Hawaii.

already here. And except for immigrants from the British Isles and Canada (excluding Quebec), these groups did not speak English. These differences often prevented people from working together harmoniously in communities where any considerable numbers of immigrants lived. Table 8-9 shows the heterogeneity of United States's foreign-stock population in 1960.[7] Such a diversity of

[6] The admission of Alaska and Hawaii to the United States and the classification of foreign-born population into white and nonwhite groups in the 1960 census can lead to confusion unless the different populations discussed are carefully identified. For example, the total foreign-born population (without regard to color) of the 50 states was 9.7 million in 1960, or 5.4 percent of the total population. In the 48 states, the total number of foreign-born whites was 9.3 million, or 5.9 percent of the total white population.
[7] In the 1960 census, the foreign-born population is combined with the native population of foreign and of mixed parentage in a single category termed "foreign stock." This category thus comprises all first- and second-generation Americans.

TABLE 8-9.   COUNTRY OF ORIGIN OF THE FOREIGN STOCK, FOR THE UNITED STATES: 1960

Region and country of origin	Number	Percent
Total........................	34,050,406	100.0
Western Europe...............	7,892,402	23.2
United Kingdom............	2,884,651	8.5
Ireland (Eire)..............	1,773,312	5.2
Norway....................	774,754	2.3
Sweden....................	1,046,942	3.1
Denmark..................	399,350	1.2
Netherlands...............	398,658	1.2
Switzerland...............	263,054	0.8
France....................	351,681	1.0
Central Europe...............	10,267,290	30.2
Germany..................	4,320,664	12.7
Poland....................	2,780,026	8.2
Czechoslovakia............	917,830	2.7
Austria...................	1,098,630	3.2
Hungary......	701,637	2.1
Yugoslavia................	448,503	1.3
Eastern Europe...............	2,933,940	8.6
U.S.S.R..................	2,290,267	6.7
Lithuania.................	402,846	1.2
Finland...................	240,827	0.7
Southern Europe..............	5,433,728	16.0
Romania...................	233,805	0.7
Greece....................	378,586	1.1
Italy.....................	4,543,935	13.3
Portugal..................	277,402	0.8
Other Europe.................	492,386	1.4
Asia........................	1,141,839	3.4
Canada.....................	3,181,051	9.3
Mexico.....................	1,735,992	5.1
Other America...............	580,679	1.7
All other....................	140,309	0.4
Not reported................	250,790	0.7

Source: U.S. Bureau of the Census, *U.S. Census of Population: 1960, General Social and Economic Characteristics, United States Summary,* PC(1)-1C, p. 1-203.

origins in our population was bound to create a wide variety of views on political and social questions.

Table 8-10 shows the linguistic diversity of our population in 1910 and in 1960. The figures for the two dates are not exactly comparable, since the 1910 figure is for the foreign-born white population and the 1960 figure is for the total foreign-born population. (The difference between total foreign-born and

TABLE 8-10.   PERCENT DISTRIBUTION OF THE FOREIGN BORN, 1960, AND FOREIGN-BORN
WHITE, 1910, BY MOTHER TONGUE, FOR THE UNITED STATES

Mother tongue	1960, foreign born	1910, foreign-born white
English.................	19.0	25.2
Norwegian..............	1.4	3.0
Swedish................	2.2	5.1
Danish.................	0.8	1.4
Dutch..................	1.3	0.9
French.................	3.4	4.0
German................	13.1	20.7
Polish.................	6.0	7.1
Czech.................	0.9	1.7
Slovak.................	1.3	1.2
Hungarian..............	2.2	1.7
Serbo-Croatian..........	0.9	0.8
Slovenian..............	0.3	0.9
Russian................	2.8	0.4
Ukrainian..............	1.1	*
Lithuanian.............	1.0	1.1
Finnish................	0.5	0.9
Romanian..............	0.4	0.3
Yiddish................	5.2	7.9
Greek.................	1.8	0.9
Italian................	12.6	10.2
Spanish................	7.9	1.9
Portuguese..............	0.9	0.5
Japanese...............	1.0	*
Chinese................	0.9	*
Arabic.................	0.5	0.2
All other..............	3.2	0.9
Not reported...........	7.3	0.9

* Not available.
Source: U.S. Bureau of the Census, U.S. Census of Population: 1960, General Social
and Economic Characteristics, United States Summary, PC(1)-1C, p. 1-203.

foreign-born white population is not significant. In 1960 there were about
444,000 nonwhite foreign born out of a total of 9.7 million foreign born.) In
1910, 75 percent of the foreign born reported a language other than English as a
mother tongue, and in 1960 this was true of 81 percent, although the foreign-
born population had decreased. Between 1910 and 1960 the percent of foreign-
born whites reporting English and German as their mother tongue dropped
quite rapidly; the English-speaking group dropped from 25 percent to 19
percent, and the German-speaking group from 21 percent to 13 percent. Those

reporting Italian as their mother tongue increased from 10.2 to 12.6 percent during this period, and those reporting Spanish increased from 1.9 to 7.9 percent. The increase in the proportion giving Spanish as their mother tongue was primarily a result of increased migration from Mexico and from areas included in the category of "other America" (Table 8-9).

TABLE 8-11.   NATIVITY AND PARENTAGE OF THE POPULATION OF THE UNITED STATES FOR REGIONS AND SELECTED STATES: 1960

Area	Foreign born (In thousands)	Percent distribution				
		Total	Native born			Foreign born
			Total	Native parentage	Foreign or mixed parentage	
United States...........	9,738	100.0	94.6	81.0	13.6	5.4
Region:						
Northeast..........	4,575	100.0	89.8	66.5	23.3	10.2
North Central......	2,277	100.0	95.6	81.5	14.1	4.4
South.............	963	100.0	98.2	94.1	4.2	1.8
West.............	1,924	100.0	93.1	77.7	15.5	6.9
States (highest percent foreign born):						
New York..........	2,289	100.0	86.4	61.3	25.0	13.6
Massachusetts......	576	100.0	88.8	60.0	28.8	11.2
Hawaii............	69	100.0	89.1	61.7	27.4	10.9
Connecticut.......	276	100.0	89.1	61.3	27.9	10.9
States (lowest percent foreign born):						
Arkansas..........	7	100.0	99.6	98.1	1.5	0.4
Mississippi........	8	100.0	99.6	98.7	0.9	0.4
Tennessee.........	16	100.0	99.6	98.3	1.2	0.4

Source: U.S. Bureau of the Census, U.S. Census of Population: 1960, General Social and Economic Characteristics, United States Summary, PC(1)-1C, p. 1-251.

Regional Distribution of the United States's Foreign-born Population. The foreign-born population has never had the same regional and rural-urban distribution as the total population. Table 8-11 shows that in 1960 the foreign born were heavily overrepresented in the Northeast region and heavily underrepresented in the South, as compared with the proportion of foreign born in the United States as a whole. Thus, in 1960 nearly one-half (47 percent) of all the foreign born lived in the Northeast, while only one-fourth (24.9 percent) of the total population lived there. On the other hand, only one-tenth of the foreign-born population (9.9 percent) lived in the South, while 31.3 percent of the total population lived in this region. The states with the largest percent of foreign born in their populations are as follows: New York, 13.6 percent; Massachusetts, 11.2 percent; Connecticut, 10.9 percent; and Hawaii, 10.9 percent.

TABLE 8-12.   NUMBER AND PERCENT OF FOREIGN-BORN WHITE AND FOREIGN-BORN NONWHITE, LIVING IN DIFFERENT TYPES OF COMMUNITIES, UNITED STATES:* 1960 (Numbers in thousands)

Color and residence groups	Foreign born	
	Number	Percent
White..........................	9,294	100.0
Urban.......................	8,131	87.5
Rural-nonfarm................	951	10.2
Rural-farm..................	212	2.3
Nonwhite......................	444	100.0
Urban.......................	379	85.4
Rural-nonfarm................	57	12.8
Rural-farm..................	8	1.8

* Excluding Alaska and Hawaii.
Source: U.S. Bureau of the Census, *U.S. Census of Population: 1960, General Social and Economic Characteristics, United States Summary,* PC(1)-1C, p. 1-201.

Urban-Rural Distribution of United States's Foreign-born Population. Not only is the foreign-born population concentrated rather heavily on the East and the West Coasts of the United States, but it is also concentrated in urban rather than rural areas. In 1960, 69.9 percent of our total population was urban, 22.6 percent was rural-nonfarm, and 7.5 percent was rural-farm. At the same time, the foreign-born white population was 87.5 percent urban, 10 percent rural-nonfarm, and only 2.3 percent rural-farm. Although the foreign-born population is overwhelmingly urban, it is not evenly distributed among urban places in the several regions and states. Table 8-13 shows how the proportion of the population which is foreign born varied in our 10 largest cities in 1950 and in 1960. In 1960 almost one-fifth (18.8 percent) of New York City's population consisted of foreign-born whites. In four other Northern cities this group constituted 11 to 12 percent of the total population, while in Baltimore, the District

of Columbia, Houston, and St. Louis the proportion of foreign-born whites was
less than 5 percent.

TABLE 8-13.   PERCENT THE WHITE FOREIGN BORN CONSTITUTE OF THE TOTAL
POPULATION IN THE TEN LARGEST CITIES IN THE UNITED STATES: 1950
AND 1960

Cities	Percent white foreign born	
	1960	1950
New York................	18.8	22.6
Chicago..................	12.1	14.5
Los Angeles..............	11.6	12.5
Philadelphia..............	8.7	11.2
Detroit..................	11.8	14.9
Baltimore................	4.1	5.4
Houston.................	2.5	2.9
Cleveland................	10.9	14.5
District of Columbia......	4.4	4.9
St. Louis................	3.5	4.9

Source: U.S. Bureau of the Census, *U.S. Census of Population: 1960, General Social
and Economic Characteristics*, State Reports PC(1), ser. C, table 72.
U.S. Bureau of the Census, *U.S. Census of Population: 1950*, vol. II, *Characteristics
of the Population*, part I, United States Summary, table 86.

RELIGIOUS COMPOSITION

Religious differences within countries are important because they often determine the national loyalty of certain groups and also play an important part in
the making of decisions. In the United States, however, religious influences have
generally been so subtly interwoven with other cultural patterns that few people
realize the influence which religious beliefs exercise over their daily conduct.
In some countries, religious adherence is a direct influence. In India, which was
divided into the Indian Union and Pakistan on the basis of religion, adherence
to the Hindu or Muslim religion apparently took precedence over adherence to
any political body or to the feeling of belonging in any given geographical area.
In most Western countries, membership in a particular religious body is a less
significant factor in political behavior than it is in India, but religious adherence
is still a powerful influence in much of the world.

Because the census of the United States has never asked people whether they
belong to any church, such information is available only through reports made
to the National Council of Churches by various religious bodies. Since the rolls

TABLE 8-14. PERCENT DISTRIBUTION OF THE POPULATION BY BROAD RELIGIOUS GROUPS, SELECTED COUNTRIES, LATEST YEAR AVAILABLE

Broad religious groups	Brazil (1950)	Canada (1951)	Egypt (1947)	India* (1951)	Netherlands (1947)	Pakistan (1951)
Total....................	100.0	100.0	100.0	100.0	100.0	100.0
Buddhist.................	0.3	0.1	——	0.1	——	0.4
Christian................	96.9	97.1	7.9	2.3	80.8	0.7
Protestant............	3.4	50.5	——	——	42.3	——
Roman Catholic.........	93.5	44.7	——	——	38.5	——
Eastern Orthodox.......	0.1	1.2	——	——	——	——
Hindu...................	——	——	——	85.0	——	12.9
Jewish..................	0.1	1.5	0.3	0.0	0.1	——
Muslim..................	0.0	——	91.7	9.9	——	85.9
Other...................	1.9	0.9	0.0	2.7	2.0	0.1
None†...................	0.8	0.4	——	——	17.1	——

* In India, there were 6,219,000 (1.7 percent) Sikh and 1,618,000 (0.5 percent) Jain.
† No organized religion; includes persons reported as "pagan," "heathen," "atheist," and so forth (p. 33).
Source: United Nations, *Demographic Yearbook, 1956,* table 8.

TABLE 8-15. NUMBER OF CHURCHES AND OF MEMBERS, BY RELIGIOUS GROUPS, UNITED STATES: 1963

Religious groups	Number of bodies reporting	Number of churches	Number of members (In thousands)
Buddhist.....................................	1	55	60
Old Catholic, Polish National Catholic, and Armenian Church of North America, Diocese.	7	348	597
Eastern Churches...........................	20	1,454	3,002
Jewish Congregations*......................	1	4,079	5,509
Roman Catholic.............................	1	23,412	43,848
Protestant.................................	222	289,892	64,930
Totals.................................	252	319,240	117,946

* Includes Orthodox, Conservative, and Reform.
Source: Benson Y. Landis (ed.), *Yearbook of American Churches,* National Council of the Churches of Christ in the U.S.A., New York, 1964, p. 252.

of most religious organizations in this country contain the names of many people who are no longer active members, such a census usually overstates the number of active adherents in every religious group.

TABLE 8-16.   CHURCH MEMBERSHIP AS PERCENTAGE OF POPULATION FOR THE UNITED STATES: 1850 TO 1962

1850	16	1920	43
1860	23	1930	47
1870	18	1940	49
1880	20	1950	57
1890	22	1955	61
1900	36	1960	63.6
1910	43	1962	63.4

Source: Benson Y. Landis (ed.), *Yearbook of American Churches,* National Council of the Churches of Christ in the U.S.A., New York, 1964, p. 280.

According to the 1964 *Yearbook of American Churches,* published by the Nationa Council of Churches and based on statistics from 252 religious bodies, church membership in the United States stands at an all-time high of 117,946,000, or 63.4 percent of the total population. However, a majority of America's population has not always belonged to a church. Table 8-16 shows that between 1850 and 1900 our church membership comprised only about 20 percent of the population. It increased sharply during the 1890s and climbed slowly for 40 years until 1940, when 49 percent of the population declared adherence to some religious body. Church membership climbed sharply during the 1940s, reaching a high of 63.6 percent in 1960. During the decade following World War II, Protestant membership increased at the rate of 3.6 percent per year, but the 1962 increase was only 1.2 percent. Protestant membership increased by only 0.8 percent during 1963, while Roman Catholic membership increased by 2.3 percent.

MARITAL COMPOSITION

There are important differences between communities and within communities with respect to marital composition. In many cases, the marital composition has changed significantly through time.

Table 8-17 shows that a great change took place in the marital composition of our population aged 14 and over between 1940 and 1960, most of it occurring between 1940 and 1950. In the United States as a whole, the proportion of single women 14 years of age and over declined from 27.6 percent in 1940 to 20.1 percent in 1950, and to 19.1 percent by 1960. The proportion of married women increased from 59.5 in 1940 to 65.7 percent in 1950; it had increased very little by 1960, reaching 65.9 percent. Similarly, the proportion of single males 14 years of age and over declined by about the same amount as that of females, from 34.8 percent in 1940 to 26.2 percent in 1950, and then declined only slightly to 25.1 percent by 1960. (In this section, unless otherwise specified,

TABLE 8-17.   **PERCENTAGE DISTRIBUTION OF THE POPULATION 14 YEARS OLD AND OVER, BY SEX AND MARITAL STATUS, UNITED STATES, CONNECTICUT, AND IOWA: 1940 TO 1960**

Area	Male			Female		
	Single	Married	Widowed or divorced	Single	Married	Widowed or divorced
1960						
United States..............	25.1	69.1	5.7	19.1	65.9	15.0
Connecticut...............	25.1	69.7	5.3	20.9	65.4	13.7
Iowa.....................	23.9	70.4	5.6	18.7	66.6	14.7
1950						
United States..............	26.2	67.6	6.1	20.1	65.7	14.2
Connecticut...............	27.3	66.9	5.8	23.3	63.7	13.0
Iowa.....................	25.5	68.2	6.3	19.5	66.9	13.5
1940						
United States..............	34.8	59.7	5.5	27.6	59.5	12.9
Connecticut...............	37.6	57.5	4.9	32.8	55.9	11.3
Iowa.....................	33.7	60.5	5.8	26.8	61.0	12.3

Source: U.S. Bureau of the Census, *U.S. Census of Population: 1960, General Social and Economic Characteristics, United States Summary,* PC(1)-1B, table 61, p. 1-174. Other years, earlier censuses were used.

the population referred to will be 14 years of age and over.) The proportion of males married rose from 59.7 percent in 1940 to 67.6 percent in 1950 and was only a little higher (69.1 percent) in 1960. Although there was a large increase in the proportion of married people between 1940 and 1950, the proportion married had been increasing for several decades prior to 1940. In 1890 the proportions of males and females who were married were only 52.1 percent and 54.8 percent, respectively.

The differences between states with respect to marital status diminished between 1940 and 1960. In all states the rise in proportion married was large during this period; as will be noted in Chapter 9, this increase has been an important factor in the rise in the crude birth rate since 1940.

Differences in marital status have demographic significance chiefly because of their effect on fertility and mortality rates, especially on the fertility rates.

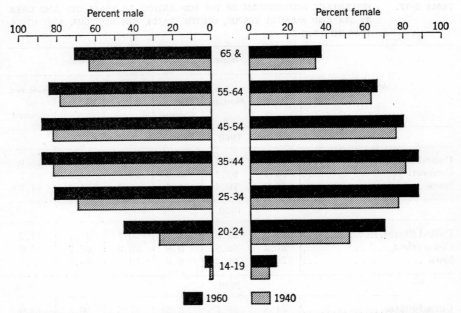

FIGURE 8-1. **Percent of the population married, by age and sex, United States, excluding Alaska and Hawaii: 1960 and 1940.** (U.S. Bureau of the Census, *U.S. Census of Population: 1960, Detailed Characteristics, United States Summary,* PC(1)-1D, pp. 1-436 and 1-437.

Obviously, a community in which a high proportion of females is married has a higher crude birth rate than a community with a lower proportion of married women. Also, both males and females who are married have lower death rates than single, widowed, and divorced persons of the same ages. Naturally, therefore, a knowledge of the marital composition of a population will aid in understanding its vital statistics.

In 1960, 69 percent of all the males and 66 percent of all the females 14 years of age and over were married. Age groups differ from each other in proportion married, however, and the sexes at the same age also differ. In 1960, 13.2 percent of the females under 20 years of age were married, but only 3.2 percent of the males in this age group were married. Women 25–34 years of age had the largest proportion married (approximately 87 percent); among men, the group 35–44 years of age had the largest proportion married (approximately 88 percent). Figure 8-1 shows the proportions of the various age groups, male and female, which were married in 1940 and 1960. (Since the biggest changes took place between 1940 and 1950, some of the 1950 statistics will be presented, although they do not appear in either tabular or figure form.) To understand the changes in the crude birth rate which took place after 1940, it is necessary to know how the proportions married changed in the various age groups between 1940 and 1960. In brief, there was a rather large increase in the proportion of both men and women under 35 years of age who were married, the increase being especially large at ages 14–19 and ages 20–24. In 1940 only 1.4 percent of the men aged 14–19 and 27.4 percent of those aged 20–24 were married. By 1950 these proportions had risen to 2.5 percent and 43.6 percent, however, and by 1960 they reached 3.2 percent and 45.9 percent. Among women in the age group 14–19 the proportion married increased from 9.8 percent in 1940 to 14.8 percent in 1950; by 1960 the proportion had decreased slightly, to 13.2 percent. The proportion of women married in the age group 20–24 increased from 51.3 percent in 1940 to 66.1 percent in 1950, and reached 69.5 percent in 1960.

In Chapter 9 we shall discuss in more detail the relationship between change in the proportion of young people married, change in the crude birth rate, and change in the average size of the family.

There are differences between countries in the proportions of married, single,

TABLE 8-18.   PERCENTAGE DISTRIBUTION OF THE POPULATION 15 YEARS OF AGE AND OVER BY SEX AND MARITAL STATUS, SELECTED FOREIGN COUNTRIES, LATEST YEAR AVAILABLE

Country	Year	Male			Female		
		Single	Married	Widowed or divorced	Single	Married	Widowed or divorced
England and Wales.......	1951	26.5	68.4	5.1	24.8	61.6	13.6
Ireland.................	1951	52.9	41.9	5.2	42.8	44.8	12.4
Italy...................	1951	37.1	58.8	4.1	32.0	55.2	12.7
France.................	1954	28.7	64.6	6.7	23.2	57.5	19.4
Sweden.................	1950	32.8	61.0	6.2	28.4	59.6	12.0
United States...........	1950	24.9	68.9	6.2	18.5	67.0	14.5

Source: United Nations, *Demographic Yearbook, 1958.*

widowed, or divorced persons, differences which are similar to those between regions within the same nation (Table 8-18). In Ireland an exceptionally low percentage of the population aged 15 and over is married; among males the percent married is 42, and among females it is 45. As we shall see later, these figures help to explain the low birth rate in Ireland. France and the United States have much higher percentages of widowed or divorced women than any of the other countries in the table, and slightly higher percentages of divorced or widowed men.

MISCELLANEOUS ELEMENTS IN THE COMPOSITION OF A POPULATION

The differences between the characteristics of various communities to which attention has been directed above by no means exhaust the list. Practically every community having more than a few thousand people has a prison population, and even small communities have some people who cannot fit into the normal life of the home and the community—the mentally ill, the feebleminded, the indigent, the deaf, the blind, and so forth. Many of these people do not remain in the local community, but some do. These people who are unable to live a normal life and therefore cannot be allowed the same freedom as normal persons, constitute a significant proportion of the population. In most modern communities the effort consumed in the care of such "abnormal" groups takes the form of taxes paid to support the services needed to care for them. People requiring custodial care not only cost the community a great deal economically but interfere seriously with the efficient operation of many community activities and institutions. The community needs to know how many of its people require special care and the type of care which will be best for them and for the community.

CONCLUSION

People can be separated into a number of groups on the basis of their demographic and social characteristics. For many purposes it is not only convenient but essential to make such categorization. However, we should take great care not to overemphasize any particular trait or characteristic when classifying the people in a community for purposes of studying the community's structure and operation. Although almost any social situation is easier to understand if we know the composition of the community's population, composition is only one of the elements to be considered. In studying the differences in the death rates of two communities, for example, after we have taken account of the sex and age differences between these communities and have allowed for differences in occupational make-up and in economic status, we shall quite possibly find a residue of differences which seem to have no relation to the composition of the populations involved. We may have to conclude that some of the difference between the two death rates must be attributed to differences in social attitudes toward sanitation and hygienic practices, differences which cannot now be measured and which do not seem to have any significant relation to the measurable differences between groups.

The same may be said for many other kinds of group differences. Criminality is connected to some extent with the age and sex composition of a population, but in some cases only a minor part of the difference between two communities in amount of criminal activity can be thus accounted for. Subtle differences between the social attitudes of two communities may be responsible to a significant degree for differences in criminality, but we are as yet unable to connect them with measurable differences in composition.

We cannot hope to understand many aspects of life in a community if we do not know the characteristics of the people who live in it, i.e., if we do not know its demographic and social composition; on the other hand, we must be very careful not to try to explain social conditions in a community or differences between conditions in different communities solely by differences in composition. While community differences in population composition are important in helping to explain many other differences between the communities, in many cases an explanation of behavior based only on a knowledge of a community's composition would be misleading; it would tend to hinder the search for other related factors, the knowledge of which is essential to the intelligent control of social change.

SUGGESTIONS FOR SUPPLEMENTARY READING

Berry, Brewton: *Race and Ethnic Relations*, Houghton Mifflin Company, Boston, 1958.

Blood, Robert O.: *Marriage*, The Free Press of Glencoe, New York, 1962.

Collver, Andrew: "The Family Cycle in India and the United States," *American Sociological Review*, vol. 28, no. 1, pp. 86–96, 1963.

Gaustad, Edwin S.: *Historical Atlas of Religion in America*, Harper and Row, Publishers, New York, 1962.

Glick, Paul C.: *American Families*, John Wiley & Sons, Inc., New York, 1957.

Higbee, Edward C.: *The Squeeze: Cities without Space*, William Morrow and Company, Inc., New York, 1960.

Hutchinson, E. P.: *Immigrants and Their Children*, John Wiley & Sons, Inc., New York, 1956.

Jacobson, Paul H.: *American Marriage and Divorce*, Rinehart & Company, New York, 1959.

Jones, Maldwyn, A.: *American Immigration*, The University of Chicago Press, Chicago, 1960.

Landis, Benson Y.: "Trends in Church Membership in the United States," *Annals of the American Academy of Political and Social Science*, vol. 332, pp. 1–8, 1960.

Lee, Rose Hum: *The Chinese in the United States of America*, Oxford University Press, Fair Lawn, N.J., 1960.

Lenski, Gerhard E.: *The Religious Factor: A Sociological Study of Religion's Impact on Politics, Economics, and Family Life*, Doubleday & Company, Inc., Garden City, N.Y., 1961.

Simpson, George E., and J. Milton Yinger: *Racial and Cultural Minorities*, 2d ed., Harper & Brothers, New York, 1958.

Taeuber, Irene B.: "Migration, Mobility, and the Assimilation of the Negro," *Population Bulletin*, vol. 14, no. 7, pp. 127–151, 1958.

Zelinsky, Wilbur: "An Approach to the Religious Geography of the United States: Patterns of Church Membership in 1952," *Annals of the Association of American Geographers*, vol. 51, no. 2, pp. 139–193, 1961.

Measures of
Fertility

PART THREE

Major
Demographic
Processes

CHAPTER NINE

Measures of Fertility

INTRODUCTORY

The fertility of women has always been a matter of vital concern to all peoples. But the overt expression of this interest, until about three centuries ago, had been confined largely to glorifying the fertile woman and to devising rites, potions, and diets of many kinds intended to render the barren woman fertile. When these measures to ensure blood descendants failed, many peoples devised customs and practices to ensure descendants that were socially acceptable. Such customs as the levirate (the marriage of a brother's widow), concubinage, and polygamy have been very widespread, and they have quite generally been concerned with the continuance of a particular line of descent. Although this interest in descendants may appear at first to be a family or private matter, it found effective expression largely in the customs and traditions which more or less unconsciously recognized that the survival of the community was of paramount interest to the individual and his family.

In spite of this very general concern for maintaining high fertility among women, many populations at times felt that fertility was so high that it threatened the welfare of the community and, indeed, its very survival. How else can we account for the many practices found among peoples aimed at reducing fertility and/or the effects of high fertility on population growth? Only a few of these restrictive practices can be mentioned here. Varying amounts of abortion have been found among most peoples. The prolonged segregation, sometimes lasting for a year or two, of women after childbirth for "purification" has also been common. At times, children have been breast-fed for several years, thus reducing the rate of conception, although this may not have been the prime purpose of the custom. Moreover, when the practices reducing fertility did not sufficiently restrain population growth, infanticide, especially of girl babies, was frequently resorted to, thus reducing the proportion of childbearing women in the population. But because of the terrific wastage of child life even when every possible effort was made to preserve all the children born, it has seemed to most peoples essential for every woman to have as many births as possible, and the cultural patterns of reproductive behavior have, as a rule, encouraged and glorified high fertility.

GROWTH OF KNOWLEDGE OF VITAL EVENTS

As a result of the growth of the knowledge of social events and changes among literate Europeans, especially after the invention of printing in Europe (about A.D. 1450), it is not surprising that by the latter part of the seventeenth century, occasional men in Western Europe and England became curious regarding the frequency of the two absolutely assured events in the life of every person—birth and death. During the 1600s and 1700s, several men investigated the number of births and deaths and marriages in particular populations and found a degree of regularity in their occurrence that suggested to them a natural law determining these *vital* events. Even in these relatively early studies of vital events, a need was felt for expressing their frequency of occurrence in a form that made possible comparisons in the same population at different times as well as between different populations at the same time. Süssmilch, in his *Die Göttliche Ordnung*, used the simple ratio obtained by dividing the number of births, deaths, and marriages in a given year into the total population and expressing the result as one birth, or death, or marriage to a given number of persons.[1] This made possible a comparison of the births and deaths in one population with those of another which was more significant than that obtained by using the actual figures. For example, there is little meaning in comparing 775 births in a specified year in a population of 25,500 with 1,250 births in a population of 36,800; but when the births in each population are divided into the number of that population we get a ratio of 1 : 32.9 in the former population and 1 : 29.4 in the latter. Clearly, the latter population has a significantly larger number of births for a population of a specified size than the former; but it is not easy to appreciate this difference even from such ratios. Moreover, as has been shown (see Chapters 4–8, Composition), no two populations of any significant size are exactly alike in age, sex, proportions married, etc. Hence, such a simple ratio as that of Süssmilch, although a great improvement over the mere statement of numbers of births, or deaths, or marriages, is far from providing an adequate measure of differences in the frequency of these events in different

[1] Johann Peter Süssmilch, *Die Göttliche Ordnung* [The Heavenly Order], Berlin, 1741. Süssmilch was an early and important investigator of vital events.

populations and in the same population at different times. It has the same defects as the *crude* birth rate (see below).

FERTILITY AND FECUNDITY

Fertility. Before discussing further the chief natality (or fertility) rates in use today, we shall find it advisable to state again how the terms "fertility" and "fecundity" are used in this book, even though we have used and explained these terms briefly in preceding chapters. Most students of population use the term fertility to indicate the actual reproductive performance of a woman or group of women. Thus, if in any specific group of women who had completed the reproductive period, 1,000 of them had borne 2,900 living children, this figure would measure their completed fertility. It might equally well be expressed as an average of 2.9 children per woman. But a woman is considered fertile if she has ever borne a live child.

Fecundity, on the other hand, denotes the physiological capacity to conceive and bear children. The proportion of all women who are fecund or infecund is not known with any precision. In some societies where practically all women are married and where there is strong social pressure to have children, it has been found that as few as 1 or 2 percent of those married have been childless after several years of married life. In most populations, however, the proportion appears to be somewhat higher. Under the conditions just mentioned, there is a strong presumption that a very large proportion of the infertile women are also infecund. However, even in such societies, infertility is not clear proof of infecundity. There is some reason to believe that the proportion of infecund married women is somewhat larger in the United States today than it was in the past and may amount to between 4 and 6 percent of all married women, but this cannot be stated positively, for the data available relate to childlessness and not to infecundity. Childlessness may be due to the voluntary control of conception or to the sterility of the husband as well as to the infecundity of the wife.

In the United States in 1940, of all native white rural-farm women aged 45–49 and married under 18 years of age, only 2.4 percent of them reported they had never borne a child. In cities of 250,000 or more, 5.8 percent of all native white women aged 45–49 who were married under 18 years of age were childless. Childlessness increased rapidly in both these groups as age at marriage rose. Among both the farm women and the city women, almost three times as large a proportion were childless when married at 20 and 21 years of age as when married under 18 years of age—6.9 percent and 14.7 percent, respectively.[2]

Until quite recently, the involuntarily childless marriage was almost always

[2] Wilson H. Grabill, Clyde V. Kiser, and Pascal K. Whelpton, *The Fertility of American Women,* Census Monograph, John Wiley & Sons, Inc., New York, 1958, p. 291.

assumed to be due to the infecundity of the wife. We now know, however, that childlessness is not proof of the infecundity of the wife but may be due to the sterility of either the wife or the husband or may arise from the fact that the spermatozoa of a particular male cannot fertilize the ova of a particular female, i.e., to the mutual incompatibility of the individuals' germ cells. In our discussion here we are interested primarily in fertility and will refer only occasionally to fecundity.

MEASURES OF NATALITY[3]

Ratios of Children to Women. In countries like the United States, which had relatively good census data showing age groups by sex for a number of population groups long before the registration of births became reasonably complete, the number of children 0–4 years of age per 1,000 women most likely to be their mothers, usually women 20–44 or 20–49, has proved useful. Such data can be used to show the trend in fertility over a substantial time period and also to measure differences in fertility between different populations, e.g., residence groups, races, and all other types of groups that can be clearly distinguished in the census data. The ratio of children to women has been most used in the United States, where only a few states had reliable registration of births before 1915 and where not all the states were admitted to the birth registration area until 1933.[4]

However, this method of measuring fertility has its limitations. Since it takes no account of the children dying before they reach the age of five years (0–4), any differences in the death rates of children in the different population groups at a given census date would affect the accuracy of comparisons between the fertility of these groups. Also, comparisons of the ratios of similar groups at different censuses would tend to understate the decline in fertility if there had also been a decline in the death rate of children during the interval. In addition, it takes no account of the differences in the age distribution of the women within the age limits (20–44 or 20–49) used; nor does it take into account any differences in marital status between the women in the groups being compared. In these respects it has many of the shortcomings of the crude birth rate (see below).

In spite of these limitations of the ratios of children to women as a measure of fertility, they were very useful in the absence of even crude birth rates, to say nothing of more refined fertility measures. For example, the ratios of children

[3] The most comprehensive study of the fertility of American women now available is that by Grabill, Kiser, and Whelpton (see footnote 2). It will be drawn upon extensively here.

[4] As far as the authors know, this method was first used by Prof. Walter F. Willcox of Cornell University. He worked closely with the census for many years after about 1885.

0–4 years of age to white women aged 20–44, which showed an almost steady decline from 1800 to 1940 in the United States as a whole,[5] left no doubt about a long and gradual decline in our birth rate. Moreover, as early as 1800, there were substantial differences between the several geographic divisions having relatively large populations. In this year (second census) New England had the lowest ratio, followed by increasingly higher ratios in the Middle Atlantic, the South Atlantic, and the East South Central divisions, the last having a ratio two-thirds higher than that of New England. The number of children under 5 years of age per 1,000 women declined in both urban and rural populations after 1800, but the ratios were at all times and in all divisions higher in the rural populations than in the urban and were highest in those divisions having the lowest proportion of urban population. As it became possible to calculate the ratios of children to women for more residence groups and also for racial and nativity groups, additional significant differentials in fertility were found. In addition, when fairly reliable life tables became available, because of improved registration of deaths, it became possible to use the ratios of children to women with some assurance to tell whether the ratio was high enough to replace the parent population, or whether, if this ratio was maintained, there would be a decrease or an increase in the population as long as the death rates on which the life table was based remained unchanged.[6] (See Chapter 12, pages 340–348, for an explanation of life-table death rates.)

Crude Birth Rate. The crude birth rate for any specified population is obtained by dividing the number of births recorded in that population during a specified year by its total numbers, which gives a fraction of birth per person. When this fraction is multiplied by 1,000 the result is the number of births per 1,000 of population.[7] This rate is called "crude" because all differences in composition between populations are ignored in calculating it. The *crude* birth rate stands in contrast to *refined* birth rates, the discussion of which occupies most of the remainder of this chapter. The process of refinement of fertility rates may be regarded as essentially an effort to find out how the different characteristics (composition) of populations affect their birth rates, or, if one prefers, their fertility.

It may also be noted here that the term "adjusted" is sometimes used officially in the same sense as corrected (see below). However, in refined rates the term generally means that differences between populations in a certain charac-

---

[5] Grabill et al., *op. cit.*, p. 17.

[6] Warren S. Thompson, *Ratio of Children to Women, 1920*, Census Monograph XI, U.S. Bureau of the Census, 1931.

[7] Since crude birth rates are relatively easy to calculate and are readily understandable and since the data are generally available within a few months after the end of each year, they are the rates most widely used and publicized.

teristic(s) have been taken into account in making the refinement. Thus an "age-adjusted" birth rate is one in which age differences between women in different populations have been allowed for so that the age-adjusted rate tells us in effect that if the groups had exactly the same age composition their birth rates would be as given (see below).

In the United States for many years a crude rate was distinguished from a *corrected* birth rate by increasing the number of births to allow for the fact that not all births are recorded.[8]

An accurate crude birth rate makes annual comparisons possible for the same population and also comparisons of the same character between different populations. Likewise, comparisons over periods of time are possible if, as in Sweden, accurate birth rates are available over a long period. However, the crude birth rate carries no implication as to why the birth rates are different in different years or between different populations at the same date.

Table 9-1 shows the crude birth rates for the total, the white, and the nonwhite population in the United States, adjusted for underregistration from the time such data became reasonably reliable through 1962. Figure 9-1 presents these same data in graphic form.

These crude birth rates show that the rather slow long-time downward trend in the birth rate of the United States shown by the ratios of children to women continued up to 1924–1925. It was then just over 25 per 1,000. In the late 1920s the rate of decline was substantially accelerated and stood at about 21.2 in 1929 and 1930, a decline of almost one-fifth in a little over five years. This decline continued to be rapid until 1933 (18.4), and after a slight recovery in 1934 and 1935, it was again 18.4 in 1936. After this it again began to recover but was still only 19.4 in 1940. In 1942 and 1943 it averaged 22.5. It then declined to slightly less than 21.0 in 1944 and 1945, the last years of the war. It rose very rapidly to 24.1 in 1946 and to 26.6 in 1947, the highest rate since 1921.

The birth rates for whites followed this pattern very closely because whites constituted about 90 percent of the total population, but at a somewhat lower level. The birth rates for the nonwhites, on the other hand, showed no clear downward trend from the time they became available until after 1925. During this period, 1917 to 1925, they averaged about 8 points higher than those of the whites. After 1926, the nonwhite birth rate fell very rapidly and averaged only a little over 26 for the decade 1931 to 1940. However, the white-nonwhite birth differential remained nearly the same as in the years 1917 to 1926—about 8 points. In the early 1940s, the nonwhite birth rate did not rise quite as rapidly as that of the whites, but after 1945 it rose very rapidly and from 1950 to 1960 averaged 9 to 10 points higher than that of the whites.

[8] Beginning with 1960, the National Vital Statistics Division of the U.S. Department of Health, Education, and Welfare (Public Health Service) abandoned the correction of birth and death rates because the registration of these events had become practically complete.

TABLE 9-1.   BIRTH RATES ADJUSTED FOR UNDERREGISTRATION, BY COLOR, UNITED STATES, 1909–1962

Year	Birth rate			Year	Birth rate		
	Total	White	Nonwhite		Total	White	Nonwhite
1962*	22.4	—	—	1934	19.0	18.1	26.3
1961	23.2	22.2	31.6	1933	18.4	17.6	25.5
1960	23.7	22.7	32.1	1932	19.5	18.7	26.9
				1931	20.2	19.5	26.6
1959	24.3	23.1	34.0	1930	21.3	20.6	27.5
1958	24.6	23.4	34.2				
1957	25.3	24.1	35.2	1929	21.2	20.5	27.3
1956	25.2	24.0	35.4	1928	22.2	21.5	28.5
1955	25.0	23.8	34.7	1927	23.5	22.7	31.1
1954	25.3	24.1	34.9	1926	24.2	23.1	33.4
1953	25.0	24.0	34.1	1925	25.1	24.1	34.2
1952	25.1	24.1	33.6				
1951	24.9	23.9	33.8	1924	26.1	25.1	34.6
1950	24.1	23.0	33.3	1923	26.0	25.2	33.2
				1922	26.2	25.4	33.2
1949	24.5	23.6	33.0	1921	28.1	27.3	35.8
1948	24.9	24.0	32.4	1920	27.7	26.9	35.0
1947	26.6	26.1	31.2				
1946	24.1	23.6	28.4	1919	26.1	25.3	32.4
1945	20.4	19.7	26.5	1918	28.2	27.6	33.0
1944	21.2	20.5	27.4	1917	28.5	27.9	32.9
1943	22.7	22.1	28.3	1916	29.1	28.5	—
1942	22.2	21.5	27.7	1915	29.5	28.9	—
1941	20.3	19.5	27.3				
1940	19.4	18.6	26.7	1914	29.9	29.3	—
				1913	29.5	28.8	—
1939	18.8	18.0	26.1	1912	29.8	29.0	—
1938	19.2	18.4	26.3	1911	29.9	29.1	—
1937	18.7	17.9	26.0	1910	30.1	29.2	—
1936	18.4	17.6	25.1	1909	30.0	29.2	—
1935	18.7	17.9	25.8				

* U.S. Department of Health, Education, and Welfare, *Monthly Vital Statistics Report,* vol. II, no. 12, Feb. 19, 1963, (provisional statistics for 1962). The correction or adjustment of birth rates and death rates in the United States has generally been made by the Federal office charged with the duty of gathering the basic data from the state offices and processing these data. This office has in the past made numerous specific studies to determine the relative completeness of the registration of births and deaths in the several states and has then corrected the registration data in the light of this knowledge. Such corrections or adjustments are no longer necessary because the registration is now practically complete.

Source: U.S. Department of Health, Education, and Welfare, *Vital Statistics of the United States, 1960,* vol. 1, table 1-8, p. 1-17. (See this citation for notes.)

The fluctuations in crude birth rates occurring within two or three years and amounting to as much as 2 to 3 points can generally be explained rather satisfactorily by their association with contemporary specific events or conditions, such as sudden changes in the level of employment and the even more sudden

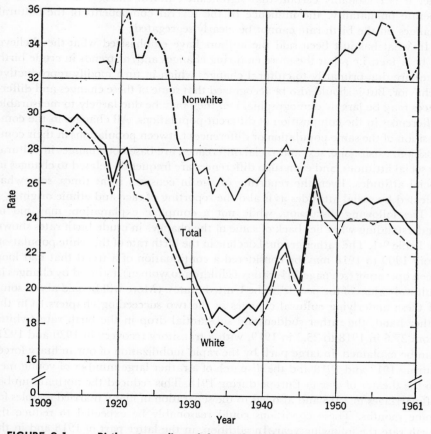

FIGURE 9-1. Birth rates adjusted for underregistration, 1909 to 1959, unadjusted 1960 and 1961, by color, United States. (Table 9-1.)

changes arising from the mobilization and demobilization of large military forces within a year or two. The more enduring changes, however, either upward or downward in birth rates are apparently associated with much less obvious social changes, such as changes in preferred age for marriage and what is regarded as the *proper* size of family and the *best* interval between births; and at a greater distance these changes themselves may arise from the broad cultural changes that attach to increased suburban living, to doing what is expected of the "organization family," or to other changes in cultural values. We are often unaware at the time of how our cultural values are changing. Moreover, even after it is reasonably certain that significant cultural changes have begun to operate on natality, the influence of the several components of the cultural changes on the birth rate cannot be clearly segregated.

In what has just been said the authors have emphasized what they believe to be a fact, i.e., that the more enduring changes and/or trends in crude birth rates are due primarily to cultural changes which in turn modify reproductive behavior. But it should also be recognized that some of these changes and differences may be largely demographic, i.e., they may be due largely to measurable differences in the composition of different populations. All changes in the composition of the same population or differences between populations in their composition, except age, sex, and racial differences, are based on changes in cultural or social attitudes, and even such differences are frequently related to changes in social attitudes. Even the reporting of age in censuses is, at times, somewhat affected by social attitudes as is also the reporting of race and ethnic origin.

The following discussion, while not a complete explanation, may aid in understanding what lies back of some of the changes in crude birth rates shown in Table 9-1. The rather gradual decline in the birth rate of the white population from 1909 to 1918 may be considered a continuation of a trend that had long been operating (see page 241, ratio of children to women), induced by changes in cultural values of the people in the United States. (More will be said about some of these underlying cultural changes in the two succeeding chapters.) On the other hand, the rather sudden and substantial drop in the birth rate (white) from 27.6 in 1918 to 25.3 in 1919, with a transitory recovery in 1920 and 1921, can be explained, in large part, by the rapid mobilization of our military forces during 1917 and 1918 and the dispatch of a rather large number of young men to the theater of war in Europe during 1918. This reduced the normal number of marriages in 1918 and also led to the separation of many married couples for some months. These conditions could reasonably be expected to reduce the birth rate the following year. In addition, in the latter part of 1918 and in the early months of 1919, a severe influenza epidemic spread over the country, causing perhaps 450,000 more deaths than would normally have been expected. There can be no reasonable doubt that some women who would have become mothers in 1919 if they had lived, died during this epidemic; also that some marriages were postponed because of severe illness. Besides, it may well be that the rate of conception was somewhat below normal during the months when the epidemic was most virulent. All these factors may have contributed to the reduction of the birth rate in 1919 by temporarily but substantially changing the composition of our population in several respects, but chiefly in changing the sex and age distribution in many communities.

By 1921, however, crude birth rates had risen again to about their 1918 level. This may be explained as due very largely to the demobilization of the Armed Forces in 1919 and the return to a more normal sex composition in most communities by 1920. The change resulted in an increase in marriages in 1919 and 1920 and the making up, in 1921, of some of the births postponed during the war.

The growing economic instability of the 1920s, especially after 1925, which was followed by the Depression of the 1930s, will explain in large part the rapid decline of the birth rate after 1925 and its continued low level up to 1940.

The recovery of the crude rate for a few years after 1945 (end of World War II), like that after 1919, was to be expected, but it is much more difficult to explain why it remained at a level of 24 or above through 1959. Some of the more refined measures of natality discussed below will show more precisely in what sex and age groups these changes occurred and will serve to emphasize the importance of social attitudes in determining changes in the level of fertility of the population.

The General Fertility Rate. This rate uses the number of women of childbearing age (15–44 or 15–49) in a population as a base for the calculation of a birth rate rather than the total population. The rate is the number of births per 1,000 women of these ages. This rate is somewhat more refined than the crude rate in that in addition to eliminating the influence of differences in size between populations it also eliminates the effect of certain compositional differences which might exist in the populations being compared. For example, it eliminates the influence of any differences in the proportion of males in the populations that are compared, a difference which may be quite large after a war and may also be significant when emigrations or immigrations have been large and prolonged, as they have been frequently when peoples have emigrated from the United Kingdom into the United States. This rate also eliminates the effect of differences in the proportion of all women who are between the ages of 15 and 44 or 49. It does not take into account, however, differences in the age distribution of women aged 15–44 or 49 in different populations, nor does it allow for the fact that a larger proportion of the women 15–44 in group A than in group B may be married.

Table 9–2 shows the *general fertility rates* (the number of births per 1,000 women aged 15–44) for the same population groups as in Table 9-1. This general fertility rate is usually four to five times as high as the crude rate in the same population because the women of these ages normally constitute from one-fifth to one-fourth of the total population. A large and sudden change in the proportion of women in a population is not likely except in wartime, when great

TABLE 9-2.   GENERAL FERTILITY RATES (NUMBER OF CHILDREN BORNE ANNUALLY BY 1,000 FEMALES AGED 15–44) ADJUSTED FOR UNDERREGISTRATION, BY COLOR, UNITED STATES, 1909–1962

Year	Fertility rate			Year	Fertility rate		
	Total	White	Nonwhite		Total	White	Nonwhite
1962*	112.1						
1961†	117.3	112.3	153.8	1933	76.3	73.7	97.3
1960	118.0	113.2	153.6	1932	81.7	79.0	103.0
1959	120.2	114.6	163.0	1931	84.6	82.4	102.1
1958	120.1	114.8	161.2	1930	89.2	87.1	105.9
1957	122.7	117.4	163.4	1929	89.3	87.3	106.1
1956	120.8	115.6	161.0	1928	93.8	91.7	111.0
1955	118.0	113.2	155.1	1927	99.8	97.1	121.7
1954	117.6	113.1	152.9	1926	102.6	99.2	130.3
1953	114.7	110.6	147.0	1925	106.6	103.3	134.0
1952	113.5	109.8	143.1	1924	110.9	107.8	135.6
1951	111.3	107.4	141.9	1923	110.5	108.0	130.5
1950	106.2	102.3	137.3	1922	111.2	108.8	130.8
1949	107.1	103.6	135.1	1921	119.8	117.2	140.8
1948	107.3	104.3	131.6	1920	117.9	115.4	137.5
1947	113.3	111.8	125.9	1919	111.2	——	——
1946	101.9	100.4	113.9	1918	119.8	——	——
1945	85.9	83.4	106.0	1917	121.0	——	——
1944	88.8	86.3	108.5	1916	123.4	121.8	——
1943	94.3	92.3	111.0	1915	125.0	123.2	——
1942	91.5	89.5	107.6	1914	126.6	124.6	——
1941	83.4	80.7	105.4	1913	124.7	122.4	——
1940	79.9	77.1	102.4	1912	125.8	123.3	——
1939	77.6	74.8	100.1	1911	126.3	123.6	——
1938	79.1	76.5	100.5	1910	126.8	123.8	——
1937	77.1	74.4	99.4	1909	126.8	123.6	——
1936	75.8	73.3	95.9				
1935	77.2	74.5	98.4				
1934	78.5	75.8	100.4				

* U.S. Department of Health, Education, and Welfare, *Monthly Vital Statistics Report*, vol. II, no. 12, February, 1963 (provisional statistics for 1962).

† U.S. Department of Health, Education, and Welfare, *Advance Report, Vital Statistics of the United States*, 1961, November, 1962.

Source: U.S. Department of Health, Education, and Welfare, *Vital Statistics of the United States, 1960*, vol. I, table 1-B, p. 1-17. (See this citation for notes.)

numbers of men are being killed or are mobilized away from home. However, there are often significant differences in the proportions of women of these ages in particular segments of any national population and in different national populations, e.g., in urban and in rural communities, in cities of different sizes, and in other areas having a considerable net in-migration or out-migration as well as in nations having large amounts of emigration or immigration. (See Chapters 4 to 8, Composition.)

The general fertility rate of the United States, like the crude birth rate, shows significant changes from year to year, and since the changes in these two rates are generally much alike, what is said about one applies, in large measure, to the other. However, in the United States about 1950, the general fertility rate began to diverge significantly from the crude birth rate. The crude rate remained relatively constant at around 24 to 25 for the total population through 1959, whereas the general fertility rate rose from about 106 to about 120, an increase of almost one-eighth. Such an extensive divergence in these rates in a large population signalizes a significant change in the age pattern of fertility, i.e., in age-specific birth rates. (See this topic below.) Only these more refined rates will show this change with precision. Such an increase in the number of births may be brought about by changes in the age at marriage, or by the making up of births postponed during a war or a depression, or by the shortening of the interval between marriage and a first birth, between a first birth and a second, etc., and is not necessarily accompanied by an increase in the average size of family. On the other hand, it may be accompanied by an increase in the average number of births per woman. This matter of the "timing" of births is of much importance but will not be treated here until age-specific birth rates have been discussed in some detail.

Age-specific birth rates probably constitute the most important basic refinement in the measurement of natality that has ever been made. Without such rates, most of the other refinements could not be made. Age-specific birth rates for any year are obtained by dividing the number of births to mothers of each age in that year by the number of women of this age in the population at that date and multiplying this figure by 1,000. An age-specific birth rate, then, is the number of births per 1,000 women of a given age per year. In Table 9-3 the rates are given for five-year age groups. To interpret this table and others like it, we must understand certain things at the outset. As the first line in this table shows, there were 528,536 women aged 15–19 in California at the time of the 1960 census. There were 54,770 live births to women of these ages in California during the year 1960. If this *number of births* to women 15–19 (54,770) is divided by the *number of women* aged 15–19 (528,536), the quotient, 0.1036, is the *number of births per woman* 15–19. This number multiplied by 1,000 gives us 103.6, which is the *number of births per thousand women aged 15–19 in California in 1960* (see notes to Table 9-3).

The information essential to the calculation of this rate, beyond the mere recording of the births, is the age of the mother at the time of the birth. Certain other refinements would be possible if the age of the mother at marriage were recorded and if the order of birth, i.e., whether this particular birth was a first

TABLE 9-3.   AGE-SPECIFIC BIRTH RATES, TOTAL FERTILITY, AND GROSS REPRODUCTION RATE, CALIFORNIA AND NEW YORK, 1960

Age of mother	California			New York		
	Births to women of specified ages*	Female population 4-1-60†	Age-specific birth rate	Births to women of specified ages*	Female population 4-1-60†	Age-specific birth rate
(1)	(2)	(3)	(4)	(5)	(6)	(7)
15–19‡......	54,770	528,536	103.6	31,950	560,467	57.0
20–24.......	128,340	480,152	267.3	113,136	501,354	225.7
25–29.......	94,596	500,265	189.1	103,398	529,485	195.3
30–34.......	57,746	558,514	103.4	68,332	601,747	113.6
35–39.......	29,402	608,699	48.3	34,382	632,113	54.4
40–44.......	6,994	536,677	13.0	7,878	601,567	13.1
45–49§......	362	484,455	0.7	376	583,614	0.6
Total......	372,210	——	725.4	359,452	——	659.7

Total fertility: $725.4 \times 5 = 3{,}627.0$
Gross reproduction rate:¶ $3{,}627.0 \times 48.8\% = 1{,}770.0$

$659.7 \times 5 = 3{,}298.5$
$3{,}298.5 \times 48.8\% = 1{,}609.7$

* U.S. Department of Health, Education, and Welfare, *Vital Statistics of the United States,* 1960, vol. 1, sec. 2.
† U.S. Bureau of the Census, U.S. Census of Population, 1960, *General Characteristics.*
‡ Births to mothers aged 15–19 include those to mothers aged 10–14.
§ Births to mothers aged 45–49 include those to mothers aged 50–54.
¶ The gross reproduction rate as given here is for 1,000 women. For practical purposes, all such rates may be rounded to the nearest whole numbers.

births per 1000 women thru gross the reproductive years

birth, a second birth, etc., were stated. However, very few countries record all these data. If, as has been the case in the United States until recently, the number of unregistered births is significant, the adjusted or corrected number of births should be used, and the unregistered births should be distributed by age of mother in the same proportion as shown by the registered births. Where the age of the mother is not stated on the birth certificate, these mothers should be distributed by age in the same proportion as those whose age is known.

When age-specific birth rates are available, the age differences of women in different populations can be allowed for, and both of the reproduction rates and standardized birth rates (see below) can be calculated. The actual process of calculating age-specific birth rates, *total* fertility as distinguished from *general* fertility, and the gross reproduction rate are shown in Table 9-3.

Because five-year age groups are used instead of single years in Table 9-3, the age-specific birth rate of 103.6 for women aged 15–19 is the *average* for the whole group, and it is assumed that the women in each year of age within the age class will have births at this average rate. (Using single-year age groups adds greatly to the time spent in calculation, without significantly improving the usefulness of the table.) At this rate, therefore, 1,000 women going through the years 15–19 will have 103.6 births multiplied by 5, the number of years each woman spends in this five-year age group. The total fertility for all women aged 15–49 may be calculated by adding the age-specific rates of the seven five-year groups and multiplying this *total* by 5.

The total fertility for the California women in the table, using this method, turns out to be 3,627. This same figure can be obtained by multiplying the age-specific birth rates for each five-year age group by 5 and then summing the resulting products. The procedure shown in the table is the easiest one to carry out. In other words, if 1,000 women gave birth at each age from 15–49 at the same rate as California women *actually* did in 1960, they would have a total of 3,627 births. The assumptions underlying the calculation of this rate are that (1) 1,000 women go completely through the childbearing period (15–49 years of age) without any mortality, and that (2) while passing through these years, these women will have births at the same age-specific rates as women of *all* these ages at a given moment in time (the year 1960 in this instance). Thus, although women aged 35–39 in 1960 were aged 15–19 in 1940, they are assumed to have had the same age-specific birth rate when they were 15–19 as did the women who were 15–19 in 1960. This might or might not be true. In any event, this total fertility rate is a hypothetical rate for the women involved and would be the same as the completed fertility of these women (see below) only if there were no change in any of the age-specific birth rates during a generation.

The Gross Reproduction Rate. Whereas total fertility includes all births, both male and female, the gross reproduction rate shows how many girl babies— potential future mothers—would be born to 1,000 women passing through their childbearing years if the age-specific birth rates of a given year remained constant and if no women entering the childbearing period died before reaching menopause. This rate may be calculated by multiplying total fertility by the percent (approximately 48.8 percent in recent years in the United States) of all births that are female births (see total fertility in Table 9-3). If the product is 1,000 or more, it means that 1,000 or more daughters are being borne by each 1,000 women of childbearing age when no account is taken of the deaths of the women during their reproductive period. The same assumptions are used in calculating the gross reproduction rate as were used in calculating total fertility. In our example it is assumed that the sex ratio at birth is the same in California and New York as in the United States.

TABLE 9-4.   NET REPRODUCTION RATE, CALIFORNIA AND NEW YORK, 1960

Age of mother	Number of years lived in age interval by a birth cohort of 100,000 females*	California		New York	
		Age-specific birth rate†	Calculated number of births	Age-specific birth rate†	Calculated number of births
(1)	(2)	(3)	(4)	(5)	(6)
15–19.....	484,208	102.8	49,777	56.5	27,358
20–24.....	482,693	267.3	129,024	225.7	108,944
25–29.....	480,803	189.1	90,920	195.3	93,901
30–34.....	478,259	103.4	49,452	113.6	54,330
35–39.....	474,665	48.3	22,926	54.4	25,822
40–44.....	469,409	13.0	6,102	13.1	6,149
45–49.....	461,537	0.7	323	0.6	277
Total...	——	——	348,524	——	316,781

Net reproduction rate (average per woman):

$$\frac{348,524 \times 48.8\%}{100,000} = 1.701$$

$$\frac{316,781 \times 48.8\%}{100,000} = 1.546$$

* U.S. Department of Health, Education, and Welfare, *Vital Statistics of the United States, 1959*, sec. 5, *Life Tables*.

† U.S. Department of Health, Education, and Welfare, *Vital Statistics of the United States, 1960*, vol. 1, sec. 1, pp. 1-37 and 1-38. Births to women under 15 years of age and over 49 years of age are not included in this table, which explains the slight differences in the age-specific birth rates for women 15–19 between Table 9-3 and Tables 9-4 and 9-5.

The Net Reproduction Rate. The net reproduction rate takes account of the deaths occurring during each five-year age period as women pass through the childbearing years; it constitutes the next step in refinement of fertility measures. (See Table 9-4). This is accomplished by using a life table for females (see Chapter 12 for an explanation of the life table) which shows how an original cohort of 100,000 girl babies at birth diminishes year by year (or by five-year periods) because of deaths. From these data the total number of years the survivors from the original cohort (100,000) will spend in each five-year class during the childbearing years can be readily calculated. The process is illustrated in column 2 of Table 9-4 for California and New York State. This figure is then multiplied by the appropriate age-specific rates in the year for which the calculation is being made (columns 3 and 5) to secure the number of births these surviving females would have (columns 4 and 6). These *calculated* births are then summed, multiplied by the proportion of these births that would normally be female (48.8 percent), and divided by 100,000 (the size of the cohort at birth) to reduce the figure to female births per woman. In the example given here, if the result is multiplied by 1,000, we can say that 1,000 females living in California and having the death rates of 1960 would have borne 1,701 daughters, while 1,000 New York State females would have borne 1,546 daughters. At the age-specific birth rates and death rates prevailing in 1960, both of these populations had far more than enough daughters to maintain the population. The chief defect in the net reproduction rate lies in its assumption that the age-specific birth rates and death rates of a particular year will remain constant during a generation. This is a very serious defect, and these rates should not be used in making a prognosis of probable future growth of population.

Standardized Birth Rates. In general, a standardized birth rate takes account of the differences between populations in a given characteristic—demographic, social, or economic—which is believed to have some effect on natality. The process of calculating a standardized rate (Table 9-5) is as follows: If we are interested in the effect of the differences in age composition of two populations on their fertility, for example, then the age distribution of the women in some population either actual or hypothetical, such as a life table population, is chosen as a "standard" distribution. When we are standardizing for age, the question to which we are seeking an answer is: If the women in populations A, B, C, etc., in our example California and New York, aged 15–49 years, were distributed by age in exactly the same proportions as the women in the "standard" population, would their natality rates bear the same relation to one another as do their *crude* rates or their *general* fertility rates or their total fertility rates in Table 9-3? This question is answered by multiplying the age-specific birth rates of each of the populations A, B, C, etc., by the number of women in each age group of the "standard" population and summing these births for each population to secure the total number of births a standard population would have if its women had had the different age-specific rates of populations A, B, C, etc.

For methodological reasons, this calculation is made by setting up a population of 1 million persons having the age composition of some population designated as a "standard million." In this standard million a definite number are, of course, women aged 15–19, 20–24, etc. The total number of births this standard million would have in a specified year if it had the age-specific birth rates of populations A, B, C, etc., is then obtained by multiplying the age-specific birth rates of these populations by the number of women of each age in the standard population, which is then divided by 1 million (Table 9-5) and multiplied by 1,000 (or more simply, divided by 1,000) to secure an age-standardized birth rate per 1,000 for each of the populations being studied. The differences between these standardized rates for populations A, B, C, etc., are differences in fertility which are not the result of differences in the age distribution of the

TABLE 9-5.   STANDARDIZED BIRTH RATE, CALIFORNIA AND NEW YORK, 1960

Age of mother	Number of females in standard million*	California		New York	
		Age-specific birth rate	Calculated number of births	Age-specific birth rate	Calculated number of births
(1)	(2)	(3)	(4)	(5)	(6)
15–19.....	33,893	102.8	3,484	56.5	1,915
20–24.....	33,787	267.3	9,031	225.7	7,626
25–29.....	33,655	189.1	6,364	195.3	6,573
30–34.....	33,477	103.4	3,462	113.6	3,803
35–39.....	33,225	48.3	1,605	54.4	1,807
40–44.....	32,857	13.0	427	13.1	430
45–49.....	32,306	0.7	23	0.6	19
Total...	——	——	24,396	——	22,173

Standardized birth rate per 1,000 population:

$$\frac{24,396 \times 1,000}{1,000,000} = 24.4 \qquad \frac{22,173 \times 1,000}{1,000,000} = 22.2$$

* Calculated from the 1959 United States life-table population, assuming 105 male births to 100 female births.

Sources: see notes to Table 9-4.

women involved. By standardizing for age on the basis of a particular standard million, we have prevented the difference in age composition of the women in the various populations from having any effect on the birth rates of these groups when compared with one another. If a different standard million were used, the resulting standardized rate for populations A, B, C, etc., would be different, but the new standardized rates would still indicate true differences in fertility in these populations. In our example, the age standardized rates show that California's women were approximately 10 percent more fertile than New York's women.

Another example of age standardization to secure a more accurate measure of the fertility of different occupational groups may be made. In such a calculation, the age distribution for *all* women aged 15–49 "married once and husbands present" in *all* the occupation groups being studied is used as the *standard* distribution. (This total group of women has certain definite proportions at ages 15–19, 20–24, etc.). The age-specific birth rates of the women having husbands in each occupational group are then multiplied by the number of women in the appropriate age group in the standard population to secure the total number of children borne by the women in the standard population if they had had these different age-specific birth rates. The sum of the children born to the women in the standard population on the basis of each set of age-specific birth rates, translated into births per 1,000 women (a simple problem in arithmetic), shows what the differences in the birth rates between the occupational groups would be if all wives in each group had had the same age composition. Hence these differences in rates are related to occupational differences and not to differences arising from differences in age make-up (composition) of the several groups of women involved.[9]

Birth rates may also be standardized for other characteristics of the population to aid in the more precise measurement of the association of these characteristics with differences in natality, for example, for the natality differences between populations differing in place of residence (urban, rural, states, etc.), for the amount of education of both husbands and wives, for the occupation of husbands, for the occupational status of wives, i.e., whether or not they belong to the labor force, and for certain other characteristics.

Completed Fertility. As the name indicates, "completed fertility" is a measure showing the total number of live births per woman, or per 1,000 women, who have passed through the childbearing period. It is generally stated as the number of children ever born per 1,000 women at ages 45–49, 50–54, etc., or for all ages 45 or over, on a specified date. In the United States, data needed to calculate a considerable variety of such rates are available in the 1910, 1940, 1950, and 1960 censuses.

Since the census data on completed fertility generally distinguish between *all women*, *mothers*, and *married women*, and are also available in these four censuses for certain important residence groups, such as urban and rural, cities and states, and for occupation of husband, duration of marriage, and for white and non-white, it is possible to calculate completed fertility rates for a considerable number of different segments of the population. In addition, in the censuses of 1910 and 1940 the data on completed fertility enable us to divide the women aged 45 and over into 5-year age groups up to 70–74 years of age. This enables us to ascertain completed fertility for women whose families were completed during the 25 to 30 years preceding the censuses of 1910 and 1940. For example, the data gathered in 1910 show the size of completed families from about 1885 to

[9] Grabill et al., *op. cit.*, p. 130.

1910 (women aged 70–74 in 1910 to those aged 45–49 in 1910). Likewise, the 1940 census contains data for women completing their families between 1910 and 1940. A few of the results from these censuses may be given here (Table 9-6; Figure 9-2).

In 1910, each 1,000 "ever-married" women 45–49 years of age in the United States, white and nonwhite, had borne an average of 4,744 children; 1,000 white

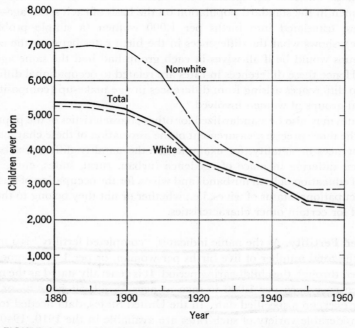

FIGURE 9-2.   Number of children ever born, per 1,000 women ever married, aged 45–49, by color, United States: 1880 to 1960. (Table 9-6.)

women had borne 4,594 children, and 1,000 nonwhite women 6,183 children. For all ever-married women 50 years of age and over, regardless of color, at this census (1910) there was a steady rise in the number of children ever born per 1,000 women from that of the age class 45–49 (4,744) to that of the age class 70–74 in which the number was 5,395 (see 1880 in Table 9-6). This rise held for both white and nonwhite women with one minor exception. The proportion of women ever married increases among women over 50 years of age as we go back in time to 1880. The 1940 data show the same pattern of declining completed fertility of ever-married women aged 45–49 from 1910 to 1940, and the completed fertility rates for 1950 and 1960 were substantially lower than the 1940 rates for all ever-married women and for both white and nonwhite women. (Childlessness will be discussed in some detail in Chapter 11.)

TABLE 9-6.   NUMBER OF CHILDREN EVER BORN, PER 1,000 WOMEN EVER MARRIED, AGED 45–49, BY COLOR, UNITED STATES, 1880–1960

Year	Children ever born		
	All women	White	Nonwhite
1960	2,402	2,354	2,824
1950	2,492	2,456	2,803
1940	3,052	3,020	3,385
1930	3,367	3,330	3,875
1920	3,700	3,630	4,517
1910	4,744	4,594	6,183
1900	5,218	5,082	6,874
1890	5,364	5,237	7,021
1880	5,395	5,278	6,935

Sources: 1880–1940, U.S. Bureau of the Census, 1940, *Special Reports, Differential Fertility, 1940 and 1910, Fertility for States and Large Cities*, tables 3 and 4. The data for 1880 are for women aged 70–74 in 1910; those for 1890 are for women aged 65–69 in 1910; and those for 1900 are for women aged 55–59 in 1910. The data for 1920 are for women aged 65–69 in 1940; those for 1930 are for women aged 55–59 in 1940. 1950 data from U.S. Bureau of the Census, 1950, *Special Reports, Fertility*, P-E, no. 5 C, table 1. 1960 data from photostat supplied to Scripps Foundation in advance of publication, table 190, P-C (S 1)-42, p. 3.

There may be an error in these data which somewhat minimizes the decline in the number of children ever born to women of completed fertility during the period from 1885 to 1940. The older women, 65 and over at the time of the census, are more likely to forget how many births they have had and/or to regard a child that died shortly after birth many years before as a stillbirth. In the days when a large proportion of the births were not attended by a physician and when there were no well-established criteria for distinguishing a live birth from a stillbirth, the actual number of live births per 1,000 women of completed fertility aged 65 or over at the time of the census was probably somewhat higher than the census figures.

Cohort Fertility. Cohort fertility is a relatively new refinement of fertility rates now coming into use. The measure takes its name from the fact that it uses as its base of calculation—all the women born in a given year—called a cohort—and follows the reproductive experience of these same women through their child-bearing years, generally the years 15–49, or such of those years as they may have attained at a specified date. A group of cohorts, e.g., the women aged 15–19 constituting five cohorts, may also be used and is quite satisfactory for many purposes. The *minimum of data* needed to calculate cohort birth rates are the same as those needed to calculate the age-specific birth rates described above, viz., number of women surviving from each cohort in each year of age 15–49, and the children borne each year by age of mother. If other data, such as order of birth of child, viz., a first child, second child, etc., and/or age of mother at marriage and date of marriage, are available, additional useful rates can be calculated.

In the United States the word *cohort* is used to designate the group of females born from July 1 of one year to June 30 of the following year and is designated as the cohort of the latter date. Thus, the women born from July 1, 1919 to June 30, 1920 constitute the cohort of 1920. All the women in each cohort are assumed to be of the same exact age on January 1 of their cohort year. The same general procedure is standard in the computation of life tables (Chapter 12).

From the minimum data, two types of cohort birth rates can be calculated: (1) age-specific cohort rates, which are calculated in the same manner as the age-specific rates already described but which apply to a cohort on January 1 of a specified year; and (2) cumulative cohort rates, which are obtained by adding the appropriate age-specific cohort rates up to a given point in time, i.e., until the women of a given cohort have attained a specified age on January 1 of a specified year. This cumulative cohort rate becomes a measure of the completed fertility of a cohort when the women in that cohort have reached menopause at about 45 years of age. Groups of cohorts, e.g., those of 1939 to 1943 or any other convenient grouping, can be used to reduce the number of rates calculated, but in this method some significant changes in rates in particular cohorts may be somewhat obscured. A similar obscuring of changes may occur when sample cohorts are chosen for study as has been done in Table 9-7. Since cohort age-specific rates are the actual rates of a specified cohort of women, as they pass through the childbearing years, they may be said to be longitudinal rates in contrast to the customary age-specific rates, which are cross-sectional and hence yield rates only for a particular point in time for specified ages (15–19, etc.) of women. A cumulative cohort birth rate shows the actual number of births per 1,000 women in a particular cohort when they have attained the specified age. Such rates for women 45 years of age would, of course, when multiplied by the percent of female births in a population (48.8 percent in recent years in the United States) tell us whether that cohort is reproducing itself, i.e., is bearing 1,000 daughters or more. As we shall see shortly, several recent cohorts even at ages as low as 35–39 have already had enough or more than enough children to replace themselves. Precise changes in the age pattern of fertility, i.e., the exact ages at which mothers bear their children, are shown most effectively by cohort rates.

The data in Table 9-7, section A, show the cumulative birth rates for *all* women in the United States, i.e., the total number of children born to 1,000 women in each of the cohorts listed in column 1, by the time they had attained the exact ages standing at the top of columns 3–9. The data for every fifth cohort are shown here, working backward from the latest (1943) to attain 19 years of age on January 1, 1962, to the cohort of 1878 (the earliest cohort in this series). The blank spaces for the cohorts of 1923–1943 for ages 44 and under cannot be filled because these women have not yet attained the specified ages. For the cohorts of 1893–1878 the blank spaces can never be filled because the age of mothers at the birth of their children was not called for on birth registration forms until 1917.

Section B of Table 9-7 shows the proportion (percent) of the completed cumulative birth rate to 1,000 women in each cohort at the specified ages on the assumption that women of exact age 44 in each cohort had completed their childbearing, i.e., had borne 100 percent of their children. This is not strictly accurate, but in no cohort except that of 1878 is the cumulative rate at age 49 as much as 1 percent higher than at age 44, and in most of them it is less than 0.5 percent higher. The cumulative birth rates of each cohort at each specified age are also shown graphically on Figure 9-3.

Reading vertically, we see that the cumulative birth rates for women of the specified age (Table 9-7, section A) show the differences in these rates between the cohorts (see also Figure 9-3, which, read along the horizontal line, shows the same cohort differences). Thus 1,000 women, aged 24, in the cohort of 1938 had a cumulative rate of 1,493, whereas 1,000 women at the same age in the cohort of 1913 had a rate of only 749, and 1,000 women at the same age in the cohort of 1893 had a rate of 991. Read horizontally (Table 9-7 or vertically in Figure 9-3), these rates show the reproductive experience of a given cohort at the specified ages. Thus the women in the cohort of 1918 (the latest to attain age 44 by January 1, 1962) had a cumulative rate of 2,070 at age 34 and a rate of 2,513 at age 44 when their families were practically completed. On the other hand, the women in the 1928 cohort at age 34 (2,736) had substantially exceeded the rate for the women aged 44 in the 1918 cohort. A glance at Figure 9-3 shows these differences in the cumulative rates of cohorts very clearly. Following the curve for the several age groups horizontally, the eye at once detects a downward movement of all cumulative rates in each successive cohort, beginning with the earliest cohort for which data are given here up to a low point which was reached by the cohort of either 1908 or 1913 at every age, except at age 19 by the cohort of 1918. This general downward movement of cohort rates from 1878 to the cohorts of 1898 or 1903 may be regarded as another and more revealing way of showing

TABLE 9-7.   SECTION A: CUMULATIVE BIRTH RATES TO ALL WOMEN IN THE UNITED
STATES IN EVERY FIFTH COHORT, 1878–1943
SECTION B: PERCENTS SHOWING PROPORTIONS OF CUMULATIVE BIRTH
RATES AT SPECIFIED AGES*

Date of cohort (birth year)	No. of child-bearing years completed to 1-1-62 or age 45+	Exact age						
		19	24	29	34	39	44	49
(1)	(2)	(3)	(4)	(5)	(6)	(7)	(8)	(9)
Section A: Cumulative birth rates								
1943	5	256	—	—	—	—	—	—
1938	10	278	1,493	—	—	—	—	—
1933	15	255	1,378	2,464	—	—	—	—
1928	20	164	1,107	2,095	2,736	—	—	—
1923	25	161	881	1,772	2,408	2,747	—	—
1918	30	148	770	1,504	2,070	2,404	2,513	—
1913	30+	163	749	1,369	1,893	2,208	2,318	2,328
1908	30+	181	848	1,440	1,867	2,162	2,269	2,279
1903	30+	183	950	1,633	2,058	2,312	2,414	2,425
1898	30+	185	958	1,754	2,259	2,540	2,642	2,653
1893	30+	—	991	1,848	2,464	2,824	2,954	2,970
1888	30+	—	—	1,885	2,567	3,030	3,202	3,224
1883	30+	—	—	—	2,652	3,147	3,353	3,381
1878	30+	—	—	—	—	3,355	3,592	3,629
Section B: Distribution of cumulative birth rates†								
1918	—	5.9	30.6	59.8	82.4	95.7	100.0	—
1913	—	7.0	32.3	59.1	81.7	95.3	100.0	—
1908	—	8.0	37.4	63.5	82.3	95.3	100.0	—
1903	—	7.6	39.4	67.6	85.3	95.8	100.0	—
1898	—	7.0	36.3	66.4	85.5	96.1	100.0	—
1893	—	—	33.5	62.6	83.4	95.6	100.0	—
1888	—	—	—	58.9	80.2	94.6	100.0	—
1883	—	—	—	—	79.1	93.9	100.0	—
1878	—	—	—	—	—	93.4	100.0	—

* All the rates in this table have been rounded to the nearest whole number. The cohort
of 1943 is the latest to attain age 19 on Jan. 1, 1962. Every fifth preceding cohort has
been used in order to shorten the table. The dashes left in the table for the cohorts
1923–1943 cannot yet be calculated. Some estimates for them will be referred to in
Chap. 17, The Future Population of the United States. The dashes for the cohorts of
1893–1878 are due to the fact that the ages of mothers at the time of birth of their
children were not completely registered until 1917.

† The percentages in Section B are calculated on the assumption that the cumulative rate
for each cohort at age 44 equals 100 percent.

Sources: *Fertility Tables for Birth Cohorts of American Women,* part I, by Pascal K.
Whelpton and Arthur A. Campbell, Scripps Foundation. U.S. Department of Health,
Education, and Welfare, Special Reports, vol. 51, no. 1, table 4, pp. 78–104. Data
for the years 1959–1962 kindly supplied by Scripps Foundation.

the long-time downward trend in birth rates referred to above. The concentration of the lowest cumulative cohort rates at all ages, except as just noted, in the cohorts of 1908 and 1913 is almost certainly due in large part to the fact that the women in the cohorts in the vicinity of these dates passed relatively large proportions of their most fertile years during the Depression of the 1930s and the war years which followed. Women born in 1908 were 20 to 30 years of age between 1928 and 1938, while the 1913 cohort of women were 20 to 30 years of age between 1933 and 1943. In somewhat lesser degree, the Depression also

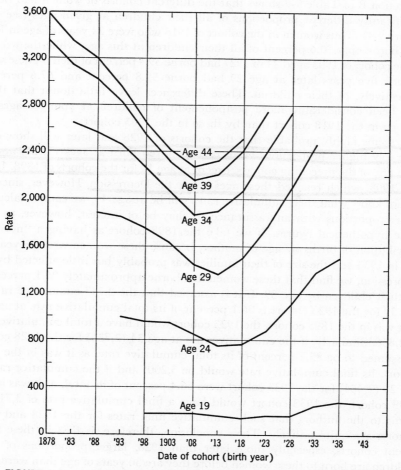

FIGURE 9-3.   **Cumulative cohort birth rates: 1878 to 1943. (Table 9-7, sec. A.)**

had an effect on the cumulative fertility of the cohorts of 1898 and 1903. The marked upswing in the cumulative cohort rates in the cohorts of 1918 and later, at all ages except at 19 years of age (where it remained low until after the cohort of 1928), probably represents in large part, for women aged 29 and over, a making up of births and/or marriages postponed during the Depression and the war. For younger women at ages 19 and 24 and especially at the latter age, the rapid rise in the cumulative cohort rates represents chiefly an earlier contribution made to births by these more recent cohorts because of marriage at younger ages and shorter intervals between births.

Section B of Table 9-7 shows that the different cohorts of women had borne significantly different proportions of all their children at given ages (see also Figure 9-4). Thus women in the cohort of 1918 who were 24 years of age in 1942 had borne only 30.6 percent of all their children at this age, while the women of the cohort of 1903 aged 24 in 1927 had borne 39.4 percent of theirs. These same cohorts five years later at age 29 had borne 59.8 percent and 67.6 percent, respectively, of their children. These differences leave little doubt that there had been considerably more postponement of children at younger ages by women in the 1918 cohort than by those in the 1903 cohort.

It seems highly probable that the cohorts of 1928 and later will show considerably higher proportions of all their children born at ages 19, 24, and 29 than any of the preceding cohorts, except at age 19 for the cohorts of 1898, 1903, and 1908, which reached these ages before the Depression. However, since we do not know what their cumulative rates will be at age 44, we cannot calculate such proportions with any assurance. It may be of interest, however, to give some hypothetical figures. If we take the 1898 cohort as having a "normal" distribution of births by age of mother, because these women were 35 years of age in 1933 and the size of their families was probably but little affected by the Depression, we find that these women had borne approximately 96.1 percent of all their children by age 39. If it is assumed that the 2,747 cumulative rate at age 39 for the 1923 cohort is 96.1 percent of its total cumulative rate at age 44 as it was in the 1898 cohort, the 1923 cohort would have a total cumulative rate of 2,856. Similarly, if the cumulative rate at age 34 (2,736) for the 1928 cohort is assumed to be 85.5 percent of its total cumulative rate, as it was in the 1898 cohort, its final cumulative rate would be 3,200; and if the cumulative rate at age 29 (2,464) for the 1933 cohort were 66.4 percent of its total, as it was in the 1898 cohort, the 1933 cohort would have a final cumulative rate of 3,711. It seems to the authors that such cumulative final rates for the 1928 and 1933 cohorts are quite unlikely. Their conclusion, therefore, is that in these more recent cohorts, especially those later than 1928, larger proportions of their children are born to these women before they are 30 years of age than were born to the women in any of the preceding cohorts.

Table 9-8, section A, shows the cumulative rates for *first* births for the same

TABLE 9-8.   SECTION A: CUMULATIVE FIRST-BIRTH RATES TO ALL WOMEN IN THE UNITED
STATES IN EVERY FIFTH COHORT, 1878–1943
SECTION B: PERCENTS SHOWING PROPORTIONS OF CUMULATIVE FIRST-BIRTH
RATES AT SPECIFIED AGES

Date of cohort (birth year)	No. of child-bearing years completed to 1-1-62 or age 45+	Exact age						
		19	24	29	34	39	44	49
(1)	(2)	(3)	(4)	(5)	(6)	(7)	(8)	(9)
Section A: Cumulative first-birth rates								
1943	5	193	——	——	——	——	——	——
1938	10	212	711	——	——	——	——	——
1933	15	196	686	869	——	——	——	——
1928	20	133	609	820	877	——	——	——
1923	25	131	518	783	858	880	——	——
1918	30	125	455	693	797	826	832	——
1913	30+	136	439	644	752	793	801	802
1908	30+	152	485	648	732	771	781	782
1903	30+	156	527	700	761	786	794	795
1898	30+	154	531	717	780	798	803	804
1893	30+	——	524	722	791	813	818	818
1888	30+	——	——	710	783	809	815	816
1883	30+	——	——	——	784	809	816	816
1878	——	——	——	——	——	819	826	826
Section B: Distribution of first births								
1943	——	21.4	——	——	——	——	100.0	——
1938	——	23.6	79.0	——	——	——	100.0	——
1933	——	21.8	76.2	96.6	——	——	100.0	——
1928	——	14.8	67.7	91.1	97.4	——	100.0	——
1923	——	14.6	57.6	87.0	95.3	97.8	100.0	——
1918	——	15.0	54.7	83.3	95.8	99.3	100.0	——
1913	——	17.0	54.8	80.4	93.9	99.0	100.0	——
1908	——	19.5	62.1	83.0	93.7	98.7	100.0	——
1903	——	19.6	66.4	88.2	95.8	99.0	100.0	——
1898	——	19.2	66.1	89.3	97.1	99.4	100.0	——
1893	——	——	64.1	88.3	96.7	99.4	100.0	——
1888	——	——	——	87.1	96.1	99.3	100.0	——
1883	——	——	——	——	96.1	99.1	100.0	——

Sources: See notes to Table 9-7. For the cohorts 1878–1918, inclusive, it is assumed
that the cumulative first births at age 44 = 100%. The proportions at younger ages
are calculated from this base. For cohorts 1923–1943, the base is 900 = 100%. This
is the assumed maximum number of first births possible per 1,000 women in any cohort.
See text for basis of this assumption.

cohorts used in Table 9-7. Figure 9-4 displays the same data graphically. Obviously no cohort of women can have more than 1,000 first births per 1,000 women surviving through the reproductive ages. The highest cumulative rate for first children borne by 1,000 women in any cohort is found in the cohort of 1923 at

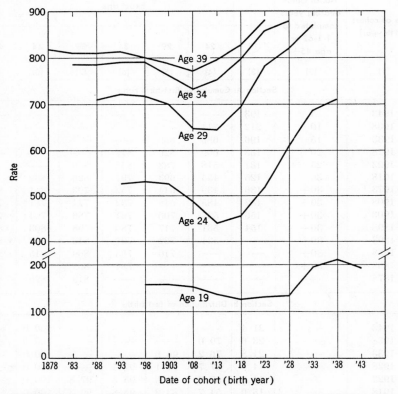

FIGURE 9-4.   Cumulative first-birth rates, cohorts of 1878–1943. Cumulative first-birth rates at age 44 are not shown because those at age 39 are so nearly the same that the curve would almost be a retrace. (Table 9-8, sec. A.)

age 39 in 1962 (880). It is possible that the women in some of the more recent cohorts may slightly exceed this rate at age 44, but it does not seem likely that the women in any cohort will exceed 900 to any significant extent. In the first place, in no cohort did the increase in the cumulative rate of first births at age 44 exceed that of women at age 39 by more than 10 points. In the second place, as of 1960, only 93.9 percent of the women reaching the ages 40–44 reported themselves ever married. Since our census treats all mothers as "ever-married" women, it would appear highly probably that *at least* 5 percent of all women will remain unmarried and will never have had a first birth. Third, the best available information leads the authors to believe that about 4 to 5 percent of the married women are sterile. (This figure cannot be considered precise but it cannot be much in error.) Fourth, in 1960, 14.1 percent of the *ever-married* women aged 40–44 had never borne a child (this, of course, includes sterile women). In view of these facts, an estimate that only 10 percent of each 1,000 women 40–44 years of age will never bear a child seems quite conservative.

In section B of Table 9-8 the percentage distribution of *cumulative first births* is given for the same cohorts and ages as in Table 9-7. In the calculation of these percentages, it is assumed that in the cohorts of 1898 to 1918 the actual cumulative rates at age 44 (see section A) represent all first births the women in these cohorts ever had, and this figure is used as the base (100 percent) in calculating the percentage of the total first births that had taken place at each younger age in each of these cohorts. For cohorts 1923 to 1943 it is *assumed* that 900 first births is the cumulative total for each cohort, and therefore this is used as the base (100 percent) to calculate the proportion of all first births in each of these cohorts that had already occurred at the ages attained by January 1, 1962.

These percentages show beyond question that the women in the more recent cohorts are bearing a much larger proportion of their possible first children at ages 19, 24, and 29 than the women in earlier cohorts. This upward trend is, of course, of longer duration for women aged 24 than for those aged 19, and for those aged 29 than for those aged 24. Furthermore, if these more recent cohorts do not have approximately 900 first children by age 39, the actual proportions born by ages 19, 24, and 29 will, of course, be larger than those shown here. The women in cohorts of 1918, 1923, and 1928 in particular postponed the bearing of first children beyond age 19 as compared with the earlier cohorts of 1898, 1903, and 1908, and even more as compared with the women of the same age in the 1933, 1938, and 1943 cohorts. At age 24 the largest postponement of first births occurred in the cohorts of 1908, 1913, and 1918. At age 29, these same cohorts showed relatively low proportions of first births, and their total cumulative rates for first births were also low at age 44. In the cohorts of 1923 to 1943, where the possible base of 900 first births is used for calculating the proportions of first births, the cohorts of 1928 and 1933 had almost attained this number (900) by ages 34 and 29, respectively.

In this connection, it is of some interest to compare the likely maximum cumulative cohort rate for first births (900) with the rate that would be found if we took a year in which births were unusually high, e.g., 1947, and calculated the age-specific rate for first births to women of each age group (15–19, 20–24, to 40–44) and add these six age-specific first-birth rates to secure a total first-birth rate for the year 1947. When this is done, it is found that this first-birth rate was

257.2 per 1,000 women aged 15–44 in 1947. Since each woman spends five years in each of these six 5-year groups, the total number of first births to 1,000 women at the age-specific first-birth rates of 1947 would be 257.2 × 5, or 1,286. Such a rate could be obtained only in a year when an unusually large proportion of the women aged 15–44 were highly likely to have a first birth. The year 1947 was chosen for this calculation because it seemed probable that the proportion of women having first births would be large in that year. The

TABLE 9-9.   PERCENT OF WOMEN EVER MARRIED, BY FIVE-YEAR AGE GROUPS, 15–44, AND MEDIAN AGE AT FIRST MARRIAGE, UNITED STATES, 1890–1960

Year	Age*							Median age at first marriage†
	15–44	15–19	20–24	25–29	30–34	35–39	40–44	
1960	75.5	16.1	71.6	89.5	93.1	93.9	93.9	20.3
1950	74.9	17.1	67.7	86.7	90.7	91.6	91.7	20.3
1940	65.0	11.9	52.8	77.2	85.3	88.8	90.5	21.5
1930	65.5	13.2	54.0	78.3	86.8	89.6	90.5	21.3
1920	64.8	13.0	54.4	77.0	85.1	88.6		21.2
1910	61.9	12.1	51.7	75.1	83.9	88.6		21.6
1900	60.0	11.3	48.4	72.5	83.4	88.9		21.9
1890	59.2	9.7	48.2	74.6	84.8	90.1		22.0

* U.S. Bureau of the Census, *1950 Census of Population*, vol. II, part 1, pp. 1-179 to 1-181, and *1960 Supplementary Reports*, PC (S1)-39.

† U.S. Bureau of the Census, *Current Population Reports*, ser. P-20, no. 105.

conditions which appeared likely to contribute to an extremely high first-birth rate in 1947 and to relatively high cumulative cohort birth rates for some years after 1947 are as follows:

1. By the end of World War II, a large deficit of marriages had accumulated because of the postponement of marriages during the war and the late Depression years. Following the war, this deficit was rapidly reduced. Thus a very considerable number of women who would normally have been married and started families during the years 1940 to 1945 were married in late 1945 and in 1946 and began to have children in 1947.

2. There was a considerable postponement of births as well as of marriages during the years 1940 to 1945. To a significant degree this was due to the prolonged but temporary separation of wives and husbands during military service.

3. Another rather sudden social change likely to raise the birth rate in the postwar years but probably not closely associated with the war was the substantial reduction of the age at first marriage for a large number of women. The evidence that such a change in age at first marriage took place is of several kinds.

In Table 9-9 we find that the proportion of the women aged 15–19 in 1940 who were ever married was only 11.9 percent but that by 1950 it had risen to 17.1 percent. This is a very large proportional increase—43.6 percent. At ages 20–24 the increase was from 52.8 percent in 1940 to 67.7 percent in 1950, or a proportional increase of 28.2 percent, and at ages 25–29 the increase was from 77.2 percent in 1940 to 86.7 percent in 1950, and the proportional increase was 12.3 percent.

Another type of rate which shows the increase of first marriages at younger ages is the cumulative cohort first-marriage rate. This is similar to the cumulative cohort birth rate in that it shows the cumulative number of first marriages per 1,000 women in each cohort at given ages (Table 9-10).[10] These rates prove beyond doubt that women have been marrying younger since World War II than they did during the Depression and even during the four decades preceding the Depression. Of 1,000 women in the cohort of 1899 and 19 years of age in 1918, 261 had already contracted first marriages. This was the largest number per 1,000 of first marriages at age 19 before the cohort of 1929. In this latter cohort it rose to 293. It then rose to 334 in the cohort of 1934. After that, it declined slightly to 325 in the cohort of 1939 and to 314 in the cohort of 1943 (the latest cohort to attain the age of 19 in 1962). Expressed somewhat differently, 26.1 percent of each 1,000 women in the cohort of 1899 had contracted a first marriage by age 19. In the cohorts which arrived at age 19 since 1945 (this would include the cohorts 1929 to 1943 in Table 9-10) the proportion of women of age 19 married for the first time is much higher than in all the earlier cohorts. The situation is the same for women aged 24. Here the women in the 1934 cohort at age 24 had a higher proportion of first marriages per 1,000 women (825 per 1,000 or 82.5 percent) than the cohorts of 1909 and earlier had when the women were five years older, i.e., were aged 29. Moreover, the women aged 29 in 1958 (cohort of 1929) had closely approximated (906 per 1,000, or 90.6 percent) the highest cohort first-marriage rate for women aged 45 (940 per 1,000, or 94 percent) shown in these tables.

Still another measure often used to indicate the changing age at marriage is the "median age at first marriage" (Table 9-9). This is the age which divides all women at first marriage into two equal parts, i.e., the age at which one-half marry below this median age and one-half marry at ages above it. This median age declined from 21.5 years in 1940 to 20.3 in 1950 and 1960. These changes in the ages of women at first marriage have an important and rather abrupt effect on most measures of fertility when they take place rather quickly, as was true in this country after 1945.

---

[10] These cohort marriage rates in Table 9-10 are taken from a table prepared by Arthur A. Campbell of the Scripps Foundation. They are used here with his permission. The complete table will be published as a part of the report being prepared by the Scripps Foundation on the 1960 survey of the *Growth of American Families* (GAF).

4. A fourth change which may significantly affect fertility rates, especially at younger ages, is the change in the spacing of children by married couples. There has been a marked reduction in the interval from marriage to a first birth and/or in the intervals between a first and a second birth and between subsequent births. These interval reductions alone might very well raise the average number

TABLE 9-10.   CUMULATIVE FIRST-MARRIAGE RATES AS OF JANUARY 1, FOR ALL WOMEN, BY EXACT AGES 19, 24, AND 29, IN SELECTED COHORTS FROM 1889–1943, UNITED STATES

Cohort	Exact age		
	19	24	29
1889	——	——	803
1894	——	640	816
1899	261	653	824
1904	260	652	804
1909	251	622	800
1914	195	636	827
1919	220	679	877
1924	256	775	894
1929	293	807	906
1934	334	825	——
1939	325	——	——
1943	314	——	——

of children borne during the first five years of married life by one-half (0.5) a child or more. As a consequence, the average age of the mother having three children might very well decline by two years or more because of earlier marriage and shorter intervals between marriage and a first birth and between a first birth and subsequent births.

The data showing the combined effect of these four changes affecting the timing of births in family formation are believed by Whelpton to show "that the age at delivery is declining significantly from the cohorts of 1910–1919 to those of 1930–1934 or 1935–1939. It now appears that the median age will decrease two or three years for first births, 2.5 to 3.5 for second births, and 2.5 to 4.0 for third births."[11]

[11] This quotation was made available to the writers by P. K. Whelpton, Director of the Scripps Foundation. It comes from a paper, "Trends and Differentials in the Timing of Births," read before the meeting of the Population Association of America, April, 1963. The data come, in part, from U.S. Bureau of the Census, *Current Population Reports, Population Characteristics, Marriage Fertility and Child Spacing*, ser. P-20, no. 108, August, 1959, and in part from surveys of the *Growth of American Families*, the second report on which is now being prepared by the staff of the Scripps Foundation.

It should be remembered, however, that these changes in the timing of births need not always consist in a downward movement in the median age of women at a given order of birth. A postponement of marriages and births such as took place during the Depression and war years raises the median age of mothers for any specified order of births. Moreover, considerable changes in the timing of births may take place without resulting in any change, or at least, in any substantial change in the average size of the completed family. In all highly industrialized countries, the size of the average completed family has been declining for some years, and considerable evidence shows that in the United States an average of about three births or slightly under three are now expected by the women interviewed in the *Growth of American Families* surveys. One can say with some assurance that in the United States the expected children and the actual completed fertility of women are approaching each other more and more closely. Under these circumstances, it seems reasonable to conclude that the timing of conceptions is not to any appreciable extent a *cause* of the increase or decrease in the *actual* size of the average family; rather it is the desired or expected size that determines the timing of the children. These timing changes are to be regarded largely as matters of convenience for an increasing proportion of couples. Timing increasingly represents the judgment of a couple as to when it is best for them to start raising their family and how the children should be spaced. This judgment of the best timing is largely determined by an intricate complex of social and economic conditions in the United States and in most other highly industrialized countries, which leads couples to prefer a certain size of family. If 100 couples prefer three-child families and another 100 prefer five children, it is reasonably certain that the timing of marriage and birth intervals will be quite different in these two groups.

Although some of the cohorts passing through their most fertile ages since the war will have larger average completed families than most of the cohorts passing through their most fertile years during the Depression and the war, there is no clear evidence yet, as was noted above, that any of these later more fertile cohorts are bearing an average of three children per woman. Some of these more fertile postwar cohorts may attain this level before their fertility is completed. However, the authors think this event unlikely.

Furthermore, such timing changes cannot continue indefinitely. For example, a considerable number of women from the cohort of 1927, who would have married at age 20 in 1947 under the conditions that had prevailed before the Depression, may have married at age 18 in 1945, and still more may have married at age 19 in 1946; but this process may be continued in a particular cohort for only a few years until all the women in the cohort would be marrying at a median age under 20, when further reduction in the age at marriage would have no significant effect on the crude birth rate or on the general fertility rate and, of course, little or no effect on the size of completed family, unless the desired or expected size rose. Likewise, the reduction of birth intervals would also soon exhaust its effect on crude measures of fertility, again unless the expected or desired size changed.

Some of the principal factors of a special character which operate to determine the size of the family and the spacing of children in highly industrialized societies will be discussed in Chapter 11.

SIZE OF FAMILY AND THE REPLACEMENT OF POPULATION

In closing this chapter, we think it may be of interest to consider in very simple terms what the average size of the completed family in the United States should be to ensure the replacement of the population as of 1960. Expressed in a somewhat different form: If a young married couple wanted to know how many children they should have to contribute their share to the maintenance of the population at a constant size, what considerations should they take into account?

In the first place, if we assume that the average young woman asking this question is 20 to 22 years of age, we find that for each 1,000 girls born, about 30, or 3 percent, have already died by age 22 and that another 10 (1 percent) will die by age 35. Let us say that approximately 3.5 percent, or 35 out of each 1,000 girls born, will die before they are likely to contribute to the next generation. This leaves about 965.

In the second place, a certain number of women never marry. In the United States during the past several decades the percent of women not contracting a first marriage by 45 years of age has been declining. It was about 9 percent in 1920 but fell to about 6 percent in 1960. It would appear conservative to estimate that about 6 percent (58) of the 965 women living to about 35 years of age have never married and have never borne a child. (In our census, any woman who reports she has never married is not asked whether she has ever borne a child.) Hence, 58 out of each 1,000 females born and surviving through the years of reproduction are barred from participating in replacement of the population because they never married and never bore a child (965 − 58 = 907).

In the third place, a further subtraction must be made from this 907 married women out of 1,000 births because a certain proportion of married couples are sterile, i.e., physiologically unable to have a live birth. As has been explained earlier in this chapter, this proportion is uncertain, but a conservative estimate would seem to be 4 or 5 per cent. (This does not include any couples who are fecund but choose not to have children.) If we assume, then, that 4 percent of all married couples are infecund, we get 36 married women who do not have children (907 − 36 = 871). If we add another 1 percent of this group of women who are fecund but because of accidents and illnesses never have a child (871 − 9 = 862) we find that only 862 out of each 1,000 born survive who are likely to contribute to the next generation. Since these 862 women must, on the average, have 1,000 daughters to replace themselves and will necessarily have approximately 1,050 sons (2,050 ÷ 862 = 2.38), every 1,000 females born and at all likely to have children would need to have approximately 2,380 children (an average of 2.38 per woman) to maintain the population at a stationary level. It should be made clear that these calculations are only *approximate* and that any substantial change in the death rates, or in the proportion of infecund couples, or in the proportion of young women married would change in some small degree the number of births needed per "likely" fertile woman to maintain the population.

SUGGESTIONS FOR SUPPLEMENTARY READING

Benjamin, Bernard: *Elements of Vital Statistics*, George Allen & Unwin, Ltd., London, 1959. A successor to the second version of the work of the same title by Sir Arthur Newsholme (1923).

Coale, Ansley J., and Edgar M. Hoover: *Population Growth and Economic Development in Low-income Countries*, Princeton University Press, Princeton, N.J., 1958.

Freedman, Ronald, David Goldberg, and Harry Sharp: "'Ideals' about Family Size in the Detroit Metropolitan Area: 1943," *Milbank Memorial Fund Quarterly*, vol. 33, pp. 187–197, 1955.

Freedman, Ronald, Pascal K. Whelpton, and Arthur A. Campbell: *Family Planning, Sterility, and Population Growth*, McGraw-Hill Book Company, New York, 1959.

Glick, Paul: *American Families*, John Wiley & Sons, Inc., New York, 1957.

Grabill, Wilson H., Clyde V. Kiser, and Pascal K. Whelpton: *The Fertility of American Women*, John Wiley & Sons, Inc., New York, 1958.

Great Britain, Census Office: *Fertility of Marriage*, H.M. Stationery Office, London, 1917. (Census of England and Wales, 1911, vol. 13.)

Kuczynski, Robert R.: *The Balance of Births and Deaths*, The Macmillan Company, New York, 1928–1931. (Brookings Institution, Institute of Economics.)

Sauvy, Alfred: *Fertility and Survival: Population Problems from Malthus to Mao Tse-Tung*, Criterion Books, New York, 1961.

United Kingdom, Royal Commission on Population: *Report*, H.M. Stationery Office, London, 1949.

Westoff, Charles F., Robert G. Potter, Jr., Philip C. Sagi, and Eliot G. Mishler: *Family Growth in Metropolitan America*, Princeton University Press, Princeton, N.J., 1961.

Whelpton, Pascal K.: *Cohort Fertility: Native White Women in the United States*, Princeton University Press, Princeton, N.J., 1954.

Willcox, Walter F.: *Studies in American Demography*, Cornell University Press, Ithaca, N.Y., 1940.

CHAPTER TEN

Differential
Birth Rates
(Fertility)

INTRODUCTORY

Probably significant differences have always existed among the birth rates (fertility) of different populations. In the preceding chapter we have placed emphasis on the measures which would help an investigator to arrive at a more accurate appreciation of the level of fertility than is provided by the *crude* and *general* birth rates. We showed there that more refined measures require a relative abundance of accurate data and good methods of processing these data. Until quite recently only a few countries have had such data, and even now the great majority of the people in the world live in areas where not even a precise crude rate can be calculated. In Table 10-1 the present crude birth rates of a few countries are shown with a code used by the United Nations in its *Demographic Yearbook* designating in some degree the reliability of the rates. These rates show that there are large differences in the crude birth rates of populations today even if great allowance is made for incompleteness of the data and the casual manner in which many countries treat their censuses and the registration of births and deaths.

In Chapter 2 we noted that Malthus found birth rates varying rather widely in the countries of Europe in which he traveled at the close of the eighteenth century—rates which, when stated in terms of births per 1,000 of the population, varied from about 28 in Norway to over 40 in Prussia and Russia. Malthus also devoted considerable attention to what he called the preventive checks to population, by which he meant chiefly the postponement of marriage. In his analysis of the preventive check, he showed that it prevailed more widely in certain classes of a given population than in others and also in some countries than in others. He definitely recognized the existence of differential birth rates.

In this chapter we are not particularly concerned with the differences between the birth rates of national populations as shown in Table 10-1. However, it is of some interest to note the rather large differences in crude birth rates between the European peoples wherever they may be found, except in a few Latin American countries and among the peoples living in the underdeveloped countries of the world. We shall have frequent occasion to call attention to such differences in birth rates in following chapters.

TABLE 10-1.   CRUDE BIRTH RATES FOR SELECTED COUNTRIES

Country	Code*	Average crude birth rate†	Country	Code*	Average crude birth rate†
Algeria:			Iran	U	43.0
European	C	20.8	Ceylon	U	36.4
Muslim	U	32.2	China (Mainland)	S	33.0
Ghana:			Formosa	C	41.4
Registration area	C	52.4	Singapore	C	41.2
Madagascar	U	33.4	India	S	39.1
Union of South Africa:			Philippines	U	22.6
Colored (mixed)	C	47.4	Albania	U	41.8
White	C	25.0	Austria	C	17.4
Egypt	U	41.6	Denmark	C	16.4
British Honduras	C	45.5	France	C	18.3
Canada	C	27.6	West Germany	C	17.3
Guatemala	C	49.2	Poland	C	25.6
Mexico	C	45.9	United Kingdom	C	16.8
United States	C	24.2	Australia	C	22.6
Argentina	C	22.7	Guam	C	62.4
Chile	C	35.4	New Zealand	C	26.6
Ecuador	U	46.5	Western Samoa	C	38.4
Japan	C	17.8			

* Data said to be relatively complete are coded C, those unreliable, incomplete, or of unknown completeness are coded U. S means that the estimate is based upon a special study or studies of unknown reliability or representativeness.

† Latest two years (usually 1958–1959) for which data are given.

Source: United Nations, *Demographic Yearbook, 1960,* table 13.

At this point we should again call attention to the fact that as far as we now know, the differences in birth rates within all relatively large populations arise from social and economic differences and not from biological differences. In other words, there is no convincing evidence that *physiological capacity to reproduce* differs significantly as between racial, ethnic, and national populations, e.g., those shown in Table 10-1, nor as between subgroups of these populations.

However, there is abundant evidence that actual reproduction (fertility) does differ greatly between population groups having different cultural values and between groups having the same broad cultural background but differing in social and economic status.

Here our interest is centered on those differences which are found between subpopulations, or classes, within a larger population that has a similar cultural background. This emphasis on differential birth rates in subpopulations should not be taken as implying that national and regional differences in birth rates are of little importance. They are, in fact, of very great importance. China is a good example of a people among whom certain aspects of their culture have long supported man's natural propensity to maintain high fertility. For centuries the Chinese had been taught to have great respect for their ancestors and to subordinate many personal inclinations and values to the basic cultural value of providing male descendants to carry on the worship of ancestors. At least, this has long constituted one of the chief cultural values of their civilization. Under such a universal and strong cultural pressure it is not surprising that early marriage was the rule and that the birth rate was very high, perhaps approaching the upper physiological limit, although abortion was by no means unusual after male descendants had been provided. Likewise, a widely different culture, that of Western Europe in the seventeenth century, also produced a population subgroup, the settlers in the North American colonies, who soon began to fulfill the Biblical injunction to "be fruitful and multiply and replenish the earth" by having very high birth rates which continued for about two centuries.

On the other hand, there have been "primitive" cultures in which birth rates have been rather low, i.e., in which only a fraction, perhaps two-thirds to three-fourths, of the physiological capacity to reproduce has been realized in actual fertility. The reasons for this, in broad terms, have been the development of cultural values which resulted in relatively infrequent conception, such as prolonged segregation of women after childbirth for "purification," and breast feeding of children for several years, or in practices which destroyed a significant proportion of female infants, thus leaving relatively few to reproduce.

DIFFERENTIAL FERTILITY IN THE UNITED STATES

Until the census data of the United States were used to show the number of children aged 0-4 per 1,000 women of ages likely to be their mothers (ages 20–44 or 20–49) and until it was suggested by General Walker in 1891 (see page 490) that immigration may have had little effect on the growth of population in the United States but was having a highly deleterious effect on the *quality* of the American population. There were, up until that time, almost no studies of differential birth rates in this country. Consequently, little was known regarding regional, racial, and native-born and foreign-born or other differentials in reproduction. In 1905 Prof. Walter F. Willcox used census data[1]—the number of children aged 0–4 per 1,000 women 15–49 years of age—to show that there were substantial differentials in fertility in this country and that they had existed at least since 1850. He further found that these ratios of children to women had declined steadily since 1860 (probably since 1850), and that the decline had been greatest in those states and regions where industrialization and urbanization had been most marked. He also noted that from 1830 to 1900 there had been a steady decline in the proportion of children under 10 years of age in the total population.[2]

Using the 1910 census data, unadjusted for underenumeration of children 0–4, Thompson was able to show that the number of children under 5 years of age per 1,000 women 15–44 years of age in both white and nonwhite populations not only varied considerably from one geographic division to another but that there were also large differences between urban and rural populations and that quite low ratios already prevailed in many of our larger cities.[3]

In the United States as a whole in 1910 in the white population, there were 382 children aged 0–4 per 1,000 women aged 15–44 in the urban population (places having a population of 2,500 or over) and 603 in the rural population. Thus the rural ratio was 221, or about 58 percent, higher than the urban. There was a surprising uniformity in the urban ratio throughout the United States. The only geographic division having urban ratios rather widely different from the national average (382) included the West North Central states (344) and the Pacific states (301). On the other hand, the rural ratios varied from a low of 458 in the New England states to 729 in the West South Central states, a difference of approximately 60 percent. (In 1910 approximately 54 percent of our population was rural—living in places of less than 2,500 population.)

It was also possible in 1910 to calculate these ratios of children to women for the white population in our larger cities. (There were relatively few Negroes in these cities at that time.) Only a few of these cities had ratios equal to or higher than the national urban average (382), and in most of these cities with the higher ratios of children, the proportion of the white population that was

[1] Walter F. Willcox, U.S. Bureau of the Census, *Proportion of Children in the United States*, p. 13, 1905.

[2] Since we have good reason to believe that the death rate was declining during most of this period, almost certainly after 1850, we have also a very good reason to believe the birth rate was also declining. The decline would occur in spite of the increase in the proportion of older people, which would automatically act to reduce the proportion of children.

[3] At that time the Negroes were still so heavily concentrated in the three Southern divisions that no child-woman ratios were calculated for Negroes in the other six divisions. Warren S. Thompson, "Race Suicide in the United States," *Scientific Monthly*, vol. 5, pp. 22–35, 154–165, 258–269, July, August, September, 1917.

native born of native parents was quite low. Thus the important differentials in birth rates shown by these data were: (1) the divisional differences, which confirmed Professor Willcox's earlier studies relating to them, but called attention to urban-rural differences in birth rates as the reason for most of the

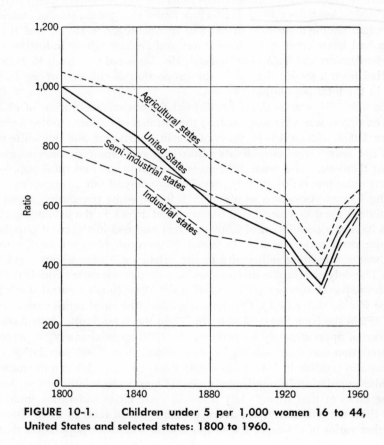

FIGURE 10-1.   Children under 5 per 1,000 women 16 to 44, United States and selected states: 1800 to 1960.

divisional differences, and (2) the differences between whites of native parentage and whites of foreign parentage, chiefly in the cities.[4]

That some of these differentials in fertility had existed for longer than had generally been realized is shown clearly in the study summarized in Figure 10-1.

[4] For data from 1800 to 1950 more recently calculated for ratios of children aged 0–4 to women aged 20–44, see Wilson H. Grabill, Clyde V. Kiser, and Pascal K. Whelpton, *The Fertility of American Women,* John Wiley & Sons, Inc., New York, 1958, pp. 13–21.

When states were classed as agricultural or industrial, large differences between them in the ratios of children to women were shown to have existed ever since 1800, and since the semi-industrial states stood in an intermediate position, it seemed safe to conclude that fertility in the United States had long varied inversely with the degree of industrialization and urbanization of the population; i.e., the more urban and industrial the state the lower its fertility.[5] However, it should be noted that these urban-rural differentials have been decreasing steadily in absolute amounts and are now significantly smaller than in the past. In 1959 the number of children ever born per 1,000 of *all* urban women aged 15–44 was 1,630, and per 1,000 for *all* rural-farm women it was 2,101. When these rates were standardized for age of women, the number of children per 1,000 urban women remained almost unchanged (1,629), but for 1,000 rural-farm women it rose to 2,298. Thus, standardizing raised the number of children ever born per 1,000 rural-farm women from 471 above that for urban women to 669 above it, or in terms of percentage from 28.9 percent larger for rural-farm women to 41.1 percent excess when the less favorable age composition of rural-farm women was taken into account.[6]

With the coming of large numbers of immigrants, chiefly from Eastern and Southern Europe after about 1890, there was increasing interest in the relative rates of growth in these newer groups and the older settlers from Western Europe. Many people believed that these new immigrants were "inferior" and were afraid the older stock, which was chiefly British and German, would be swamped by the newcomers. Consequently, many of the earlier studies of differential fertility were concerned with showing that these newer immigrants were more fertile than the older native stock. This interest was largely concentrated in the Northeastern part of the country, probably because the people interested in such matters also lived in that region.

Hoffman (1909) showed that the average number of children born to a native-born married white woman in Rhode Island in 1885 was 3.49, whereas for a foreign-born woman it was 5.38.[7] (In 1885 the native-born white women of completed fertility in Rhode Island were probably of British origin, and the foreign born were likely to be chiefly of Irish descent.) A little later (1915), Crum stated on the basis of the data in Table 10-2 that "other careful investigators on this subject . . . all interpret the best available data in the same way [as himself] and all arrive at the same general conclusion, namely, that the native element is failing to contribute anything like its proper quota to the new

[5] P. K. Whelpton, "Industrial Development and Population Growth," *Social Forces*, vol. 6, pp. 458–467, 629–638, 1928.
[6] Wilson H. Grabill and Robert Parke, Jr., *Marriage, Fertility and Childspacing*, August, 1959, *Current Population Reports*, ser. P-20, no. 108, July 12, 1961, table 3.
[7] F. L. Hoffman, "The Decline in the Birth Rate," *North American Review*, vol. 189, p. 677, 1909.

population of this country." These New England data probably exaggerated the differences between the *older* and the *newer* stock in the United States as a whole because they ignored such a large proportion of the older stock which still lived on farms in Western states.

TABLE 10-2.   AVERAGE NUMBER OF CHILDREN PER WIFE AMONG PIONEER FAMILIES WHO ORIGINALLY SETTLED IN NEW ENGLAND, BY MARRIAGE PERIODS, 1700–1879

Marriage periods	Average number of children per wife
Total	4.80
Previous to 1700........	7.37
1700–1749	6.83
1750–1799	6.43
1800–1849	4.94
1850–1869	3.47
1870–1879	2.77

Source: Frederick S. Crum, "The Decadence of the Native American Stock," *American Statistical Association Journal*, vol. 14, n.s., no. 107, p. 216, 1914.

As interest in group differentials in birth rates increased, a number of other studies were undertaken, which were motivated only by the desire to find the facts. In 1930 and 1931 Notestein and Sydenstricker (see Table 10-3) showed that there were large differences in size of family as between social and economic classes.[8] The proportions of wives aged 40–44 in 1910 who had borne one or two children, or none, was significantly higher in the business and professional classes (63.1 percent) than in farmer and unskilled laborer classes (42.3 percent). On the other hand, the proportion of wives of business and professional men who had borne five or more children (9.6 percent) was much lower than for the wives of farmers and unskilled laborers (30.8 percent). There was little difference between the wives in these occupational groups in the proportions who had borne three or four children.

Such differences were considerably smaller for wives aged 60–64 in 1910 who had completed their families about 20 years earlier. However, the differences were still highly significant; 46.2 percent of the wives (60–64) of business and

[8] Frank W. Notestein, "The Decrease in Size of Families from 1890 to 1910," *Milbank Memorial Fund Quarterly*, vol. 9, pp. 181–188; Frank W. Notestein and Edgar Sydenstricker, "Differential Fertility According to Social Class: A Study of 69,620 Native White Married Women under 45 Years of Age, Based upon United States Census Returns of 1910," *American Statistical Association Publication*, vol. 25, pp. 9–32, 1930; see also Clyde V. Kiser, "Fertility Trends and Differentials in the United States," *American Statistical Association Journal*, vol. 47, pp. 25–48, 1952.

professional men had borne two children or fewer, while only 29.4 percent of
the wives of farmers and unskilled laborers had borne two or fewer children.
On the other hand, only 24.1 percent of the wives (60–64) of business and
professional men had borne five children or more as compared with 42 percent
of the wives of farmers and unskilled laborers. These data left little doubt that
in the United States occupational differentials in fertility had existed for some
decades and that during the decades 1890 to 1900 and 1900 to 1910, the voluntary control of the size of the family was proceeding more rapidly in the business
and professional groups than in the farmer-laborer groups.

TABLE 10-3. | **PERCENT OF WIVES AGED 40–44 AND 60–64 IN SELECTED SOCIAL CLASSES WHO HAD BORNE SPECIFIC NUMBERS OF CHILDREN, UNITED STATES, 1910**

Total children born	Professional		Business		Skilled		Unskilled		Farm owner	
	60–64	40–44	60–64	40–44	60–64	40–44	60–64	40–44	60–64	40–44
Total	100.1	100.1	99.9	100.0	100.1	100.1	99.9	100.0	100.3	100.0
0	14.7	19.8	9.6	17.9	8.8	17.4	4.4	16.3	9.0	10.6
1	13.3	19.6	14.0	21.5	13.3	17.0	12.4	14.9	8.8	10.1
2	19.8	24.5	21.1	22.9	16.7	18.0	12.4	16.1	11.8	16.6
3	15.5	18.4	16.7	17.1	15.5	16.2	16.8	14.4	14.8	16.4
4	14.1	9.6	13.0	9.7	12.2	11.0	13.1	9.9	12.7	13.2
5	8.8	4.0	9.8	5.0	9.9	7.2	9.5	6.9	12.5	9.6
6	6.5	2.5	6.8	3.0	7.9	5.2	10.2	5.9	7.9	7.8
7 or more*	7.4	1.7	8.9	2.9	15.8	8.1	21.1	15.6	22.8	15.7

* Percent for 7 or more combined by the authors.
Source: Frank W. Notestein, "The Decrease in Size of Families from 1890 to 1910,"
Milbank Memorial Fund Quarterly, vol. 9, pp. 181–188.

Using 1930 census data for the East North Central states, Notestein also
showed that there was an inverse relationship between the value of the home
and the number of children when the value of the home was less than $10,000:
The lower the value of the home the larger the number of children. When the
home was valued at over $10,000, the number of children was slightly higher
than in homes valued at $5,000 to $9,999 but smaller than in homes valued at
under $5,000. Notestein suggested that the slightly larger number of children
in the more costly homes might represent a reversal of the inverse relation
between economic status and size of family which had prevailed in the past.[9]

[9] Frank W. Notestein, "Differential Fertility in the East North Central States," *Milbank
Memorial Fund Quarterly*, vol. 16, pp. 173–191, 1938.

Kiser,[10] using data collected in urban communities in the National Health Survey (1935), found substantial fertility differentials (standardized birth rates) as between occupational groups, educational groups, and groups having different incomes; also for native whites, foreign-born whites, and nonwhites sepa-

TABLE 10-4.   FERTILITY RATES AMONG WHITE AND NONWHITE WIVES OF CHILDBEARING AGE, BY OCCUPATION, EDUCATION, AND INCOME, 1935* (STANDARDIZED FOR AGE)

Occupation, education, and income	Live births per 1,000 wives		
	White		Nonwhite
	Native	Foreign-born	
Occupational class of head, total............	96	111	86
Professional............................	94	86	79
Business................................	86	109	81
Skilled and semiskilled....................	100	111	85
Unskilled...............................	115	122	86
Educational attainment of wife, total.........	96	111	86
College................................	87	82	64
High school............................	91	108	85
Seventh and eighth grade..................	105	109	85
Under seventh grade......................	118	125	87
Family income, total.......................	96	111	86
$5,000 and over.........................	78	—	—
$3,000–$4,999...........................	77	83	—
$2,000–$2,999...........................	76	90	45
$1,500–$1,999...........................	81	102	60
$1,000–$1,499...........................	90	104	73
Under $1,000 and total relief..............	117	128	90
Under $1,000 and nonrelief................	96	108	69
Total relief.............................	147	155	126

* These data relate to New York City.
Source: Clyde V. Kiser, Group Differences in Urban Fertility, The Williams & Wilkins Company, Baltimore, 1942, pp. 56, 91, and 124.

rately. Although no clear pattern of fertility differences among nonwhites by social status emerges from these data, there is a definite inverse relation between income and fertility (see Table 10-4).

Without making any attempt at evaluation of the relative importance of the factors in producing the differentials in the birth rates shown here, one can say

[10] Clyde V. Kiser, Group Differences in Urban Fertility, The Williams & Wilkins Company, Baltimore, 1942.

that among the whites, occupation, income, and education clearly had a significant influence on fertility whether as direct causes or as causes of conditions which encouraged the voluntary control of the size of the family.

Kiser and Whelpton[11] in reporting the results from the preliminary survey of the Indianapolis study found several differentials in fertility which will be summarized very briefly:

1. Substantial differences in size of completed family were found between Protestant and Catholic couples in respect of all social and economic factors considered. Of the Protestant couples, 67.0 percent had had two or fewer children, while of the Catholic couples 52.0 percent were in this group. The average number of children to Protestant couples was 2.19 and to Catholic couples 2.74. For both Protestant and Catholic couples, the number of children declined steadily as rent rose from $15 toward $50–$59, the smallest number of children in both groups being found in families paying rents of either $50–$59 or $60–$79. The number of children rose somewhat in both religious groups at rents of $80 and over as compared with those paying $50–$79. The increase in the proportion of families having five or more children with the decrease in rents is striking for both Protestants and Catholics; however, the differences are somewhat more pronounced for Protestants.

2. The proportion of couples with five or more children also decreased as the amount of education increased for both Protestants and Catholics, but as in the case of increasing rentals, the decrease in number of children was more pronounced for Protestants than for Catholics. In other words, for Catholics, religion tends to reduce somewhat the effects of economic and educational differences in determining the size of the family.

3. The region of birth of the couples was also related to the size of the family. In general, fewer couples born in the South were childless, and more had five or more children than those born in the North. The Protestant couples born in the South had substantially larger families than the Catholic couples, practically all of which were born in the North. Couples born in the South were probably of lower than average economic status and had less education than those born in the North.

In a study of fertility in the different census tracts[12] of eight large cities,

[11] Clyde V. Kiser and P. K. Whelpton, "Social and Psychological Factors Affecting Fertility: Variations in the Size of Completed Families of 6,551 Native White Couples in Indianapolis," *Milbank Memorial Fund Quarterly*, vol. 22, no. 1, pp. 72–105, 1944. This paper is of primary interest here although it is only an incidental by-product of this Indianapolis study. The central concern was the evaluation of the social and psychological factors which influenced people in determining the size of their families when voluntary control was widespread in a community. See Chap. 11 for more detailed information about this study.

[12] Warren S. Thompson, "Some Factors Influencing the Ratios of Children to Women in American Cities," *American Journal of Sociology*, vol. 45, pp. 193–194, September, 1939. (See also U.S. Bureau of the Census, *Ratio of Children to Women in the United States, 1920*, Census Monograph, no. 11.)

Thompson found that the tracts with the higher ratios of children under 5 years of age to women aged 15–44 were the tracts with: (1) lower than average rentals; (2) lower proportions of employed women; (3) larger proportions of the employed population engaged in manufacturing; and (4) a higher proportion of married women. The proportion of married women was at that time no doubt closely related (inversely) to the proportion of women employed; hence, the tracts with a high proportion of married women would also have low proportions of women employed.

This study also showed that in seven of the large cities (Pittsburgh was the exception) less than 42.0 percent of white women lived in tracts where the ratio of children was high enough to replace the existing population, while in Chicago only 10.9 percent of the white women lived in such tracts. Thus it appeared that there were significant differences in fertility within cities and between cities. These differences unquestionably arose from the differences in fertility associated with differences in social, economic, and educational status which prevailed at the time the data were gathered. The fact that the differences in fertility associated with differentials in social, educational, and economic status appear to be changing somewhat will be discussed below.

Fertility Differences in Completed Families. Information regarding differentials in fertility as measured by the number of children ever born per 1,000 women of completed fertility, 45 years of age and over, in the United States is relatively good and abundant. The data used come chiefly from samples chosen from the 1910, 1940, 1950, and 1960 censuses and from several surveys relating to fertility taken by the Bureau of the Census during the 1950s and reported in its Current Population Reports.[13]

In the United States as a whole, 1,000 native white women aged 70–74 in 1910 who had been married once and whose husbands were still living had borne 5,152 children. These women had completed their families about 1880–1885. One thousand white women 45–49 years of age, who had only recently completed their families at the time of the 1910 census, had borne 4,512 children. The decline in the size of their completed families between 1885 and 1910 was

---

[13] U.S. Bureau of the Census, *Population, Differential Fertility, 1940 and 1910, Women by Number of Children Ever Born*, 1945–1947; 1950, *Fertility, Special Reports*, vol. IV, part 5, chap. C, 1955.

Since 1950, several surveys made by the Bureau of the Census also contain much pertinent information on fertility. Presumably there will be a report on fertility based on the 1960 census; but only a few data were available at the time of writing. [See U.S. Bureau of the Census, 1960, *Supplementary Reports*, PC(S 1)—42.]

In addition to providing data on the size of completed families, some of these reports also contain many other data bearing on various aspects of fertility, e.g., cumulative number of children born per 1,000 women under 45 by 5-year age groups. This in effect provides data somewhat similar to cumulative cohort birth rates for 5-year groups of cohorts (see preceding chapter).

therefore about 12 percent, which probably understates the size of the decline because of the tendency of older women to forget births or to regard as a still-birth a child that died shortly after birth many years before.

Residential Differentials. As we have already noted, one of the early differentials in fertility to attract attention in the United States was that between urban and rural residents. The 1910 and 1940 data just mentioned contain much interesting information on this and several other types of differential fertility. Only a few of the more salient points can be presented in tabular form.

When the number of children ever born to 1,000 women aged 45–49 in 1885 but aged 70–74 in the census of 1910, residing in different types of communities, was compared with that for women in the same type of communities who were aged 45–49 in 1910, very substantial differences by residence were found. This was to be expected from the data on the ratio of children to women presented earlier in this chapter. Native white women 45–49 years of age in 1885 had borne 4,576 children per 1,000 women when they lived in urban communities, 5,222 when they lived in rural-nonfarm communities, and 5,579 when they lived in rural-farm communities. The corresponding numbers for women 45–49 in 1910 were 3,665, 4,404, and 5,542 (see Table 10-5, all occupations, 1910).[14] The decline during this interval (1885–1910) was 20 percent for urban women, 16 percent for rural-nonfarm women, but only 0.7 percent for rural-farm women. The line "all occupations" in this table brings this comparison of the fertility of married white women up to 1950. No data on the fertility of white married women by occupation of the husband are yet available for 1960. (At this point we are concerned only with the residence data in Table 10-5 showing all occupations.) However, data are available showing children ever born for all ever-married (in census parlance "ever married" includes widowed and divorced) white women aged 45–49 in 1960, living in these three types of communities, which are comparable with these "all-occupation" figures for earlier years. They are as follows: for urban women 2,133; for rural-nonfarm women 2,787; and for rural-farm women 3,161.

Table 10-5 also shows the number of children ever born per 1,000 native white women aged 45–49 for nine broad occupational groups of the husbands by community of residence for 1950, 1940, and 1910; but here we are dealing only with the line "all occupations." When the three residence groups on each date are combined to yield a total, e.g., when the women in these three residence groups in 1950 are added together and divided into the total number of their children, we get the figure 2.525 children per woman. This means that each white woman of specified ages (45–49) had borne this average number of children. When this number is multiplied by 1,000, we can say that 1,000 women

[14] At this point only the data relating to residence will be considered. The occupational differentials in Table 10-5 will be discussed in the following section.

TABLE 10-5. NUMBER OF CHILDREN EVER BORN PER 1,000 WHITE WOMEN* AGED 45–49, BY MAJOR OCCUPATION GROUP OF HUSBAND, BY URBAN AND RURAL RESIDENCE, UNITED STATES, 1950, 1940, AND 1910

Occupation group of husband	Community of residence											
	1950				1940				1910			
	Total	Urban	Rural-non-farm	Rural-farm	Total	Urban	Rural-non-farm	Rural-farm	Total	Urban	Rural-non-farm	Rural-farm
All occupations..........	2,525	2,191	2,796	3,608	3,022	2,449	3,196	4,136	4,512	3,665	4,404	5,542
1. Professional, technical, and kindred workers........	1,751	1,678	1,873	2,994	2,069	1,964	2,325	2,906	3,079	2,759	3,569	4,282
2. Managers, officials, and proprietors, except farmers........	1,978	1,897	2,215	2,726	2,283	2,128	2,502	3,444	3,493	3,261	3,810	4,772
3. Clerical, sales, and kindred workers.....	1,928	1,866	2,079	2,781	2,108	1,999	2,443	2,991	3,242	3,094	3,627	4,699
4. Service workers, including private household........	2,416	2,283	2,915	3,482	2,737	2,507	3,445	—	4,027	3,883	4,512	—
5. Craftsmen, foremen, and kindred workers........	2,480	2,320	2,793	3,461	2,847	2,630	3,182	3,976	4,224	4,008	4,600	5,182
6. Operatives and kindred workers.........	2,753	2,514	3,107	4,158	3,037	2,679	3,538	4,399	4,496	4,121	5,243	5,621
7. Laborers, except farm and mine.........	3,356	3,127	3,515	4,414	3,627	3,230	3,922	4,431	4,869	4,794	4,916	5,531
8. Farmers and farm managers.........	3,510	3,100	2,843	3,568	4,104	2,701	3,506	4,144	5,551	4,176	5,068	5,603
9. Farm laborers and foremen.........	4,222	3,607	4,456	4,235	4,270	—	4,332	4,385	5,176	4,424	5,311	5,130

* For 1950, white women married once, husband present, by major occupation group of husband in the experienced labor force; for 1940 and 1910, native white women, by occupation of husband. For 1960, no data for occupational status were available at time of writing.

Source: U.S. Bureau of the Census (1) 1950, *Special Report, P-E, No. 5C, Fertility*, table 28; and (2) 1940 and 1910, *Fertility by Duration of Marriage*, 1947, tables 11 and 13.

aged 45–49 in the United States in 1950 and having the other characteristics specified (age, white, etc.) had borne 2,525 children. In order to measure the differences between the size of the completed families in these three residence groups, we shall use these totals at each census (1950, 1940, and 1910) as the base figures. It is customary to give this base number the value of 100 and to measure the variations between the subpopulations from this value. In 1950 the number 2,525 equals 100 (see the line "all occupations," 1950, in Table 10-5). If then we divide this base number (2,525 = 100) into each of the numbers showing the average size of completed families for women in the urban population (2191 ÷ 2525 = 87 percent), the rural-nonfarm population (2796 ÷ 2525 = 111 percent), and the rural-farm population (3608 ÷ 2525 = 143 percent), we get the index numbers shown in Table 10-6, line "all occupations." This process is repeated for each census. The 87 (in the urban column, 1950) means that 1,000 women of completed fertility living in urban communities in 1950 had borne only 87 percent as many children as 1,000 of *all* women, while the rural-nonfarm women had borne 111 percent as many children as 1,000 of all women, and the rural-farm women had borne 143 percent as many as 1,000 of all women. These index numbers show at a glance the ratio of the number of children in completed families in each residence group to *all* women in the three residence groups combined. In 1910, 1,000 rural-farm women had borne 23 percent *more* children (index 123) than 1,000 "total" women (index 100), while 1,000 urban women had borne 19 percent fewer than the total (index 81). The direct comparison between urban women and rural-farm women in 1910 shows that 1,000 of the latter had borne 51 percent more children than 1,000 of the former (index 123 ÷ 81 = 151 percent). In 1940 the corresponding figures for rural-farm women are 37 percent above the total (index 137) but 69 percent above that for urban women (index 137 ÷ 81 = 169 percent). In 1950 rural-farm women had an index 43 percent above the total (index 143) and 61 percent above that for urban women. In 1960 the rural-farm women had an index (134) 34 percent above that for total women and 48 percent above that for urban women (for the 1960 data, see the following text table at ages 45–49). Thus the difference between the average size of the completed families of rural-farm women as compared with those of urban women rose substantially from 51 percent in 1910 to 69 percent in 1940 and then declined to 61 percent in 1950 and to 48 percent in 1960, which was only slightly below what it was in 1910 (51 percent). During all this time (1910–1960), there has been a steady rise in the index showing the relation of the average size of families of rural-nonfarm women in comparison with that of *all* women (100 at each date)—from 98 in 1910 to 106 in 1940, to 111 in 1950 and to 118 in 1960. However, the index for rural-nonfarm women on the basis of 100 for rural-farm women was practically stationary, 77 to 79, until 1950. It then rose to 88 in 1960.

Taking only the beginning and the end of the 50-year period 1910 to 1960, we see that the number of children ever born per 1,000 rural-farm white married women in 1960 declined to 57 percent of their 1910 level, while that for urban women declined to 58 percent of their 1910 level. Thus, during this half century, the proportional decline was approximately the same in both these residence groups. As we have just seen, however, the sharp decline in the number of children ever born came three decades later for rural-farm women than for urban women.

The rural-nonfarm women generally stood in an intermediate position between rural-farm and urban women; however, between 1950 (2,796) and 1960 (2,787) there was almost no change in the number of children ever born per 1,000 rural-nonfarm women aged 45–49, and in 1960 they had borne only 12 percent fewer children than the rural-farm women but 31 percent more than the urban women. Their fertility appears to be approaching the level of the rural-farm women.

Another very interesting point appears in the 1960 data given just below; viz., 1,000 white women ever married aged 35–39 in 1960 in each residence group had already borne more children than 1,000 women of the same marital group aged 45–49 at that date.

Age in 1960	Total	Community of residence		
		Urban	Rural-nonfarm	Rural-farm
35–39	2,629	2,481	2,924	3,265
45–49	2,354	2,133	2,787	3,161

The above data show clearly that a rise in the size of completed families will be found in all three residence groups in 1970 as compared with the size in 1960. This increase is the consequence of the changes in age at marriage and in the timing of births noted at several points in the preceding chapter, as well as of a change in the desired size of family after the war. But it should be noted that whereas the number of children ever borne by 1,000 urban white married women aged 45–49 in 1960 was only 67 percent of that of rural-farm women in the corresponding group (2,133 ÷ 3,161 = 67 percent), urban women aged 35–39 in 1960 had already borne 76 percent as many children as rural-farm women of the same ages in that year. This may indicate a still further narrowing of the urban-rural differentials in size of completed families, although it may be due largely to differences in the timing of births in these two residence groups. It will be several years before we can be certain on these points.

We may note here some of the differences in number of children ever born by place of residence of mothers for different occupational groups, although we should find it equally satisfactory to treat them in the following section. These differences are also shown in Table 10-6, where the total number of children per 1,000 white women aged 45–49 in each occupational group (1–9) at each census is given the value of 100, and this number (see Table 10-5) is divided into the number of children per 1,000 women in the urban, in the rural-nonfarm, and in the rural-farm populations, to secure indices for these residence groups. (The process for each occupational group is the same as that described above for "all occupations.") For example, in occupation class 1, professional, technical, and kindred workers, in 1950, 1,000 "total" women with husbands in this class had borne 1,751 children (see Table 10-5). This is the 1950 base (100) for this class, 1. When these women lived in the urban areas, 1,000 of them had borne only 1,678 children, or 96 percent as many children as the total women (Table 10-6). When they lived in rural-nonfarm communities, they had borne 107 percent as many as the same number of total women, and when they lived in rural-farm communities, they had borne 171 percent as many children as 1,000 total women. Likewise, the number of children ever born to 1,000 total women in each occupational class is considered 100, which becomes the base for the indices for children ever born to 1,000 women in each residence group. These indices show that in every occupational group, when the families lived in urban communities, the index was below 100, i.e., was below that of the occupational class total. (This means little for occupational groups 8 and 9, because few men in these two occupational groups live in urban communities.) Moreover, in all occupational groups except 8 and 9, there was a very large difference between the indices for urban women and rural-farm women. This was especially large for group 1 (professional, technical, and kindred workers).

The very high indices of children ever born per 1,000 women whose husbands belonged to occupational group 1 (see Table 10-6) and who lived in rural-farm communities is of interest but has had little quantitative significance in the past because the number of group 1 families living in rural-farm communities was quite small until after World War II. However, if these residence differences within occupational groups persist as more and more in professional occupations move into rural-farm areas, these residential differentials may become of increasing importance. The same situation prevailed in 1950 in groups 2–7, although the residence differentials were not quite as large as in group 1. But there was an urban–rural-farm differential of between 40 percent and 50 percent between all of these groups. Moreover, the 10 to 25 percent residence differentials between urban families and rural-nonfarm families will become of increasing importance as more and more people in occupation groups 2–7 move into rural-nonfarm areas. As yet, however, little is known as to whether city couples with larger families seek rural-nonfarm residence *because they have*

TABLE 10-6. INDICES SHOWING THE RELATION OF THE NUMBER OF CHILDREN EVER BORN PER 1,000 WHITE WOMEN AGED 45—49 IN URBAN AND RURAL RESIDENCE GROUPS TO THE NUMBER BORN TO 1,000 WOMEN IN THE TOTAL POPULATION, BY MAJOR OCCUPATION GROUP OF HUSBAND, UNITED STATES, 1950, 1940, AND 1910

Occupation group of husband	Community of residence											
	1950				1940				1910			
	Total	Urban	Rural-non-farm	Rural-farm	Total	Urban	Rural-non-farm	Rural-farm	Total	Urban	Rural-non-farm	Rural-farm
All occupations	100	87	111	143	100	81	106	137	100	81	98	123
1. Professional, technical, and kindred workers	100	96	107	171	100	95	112	140	100	90	116	139
2. Managers, officials, and proprietors, except farmers	100	96	112	138	100	93	110	151	100	93	109	137
3. Clerical, sales, and kindred workers	100	97	108	144	100	95	116	142	100	95	112	145
4. Service workers, including private household	100	94	121	144	100	92	126	—	100	96	112	—
5. Craftsmen, foremen, and kindred workers	100	94	113	140	100	92	112	140	100	95	109	123
6. Operatives and kindred workers	100	91	113	151	100	88	116	145	100	92	117	125
7. Laborers, except farm and mine	100	93	105	132	100	89	108	122	100	98	101	114
8. Farmers and farm managers	100	88	81	102	100	66	85	101	100	75	91	101
9. Farm laborers and foremen	100	85	106	100	100	—	101	103	100	85	103	99

Source: Calculated from children ever born per 1,000 women in Table 10-5.

such families, or whether couples moving from city to rural-nonfarm areas have larger families *because rural-nonfarm residence encourages such families.*

Occupational Differentials. Table 10-7 shows how the size of the completed families of women whose husbands belong in different occupational groups varies from occupation to occupation when they live in the same type of community—urban, rural-nonfarm, and rural-farm. In this table the number of children ever born per 1,000 white women aged 45–49 whose husbands were engaged in all occupations is given the index value 100 for the column headed "total." For the columns showing residence, the index (100) is the number of children ever born per 1,000 white women aged 45–49 for all women living in that type of residence. (The actual figures are given in Table 10-5.) When the base figure, given the value 100, is divided into the figure for each occupation in each column, we get the indices shown in Table 10-7. These figures show that with only a few exceptions, the indices rise in all these types of communities as we proceed from occupational group 1 to group 9. Just as we could say above (see Table 10-6) that in each occupational group there were substantial differences among residence groups, we can now also say that in the same residence groupings there are substantial differences between the occupational groups.

These differentials stand out even more clearly if we again combine the nine occupational groups into three broad groups: the white-collar group, the blue-collar group, and the farmer-laborer group. When place of residence is the same, we get the following percents showing the relation of the number of children ever born to 1,000 wives aged 45–49 (see following tabulation): (1) the number of children ever born to 1,000 wives in the white-collar group as a percentage of the number of children born to wives in the blue-collar group; (2) the number of children born to wives in the white-collar group as a percentage of those born to wives in the farmer-laborer group; and (3) the number of children born to wives in the blue-collar group as a percentage of those born to wives in the farmer-laborer group.

Relationship	1950	1940	1910
1	74.3	75.2	78.4
2	54.3	54.0	61.7
3	73.0	71.8	78.7

During this 40-year period there was a comparatively small decline (line **1**) in the relative number of children born per 1,000 wives in the white-collar

TABLE 10-7. INDICES SHOWING THE RELATION OF THE NUMBER OF CHILDREN EVER BORN PER 1,000 ALL WHITE WOMEN AGED 45–49 HAVING HUSBANDS IN ALL OCCUPATION GROUPS COMBINED TO THAT OF WOMEN IN EACH OF THESE GROUPS, BY COMMUNITY OF RESIDENCE, UNITED STATES, 1950, 1940, AND 1910

Occupation group of husband	Community of residence															
	1950				1940				1910			
	Total	Urban	Rural-non-farm	Rural-farm	Total	Urban	Rural-non-farm	Rural-farm	Total	Urban	Rural-non-farm	Rural-farm
All occupations....................	100	100	100	100	100	100	100	100	100	100	100	100
1. Professional, technical, and kindred workers...................	69	77	67	83	68	80	73	70	68	75	81	77
2. Managers, officials, and proprietors, except farmers............	78	87	79	76	76	87	78	83	77	89	87	86
3. Clerical, sales, and kindred workers..	76	85	74	77	70	82	76	72	72	84	82	85
4. Service workers, including private household...............	96	104	104	97	91	102	108	—	89	106	102	—
5. Craftsmen, foremen, and kindred workers...................	98	106	100	96	94	107	100	96	94	109	104	94
6. Operatives and kindred workers......	109	115	111	115	100	109	111	106	100	112	119	101
7. Laborers, except farm and mine......	133	143	126	122	120	132	123	107	108	131	112	100
8. Farmers and farm managers.........	139	141	102	99	136	110	110	100	123	114	115	101
9. Farm laborers and foremen.........	167	165	159	117	141	—	136	106	115	121	121	93

Source: Calculated from children ever born per 1,000 women in Table 10-5.

group as compared with that born to wives in the blue-collar group—from 78 percent as many in 1910 to 75 percent as many in 1940 and to 74 percent as many in 1950. Most of this decline took place between 1910 and 1940. There was, however (line 2), a rather sharp decline in the number of children born to 1,000 wives in the white-collar group as compared with the farmer-laborer group between 1910 and 1940, from 61.7 percent to 54.0 percent, with a very small rise between 1940 and 1950. There was (line 3) a significant decline in the number of children born to 1,000 wives in the blue-collar group as compared with the farmer-laborer group between 1910 and 1940, from 78.7 percent to 71.8 percent, and then a small rise between 1940 and 1950 (to 73.0 percent). If the number of children ever born to 1,000 wives in each of these three broad occupational classes in 1910 is given the base value of 100, the white-collar wives in 1940 had only 65.1 percent as many children as in 1910, and by 1950 this had fallen to 57.1 percent. In 1940 the blue-collar wives had 67.9 percent as many children as in 1910, and in 1950 this proportion had fallen to 60.3 percent as many. By 1940 the farmer-laborer wives still had 74.4 percent as many children as in 1910, but by 1950 this had fallen to 65.0 percent. Thus, on the 1910 base (100) for number of children ever born to 1,000 women aged 45–49 in each of these three occupational groups, the white-collar wives in 1950 had only 57.1 percent as large families as in 1910; the blue-collar wives had families 60.3 percent as large, and the farmer-laborer wives had families 65.0 percent as large. These declines are large for all occupational groups, but are significantly smaller for the farmer-laborer group than for either the blue- or white-collar groups. Similar data for 1960 are not yet available.

In default of these 1960 census data, we may cite the findings of the 1955 survey of the *Growth of American Families* (GAF), *Family Planning, Sterility and Population Growth*.[15] Although these data are not strictly comparable to those just given, they are suggestive. In the sample surveyed in this study *all* wives in the age classes 15 to 39 had borne the following average number of children by 1955 when their husbands were classified as belonging to the following specified occupational groups: (1) upper white-collar, 1.9; (2) lower white-collar, 1.9; (3) upper blue-collar, 2.1; (4) lower blue-collar, 2.2; (5) farm, 2.7. When only women aged 35–39 in 1955 were considered (their families were more nearly complete than those of younger women), the following average number of children had been borne: (1) upper white-collar, 2.3; (2) lower white-collar, 2.2; (3) upper blue-collar, 2.4; (4) lower blue-collar, 2.7; (5) farm, 3.8. The average for *all* these occupational groups of women aged 35–39 combined was 2.6 children. If this average is given the value of 100, the indices for women in the several occupational groups are: (1) 88, (2) 85, (3) 92, (4) 104, (5) 146.

[15] Ronald Freedman, Pascal K. Whelpton, and Arthur A. Campbell, *Family Planning, Sterility, and Population Growth*, McGraw-Hill Book Company, New York, 1959, pp. 306–307. This study relates only to white married women.

Clearly, there are still substantial occupational differences in fertility in this sample group. How these differences might change by the time these women reached 45 years of age cannot be told.

Educational Differentials. Another important differential in completed fertility in the United States is that between women having different amounts of education. Although special studies (see Kiser, above) had frequently called attention to this differential, showing an inverse relation between education and fertility,

TABLE 10-8.   NUMBER OF CHILDREN BORN PER 1,000 WOMEN AGED 45–49, WITH INDICES, BY AMOUNT OF EDUCATION, BY COLOR, UNITED STATES, 1950 AND 1940

	1950				1940			
Amount of education	White		Nonwhite		Native white		Negro	
	No.	Index	No.	Index	No.	Index	No.	Index
4 years college or more.....	1,079	100	1,071	100	1,231	100	1,355	100
1–3 years college...........	1,513	140	1,828	171	1,701	139	1,862	137
4 years high school.........	1,643	152	1,850	173	1,747	142	2,032	150
1–3 years high school.......	2,148	199	2,376	222	2,370	193	2,669	197
8 years elementary.........	2,487	230	2,536	237	2,780*	226	2,760*	206
Less than 8 years elementary	3,232	300	2,896	270	3,948†	321	3,444†	254

* 7 and 8 years elementary.
† Less than 7 years elementary.
Source: U.S. Bureau of the Census, 1940, Differential Fertility 1940 and 1910, Women by Number of Children Born, tables 49 and 50; 1950 Census, Population, Fertility, Special Report P-E, no. 5-C, tables 20 and 22.

i.e., the more education women had, the fewer children they had borne, it was not until samples from the 1940 and 1950 censuses bearing on this point were tabulated that comprehensive data became available.

Table 10-8 shows the number of children ever born per 1,000 women 45–49 years of age, by color, 1940 and 1950, who had completed different amounts of schooling (see notes to this table for the specific differences in other characteristics of the 1950 and 1940 groups), and it gives indices showing the relative differences in fertility between educational groups for whites and for nonwhites. when the number of children ever born per 1,000 women who had completed college or more is given the index value of 100. These indices for both white and nonwhite women rise rapidly as the number of years of schooling decreases.

With only two exceptions large enough to be significant, 1,000 nonwhite women had borne substantially more children than 1,000 white women when both had the same amount of education, both in 1950 and 1940.

The fertility of both white and nonwhite women is relatively much greater for those who attended college for one to three years but who did not graduate than for those who graduated from college, while there was a relatively small increase in fertility between those who graduated from high school and those who attended college for one to three years but did not graduate (see indices in Table 10-8). In the next lower educational group, women completing only one to three years of high school, the relative increase in fertility was large as compared with that of the women who had completed high school. Finally, even though the women who had completed either seven or eight years of elementary school had borne a substantially larger number of children per 1,000 than those with one to three years of high school, they had borne considerably fewer than those women who had completed less than seven or eight years of elementary school. In this latter group with the least schooling, both in 1940 and 1950, the nonwhite women had borne fewer children than the white women. It is possible that this may be merely the consequence of a considerable proportion of nonwhite women with almost no schooling forgetting to report all births and/or considering as stillbirths an appreciable proportion of their births which the corresponding educational class of white women reported as live births.

It is also of some interest that with the same amount of education, urban-rural differences still persist. For example, in 1950, 1,000 urban white women aged 45–49 with college education had borne 1,009 children; 1,000 rural-nonfarm women had borne 1,224; and 1,000 rural-farm women had borne 1,591. Similar data for nonwhite women were not available.

Labor-force Status and Differences in Fertility. The following data show that labor-force status, i.e., whether or not women belonged in the labor force, was associated with a substantial difference in their fertility. These data also show

Residence	Women in the labor force		Women not in the labor force	
	White	Nonwhite	White	Nonwhite
Total..................	1,956	2,277	2,658	3,225
Urban.................	1,782	1,949	2,309	2,580
Rural-nonfarm..........	2,264	2,818	2,967	3,338
Rural-farm.............	2,981	4,550	3,695	4,971

the number of children ever born per 1,000 women ever married and aged 45–49 by color and type of community of residence.[16] Both the white and nonwhite women in the labor force had borne substantially fewer children than those not in the labor force. When the women were also classified by community of residence (urban, rural-nonfarm, and rural-farm) similar differences were found for each type of community. Both in the labor force and not in the labor force, the fertility of the nonwhite women was much higher than that of white women in each type of community.

Economic Status and Differences in Fertility. Data from the 1940 census showing monthly rental for homes and number of children ever born per 1,000 native white women show an almost steady increase in the number of children as rents fall below $75–$99 per month. However, the number of children ever born is slightly higher when the monthly rental is over $100 than when it is between $50 and $100.

In 1950 the number of children ever born per 1,000 women (white and non-white combined) 45 years of age and over showed a steady increase as husband's yearly income declined from $7,000 and over to under $1,000, except where husband's income was $4,000–$4,999. In this income class, the number of children ever born was slightly smaller than in the $5,000–$6,999 class but still slightly above the number in the income class of $7,000 and over. When only the urban and rural-nonfarm population was considered, this inverse relation between number of children ever born per 1,000 women and income was consistent without exception.[17] (Rural-farm families seldom pay cash house rental.)

There is some evidence, however, in this same study that this inverse relation between income of husband and number of children ever born may be undergoing a change. In the United States as a whole (all color, occupation, and residence groups combined), when the number of children ever born per 1,000 women 15–44 years of age is standardized on the distribution by age of married women, husband present, in the United States in April, 1952, 1,000 women whose husbands had incomes of $7,000 and over in 1951 had borne somewhat more children than those in the income classes of $3,000–$6,999. In the urban and rural-nonfarm population (combined) there was almost no difference in number of children between the $7,000 plus, the $5,000–$6,999, and the $2,000–$2,999 income classes (almost 1,890 in all these classes); the lowest number of children was found in the $4,000–$4,999 class and the highest (2,112) in the under $1,000 class.

[16] See U.S. Bureau of the census, 1950, *Special Report*, P-E, no. 5 C, Fertility tables 24 and 26.
[17] U.S. Bureau of the Census, "Fertility of the Population: April, 1952," *Current Population Reports*, ser. P-20, no. 46, p. 13.

Differences in Completed Fertility of Foreign-born Women. It is also of considerable interest that when the number of children ever born per 1,000 foreign-born white women 45–74 years of age in the United States was considered by nationality groups, in 1910 and 1940 very substantial differences were found. (See Table 10-9.) There were also very large proportional declines during this period in the number of children ever born per 1,000 ever-married women in all nationality groups shown in this table. The smallest declines were for women from Italy and Mexico, these declines being only 16 percent and 13

TABLE 10-9.   NUMBER OF CHILDREN EVER BORN PER 1,000 FOREIGN-BORN WHITE WOMEN 45–74 YEARS OLD, EVER MARRIED AND REPORTING ON CHILDREN, BY COUNTRY OF BIRTH OF WOMAN, FOR THE UNITED STATES: 1940 AND 1910

Country of birth of woman	1910	1940	Decline	Percent decline
England and Wales..........	5,107	2,689	2,418	47
Ireland*....................	5,428	3,332	2,096	39
Germany...................	5,785	3,342	2,443	42
Poland....................	7,422	4,689	2,733	37
Russia†....................	7,156	3,777	3,379	47
Italy......................	5,942	4,984	958	16
Canada:				
French..................	7,382	4,352	3,030	41
Other...................	4,366	2,627	1,739	40
Mexico....................	6,507	5,664	843	13

* Eire in 1940.
† U.S.S.R. in 1940.
Source: U.S. Bureau of the Census, *Population, 1940, Differential Fertility 1940 and 1910, Women by Number of Children Ever Born,* Introduction, table V.

percent, respectively. Moreover, except for women from these two countries, the percentage declines for women born in the other countries listed here were significantly larger (41.8 percent) than for native white women of the same ages (31.8 percent).[18] However, the percentage decline for all foreign-born white women between 1910 and 1940 was almost the same (32.7 percent) as for all native white women.

Table 10-10 shows that the residence differentials in the number of children ever born per 1,000 Negro women in the South in 1940 and 1910 and per 1,000

[18] U.S. Bureau of the Census, *Population, 1940, Differential Fertility 1940 and 1910, Women by Number of Children Ever Born.* Percentages calculated from table III.

nonwhite women in 1960, 1950, and 1940 had the same residence pattern as those for native white women, viz., relatively low fertility for urban women and much higher fertility for rural-farm women, with that for rural-nonfarm women in an intermediate position; but at all dates and in all residence groups, the fertility for any fairly large group of nonwhite women has been higher than that of native white or all white women in the corresponding age and residence groups. The same may be said regarding the pattern of occupation differences in number of children ever born per 1,000 Negro women aged 45–49 whenever such comparison can be made.

TABLE 10-10.   NUMBER OF CHILDREN EVER BORN PER 1,000 NONWHITE WOMEN EVER MARRIED, AGED 45–49, UNITED STATES, 1960, 1950, 1940, AND 1910

Residence	1960	1950	1940	1910
Total..........	2,824	2,803	3,288 (3,580)*	6,161 (6,191)*
Urban..........	2,323	2,241	2,397 (2,557)	(4,507)
Rural-nonfarm..	4,072	3,113	3,671 (3,588)	(5,808)
Rural-farm......	5,307	4,861	4,900 (4,837)	(7,386)

* Figures in ( ) for 1940 and 1910 are for all Negro women aged 45–49 in the South, except ever married not reporting on children.
Source: U.S. Bureau of the Census, *Population, 1940, Differential Fertility, 1940 and 1910, Women by Number of Children Ever Born,* tables 71 and 74; and U.S. Bureau of the Census, *Population, 1950, Special Report* P-E, no. 5 C, table 6; 1960 *Supplementary Report,* PC (S 1)-42, table 190.

DIFFERENTIAL FERTILITY IN ENGLAND AND WALES

The study of fertility in England and Wales based on data gathered in the 1911 census also dealt with differential fertility, and until about 1949 (see Glass and Grebenik, as listed in supplementary readings for this chapter) provided most of the data available on this subject in England and Wales. In this study, the age of women at marriage as well as the number of children they had borne and the number surviving were obtained for every woman in the country. This information, when used in conjunction with the other information on the census schedule, made possible an exhaustive study of the fertility of women in England and Wales as it was 50 to 100 years ago. The findings of this study were not startling, but they gave a more exact picture of differential fertility in a larger population than had previously been investigated in detail. Some of the more significant facts are given in Table 10-11.

Table 10-11 shows the number of children born to each 100 couples of completed fertility classified by social status, by duration of marriage in 1911, and by decade of marriage. There were very large differentials in the number of children born to women in the different social classes when they had completed their families shortly before 1911, i.e., women who were married 25 to 30 years earlier, or about 1881–1886. However, these differentials diminished as the duration of marriage increased, i.e., as families were completed at earlier dates (from about 1885–1905). One hundred women married in 1881–1886 and

TABLE 10-11. **NUMBER OF CHILDREN BORN PER 100 COUPLES WHERE THE WIFE WAS 45 OR OVER AT TIME OF CENSUS, BY DATE OF MARRIAGE, SOCIAL CLASS, AND DURATION OF MARRIAGE: ENGLAND AND WALES, 1911**

Date of marriage	Dura-tion of mar-riage, yrs.	Total popu-lation	Occu-pied only	Social classes*							
				I	II	III	IV	V	VI	VII	VIII
1881–1886	25–30	551	554	422	493	556	562	609	513	684	632
1871–1881	30–40	605	611	497	567	615	616	652	567	717	667
1861–1871	40–50	662	673	593	650	679	673	698	633	760	702
1851–1861	50–60	690	701	625	700	707	700	718	654	759	738
1851 or earlier	over 60	697	700	605	728	681	740†	698†	‡	‡	746

> * Class I, upper and middle classes; class II, retired and unoccupied, living on private means; class III, skilled artisans; class IV, intermediate between classes III and V; class V, unskilled workers; class VI, textile workers; class VII, miners; class VIII, agricultural laborers.
> † Rates based on less than 100 couples.
> ‡ Less than 10 couples.
> Source: Great Britain, Census Office, *Fertility of Marriage*, Pt. 2, p. xcviii, table 44, H.M. Stationery Office, London, 1925. (Census of England and Wales, 1911, vol. 13.)

over 45 years of age in 1911 had borne only 422 children if they were in the upper and middle classes (I), while 100 women of the unskilled laborer class (V) had borne 609 children, 100 miners' wives (VII) had borne 684 children, and 100 wives of agricultural laborers (VIII) had borne 632 children; but 100 wives of textile workers (VI) had borne only 513 children. At this time (1906–1911), then, the average number of children born to 100 women in the working-class groups V, VII, and VIII was over one-half higher than the number born to women in the upper and middle classes. For the women marrying from 1851–1861, whose families were for the most part completed in the decade 1875–1884, these three working-class groups of women with highest fertility averaged only about one-sixth more children per 100 couples than the upper- and middle-class women. Even at this time the wives of textile workers (VI) had only slightly larger families than class I women. The larger families of women in classes V, VII, and VIII (manual workers) as compared with women in class I may be due in part to earlier marriage of the women in these laboring classes, but they are probably due in larger measure to the fact that these working-class women did not learn about contraception as early as upper-class women, nor did they have the facilities to practice it as effectively. The relatively low fertility of textile workers' wives married as early as 1851–1861 and completing their families about 25 to 30 years later (1875–1884) is generally believed to be due largely to the fact that many of these women were also textile workers and that the knowledge of how to limit the size of the family spread rapidly in this particular occupational group after about the mid-1800s.

The class differentials in completed fertility doubtless increased rapidly from about 1880–1911. The voluntary control of fertility had probably begun in the upper and middle classes and among textile workers in England and Wales by about the middle 1800s, and the differentials between classes kept increasing at least up to 1911. There are no strictly comparable data for the period since 1911, but the report of the Royal Commission on Population based on the Family Census (1946)[19] gives the estimated size of the average completed family for persons marrying from 1900–1929, classified as manual workers and non-manual workers. These data show a continuous decline in both groups in the size of the completed family, but since it declined at nearly the same rate in both groups, the size of the manual worker's family remained 41 to 44 percent larger than the non-manual worker's family during this period, ending in 1946.

Figure 10-2, from the 1911 study of fertility, also shows the proportions of all the children produced by different proportions of marriages when the latter were arrayed by size of family. Unfortunately for our purposes, it does not cross-classify these data by social class. It is of much interest, however, that at the time of the 1911 census, the least fertile 25 percent of marriages of completed fertility had produced only 2.1 percent of all births, while the most fertile 25 percent had produced 52 percent of all births. We can reasonably assume that the women in the upper and middle classes constituted an increasing proportion of the least fertile 25 percent of women after about 1880. On the whole, apparently, the group differentials in fertility in England and Wales up to 1946 were of much the same character as those in the United States. Since the war the crude birth rate in England and Wales (1945–1949, 18 per 1,000) has not attained the level prevailing before the war (1935–1939, about 20 per 1,000), and in the five years 1957 to 1961 it averaged only 16.7. This may also indicate a stabilization at a slightly lower level of the prewar differentials, but the authors cannot

[19] Royal Commission on Population, H.M. Stationery Office, London, 1949, p. 28. See also Glass and Grebenik in Supplementary Readings.

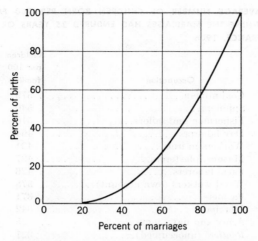

FIGURE 10-2.   Percentage distribution of births to marriages of completed fertility, England and Wales: 1911.

state this positively, since recent data regarding class differentials have not been found.

DIFFERENTIAL FERTILITY IN FRANCE

At the beginning of this century, differential fertility by occupation appears to have been much the same in France as in the United States and in England and Wales (Table 10-12). It should be noted, however, that in France families of farmers and farm laborers were relatively small (marriages of 25 or more years' duration) as compared with such families in the United States and in England and Wales, and also as compared with other hand-working groups in France. In addition, the proportion of marriages in which no child was born increased as the socioeconomic status of the family improved (see Figure 10-3).

Later data for France strictly comparable with those in Table 10-12 are not available. In 1936 the number of children per 100 families for certain occupational groups where the heads had not yet passed 55 years of age (average 38 to 39 years) was as follows:

Extractive industries	211	Public service	152
Agriculture and forestry	203	Manufacturing	151
Fishing	194	Commerce	130
Transportation	165	Liberal professions	129

TABLE 10-12.   AVERAGE NUMBER OF CHILDREN BORN PER 100 FAMILIES WHERE THE MARRIAGES HAD ENDURED 25 YEARS OR MORE, FRANCE, 1906

Occupation	Children per 100 families
Coal miners	579
Spinners	540
Fishermen and sailors	510
Day laborers	464
Workers in iron	431
Masons, plasterers	427
Farm laborers	426
Wood workers (own account)	378
Farmers	371
Merchants	342
Army and navy men	325
Rentiers (unoccupied)	321
Professions	312
Office employees	294

Source: France, Bureau de la Statistique Générale, *Statistique des familles en 1906*, Imprimerie Nationale, Paris, 1912, p. 115.

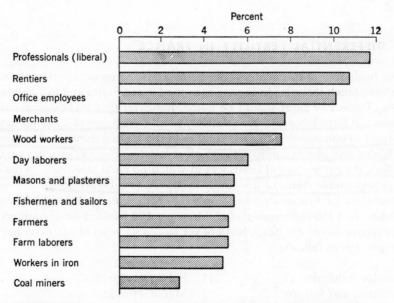

FIGURE 10-3.   Percent of couples married over 25 years with no children, France: 1906. (Source same as Table 10-12.)

These data do not relate to families that were practically completed as do those in Table 10-12, but they do indicate there were still significant differentials in fertility between white-collar workers and hand workers.

A sample of married women drawn from the 1954 census of France, supplemented by special reports from a sample of about 50,000 women born 1899 to 1908, whose families would have been completed by 1954 when they were aged 45–54, showed that there were still substantial differences in fertility of wives when their husbands were classified by occupation.[20] This age group of women was chosen because most of the women were too young at the time of World War I to have had their fertility directly affected by it and had practically completed their families before the outbreak of World War II. Farmers' and farm laborers' wives had the largest families, approximately 3.5 children, but wives of employers in agricultural enterprises had only 2.73 children. Miners' and laborers' wives had the next highest numbers of children, 3.23 and 3.11, respectively. At the other extreme, wives of employees in trade had only 1.70 children; office employees 2.06; employers in trade 1.96; overseers and foremen 1.99; and middle-class clerical workers 1.89. The wives of men in the liberal professions had 2.38 children; the wives of higher-class clerical workers had 2.12 children; and the wives of skilled workers and those with specialized trades combined had 2.46 children. It is of interest that the families of people in the liberal professions and of the employers in agriculture were substantially larger than a number of other white-collar groups of lower economic status. Similar differences, we remember, have been found between the better-paid and poorly paid white-collar groups in the United States.

Another interesting fact brought out in this study was that the women married in 1944, who had been married 10 years when the census of 1954 was taken, actually had already borne more children in several of the occupational groups than the women in these same occupational groups whose families were completed by that date (1954). In general, this held for the occupational groups which had the smallest completed families in 1954. These groups are also, for the most part, those who have benefited most economically from the family code of 1939, which granted subsidies based on the number of children in the family to certain classes of workers. The statistical projection of the size of the families of women who had been married 10 years in 1954 shows an average increase in size of family amounting to about 25 percent for all occupational groups combined. Like all such projections, this is based on the assumption that a certain age pattern of fertility (age-specific birth rate) will persist through the period for which the projection is made, in this case through the remaining years of childbearing for the women married in 1944. To the authors, these later data on occupational fertility in France seem to indicate that there is still a significant

[20] Maurice Febvay, "Level and Trend of Fertility by Socio-occupational Groups in France," *Population*, vol. 14, no. 4, pp. 729–739, October–December, 1959.

inverse relation between economic status and the size of the family in that country.

DIFFERENTIAL FERTILITY IN GERMANY

In Germany, as in these other countries, the birth rate has varied considerably from class to class and from one residence group to another. Bertillon's data (Table 10-13) show how different quarters in Berlin and in three other European capitals differed from one another about 75 years ago. In the 1933 census, the

TABLE 10-13.   BIRTHS PER 1,000 WOMEN 15–50 YEARS OF AGE IN SECTIONS OF CITIES RATED ACCORDING TO ECONOMIC CIRCUMSTANCES

Economic circumstances	All women				Married women	
	Paris, 1889–1893	Berlin, 1886–1894	Vienna, 1890–1894	London, 1881–1890	Paris, 1889–1893	Berlin, 1886–1894
Very rich............	34	47	71	63	65	121
Rich................	53	63	107	87	94	145
Very comfortable.....	65	96	153	107	96	172
Comfortable.........	72	114	155	107	109	192
Poor................	95	129	164	140	128	198
Very poor...........	108	157	200	147	143	214

Source: Data furnished by Bertillon to Sir Arthur Newsholme and T. H. C. Stevenson for an article on "The Decline in Human Fertility as Shown by Corrected Birth Rates," *Royal Statistical Society Journal,* vol. 69, pp. 34–38, 1906.

German Statistical Office made a very comprehensive study of fertility, the results of which are of much interest.[21] In the first place, it showed that the differences in fertility between cities and small communities were still large. Thus women who lived in communities of less than 2,000 inhabitants and who had been married 21 to 25 years at the time of the 1933 census had borne an average of 3.95 children, while the women of the same duration of marriage who lived in cities of over 100,000 had borne an average of only 2.41 children. In this same duration-of-marriage group of women, 34.7 percent had families of five or more children when they lived in communities of less than 2,000, but only 12.1 percent of them had families of this size when they lived in the larger

[21] Germany, Statistisches Reichsamt, *Volkszählung vom 16 Juni 1933,* vol. 432, no. 1, Paul Schmidt, Berlin, 1937, pp. 14–41.

cities. In Berlin, only 5.1 percent of this group married 21 to 25 years had borne five or more children.

When Protestant and Catholic groups in communities of the same size were compared, it was found that a larger proportion of the women in the latter group had families of five or more than in the former. There were also fewer childless marriages among the Catholics. Unfortunately, the average number of children born to women of different religious faiths, married a given length of time, is not given.

Table 10-14 shows that there were also large differences between occupational classes in the proportion of women, married 20 years or more in 1933, who had

TABLE 10-14.   PERCENT OF MARRRIED COUPLES LIVING TOGETHER AND MARRIED IN 1913 AND EARLIER THAT HAD A GIVEN NUMBER OF CHILDREN, BY OCCUPATIONAL CLASS, GERMANY, 1933

Occupational class	Number of children					
	0	1	2	3	4	5 or more
Independent peasants........	5.3	7.7	13.1	14.3	13.1	46.5
Agricultural workers.........	5.5	6.7	10.0	11.6	12.0	54.2
Agricultural officials.........	7.8	15.0	24.8	19.6	12.6	20.2
Independent workers.........	8.6	12.8	19.6	17.4	13.0	28.6
Independent workers in trade and commerce............	12.4	16.6	22.1	17.3	11.2	20.4
Professions.................	13.5	17.9	24.6	18.5	10.8	14.7
Administrative officials......	10.3	20.0	26.3	18.5	10.9	14.0
Laborers...................	7.9	11.6	16.8	15.9	12.9	34.9

Source: Germany, Statistisches Reichsamt, *Volkszählung vom 16 Juni 1933*, vol. 452, no. 1, Paul Schmidt, Berlin, 1937, p. 33.

borne given numbers of children. Among the wives of white-collar workers large proportions had borne no child or only one or two children, and small proportions had borne four children or more, while among the hand workers (including farmers) smaller proportions had borne none or one or two children and much larger proportions had borne four or more.

A close association also appeared between the ownership of land and the size of the family, even in the nonagricultural occupations, where the duration of marriage was 20 years or more. Thus, even in the professions, only 9.7 percent of the women were childless if the couples owned land, while 15.2 percent were childless if the couple did not own land. Moreover, 53.5 percent of the landowning couples had three or more children, while only 39.7 percent of the couples not owning land had three or more children. The differences in fertility between owners and nonowners of land were proportionally much the same for most occupational groups; even the laborers in agriculture had larger families when they owned land than when they did not. Land ownership may not be a cause of these differences. They may be the effect of differences in age and economic status associated with ownership.

These studies of fertility in Germany leave no doubt that rather large differentials in fertility still existed between social classes and area groups in Germany as late as 1933 and that in general, the lower the economic and social status, the greater was the fertility. Some income data given by Burgdörfer, however, led him to believe that in the cities this pattern might be undergoing a change.[22] He found that the number of children increased as the size of the taxable income increased if the community had 10,000 or more inhabitants. He believed this increase was sufficiently consistent to warrant the statement that the number of children for whom tax exemption could be claimed increased as income increased in these communities. However, since the age of the people in the different income classes and the length of time they had been married were not standardized, some uncertainty must remain as to this positive relationship between size of family and size of income—the larger the income the larger the family. There would seem to be little doubt, however, that the differentials in fertility between the poorer and the well-to-do classes in German cities were diminishing. They may even have been positive by 1933, as regards certain occupational and income classes.

DIFFERENTIAL FERTILITY IN SWEDEN

In connection with the development of a national population policy (see also Chapter 20), a special study of fertility was made in Sweden in 1936, the results of which are summarized in Table 10-15. This table shows some small variations from the usual inverse relation between income and the size of family. The largest number of children born alive was found, as a rule, in the income class $250 to $375 (1,000 to 1,500 crowns), although among farmers, farm laborers, and salaried employees in cities the maximum size of family was reached at the next higher income level ($375 to $500) but in no case at an income level in excess of $500 (2,000 crowns), except among farmers, where the maximum occurred at the level of $500 to $750. (The excess at this higher income was extremely small, 0.03 of a child.) From the maximum at these relatively modest incomes the number of children generally declined in the income classes $750 to $1,250 and $1,250 to $2,500 and was lowest of all in the latter class, except for farmers. In several groups, however, when the income was in excess of $2,500— the well-to-do group—the number of children rose slightly above that in the

[22] Friedrich Burgdörfer, *Volk ohne Jugend*, 3d ed., Vowinkel, Berlin, 1935, p. 59.

$1,250–$2,500 level, but in no case did it rise as high as in the $750–$1,250 income group. Thus, while the inverse relation between income and size of family in Sweden was much more common in 1936 than the positive relation, it can be said that there are enough exceptions as between the group with an income in excess of $2,500 and the next lower ($1,250–$2,500) income group

TABLE 10-15. AVERAGE NUMBER OF CHILDREN BORN ALIVE IN MARRIAGES HAVING A DURATION OF 20 TO 35 YEARS, BY OCCUPATION, RESIDENCE, AND INCOME OF HUSBAND, SWEDEN, 1936

Occupation	Residence	Income of husband							
		Under $150	$150–$250	$250–$375	$375–$500	$500–$750	$750–$1,250	$1,250–$2,500	$2,500 and over
All classes........	Country	4.12	3.85	4.33	4.31	4.01	3.60	3.12	3.32
	City	3.12	3.01	3.38	3.31	3.28	2.92	2.53	2.68
Farmers, agricul-	Country	4.30	3.98	4.35	4.69	4.72	4.38	3.97	4.35
tural patrons	City	4.30	3.17	3.39	3.85	3.78	3.79	——	
Farm laborers.....	Country	4.92	3.83	5.04	5.39	5.08	——	——	——
	City	——	——	5.09	4.40				
Other independent	Country	3.73	3.62	3.86	3.76	3.55	3.33	3.16	3.14
patrons	City	3.18	3.07	3.34	3.29	3.06	2.88	2.72	2.76
Officials and sala-	Country	3.63	2.86	4.07	3.38	3.21	3.27	2.75	3.04
ried employees	City	2.70	2.77	2.62	3.09	2.85	2.84	2.55	2.64
Laborers in indus-	Country	4.16	3.93	4.25	3.96	3.95	3.62	3.37	——
try	City	3.61	3.49	3.82	3.51	3.44	3.04	2.33	——
Other laborers.....	Country	4.55	4.00	4.48	4.37	3.75	3.33	2.67	——
	City	3.33	3.29	3.40	3.43	3.36	2.90	2.26	——

Source: Sweden, Statistiska Centralbyrån, Statistisk Årsbok for Sverige, 1941, P. A. Norstedt & Söner, Stockholm, 1941, pp. 32–34. The Swedish crown has been converted into dollars at the rate of 4 to 1. It should not be inferred, however, that the level of living at a given income in Sweden is the same as at this same income in the United States. Four crowns would undoubtedly buy considerably more of many kinds of goods in Sweden in 1936 than 1 dollar would buy in the United States.

to suggest that these differentials in fertility according to income may be positive for certain occupational groups.

The chief points made in an earlier careful and detailed investigation of the relation of fertility to social and economic status in Stockholm just after World War I may be quoted here.[23]

[23] Karl A. Edin and Edward P. Hutchinson, Studies of Differential Fertility in Sweden, P. S. King & Staples, Ltd., London, 1935, pp. 85–90.

The observed fertility rates increased without exception from the lowest to the highest educational groups. The validity of this observation was confirmed by demonstrating:

1. That the fertility differentials were not produced by a more favorable age distribution or a less frequent employment of wives in the more educated groups

2. That they were not merely a result of the better economic position of the more educated

3. That they were not a product of temporary changes in fertility during the postwar years (World War I)

4. That in all probability they were not the result of social-class differences in the number of children born to wives before the observed marriages (illegitimate children plus children of former marriages)

These findings are very significant, for they strongly reinforce other data indicating that a change from an inverse to a positive relation between social status and income, on the one hand, and fertility, on the other, may be taking place; but certainly for Sweden as a whole this change is not as well established as for Stockholm shortly after World War I.

SUMMARY

We do not need to add further facts regarding the differential birth rate. Everywhere in Europe and in countries settled by Europeans there are still marked differentials between the different economic and social classes in the population. The latest data available indicate that these differentials are still preponderantly inverse, namely, that the lower the socioeconomic status, the larger is the family.

At present, the chief differentials in most countries appear to be as follows: (1) If the population is divided into hand workers and white-collar workers, the former have significantly higher fertility. (2) If hand workers are divided into farmers and others, the farmers generally have the higher fertility, although this may not hold as regards some particular groups of nonagricultural hand workers, e.g., miners and unskilled laborers. (3) Within this group of nonagricultural hand workers it would appear that the less skilled and those whose work is harder and dirtier—who in general have a lower socioeconomic status—have larger families than those whose work is more skilled, less onerous, and cleaner— the upper blue-collar class. (4) Within the white-collar class it appears that some of the lower-paid groups not infrequently have smaller families than the better-paid groups. (This appears to us a partial explanation of the lower average size of the family at some of the middle-income and rental intervals than at the higher-income intervals such as was found in several studies for different countries.) (5) When amount of education is taken as a criterion for classifying people by socioeconomic status, those with smaller amounts of schooling generally have larger families than those with more education.

It is the authors' opinion that the differentials in fertility discussed here—those which have prevailed for two or three generations in most Western countries and which still predominate—are largely the consequence of the fact that certain classes in the community were more strongly motivated to limit the size of their families than other classes and that these same classes were also possessed of the best facilities to control conception effectively. The classes that first gained control over fertility lived predominantly in the cities and were generally of better-than-average socioeconomic status. However, the knowledge of conception control spread gradually and with unequal speed—first to other urban groups of lower socioeconomic status, and later to rural groups. As this took place, fertility declined in all classes, but for some time it continued to decline more rapidly in the upper socioeconomic classes. There is some evidence that more recently the decline in fertility has become more rapid in the less-favored socioeconomic classes and that as a consequence, the differentials in fertility have become smaller.

SUGGESTIONS FOR SUPPLEMENTARY READING

Berent, Jerzy: "Fertility and Social Mobility," *Population Studies*, vol. 5, no. 3, pp. 244–260, 1950.

Carr-Saunders, A. M.: *A Survey of Social Conditions in England and Wales as Illustrated by Statistics*, Oxford University Press, Fair Lawn, N.J., 1958. (A revised and enlarged 3d edition of *A Survey of the Social Structure of England and Wales*, 1927 and 1937.)

Carter, Cedric O.: "Changing Patterns of Differential Fertility in Northwest Europe and in North America," *Eugenics Quarterly*, vol. 9, no. 3, pp. 147–150, 1962.

Glass, D. V., and E. Grebenik: *The Trend and Pattern of Fertility in Great Britain: A Report on the Family Census of 1946*. Papers of the Royal Commission on Population, H.M. Stationery Office, London, 1954, part I, Report; part II, tables.

Hatt, Paul K.: *Backgrounds of Human Fertility in Puerto Rico*, Princeton University Press, Princeton, N.J., 1952.

Innes, John Warwick: *Class Fertility in England and Wales*, Princeton University Press, Princeton, N.J., 1938.

Rosenthal, Eric: "Jewish Fertility in the United States," in American Jewish Committee, *American Jewish Yearbook, 1961*, vol. 62, pp. 3–27, 1961. (A summary and analysis of recent data on fertility by religious groups, in relation to demographic and socioeconomic characteristics, in the United States; international comparisons. Review of current Jewish attitudes toward family planning and prospective trends.)

CHAPTER ELEVEN

Some Factors Affecting Fertility

As we have already noted at several points in preceding chapters, there is no convincing evidence of any biological change in any population regarding which we have knowledge that would inevitably result in a lower fecundity than has prevailed for ages past. The well-proved changes in fertility were, until very recently, confined largely to peoples of Europe living west of a line drawn, let us say, from Trieste on the Adriatic to Danzig on the Baltic and to the people who migrated from this region during the past three centuries to settle other parts of the world. Several exceptions must be made to this general statement. The Latin American countries in Central and South America still have some of the highest authenticated birth rates in the world. On the other hand, the populations of Poland, the U.S.S.R., and Japan must now be added to the peoples whose fertility has declined greatly during the past century. As of 1962, one is probably justified in saying that about one-third of the world's people now have crude birth rates of around 25 per 1,000 or under. These are the low-birth-rate peoples at the present time. In many of them the rates are in the lower twenties and higher teens. People with birth rates of 26 to 34 inclusive may conveniently be regarded as having medium rates. These medium-birth-rate peoples constitute a comparatively small proportion of the world's population today, perhaps from 6 to 10 percent. Much the largest part of the world's people still have high birth rates, i.e., birth rates of 35 and over. These peoples probably constitute about 60 percent of the total.

It is important to note that although in most of the West declining birth rates have been closely associated with the increasing and more effective practice of contraception, this practice is not the cause of the decline in the birth rate; it is only the means most generally employed by the low-birth-rate peoples to keep the size of their families within the range considered desirable. In very general terms, the cause of the decline in fertility consists of all those changes in social and psychological factors that lead people to want fewer births in their own families than would occur if nature were allowed to take its course. We cannot even enumerate the reasons that have led great masses of people to adopt, voluntarily, measures for the control of conception. Motives vary greatly from couple to couple and from group to group. Thus, in spite of considerable investigation of the social and psychological factors affecting fertility, only a little is known about them as yet. We shall discuss here only a few of those changes which appear to be of prime importance in helping to determine the size of the family desired in modern industrial societies.

DECLINE IN THE DEATH RATES

In the first place, we would call attention (Chapters 12 and 13) to the great decline in the death rate which has taken place in the West. This began perhaps as much as a century and a half or two centuries ago in some countries, but most of the decline has taken place since about 1850. Since World War II, most other countries in the world have also had rapidly declining death rates. (See Chapters 15 and 16.) This decline in the death rate has unquestionably been an important factor leading many people in the more industrialized countries to undertake the voluntary control of the size of their families. The significance of a high death rate for reproduction can be shown quite briefly and clearly by comparing the number of female survivors at selected ages from 1,000 female births for several countries at different dates. A decimal point preceding the last figure will give the percent of survivors.

Country	Female life-table survivors by age from 1,000 female births			Life expectancy at birth in years
	15	30	45	
United States:				
1900–1902	803	734	641	51
1960	970	960	932	73
Sweden:				
1816–1840	719	652	553	44
1959	981	974	955	75
Ceylon:				
1920–1922	576	466	346	31
1954	848	810	758	59
Mexico:				
1930	581	507	416	34
1940	671	595	498	40

The earliest fairly reliable life tables for the United States are those of 1900–1902, and even these are based on data from a few states only and must be regarded with some reservations as giving a true picture of survival in the country as a whole. These tables show that approximately 803 out of each 1,000 females born would live to 15 years of age at the death rates then prevailing and that only about 734 would survive to 30 years of age and 641 to 45 years of age, i.e., through their childbearing period. The expectation of life at birth for white females was only 51.08 years. The corresponding figures for nonwhite females are 624, 496, and 423, respectively,[1] and their expectation of life at birth was only 35.04 years. Stolnitz[2] has calculated a life table for the native white women in the United States, 1885 to 1889, which shows survival rates about 6 percent lower than in 1900. Such survival rates, low as they seem to us now, were high as compared with all but a few other countries at that time.

Sweden and Norway probably had the best health conditions in Europe from 1751 onwards, but in spite of this in Sweden, from 1816 to 1840, of 1,000 females born, only 719 lived to 15 years of age and only 652 to age 30, while only 553 lived to the end of their childbearing period. In the 50 to 60 years following 1840 (1891 to 1900) these numbers rose to 809, 744, and 668, respectively (not shown in preceding tabulation), and at this later date in Sweden, the expectation of life for females at time of birth was only a little over 52 years but was from 5 to 10 years higher than in most other Western European countries.[3] In 1960 in the United States, out of each 1,000 white females born, 970 survived to age 15, 960 to age 30, and 932 to age 45. The survival rates in Sweden (1959) at the same ages were 981, 974, and 955, respectively.

In contrast to the survival rates in Sweden and the United States, it will be of interest to note those for Ceylon and Mexico.[4] In Ceylon in 1920–1922, only 576 out of each 1,000 females born lived to 15 years of age, only 466 lived to 30 years of age, while only 346 survived to 45 years of age. In Mexico in 1930, the corresponding figures were 581, 507, and 416. Although these figures should be regarded as only approximate, they show clearly that in Ceylon and Mexico only a few years ago scarcely more than one-half of the females born lived to reproductive age and that during the early reproductive years the wastage of life was still very high.

Furthermore, if age-specific birth rates in Ceylon have remained constant from 1920–1922 to 1954, as is highly probable, most families with mothers married five to ten years in 1954 have more young dependents to support than

---

[1] U.S. Department of Health, Education, and Welfare, *Vital Statistics of the United States, 1958*, vol. 1, pp. 3–5.
[2] George J. Stolnitz, *Life Tables from Limited Data: A Demographic Approach*, Princeton University Press, Princeton, N.J., 1956, p. 144.
[3] Axel Gustav Sundbärg, *Bevölkerungsstatistik Schwedens*, 1750–1900, P. A. Norstedt & Söer, Stockholm, 1907, pp. 152 and 154.
[4] United Nations, *Demographic Yearbook, 1957*, pp. 593 and 597.

did families with mothers of the same duration of marriage in 1920–1922. This point is not generally realized by the people who have heretofore had high birth rates and high death rates. But even in many of these countries and also in those which have been slowly industrializing for decades, the declining death rate is and has been raising the practical problem of how to support the larger family, although the great majority of the people may not realize that young dependents are more numerous than in the past. This increase in young dependents is by no means the only change, and perhaps not the chief change, that leads economically developing peoples to desire to control their families. But the daily problems it creates for the family are widely felt. There are many other social and economic factors that promote interest in the control of the size of the family more directly than the decline in the death rate, but this decline must be regarded as one of the underlying factors in the whole social complex which has led to the increasing adoption of voluntary control of the size of the family in modern industrializing societies. (See Chapter 5.)

ABORTION

Abortion has always been and still is a significant factor in determining the birth rate.[5] It is discussed here as a *social* factor of importance because the extent to which it is used in any society depends upon the cultural values of that society.

The Extent of Abortion.   Dr. Wiehl, who reviewed the evidence on abortion in the United States in 1938, concluded that about 15 percent of all pregnancies terminated in abortions and that about two-thirds of these were spontaneous and one-third were induced.[6]

Taussig shows that there are wide variations in the estimates of the amount of induced abortion in different countries and regions. He believes that in the United States about one-third of all abortions were induced and that somewhat over one-half of these were illegal, while somewhat fewer were therapeutic. Since therapeutic abortions are generally performed where the life or health of the expectant mother is at stake, they may be assumed to have comparatively little effect on the size of the population; often one life is saved while the other is lost, and there is no net change. Most illegal abortions and many spontaneous abortions, on the other hand, not only result in direct pregnancy wastage and thus reduce the birth rate but in many cases affect the health of the woman adversely and not infrequently result in permanent sterility or death.[7]

[5] In medical parlance, abortion includes spontaneous miscarriage as well as induced abortion.
[6] Dorothy G. Wiehl, "A Summary of Data on Reported Incidence of Abortion," *Milbank Memorial Fund Quarterly*, vol. 16, p. 88, 1938.
[7] Frederick J. Taussig in "The Abortion Problem," *Proceedings of the Conference Held under the Auspices of the National Committee on Maternal Health, Inc.*, The Williams & Wilkins Company, Baltimore, 1944, p. 39.

It is not possible to estimate the total number of abortions in any Western population with accuracy, but if 15 percent of *all* pregnancies end in abortion in the United States this means approximately 18 abortions per 100 live births; then with about 4,258,000 live births in 1960, there would have been over 766,000 abortions. It is not known how many of the spontaneous abortions, which constitute much the largest class, are preventable or how many of the illegal and therapeutic abortions prevented a normal live birth. But there can be no reasonable doubt that the number of live births would be significantly larger if all preventable spontaneous abortions were eliminated and if there were no illegal abortions; at a guess, there might be an increase of between 300,000 and 500,000 more live births in the United States annually. We would not minimize the importance of abortion in reducing the birth rate or its injurious effects on the health of women, but we can be reasonably certain that abortion has only a small effect in reducing the birth rate as compared with the practice of contraception. Moreover, abortion is probably becoming less and less important as the *effective* use of contraception increases.

The authors know of no reliable evidence that the rate of abortion has been increasing over what it was in the past in those countries where the birth rate has been falling (except Japan). Hence there is no basis for regarding it as a highly important factor in the decline of the birth rate in these countries in recent decades. In Japan, though, until the Restoration (1868), it had long been sanctioned by public opinion, and since World War II it has been legalized and is performed for the most part by physicians in public hospitals (see Chapter 20). It should be said in passing that most of the people in Japan who believe that a relatively slow growth of population is of benefit to the nation would much prefer to see contraception replace abortion as the dominant means of limiting the size of the family, but they accept abortion as a lesser evil than the overpopulation which would certainly soon become more burdensome if abortion were made illegal. Most Japanese physicians believe that the legalization of abortion for personal and for social and economic reasons has greatly reduced the health hazards accompanying illegal abortion in the past, since most abortions are now performed openly, under good sanitary conditions, and before the end of the third month of pregnancy. (See Japan in Chapter 20.)

CHILDLESSNESS IN THE UNITED STATES

There can be no reasonable doubt that in most Western countries the proportion of all married couples who were childless had been increasing for some decades preceding World War II and that childlessness was a factor of importance in reducing birth rates. The recent rise in the birth rate in several of these countries has been accompanied by a decrease in childlessness. As far as the authors know, no thorough investigation has ever been made which shows "normal" childlessness among married couples where there was no voluntary control of conception. Some data, however, show childlessness under conditions more or less closely approximating uncontrolled conception. These seem to indicate that under certain conditions the normal proportion of childless couples may be as low as 2 or 3 percent, although most figures are somewhat higher. Only a few data from such studies can be given here, and their results do not enable us to say positively what proportion of married couples are involuntarily childless (infecund).

Crum, in examining genealogical records of New England families, found: "In the seventeenth and eighteenth centuries less than two per cent of the wives were childless; in the first half of the nineteenth century the proportion jumped to over four per cent, and this latter figure had doubled by 1870 to 1879."[8] Certainly by 1870 to 1879, voluntary childlessness must have become a factor of some importance in lowering the birth rate in New England, and it may well have entered the picture at an earlier date in the group Crum was studying.

In the report of the Immigration Commission,[9] Hill found that 7.4 percent of all women included in his sample, married 10 to 20 years and under 45 years of age at the time of the census of 1900, had never borne a child. But he also found great differences in the proportions in rural and urban areas and between native and foreign-born women. In Cleveland 8.1 percent of all the women in the tabulation who were under 45 years of age at the time of the 1900 census, and who had been married 10 to 20 years, reported that they had never borne a child. In the rural areas of Ohio the percentage for the group with the same characteristics was 5.2. In Minneapolis the proportion of all such women who were childless was slightly higher than in Cleveland, 8.5 percent, but in rural Minnesota it was only 3 percent.

The results of the Indianapolis study bearing on the proportion of voluntary and involuntary childlessness which are of interest to us here may be summarized as follows:[10] There were 322 couples, or 16.3 percent of all couples, who never had a conception. Of these 194, or 9.8 percent, were judged to be unable to conceive, while 128 could have conceived if they had never made any effort to prevent conception. Thus only about 60 percent of the childless couples in this study were judged to be infecund, while 40 percent were voluntarily childless. It should be noted here that the basis on which these couples were selected— white, Protestant, a minimum of 8 years elementary education, living in

[8] Frederick S. Crum, "The Decadence of the Native American Stock," *American Statistical Association Journal*, vol. 14, n.s., no. 107, p. 218, 1914.

[9] Joseph A. Hill, "Comparative Fecundity of Women of Native and Foreign Parentage in the United States," *Publications of the American Statistical Association*, vol. 13, pp. 583–604, 1913.

[10] P. K. Whelpton and Clyde V. Kiser, "Social and Psychological Factors Affecting Fertility: VIII. The Comparative Influence on Fertility of Contraception and Impairments of Fecundity," *Milbank Memorial Fund Quarterly*, vol. 26, no. 2, pp. 224–225, 1948.

Indianapolis, women married under 30, a marriage duration of 12 to 15 years, and most of their married life spent in a city—probably resulted in a larger proportion of infecund couples than would have been found in a representative sample of the city's population.

In the United States since the Indianapolis study was made, we have obtained a large amount of information regarding childlessness in the studies by the Bureau of the Census on fertility already referred to in the preceding chapter. Some of the findings are highly pertinent here and will be used though their citation involves some repetition.

In 1910 in the United States as a whole, 10 percent of the ever-married native white women 45–49 years of age were childless; by 1940, for the women having

TABLE 11-1.   PERCENT OF NATIVE WHITE WOMEN EVER MARRIED, 45–49 YEARS OF AGE, FOR WOMEN REPORTING ON NUMBER OF CHILDREN EVER BORN, WHO WERE CHILDLESS; BY RESIDENCE, UNITED STATES, 1960, 1950, 1940, AND 1910

Year	Total	Urban	Rural-farm
1960*	17.1	18.3	11.5
1950†	18.2	19.9	12.1
1940‡	15.7	19.0	9.0
1910‡	10.0	12.9	6.4

* U.S. Bureau of the Census, *Population, 1960, Detailed Characteristics,* United States Summary, table 190.
† U.S. Bureau of the Census, *Population, 1950, Fertility,* Special Report P-E, no. 5 C, table 3, white women married once and husband present.
‡ U.S. Bureau of the Census, *Population, 1940, Differential Fertility 1940 and 1910,* tables 7 and 10, native white women ever married by number of children ever born.

the same characteristics, the percentage had risen to 15.7; and in 1950, for all white women of the same ages married once, husband present, it was 18.2 percent. In 1960, for all white women of the same ages ever married, 17.1 percent were childless (Table 11-1). Although some difference exists between native white (1910 and 1940) and all white women (1950 and 1960), this difference is probably too small to be of any significance. The small decline in childlessness between 1950 and 1960 is significant, and there can be little doubt that when the women marrying since 1945 reach the ages 45–49, we may expect a significant decline in the proportion childless both because of the larger proportion ever married and a real decline in voluntary childlessness.

When the native white women aged 45–49 in Table 11-1 are grouped by age at marriage (Table 11-2), the differences in the percentages childless are quite striking. When married under 18 years of age, only 2.4 percent of the rural-farm women were childless, whereas 4.6 percent of the urban women were childless. The proportion of childless women in both rural and urban populations rose quite rapidly as age at marriage rose, 60 percent to 80 percent higher at 18 and 19 than at under 18, and was almost three times as high when marriage took place at 20 and 21 years of age as when it took place under 18 years of age. The proportion childless when the women married at 25 and 26 years of age was practically double that when they married at 20 and 21 years of age. So far as the authors know, we have no sound basis for attributing this rapid rise in childlessness as age at marriage rises solely to biological causes. Social (cultural) factors must certainly become increasingly operative as age at marriage rises,

TABLE 11-2.   PERCENTAGES OF CHILDLESS NATIVE WHITE WOMEN AGED 45–49, MARRIED ONCE, HUSBANDS PRESENT, BY AGE AT MARRIAGE, BY URBAN AND RURAL-FARM RESIDENCE, UNITED STATES, 1940

Age at marriage	Total	Urban	Rural-farm
Under 18	3.6	4.6	2.4
18–19	6.1	7.3	4.3
20–21	10.3	12.6	6.9
22–24	13.5	15.4	8.3
25–26	19.8	22.1	12.4
27–29	25.0	27.5	18.2
30–34	36.2	40.0	24.0

Source: U.S. Bureau of the Census, Population, 1940, Differential Fertility, 1940 and 1910, table 21.

but the differences in childlessness between women who married under 18 and those who married at 18 and 19 and at 20 and 21, although no doubt due in part to premarital conceptions, are so large proportionally that we cannot help asking whether very early marriage may not have some physiological effect on fecundity as well as on fertility. In any event, there can be no reasonable doubt: (1) that the proportion of white women in the United States aged 45–49 who were childless had been increasing for several decades up to about 1950; (2) that there had long been substantial differences between urban and rural-farm married women in the proportions who had never borne a child; (3) that any substantial increase in the proportion of women marrying under 22 years of age would tend to reduce childlessness. That such a change has been taking place was shown in Table 9-10. The authors believe that the substantial increase in childlessness in the United States from about 1910 to 1945 or 1950 and the present decline in childlessness is to be regarded primarily as the consequence of changes in social attitudes regarding premarital sexual relations, desirability of early marriage, and childbearing shortly thereafter rather than as the consequence of any biological change in fecundity.

The study, *Family Planning, Sterility, and Population Growth*,[11] indicates that as many as 10 percent of the older women in this study, i.e., the women 35 to 39 years of age, have some impairment of fecundity of whom one-half were definitely sterile at the time of the study (1955). But a number of these had already had children and hence were not infecund. Probably childlessness from physiological causes lies somewhere within the range of 5 to 10 percent, but that still leaves us uncertain how many were infecund.

As we have just noted, recent experience in the United States shows that childless marriages have decreased somewhat since World War II, but impairments of fecundity arising during married life do appreciably affect the fertility of particular couples. However, "Fecundity impairments have a minor effect on birth rates in the United States. The major force keeping American families relatively small is contraception rather than subfecundity. . . . Relatively few [couples] will be unable to have any children."[12]

If earlier marriage becomes more general and remains so, the proportion of involuntarily childless couples will almost certainly decline substantially, so that childlessness will have a decreasing effect in keeping the birth rate low in the United States.

CHILDLESSNESS IN OTHER COUNTRIES

In general, European studies on childlessness, where fairly comparable with the American studies, show somewhat higher proportions of married women who are childless. In 1910 Körösy[13] found that in Budapest 22.3 percent of the marriages broken by death (1879 to 1900), where the women had been married 10 years or more, were childless. Even where the marriage had endured 30 years or more, 16.6 were childless. In Copenhagen in 1900, where the average duration of marriage was 13.5 to 15.5 years, the proportion of childless wives varied from 9 percent among workers to 11 percent among government employees and professional families.[14] In three sections of Paris (census of 1901), when the women were married at 20 to 25 years of age and had been married

[11] Ronald Freedman, Pascal K. Whelpton, and Arthur A. Campbell, *Family Planning, Sterility, and Population Growth*, McGraw-Hill Book Company, New York, 1959, p. 47.

[12] *Ibid.*, p. 55.

[13] Josef Körösy, "Weitere Beiträge zur Statistik der ehelichen Fruchtbarkeit," *Bulletin de l'institut international de statistique*, vol. 13, part 3, pp. 1–20, 1901.

[14] Lucien March, "Les Statistiques de familles," *Bulletin de l'institut international de statistique*, vol. 17, p. 218, 1907.

15 years, the proportions of families without living children varied from 14 percent in a workers' section to 21 percent in a section classed as comfortable and to 23 percent in a rich quarter. In 1901 the proportion of couples in France married more than 15 years having no living child rose steadily as the size of the community increased, from 9.6 percent of those living in communities having under 2,000 inhabitants to 17.4 percent in Paris. It should be noted that "having no living child" is not the same as "childlessness," nor does "married 10 years or more" exclude the possibility of future births.

Data on number of children borne by each woman were collected in the 1912 census of Romania.[15] Of the rural women in Romania who were married, widowed, or divorced and aged 35 to 39 at the census, only 5.4 percent were childless, while in urban communities the proportion was 18.2 percent.

A study showing childlessness among married women in Italy was made in connection with the 1931 census.[16] The following data refer to women married under 25 years of age who had lived with their husbands until the time of the census (1931) and were 45 or over at that time. In the whole of Italy, 5.2 percent of such women were childless, but the proportion childless varied from 4 percent among people attached to agriculture to 9.2 percent among professional people.

The study of fertility based on the 1911 census for England and Wales, referred to in Chapter 10, showed that 16.2 percent of the married women over 45 had never had a child.[17] This is a high proportion at that time for an entire country, but it is not surprising if we remember that even then England and Wales were more urbanized than any other country and that the proportion of childlessness among urban women is generally much higher than among rural women. The 1946 Family Census of England and Wales shows that of women "whose reproductive history was completed (women married 1900–1924) 12 percent were childless."[18]

The 1933 German data throw more light on childlessness in that country than do the data for most other countries, since both the age at marriage and the duration of the marriage are known.[19] These data show that: (1) the proportion of childless wives had been increasing since early in this century and

---

[15] Romania, Direction Générale de la Statistique, *Bulletin statistique de la Romaine,* ser. 4, vol. 16, no. 6-7, p. 102, 1921.

[16] Italy, Instituto Central de Statistica, *Notiziario demografico, Rassegna mensile dati e noticie sulle populazioni dell' Italia e degli altri paesi,* vol. 8, no. 8, p. 221, Rome, 1955.

[17] Great Britain, Census Office, *Fertility of Marriage,* part 2, p. xliii, H.M. Stationery Office, London, 1923. (Census of England and Wales, 1911, vol. 13.)

[18] E. Lewis-Faning, *Report on an Enquiry into Family Limitation and Its Influence on Human Fertility during the Past Fifty Years,* Papers of the Royal Commission on Population, vol. 1, H.M. Stationery Office, London, 1949, p. 85.

[19] Germany, Statistisches Reichsamt, *Volkszählung vom 16 Juni 1933,* vol. 452, no. 1, Paul Schmidt, Berlin, 1937, pp. 9–48.

that the increase was far more rapid in large cities than in rural areas; (2) the proportion of childless wives mounted very rapidly as age at marriage increased, especially at ages above 25; (3) in the same areas there was little difference in the proportion of childlessness among Evangelical and Catholic populations; (4) the proportion of childless women increased steadily and rapidly as social status improved, social status being measured here by type of occupation, beginning with the peasantry and agricultural labor as the lowest and proceeding to the professions and those of independent means; (5) fewer wives of landowners than of nonlandowners were childless; and finally, (6) the proportion of childless wives apparently had been mounting rapidly in the 10 to 15 years prior to 1933, if it is assumed that women married 10 to 15 years and still childless at that time (1933) would never have a child. The proportion of wives married in 1918 and childless in 1933 was 17.4 percent and of those married in 1923, the percentage had risen to 28.8.

The most recent data which the authors have been able to find showing the proportions of childless women in a number of countries are those in the United Nations *Demographic Yearbook*, 1959, Tables 6 and 7, pages 168 to 194. Unfortunately the data given there are not highly comparable, since those for some countries are for *all* women, while for other countries they relate only to *ever-married* women. The lowest proportion of women childless in a fairly large population was 3.2 percent in the Philippines and relates to *ever-married* women only, 45 years of age and over in 1958. This came from a sample study of the population. Other very low proportions were: 5.7 percent in Guinea (1955) for *all* women 45–49; 7.1 percent in Malaysia (1957), *all* women 45–49; and 8.9 percent *ever-married* women, Japan, 1950. At the other end of the range, the highest proportion of *all* women aged 45–49 who were childless was found in Cuba, 23.1, followed closely by Mexico (1950), 21.4 percent, and Venezuela (1950), 21.5 percent. These latter proportions are substantially higher for *all* women than those of France (1954), 17.4 percent, and Hungary (1949), 15 percent, and slightly higher than for the United Kingdom (1951), 20.6 percent. The authors doubt that Cuba, Mexico, and Venezuela have a substantially higher proportion of *all* women aged 45–49 who are childless than do most European countries.

GROWTH OF INTELLECTUAL FREEDOM

Many very significant changes in the social and intellectual atmosphere of Western Europe, which had been gaining momentum since the Renaissance, became even more potent in the eighteenth and nineteenth centuries as industrialization proceeded. A growing body of people was coming to realize that man could exercise a large measure of control over many events of the utmost importance to his welfare. As long as men followed tradition and regarded a large part of what happened to them as outside the field of human control, they had little incentive to undertake deliberately significant economic and social changes. Intellectually, there had been little interest in the causal relations between social and economic events and human behavior. Morally, the man of the Middle Ages was conditioned to accept tradition and dogma unquestioningly. The development of an atmosphere favorable to freedom of thought and experimentation had taken place, and gradually it became a basic factor in the modern era of scientific achievement and of the use of science to increase human welfare.[20] This greater freedom of thought in due course led to the agricultural and industrial revolutions, to the French Revolution, and to a new type of political organization.

- This growth of a new intellectual atmosphere may at first seem irrelevant to the explanation of how a large part of the people in the Western world have come to look favorably upon the voluntary control of the size of the family. We believe, however, that this gradual emancipation of the human mind from the fetters of tradition and dogma was a very important factor in changing the attitudes of many Western peoples toward reproduction in the eighteenth and nineteenth centuries. To mention only one important change, the "emancipation" of women and all that this term implies as to change in woman's place in Western civilization will leave no one in doubt that such a transformation in woman's status could not have taken place as rapidly as it did after about 1850 without long intellectual preparation. When women began to demand personal rights analogous to those of men, they needed to take only a relatively short step to the demand that they have a vote in determining how many children they would bear. To ignore the change in the general intellectual atmosphere which made women demand rights as persons is to overlook one of the underlying causal factors in the decline in the birth rate.

GROWTH IN PRODUCTIVITY

As science was applied to the problems of production in the eighteenth and early nineteenth century, great progress was made in reducing the amount of human labor needed to yield a given amount of goods both in agriculture and in industry and also in the labor required to move these goods from place to place. These revolutions soon made possible a slow change in the distribution of labor. Less labor was needed for the mere necessities of life; hence more labor could be devoted to science and to the arts and to the services and goods which contributed to man's welfare and thus tended to reduce the death rate. But such a change for the better could not be permanent unless it was accompanied by a

[20] See quotation from Malthus in Chap. 2, p. 34.

reduction in the birth rate. This principle is the point Malthus was intent upon hammering home.

SCIENCE AND HEALTH

In addition to the reduction in the death rate arising from the improvement of economic conditions, science began in due time to study the problems of health directly and after about 1850, but especially after 1880, contributed to the control of the infectious diseases with a degree of effectiveness not hitherto dreamed of.

Under the conditions prevailing in Western Europe in the latter half of the eighteenth and the first half of the nineteenth century, it is not surprising that an increasing proportion of the people began to discuss more and more openly the control of the size of their own families as a means of avoiding the hardships which Malthus and a number of other thoughtful persons regarded as more or less inevitable if the birth rate remained uncontrolled. Had there not been a rapidly growing appreciation of the value of science in making good health possible and of the importance of an economic minimum for maintaining a healthy family, the voluntary control of the size of the family by the use of contraception almost certainly could not have developed as rapidly as it did from about 1850 to the present time.

AMBITION

It is quite generally recognized that most people who have a good social and economic status are highly desirous of maintaining it and will strive hard to prepare their children to maintain a similar status. Likewise, as freedom of thought increases, many people who have a less desirable position will revolt against their lowly status and will try hard to improve it and to enable their children to enjoy the benefits of a better status even though they themselves cannot achieve it. If we call this urge to maintain or secure a good social status "ambition," then we may say that ambition is one of the most important of all factors leading to the voluntary control of the size of the family. Dumont (see Chapter 3) called this process of moving upward in the social system "social capillarity." It is also probable that the differences in the degree of ambition found in different countries and in different social and economic groups will go far to explain the differentials in fertility described in the preceding chapter. It requires little argument to convince anyone that the great majority of couples with a good social and economic status will much more easily prevent the loss of that status or maintain it and ensure somewhat the same status to their children if families are relatively small. This is even more true of couples that are themselves trying to rise in social position and to ensure an improved status to their children. Therefore, in a society where there is strong competition to maintain and/or improve social status and where safe and simple means of preventing conception are widely known, the restriction of the size of the family is likely to spread rather rapidly.

Rural-Urban Differentials. One of the most important differentials in fertility has been shown to be that between farm people and city people. A scrutiny of some of the differing effects of ambition in rural and urban populations may help us to understand the differences in fertility between these residence groups during the past several decades.

In the United States, a large proportion of city dwellers, both native and foreign-born, have been migrants or the children of migrants from rural-farm communities. The completely different situations in which these migrants to cities found themselves rendered their traditional beliefs and modes of conduct quite inadequate as guides to many types of behavior of vital importance in their new abode. Under such conditions they were assailed by a vast number of new suggestions which might or might not contribute to a reasonably satisfactory personal and family adjustment in their new and more complex urban environment. They saw differences in modes of living, in incomes, in types of work, in power wielded, in leisure, and in opportunity which the stay-at-home rural dweller or the second-generation city dweller did not encounter in such compulsive and distracting forms, if at all.

The complexities of modern city life are highly stimulating and offer many opportunities for personal development and advancement which do not exist in agricultural communities, but at the same time they are highly confusing to a great many people because they put so many decisive choices up to individuals who can count on little guidance from tradition or experience in making their choices. It is not surprising, therefore, that personal ambitions (using this term in a broad sense) all too often provide the dominating motive in establishing the pattern of family life and hence exercise much influence in determining the size of the family.

We have already pointed out in other connections that the fertility differential between urban and rural women and especially between city and farm women is highly persistent and remains proportionally large in spite of a decline in the absolute size of this differential. This fact is dismissed by too many people with the simple statement that the differential is diminishing and will therefore probably soon vanish. This may be true. However, in 1960 *all* ever-married *urban* women in the United States aged 45–49 had borne 2,153 children per 1,000 as compared with 3,347 per 1,000 for the same category of women in the *rural-farm* population—a difference of 55 percent. Rural women, and especially farm women, have long been and are still contributing a substantially larger proportion of children to the next generation than they themselves constituted of their own generation. One of the important reasons for this difference may be found in the differing intensity of ambition or in the different types of ambition in these groups of the population. Naturally, as the urban population becomes an increasing proportion of the total, the absolute growth of the total depends more and more on the average size of the urban family. The important point is that modern urban life more quickly and more basically disturbs the values and patterns of family life than does a simpler, more traditional agricultural environment. City people are more ready to adopt the small-family pattern because it is more conducive to the realization of their ambitions than is the larger-family pattern, which still exercises significant influence among farm people. There are a number of other reasons to expect the continuation of substantial urban-rural differentials in fertility even though they continue to diminish in absolute amount. Only a few can be mentioned here.

The higher grades of white-collar work require a long period of rather intensive training, and the incomes of workers in such jobs are relatively small until they become well established. Since most young people are eager to live as do other members of their class, and since in a great many cases they cannot possibly do so if they have children, many of them find it decidedly advantageous to postpone both marriage and/or children until they are well started on their careers. There is some evidence that this situation has been less decisive as to age at marriage and the size of the family since 1945. However, the point is worthy of a brief parenthetical note here.

We have shown in Chapter 9 that in the United States the recovery from low birth rates of the 1930s and the war years was more rapid in the cities (urban population) than in the farm population. Since the decline in the birth rate had also been greater in the urban population than in the farm population, it would be reasonable to expect a somewhat earlier birth-rate recovery in the urban and rural-nonfarm population than in the rural-farm population. Moreover, in our opinion there has been a strong element of "keeping up with the Joneses" in the rise of the birth rate after the war and its continuance at about the same level until 1959. It became fashionable to marry young and to have children—often three or four—almost as fast as was physiologically possible. It is not surprising, therefore, that temporarily this fashion in family formation first became manifest in the urban population or that it most quickly prevailed there over the longer-run interest in maintaining social and economic status and in giving one's children adequate educational opportunities. Even so, in 1955 the GAF study[21] showed that the *expected* size of family for couples living on a farm was 3.7 children as compared with 3.1 for the rural-nonfarm couples and 2.9 for the urban couples. Thus the expected families of farm women were

[21] Freedman et al., *op. cit.*, p. 314.

28 percent higher than those of urban couples and 19 percent higher than those of rural-nonfarm couples. It is also probable that urban couples practice contraception somewhat more effectively than do farm couples. If so, the expected differences may be less than the actual differences.

A steadily growing amount of information, as yet unorganized and inconclusive, indicates that many of these urban and rural-nonfarm couples, whose children are now reaching high school and college age, are beginning to realize that the cost of giving three or four children, closely spaced, the education and training they need to maintain the family's social and economic status is beyond their means. Although it cannot be stated as a fact, it may very well be that this realization is now reaching back to younger couples and is one of the important factors in the current decline in the crude birth rate of the United States. In the year ending August 31, 1963, the crude birth rate was 21.9, whereas it was 24.3 for the calendar year 1958, a decline of 10 percent in five years. That younger couples are probably being influenced by the considerations noted above is also suggested by the fact that in the 1960 GAF study the younger women (under 25 years of age) desired somewhat smaller families than did women of the same age in the 1955 GAF study.[22]

In contrast to the young man getting a start in the city, the young man in the country is more likely to be quite as able to start his family in his early twenties as he will ever be. His physical vigor is near the maximum, and he has generally acquired sufficient training to enable him to handle his job satisfactorily. Furthermore, not only are his wife and children not a handicap to his success, as is often true in the city, but his wife is the economic equivalent of the working wife in the city. In addition, the farm woman's children do not constitute so serious a handicap to her in making a substantial contribution to the economic well-being of her family. The handicap of children from the standpoint of the attainment of the respect of the community is therefore a less compelling reason for family limitation among farm people than among many classes of city people.

The farm family also remains a more closely knit economic and social unit than the city family. All members of the farm family work at a common task, and each can readily see that his particular work contributes to the welfare of all members of the family and that in return he receives many services from the others. This cooperation contributes substantially to the feeling of family unity. Besides, the social life of farm communities is still organized around the family unit to a greater extent than in the city, although this situation, too, is changing somewhat.

[22] This 1960 GAF study has not yet been published. Professor Whelpton of the Scripps Foundation provided this information and authorized its mention here. For certain other aspects of recent changes in the United States birth rate see P. K. Whelpton, "Why Did the United States' Crude Birth Rate Decline during 1957–1962?" *Population Index*, April, 1963.

Another point to be considered is that general farming, which still supports the great majority of our farmers, is a 365-day job and that 8-hour days are unknown during the greater part of the year. Such farming requires that the farmer and his wife be at home most of the day and almost every day. Since they must be at home nearly all the time in any event to look after crops and stock, they do not find that children add materially to their immobility. Among city people, however, and in spite of automobiles, children do add considerably to the immobility imposed upon the parents by the nature of their jobs and hours of work and by the added imposition of the children's regular school attendance.

It should be said, however, that specialty farming as contrasted with general farming is steadily growing in importance and that the portion of the farm population so engaged tends more and more to approximate the rural-non-farm population in mode of life and family interests. The consolidation of farms into larger units also tends to maintain a flow of young people into semiurban or urban communities, although this stream is of decreasing importance both in absolute numbers and as a proportion of the persons needing training for urban types of work.

Other differences between urban and farm living which seem to the authors likely to be of some importance in deciding upon the size of the family are that: (1) congenial occupations for women, aside from home-making, are found largely in the city, and (2) work for the children which will be good for them both physically and morally can be provided much more readily at home in the country. If city children do any work other than attend school they must generally do it away from home where they cannot be supervised by the parents and where the parents have little or no control over the conditions of work or their companions while at work. The scarcity of useful tasks for children not only increases the economic cost of children in the city but also adds to the moral responsibility of the parents without providing them with enhanced means of discharging this responsibility.

Finally, in pointing out the differences between the country and the city which make for smaller families in the city, we should not forget that information regarding contraceptives has been until quite recently more widely disseminated in the cities than in the country. This situation has changed rapidly in recent years, although there are still many pockets in rural areas where little or nothing is known about contraception. However, even when contraception becomes as general and effective in rural areas as in urban areas, the authors doubt that the restriction in the size of the family will become as drastic in farm communities as in many groups of our city population. A family of four or five children will always interfere less with most country people living as they desire than with most city people. It should be noted, however, that with the increased use of the automobile by city workers and with the spread of utilities into rural areas, a larger and larger proportion of the nonagricultural workers are moving into suburban and even into agricultural areas where they can live a semirural life, so that the differences in living conditions between farmers and village residents on the one hand and city workers on the other are probably becoming less important than they have been during the past several decades in determining the size of the family; but the nature of farm work and farm living still remain quite distinctive.

SOME REASONS FOR THE DIFFERENTIAL BIRTH RATE IN CITIES

Ambition

When we turn to the consideration of the differences in birth rates between groups or classes within the city, these differences, too, may be explained to a significant degree by the way in which the number of children in the family affects the attainment of ambitions by the members of the different groups in the city population. It will be recalled (Chapter 10) that, in general, unskilled laborers have the largest families and that families decline in size as we pass from this group to the semiskilled, skilled, and white-collar occupations, the professional and clerical workers having the smallest families. It should not be forgotten, however, that these differences are decreasing in absolute size and that the urban people in more comfortable circumstances occasionally have somewhat larger families than do those somewhat below them on the social and economic scale.

Few people will question that the desire to maintain a good social and economic status and to ensure such a status to one's children is a more potent determinative of behavior, by and large, in the white-collar class than in the hand-working group. Moreover, in the more poorly paid white-collar groups (clerical and sales workers), the desire to have their children move into a higher social and economic position is a very powerful motive for restricting the size of the family. Hence, the additional expense involved in rearing more than one or two children is likely to prove a very heavy handicap to this lower-income segment of the white-collar class. Most of these people find it far easier to keep the family small and thus have more to spend per capita on education and the maintenance of social status than to increase their income sufficiently to care for a larger family at the desired level of living. In the past, this has also been the more certain way to assure oneself of the savings which would guarantee reasonably good living conditions in old age. With the development of social security, however, this motive may no longer be so important. But it is true that for most urban dwellers mere existence depends upon such a variety of factors—employment, prices, ability to continue at work, employer-employee relations—over which the individual has little control that each additional child adds considerably to the uncertainties of family life among a large proportion of the white-collar workers.

The extent to which life is complicated and made more difficult economically by children and particularly by more than two would seem to vary more or less directly with the difference between the way one wants to live and the kind of start he wants to give his children and the means at his disposal. Obviously, the hand laborer, who has a very modest manner of life to maintain and whose children are more often expected to follow his pattern of life with little more than the required minimum of education, has less incentive to keep his family small than does the clerical worker, who often has even less income but has to dress better, is expected to live in a higher-rent area, and in other ways must at least appear to live at a higher level. If, in addition, the clerical worker, feeling the general insignificance of his position more than the laborer because of his closer contact with the better-paid managerial and supervisory groups, decides that his children must have a rather long and expensive training for a better job than he himself holds, he has a further strong incentive to keep the family small.

Today, however, with machinery, some of it automated, taking over many of the jobs formerly held by unskilled hand workers and even by skilled workers and with the growing need of their children for more education if they are to find steady and better-paid employment, these groups may very probably soon come to feel a more urgent need to reduce the size of their families.

A large number of other situations and motives probably play a part in determining the size of families people may want. Some of these are of such a character that they operate decisively in the control of the size of the family only under particular circumstances, e.g., when the health of some member of the family is occasioning serious concern, or when some serious break in the regularity of the family income takes place. Others are of a more general character and are likely to affect large numbers of people almost simultaneously, e.g., changes in attitudes in a large population as regards the most desirable age at marriage and the best ages for the bearing of children—such changes as took place, or at least became apparent, in the United States shortly after World War II. They were in sharp contrast with the social attitudes determining age of marriage and the spacing of children which had prevailed for several decades prior to World War II and which were especially pronounced during the Depression of the 1930s. It scarcely need be said that social conditions and the attitudes they generate affect different couples quite differently, but in the aggregate they may determine decisively the level of fertility in a population in which the practice of contraception has become accepted. Under such conditions, we may expect more and quicker changes in fertility than were to be anticipated in the past.

We may convey some idea of the multiplicity of the social and psychological attitudes which it was believed might be important in determining the fertility of families by quoting the hypotheses used in the Indianapolis study which has already been referred to in several places. The number of questions in the schedule assigned to each hypothesis is indicated in each case.[23] The number of questions assigned to each hypothesis does not necessarily indicate the relative importance of the hypothesis or that these questions were used only in the study of the hypothesis to which they were considered most pertinent. This was a pioneering and exploratory study, and as such its contribution consisted more in helping to define the field of research and in demonstrating the feasibility of intensive interviews with couples (chiefly the wives) regarding the conditions which they believed played an important role in determining the size of their families than in definitely measuring the relative significance of the numerous factors regarding which information was obtained.

HYPOTHESES OF THE INDIANAPOLIS STUDY

1. The greater the difference between the actual level of living and the standard of living desired, the higher the proportion of couples practicing contraception effectively and the smaller the planned families. 19 questions.

2. The greater the feeling of economic insecurity, the higher the proportion of couples practicing contraception effectively and the smaller the planned families. 12 questions.

3. The higher the socioeconomic status, the higher the proportion of couples practicing contraception effectively and the smaller the planned families. 55 questions.

4. The greater the extent of doubling-up within families, the higher the proportion of couples practicing contraception effectively and the smaller the planned families. 10 questions.

5. The stronger the interest in, and liking for, children, the lower the proportion of couples practicing contraception effectively and the larger the planned families. 24 questions.

6. The interest of children in, and their desire for, brothers and sisters affects the size of the family. 4 questions.

7. The stronger the feeling that children interfere with personal freedom, the higher the proportion of couples practicing contraception effectively and the smaller the planned families. 23 questions.

8. The belief that an only child is handicapped is an important reason for having a second child. 4 questions.

[23] P. K. Whelpton and Clyde V. Kiser, "Social and Psychological Factors Affecting Fertility: IV. Developing the Schedules and Choosing the Type of Couples and the Area to be Studied," *Milbank Memorial Fund Quarterly*, vol. 25, no. 4, pp. 394–396, 1945.

9. The desire to ensure against childlessness is an important reason for having a second child. 4 questions.

10. Preferences regarding the sex of children affect the size of the family. 11 questions.

11. The number, size, and location of communities in which couples have lived affect the proportion practicing contraception effectively and the size of planned families. 20 questions.

12. Family and childhood situations and attitudes affect the proportion of couples practicing contraception effectively and the size of the planned families. 66 questions.

13. Conformity to group patterns affects the proportion of couples practicing contraception effectively and the size of the planned families. 16 questions.

14. The greater the adherence to traditions, the lower the proportion of couples practicing contraception effectively and the larger the planned families. 28 questions.

15. The greater the interest in religion, the lower the proportion of couples practicing contraception effectively and the larger the planned families. 28 questions.

16. The stronger the feeling of personal inadequacy, the higher the proportion of couples practicing contraception effectively and the smaller the planned families. 35 questions.

17. The greater the tendency to plan in general, the higher the proportion of couples practicing contraception effectively and the smaller the planned families. 18 questions. (Note: Hypothesis 18 has been intentionally omitted.)

19. That member of the couple who is dominant in general family matters tends also to be dominant in determining whether conception shall be controlled and the size of the planned family. 26 questions.

20. The more satisfactory the marital adjustment, the higher the proportion of couples practicing contraception effectively and the larger the planned families. 32 questions.

21. The poorer the health of the husband and/or wife, the higher the proportion of couples practicing contraception effectively and the smaller the planned families. 16 questions.

22. The poorer the health of the children, the higher the proportion of couples practicing contraception effectively and the smaller the planned families. 6 questions.

23. The greater the fear of pregnancy, the higher the proportion of couples practicing contraception effectively and the smaller the planned families. 10 questions.

In addition to the questions assigned to a hypothesis, others related to the following topics:

1. Attitudes toward hypothetical inducements to have more children. 16 questions.

2. Demographic information about the couple and each child. 27 questions.

3. Contraceptive practices, menstruation, and lactation. 23 questions (many of them repeated for each practice and for each interpregnancy interval).

To supplement the information obtained by questioning the wife and husband, the interviewer herself recorded certain facts and opinions. While the wife and husband were checking categories on the questionnaires, the interviewer checked the items on Chapin's Social Status Scale. Soon after the last schedule (Form E) was completed for each couple, she rated the husband and wife with respect to ten of the hypotheses and three other items. Finally, she wrote a short analytical summary of the case.

The results of this study, while less conclusive than could be desired, are perhaps not much less so than was reasonable to expect in view of the pioneering character of the investigation. The results relating to several hypotheses are noted briefly below.

SOME CONCLUSIONS FROM THE INDIANAPOLIS STUDY[24]

Whelpton and Kiser in their analysis of hypothesis 2 (economic insecurity and fertility) say:

> The first part of the hypothesis (the greater the feeling of economic insecurity the greater the effective practice of contraception) is not borne out by the data. Among the couples studied, success in fertility planning is directly associated with economic security but this relation virtually disappears when socioeconomic status is held constant. The second part of the hypothesis (the greater the feeling of insecurity the smaller the planned families) is supported by the data. The size of "planned families" and particularly the size of "number and spacing" families is directly associated with economic security regardless of differences in socioeconomic status. There is a particularly strong tendency for childlessness to be associated with economic insecurity among "number and spacing" families. This accounts for much of the direct relation of fertility to economic security among these families. It accounts for virtually all of this type of relation among the total group of "planned families" in the Indianapolis Study.[25]

[24] Clyde V. Kiser and P. K. Whelpton, "Social and Psychological Factors Affecting Fertility, XXXIII. Summary of Chief Findings and Implications for Future Studies," *Milbank Memorial Fund Quarterly*, vol. 36, no. 3, May, 1958; also see vol. 5, pp. 1325–1372.

[25] Clyde V. Kiser and P. K. Whelpton, "Social and Psychological Factors Affecting Fertility: XI. The Interrelation of Fertility, Fertility Planning, and Feeling of Economic Security," *Milbank Memorial Fund Quarterly*, vol. 29, no. 1, p. 112, 1951.

Hypothesis 3 (socioeconomic status and fertility) has also been reported upon by Whelpton and Kiser. The following briefly summarizes their findings:

> Despite the relatively low fertility of the "number and spacing" planned group, the fertility rates within this group tend to increase rather than to decrease with rising socioeconomic status. Descending the scale by planning status, one finds from these data a rather systematic transition from a direct association of fertility to socioeconomic status in the "number and spacing planned" group, to an inverse relation of these variables within the "excess fertility" group. . . .
>
> Finally, with reference to the hypothesis considered in this article, "the higher the socioeconomic status, the higher the proportion of couples practicing contraception effectively, and the smaller the planned family," the first part is definitely confirmed by the Indianapolis data but the second part is not. The hypothesis has reference to the "number and spacing planned" and "number planned" groups combined. However, these two groups exhibit marked contrasts in class differences in fertility, and therefore a combination of the two tends to conceal the actual relationships. The second part of the hypothesis is partially confirmed by the experience of the "number planned" but not by the "number and spacing planned" group.[26]

It should be noted, however, that although the highest fertility in the "number-and-spacing-planned" group was found in the group having the highest social status, in the "number-planned" group the relation was only partially inverse, while in the "quasi-planned" and "excess-fertility" groups, the inverse relation was clearly marked. It may be that the association of socioeconomic status with fertility as shown in past studies is, in part, another aspect of urban-rural differentials; but it may also be that as the adulteration of the urban population by rural migrants wanes, urbanites will develop a firm direct relation between socioeconomic status and fertility. As yet the data do not warrant any definite conclusion on this point. The study of American families shows that even some farm experience by both husband and wife, although not on a farm at the time of interview, leads to a larger average number of births expected than when neither has any farm experience but a substantially smaller number of children than when they were on the farm at the time of interview.[27]

Hypothesis 20 (marital adjustment and fertility) was reported on by Dr. Reed, who summed his findings as follows:

1. A decline in marital adjustment with increasing family size
2. An increase in marital adjustment with increasing success in controlling fertility according to the desires of the couple

[26] Clyde V. Kiser and P. K. Whelpton, "Social and Psychological Factors Affecting Fertility: IX. Fertility Planning and Fertility Rates by Socioeconomic Status," *Milbank Memorial Fund Quarterly*, vol. 27, no. 2, pp. 242–245, 1949.
[27] Freedman et al., *op. cit.*, pp. 314–315.

3. An increase in success in controlling fertility with increasing willingness of both wife and husband to take responsibility for fertility control[28]

He concludes that the relation of marital adjustment and fertility found here may be affected by other variables:

> Although this discussion has been in terms of marital adjustment and fertility without reference to other variables, it is obvious that additional factors are present in the problem. High economic status, for example, has been shown in the past to be associated with low fertility. It is also associated to some extent with good marital adjustment and probably with success in controlling fertility. Thus, differences in economic status or some similar variable may account, in part, for the relationships found between marital adjustment, size of family, and fertility control. It is hoped that further analysis of the couples will throw some light on the influence of the economic and other factors.[29]

Freedman in his analysis of hypothesis 15 (interest in religion and fertility) says:

> A slight negative relationship exists between the effective practice of contraception and degree of religious interest as determined in this study. However, this relationship is mainly a function of socioeconomic status. It is not maintained with any consistency within the categories based on an Index of Socio-Economic Status. Religious denomination is more related to effective planning than is any of the other indices of religious interest or activity which were utilized. . . .
>
> Four denominations have a sufficiently large number of couples to make it worth while to compute fertility rates separately for each fertility planning status. The most significant finding here is that the Presbyterian group, which has the lowest total fertility rate among the four denominations compared, has the highest fertility rate in the two effective-planning categories. This is consistent with a Kiser-Whelpton finding that the negative relationship between socioeconomic status and fertility is reversed for effective planners. The Presbyterian group has a much higher socioeconomic status than any of the three other groups.
>
> On the whole, the findings do not indicate that religious interest is of great importance in explaining variations in reproductive behavior. Neither planning status nor fertility vary in regular gradation with religious interest or participation. It is only when comparisons of extreme religious interest groups are made that findings indicate a small relationship consistent with the hypothesis. Even the small inverse relationship between fertility planning and religious interest has been shown to be mainly a function of socioeconomic status.
>
> It is important to emphasize that the generality of the findings is limited by the

[28] Robert B. Reed, "Social and Psychological Factors Affecting Fertility: VII, The Interrelationship of Marital Adjustment, Fertility Control, and Size of Family," *Milbank Memorial Fund Quarterly*, vol. 25, no. 4, p. 432, 1947.
[29] *Ibid.*, p. 425.

nature of the sample—a group of urban native white Protestants with at least a grammar school education.[30]

In the preceding chapter attention was called to the fact that the preliminary survey of families in Indianapolis made for the purpose of selecting those couples which met the requirements for inclusion in the sample which was to be studied intensively showed that Protestants had somewhat smaller families than did Roman Catholics under quite similar conditions. Thus, while differences between Protestant denominations in religious activities and interests showed but little relation to size of family, the differences in size of family between Protestants and Roman Catholics in the same socioeconomic groups would probably have been shown to be of considerable importance if Catholics had been included in the sample studied intensively. (At the time the study was planned, it did not appear feasible to interview Catholic families.) That Catholic families are somewhat larger than Protestant families now seems to be well established by later intensive studies in which Roman Catholics were included. But the term *larger* must be understood to mean perhaps an average of about one-half a birth more per wife. Furthermore, Roman Catholic families vary in size by socioeconomic status in much the same way as Protestant families.

A GENERAL CONCLUSION

The most general conclusion the authors draw from the many studies of fertility that have been made during the past seven decades is about as follows: Once the traditional cultural patterns of reproductive behavior in preindustrial societies begin to give way under the stress of adjusting family life to the social and economic changes involved in developing an industrial and commercial society, a great multiplicity of new social and psychological factors come into play in determining the size of families. These factors modify reproductive behavior in a great variety of ways and act at different rates of speed in different societies. This is because reproductive behavior, like all other socially controlled behavior in any society, has its roots in the historical-cultural past. It is not to be expected that changes in reproductive behavior, in India for example, which will bring about a reasonably satisfactory adjustment of numbers to production, will follow the same pattern or the same time schedule as that which has taken place in many Western countries during the past 100 to 150 years, nor that it will follow the pattern of Japan.

As the people in any society come to believe, for whatever reason(s), that it is desirable to keep families rather small if they are to assure a decent level

[30] Ronald Freedman and P. K. Whelpton, "Social and Psychological Factors Affecting Fertility: X. Fertility Planning and Fertility Rates by Religious Interest and Denomination," *Milbank Memorial Fund Quarterly*, vol. 28, no. 3, pp. 333–334.

of living to their families and good opportunities to their children, they will adopt the measures to achieve this end which are most compatible, perhaps we should say least incompatible, with their cultural values and with the existing practices that have been used to achieve these values. There are probably many ways to achieve the aim of adjusting the size of a population to its economic bases of support and at the same time to assure as far as is possible the continuous cultural and personal development that appear desirable in modern societies. The authors believe, however, that keeping population within the bounds determined by the ability of the society to ensure a decent living to all its people is now or will gradually become one of the greatest values in all societies. Finally, we believe that no one pattern of adjustment will be *best* for every society, but that each will develop suitable means of achieving this adjustment in its own way.

SUGGESTIONS FOR SUPPLEMENTARY READING

Bachi, Roberto, and Judah Matras: "Contraception and Induced Abortions among Jewish Maternity Cases in Israel," *Milbank Memorial Fund Quarterly*, vol. 30, no. 2, pp. 207–229, 1962.

Blacker, J. G. C.: "Social Ambitions of the Bourgeoisie in 18th Century France, and their Relation to Family Limitation," *Population Studies*, vol. 11, no. 1, pp. 46–63, 1957.

Fagley, Richard M.: *The Population Explosion and Christian Responsibility*, Oxford University Press, Fair Lawn, N.J., 1960.

Freedman, Ronald, Pascal K. Whelpton, and Arthur A. Campbell: *Family Planning, Sterility, and Population Growth*, McGraw-Hill Book Company, New York, 1959.

Guttmacher, Alan F., and the Editors of Consumer Reports: *The Consumers Union Report on Family Planning*, Consumers Union of U.S., Inc., Mount Vernon, N.Y., 1962.

Hajnal, John: "The Marriage Boom," *Population Index*, vol. 19, no. 2, April, 1955, pp. 80–101.

Kiser, Clyde V.: "Voluntary and Involuntary Aspects of Childlessness," *Milbank Memorial Fund Quarterly*, vol. 17, pp. 50–68, 1939.

Lorimer, Frank, and Frederick Osborn: *Dynamics of Population: Social and Biological Significance of Changing Birth Rates in the United States*, The Macmillan Company, New York, 1934. Contains much material of general interest.

Pearl, Raymond: *The Natural History of Population*, Oxford University Press, Fair Lawn, N.J., 1939.

Popenoe, Paul: "Motivation of Childless Marriages," *Journal of Heredity*, vol. 17, no. 12, pp. 469–472, 1936.

United Nations: *Recent Trends in Fertility in Industrial Countries*, Population Studies, no. 27, Department of Economic and Social Affairs, New York, 1958.

Whelpton, P. K., and Clyde V. Kiser (eds.): "Social and Psychological Factors Affecting Fertility," *Milbank Memorial Fund Quarterly*, New York, 5 vols., 1946, 1950, 1952, 1954, and 1958.

CHAPTER TWELVE

Mortality

INTRODUCTORY

From time immemorial man has been interested in trying to control disease. The shaman, the medicine man, the priest, the granny with her herbs, and innumerable magicians with their still more numerous incantations and rites all undertook in various ways to cure man's diseases and/or to drive out the evil spirits which imperiled his health. It would not be just to say that all these practitioners were charlatans and that they contributed nothing to the alleviation of man's suffering from disease. But in the almost complete absence of scientific knowledge and with no means of collecting and organizing the knowledge that did exist, it is not surprising that until quite recently, comparatively little progress had been made in most parts of the world in controlling man's death rate. There were, of course, occasional men who searched for the causes of disease in the scientific spirit, but they seem to have been few and far apart in time and space, and generally they were less respected than those who were healing by the traditional means sanctioned by their forefathers. Even after the Renaissance and during the Age of Enlightenment in Europe, the problem of man's health received comparatively little attention. The interest in health science increased slowly during the eighteenth and early nineteenth centuries, but such information as we have on death rates before 1800 would indicate that only a little progress in reducing them had been made up to that time even in Northern and Western Europe. It seems probable that until the great plague in London in 1665, so little careful observation had been made in England of conditions which might lead to the checking of the plague that no effective measures could be taken to control the recurrence of such disasters and to prevent the spread of an epidemic once it had gained a foothold.[1] But when a few people in positions of power in England in the latter part of the seventeenth century and the early decades of the eighteenth century became convinced that overcrowding and filth (almost complete lack of sanitation) were closely asso-

[1] See the works of Cheyney, Defoe, and Hecker in Suggested Readings for Chapter 14.

ciated with outbreaks of plague and took measures to improve these conditions even a little, London never again had so deadly a visitation of the disease. (See quotation from Malthus in Chapter 15, page 412.)

Quite aside from the great epidemics, before the rise of the scientific spirit in Europe, little effort had been made to ascertain the causes of disease, and even the most enlightened peoples gave but little attention to their cure. The control of disease in the individual, as has been said, was attempted, but in general it was so little successful that a high death rate was accepted as inevitable by the great mass of the people everywhere. As might be expected, given man's powerful urge to reproduce, this high death rate evoked very widespread cultural patterns of reproduction calculated to ensure the use of man's great fecundity to offset his perpetual high death rates.

Once the growth of the scientific spirit was tolerated even to a small degree, it was only a question of time until some of the minds emancipated from the traditional thrall of accepting the inevitability of a high death rate would begin to make scientific observations regarding the causes and cures of disease. The first really great step forward in the control of particular diseases was taken when Jenner announced in 1798 the effectiveness of inoculating people with cowpox to immunize them against smallpox. For ages smallpox had yearly claimed a great toll of life in almost all parts of the world. The traditionalists were strongly opposed to any such innovation—it was "unnatural" and was an effort to thwart God's will. But the use of a cure so patently beneficial to man could be delayed for only a few decades by such arguments, and by 1825 Malthus had come to believe that the spurt in population growth in France in the early part of the nineteenth century, in spite of the Napoleonic Wars and a small decline in the birth rate, was probably due in measurable degree to the use of vaccination against smallpox.

In different parts of Europe in the late seventeenth century and in the early years of the eighteenth, a few people for varying reasons became curious about the number and the frequency of deaths and births. Some of them began to compare births and deaths to find out whether or not population was growing (or diminishing) by reason of the excess of one over the other; some were interested in finding out whether there was a regularity in the occurrence of deaths that would make it financially possible to insure lives on a sound basis; and some wanted to find out what "heavenly order" prevailed in births and deaths, for surely the Lord had some plan in permitting such events to take place.

CRUDE DEATH RATES

In the early study of deaths, as in that of births, one of the earliest methods used was to divide the number of deaths into the population under observation, e.g., population 12,000, deaths 300, gave $\frac{12,000}{300} = 40$, or 1 death to each 40 persons. But this sample measure of mortality, like the similar measure of natality noted in Chapter 9, soon gave way to the present crude death rate. This is calculated in exactly the same manner as the crude birth rate. The formula is $\dfrac{\text{(deaths) }300}{\text{(population) }12,000} = 0.025$ deaths per person; $0.025 \times 1,000 = 25$ deaths per 1,000. In turn, the crude death rate gave way to more refined death rates because some men wanted to know how many persons survived to certain ages out of 100 or 1,000 born, so that insurance premiums could be calculated; also because it soon became apparent to men studying the actual registers showing deaths in a given locality that there were great differences in deaths according to age. For example, Graunt,[2] in calculating a table of survivors, found that in London about the middle of the 1600s, of 100 babies born only 40 survived to 16 years of age and only 25 survived to 26 years of age. Since the data on which his study was based were incomplete and inaccurate in many respects, of which fact Graunt was fully aware, he considered his results as only approximations. But his work published in 1662 was of a poineering character and was a stimulus to many who followed him to improve upon it, as more abundant and reliable data became available.

Table 12-1 shows average crude death rates for specified years in the United States from 1900 to 1961 for both sexes combined and for males and females, and by color. Table 12-2 shows similar rates for selected countries.

The most important fact shown here is the steady decline in the crude death rates for some decades in the more developed countries. Thus for the total population of the United States, the average death rate for the years 1900 to 1905 was approximately 16.2 per 1,000 and for the years 1955 to 1959 it was 9.4, a decline of over 40 percent during this period. The decline during the half century 1850 to 1900 for several of the countries having such data was almost as large proportionally as from 1900 to the present, because during the latter part of the nineteenth century the role of bacteria in causing many diseases began to be appreciated, and increased sanitary precautions became more common both in the home and in public health services, especially in the cities.

AGE-SPECIFIC DEATH RATES

An age-specific death rate (number of deaths of persons of a given age per 1,000 population of that age) can be calculated with precision only if we know the size of the different age groups and if the deaths for the same groups are adequately registered. It is also highly desirable to calculate these rates by sex.

[2] See Louis I. Dublin, Alfred J. Lotka, and Mortimer Spiegelman, *Length of Life; A Study of the Life Table*, rev. ed., The Ronald Press Company, New York, 1949, pp. 26–43.

Such rates are the basis for practically all refinements in mortality rates that are in use today. They give an accurate picture of mortality for both males and females at each age. The population base is usually the population in the middle of the period under consideration. If single-year groups are used, there

TABLE 12-1.   AVERAGE* CRUDE DEATH RATES, BY COLOR AND SEX: DEATH-REGISTRATION STATES, 1900–1932, AND UNITED STATES, 1933–1961

(Data refer only to deaths occurring within the specified area and exclude fetal deaths. Rates per 1,000 population residing in area for specified group.)

Area and year	Total			White			Nonwhite		
	Both sexes	Male	Female	Both sexes	Male	Female	Both sexes	Male	Female
United States†									
1960–1961	9.4	10.8	8.0	9.4	10.8	8.0	9.8	11.2	8.4
1955–1959	9.4	10.9	8.0	9.3	10.8	7.9	10.1	11.5	8.9
1950–1954	9.5	11.0	8.1	9.4	10.9	7.9	10.8	12.2	9.5
1945–1949	10.1	11.6	8.6	9.9	11.5	8.4	11.4	12.7	10.2
1939–1944	10.6	12.0	9.3	10.4	11.7	9.0	13.1	14.4	11.9
1933–1938	11.0	12.1	9.9	10.6	11.7	9.5	14.6	15.9	13.3
Death-registration states									
1928–1932	11.4	12.3	10.5	10.9	11.8	10.0	16.1	17.1	15.1
1923–1927	11.8	12.5	11.0	11.2	12.0	10.5	17.0	17.8	16.3
1918–1922	13.4	14.2	12.7	13.0	13.8	12.2	18.4	18.8	18.0
1912–1917	13.6	14.6	12.6	13.2	14.2	12.3	20.1	20.9	19.3
1906–1911	14.8	15.8	13.9	14.6	15.6	13.7	22.6	23.2	22.0
1900–1905	16.2	17.0	15.3	16.0	16.8	15.1	24.8	26.0	23.7

* These are a simple average of the crude rates for the years indicated; hence, the rate for each year is given equal weight and obscures the importance of an epidemic of large magnitude such as that of influenza in 1918.
† Beginning with 1959; includes Alaska.
Source: *Vital Statistics of the United States, 1959,* vol. 1, table 6-A, pp. 6–11.

are about 100 rates. With such a multitude of rates, only the expert can tell at a glance and then only approximately how the mortality conditions of two populations compare. If five-year groups are used there are still about 20 different rates which make it difficult for the reader to get an overall picture. This is the reason for using ten-year age groups at certain ages as in Table 12-3.

TABLE 12-2.   CRUDE DEATH RATES FOR SEVERAL COUNTRIES SELECTED TO SHOW LONG-TIME AND CURRENT TRENDS*

Year	Algeria		Aus- tralia	Ceylon	Den- mark	England and Wales	France	Japan	Norway	Sweden
	Euro- pean	Muslim								
1956–1960	9.9†	13.6†	8.8	9.7†	9.3	11.6	11.7	7.8	8.9	9.7
1948–1952	10.2	15.3	9.6	12.4	8.9	11.6	13.0	10.7	8.8	9.9
1938–1942	14.3†	——	10.4	20.1	10.1	12.8	17.0	16.7	10.5	11.1
1928–1932	15.1	——	9.0	24.0	11.1	12.2	16.4	18.8	10.9	12.0
1918–1922	17.6	——	10.5	31.6	12.4	13.7	20.0	24.0	13.5	14.2
1908–1912	17.9	——	10.7	31.1	13.4	14.2	18.5	20.8	13.6	14.1
1898–1902	21.6†	——	12.7	28.2	16.0	17.4	20.7	20.6	15.4	16.2
1888–1892	25.8†	——	14.4	26.8	19.3	19.0	22.2	20.4	17.7	16.8
1878–1882	28.3†	——	15.2	22.7	19.2	20.3	22.4	18.1	16.6	17.6
1868–1872	26.9†	——	14.4	20.9	19.0	22.2	26.6	——	17.0	19.3
1858–1862	27.5†	——	——	——	20.1	21.9	23.4	——	18.0	19.9
1848–1852	43.7†	——	——	——	20.1	22.6	23.5	——	18.2	20.6
1838–1842	39.1†	——	——	——	20.3	22.1	23.6	——	19.3	21.7
1828–1832	39.8†	——	——	——	26.8	——	25.9	——	19.4	25.8
1818–1822	——	——	——	——	20.7	——	25.3	——	19.5	24.9
1808–1812	——	——	——	——	24.9	——	25.7	——	——	33.1

Year	Argen- tina	Brazil‡	Canada	Egypt§	Ecuador	Guate- mala	Honduras (British)	Mexico	Formosa
1956–1960	8.3	13.2†	8.0	17.8†	14.7	19.3	9.2	12.1	7.6
1948–1952	9.0	13.0	9.1	19.4	17.3	22.2	12.4	16.6	12.1
1938–1942	10.5	——	10.6	26.3	25.3¶	27.4	19.9	22.8	18.9
1928–1932	12.8	——	10.8†	26.9	——	21.1	23.0	25.2¶	21.3¶
1918–1922	17.1†	——	12.5†	29.7	——	23.1	25.6†	25.5¶	24.0¶
1908–1912	17.2†	——	12.1	27.1	——	21.4	25.2†	——	——
1898–1902	18.4†	——	11.0	26.5†	——	20.7	——	——	——
1888–1892	——	——	——	25.1†	——	28.2	——	——	——

* For the current data on death rates, the reader is referred to *Population Index* and to the late United Nations Demographic Yearbooks.
† Algeria, 1956–1959, 1931 and 1933–1935, 1901–1905, 1891–1895, 1881–1885, 1872–1876, 1861–1865, 1851–1855, 1841–1845, 1831–1835; Ceylon, 1956–1959; Argentina, 1915–1919, 1909–1913, 1899–1902; Brazil, 1956–1958; Canada, 1920–1924, 1911–1913; Egypt, 1956–1958, 1905–1909, 1901–1904; Ecuador, 1956–1959, 1937–1939; Honduras (British), 1922–1924, 1909–1911; Mexico, 1926–1935, 1921–1925; Formosa, 1926–1935, 1921–1925.
‡ State capitals only.
§ Before 1917 Bedouins were not included in population estimates.
¶ *Population Index.*

TABLE 12-3.   DEATH RATES BY AGE, COLOR, AND SEX: UNITED STATES, 1960 AND 1939–1940

(Data refer only to deaths occurring within the United States, including Alaska and Hawaii in 1960, and exclude fetal deaths. Rate per 1,000 population residing in area for specified group, enumerated as of April 1 for 1960 and estimated as of July 1 for 1939–1940.)

Year and age	Total			White			Nonwhite		
	Both sexes	Male	Female	Both sexes	Male	Female	Both sexes	Male	Female
1960									
All ages*	9.5	11.0	8.1	9.5	11.0	8.0	10.1	11.5	8.7
Under 1	27.0	30.6	23.2	23.6	26.9	20.1	46.3	51.9	40.7
1–4	1.1	1.2	1.0	1.0	1.0	0.9	1.9	2.1	1.7
5–14	0.5	0.6	0.4	0.4	0.5	0.3	0.6	0.8	0.5
15–24	1.1	1.5	0.6	1.0	1.4	0.5	1.6	2.1	1.1
25–34	1.5	1.9	1.1	1.2	1.6	0.9	3.2	3.9	2.6
35–44	3.0	3.7	2.3	2.6	3.3	1.9	6.3	7.3	5.5
45–54	7.6	9.9	5.3	6.9	9.3	4.6	13.4	15.5	11.4
55–64	17.4	23.1	12.0	16.3	22.3	10.8	27.7	31.5	24.1
65–74	38.2	49.1	28.7	37.4	48.5	27.8	47.8	56.6	39.8
75–84	87.5	101.8	76.3	88.3	103.0	77.0	76.3	86.6	67.1
85 and over	198.6	211.9	190.1	203.5	217.5	194.8	139.1	152.4	128.7
1939–1940									
All ages*	10.7	11.8	9.5	10.3	11.5	9.1	13.6	14.9	12.4
Under 1	54.4	61.1	47.5	49.8	56.0	43.4	88.0	99.9	76.3
1–4	3.0	3.3	2.8	2.7	2.9	2.5	5.1	5.5	4.7
5–14	1.1	1.2	0.9	1.0	1.2	0.8	1.6	1.7	1.5
15–24	2.1	2.3	1.9	1.7	2.0	1.4	5.1	5.0	5.1
25–34	3.1	3.4	2.8	2.5	2.8	2.2	8.0	8.6	7.5
35–44	5.3	5.9	4.6	4.4	5.1	3.7	12.4	13.3	11.6
45–54	10.6	12.4	8.6	9.5	11.3	7.5	22.5	24.1	20.8
55–64	22.0	25.6	18.1	20.9	24.7	16.9	36.9	38.4	35.2
65–74	47.0	52.9	41.1	46.7	52.8	40.8	49.6	54.1	44.8
75–84	110.4	118.9	102.7	111.5	119.8	104.0	91.8	104.0	80.4
85 and over	222.0	236.1	211.7	228.3	242.2	218.3	162.7	181.1	149.1

* Figures for age not stated included in "All ages" but not distributed among age groups.

Source: *Vital Statistics of the United States, 1960*, vol. II, sec. 1, Table 1C; *Vital Statistics of the United States, Supplement 1939–40*, part 3, p. 52.

Table 12-3 shows the age-specific death rates for the United States in 1960 and 1939–1940 for 11 age classes, by color and sex. At all ages the rates for females were lower than those for males and also lower at all ages for whites than for nonwhites, except at ages 75 and over. These data show a relatively high death rate under 1 year of age for all groups (this is not quite the same as infant mortality, which is the number of deaths under 1 year of age per 1,000 live births in the same year). The rate at ages 1–4 was only about 5.5 percent as high as the under-1-year rate in 1939–1940 and only about 4 percent as high in 1960. The rate was still lower at ages 5–14. From ages 15–24 to ages 35–44 there is a slow rise, but from 45 years of age upward the rise is more rapid, until at ages 65–74 it is as high as, or higher than, under 1 year of age, and at ages 85 and over it is about 200 per 1,000. Such age-specific rates make it abundantly clear that age differences in any two populations will have a highly significant effect on their crude death rates and will render such rates useless for many purposes. However, most of us need a single figure which takes into account age differences, if we are to get more than a very hazy idea of how mortality conditions in two populations compare or of how the conditions determining mortality in a particular population have changed over time.

AGE-STANDARDIZED DEATH RATES

The *standardized death rate*, based on age-specific death rates, supplies a simple and accurate basis for comparing the death rates of different populations (Table 12-4). Assuming that the death rate of each sex is standardized for age, we find from this rate what the rate would be if the population being studied had the same age composition as some other population which is used as a *standard*. (See Chapter 9 for explanation of process for standardizing birth rates for age.) When the death rate for males and females of two or more populations are standardized for age on the same population base (a standard population) their sex death rates can be compared with assurance that age differences do not account for any part of the difference in these rates. Rates can also be standardized for other differences in the composition of populations, e.g., education, marital status, occupation, and so forth.

LIFE TABLES

Life tables are based on knowledge of the exact age of death of persons in a specified population. Since they arose out of the need for knowing the probability of dying at, or conversely, of surviving to, any specified age if life insurance were to become a business, and since there has never been any hope of telling

TABLE 12-4.   AVERAGE* AGE-ADJUSTED DEATH RATES BY COLOR AND SEX: DEATH-REGISTRATION STATES, 1900–1932, AND UNITED STATES, 1933–1959

(Data refer only to deaths occurring within the specified area and exclude fetal deaths. Rates per 1,000 population. Computed by the direct method, using as the standard population the age distribution of the total population of the United States as enumerated in 1940. Based on age-specific rates shown in vol. I of *Vital Statistics of the United States* as follows: Rates for 1900–1939 are shown in table 8.40 of the 1950 report; for 1940–1949, in table AO of the 1954 report; and for 1950–1959, in table 6-C of this report.)

Area and year	Total			White			Nonwhite		
	Both sexes	Male	Female	Both sexes	Male	Female	Both sexes	Male	Female
United States †									
1955–1959	7.8	9.6	6.1	7.4	9.3	5.8	11.0	12.6	9.5
1950–1954	8.1	9.8	6.6	7.8	9.5	6.2	11.8	13.2	10.4
1945–1949	9.0	10.5	7.5	8.6	10.1	7.1	12.6	13.8	11.4
1939–1944	10.3	11.7	8.9	9.8	11.2	8.3	15.1	16.3	13.9
1933–1938	11.6	12.9	10.4	11.0	12.3	9.8	17.6	18.8	16.3
Death-registration states									
1928–1932	12.6	13.6	11.5	11.9	12.9	10.8	19.8	20.6	18.9
1923–1927	13.1	13.9	12.2	12.4	13.3	11.5	20.5	21.0	20.0
1918–1922	14.6	15.4	13.8	14.1	14.9	13.2	21.1	21.2	21.2
1912–1917	14.8	16.0	13.7	14.5	15.6	13.3	22.8	23.5	22.2
1906–1911	16.0	17.1	14.8	15.7	16.9	14.5	24.9	25.6	24.1
1900–1905	17.0	17.9	16.0	16.7	17.7	15.7	27.5	28.9	26.2

* These are a simple average of the age-adjusted death rates for the years indicated; hence the rate for each year is given equal weight and obscures the importance of an epidemic of large magnitude, such as that of influenza in 1918.
† Beginning with 1959; includes Alaska.
Source: *Vital Statistics of the United States, 1959*, vol. I, table 6-B, p. 6-12, with averages comparable to those of Table 12-1.

that a particular individual would live to, or die in, any specified number of years, it was necessary to resort to the calculation of the probability of living or dying of the individual as a member of a fairly large group. Such information could be used to calculate the premium any individual as a member of a group would need to pay in order to make it possible to guarantee each member of this group a specified sum of money at a given age or his heirs a specified sum upon his death. Thus, if in a group of 1,000 persons who were 25 years old it was known that together these men would live 30,000 years, i.e., would die at an average age of 55, all members of this group could be safely insured by calculating how much each one needed to pay in premiums each year for an average of 30 years to keep the undertaking solvent. The deficit of payments caused by some members dying before making 30 payments would be balanced by the excess of payments by those living beyond 55 years of age. This is a very much simplified statement of the useful calculations for insurance purposes which the life table makes possible, but it illustrates how the knowledge of the probability of dying at a given age for a fairly large group makes life insurance a business rather than a gamble for the insurer. It always remains something of a gamble for the insured. Here we are interested chiefly in certain demographic uses of the life table.

Life tables, to be useful, must be based on a fairly large population, and the basic rates used to calculate them are the age-specific death rates. As we have just noted, it has become standard practice to convert age-specific death rates to show the probability of an individual of any specified age dying in any particular interval, e.g., the probability of a male aged exactly 35 dying before reaching exact age 36, etc. (see column 2 in Tables 12-5A and 12-5C). An *unabridged* life table shows this probability for every year of age from 0 (birth) to extreme old age. The life table, as calculated in the United States, generally starts with the assumption that 100,000 babies, usually 100,000 boys and 100,000 girls separately, are born at a given moment, let us say on January 1, and proceeds to answer the question how many of them will die in each annual interval, e.g., by the time the survivors are exactly 1, or 2, or 10, or 50 years old. The processes by which the rates showing the probability of dying are arrived at are rather complicated and are not of interest at this time. Tables 12-5A to 12-5D are *abridged* life tables using 5-year age classes for whites and nonwhites. Such abridged tables are quite satisfactory for our purposes. We have already noted that there are substantial differences in the death rates of males and females and of whites and nonwhites in the United States. This is the reason for giving the four life tables (whites, males and females, and nonwhites, males and females).

Columns 6 and 7 of the tables are of special interest. Column 6 of Tables 12-5A and 12-5B, "stationary population," shows the white male and female populations that would be alive at any given time, (1) if 100,000 babies born at a given moment were added each year, and (2) if the rates for the probability of dying prevailing in 1960 applied to them throughout life and to all successive annual cohorts of 100,000, until all the individuals in the earliest cohort had died. With this fixed number of births and these fixed death rates (probabilities of dying), the white male population would remain stationary at 6,736,870 for each 100,000 boy babies and at 7,411,812 for each 100,000 white girl babies, and the birth rate would equal the death rate. It would take about 90 years to approximate these stationary populations. Since there are normally about 105.5 white male births to 100 white female births in this country, the life-table population of males would need to be increased by the addition of 5,500 (5.5 percent) boy babies to begin with, i.e., to a total of 105,500 boy babies. Using this number for white male additions each year and the same probabilities of dying, we secure a figure for male survivors at each age interval in the life table that would approximate the number of males in an actual population, assuming, of course, there were no migration. This calculation would yield a significantly different total number of white males from that given above and also in each age interval. Thus the total sex ratio of white survivors (number of males per 100 females) as shown in Tables 12-5A and 12-5B is 90.9, but starting with 105,500 white boy babies, the total sex ratio would be 95.9, and at each age interval it would also be higher by 5.5 percent than that calculated directly from male life tables starting with 100,000 births. However, because of the lower death rates of females at all ages the sex ratio in most populations for which reliable life tables are available would be under 100 (see Chapter 5).

Several other interesting comparisons can be made from the figures in column 6 in different life tables. The total stationary white male population from 100,000 births annually was 4,823,011 in the United States in 1901; by 1960 this had increased to 6,736,870—a total white male population about 40 percent larger from the same number of births. This increase is due directly to the lower age-specific death rates prevailing in 1960. The increase in white females in a stationary population during this period, because of greater improvement in their death rates, would be somewhat larger than that of males (see the population pyramids for these years in Chapter 5).

In 1901 the total stationary population of *Negro* males in their life table was 3,255,580. This must be compared with the analogous figure for *nonwhite* males in 1960—6,109,681. Although Negro and nonwhite are not identical, Negroes constitute over 95 percent of all nonwhites. Thus the gain of nonwhite males over Negro males during this period was 87.3 percent or more than twice as much as that for white males (about 40 percent). The gain of nonwhite females in a life-table stationary population in 1960 over Negro females in 1901 in numbers was from 3,504,421 to 6,628,221 in 1960, or an increase of 89 percent. Thus the general improvement of health conditions for nonwhite females was slightly larger than that for nonwhite males, and both sexes of nonwhites gained rapidly on whites between 1901 and 1960.

Another calculation of much interest can be made from the total number of survivors (column 6 in these life tables). In 1960 the total number of white males in a stationary population from 105,500 births would be the number from 100,000 births plus 5.5 percent, or 7,107,398 at the 1960 probabilities of dying. The number of white females surviving from 100,000 births would be as in the life table, 7,411,812, and the total of 14,519,210 would constitute the white

TABLE 12-5A.   ABRIDGED LIFE TABLES FOR WHITE MALES, UNITED STATES, 1960 (INCLUDES ALASKA AND HAWAII)

Age interval	Proportion dying	Of 100,000 born alive		Stationary population		Average remaining lifetime
Period of life between exact ages stated in years	Proportion of persons alive at beginning of age interval dying during interval	Number living at beginning of age interval	Number dying during age interval	In the age interval	In this and all subsequent age intervals	Average number of years of life remaining at beginning of age interval
(1)	(2)	(3)	(4)	(5)	(6)	(7)
x to $x + n$	$_nq_x$	l_x	$_nd_x$	$_nL_x$	T_x	$\overset{\circ}{e}_x$
0–1..........	0.0260	100,000	2,602	97,665	6,736,870	67.4
1–5..........	0.0041	97,398	401	388,643	6,639,205	68.2
5–10.........	0.0027	96,997	258	484,300	6,250,562	64.4
10–15.........	0.0026	96,739	254	483,112	5,766,262	59.6
15–20.........	0.0062	96,485	598	481,038	5,283,150	54.8
20–25.........	0.0082	95,887	790	477,485	4,802,112	50.1
25–30.........	0.0076	95,097	725	473,682	4,324,627	45.5
30–35.........	0.0086	94,372	814	469,917	3,850,945	40.8
35–40.........	0.0126	93,558	1,181	465,045	3,381,028	36.1
40–45.........	0.0207	92,377	1,912	456,581	2,915,983	31.6
45–50.........	0.0349	90,465	3,161	444,964	2,459,402	27.2
50–55.........	0.0577	87,304	5,040	424,713	2,014,438	23.1
55–60.........	0.0857	82,264	7,049	394,596	1,589,725	19.3
60–65.........	0.1292	75,215	9,719	352,697	1,195,129	15.9
65–70.........	0.1850	65,496	12,119	298,064	842,432	12.9
70–75.........	0.2591	53,377	13,832	232,901	544,368	10.2
75–80.........	0.3573	39,545	14,131	162,083	311,467	7.9
80–85.........	0.5031	25,414	12,785	93,751	149,384	5.9
85 and over....	1.0000	12,629	12,629	55,633	55,633	4.4

**TABLE 12-5B.   ABRIDGED LIFE TABLES FOR WHITE FEMALES, UNITED STATES, 1960
(INCLUDES ALASKA AND HAWAII)**

Age interval	Proportion dying	Of 100,000 born alive		Stationary population		Average remaining lifetime
Period of life between exact ages stated in years	Proportion of persons alive at beginning of age interval dying during interval	Number living at beginning of age interval	Number dying during age interval	In the age interval	In this and all subsequent age intervals	Average number of years of life remaining at beginning of age interval
(1)	(2)	(3)	(4)	(5)	(6)	(7)
x to $x + n$	$_nq_x$	l_x	$_nd_x$	$_nL_x$	T_x	$\mathring{e}_x$
0–1..........	0.0196	100,000	1,964	98,246	7,411,812	74.1
1–5..........	0.0034	98,036	329	391,347	7,313,566	74.6
5–10.........	0.0019	97,707	186	488,033	6,922,219	70.8
10–15........	0.0016	97,521	151	487,242	6,434,186	66.0
15–20........	0.0025	97,370	242	486,277	5,946,944	61.1
20–25........	0.0030	97,128	292	484,932	5,460,667	56.2
25–30........	0.0036	96,836	347	483,347	4,975,735	51.4
30–35........	0.0048	96,489	467	481,339	4,492,388	46.6
35–40........	0.0074	96,022	707	478,454	4,011,049	41.8
40–45........	0.0119	95,315	1,131	473,938	3,532,595	37.1
45–50........	0.0183	94,184	1,722	466,884	3,058,657	32.5
50–55........	0.0277	92,462	2,561	456,303	2,591,773	28.0
55–60........	0.0408	89,901	3,672	440,915	2,135,470	23.8
60–65........	0.0660	86,229	5,690	417,734	1,694,555	19.7
65–70........	0.1033	80,539	8,318	383,157	1,276,821	15.9
70–75........	0.1659	72,221	11,985	332,604	893,664	12.4
75–80........	0.2661	60,236	16,028	261,987	561,060	9.3
80–85........	0.4209	44,208	18,609	173,695	299,073	6.8
85 and over....	1.0000	25,599	25,599	125,378	125,378	4.9

Source: *Vital Statistics of the United States, 1960,* vol. II, sec. 2, p. 2-8.

TABLE 12-5C.   ABRIDGED LIFE TABLES FOR NONWHITE MALES, UNITED STATES, 1960 (INCLUDES ALASKA AND HAWAII)

Age interval	Proportion dying	Of 100,000 born alive		Stationary population		Average remaining lifetime
Period of life between exact ages stated in years	Proportion of persons alive at beginning of age interval dying during interval	Number living at beginning of age interval	Number dying during age interval	In the age interval	In this and all subsequent age intervals	Average number of years of life remaining at beginning of age interval
(1)	(2)	(3)	(4)	(5)	(6)	(7)
x to $x+n$	$_nq_x$	l_x	$_nd_x$	$_nL_x$	T_x	$\mathring{e}_x$
0–1..........	0.0480	100,000	4,804	95,937	6,109,681	61.1
1–5..........	0.0080	95,196	764	378,871	6,013,744	63.2
5–10.........	0.0036	94,432	340	471,239	5,634,873	59.7
10–15........	0.0040	94,092	376	469,615	5,163,634	54.9
15–20........	0.0083	93,716	779	466,836	4,694,019	50.1
20–25........	0.0136	92,937	1,263	461,667	4,227,183	45.5
25–30........	0.0171	91,674	1,566	454,553	3,765,516	41.1
30–35........	0.0209	90,108	1,886	446,006	3,310,963	36.7
35–40........	0.0304	88,222	2,679	434,705	2,864,957	32.5
40–45........	0.0424	85,543	3,630	419,113	2,430,252	28.4
45–50........	0.0619	81,913	5,074	397,538	2,011,139	24.6
50–55........	0.0910	76,839	6,991	367,454	1,613,601	21.0
55–60........	0.1179	69,848	8,232	329,120	1,246,147	17.8
60–65........	0.1847	61,616	11,380	279,730	917,027	14.9
65–70........	0.2282	50,236	11,463	222,322	637,297	12.7
70–75........	0.2812	38,773	10,904	166,264	414,975	10.7
75–80........	0.3205	27,869	8,931	116,475	248,711	8.9
80–85........	0.4363	18,938	8,262	73,221	132,236	7.0
85 and over....	1.0000	10,676	10,676	59,015	59,015	5.5

**TABLE 12-5D.   ABRIDGED LIFE TABLES FOR NONWHITE FEMALES, UNITED STATES, 1960
(INCLUDES ALASKA AND HAWAII)**

Age interval	Proportion dying	Of 100,000 born alive		Stationary population		Average remaining lifetime
Period of life between exact ages stated in years	Proportion of persons alive at beginning of age interval dying during interval	Number living at beginning of age interval	Number dying during age interval	In the age interval	In this and all subsequent age intervals	Average number of years of life remaining at beginning of age interval
(1)	(2)	(3)	(4)	(5)	(6)	(7)
x to $x+n$	$_nq_x$	l_x	$_nd_x$	$_nL_x$	T_x	$\mathring{e}_x$
0–1..........	0.0386	100,000	3,862	96,789	6,628,221	66.3
1–5..........	0.0068	96,138	654	382,939	6,531,432	67.9
5–10.........	0.0030	95,484	288	476,610	6,148,493	64.4
10–15........	0.0023	95,196	215	475,509	5,671,883	59.6
15–20........	0.0040	94,981	380	474,048	5,196,374	54.7
20–25........	0.0068	94,601	640	471,479	4,722,326	49.9
25–30........	0.0105	93,961	984	467,437	4,250,847	45.2
30–35........	0.0153	92,977	1,421	461,504	3,783,410	40.7
35–40........	0.0228	91,556	2,087	452,832	3,321,906	36.3
40–45........	0.0318	89,469	2,849	440,605	2,869,074	32.1
45–50........	0.0461	86,620	3,991	423,588	2,428,469	28.0
50–55........	0.0683	82,629	5,641	399,593	2,004,881	24.3
55–60........	0.0934	76,988	7,191	367,422	1,605,288	20.9
60–65........	0.1398	69,797	9,758	324,854	1,237,866	17.7
65–70........	0.1631	60,039	9,793	275,738	913,012	15.2
70–75........	0.2102	50,246	10,561	224,759	637,274	12.7
75–80........	0.2568	39,685	10,191	172,621	412,515	10.4
80–85........	0.3513	29,494	10,360	120,852	239,894	8.1
85 and over....	1.0000	19,134	19,134	119,042	119,042	6.2

Source: *Vital Statistics of the United States, 1960, vol. II, sec. 2, p. 2-8.*

stationary population from 205,500 births. In the United States in 1960 there were 3,600,744 white births. Since 205,500 white births divided into the total white births shows that there were 17.52 times as many white births as were needed to yield a stationary population of 14,519,210, if we multiply this latter figure by 17.52, we get the total white stationary population of 254,376,559, if the total *number of white births* and the *probability of dying* both remained constant at the 1960 level for about 90 to 95 years. Similar calculations for the nonwhite population, using the 1960 sex ratio at birth for nonwhites of 102, show that their stationary total would amount to approximately 41,834,120. Hence, our total stationary population, with the annual *number* of births for both whites and nonwhites remaining as in 1960 and the probability of dying at each age remaining as in that year, would be approximately 296 million. The crude birth rate would, of course, be declining rather steadily but slowly as the total population increased, because these calculations assumed a fixed *number* of births. By about the year 2060, both the crude birth rate and the crude death rate would be about 14.4 per 1,000. The crude death rate is now about 9.5 per 1,000; thus it would then be about 5 points, or practically one-half higher than at present, because of the age composition of the life-table population.

These data show that present age-specific death rates are already so low that if they were to remain at the 1960 level and if the absolute number of births remained constant, there would still be a considerable increase in population for several decades.

Expectation of Life. Another calculation of much interest derived from a life table shows how long, *on the average*, persons of any given age may expect to live (column 7). This is called the expectation of life. According to the probabilities of dying for 1960, the average white boy baby at birth could expect to live 67.4 years and a white girl baby, 74.1 years. For nonwhites the corresponding figures are (males) 61.1 and (females) 66.3 (the top figure in column 7 for each color and sex). At age 45, the average white male in the United States (1960) could expect to live 27.2 years (column 7, line 45–50, white male), the nonwhite male of the same age, 24.6 years. The average white woman aged 45 could expect to live 32.5 years and the nonwhite woman 28 years. These figures are secured by dividing the total number of years (column 6) remaining to be lived by all the survivors (column 3) at any age one may choose; for example, in column 6 at age 45, for white males 2,459,402 years of life remain for 90,465 survivors at this age (column 3). Thus, 2,459,402 divided by 90,465 equals 27.2 years.

The reader will have noticed that at every age, both for whites and nonwhites, the expectation of life (column 7) for females is considerably in excess of that for males. This same phenomenon reversed is seen (column 3) in the smaller number of male than of female survivors at every age from the same number of births. This greater viability of females than males goes far to account for the large excess of widows over widowers at the older ages. The fact that men generally marry women younger than themselves also adds to the excess of widows. Some of the social and economic implications of these sex differences in expectation of life in the United States are noted in Chapter 17.

It is also of some interest that the expectation of life in the population at exact age 1 is higher than at birth for both males and females. In general terms this is due to the fact that infant mortality although very greatly reduced during the last 50–75 years remains a much greater hazard (chance) for all children born than the probability of dying is to all children and adults at any age from 1 to about 45–50. Nevertheless, it is the great reduction of infant mortality that accounts for most of the increase in expectation of life during the past century. The decrease in the death rates of children 1–14 and of young people 15–25 accounts for most of the remainder of this increase.

The number of survivors at any age (column 3) from the original cohort of 100,000 is a good indicator of differences in the health conditions that have prevailed up to the age specified in the different populations and in the same population when life tables for different dates are available. If one desires to think in terms of the percentage of the population surviving at a specified age (column 3) in different populations, the comma may be thought of as a decimal point. Thus 96.5 percent of the white males born in 1960 will live to exact age 15, while only 93.7 percent of nonwhite males will live to this age.

It should also be noted that in the United States life tables for 1960, approximately 15 percent of the stationary white population would be 65 years of age and over, while only about 12 percent of the nonwhite population would fall into the same age group. This may be compared with approximately 9.4 percent at the present time for whites and 6.1 percent for nonwhites.

The life-table data show how different probabilities of dying affect the age and sex composition of a population (see Chapter 5). But, of course, if the basic data are adequate to permit the calculation of good age-specific death rates, these rates can be used directly to study the significance of differences in mortality as they affect the composition of different populations. A life table has the advantage for most of us that many of the most significant differences in mortality have already been calculated with precision in a form which makes comparisons of general health conditions between populations quite easy to understand.

It will be of considerable historical interest to compare the number of survivors, the expectation of life, and the probabilities of dying as shown by the life tables for Sweden at certain ages in 1816–1840 and in 1959 (Table 12-6), an interval of about 125 years. As the following figures show, the number of male survivors from the original cohort of 100,000 at age 15, according to the 1816–1840 life table, was 69.1 percent (this is the same as 69,080 out of 100,000).

In 1959 this had risen to 97.4 percent. For females, the corresponding proportions surviving were 71.9 percent and 98.1 percent. At age 45, slightly less than one-half (49.8 percent) of the original male cohort (1816–1840) survived; by 1959 this proportion had risen to 93.2 percent. For females, the corresponding proportions at age 45 were 55.3 percent and 95.5 percent.

TABLE 12-6.   SURVIVORS, EXPECTATION OF LIFE, AND DEATH RATES, BY SEX, SWEDEN, 1816–1840 AND 1959

Year and age	Survivors		Expectation of life		Death rate	
	Male	Female	Male	Female	Male	Female
1816–1840*						
0............	100,000	100,000	39.50	43.56	179.70†	154.90†
15............	69,080	71,940	41.23	44.65	4.90	4.60
30............	61,550	65,230	30.25	33.40	10.90	8.70
45............	49,800	55,320	20.52	22.98	19.10	14.10
60............	32,780	40,890	12.07	13.22	40.00	31.50
1959‡						
0............	100,000	100,000	71.69	75.24	17.6	13.2
15............	97,368	98,127	58.57	61.64	0.7	0.4
30............	95,741	97,418	44.43	47.03	1.1	0.7
45............	93,239	95,543	30.40	32.77	3.4	2.1
60............	83,950	89,089	17.75	19.49	14.1	10.3

* Gustav Sundbärg, *Swedish Population Statistics, 1750–1900*, Norstedt & Sons, Stockholm, 1907, pp. 152–153.
† This is infant mortality for the years 1816–1840.
‡ United Nations, *Demographic Yearbook, 1961*.

From the standpoint of fertility, the most significant fact in these tables is that of the original cohort of 100,000 females (1816–1840), only 71.9 percent survived to childbearing age, only 65.2 percent survived to age 30, and 55.3 percent lived to the end of the childbearing period. According to the 1959 life table, 98.1 percent of the original 100,000 females survived to the reproductive age of 15, 97.4 percent lived to 30 years of age, and 95.5 percent lived to age 45.

As would be expected from the numbers of survivors, there was a very large increase in the expectation of life at each age and for both sexes during this interval of about a century and a quarter. Moreover, there was a highly significant change in the expectation of life at age 15, as shown in these tables. In 1816–1840 the expectation of life for both sexes was somewhat higher at age

15 than at birth, whereas in 1959 the expectation of life at this age (15), for both males and females, was 13 to 14 years less than at birth. This difference arises largely from the great reduction of infant and child mortality, which has already been noted but is strongly emphasized by these data. Although the death rate at age 0 is *infant mortality* in the 1816–1840 data and is *probability of dying* during the first year of life in the 1959 data, no significant error is involved in saying that the infant death rate for males was about 10 times as high in 1816–1840 as in 1959 and for females was about 15 times as high. At age 15, the death rate was 7 times as high for males and 11 times as high for females in 1816–1840 as in 1959. This great wastage of life at the younger ages explains the lower expectation of life at birth than at 15 years of age in 1816–1840.

It will be of some interest to note how the expectation of life at birth would change if the present crude death rate in the United States, viz., about 9.5 per 1,000 of the total population, prevailed in a stationary population.

A life-table death rate of 9.5 (both sexes) would mean that only 9.5 persons per 1,000 in a stationary population died each year. This could happen only if the rates for probability of dying at the several ages declined to such an extent that in the aggregate the total life-table population (stationary) rose to approximately 10.5 million, which is about 3.5 million above the 1960 stationary population. Ten and one-half million is also the total number of years lived by each cohort of 100,000 babies (both sexes) entering this population. Hence, each person in such a hypothetical population would, on the average, live approximately 105 years. There is certainly no evidence in the data we possess today that we are likely to approach such an expectation of life in the foreseeable future. A life-table death rate of 12 would mean an expectation of life at birth of 83.3 years, which is one-sixth to one-fifth higher than that of today. It would be folly to say that this could not happen within three to four decades, but it certainly is not likely to be achieved within a few years. Our present low crude death rate of about 9.5 is possible only because we still have a population that is relatively young.

DEATH RATES BY CAUSE OF DEATH[3]

The death rate from a given disease is another measure of mortality which is very helpful both in evaluating the effectiveness of present health work in different communities and also in indicating in which direction the extension of health services is most needed. Rates for deaths by cause are most useful when

[3] The term "cause," as used here, is purely a medical concept, denoting the physical character of the abnormality found in the human body which led to death. It carries no direct implication as to how these causes became operative. Some environmental factors underlying these medical causes of death will be noted briefly in the following chapter.

they are also shown by age and sex, since certain of the most important diseases operate chiefly or almost exclusively at certain ages and a few diseases are found chiefly in males or females. Death rates for such diseases mean little unless differentiated by sex. For practically all the more important causes of death, the rates for males are higher than those for females.

Since advanced medical practice today recognizes several hundred diseases as "causes" of death, the death rates for most causes would usually be less than 1 per 1,000; hence death rates by cause are generally expressed in terms of the number of deaths occurring in a rather large population unit, e.g., per 100,000 or per 10,000. The usual practice in the United States is to use 100,000.

The 1960 age-adjusted mortality rates for all causes of death combined and for selected causes, for whites and for nonwhites, and for males and females (Table 12-7), show wide differences. The age-adjusted death rate for white males (918) from all causes was 65 percent higher than that for white females (555), and that for nonwhite males (1,211) was 36 percent higher than for nonwhite females (893). The age-adjusted death rate for the total white population was only 70 percent as high as that for the nonwhite population. (These racial differences in death rates will be discussed in more detail in the following chapter.) It is important to note that these age-adjusted rates (1960) should not be compared with the unadjusted rates for the total population in Table 12-8. These age-adjusted rates (Table 12-7) from all causes and for each selected cause tell us what the 1960 rates would have been if the age composition of each group (white, nonwhite, male, and female) in 1960 had been the same as in 1940. Changes in age explain the difference between the unadjusted rate for the total population in 1960 (954.7, Table 12-8) and the adjusted rate (760.9, Table 12-7). The actual age composition of the population in 1960 was much less favorable to low death rates than that of 1940.

Table 12-8 shows that ten major causes of death, not including "all other causes," accounted for 787.8 deaths per 100,000 of the population out of a total of 954.7 per 100,000, i.e., for approximately 82 percent of all deaths in 1960. The change between 1900 and 1960 in the proportion of deaths due to these causes is also shown in Table 12-8. (The death registration area of 1900 consisted of only a few states in the Northeastern part of the country.) There are two striking changes in causes of death during this period: (1) Whereas tuberculosis, influenza and pneumonia, and diseases of the digestive tract accounted for 539 deaths per 100,000 out of a total of 1,719 deaths per 100,000, or for 31 percent of all deaths in 1900, they accounted for only 5 percent of all deaths in 1960; (2) in 1900 the deaths from major cardiovascular-renal diseases and cancer accounted for only about 24 percent of all deaths but for 70 percent in 1960. In other words, infectious diseases caused almost one-third of all deaths in the United States as late as 1900 but only about one-twentieth of them in 1960. In most other highly developed industrialized countries much the same

TABLE 12-7. AGE-ADJUSTED DEATH RATES FOR SELECTED CAUSES, BY COLOR AND SEX: UNITED STATES, 1960

(Data refer only to deaths occurring within the United States, including Alaska and Hawaii, and exclude fetal deaths. Based on age-specific death rates per 100,000 population in specified group, enumerated as of April 1. Computed by the direct method using as the standard population the age distribution of the total population of the United States as enumerated in 1940.)

Cause of death	Total			White			Nonwhite		
	Both sexes	Male	Female	Both sexes	Male	Female	Both sexes	Male	Female
All causes............	760.9	949.3	590.6	727.0	917.7	555.0	1,046.1	1,211.0	893.3
Major cardiovascular-renal diseases............	399.3	500.5	308.5	386.8	493.2	291.5	513.6	564.0	467.1
Diseases of cardiovascular system............	393.5	493.6	303.7	381.9	487.3	287.6	499.0	547.8	453.8
Vascular lesions affecting central nervous system............	79.7	85.4	74.7	74.2	80.3	68.7	134.8	135.2	134.4
Diseases of heart............	286.2	375.5	205.7	281.5	375.4	197.1	324.2	368.3	283.3
General arteriosclerosis............	13.2	14.8	11.8	13.1	14.7	11.7	13.8	15.5	12.3
Chronic and unspecified nephritis and other renal sclerosis............	5.7	6.8	4.8	4.9	5.9	3.9	14.6	16.1	13.2
Malignant neoplasms, including neoplasms of lymphatic and hematopoietic tissues............	125.8	143.0	111.2	124.2	141.6	109.5	139.3	154.8	125.0
Accidents............	49.9	73.9	26.8	47.6	70.6	25.4	67.3	101.1	36.1
Motor vehicle accidents............	22.5	34.5	11.0	22.3	34.0	11.1	24.4	39.5	10.6
Other accidents............	27.4	39.3	15.8	25.3	36.5	14.4	42.9	61.6	25.5
Influenza and pneumonia, except pneumonia of newborn............	28.0	35.0	21.8	24.6	31.0	19.0	55.2	68.0	43.3
Diabetes mellitus............	13.6	12.0	15.0	12.8	11.6	13.7	21.6	16.1	26.8
Cirrhosis of liver............	10.5	14.5	6.9	10.3	14.4	6.6	11.9	14.9	9.1
Tuberculosis, all forms............	5.4	8.2	2.9	4.4	6.8	2.2	15.1	21.4	9.3

Source: *Vital Statistics of the United States, 1960, vol. II, sec. 1, table 1-J.*

change has taken place during this period although the death rates from heart and cancer diseases are somewhat higher in the United States than in most other industrialized countries. This is a very important change, to which we shall have occasion to call attention quite frequently in later chapters.

TABLE 12-8.   MORTALITY PER 100,000 FROM SELECTED CAUSES OF DEATH: DEATH-REGISTRATION STATES, 1900, AND UNITED STATES, 1960*

Cause of death	1960		1900	
	Rate	Percent	Rate	Percent
All causes.............................	954.7	100.0	1,719.1	100.0
Tuberculosis, all forms...................	6.1	0.6	194.4	11.3
Influenza and pneumonia, except pneumonia of newborn...........................	37.3	3.9	202.2	11.8
Gastritis, duodenitis, enteritis, and colitis, except diarrhea of newborn..............	4.4	0.5	142.7	8.3
Diphtheria.............................	0.0	0.0	40.3	2.3
Typhoid fever..........................	0.0	0.0	31.3	1.8
Major cardiovascular-renal diseases.........	521.8	54.7	345.2	20.1
Vascular lesions affecting central nervous system...........................	108.0	11.3	106.9	6.2
Diseases of heart......................	369.0	38.7	142.7	8.3
Other hypertensive disease and general arteriosclerosis......................	27.1	2.8	} 14.7	} 0.9
Other diseases of circulatory system......	11.0	1.2		
Chronic and unspecified nephritis and other renal sclerosis..................	6.7	0.7	81.0	4.7
Malignant neoplasms, including neoplasms of lymphatic and hematopoietic tissues...	149.2	15.6	64.0	3.7
Diabetes mellitus.......................	16.7	1.8	11.0	0.6
Motor vehicle accidents..................	21.3	2.2	——	——
All other accidents......................	31.0	3.3	72.3	4.2
All other causes........................	166.9	17.5	615.7	35.8

* See headnote to Table 12-7.
Source: *Vital Statistics of the United States, 1960,* vol. II, sec. 1, table 1-K.

Table 12-9 shows the changes in the distribution of deaths by age between 1930 and 1960. As we have just noted, the changes in the causes of deaths are to a considerable extent responsible for the large decreases in the proportions of deaths at the younger ages and the large increases in the proportions at the older ages, especially at ages 65 and over. However, it should be noted that there were very large absolute and proportional increases in persons 65 years of age and over during this period, from 6.6 million in 1930 to 16.2 million in 1960 and from 5.5 percent of the total population in 1930 to 9.0 percent in 1960. This proportional change is also an important factor in explaining the changes in the proportions of deaths occurring at the younger and older ages.

TABLE 12-9.   DEATHS AT EACH AGE AND THE PROPORTION OF THESE DEATHS OCCURRING AT DIFFERENT AGES,* UNITED STATES, 1960 AND 1930

Age	1960		1930	
	Number	Percent	Number	Percent
All ages............	1,711,982	100.00	1,343,356	100.00
Under 1..........	110,873	6.48	145,374	10.82
1–4..............	17,682	1.03	49,826	3.71
5–14.............	16,537	0.97	40,608	3.02
15–24............	25,533	1.49	72,505	5.40
25–34............	33,414	1.95	85,919	6.40
35–44............	72,103	4.21	114,590	8.53
45–54............	154,876	9.05	155,142	11.55
55–64............	270,197	15.78	197,791	14.72
65–74............	420,312	24.55	238,213	11.73
75 and over......	589,735	34.45	241,521	17.98

* The percents given here do not add to exactly 100 because the total includes deaths at unknown ages.
Source: Vital Statistics of the United States, 1960, vol. II, sec. 1, p. 1-22; Mortality Statistics of the United States, 1930, p. 266.

INFANT MORTALITY

The infant mortality rate shows the number of deaths of children under 1 year of age per 1,000 live births occurring in the same year. Of course, not all children under 1 who die in a given year were born the same year, but usually the changes in the number of births and infant deaths from one year to the next are not so great that the infant-mortality rate tells a significantly different story from the death rate of children under 1 based on the midyear population of children under 1. The infant mortality rate is generally considered a very good index of living in any population group—the lower the infant mortality rate, the better the level of living—as well as a good indication of the general health conditions prevailing in a population. This index is of less value since World

War II because of the fact that the new health services are making large use of the miracle drugs in the underdeveloped countries.[4]

Although they involve some repetition, a few historical data will be of interest in tracing the decline of infant mortality since about the middle of the seventeenth century. John Graunt, working with parish registers in London, estimated that about 1662 only 640 children out of each 1,000 born survived to age 6 and only 250 survived to age 26. Dupré de St. Maur calculated that in France prior to 1750, only 540 children out of 1,000 born alive survived to the fifth year, and only 484 to the tenth year. Halley, working on data for Breslau, 1687 to 1691, found 661 surviving to the tenth year and Süssmilch, basing his calculations on German data prior to 1775, found only 532 surviving to the tenth year. Wargentin, working on Swedish data, 1757 to 1763, found 611 surviving to age 10. At the end of the eighteenth century in Sweden, about 200 babies under 1 year of age were dying per 1,000 live births during the year. Such calculations, except those for Sweden, although based on data which were both scanty and less accurate than those to which we are accustomed today, show beyond reasonable doubt that the mortality of infants and of children during the first few years of life was very great in Europe before the agricultural and industrial revolutions had begun to exercise much influence on the economy of this region. However, by the end of the eighteenth century, such rates had begun to decline in a few countries.[5]

Table 12-10 shows the infant mortality for a few countries in recent years. In 1900 several of these countries reported rates of 190 or over, and only Sweden had a rate under 100. By 1956–1960, only Chile and the Muslim population of Algeria reported rates over 100 (120 and 103 respectively). By this time several countries (some of them not included here) had rates below 25, and Sweden had a rate of only 17.

Deaths of babies under 28 days of age are often referred to as *neonatal* deaths. They are, of course, included in infant mortality, but they are sometimes treated separately and in detail by people especially interested in health services because they arise to a considerable extent from causes over which even the best health services have comparatively little control. For example, in 1960 almost one-fifth of all infant deaths in the United States were due to congenital malformations about which practically nothing can now be done, and approximately

---

[4] The term "underdeveloped country" (or countries) will be used frequently in following chapters. It simply means a country that as yet has only a small amount of machine industry and hence only a small proportion of its workers engaged in nonagricultural tasks and living in large towns or cities.

[5] Emile Levasseur, "The Tables of Mortality and Survivorship," *Royal Statistical Society Journal*, vol. 50, no. 3, pp. 549–554, 1887. (Translated from *Journal de la société de statistiques de Paris*, March, 1887.)

TABLE 12-10.   AVERAGE INFANT MORTALITY RATES IN SELECTED COUNTRIES, 1898 TO 1960* (Deaths under one year per 1,000 live births)

Country	1956–1960	1948–1952	1938–1942	1918–1922	1908–1912	1898–1902
Sweden	17	22	38	65	75	98
Australia	21	25	39	63	73	111
England and Wales	23	31	54	85	112	152
Denmark	24†	32	54	84	104	131
Finland	24	42	70	108	115	138
United States	26	30	46	85¶	——	——
France	32	53	73	112	123	154
Formosa	34	42	——			
Germany	36‡	57‡	65	140	170	199†
Japan	36	58	96	172	159†	155
Austria	41	66	74	155	198†	220
Algeria						
European	42†	66	108†	——	——	——
Muslim	103†	88	——	——	——	——
Italy	47	68	107	141	147	167
Spain	49	69	127	158	152	190†
Argentina	61†	67	92	——	——	——
Ceylon	66†	84	145	——	——	——
Honduras (British)	75	98	107	——	——	——
Mexico	76	99	124	——	——	——
Guatemala	95	106	117	——	——	——
India	98†§	124	159	212	206†	——
Chile	120	141	214	258†	314	349

* For the current data on infant mortality rates the reader is referred to current issues of *Population Index.*

† Denmark, 1955 to 1959; Germany, 1901 to 1905; Japan, 1908 to 1910; Austria, 1909 and 1910 not included; Algeria, 1955 to 1959, 1939 to 1943; Spain, 1900 to 1902; Argentina, 1955 to 1959; Ceylon, 1955 to 1959; India, 1955 to 1959, 1911, and 1912; Chile, 1919 and 1920 not included.

‡ Federal Republic.

§ Registration area.

¶ Birth registration area.

three-fifths were due to diseases of early infancy, a considerable proportion of which, e.g., birth injuries, asphyxia, and *infections of the immature newborn*, often cannot be prevented. These two broad groups of causes accounted for one-half or more of all infant mortality in 1960. It is also of interest that in this year neonatal mortality constituted over 70 percent of all infant mortality. About one-half to three-fifths of all infant deaths in the United States now appear to be due to causes which cannot yet be controlled to any considerable extent. Hence it is unlikely that infant mortality in the near future can be reduced much more than 8 to 10 points from the level (26) it had attained in the United States in 1960. Most of the future reduction in infant mortality for the total population in the United States will take place in the nonwhite population, which now constitutes about 10–11 percent of the total and still has a high rate (43.2 in 1960) of infant mortality.

CHAPTER THIRTEEN *Some Environmental Influences on the Death Rate. Mortality Trends*

This chapter will deal chiefly with certain environmental factors that influence the death rate and will summarize mortality trends. Famines, epidemics, and wars will be discussed in Chapters 14 to 16, passim.

MORTALITY AND COMMUNITY OF RESIDENCE

Long before modern vital statistics made it possible to distinguish between deaths in rural and urban communities, cities and towns had gained bad repute as killers of men. There is little doubt that they deserved this reputation as long as the contagious and infectious diseases ran rampant and accounted for a large proportion of all deaths. The almost complete lack of sanitary measures in nearly all cities until near the end of the nineteenth century and the crowding of the great majority of city dwellers in hovels with no windows, bordering on streets where one could almost touch the structures on both sides by stretching out his arms and where the *sewage and the drinking water ran down the same open gutters*, ensured contagion and infection almost perfectly. Some remnants of such conditions were still to be found in many communities in the West as late as 1900.

During the nineteenth century vital statistics gradually improved, and it became increasingly possible to compare the death rates of urban and rural communities. These early comparisons showed in general that the death rates of rural communities were lower than those of urban communities. But the rates first used were *crude* death rates. The fact that the growing cities of the nineteenth century contained a relatively high proportion of young people from rural areas who had relatively low death rates wherever they lived obscured the actual favorable differentials in the death rates of rural communities. Age adjustments came later, when more detailed data made possible the calculations of age-specific death rates.

Dorn's study of rural-urban mortality in Ohio in 1930 (Table 13-1)[1] will serve to illustrate the points just made. This study showed that when crude death rates were used, the lowest death rate (9.3) for native white males in Ohio was found in the largest cities (100,000 and over) and the highest (11.7)

TABLE 13-1.   DEATHS PER 1,000 NATIVE WHITE POPULATION BY AGE AND SEX IN URBAN GROUPS AND RURAL AREAS, OHIO, 1930

Age	100,000 and over		10,000–100,000		2,500–10,000		Rural-nonfarm		Rural-farm	
	Male	Female	Male	Female	Male	Female	Male	Female	Male	Female
Total (crude).	9.3	8.1	10.3	9.2	11.7	10.7	10.4	9.9	11.7	11.1
0–4.........	17.2	13.6	17.1	15.0	17.2	13.2	17.3	13.7	16.8	14.0
5–9.........	2.4	1.7	1.9	1.0	1.9	1.2	1.9	1.4	1.8	1.7
10–14.......	1.5	1.2	1.7	0.9	1.5	1.0	1.4	1.4	1.5	1.3
15–19.......	2.4	1.9	2.6	1.7	2.5	2.3	2.7	2.2	1.6	1.8
20–24.......	2.7	2.7	2.7	2.5	3.8	3.4	3.6	3.5	3.6	3.1
25–29.......	3.1	3.3	3.3	3.1	3.9	3.9	3.4	3.5	4.0	3.7
30–34.......	4.4	3.8	3.7	3.3	3.9	3.4	3.5	3.4	3.3	4.3
35–44.......	6.4	5.0	5.4	4.5	4.6	4.9	5.2	4.8	4.5	4.5
45–54.......	12.3	10.0	10.6	9.0	9.6	9.6	7.8	8.6	7.2	7.5
55–64.......	25.8	19.9	24.0	19.1	23.2	17.7	17.0	17.0	16.6	16.2
65–74.......	59.1	45.9	58.8	45.1	51.2	41.4	43.9	41.2	43.8	39.5
75 and over..	135.6	114.5	140.9	122.2	140.8	122.2	117.6	123.5	118.0	110.1
Adjusted rate*......	10.7	8.7	10.3	8.5	10.0	8.4	9.0	8.4	8.6	8.0

* Based on the standard million population of England and Wales, 1901.
Source: Harold F. Dorn, *Differential Rural-Urban Mortality in Ohio, 1930*, The University of Wisconsin Press, Madison, Wis., 1933, pp. 90, 114–115. Exclusive of institutional deaths.

in the rural-farm communities and small cities (2,500 to 10,000). Males in rural-nonfarm communities and in cities of 10,000 to 100,000 had crude rates about midway between those of the other groups. The crude rates for females were also highest in the farm population (11.1) but almost as high in the smallest cities. They were lowest (8.1) in the largest cities. However, when rates were standardized for age, the above rankings were, in general, reversed. The rate for males showed a consistent decline from the largest cities to rural-farm

[1] Similar data were not available for the United States at that time.

communities. The rates for females declined in much the same manner, except that rural-nonfarm communities had the same rate as the smallest cities.

In 1940 the crude death rate of Ohio's white population, both sexes combined (see Table 13-2), was lowest (10.5) in cities of 10,000 to 100,000, next lowest in cities of 100,000 and over (11.2), followed by rural communities (11.5 in all places under 2,500), and highest in the smallest cities (11.8). When these rates

TABLE 13-2.   DEATHS PER 1,000 WHITE POPULATION BY AGE AND POPULATION-SIZE GROUPS, UNITED STATES AND OHIO, 1940

Age	United States				Ohio			
	100,000 and over	10,000– 100,000	2,500– 10,000	Rural	100,000 and over	10,000– 100,000	2,500– 10,000	Rural
Total (crude)......	10.9	11.0	12.0	9.5	11.2	10.5	11.8	11.5
Under 1...........	45.7	55.0	66.6	47.8	44.3	46.1	50.4	48.9
1–4.............	2.1	2.6	3.3	2.7	2.0	2.1	2.8	2.5
5–14.............	0.9	1.0	1.3	0.9	0.9	0.9	1.0	1.0
15–24............	1.4	1.7	2.1	1.8	1.5	1.4	1.7	1.7
25–34............	2.3	2.5	2.9	2.5	2.5	2.2	2.6	2.5
35–44............	4.7	4.4	4.9	3.9	4.9	3.9	4.1	4.1
45–54............	10.9	10.0	10.2	7.8	10.8	8.8	8.6	8.1
55–64............	24.7	22.5	22.4	17.4	24.3	19.9	19.7	18.3
65–74............	53.3	50.1	49.9	42.4	54.6	47.4	44.7	42.9
75–84............	118.0	115.8	117.4	108.9	123.0	112.3	113.9	118.0
85 and over......	210.8	238.2	259.8	241.7	231.1	251.5	264.3	254.3
Adjusted rate*....	10.8	10.6	11.2	9.3	11.0	9.7	9.9	9.6

* Based on the total population of the United States, 1940.
Source: U.S. Bureau of the Census, *Vital Statistics Rates in the United States, 1900–1940*, pp. 198 and 205.

were standardized, the different sizes of places ranked as follows in descending order of rates: 100,000 and over, 11.0; 2,500 to 10,000, 9.9; 10,000 to 100,000, 9.7; rural, 9.6.

In the white population of the United States in 1940, males and females combined, both the crude and the standardized rates were lowest in rural communities (see Table 13-2). The largest cities had the next lowest crude rates but slightly higher standardized rates than the medium-sized cities. The smallest cities had the highest rates, both crude and standardized. It should be noted here, however, that by 1940, in the white population in both Ohio and the United States, most of the age-specific death rates at ages under 35 were lower in the larger cities than in either the rural population or the smaller cities, while at ages of 35 and over the largest cities had the highest death rates, except at ages 35–44 for the smallest cities and at ages 85 and over.

Likewise, in recent years mortality rates for children under 1 year of age in the larger cities of the United States have consistently fallen below those in the rural areas, with the exception of rural communities in metropolitan counties (see below). By 1940 the death rate for whites under 1 year of age in the large cities of the United States had fallen to 45.7, while that for the rural white population was 47.8. This rate rose as the size of the city decreased, to 55.0 in cities of 10,000 to 100,000 and then to 66.6 in cities of 2,500 to 10,000 (see Table 13-2). Clearly, the death rate of babies in the largest cities was falling faster than that in the rural communities, although the highest rates were still to be found in the smaller cities. Since 1940 there has been a very large further decline in infant mortality and that of young children in all types of communities. This decline has been about the same in rural communities (34 percent in the years 1940–1949) as in cities of 2,500 to 100,000 (35 percent) and larger than in cities of 100,000 and over (28 percent).

The 1950 data on crude death rates in the United States show that once again those for the rural population (1950 definition of rural and including all races and both sexes) was 10.5 per 1,000 for the urban population but only 8.3 for the rural population and that there is about the same difference for both whites and nonwhites. This plus the information on infant mortality for 1960 in the following paragraph creates a strong probability that rural residence is again becoming more favorable to lower death rates than urban residence.[2]

In 1960 the mortality rate for white infants in the rural population of the *metropolitan* counties was 20.8. In the urban population of these same counties it was 22.7. The infant mortality rates in the *nonmetropolitan* counties corresponding to these were 23.7 in the rural population and 24.7 in the urban population.[3] Since the rural population of the metropolitan counties, especially in those counties having cities of over 100,000, probably has the advantage of better county health services than the rural population living in the nonmetropolitan counties and also the advantages that go with living in less congested areas and at a higher income level than the urban population in the same counties, it is not surprising that this rural metropolitan population has the lowest infant mortality rates.

That differences in death rates between rural and urban communities have

[2] U.S. Bureau of the Census, *Vital Statistics in the United States, 1900–1940*, p. 578, and U.S. Federal Security Agency, National Office of Vital Statistics, *Vital Statistics of the United States, 1949*, part 1, p. xlix; also, 1950, vol. I, table 8.11.

[3] *Vital Statistics of the United States, 1960*, vol. II, part B, table 9-2, pp. 9-60 and 9-61.

not been confined to the United States is shown by the data for England and Wales given in Table 13-3 for 1930 to 1932. At no period of life, except at ages 20–24 and at 85 and over, did males in the rural districts of England and Wales have as high a rate of actual to expected deaths as did males in either county boroughs or in other urban districts. (The expected rate is 1,000 because

TABLE 13-3.   RATIO OF ACTUAL TO EXPECTED DEATHS AS COMPUTED BY ENGLISH LIFE TABLES, ENGLAND AND WALES, 1930–1932

Age	Male			Female		
	County* boroughs	Urban districts	Rural districts	County* boroughs	Urban districts	Rural districts
5 and over..........	1.106	0.971	0.858	1.054	0.978	0.934
5–9...............	1.088	0.971	0.847	1.066	1.011	0.840
10–14..............	1.096	0.949	0.929	1.064	0.966	0.906
15–19..............	1.050	1.002	0.921	1.063	0.962	0.937
20–24..............	1.043	0.957	0.971	1.038	0.957	0.975
25–29..............	1.060	0.954	0.932	1.024	0.984	0.978
30–34..............	1.092	0.939	0.902	1.031	0.972	0.983
35–39..............	1.120	0.940	0.850	1.029	0.972	1.002
40–44..............	1.145	0.929	0.800	1.073	0.951	0.921
45–49..............	1.169	0.929	0.763	1.064	0.962	0.916
50–54..............	1.164	0.935	0.756	1.074	0.955	0.911
55–59..............	1.140	0.947	0.796	1.068	0.967	0.909
60–64..............	1.114	0.971	0.815	1.059	0.983	0.907
65–69..............	1.109	0.983	0.835	1.064	0.978	0.913
70–74..............	1.099	1.000	0.841	1.054	0.986	0.908
75–79..............	1.075	1.001	0.905	1.051	0.988	0.945
80–84..............	1.060	1.003	0.932	1.044	0.984	0.963
85 and over.........	1.029	0.963	1.000	1.035	0.988	0.985

* Includes London Administrative County.

Source: Great Britain, Registrar-General, *The Registrar-General's Decennial Supplement; England and Wales, 1931*, part 1, H.M. Stationery Office, London, 1936, pp. 45–47.

the rate for total males and females at each age for urban and rural communities combined is given a value of unity, 1,000.) On the other hand, this ratio among females was higher in the rural districts than in the smaller urban districts at ages 20–24 and 30–39, but at no age for either sex was this ratio as high in the rural districts as in the county boroughs (the larger cities). (See page 369 for further explanation of the ratio of actual to expected deaths.)

In Sweden before 1910 the crude death rates in the rural areas were lower than in the cities, but after that date were usually lower in the cities. In 1945–

1946, however, when the crude death rate for males in rural communities was 11.1 and that for males in urban communities was 10.1, the standardization of these rates reduced the rural rates to 10.3 but raised the urban rate to 11.2. For females in the same year, the crude rates were as follows: rural, 11.5; urban, 9.6. Standardization changed them to 10.9 and 10.4, respectively, thus leaving the urban rate for females only slightly lower than the rural rate. The pattern of age-specific death rates now appears to be much the same in Sweden as in the United States, but at a slightly lower level. In Sweden also, urban age-specific rates are generally lower at ages under 35 than rural rates but higher at older ages.

It would appear probable that city populations now possess certain advantages over rural populations in controlling deaths up to about 30–35 years of age, while at older ages living conditions in rural communities are better suited to retarding the onset of the chronic and organic diseases which develop later in life. More space, fresh air, a slower pace of life, and possible better sources of fresh foods may be of some significance in this connection.

MORTALITY AND MARITAL STATUS

The data in Table 13-4 show the age-specific death rates in the United States for 1959 and in France for 1945 by marital status. For the United States, these rates must be regarded as only approximate because the population base figures by age and the deaths by marital status and age are taken from different sources and may not be strictly comparable. Nevertheless, there can be no reasonable doubt that for both countries the death rates for married persons (both males and females) at all ages of 20 and over are very substantially lower than for single and widowed and divorced persons. These differences are usually larger for males than for females.

A similar relation between marital status and age-specific death rates is to be found in relatively recent data for Germany and Sweden (see Table 13-5), although there are differences in detail, as will be seen by studying these tables.

The explanation of these differences in death rates by marital condition appears to be somewhat as follows: In the first place, marriage is selective as regards both physical constitution and social adaptability. Young men who are in ill-health are more likely to avoid marriage than those in good health because of the difficulty they will encounter in providing for a family; they are also probably less likely to be chosen by females as mates. In addition, persons, both male and female, who for various reasons have low social adaptability and who do not get on well with other people may be more likely to remain single. The selective factors among women may be somewhat different from those among men, but reasonably good health would seem to be of great impor-

TABLE 13-4.   DEATH RATES PER 1,000 BY AGE, SEX, AND MARITAL CONDITION, FRANCE, 1945, AND UNITED STATES, 1959

Age	France, 1945			United States, 1959			Age
	Single	Married	Widowed or divorced	Single	Married	Widowed or divorced	
			Males			Males	
20–24.........	5.34	3.20	——	2.49	1.34	4.18	20–24
25–29.........	7.62	3.66	——	} 2.96	} 1.50	} 7.03	25–29
30–34.........	10.42	4.30	5.81				30–34
35–39.........	13.82	5.02	7.55	} 6.50	} 3.06	}12.80	35–39
40–44.........	14.69	6.73	10.26				40–44
45–49.........	17.81	8.83	13.33	}13.91	} 8.34	}25.09	45–49
50–54.........	23.44	12.55	17.81				50–54
55–59.........	32.88	17.75	25.07	}28.03	}20.58	}37.13	55–59
60–64.........	44.91	26.89	34.73				60–64
65–69.........	63.09	40.86	49.83	}73.41	}44.22	}68.56	65–69
70–74.........	——	——	——				70–74
75 and over.....	——	——	——	142.52	97.06	157.83	75 and over
			Females			Females	
20–24.........	3.06	2.74	——	0.92	0.58	1.97	20–24
25–29.........	3.95	3.10	5.28	} 2.16	} 0.90	} 2.76	25–29
30–34.........	5.20	3.21	4.26				30–34
35–39.........	6.60	3.45	4.19	} 3.80	} 1.95	} 4.42	35–39
40–44.........	6.87	4.03	5.04				40–44
45–49.........	8.03	5.30	6.57	} 5.62	} 4.61	} 7.63	45–49
50–54.........	11.32	7.50	8.81				50–54
55–59.........	14.40	10.63	12.52	}12.78	}10.45	}14.58	55–59
60–64.........	23.13	16.75	18.84				60–64
65–69.........	36.78	27.83	30.59	}32.72	}26.05	}34.72	65–69
70–74.........	——	——	——				70–74
75 and over.....	——	——	——	117.88	67.82	104.30	75 and over

Sources: France, Direction de la statistique générale, *Statistique du mouvement de la population*, part 1, 1945.
U.S. Department of Health, Education, and Welfare, *Vital Statistics of the United States*, 1959, vol. II, p. 17; and U.S. Bureau of the Census, *Current Population Reports*, ser. P-20, no. 96, p. 7.

TABLE 13-5.   DEATH RATES PER 1,000 BY AGE, SEX, AND MARITAL CONDITION, SWEDEN AND GERMANY, 1960

Age	Sweden, 1960			West Germany, 1960		
	Single	Married	Widowed and/or divorced	Single	Married	Widowed and/or divorced
	Males			Males		
20–24	1.17	0.64	——	1.83	1.38	4.00
25–29	1.58	0.79	2.61	2.20	1.38	7.07
30–34	2.23	1.04	2.11	3.23	1.47	6.85
35–39	3.21	1.27	4.03	5.23	2.15	7.23
40–44	3.95	2.18	5.27	7.91	2.93	8.83
45–49	5.97	3.33	8.10	10.41	5.16	14.18
50–54	8.60	5.45	11.36	16.53	8.89	18.80
55–59	13.18	10.63	16.69	23.80	15.29	25.41
60–64	22.74	17.28	24.26	34.92	24.76	37.30
65–69	34.09	28.17	39.51	——	——	——
70–74	57.91	47.64	57.65	——	——	——
	Females			Females		
20–24	0.48	0.38	——	0.64	0.53	1.36
25–29	1.17	0.51	1.03	1.30	0.73	1.74
30–34	1.49	0.71	0.72	2.16	0.96	2.44
35–39	2.42	0.97	2.34	2.88	1.50	2.93
40–44	2.97	1.56	2.60	3.54	1.96	2.59
45–49	4.97	2.78	3.89	5.71	3.47	4.15
50–54	5.86	4.23	5.16	6.42	4.93	5.61
55–59	8.35	6.45	7.81	9.93	7.78	8.64
60–64	14.13	10.71	12.42	15.91	12.93	14.59
65–69	21.15	19.62	21.13	——	——	——
70–74	44.77	37.15	39.70	——	——	——

Sources: Sweden, Statistiska Centralbyrån, *Befolkningsrörelsen År 1960.*
Germany, *Statistisches Jahrbuch für die Bundesrepublick Deutschland, 1962.*

tance. It may very well be, therefore, that a significant proportion of men and women who remain single are relatively poor health risks and hence have higher death rates than those who marry. However, the selective processes involved in marriage probably vary considerably from one population to another. In countries like the United States, New Zealand, and Australia, where a relative scarcity of women has been due to the preponderance of male

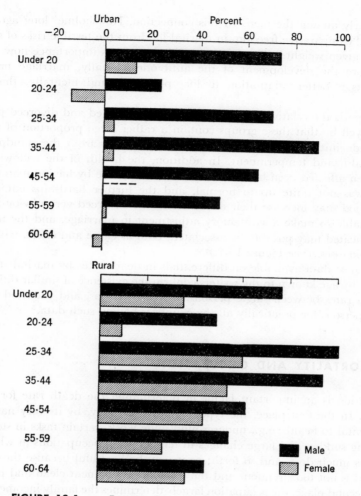

FIGURE 13-1. Percent by which death rates of single persons exceed those of married persons, urban and rural, by age and sex, United States: 1940. (Warren S. Thompson, *Population Problems*, 4th ed., McGraw-Hill Book Company, New York, 1953, p. 249.)

immigrants during much of their history, women are likely to have been more careful in selecting their mates than women in countries having considerable emigration, which have generally had a rather large surplus of women.

Another factor that may be of some importance in keeping the death rates of married persons low is the greater regularity of living among the married, particularly among the men. In this connection, Newsholme[4] long ago noted that the "comparative freedom in marital life from the terrible risks of syphilis must be given weight." This factor is probably of less importance now than it was before the development of the antibiotics. Finally, marriage probably represents a better adaptation to life, physically and mentally, than does celibacy.

As regards the relatively high death rates of widowed and divorced persons, it may well be that these groups contain a rather large proportion of persons who made initial mistakes in the selection of mates from the standpoint of both health and temperament. In addition, the health of the widowed may have been affected even before the death of the spouse by having mates whose health was not quite up to normal, and the further hardships entailed by widowhood may increase their death rates. The divorced very obviously have been unable to make a satisfactory adjustment in marriage, and the inability thus indicated may possibly be associated, both as cause and effect, with physical weaknesses. (See Figure 13-1.)

The latest data available on differentials in death rates by marital status by sex and by age known to the writers confirm the existence of similar differences in death rates between single persons, married persons, and widowed and divorced persons for practically all the countries having such data.[5]

MORTALITY AND OCCUPATION

Occupation is an important factor in determining the death rate for several reasons. In the first place, the type of work done may, by its very nature, be detrimental to health, e.g., underground mine work, certain tasks in steel mills involving sudden and large changes in temperature, occupations in which one breathes much dust, and so forth; or it may be healthful because the exercise involved is not too strenuous and the general environment clean and pleasant. In the second place, the occupation largely determines the family income and the physical surroundings of the worker and of his family at home. This being the case, it is quite surprising that more material cannot be found relating to the deaths by occupation. Most of the older material is of relatively little practical use because working conditions in many occupations have changed so fast that many of the unhealthful conditions prevailing only a few years ago are no longer of any concern. Besides, most of the earlier studies were made before any considerable body of reliable data became available, and often the methods

---

[4] Arthur Newsholme, *The Elements of Vital Statistics in Their Bearing on Social and Public Health Problems*, rev. ed., George Allen & Unwin, Ltd., London, 1923, p. 214.
[5] United Nations, *Demographic Yearbook, 1961*, table 21, pp. 588–595.

available for processing the data were inadequate to bring out the points of greatest practical significance.

Table 13-6 shows death rates per 100,000 men by broad occupational groups at ages 25 to 59 in the United States in 1950 (columns 3–7). Column 2 of this

TABLE 13-6.   DEATH RATES PER 100,000 FOR MEN 25 TO 59 YEARS OLD WITH WORK EXPERIENCE BY OCCUPATION, AGE, AND STANDARD MORTALITY RATIOS, UNITED STATES, 1960

Occupation	SMR* for ages 25–59	Death rate in age groups				
		25–29	30–34	35–44	45–54	55–59
(1)	(2)	(3)	(4)	(5)	(6)	(7)
All occupations	100	194.3	239.2	436.7	1,094.0	2,044.7
1. Professional, technical, and kindred workers.................	85	120.8	158.2	324.9	973.0	1,969.6
2. Managers, officials, etc..........	86	132.6	157.0	337.4	954.1	1,900.0
3. Clerical and kindred workers....	83	132.2	157.3	334.8	961.3	1,821.1
4. Sales workers.................	94	110.9	170.0	366.2	1,110.7	2,177.4
5. Craftsmen, foremen, and kindred workers......................	96	166.4	209.0	406.7	1,033.4	2,105.2
6. Operatives and kindred workers..	97	190.9	233.5	430.6	1,058.1	1,936.3
7. Private household workers.......	54†	108.8	328.3	235.3	612.2	915.7
8. Service workers, except private household....................	127	219.9	305.9	594.1	1,471.8	2,398.4
9. Laborers, except farm and mine..	176	409.0	546.8	917.1	1,893.6	2,928.9
10. Farmers and farm laborers.......	96	286.9	312.0	439.5	995.5	1,862.6

* "SMR," Standard Mortality Ratio.

† The number of deaths in this occupational group was only 245. The total number so employed is probably so small that this SMR is of little or no significance. The student interested in details should consult the source below.

Source: Lillian Guralnick, "Mortality by Occupation and Industry among Men 20 to 64 Years of Age: United States, 1950," *Vital Statistics: Special Reports*, vol. 53, no. 2, September, 1962, pp. 82–84.

table shows the standardized mortality ratios (SMRs) for these occupational groups. This ratio "compares the tabulated number of deaths in an occupation with the number to be expected had the death rate for the total male population with work experience prevailed in that occupation."[6] Thus the death rate for

[6] Lillian Guralnick, "Mortality by Occupation and Industry among Men 20 to 64 Years of Age: United States, 1950," *Vital Statistics: Special Reports*, vol. 53, no. 2, September, 1962, pp. 82–84.

men in all occupations is given the value 100. On this basis of comparison the lowest ratio is that of private household workers (male) and is only about one-half (54) of the rate for the total occupied male population (see note † to Table 13-6). The highest SMR is for laborers, except farm and mine laborers (176), i.e., the death rate of male laborers is three-fourths higher than for the total of employed males. The second highest ratio is for the group service workers, excluding those in private households (127). The white-collar workers, except sales workers, have relatively low death rates (83 to 86). Craftsmen and operatives have higher ratios, 96 and 97, respectively, and farmers and farm laborers (96) likewise have a ratio only a little below the total.

But ratios for such broad occupational groups as those in this table hide many very significant differences in death rates, as can easily be seen from the following comparisons. Professional workers as a whole (group 1, Table 13-6) had a low SMR for males aged 25–59 (85), but there were five specific occupations in group 1 for which the ratios were over 100, and three of these five had ratios above 115—authors, editors, and reporters (103); clergymen (104); musicians and music teachers (161); pharmacists (125); technicians, medical and dental (116). At ages 25–29 the deaths in these five specified occupations constituted 26 percent of all deaths in group 1. In group 2 (managers, officials, etc.), in which there were almost twice as many deaths as in group 1, in no particular occupation did the ratio exceed 100. The same was true for group 3. In group 4 (sales workers) two occupations had ratios in excess of 120—real estate agents and brokers (122); other specified sales workers (135). In group 5 (craftsmen and the like) there were 18 specified occupations with ratios in excess of 100, and of these, 8 had ratios in excess of 115. In group 6 (operatives and kindred workers) the situation was much the same as in group 5. Group 7 was very small, with no subdivisions and a very low ratio (54). Group 8 (service workers) had a high ratio (127), and no suboccupation had a ratio under 111 (barbers, charwomen, cooks, waiters, firemen, policemen, etc.). Group 9 (laborers, except farm), as already noted, had an extremely high ratio (176); in 7 suboccupations the ratio was above 200, and in one (transportation, except railroads) it was 301.

It seems clear from these data that as late as 1950, substantial occupational differentials were still in operation in the United States; but what proportion of these differences in death rates is due to occupational differences and what proportion to differences in economic status cannot be determined.

In the study of mortality by occupation used above, a special tabulation was also made of the deaths of miners from tuberculosis. The results were very revealing. When the number of deaths from tuberculosis per 100,000 of all males in the study was used as a standard and was given the value of 100, it was found that the TB standard mortality ratio (SMR) for miners aged 25–59 was 249, and for those aged 20–64 it was 263. Such studies pinpoint the need for special health services for workers in particular occupations and in particular communities when the workers in the community are highly concentrated in a few occupations.[7]

If we bear in mind the differences in the death rates of different occupational groups noted above and also the differences in economic status associated with the different occupations, we shall have little difficulty in understanding the differences in mortality between certain types of communities. Clearly, a section of a city, or a town, or an entire city in which certain industries or occupational groups are highly concentrated, e.g., textile workers, steel-mill workers, day laborers, will be almost certain to have different and higher age-specific death rates than a section of a city, or a city where professional men live, or a residence suburb where only white-collar people with good incomes live. As between a rural area in which miners predominate and one in which only farmers live, e.g., in some coalfields in western Pennsylvania and West Virginia on the one hand and farm areas in rural Kansas on the other, there will be large differences in death rates.

Such differences in death rates by occupation as have just been noted are by no means confined to the United States. The United Nations *Demographic Yearbook, 1961*, gives some recent data for several countries, a few of which are of interest here.[8] In Japan (1954–1956), for all male workers aged 45–54 there were 700 deaths per 100,000. The occupational groups that fell substantially below this total number were: professional workers (620), administrators and managers (445), transport and communications workers (635), and service, sport, and recreation workers (619). Those occupations in which the death rates were substantially above the total were: farmers, fishermen, and lumbermen (839), and miners (1,162); most other occupational groups had rates fairly close to the total for all workers.

In France (1955), the death rate per 100,000 for all workers aged 45–54 was 1,040. The groups having rates well below this total were: farmers (750), business employers (910), professional and administrative workers (570), and manufacturers and craftsmen (780). Those groups with rates well above the total were: unskilled workers (1,300), mariners and fishermen (1,280), and miners (1,130).

In England and Wales (1949–1955), the death rate per 100,000 for all workers aged 45–54 was 821. The occupational groups with substantially lower rates were: farmers and agricultural workers (c. 560),[9] administrative, professional, and kindred groups (c. 730), foremen (655), and shop assistants (708).

[7] *Ibid.*, p. 58.

[8] United Nations, *Demographic Yearbook, 1961*, table 25, pp. 619–620.

[9] c. = circa (approximately). Combining certain related groups makes it impossible to calculate a precise rate.

Those groups with substantially higher rates were: clerical workers (979), personal service workers (999), and unskilled workers (1,028).

The categories used here are not fully comparable in the three countries, and the rates were not calculated on exactly the same basis, but there can be no doubt that the occupations of the workers and their economic status are significantly associated with the death rates of the several groups much as in the United States. In general, the better-paid and the white-collar groups have the lowest death rates. As the economic status declines and hand labor becomes heavier and dirtier, the death rates rise, except for farmers in most countries. In Japan, however, farmers apparently have a high death rate. Because of the lack of strict comparability of these data from different countries, it is useless to attempt any general explanation of the national differences in occupational death rates.

MORTALITY AND CLEANLINESS

Today, in the more developed industrial countries, we take for granted that a high standard of personal cleanliness, household cleanliness, and public cleanliness (sanitation) have long been man's normal lot. It is not widely realized that for most peoples cleanliness is a relatively recent achievement. However, until about 1900 few people knew that filth harbors many kinds of bacteria which cause a great variety of diseases. Contaminated wells have led to untold thousands of epidemics of intestinal diseases in villages and parts of cities where wells supplied *all* the water for the household. Public water supplies, carefully managed to avoid contamination, were not provided by many towns and cities here and in Western Europe even in 1900. Until a few decades ago, careless sewage disposal was the rule rather than the exception in most communities in most parts of the world. Hence many diseases were spread by many types of carriers of bacteria, e.g., by houseflies and mosquitoes and by air from dumps and open pools into which all manner of wastes were drained and from which drinking water was drawn.

When one member of the family or of the household had tuberculosis, the infection of others in the household was almost inevitable because of the crowded, unventilated, and filthy living quarters which were very general until about 150 years ago. Inadequate food, poorly prepared, weakened the resistance of a large part of most populations to the diseases which they were likely to contact. In fact, carelessly prepared food was itself a frequent cause of intestinal diseases; it still is, in many areas.

This whole matter of cleanliness of person and home and in all manner of public services is today very closely related to the level of living of any population. It can almost be taken for granted that if the economy is such as to enable the mass of the people to live comfortably, the standard of cleanliness is good. But in the not distant past, even when a particular family or class had the economic means to live well, most people did not include cleanliness in their concept of living well. Considering what we now know about the relation of cleanliness to good health we cannot find it surprising that the grandmothers of the second half of the nineteenth century made frequent use of the statement that "cleanliness is next to godliness." They knew that cleanliness paid off in better health even though they did not know why.

Incidentally, the people interested in public health work in underdeveloped countries today are finding it more difficult to teach the village farmers and their families the essentials of village and household preventive cleanliness than to persuade them to use drugs to cure an illness they have already contracted. They will take a "shot" to cure dysentery or to prevent typhoid but are much more reluctant to clean up the village and to maintain its sanitary cleanliness by keeping the new pump in working order.

MORTALITY TRENDS

The data on crude death rates in Tables 12-1 and 12-2 show that the death rates have been declining in the United States and in most Western countries for some decades and that they are now declining quite rapidly in some of the countries for which data have only recently become available. Even now, for perhaps one-third to one-half of the people in the world, the crude death rates available must be regarded as only approximate. China, India, the Malay Peninsula, much of Africa, large areas in the Near East, and a number of countries in Central and South America belong in this group.

However, in spite of the existing deficiencies just mentioned, there can be no doubt that in most of the underdeveloped countries the death rates have been declining quite rapidly since World War II. The growth of population as shown in successive censuses in a number of such countries is sufficient to prove a substantial decline in their death rates because there is no reliable evidence of any significant increase in their birth rates.

In most of those countries where no reliable census data exist, we are forced to accept the judgment of people familiar with these areas and/or to compare living conditions in country A with those in country B or C about whose death rates something is known in order to arrive at an approximation of the death rates in A. Since about 1930 in a number of underdeveloped countries, and since World War II in most such countries, health services have so changed in character and effectiveness that it is safe to say with regard to the crude death rates in a particular country that if they stood around 20 per 1,000 during the 1950s they were almost certainly *much higher* before that time. Moreover, even where only recently a reliable census has been taken, we can tell something about the death rates of the population during the past two or three decades from the age structure of the population (see Chapter 5).

We shall try to summarize the broad trends in the death rates of most of the more developed countries of the West since about the middle of the eighteenth century largely on the basis of Swedish data. Although the dates, the length of the periods considered, and the extent of the analogous declines certainly

TABLE 13-7.   AVERAGE DEATH RATES BY AGE FOR PERIODS, SWEDEN, 1751–1959

Age	1955–1959	1945–1948	1881–1910	1811–1840	1751–1780
Total..........	9.61	10.50	16.06	24.08	28.01
0–4..........	4.17	6.98	36.29	63.16	86.61
5–9..........	0.49	0.80	5.92	8.25	13.82
10–14..........	0.36	0.65	3.60	4.92	7.23
15–19..........	0.71	1.34	4.62	5.40	6.99
20–24..........	0.83	1.95	6.05	7.58	8.53
25–29..........	0.91	1.93	6.29	8.49	10.11
30–34..........	1.13	2.07	6.47	10.67	12.17
35–39..........	1.54	2.45	7.22	12.81	12.21
40–44..........	2.25	3.22	8.25	15.48	16.57
45–49..........	3.53	4.74	9.62	17.75	17.87
50–54..........	5.67	7.28	12.15	23.58	22.97
55–59..........	9.22	11.08	16.31	30.26	27.61
60–64..........	15.19	17.47	23.49	43.29	40.58
65–69..........	25.37	28.95	35.90	61.77	56.94
70–74..........	43.50	47.71	57.22	94.07	89.17
75–79..........	74.33	82.23	93.65	138.90	123.18
80 and over.....	159.59	174.39	184.22	243.25	220.68

Source: 1955–1959, *Statistical Abstract of Sweden, 1961*, p. 30. For earlier years see earlier *Abstracts*.

varied considerably from country to country, it is permissible to use these Swedish data for illustrative purposes for two reasons: In the first place, Sweden has had reliable data since 1750, and in the second place, there is good reason to believe that the *general pattern* of change in death rates was much the same in all the more developed Western countries. The trend in the death rates in underdeveloped countries will be considered more fully at appropriate points in Chapters 14, 15, and 16.

As Table 13-7 shows, the decline in the average crude death rate for the 30-year period 1751–1780 to the 30-year period 1811–1840 was from 28.01 to

24.08. Thus in the 60 years from 1765–1825 (the midyears of these two periods) there was a decline in the crude death rate of approximately 14 percent. In the next 30-year period, 1811–1840 to the period 1881–1910, 70 years between midyears, the decline in the crude death rate was from 24.08 to 16.06. This is a decline of approximately one-third, or somewhat more than twice as large as in the preceding interval. In the third interval, midyears 1895 and 1946, about 50 years, there was also a decline of about one-third. In this connection it is important to note that within the period 1881–1910, there was a quite rapid decline in the death rate in most of the more developed Western countries because of the advances being made in the control of a number of the more deadly infectious diseases. This successful attack on the infectious diseases continued through the period 1945–1948, and by that time Sweden and most of the other more developed countries had relatively few deaths from such diseases.

If we turn our attention now to the changes in age-specific death rates in Sweden since the period 1751–1780, we find that the largest proportional declines have taken place at the younger ages. Thus the death rate for children aged 0–14 in the period 1955–1959 was only about 5 percent as high as in 1751–1780, and at ages 15–34 the rates were only about 10 percent as high as in the earlier period. On the other hand, in the period 1955–1959, at ages 45–49, the death rates were 20 percent of those in 1751–1780; at ages 55–59 they were 33 percent as high, and at ages 65–69 they were almost 45 percent as high. This general pattern of large declines in age-specific death rates at ages under 35 as contrasted with smaller and diminishing declines at ages over 35 prevailed throughout these two centuries with only minor variations.

MORTALITY CHANGES IN THE NEAR FUTURE

In the future, the decline of the death rate in any particular population will depend in large measure upon the decline already attained in that population. In those populations still having relatively high death rates, the future decline will depend largely upon the rate at which those environmental conditions and services known to be favorable to the further decline of the death rate can be supplied and maintained. Economic conditions in the underdeveloped countries may become the chief determiner of their death rates in the near future.

In general, it may be said that where crude death rates are already quite low (perhaps 8–10 per 1,000), because of the existence of relatively good living conditions and good health services, a further decline in the *crude* rate is unlikely because in most such populations the age composition is steadily becoming less favorable to the maintenance of these low crude rates. In most of these countries, although there will be further declines in the age-specific death rates, particularly at ages over 35, the death rates at the younger ages are already so low that there is little room for further reduction. In such populations the infectious diseases have already been largely eliminated. There are, of course, still appreciable differences in mortality rates between what we now think of as low-death-rate populations, but we must consider declines in the crude death rates in the next two or three decades in those now having death rates of 10 or under as almost negligible.

In 1959 approximately 84 percent of the boy babies born in Sweden could be expected to be alive at 60 years of age, and of girl babies born, 89 percent would be alive at that age. In the United States, in 1960, these proportions for white males were substantially lower, 75 percent, but only a little lower for white females, 86 percent. It would seem reasonable, however, to expect that the rates in the United States and in most other well-developed countries would approach closely to the Swedish rates within a few years. But obviously, when such high proportions of all children born survive to age 60 as in the United States today, there is comparatively little reason to expect much improvement in survival at younger ages.

The fact is that up to now the great decline in the crude death rate and most of the increase in the expectation of life *in the present low-death-rate countries* have come about chiefly because we have learned to control the infectious diseases which have always been the great killers of young people. These diseases have not been as deadly for old people. Hence the expectation of life of older people, let us say those of 60 and over, has been changed comparatively little by man's conquest of the infectious diseases. Any substantial increase in the expectation of life of persons over 60 years of age must come from learning how to keep the human organism from wearing out, and we have made relatively slow progress in this direction as yet; nor is there any clear prospect for quick progress.

What has just been said is not meant to imply that the age-specific death rates of older people will not be reduced as time goes on, but it does not appear reasonable as of now to expect a rapid reduction of the death rates at older ages. The human organism tends to function less effectively as age advances, and the causes of this exhaustion of the life force are not so specific nor so controllable as the causes of the infectious diseases.

Among the peoples where death rates are now high, there may be not only large but very rapid declines in the crude death rates due to the increasing control of infectious diseases. Such declines will certainly lead to a very rapid growth of population in these areas, much more rapid than that which took place in Europe in the nineteenth century—provided, of course, that the economic base for support of better health services and the resulting increase in numbers can be provided for in one way or another. (See Chapter 16.)[10]

---

[10] It will be necessary to give further attention to certain aspects of future changes in mortality in Chap. 16 where the "population explosion" is described and evaluated.

THE ROLE OF MORTALITY IN POPULATION GROWTH

Most peoples have long known that there were frequent "bad" years when famine and/or pestilence and/or war caused violent fluctuations in the number of deaths. The Black Death (1348–1350) devastated much of Europe. The surface causes of excessive death rates were generally quite easily recognized. It was far less commonly recognized, however, that certain causes of death operated quite regularly to maintain the death rate at a high level, generally at about the same level as the birth rate.

But even though individuals and communities have always resorted to whatever means were believed to be effective in curing the diseases or illnesses of individuals, it was not until about the end of the eighteenth century that man was in position even to begin the scientific control of his death rate. Before that, a high death rate and a widely fluctuating number of deaths from year to year was generally accepted as normal and inevitable.

The trend of the death rate in Sweden over rather long periods during the past two centuries has already been examined. However, it will be of some interest to call attention to some of the large and well-authenticated short-time fluctuations in the death rates of Sweden and Finland since about 1750, because in many underdeveloped countries there may still be rather wide fluctuations from year to year although, let us hope, not as violent as some of those mentioned below.

The death rate in Sweden rose from 27.7 in 1756 to 29.9 in 1757 and to 32.4 in 1758. It then fell to 24.8, or by almost one-fourth, in 1760. In 1762 and 1763 it again rose and was above 32 in the latter year but fell to 25.1 in 1766. In 1772 it rose to 37.4 and then jumped to 52.4 in 1773, only to fall to 22.4 in the following year (1774). In the war years 1808–1810, it averaged 35.5 but fell to an average of 27 in the ensuing five years. Variations of 3 to 4 points from year to year were by no means uncommon until the latter third of the eighteenth century. There were even larger variations lasting well into the nineteenth century in Finland. In 1868 (a war year) Finland had a death rate of 77.6, and its population declined by 96,660, or by 55 per 1,000 in a single year.

In France and England there were also rather wide fluctuations in the death rate well into the nineteenth century. In most cases these wide fluctuations can be connected rather closely with food shortages, epidemics, and war. Such data leave no doubt that within the past 150 to 200 years there have been wide fluctuations in the death rates even in those countries sufficiently well organized politically and economically to make the recording of vital events possible.

Different aspects of the role of mortality in determining the changes in the size of populations will be discussed more fully at several points in Chapters 14, 15, and 16. But we should not forget that in many of the underdeveloped countries, even their present low levels of living are in great danger because of their rapid population growth. Man cannot live long on better sanitation and antibiotics without a commensurate increase in subsistence.

SUGGESTIONS FOR SUPPLEMENTARY READING (CHAPTERS 12 AND 13)

Dickinson, Frank G., and Everett L. Welker: *Mortality Trends in the United States, 1900–1949*, American Medical Association, Chicago, 1952.

Dublin, Louis I., et al.: *Length of Life*, rev. ed., The Ronald Press Company, New York, 1949.

Durand, John D.: "Demography's Three Hundredth Anniversary," *Population Index*, vol. 28, no. 4, pp. 333–338, 1962.

Great Britain: *The Registrar-General's Statistical Review of England and Wales for the the Year 1959*, part 3, H.M. Stationery Office, London, 1961. (Mortality according to marital status chosen for special notice in this review.)

Guralnick, Lillian: "Mortality by Occupation and Industry among Men 20 to 64 Years of Age: United States, 1950," *Vital Statistics: Special Reports*, vol. 53, no. 1, pp. 45–92, September, 1962.

March, Lucien: "Some Researches Concerning the Factors of Mortality," *Royal Statistical Society Journal*, vol. 75, pp. 505–538, 1912.

Moriyama, Iwao M., and Lillian Guralnick: "Occupational and Social Class Differences in Mortality," in Milbank Memorial Fund, *Trends and Differentials in Mortality*, New York, 1956, pp. 61–73.

"Mortality and Social Class," Metropolitan Life Insurance Company *Statistical Bulletin*, vol. 40, October, 1959, pp. 9–11. (England and Wales by Sex and Social Class, 1930–1932 and 1949–1953.) Same issue gives mortality from selected causes, industrial policy holders Metropolitan Life Insurance Company, 1957, 1958, 1959.

Peller, Sigismund: "Mortality Past and Future," *Population Studies*, vol. 1, no. 4, pp. 405–456, 1948.

Rosenberg, Charles E.: *The Cholera Years: the United States in 1932, 1949, and 1866*, The University of Chicago Press, Chicago, 1962.

"Sex Differences in Mortality Increasing," Metropolitan Life Insurance Company *Statistical Bulletin*, vol. 38, September, 1957, pp. 1–4.

Shurtleff, Dewey: "Mortality and Marital Status," *Public Health Reports*, vol. 70, March, 1955, pp. 248–252. (Mortality rates for the United States by marital status, age, and sex based on the 1950 census.)

Spiegelman, Mortimer: "Mortality Trends and Prospects and Their Implications," *The Annals of the American Academy of Political and Social Sciences*, vol. 315, pp. 25–33, March, 1958. (Comparison of the mortality experience of the United States and Canada since 1900 and discussion of environmental influences, marital status, causes of death, factors in trends, and prospects.)

———: *Significant Morbidity Trends in the United States since 1900*, American College of Life Underwriters, Philadelphia, Pa., 1960.

Stolnitz, George J.: "A Century of International Mortality Trends," Part I: *Population Studies*, vol. 9, no. 1, July, 1955, pp. 24–55. Part II: *Population Studies*, vol. 10, no. 1, July, 1956, pp. 17–42.

Tarver, James D.: "Projections of Mortality in the United States to 1970," *Milbank Memorial Fund Quarterly*, vol. 37, no. 2, pp. 132–143, April, 1959. "The two major objectives of this paper are: *First*, to ascertain the projected age-sex specific mortality rates of U.S. white and nonwhite populations for the years 1960, 1965, and 1970; and *second*, to establish the future life expectancy at selected ages for these four race-sex population groups based on hypothetical life tables derived from projected death rates."

Taylor, Wallis, and Majorie Dauncey: Changing Pattern of Mortality in England and Wales; Mortality in Old Age, *British Journal of Preventive and Social Medicine*, vol. 9, no. 3, July, 1955.

Titmuss, Richard M.: *Birth, Poverty and Wealth: A Study of Infant Mortality*, Hamish Hamilton Medical Books, London, 1943.

Tomasson, Richard F.: "Bias in Estimates of the U.S. Nonwhite Population as Indicated by Trends in the Death Rates," *Journal of the American Statistical Association*, pp. 44–51, 1961.

United Nations, *Demographic Yearbook, 1948*.

Urlanis, B. Ts.: *Wars and Population in Europe. Losses of Human Lives in the Armed Forces of European Countries during the Last Three and a Half Centuries*, Social. Econ. Lit. Press, Moscow, 1960.

Whitney, Jessamine: *Death Rates by Occupation, Based on Data of the U.S. Bureau of the Census, 1930*, National Tuberculosis Association, New York, 1934.

Wigglesworth, Edward: "A Table Showing the Probability of the Duration, the Decrement, and the Expectation of Life in the States of Massachusetts and New Hampshire, Formed from Sixty-two Bills of Mortality in the Files of the American Academy of Arts and Sciences for the Year 1789," *American Academy of Arts and Sciences Memoirs*, vol. 2, o.s., pp. 131–135, 1793.

Woodbury, Robert Morse: *Causal Factors in Infant Mortality: A Statistical Study Based on Investigations in Eight Cities*, U.S. Children's Bureau Publication 142, 1925.

PART FOUR

Changing Patterns in Population Growth

CHAPTER FOURTEEN # *Population Growth before 1650*

Chiefly because the two most used estimates of world population in modern times begin with 1650, that date will be used here for convenience as the beginning of the important changes in the growth patterns of population in the Western world which we call *modern*.[1] Other dates will also be used in this and the following chapter to signalize the beginning of other important phases in the development of new patterns of population growth. But it should be recognized that any date specified to indicate the inauguration of a great social (cultural) change among any people is quite arbitrary and does not mean that a noticeable change took place suddenly, unless it is specifically stated that some catastrophe or other unexpected event occurred.

SOME GENERAL CONSIDERATIONS

In this chapter we are mainly concerned with growth before 1650. The question we shall try to answer is: Why were there no more than 600 million people in the world in 1650 although Homo sapiens had been on the earth many tens of thousands of years?

Because of the lack of reliable data, the discussion of population growth in the world before 1650 depends largely on the interpretation of descriptive materials from writings of travelers and long-time foreign residents among peoples whose cultures are, or were at the time their observations were recorded, little changed

[1] Significant changes in population growth have begun at different times among different peoples even when they have much the same broad cultural backgrounds; the rhythm of change may also be different (faster or slower) for a great variety of reasons, some of which will be noted in rather general terms at appropriate points throughout this Part Four. The phrase Western world, or simply the West, will be used here to designate Western, Northern, and Central Europe and the colonies settled by people from these regions of Europe.

from those that had long existed. The studies of anthropologists are also of much importance. More recently, a considerable number of students have been interested in the factors which appear to be determinative of the growth and changes in populations in the underdeveloped countries. In many of these countries the most important determinative factors are believed to be much the same as they were among most peoples in the world before about 1650, the date chosen here as inaugurating the *modern era* of population growth in the West.

Because of this scarcity of knowledge, it is not in the least surprising that two very careful students of population growth in the past should arrive at estimates of world population in 1650 (Table 14-1) that differ by 75 million, that of Willcox being the smaller.[2] This difference in estimates for 1650 arises chiefly because these two men attached different values to the sketchy evidence available on which to base estimates for China. The authors, with the advantage of the hindsight provided by the 1953 census of Communist China (although they do not accept this census at face value), consider the estimates of Carr-Saunders more probable. They will therefore use his estimates in calculating the rates of growth of population since 1650 (see Chapter 15). However, the authors wish to make it clear that this difference in estimates is of little or no importance in trying to understand the processes of population growth in the past. A hypothetical illustration will best serve our purposes here.

Let us assume that two countries known to have developed rather highly efficient civilizations at least 30 centuries before 1650, viz., India and China, had populations of 10 million each in 1350 b.c. If one of these countries, let us say India, had had a low but regular rate of increase amounting to 2 persons per 1,000 per year (0.2 percent per year) during these 30 centuries, it would double its numbers in approximately 346 years and thus would repeat this doubling somewhat more than 8.5 times in 3,000 years. By 1650 its population would have risen to approximately 4.1 billion. This is seven times as large as the estimate of Carr-Saunders for the world's population in 1650. If the other population of the same size in 1350 b.c. (China) added 3 persons per 1,000 each year (0.3 percent per year), this population would somewhat more than double in 230 years and thus would double between 12 and 13 times in 3,000 years. This would result in a population of about 80 billions by 1650, or about 147 times Carr-Saunders's estimate.

A population of 10 million steadily adding only 1 person per 1,000 each year would double in approximately 700 years and would, therefore, grow to about 200 million in 3,000 years. Hence, a *world* population of about 30 million in 1350 b.c., adding only 1 person per 1,000 each year in the three millennia preceding 1650, would have increased to somewhat more than Carr-Saunders's

[2] A. M. Carr-Saunders, *World Population*, Oxford University Press, Fair Lawn, N.J., 1936, p. 42; Walter F. Willcox, *Studies in American Demography*, Cornell University Press, Ithaca, N.Y., 1940, p. 45.

TABLE 14-1.   ESTIMATES OF WORLD POPULATION BY REGIONS, 1650–1960 (In millions)

Series of estimates and date	World total	Africa	Northern America[a]	Latin America[b]	Asia, excluding U.S.S.R.[c]	Europe and Asiatic U.S.S.R.	Oceania	Area of European settlement[d]
Willcox[e] estimates:								
1650............	470	100	1	7	257	103	2	113
1750............	694	100	1	10	437	144	2	157
1800............	919	100	6	23	595	193	2	224
1850............	1,091	100	26	33	656	274	2	335
1900............	1,571	141	81	63	857	423	6	573
Carr-Saunders estimates:[f]								
1650............	545	100	1	12	327	103	2	118
1750............	728	95	1	11	475	144	2	158
1800............	906	90	6	19	597	192	2	219
1850............	1,171	95	26	33	741	274	2	335
1900............	1,608	120	81	63	915	423	6	573
United Nations estimates:[g]								
1920............	1,811	141	117	91	966	487	9	704
1930............	2,015	157	135	109	1,072	532	10	786
1940............	2,249	176	146	131	1,212	573	11	861
1950............	2,510	206	167	162	1,386	576	13	918
1960............	2,995	254	199	206	1,679	641	16	1,062

[a] United States, Canada, Alaska, and Saint Pierre and Miquelon.

[b] Central and South America and Caribbean Islands.

[c] Estimates for Asia and Europe in Willcox's and Carr-Saunders's series have been adjusted to include the population of the Asiatic U.S.S.R. with that of Europe rather than Asia. For this purpose, the following approximate estimates of the population of the Asiatic U.S.S.R. were used: 1650, 3 million; 1750, 4 million; 1800, 5 million; 1850, 8 million; 1900, 22 million.

[d] Includes Northern America, Latin America, Europe and the Asiatic U.S.S.R., and Oceania.

[e] Walter F. Willcox, *Studies in American Demography*, Cornell University Press, Ithaca, N.Y., 1940, p. 45. Estimates for America have been divided between Northern America and Latin America by means of detailed figures presented, pp. 37–44.

[f] A. M. Carr-Saunders, *World Population*, Oxford University Press, Fair Lawn, N.J., 1936, p. 42.

[g] United Nations (Department of Economic and Social Affairs), *Demographic Yearbook, 1961*, p. 120.

estimate for 1650. Such a rate of growth in any particular population would have been practically imperceptible during the adult life of any person interested in population growth in his own community or country. Moreover, since we now know that there were several very important civilizations having moderately large populations long before 1350 B.C., it is obvious that in the world as a whole even the extremely low rate of growth of 1 person per 1,000 per year had not prevailed continuously for any considerable period of time. A population of only 5 million in the world in 3500 B.C. at even this low rate of growth would have numbered 640 million by A.D. 1400 and well over 850 million by 1650. This is over one-half larger than Carr-Saunders's estimate for this date.

In terms of probable crude birth rates and death rates, we may say that a rate of growth of 2 per 1,000 per year would result from a crude birth rate averaging 43 to 45 live births each year for each 1,000 of the population and about 41 to 43 deaths per 1,000. However, we now know enough about the factors which largely determine both birth rates and death rates in preindustrial societies to justify the statement that in all probability before 1650 no population having a relatively homogeneous culture and consisting of even 1 million persons at a given initial date three or four millennia prior to 1650 ever grew regularly even at a rate of 2 or 3 per 1,000 per year over any considerable period of time, to say nothing of growing regularly during several millennia.

BIRTH RATES AND DEATH RATES BEFORE 1650

We know very little about the birth rates and death rates before 1650. However, we do have several studies among peoples who have exercised little or no voluntary personal control over conception that show an *average* fertility of 7 or 8 to 10 or more live births per woman living to menopause. It is important to remember that this is an average number of children *actually* borne and hence is certainly somewhat below the *potential* fertility of the average female in these populations. Most of these studies also show that some women, although married relatively young and always living with their husbands, had borne no children and that at the other extreme some women under similar conditions had borne a dozen and even twenty children or more.

No evidence justifies the assumption that fecundity differs from race to race, from nation to nation, from class to class within any society, or that it has changed within historical time. There is abundant evidence, however, that fertility, the actual number of children borne by a woman, varies substantially from woman to woman in practically all cultures and also varies from one culture group to another. Hence we must conclude that for all meaningful thinking about population growth now or in the past, fecundity must be considered a constant factor which has determined the possible upper limit of human reproduction. On the other hand, fertility is a highly variable factor and is determined to a greater or lesser extent in all population groups by their cultural patterns of behavior associated with reproduction. Possibly no society has ever realized its full fecundity because its cultural patterns of behavior which made a group of persons into a society—a social organization—have restricted fertility in some respect, although in most larger societies this restriction has been relatively small. In some tribal groups these restrictions may have been rather severe.

Only a few such restrictive customs can be mentioned here: (1) Abortion has been practiced more or less among all peoples; (2) segregation of women for relatively long periods of purification following childbirth long prevailed in many societies, especially in tribal groups; (3) exposure of female infants or the inferior care given them has reduced the number of females reaching the age of reproduction; (4) polyandry (several husbands to one woman) has been found in a number of societies; (5) polygamy and concubinage, which if widely practiced deprive many young men of wives at the most fertile ages, have had an equivalent effect on reproduction; (6) marriage customs which postpone family formation until several years after puberty, such as the accumulation by young men of the scalps or heads of the tribal enemies before marriage is permitted, inevitably result in fewer possible husbands in the clan or tribe.

In spite of these and many other practices which actually reduce fertility somewhat below fecundity, the birth rates in most preindustrial societies organized on a civil basis (territorial) have generally been relatively high, probably 40 or more per 1,000 per year. This was almost certainly the case in most of the more developed agricultural societies prior to 1650. Moreover, such societies then comprised a very large proportion of the world's population. Since a number of these agricultural societies had undergone only minor social and economic changes until a few decades ago, we possess considerable knowledge regarding the conditions determining population growth in such societies, although we have no precise data.

Some of the tribal peoples that depended largely on hunting and fishing, on gathering fruits, roots, and such vegetable food, and on their flocks and herds for their sustenance may not have had as high birth rates as the more settled agricultural peoples. However, we do not know enough to justify any positive statement on this point. Even three centuries ago the societies depending on hunting, fishing, and gathering constituted only a small proportion of mankind; hence we are justified in basing our discussion of preindustrial population growth before 1650 on the assumption that the birth rate of the total population was high, i.e., was generally about 40 per 1,000 per year.

What we know about the death rate, the other basic factor in determining the rate of natural increase in every population, in preindustrial societies is of the same hazy character as our knowledge of the birth rate. Much historical material shows that the number of deaths has varied greatly in the same society from time to time. Even from one year to another the variations in the death rate have often been quite startling. (See data for Finland and Sweden in Chapter 12, Figure 12-1.)

The reader will recall that Malthus divided the *checks* to population growth into two classes: (1) the positive checks, those that cut short life already in being; (2) the preventive checks, those that reduced the birth rate and/or the number of births per female. We have already noted some of these checks that reduce fertility and shall note others in their appropriate setting. In the three following sections we shall focus attention on the positive checks which have long operated in preindustrial agricultural societies. Malthus stressed three such checks, viz., lack of food, disease, and war (see Chapter 2). We shall give some illustrations of the operation of these factors.

HUNGER AND FAMINE

Those of us who have always lived in a society where food was plentiful can hardly realize how the lack of adequate food has always affected the death rate in the greater portion of mankind. It has been a potent check on population growth among all preindustrial peoples and still operates to check growth in a considerable portion of mankind.

The folklore of almost every agricultural people, as well as that of people who may be called preagricultural because they depend so largely on hunting, fishing, and gathering wild vegetable foods, contains many references to seasons unfavorable to the production and storage of food. The particular causes of short crops and of wild foodstuffs, of course, vary from region to region and from time to time, but the lack of rain (drought) has probably been the most common cause of such shortages. However, there have always been and still are many other causes of shortages in cultivated crops, such as too much rain with accompanying floods, the inability to harvest crops at the proper time resulting in substantial losses, the spoilage of grain already in storage, plagues of grasshoppers and locusts and insects, blights of plant diseases, unusually early or late frosts, and above all, the great inefficiency of agricultural labor due chiefly to the highly traditional character of agricultural knowledge and practices among most preindustrial peoples.

Among peoples dependent for their livelihood upon hunting and fishing, upon their flocks and herds, and upon gathering wild crops, the same story is told in somewhat different terms—a failure of the salmon run in a particular coastal area, a bad season for game in the forest and on the prairie, disease among the cattle or the sheep, and always and everywhere rather frequent and severe drought, which has affected the food supply of hunters, gatherers of wild crops, and pastoral peoples in much the same way as the failure of the crops of the agriculturalists affected their death rates. Food shortage has been one of the most constant hardships of mankind in all past ages, and, let us not forget, is still a constant threat in *many* parts of the world. Witness China's troubles in the past few years, India's present need for imported foods (rice and wheat) for which she has little to exchange, and the 1963 wheat buying of the Communist countries of Europe.

The shortage of food takes two main forms: (1) *chronic* and (2) *acute*. Of these, the former probably has been the most deadly to man, although the latter, being more spectacular, has received more than its due meed of attention.

Chronic Lack of Food. The chronic lack of adequate food, although it does not kill outright, has undoubtedly been indirectly responsible for untold tens of millions of premature deaths. This point can be illustrated by citing the results of a postwar survey by the Food and Agriculture Organization (FAO) of the United Nations.[3] This survey showed that over one-half of the people in the world had a daily per capita intake of food providing less than 2,250 calories— a minimum for the maintenance of health. Most of these peoples had a crude death rate (as estimated for about 1930) of 30 and over per 1,000. The relatively small proportion of this group which had death rates of 25 or less was found to live in well-managed colonial areas, or in Central and South America.

On the other hand, those peoples having over 3,000 calories available had death rates of 14 or under. Most of the countries with 2,250–2,499 calories available per capita also had very high death rates, although only about 35 percent of this group of peoples had death rates above 30. In general, the death rate declined as the number of calories available per person per day increased. A very rough estimate of the *annual* excess of deaths in the countries having less than 2,250 calories available per capita as compared with those which would have occurred if the people had lived in countries having 3,000 or more calories per capita available is 18 million. This is over twice as many as would have occurred in the countries where the people are well fed. Of course these data do not relate to the preindustrial peoples before 1650, but there is very good reason to believe that similar conditions did prevail among the same peoples from time immemorial.

One should be careful, however, *not to assume* that the very low calorie intake in these poor countries is the *sole* cause of their excess mortality over that of well-fed peoples, and it may not even be the chief cause at any particular time; but one cannot doubt that the inadequacy of food in poor countries has always contributed directly to a high death rate. Almost all the people in almost every part of the world have suffered chronically from inadequate food until two or three centuries ago. Only a favored few in any country ever had food adequate to the

[3] "Food, Income, and Mortality," *Population Index*, vol. 13, no. 2, pp. 96–103, 1947; Food and Agricultural Organization of the United Nations, *World Food Survey*, Washington, D.C., 1946.

maintenance of good health. Because in particular situations it is often impossible to distinguish with any precision between deaths which should be attributed to disease, to war, and to physical weakness due to chronic hunger, we must recognize that a great many of the people who died of intestinal diseases and from many other infectious diseases would not have died when they actually did if they had not been suffering from chronic undernourishment; i.e., because they were already greatly weakened by an inadequate diet they died prematurely, and at times of great epidemics they would always be the first to succumb.

The United Nations made another survey of the world's food supply in 1952. There are different interpretations of its findings largely because different people evaluate them on different bases.[4] Only a few of the more significant findings as they affect population growth in the past can be given here. To attain a fairly satisfactory nutritional level, most of the peoples of the Far East would need to raise the *per capita* food supply by 2 percent annually for some years and the *total food* supply by 5 percent annually because of the increases in population that appear to be taking place since World War II. Actually, the per capita supply has been increasing by only about 1 percent in recent years. The situation is somewhat different in other parts of the world greatly in need of more and better food, but in the Near East, in Africa, and in Latin America very large annual increases in the total food supply are needed if the masses of the people are to experience any substantial improvement in their diet, assuming that the population will grow at the rate of 1.5 percent to 2 percent per year. Failing such an increase in the food supply in quantity and also in nutritional adequacy, the death rates of these peoples are unlikely to continue to fall as fast as they have during the past few years. Hence, the rate of population growth may be somewhat checked in spite of further improvements in their health services. In the past, such large increases in the per capita supply of food have seldom taken place regularly or for any considerable length of time.

Famine. Famine may be described as an acute shortage of food in contrast to a chronic shortage of calories and/or of vitamins and such food values. The history of many countries shows that frequent famines have been the lot of man from time immemorial. Only a few examples can be given here. Walford[5] lists only 350 famines; 201 of these occurred in the British Isles between A.D. 10 and 1846. Seventy others occurred in other parts of Europe. Thirty-one occurred in India between 1769 and 1878, and 17 more occurred around the Mediterranean

---

[4] For an evaluation of these new findings, see the paper of P. F. Sukhatme, "The World's Hunger and Future Needs in Food Supplies," *Journal of the Royal Statistical Society*, ser. A (General), vol. 124, part 4, 1961, pp. 463–508. This is followed by a long discussion of the paper by a number of persons, pp. 508–525.

[5] Cornelius Walford, "The Famines of the World: Past and Present," *Journal of the Royal Statistical Society*, vol. 41, pp. 433–526, 1878.

Sea, but not in Europe. This leaves only about 30 occurring in other parts of the world or in India and China before 1769. Clearly, Walford's list, though it may be fairly complete for the British Isles even if it does not include the great Irish famine of 1846 to 1851,[6] is far from complete for most other countries even in Europe. In about one-third of these famines, severe epidemics followed, and in a few cases severe famines followed great epidemics.

The restricted coverage of Walford's list of world famines is shown by studies of Chinese famines. Mallory refers to a study made by students at the University of Nanking listing 1,828 famines in China between 108 B.C. and A.D. 1911.[7] These famines were both great (affecting a large territory with great population) and small (more or less local shortages affecting relatively few people), but often even local famines were quite deadly because of the inability of the government to transport food from areas of relative abundance to areas of crop failure.

The authors know of no historical study of famines in India comparable to that cited by Mallory to describe the effects of famine on population growth in China. However, in view of the 31 famines in India between 1769 and 1878 listed by Walford and the records available regarding more recent famines in India, and because India's rainfall is of much the same general character (monsoon) as that of China, it seems reasonable to assume that India, too, has had many hundreds of famines during the past 2,000 years and that untold millions of people have died as the consequence, both direct and indirect, of these famines. It is also highly probable that direct famine losses have always been highest in the areas in which chronic lack of food was greatest. Such areas almost never have food reserves sufficient to tide them over even short periods of unusual shortage.

Effects of Particular Famines. Since famine has been such an important factor in determining the growth of population in the world, we may profitably give some estimates of deaths in a few great famines of relatively recent date about which considerable is known. We know very little about the death losses of most of the famines in these countries, but we do know that living conditions in China and India until quite recently resembled rather closely those in the West two or three centuries ago, and we are justified in inferring that the famines in other parts of the world in the past were also deadly, even though they may not have been so deadly as those of China and India, largely because of climatic differences.

The worst famine in China in the past century appears to have been that

[6] S. H. Cousens, "Regional Death Rates in Ireland during the Great Famine, from 1846 to 1851," *Population Studies*, vol. 14, no. 1, pp. 55–74, 1960.
[7] Walter H. Mallory, *China: Land of Famine*, American Geographical Society, New York, 1926, p. 1.

which occurred as the result of a great drought in the northwest in the years 1876 to 1879. The area affected included about 300,000 square miles (about the area of New England, the Middle Atlantic States, Ohio, Indiana, and Illinois). Somewhere between 9 and 13 million people are supposed to have perished from hunger and the disease and violence accompanying prolonged famine. What the population was at this time is not known, but possibly as many as one-fifth of the people died. More recently, in 1920 and 1921, not less than 20 million people in the northwest provinces of China were made destitute by crop failure, and in spite of the most efficient famine relief ever known in China, by which more than 7 million people were given public relief, at least 500,000 died of want. During 1929 and 1930 the newspapers reported that millions died of starvation and disease, again in northwestern China. Some reports placed the number of deaths as high as 4 million, or about one-fifth of those affected by it.

Scarcely had a fair crop in this region eased matters there, when the most disastrous flood ever known covered many thousands of square miles along the Yangtze River and its tributaries. Over vast areas the crops were totally destroyed and where not destroyed were badly damaged. The number of deaths was very large, although the fact that relief could be brought to much of this area by water transport kept the death toll far below what was usual in the more remote regions of the country.

Mallory is fully justified when he says: "In fact, the normal death rate [in China] may be said to contain a constant famine factor. Depleted vitality following years of want tends to increase the death rate."[8]

The story is much the same for India as for China. Droughts are common, and almost every year some region suffers more or less from the shortage of food. In 1769 to 1770 there was a great famine in Bengal, which is said to have carried off one-third of the total population, or about 10 million people.[9] Other great famines occurred in 1803 to 1804 and in 1837 to 1838. The mortality resulting from them can only be guessed at, but the victims must certainly be counted by millions, if we also take into account the incidental effects of these periods of want. A brief description of the great India famine of 1837 to 1838 will help us to understand the profound effects of such a calamity upon the growth of population in the past. The following description was written by an official who not only had access to all the official reports but was himself an on-the-spot observer of events:

The famine of 1837 to 1838 was the last of the great desolating famines which characterized this epoch; like the Doji Bara in the Deccan, and the Chalisa in Upper India, it loosened the bonds of society, laid waste large tracts of country, and perma-

---

[8] *Ibid.*, p. 1.
[9] Theodore Morison, *The Industrial Organization of an Indian Province*, John Murray (Publishers), Ltd., London, 1918, p. 253.

nently modified the development of industry. It is the one famine of the old type of which we possess adequate detailed records; the reports of the local officers at various stages of the famine are, in many cases, still extant, and Mr. Girdlestone, in his "Past Famines in the Northwest Provinces," has given a history of it which covers 28 pages. The main features of the famine may be clearly traced, and they are unmistakably characteristic of the worst famines of this epoch. There had been a succession of bad harvests since 1832 which had caused considerable distress in various localities. The summer of 1837 brought a terrible drought. . . . July and August are described as being absolutely rainless, and such were the anticipations of dearth that "in Aligarh the *baniyas* would not produce grain even when payment was offered at their own exorbitant prices." With the prospect of inevitable starvation at their homes, the people naturally began to wander; in August Bulandshahr was already being overwhelmed with emigrants from Marwar and Hariana. In September there were a few partial showers toward the south, but in the upper Doab this month was practically rainless. "The utter hopelessness of their case was enough in the minds of the lower classes to justify recourse to violence, and soon . . . neither grainboats nor storehouses were safe from attack, whilst the public roads were dangerous to travelers, owing to the number of armed men who were roaming about in quest of plunder." On October 20, John Lawrence wrote from Gurgaon: "I have never in my life seen such utter desolation as that which is now spread over the pargunnahs of Horul and Pulwul. The people have been feeding their cattle for the last two months on the leaves of trees, and, since this resource has failed are driving them off." The difficulty of feeding the cattle is often mentioned. From Cawnpore in the beginning of 1838 Mr. Rose wrote: "There was not, I am told, in 1783 that total absence of vegetation which has caused the present dearth of cattle, and in milk the people then possessed a valuable article of food which is now wanting. . . . To those who have not witnessed the melancholy change it will scarcely be credible that an extensively-cultivated and thickly-populated country like the Doab could, by one year's drought, be reduced to its present state of waste and desolation. Flourishing villages, which last year contained from 300 to 400 cultivators, are now occupied by half a dozen starving beggars, and I have travelled for 20 miles in the pergunnahs adjoining the Jumnal, where there are no wells, without seeing a vestige of cultivation." . . . So long as the rich zemindars had the means, they fed their poor neighbors, and even went to the length of selling jewels and ornaments to raise money for the purchase of food. When their resources were exhausted and the baniyas proved inexorable, the poorer classes resorted to the jungle, in the hope of securing a meal from some of the wild trees. . . . Women were ready to sell their children for 2 or 3 seers of wheat, whilst their husbands and brothers waylaid and plundered travellers. Gold and silver were parted with at half their ordinary value, and brass and copper were esteemed worth their weight in grain. Artisans disposed of their tools at a quarter of their cost price.[10]

The terrible destruction of life under the conditions described above must have recurred many times in many countries over many centuries, and minor

[10] *Ibid.*, pp. 262–264.

local famines were annual events in almost all regions. But since almost nothing is known about most of these local famines, it is impossible to evaluate the relative importance of the *great* and the *small* famines as destroyers of human life just as it is impossible to evaluate with any precision the relative importance of chronic hunger and famine in this respect. But attention will shortly be called to the effect on population growth of a relatively small but constant addition to the rate of mortality as a consequence of chronic food shortages. It is easy to overestimate the effect of catastrophic events like great famines and great epidemics in contrast to chronic hunger and the customary attrition due to infectious diseases.

But lest we think of the effects of famine as being confined almost exclusively to the more densely settled areas of the Far East in relatively recent times, attention should again be called to the large number of famines in the British Isles listed by Walford, 201 between A.D. 10 and 1846 and 70 in other parts of Europe during the same period.

The most significant facts regarding the great famine of 1918–1922 in the U.S.S.R. and the probable losses in that of 1934 and 1935 will be summarized very briefly because they are illustrative of the great losses of life that may occur even when relatively large famine relief has been available. The American Relief Administration took the most active part in supplying outside help to the stricken area of the U.S.S.R. At the time of its greatest activity in August, 1922, the ARA was feeding 10,491,297 people, and famine deaths had fallen to comparatively small figures. It has been estimated that out of 30 to 40 million people who were affected by this famine, from 2 to 5 million perished from hunger. In some communities mortality was unbelievably high, running from 4 to 6 percent *a month* when conditions were at their worst.[11] In other communities 25 to 50 percent of the total population is supposed to have perished.

In 1934 to 1935 there was another famine in Russia which seems to have killed millions but about which comparatively little is known because of the stringent censorship maintained. The census of January 17, 1939, counted about 5.5 million fewer persons than would have been expected, carrying forward the population from 1926 by the addition of births and subtraction of deaths at normal rates.[12] By no means all of these died of famine, but there is no doubt that famine contributed significantly to this deficit of population between 1926 and 1939. But Russia had been no stranger to famines. In the three decades before the revolution there were three severe famines: 1891, 1906, and 1911. As we shall see in the following section, there is generally a close connection between famine and disease.

We should remind the reader again that our discussion of hunger and famine here has perforce been limited to definite examples of relatively recent date.

[11] *Epidemiological Intelligence*, part II, no. 5, League of Nations, Geneva, 1922, pp. 54–55.
[12] *Ibid.*, pp. 133–137.

However, there is good reason to believe that somewhat similar conditions as regards shortage of food and famine have prevailed for many millennia in all types of societies. But, of course, in small societies, both tribal and civil, the absolute numbers dying prematurely from these causes was also small, even though the proportion may have been as large as in the larger societies.

DISEASES AND EPIDEMICS

Infectious Diseases. From time immemorial, the infectious diseases which we now know to be preventable have taken a heavy toll of human life. This has been most noticeable in those areas and regions where there was any considerable concentration of population. It is important to remember in this connection that over most of the world most of the people have lived in villages or small tribal camps, so that infectious diseases were rapidly spread through local groups by personal contact and by the use of community sources of water and food which often became contaminated at certain seasons because of the customary practices of waste disposal and manuring. They were also spread from village to village by insects and by the constant movements of the people to markets, temples, or shrines and through visits to neighboring villages. Moreover, at times of famine the local groups most affected by the dearth would migrate toward areas where rumor had it that food could be procured. These migrants not only carried with them any of the infectious endemic diseases they already had, e.g., typhoid, smallpox, dysentery, pneumonia, tuberculosis, etc., but also contracted any diseases prevalent in the communities they passed through. Besides, many of these migrants, already weakened by hunger and quite possibly by disease, died along the way or in camps where they gathered and thus helped to spread disease wherever they went. Hence, it is not surprising that severe famine generally bred epidemics and that the ensuing deaths, even if they were known, could not be allotted accurately to hunger or to disease.

But even aside from the very intimate relation of hunger and disease, it was so usual for people to die of these infectious diseases that until 150 to 200 years ago almost no one thought of trying to do anything about them, and if their *prevention* was given consideration there was no scientific knowledge on which plans for their control could be based. Probably the intestinal diseases took the heaviest toll of lives year after year, although tuberculosis was almost certainly a close second among many peoples. These kinds of diseases were made more deadly by the debilitating effects of inadequate food and crowded living quarters. In many regions the almost universal incidence of malaria not only caused deaths directly but also so debilitated great masses of people that they became easy victims of other diseases and very inefficient producers of food. Practically every mother expected to lose a large proportion of her babies from enteritis and respiratory ailments before they reached the end of their first year (see Chapter 12, section on Infant Mortality). Frequently, from one-fourth to one-third of the babies died before completing their first year. Further great losses took place in the next four years from enteritis and the children's diseases that were rampant in almost every community—measles, whooping cough, scarlet fever, diphtheria, etc. Then came typhoid fever, smallpox, and in some regions yellow fever, typhus and plague, and of course, respiratory ailments took a heavy toll not only among young children but among youth and young adults.

Swedish death statistics, which are generally considered the best available in the middle of the eighteenth century and are also generally considered the lowest rates in Europe at that time, show clearly that the situation just delineated is not exaggerated. The following data show the average death rates of children in Sweden at ages under 10 in the 20 years from 1751–1770 and in 1960.[13]

Deaths	1751–1770	1960	Percent col. 2 is of col. 1
Infant mortality (deaths under 1 year of age per 1,000 births in the same year)	210.4	16.5	7.8
Deaths of children aged 1 and 2 per 1,000 children aged 1 and 2	51.42	1.04	2.0
Deaths of children aged 3 and 4 per 1,000 children aged 3 and 4	27.27	0.69	2.5
Deaths of children aged 5–9 per 1,000 children aged 5–9	12.89	0.42	3.2

If one uses the rate in 1751–1770 at each of the ages given here as the base (100), the largest proportional decline between 1751–1770 and 1960 was from 100 to 2 at ages 1 and 2; at ages 3 and 4, it was from 100 to 2.5; at ages 5 to 9, it was from 100 to 3.2, and at under 1 year of age (infant mortality) it was from 100 to 7.8. However, from the standpoint of the number of lives saved out of each 1,000 children born to the age when they were likely to contribute to the next generation, the truly great saving of life was through the reduction of infant mortality. In 1751–1770 out of 1,000 babies born, only 790 (about 79 percent) (1,000 − 210 = 790) lived to 1 year of age. In 1960 approximately 983 (98.3 percent) lived to this age. In 1751–1770 only about 620 out of each 1,000 babies born lived to 15 years of age, while in 1960 slightly over 975 lived

[13] Sweden: Central Bureau of Statistics, *Statistical Abstract of Sweden*, 1932, pp. 52–53; 1962, pp. 36 and 38.

to this age. Thus, out of each 1,000 children born there were over one-half (56 percent) more reaching reproductive age in 1960 than in 1751–1770.

It is also clear from these data that nearly all (about 93 percent) of the deaths of children from birth to 15 years of age in the period 1751–1770 have been found preventable. This is largely due to the increasing control over the infectious diseases. Furthermore, it should not be forgotten that these death rates of babies and children in Sweden in the middle of the eighteenth century were undoubtedly somewhat below those in Western Europe as a whole and still more below those which prevailed in most parts of the world before 1650. Even today, the United Nations Demographic Yearbook publishes infant mortality rates for a few countries rising to 250–300 per 1,000 live births, although it is careful to indicate that these rates are estimates and cannot be vouched for. However, there can be no reasonable doubt that before about 1650, close to one-half of all babies born died before reaching 10 years of age. As we shall have occasion to note later, it is chiefly the control of the infectious diseases among babies and children that is now leading to the rapid growth of population since World War II in most of the underdeveloped countries.

Great Epidemics. In great epidemics we should include only those epidemics of diseases which, although rather unusual, occasionally visited most peoples and were generally very deadly when they did. Such epidemics, like famine, have always attracted much attention, but there can be little doubt that, by and large, they usually had far less effect on population growth than the infectious diseases which were always present (endemic) and took their heavy toll year after year, for example, intestinal and respiratory diseases of children, smallpox, and tuberculosis. We shall, however, devote a few paragraphs to several of these great epidemics.

The Black Death. Hecker in his account of the Black Death (1348–1350) gives figures which seem incredible, but they are so generally used that we may repeat a few of them here.[14] All Europe was devastated. London is supposed to have lost 100,000; Venice, 100,000; Florence, 60,000; and Paris, 50,000. The populations of these cities at that time are not known, but it is not at all unlikely that nearly one-half or even more of their people perished within a period of several months, while in rural areas the losses were somewhat less proportionally. The island of Cyprus is said to have been practically depopulated; Italy as a whole is thought to have lost one-half of its total population; England about one-third; and France about one-third. Eastern Europe did not suffer so severely as Western and Southern Europe; probably the lesser density of the population in Eastern Europe will help to explain this difference. For the

[14] J. F. K. Hecker, *The Epidemics of the Middle Ages*, translated by B. G. Babington, George Woodfall (The Sydenham Society), London, 1844, pp. 22–24.

entire continent, it is quite generally believed that not less than one-fourth of the people and quite possibly one-third perished during this epidemic. The loss may very well have amounted to 25 to 35 million.

Imagine, if you can, what it would mean if the population of the United States fell from 180 million to 120 million within two or three years and if many of our great cities lost half of their populations in a few months.

Influenza, 1918–1919. Those of us who were adult in 1918 can recall how, in the autumn of that year, people died in our own neighborhoods without being able to secure the services of a physician, how whole families were stricken suddenly and were unable to call aid of any kind, and how helpless even the most industrialized countries appeared in the grip of this disease. But in spite of what seemed to us in the industrialized countries the terrible ravages of influenza, we suffered little compared with a number of the preindustrial countries. In the registration area of the United States, the death rate for 1918 was only 4 or 5 per 1,000 above normal, and the total number of deaths was only about 450,000 more than were to be expected. This was less than one-half of 1 percent (0.5 percent) of our population at that time. We would not minimize the ravages of this disease in the United States and other of the more industrialized countries, but when we compare our experience with India's[15] at the same time and with the ravages of recurrent great epidemics in preindustrial countries in the past, we realize that we suffered comparatively little.

In India the number of influenza deaths will never be known, but the lowest estimate is about 8 million. The senior author's estimate, made in 1944 after he had studied the Indian data very carefully, was that the minimum must have been in the neighborhood of 15 million. Even such an estimate allows for some famine deaths and for deaths from other minor epidemics aggregating 10 million or more if it is assumed that a "normal" increase between 1911 and 1921 would have been the average of the increases in the decades 1901–1911 and 1921–1931.

In a Chinese community[16] where an experiment in the registration of births and deaths was carried out under the senior author's direction during the four years, September 1, 1931 to August 31, 1935, the death rate for the year September 1, 1933 to August 31, 1934 was 52 per 1,000 or about 8 per 1,000 in excess of the average birth rate for the four years. The field worker living in the community said that though this was considered a bad year, it was not regarded as *especially* bad. The year in which there was not a local epidemic of typhoid or dysentery or smallpox or of some respiratory disease was the unusual year. Epidemics of bubonic plague or pneumonic plague or influenza or typhus would

[15] At that time India and Pakistan were one country under British control.
[16] Warren S. Thompson and C. M. Chiao, *An Experiment in the Registration of Vital Statistics in China*, Scripps Foundation for Research in Population Problems, Oxford, Ohio, 1938, p. 49.

be worthy of remembrance, but not a local epidemic of those diseases which were always with them (endemic) and which resulted in an increase in the "normal" death rate of only one-third or one-half for one year only.

The brief description given above of the almost regular losses of human life due to scarcity of food and to the ever-present infectious diseases will go far toward enabling us to understand why for many thousands of years man's numbers grew slowly and irregularly and in some regions even declined from time to time, although his rate of reproduction (birth rate) was generally high enough to double his numbers every three or four decades if his death rate was only moderately high. But there was still another positive check to population growth which reinforced hunger and disease in their deadly effects on human life.

WAR

The effects of war in retarding population growth during most of man's preindustrial existence were probably greatest in tribal society. Intertribal war was quite different from the type which was from time to time carried on between 1700 and 1900 in Europe and the West. It consisted largely of one tribe, or sometimes a group of tribes, carrying on an almost steady feud with its neighbors. Sometimes these tribal wars lasted for generations. In the beginning, all the tribal groups involved probably needed the additional food they might secure from the control of a larger land area by hunting, fishing, and gathering wild crops. Some tribal peoples also practiced a rather primitive agriculture. In the course of time, many such wars must have developed such cultural practices as head hunting, wife stealing, or scalp taking or other socially sanctioned practices leading to prolonged decimation of the populations involved and not infrequently to the extinction of one and sometimes of both of the conflicting parties at the hands of a third party. The women of the vanquished tribe(s) often became the additional wives and/or slaves of the conquerors.

These wars between relatively small tribal groups frequently led to the destruction of a significant portion of the annual food supply of both parties and thus increased the deaths from hunger and famine. Such wars were also likely to intensify and to spread local epidemics of the infectious diseases with which either party was afflicted.

Wars between relatively small neighboring groups organized on a civil basis had much the same effects on population growth as tribal wars, for example the wars between the Greek states. But where tribal nomads vanquished agriculturalists, although oftentimes all the men in the latter population may have been slaughtered, the conquerors often used their widows as tillers of the soil and also as breeding stock, so that the conquered land would soon have been replenished with people to the extent its food supply would permit.

It must be recognized that this brief account of the effects of war on population growth in the rather distant past is speculative, but the authors believe that the picture drawn of the devastating effects of prolonged tribal wars and even of the wars of small groups of peoples organized on a civil basis is essentially correct and that Malthus was fully justified in regarding war as a third very important factor in determining man's growth in numbers over long periods of time in the past. Further, it should be remembered that until quite recently even in war between civil states, all armies "lived off the land," and that all property that could be carried off was considered the legitimate booty of the armies, both friends and foes. Besides, on enemy territory the armies nearly always destroyed the property they could not carry off. But even so, the armies were generally small according to present-day standards, and the lines of march were relatively narrow, so that the majority of the people often lived beyond the radius within which it was feasible for armies to plunder thoroughly. Nevertheless, such wars led to many local famines through their levies on the food on hand (grain and livestock, for example), and their destruction of the growing crops and of the implements used in agriculture. Moreover, armies were always the carriers of disease as were the famine wanderers in the famines of India and China noted above. There cannot be the least doubt that these wars between preindustrial states, even if they were less obstructive of population growth than tribal wars, took an enormous toll of life over long periods of time, and hence played an important role in preventing the more rapid growth of man's numbers in many places and at many times. The effects of World Wars I and II on population growth will be discussed in the following chapter.

SUGGESTIONS FOR SUPPLEMENTARY READING

Buer, M. C.: *Health, Wealth, and Population in the Early Days of the Industrial Revolution (1760–1815)*, George Routledge & Sons, Ltd., London, 1926.

Cheyney, Edward P.: *An Introduction to the Industrial and Social History of England*, rev. ed., The Macmillan Company, New York, 1925.

Cousens, S. H.: "Regional Death Rates in Ireland during the Great Famine, from 1846 to 1851," *Population Studies*, vol. 14, no. 1, pp. 55–74, 1960.

Defoe, Daniel: *History of the Plague in London, 1665* . . . , George Bell & Sons, Ltd., London, 1905.

Goldner, Frank Alfred, and Lincoln Hutchinson: *On the Trail of the Russian Famine*, Stanford University Press, Stanford, Calif., 1927.

Hecker, Justus Friedrich Karl: *The Epidemics of the Middle Ages*, translated by B. G. Babington, George Woodfall (The Sydenham Society), London, 1844.

Mallory, Walter H.: *China: Land of Famine*, The American Geographical Society, New York, 1926.

Morison, Theodore: *The Industrial Organization of an Indian Province*, John Murray (Publishers), Ltd., London, 1918.

Thompson, Warren S., and C. M. Chiao: *An Experiment in the Registration of Vital Statistics in China*, Scripps Foundation for Research in Population Problems, Oxford, Ohio, 1938.

Walford, Cornelius: "The Famines of the World: Past and Present," *Royal Statistical Society Journal*, vol. 41, pp. 433–526, 1878.

Zinsser, Hans: *Rats, Lice, and History*, Little, Brown and Company, Boston, 1935.

CHAPTER FIFTEEN *Population Growth in the Modern World, 1650–1930*

At several points in the preceding chapter reference has been made to the relatively inefficient techniques of production in use in preindustrial societies. This discussion also called attention to the fact that practically all societies organized on a civil basis as contrasted with those organized on a tribal basis were also agricultural societies and had their crops and often some livestock available for food and clothing materials as well as any wild game and grain and other vegetable products they might gather. On the whole, civil-agricultural societies were a few steps in advance of tribal societies in the amount and the certainty of food available within a specified area and therefore were more populous and probably slightly less subject to food shortages, although this latter surmise cannot be stated as an established fact. It was further noted, however, that because of the relatively static agricultural practices prevailing in such societies during most of their existence, hunger was almost as constant a check to population growth among them as among tribal peoples. Moreover, within historical times, the vast majority of the people in the world had long been organized on a civil basis, i.e., as inhabitants of a particular territory rather than as members of tribal groups. Here we are primarily concerned with the changes in the structure of society, especially in the West, which began in the seventeenth century and which led to a more steady and a somewhat higher rate of population growth than had formerly been customary. Just as the chief purpose of Chapter 14 consisted in giving an answer to the question why the population of the world almost certainly did not exceed 600 million in 1650, this chapter attempts to answer the question, Why did the population of many Western countries, and possibly of China, begin to grow a little faster and more steadily after about 1650?

IMPROVEMENTS IN PRODUCTION TECHNIQUES AND POPULATION GROWTH

The authors should say at once that when they speak of the inefficiency of the techniques of production in preindustrial societies and emphasize particularly the inefficiencies of agricultural techniques and practices, they do not mean to imply that all such societies have been equally inefficient or that agriculture was the only productive activity in which they engaged. Societies have always differed in the efficiency of their productive techniques both agricultural and nonagricultural. Moreover, no date can be used with any precision to indicate when different societies began to improve their techniques of production. It is important to realize, however, that in all preindustrial societies, even in those in which agriculture was most highly developed, only a small proportion of the people could be spared from the production of food and a few other essential goods, e.g., clothing and shelter, simple agricultural implements, and weapons. It is doubtful whether as many as one-fourth of the people in such societies could ever be spared from the production of the absolute necessities of life. Indeed, very few past civilizations could have supported this proportion of their people to carry on the government, to build public works, to perform religious services, to engage in the arts and sciences, to provide for defense and police activities, or to join a leisure class from which no productive service was required.

Moreover, even when better methods of production had been developed, as must have happened occasionally in all the great civilizations of the past, it took a long time to secure the widespread adoption of the new techniques and practices and to organize society for the effective use of these improvements. This was especially true of agricultural improvements. However, during periods when improvements in production were in process of being adopted, probably a slow but significant growth took place in those populations producing more efficiently, if famine and war and disease did not intervene too frequently. An increased per capita food supply generally acted to reduce the death rate to some extent. But unless there was a continuous increase in production, the growth in numbers was soon checked by want and the increased debility it produced. Apparently, a relatively continuous improvement in the methods of production and in the management and distribution of the increasing product was never achieved over any considerable period of time in preindustrial societies. In addition, most preindustrial societies have never been so favorably situated that they could continue to expand the area of tillage substantially during long periods. However, occasionally and for some decades some societies were no doubt able to expand their agricultural production by the acquisition of new lands and the reclamation of land hitherto not tillable, e.g., by building an irrigation system. But for the most part, both the improvements in agricultural practices and the increase in tilled area were not sufficient to ensure even a moderate growth, let us say, by 3 or 4 per 1,000 per year, nor for more than a few decades.

On the whole, before about 1650 to 1700 improvements in agricultural production were apparently few and far between and added only modest increments to the food production of the societies in which they took place. The real Agricultural Revolution in the West began about 1700. It should also be noted that the greater the changes in the agricultural techniques and practices required to secure larger production for the same labor on the same tilled area, the greater was the reluctance of the farmers to adopt these practices because such improvements required a definite break with traditional practices and the expenditure of new capital. Hence the adoption of improved agricultural practices generally took place quite slowly.

For our discussion here the important point to remember is that by the latter part of the seventeenth and the early part of the eighteenth century the intellectual atmosphere in some classes in several countries in Western Europe had become somewhat more tolerant of new ideas, i.e., of departures from tradition, than it had been in the past. In these countries some men were coming to believe that the secrets of nature could be probed and that man could make use of the knowledge thus required to improve his manner of life. In other words, the power of tradition to keep man's thought and actions in the straight and narrow paths blocked out by his ancestors was slowly weakening in a few societies in the West.

A brief quotation from an historian of English farming will help us to appreciate how the developing willingness to modify traditional agricultural practices was leading to improvements in farming in some of the countries in Western Europe during the eighteenth century:

> The gigantic advance of agriculture in the nineteenth century dwarfs into insignificance any previous rate of progress. Yet the change between 1700 and 1800 was astonishing. England not only produced food for a population that had doubled itself, as well as grain for treble the number of horses, but during the first part of the period became, as M. deLavergne has said, the granary of Europe. [The advances in agriculture during this period] may be summed up in the adoption of improved methods of cultivation, the introduction of new crops, the reduction of stock breeding to a science, the provision of increased facilities of communication and transport, and the enterprises and outlay of capitalistic landlords and tenant farmers.[1]

Once the application of science to the techniques of agriculture (using "techniques" in a very broad sense) was begun and the better farmers and landholders became interested in increasing production (per unit of labor and of

[1] Roland Edmund Protheroe, First Baron Ernle, *English Farming, Past and Present*, Longmans, Green & Co., Inc., New York, 1922, p. 148.

land), a new era was under way. However, the rate of improvement and the period within which these improvements were widely adopted, even in Western Europe, varied considerably in different countries and at different periods. This Agricultural Revolution had begun as early as 1700 in England and in a few other countries in Europe. It later spread to other countries and is still in process, and some of its greatest achievements in terms of reduction of the labor cost for a specific unit of agricultural product have been attained by a number of peoples during the past few decades. Only now are the underdeveloped countries of the world beginning to revolutionize their traditional systems of agriculture, and their progress is slow, as was ours in the past.

Although the effects of innovations in the techniques of nonagricultural production and of transportation are much more widely known than those in agriculture, it will still be in order to call attention to two or three of the basic nonagricultural innovations of the eighteenth century because of their subsequent effects on agriculture as well as on productivity in other sectors of the economy. Perhaps the most important of all the innovations was the steam engine. In 1698 Thomas Savery invented a steam engine which could be used to pump water from mines. This soon led to a cheapening of the cost of coal, which in turn cheapened steam power. Numerous improvements in this engine were made by Newcomen in 1705–1711 and by Watt and others in the latter half of the eighteenth century. For several decades after 1700, the use of steam power spread only slowly to the operation of machinery and to the propelling of vehicles for transportation. It was not until 1804 that Richard Trevithick built an engine that successfully pulled "ten tons of iron, five waggons, and seventy men" on a prepared track. The efficiency of vehicles and boats was rapidly improved. By 1819 a sailing ship using a steam engine as auxiliary power crossed the Atlantic, and in 1825 the Darlington Railway in Britain, 38 miles long, was opened for public use.

In the meantime other innovations in machinery built to use steam power were being perfected. Among the most important of these, during the last quarter of the eighteenth century, were the inventions of Edmund Cartwright and others applying power to the manufacture of textiles, which then constituted one of the most important of British industries. Whitney's invention of the cotton gin in 1794 was another great step forward in supplying cheaper cotton cloth to the people of the West because it reduced greatly the labor of separating the fiber from the seed.

The most significant aspects of these technical innovations in agriculture, industry, and transportation, which became effective in the eighteenth century or even a little earlier in some countries, are that (1) they increased the efficiency of man's labor in producing food; (2) they had the same effect on his supply of certain other necessities and also made possible some heretofore unattainable comforts for a larger number of people; (3) they aided in opening, because of improved transport, vast new areas of land, particularly in the Western Hemisphere and in Oceania, some of them very rich in agricultural and other natural resources. Thus these revolutionary improvements in the techniques of production and in transport by making life a little easier for a slowly increasing proportion of the populations of the West prepared the way for a larger and more steady increase in their numbers.

An example from our own history will aid in understanding this very intimate relationship between the state of a people's technology and social organization, on the one hand, and the size of the population that it could support at any given level of living in a specified area, on the other.

North America. The most reliable estimates of the Indian population in America, north of Mexico, at the time (1650) that European settlement was becoming well established on the East Coast of the United States range between 500,000 and 1 million. In most of this region the Indians' techniques of hunting, of agriculture, and of housing were so primitive that even this small population suffered frequently from hunger and cold. Moreover, they carried on highly destructive wars with neighboring tribes in their efforts to ward off encroachment on the lands they needed for their support and/or to acquire more land to support a small increase in numbers.

The area on which at most a million Indians eked out a miserable existence, so repressive of growth that their numbers were practically stationary, now supports over 185 million (1962) people at a very high level of living, although the *natural resources* in absolute amounts are less today than they were three centuries ago. The difference in the productive power of the Indians and that of the present population of the United States is due in large measure to improvements in the techniques of production, although one should not overlook the fact that the maintenance of peace and the establishment of the forms of political and social organization brought by the European settlers from their home lands made it possible for these settlers and their descendants to apply these new techniques to the abundant natural resources more rapidly and more effectively; so effectively as regards the use of the land (agriculture) that only about 8 percent of the population of the United States is now engaged in agriculture.

WORLD POPULATION GROWTH, 1650–1800

This period (1650–1800) has been chosen to illustrate the beginning of a new era of population growth in part because we know so little about population growth before 1650 even in Europe and still less in the other continents, and in part because we do know that between about 1650 and 1800 some very important social and economic changes closely affecting population growth were taking place in several parts of the world. However, it is important for the reader to realize that even as late as 1650 there was almost total ignorance regarding the rate of population growth, if any, in practically all parts of the world and that in only a few countries was there a fairly good basis for making estimates of the size of the population. Hence the best estimates of the population of the world in 1650 were necessarily conclusions based on a careful study of the scanty materials available. (See Table 14-1.) Even in 1800 only a few countries had reliable data regarding the size of their populations. Carr-Saunders's figures will be used here in our discussion of world population growth since 1650 because, in the light of the 1953 census of Communist China, we prefer his estimates for 1650 and 1750 to those of Willcox.

During the period 1650–1800, the development of new techniques in agriculture, in manufacturing, and in transportation and communication, as well as the development of more stable political conditions doubtless, had increasingly important effects on population growth in the West.[2]

Carr-Saunders's data in Table 14-1 show a growth in the world population of 185 million between 1650 and 1750. The average *annual* rate during this century on this basis would be a little over 3 per 1,000 per year, or 0.3 percent. It should not be forgotten that the data for 1650 are at best only carefully informed estimates for most of the world. Those for 1750 have a somewhat more substantial basis, although they still leave much to be desired. But whether the annual rate of growth during this century was 3 per 1,000, or a little more or a little less, it is reasonable to assume that the growth of population during this century was both more regular and at a somewhat higher rate in certain parts of the world than that which had prevailed for any considerable portion of man's life on earth. (See the hypothetical calculations of population growth during such a period at varying rates in Chapter 14.) Carr-Saunders also found evidence that led him to believe the rate of population growth in the world during the half century 1750–1800 was about 4.5 persons per 1,000 per year, or an annual rate almost one-half higher than in the 100 years preceding 1750.

When the continents are considered as wholes, Asia is accorded the highest rate of growth between 1650 and 1750, about 45 percent, or slightly under 4 persons per 1,000 per year.[3] Europe's rate was only slightly smaller (40 percent).

---

[2] Since we shall have frequent occasion to refer to the "area of European settlement" from this point on, the reader is referred to notes *c* and *d* appended to Table 14-1 for the definition of this area. Since the phrase "area of European settlement, *except Latin America*" is also used frequently, the reader should try to recall the approximate population of Latin America at the given period by referring to Table 14-1.

[3] See the discussion of the probable growth of population in China during this period later in this chapter.

However, during the 50 years (1750–1800) Asia had a rate of growth of only 25 percent, an annual rate somewhat under 5 per 1,000 per year, while in Europe the rate of growth (1750–1800) was 35 percent in this 50 years, or about 6 per 1,000 per year as compared with its rate of less than 4 per 1,000 per year from 1650–1750. Although these figures cannot be regarded as precise, especially those for Asia, two general conclusions appear permissible: (1) In the entire period 1650–1800 the world's population was growing, although the rate of growth was rather slow; (2) the *rate of growth* during the 50 years 1750–1800 was rising significantly in Europe and in the area of European settlement as a whole. Quite probably it was not rising so much in Asia, although there is less certainty on this point. We have no basis for believing that there was any growth in Africa during this period, but Latin America was probably growing fairly rapidly, especially from 1750–1800. The reasons for this larger and more steady growth of population during this period can be best understood by a brief description of the conditions favoring or hindering its growth in several regions.

North America. During the 50 years preceding 1660, a number of colonies had been established along the Atlantic coast of what is now the United States, chiefly by people from the British Isles. The population in these colonies grew from about 210 persons in 1610 to an estimated 84,800 in 1660.[4] Immigration contributed a large part of the increase during this early period. After 1660, however, immigration became of decreasing importance as a source of growth. The reference just noted estimates the 1750 population of the colonies at 1,207,000. This is approximately a fourteenfold increase in 90 years. Moreover, during this time (1660–1750) the rate of increase remained remarkably constant at about 35 percent decade after decade, or 30 per 1,000 per year, a rate of growth that would double the population in 23 to 24 years. Immigration was never very large between 1660 and 1750. Since the population of the United States at the first national census (1790) was almost 4 million, i.e., about 3.25 times as large as it was in 1750, and since it is known that there was comparatively little immigration between 1750 and 1790, because of the French and Indian Wars and the Revolution, it appears reasonable to conclude that the natural increase of the population from 1660 onwards amounted to about 28 to 30 per 1,000 per year (2.8 to 3 percent) during the period 1660–1790, and we know that the natural increase remained at about the same level between our first and second censuses (1790–1800). Hence, although the total increase of population in the United States was too small to have any appreciable effect on the increase of the world's population during this period, its rate of increase did prove that probably any population could grow very rapidly under certain conditions. Moreover, we also know that in spite of the considerable emigration

[4] U.S. Bureau of the Census, *A Century of Population Growth in the United States, 1790–1900,* 1909, p. 9.

from the British Isles, chiefly from England, the population in the home country increased more regularly and faster after 1700 than in the preceding century.

These favorable conditions prevailing in the American Colonies may be described very briefly. Since there is no reason to assume that the fecundity of the American colonists, i.e., their physiological capacity to reproduce, was any greater than that of the people in the areas from which they migrated, there remain only two possible demographic changes to account for this very high natural increase: (1) an increase in fertility, i.e., in the average number of live births per woman; and (2) a decrease in the death rate. As regards the actuality of these two demographic changes, it is certain that the fertility of the women in the American Colonies was considerably higher than that of the women in the countries from which the migrants came. It may also have been that the easier economic conditions in the colonies reduced somewhat the practice of abortion, although there is no proof whatever that this was the case. Attention may also be called to the fact that once a population has begun to grow by natural increase, the proportion of young adults also begins to increase within a few years and remains relatively large so long as the birth rate remains high.

We can say with much less certainty that there was any substantial decline in the death rate in the colonies as compared with that in the countries of origin. However, several reasons will be given shortly which seem to the authors to justify the belief that there may have been some decline in the death rate in the colonies at an early date, particularly in the mortality of infants and young children. The causes of the demographic changes just mentioned are to be found chiefly in the social and economic conditions prevailing in these colonies, which led to changes in the customary patterns of behavior determining reproduction.

The chief reason for the increase in fertility in the colonies is probably to be found in the fact that colonial economic conditions encouraged a larger proportion of the people to marry than in the mother countries and also to marry at earlier ages than had been customary. The abundance of new and fertile land available on easy terms, a climate well adapted to the production of the chief grain crops of Europe, the acquisition of a new but very important native crop (corn) plus the ready adaptability of the agricultural practices of Europe to the lands of North America, all combined to contribute to "the Ease and Convenience of Supporting a Family" as Franklin said.[5]

It is reasonably certain that the conditions just enumerated encouraged early marriages in colonial America and that early marriages in turn raised the birth rate considerably above that in the countries from which the settlers came. In practically all of these European countries there had long been serious economic obstacles to early marriage which in due time crystallized into customs leading to postponement of marriage for several years after puberty. These customs

[5] Benjamin Franklin, "Observations Concerning the Increase of Mankind, The Peopling of Countries, &c.," *Magazine of History, with Notes and Quotes*, extra number, no. 63, 1775.

were soon modified and earlier marriages were made easier under the more open opportunities prevailing in colonial America. In most older and more closely settled countries, the young people growing up on farms, who constituted 80 percent or more of all young people, had little chance of renting a farm, to say nothing of owning one, until their parents had died or retired. Moreover, there were relatively few long-time household servants in the colonies and almost none on colonial farms. Since such servants usually married late, if at all, their transformation into farmers tended to raise the birth rate.

Because of the relative ease of acquiring a farm that prevailed in the American Colonies from 1660 onward, the student of population is not surprised to find a much higher birth rate among the colonists than in the countries of their origin. This change in the birth rate receives strong confirmation from calculations for the United States around 1800, based on census data, showing age and sex, which yield a crude birth rate in the United States of about 55 per 1,000.[6] The highest European birth rates about 1800 which can be vouched for were 33 to 35 for Sweden and 38 to 39 for Finland. Malthus, however, believed birth rates of 40 or more prevailed in Prussia and Russia at that time. He based his opinion on information gained from travel in these countries about 1800. It would also appear that the birth rate in the British Isles was about 38 at that time, although this estimate is somewhat less certain.

We can make no equally good estimate of the level of the death rate in the American Colonies during the latter part of the seventeenth and the first half of the eighteenth centuries. But as we have shown, there is good evidence that their populations grew very rapidly and that comparatively little of this growth was due directly to increase by immigration from about 1750 to about 1820. The doubling of any population from natural increase in about 25 years, as was happening in America, requires a difference of 27 to 28 per 1,000 per year between the birth rate and the death rate. Hence, a crude birth rate in the vicinity of 55 per 1,000 and a crude death rate of 27 to 28 would account for practically all the rapid rate of growth in colonial America and in the United States up to 1800 or a little later. Such a death rate is much the same as the death rate of Sweden (27.4) in the period 1751–1760. These Swedish data are considered quite reliable.

Incidentally, it may be pointed out in this connection that by 1751–1760 Sweden had a population growing at a rate of 8 per 1,000, or 0.8 percent per year, a rate which could not possibly have endured for long in the past. The proof of this statement is the fact that Sweden's population in 1600 is known to have been approximately 950,000 or 53.4 percent as large as in 1750. A steady rate of growth of about 4 persons per 1,000 per year during the 150 years (1600–1750) would account for Sweden's population increase during this period.

[6] Warren S. Thompson and P. K. Whelpton, *Population Trends in the United States*, McGraw-Hill Book Company, New York, 1944, p. 263.

Moreover, in the two centuries 1600–1800, Sweden's population grew considerably faster than Europe's as a whole. Since Sweden's crude birth rate appears to have been lower than that of a number of other European countries during much of this time, it would appear that Sweden's crude death rate even for some time before 1750 had been somewhat below that of most other European countries.[7]

For several reasons the authors believe it is not unreasonable to assume that the death rate in the American Colonies quite soon after settlement was established did not exceed that of Sweden in 1750 (27.4 per 1,000). The chief reason for this belief is implied in Franklin's phrase quoted above. An adequate and highly dependable food supply, which could readily be increased as fast as population grew, has always been favorable to regularizing the death rate and keeping it at a lower level than when food was scarce and difficult to increase. In the colonies good land was easy to find and to own.

In the second place, as fast as the menace of the Indians to the isolated frontier settlements was removed—and this took place rather shortly in most areas—the farmers began to live on the land they tilled rather than in villages, as was customary in Europe. It seems probable that this relative isolation of the farm family in a country where only about 5 percent of the population lived in places having a population of over 2,500 as late as 1790 had a significant effect in preventing the spread of epidemics which were especially deadly to young children. It also probably reduced the number of contagious intestinal infections arising from the use of water from contaminated village wells. Village wells were common in most of Europe. Moreover, this isolation of families also mitigated the spread of infections by passing strangers.

China. Although we have no reliable evidence regarding the growth of China's population from 1650–1800, several reasons lead us to conclude that its population may have grown significantly faster during this period than was customary. China's development may account for the somewhat more rapid growth of population in Asia between 1650 and 1750 than in Europe during the same period as estimated by Carr-Saunders (see Table 14-1). By about 1650 the Manchu conquerors of China had firmly established their rule and appear to have been able to maintain an unusually high degree of peace and political stability for about a century and a half. Moreover, during the first several decades of this period the emperors and high administrative officials appear to have taken great interest in improving agriculture and in informing farmers of these improvements. Less oppressive and less arbitrary tax policies than had prevailed before the Manchu conquest also appear to have been adopted. This relaxation of severity in management increased the incentive of the farmers both

[7] Axel Gustave Sundbärg, *Bevölkerungsstatistik Schwedens, 1750–1900*, Norstedt and Söner, Stockholm, 1907, pp. 2 and 5.

to make use of the better methods of cultivation being developed and to till more land where it was available.

All these conditions combined—peace, improvements in agriculture (China's agriculture probably became the most efficient in the world at that time), efficient and fairly honest civil administration, a considerable addition to the tilled areas made possible by moving into less densely settled areas in the southern parts of the country and by an increase in irrigation—were favorable to a reduction in the death rate for some decades.

Although little is known about the birth rate in China at that time, we have no good reason to suppose that it was much different from what it had been for centuries past or from what it has been during the past several decades, except as the conditions just noted may have contributed to age changes (a larger proportion of young women) which were favorable to a somewhat higher birth rate during the latter part of the seventeenth century and most of the eighteenth century. In the early decades of the twentieth century, a few studies were made in widely scattered communities in China which showed that the birth rate was probably in the range of 40 to 45 per 1,000. The teachings of the Chinese moralists and philosophers had long encouraged a high birth rate to ensure the continuance of the family line and thereby maintain the traditional worship of ancestors. Thus, with prevailing economic and political conditions rather favorable to some reduction of the usual death rate and with the possibility of a slightly increased birth rate, it would not be unreasonable to expect an average growth rate of 4 to 6 per 1,000 per year, e.g., a birth rate of 42 to 43 and a death rate of 36 to 38. The actual fluctuations in the death rate from year to year would, however, be much larger than the variation of three points suggested here for the average.

India. It would appear that economic and political conditions in India during the century and a half (1650–1800) were much less favorable for population growth than in China. Political conditions were highly unstable over much of the subcontinent. The empire of the Moguls was breaking up, and the control of the British was not yet firmly established. Much internal strife existed between the scores of governments, each controlled by an independent ruler. Moreover, the rulers and their administrators appear to have shown very little interest in the improvement of agriculture, which was the sole source of livelihood for the vast majority of the people. Civil strife, with the consequent insecurity of life and property, the stagnation of agriculture, arbitrary taxation, and personal government, have always had an unfavorable effect on the death rate. Birth rates probably were in the range 40 to 45 and death rates about the same. Furthermore, there was probably less new land readily available for settlement in India in 1650 than in China. Hence it appears likely that India's population grew very slowly, if at all, during much of this period.

Europe. In Europe after about 1650, a number of social and economic changes were beginning to produce somewhat more favorable conditions for population growth than those that had prevailed in the past. This was especially true after about 1700. Sundbärg's study indicates that Europe's population grew by somewhat over 35 percent between 1600 and 1700.[8] This would mean an average annual rate of 3 per 1,000. Moreover, at that time Sweden's population was growing at a somewhat faster rate than that of Europe as a whole. Hence, Sweden's population was becoming an increasing proportion of Europe's total, rising from 10 percent in 1600 to 11.4 percent in 1700 and to 12.5 percent in 1800.

In 1650 in most of the countries of Europe, there was still a considerable amount of unused land or grazing land that could be brought into tillage. The disintegration of the feudal system also enabled an increasing number of the farmers and business men with capital to acquire control of land either through ownership or long-time leases. Moreover, as we have already noted, the scientific knowledge of agriculture increased significantly during the eighteenth century, and the Agricultural Revolution was going strongly by 1800. In addition, in some parts of Europe by 1750, transport both by water and by land had become slightly more efficient, so that local food shortages could occasionally be relieved by moving grain from areas of plenty to areas of scarcity.

Certain other changes were also taking place in Western Europe which tended to reduce the customary average death rates. For example, there had been no repetition in Europe of a plague as deadly as the Black Death (1348–1350). Even though the plague of 1665–1666 was extremely severe in London,[9] its ravages in England as a whole were not to be compared with those of the Black Death three centuries earlier.

Malthus, probably writing about 1800–1802, believed that this plague of 1665–1666 had taught the English some very valuable lessons in urban sanitation (cleanliness), and thereby helped to prepare the way for more substantial population growth after about 1700. He wrote:

> The prevalence of the plague in London till the year 1666 operated in a proper manner on the conduct of our ancestors; and the removal of nuisances, the construction of drains, the widening of streets, and the giving more room and air to the houses, had the effect of eradicating completely this dreadful disorder, and of adding greatly to the health and happiness of the inhabitants.[10]

[8] *Ibid.*, pp. 2 and 3.

[9] Daniel Defoe, *History of the Plague in London, 1665* . . . , G. Bell & Sons, Ltd., London, 1905, pp. 69–71.

[10] Thomas Robert Malthus, *An Essay on Population*, vol. 2, J. M. Dent & Sons, Ltd., London, p. 155; E. P. Dutton & Co., Inc., New York, n.d. (Everyman's Library, no. 692, reprinted from the 7th ed.).

Clearly some of the Western Europeans were beginning to appreciate the benefits of better sanitary arrangements even though the bacterial origin of local
epidemics and of plagues was not yet known. It is not surprising, then, that in
spite of rather severe calamities (chiefly droughts and local epidemics) during
the period 1650–1800 Europe's population began to grow a little faster and a
little more regularly than it had previously, perhaps from 3 to 5 per 1,000 per
year. (See above.) The growth of Asia's population at a slightly higher rate than
that of Europe during this period also appears probable.

However, by and large, both in Europe and in Asia the poverty and the
disease and the unsettled political conditions, which from time immemorial had
done much to keep man's death rates at almost as high a level as his birth rates,
and also rendered the death rate highly variable from time to time, had abated
only a little during this period. By 1800 it was increasingly clear to the better-
informed Europeans that their agriculture and industry were becoming more
efficient and that widespread famines and epidemics were also becoming less
frequent. Hence such people could reasonably expect that death rates would
continue to decline slowly and that population would grow a little faster since
there was then no rational expectation of a decline in the birth rate (see Chapter
2). On the other hand, there were some indications that living conditions in Asia
and particularly in China would grow more difficult as internal dissension
increased, as agriculture stagnated, and as new land became scarcer. Europe
and North America were expanding their production of the necessities of life
and adding some non-necessities faster and rather more steadily, but there was
no evidence that this was happening to a significant degree in other parts of the
world. The evidence of the hopeful outlook for improving living conditions in
Europe is found in the writings of the "perfectionists," whose views stimulated
Malthus's first *Essay* (see Chapter 2).

WORLD POPULATION GROWTH, 1800–1850

In the half century from 1800–1850 the world's population increased slightly
faster than between 1750 and 1800 (about 29 percent or almost 5 per 1,000 per
year). The population of Europe, however, grew by almost 43 percent, i.e., at a
rate slightly over 7 per 1,000 per year (0.7 percent), or about 50 percent faster
than that of the world as a whole. Furthermore, there is convincing evidence in
the good data of the Scandinavian countries that during the period 1800–1850
their populations grew at relatively high rates as compared with the preceding
50 years and as compared with the remainder of Europe during the same period.
It would appear that an improvement of political and economic conditions consisting chiefly of a more secure and more adequate food supply, of somewhat
better sanitation, and, by the second quarter of the nineteenth century, the

reduction in some areas of the ravages of smallpox, were slowly becoming effective in reducing the death rates in Western Europe. In the areas of European settlement in North America, the relatively easy living conditions remained effective in keeping the birth rate high and in keeping the crude death rate in line with the death rates in Western Europe in spite of the large volume of infant mortality always accompanying a high birth rate in those days.

In the entire area of European settlement (for definition see Table 14-1, notes *c* and *d*), Carr-Saunders's estimates show that the population grew by 53 percent between 1800 and 1850, or somewhat less than 10 per 1,000 per year. By this latter date (1850), the United States was becoming a substantial contributor to the population of this area (United States population in 1800—5.3 million, in 1850—25.2 million). On the other hand, in the remainder of the world the total increase (1800–1850) was only about 25 percent, and the annual rate was about one-half as large as in the area of European settlement and perhaps one-sixth to one-seventh as high as in the United States. Even in 1850, outside of Europe and North America, all population data were still estimates and should be thought of as only approximations.

In a word, it may be said that in parts of Western Europe the beginnings of a more efficient economy, which were noted in the latter part of the period 1650–1800, slowly became a full-fledged revolution and were steadily expanding. The cultivated area continued to increase, and the efficiency of agricultural labor gradually rose through the increasing acceptance of better agricultural practices and improved implements. Interest in cleanliness (sanitation) both in the home and in the community was slowly increasing. To these factors favoring the reduction of the death rate must be added the increasing efficiency of labor in the nonagricultural pursuits, especially in manufacturing and transportation, which helped to mitigate the rigors of life. Finally, after about 1825 in Europe and North America, the increasing use of vaccination against smallpox began to contribute significantly to the decline in the death rate.

The vital statistics of European countries having reliable birth rates and death rates in the first half of the nineteenth century show clearly that in most of them the increasing rate of population growth was due to the decline in the death rate rather than to any change in the birth rate. In Sweden the death rate for the ten years 1800–1810 was 27.9 and by 1851–1860, a half century later, it had fallen to about 21.7, while the birth rates for those periods were 30.9 and 32.8 respectively. This *pattern of a lag in the decline in birth rates* as compared with that in the death rates varied somewhat from country to country. In Europe, however, the decline in the death rate preceded any significant decline in the birth rate by several decades, and the irregularities in the death rate within short periods of time remained much more marked than those in the birth rate.

However, in France it appears that contraception was practiced to a slight extent as early as 1750 and by 1800 was having a small but noticeable effect on the birth rate. By 1850 it had become a significant factor in keeping the growth of population in France somewhat below that in most other countries in Western Europe. In the United States the censuses from 1810 on show a declining ratio of children aged 0–4 to 1,000 women aged 20–44 (see Chapter 9) which is *definite proof* of a declining birth rate, unless we assume that the death rates of children under 5 were rising rather rapidly and thus reducing the number of children aged 0–4. There is no evidence of such a rise in infant and child death rates. This decline in the birth rate in the United States after 1810 did not have much effect on the rate of population growth until after 1860. This was due, in part, to the arrival of large numbers of immigrants from Europe during the period 1820–1860 and in part to the decline in the death rate which began somewhere around the middle of the century. It is of interest in this connection to note that the increased emigration from Europe after about 1820 did not prevent the populations of the countries which sent out the immigrants from growing more rapidly during the first half of the nineteenth century than they had ever grown in the past.

The period from 1800–1850 was one of increasing growth differentials among countries, regions, and continents. What was just hinted at in the preceding period became established—the death rate came increasingly but slowly under control, and death rates were pushed gradually downward in most of the countries in Europe. But so far as we know, there was little change in North America. During this period (1800–1850) in the West as a whole, the aggregate death rate fell to the lower 20s per 1,000, whereas the aggregate birth rate probably remained almost stationary. The aggregate rate of natural increase probably averaged 11 or 12 per 1,000 per year. However the variations in these rates from country to country were considerable. There is little or no evidence of any significant spurt in population growth in the non-European populations during this half century (1800–1850), although Asia is estimated to have grown by about 25 percent, or slightly more than 4 per 1,000 per year.

WORLD POPULATION GROWTH, 1850–1900

During the period from 1850–1900 more and more countries were taking censuses, so that data showing changes in population growth became more abundant and also more reliable. Moreover, the technical revolutions in agriculture and in the nonagricultural industries were spreading quite rapidly in the West and were becoming more and more effective in raising man's productivity and thus in alleviating the pressure of population on the necessities of life. These revolutions were also beginning to modify more rapidly the social and economic organization of the Western peoples by changing the mode of living especially among their rapidly growing urban populations. From the standpoint of population growth, the most significant change during this period was the fairly rapid reduction in the birth rate. In general, it may be said that during the period 1850–1900 it became clear to most European peoples that man could control his rate of population growth by controlling both his birth rate and his death rate. Vaccination against smallpox became quite general. Transportation developed in most of the Western world, except Latin America, to the point where local crop failures had less and less effect on the death rate than in the past because shortages, both local and regional, could often be relieved with comparatively little difficulty. The value of sanitary cleanliness, both private and public, in maintaining health was more widely appreciated because, toward the end of this period (1850–1900), the knowledge that many diseases were caused by bacteria spread rather rapidly.

In the European countries that possess reliable data there is not the least doubt that their death rates, which had begun to fall after about 1800, continued to fall during this half century (see Table 12-9) at a somewhat more rapid rate than before 1850. In the United States most students of population tend to use 1850 as an approximate date to indicate the beginning of a more rapid decline in the death rate. Declines in crude death rates in the more economically developed Western countries fell in widely varying amounts, from around 24 to 22 in 1850 to 20 to 16 per 1,000 by 1900. Increasing urbanization probably tended to retard the decline in the death rate in some countries until public sanitation became more general about 1900. In a number of countries, however, death rates of 16 to 18 per 1,000 had been attained by that time. This indicated excellent progress in the improvement of health, even though the discoveries of the nineteenth century bacteriologists were far from being fully used by 1900.

The data in Table 14-1 show the results of these lower death rates on population growth. Using Carr-Saunders's figures, we see that Europe's population (excluding the Asiatic possessions of Russia) increased by about 51 percent, a little less than 7.5 persons per 1,000 per year during the half century 1850–1900. The population in the area of European settlement (including Latin America) increased by about 69 percent, or a little less than 11 persons per 1,000 per year. The increase in the remainder of the world, i.e., all except the area of European settlement, was about 30 percent, or less than one-half as much.

Although there is clear evidence (see Chapter 9) that between 1850 and 1900 the birth rate had declined substantially in most of Western Europe and also in the other areas of European settlement, except Latin America, the relatively more rapid growth of population in the area of European settlement must be attributed to the lag of the decline in the birth rate behind that of the death rate. France alone of all the European countries having reliable vital statistics in 1900 and in 1850 had a lower rate of natural increase in 1900 than in 1850. This was probably due in large measure to the fact that voluntary control of the size of the family prevailed more widely in France than in most other Western countries. With the possible exception of France, the declines in the birth rates of the countries in the area of European settlement during the latter half of the nineteenth century were very closely associated with the spread of the Industrial Revolution and the increasing urbanization of the population.

WORLD POPULATION GROWTH, 1900-1930

Because the facts regarding the decline of the death rate in various parts of the world since 1900 are relatively abundant and because they seem to the authors to show quite clearly that there have been two rather different phases in the control of the death rate during the period 1900–1960, our treatment of population growth since 1900 will be divided into two parts, viz., 1900–1930 and 1930–1960. Population growth since 1930 will be accorded a separate chapter, Chapter 16.

Between 1900 and 1930, in the area of European settlement, excluding Latin America, for which reliable population data were still scanty and rather unreliable, population continued to grow at a fairly rapid rate (over 30 percent, or slightly less than 10 per 1,000 per year) in spite of the great losses in World War I, which will be described presently. For the remainder of the world the rate of growth was about 22 percent, or a little less than 7 per 1,000 per year. During this period the area of European settlement, excluding Latin America, witnessed a rapidly increasing control over more and more of the infectious diseases which had hitherto taken a heavy toll of life among all peoples. The decline in the death rate in most of the countries in the West was truly amazing. Even in the countries already having what were considered low crude death rates in 1900 (16 to 18 per 1,000) these rates declined by one-fourth to one-third during these 30 years, and the relative importance of the infectious diseases as causes of death (see Chapter 12) declined almost year by year in the more developed countries until for many of them it was only a small fraction in 1930 of what it had been in 1900. Nevertheless, the annual rate of population growth in this area declined somewhat because the birth rate had begun to fall even faster than the death rate in a number of countries, and World War I took a heavy toll of births as well as of deaths in most of Europe.

During the period 1900–1930 the rate of population growth varied greatly between different countries and peoples. In Japan the population grew from 43.8 million in 1900 to 63.9 million in 1930 or by approximately 46 percent in 30 years or a little less than 13 per 1,000 per year. This is considerably faster than in the area of European settlement (excluding Latin America). The Philippine population grew by almost 2 percent (20 per 1,000) a year after the first census, under United States auspices, increasing from about 7.6 million in 1903 to about 13 million in 1930. In India (present area) the population grew by only about 17 percent during this period, or a little over 5 per 1,000 per year. The growth rate would probably have been nearly twice as great if it had not been for the terrific loss of life in the influenza epidemic of 1918. There is no reliable information regarding the growth of population in China during this period. The population of Latin America, according to the best data available, grew by 75 percent, or somewhat less than 2 percent per year, but data from this area for 1930 must still be used with caution because more adequate enumeration and better estimates had an unknown amount of influence on the data used in this calculation.

On the whole, it may be said that the large measure of control over the infectious diseases which came to prevail in the area of European settlement by 1930, excluding Latin America, was, at best, only beginning to manifest itself in most other parts of the world. Indeed, in the regions containing a large part of the non-European population of the world, the scarcity of food and/or the wide prevalence of the infectious diseases were still the great killers of men and determined in large measure the death rates in these regions.

Nevertheless, by 1930 it seemed clear to the senior author[11] that the future growth of population in the world would assume a quite different pattern from that which had prevailed during the past century or two. The death rates in the limited area of European settlement, excluding Latin America, had reached such a low point in many countries that future declines were certain to be small when compared with past declines and were likely to take place slowly. Moreover, in a number of these same populations the birth rates had also declined to such low levels that the margin between births and deaths was diminishing fairly rapidly. On the other hand, as we have just stated, there was evidence that death rates in a few non-European populations were declining, but the prospect seemed clear that this decline would spread at varying speeds to all these peoples in the not too distant future. Since there was no evidence whatever that the birth rates of most non-European peoples had yet begun to decline significantly, it seemed reasonably certain that the first effect of the increasing control of the death rate among practically all these peoples would be a more steady and a more rapid increase in their rates of growth than in the past. This judgment assumed, of course, that their food supplies could be increased fast enough to care for their growing numbers, at least at no lower per capita levels than those then prevailing.

The probable trend of world population growth as conditions were in 1930 justified dividing the peoples of the world into three broad groups as regards probable future population growth.

[11] Warren S. Thompson, *Danger Spots in World Population*, Alfred A. Knopf, Inc., New York, 1929.

Group I. All the Western peoples who had been exercising a large measure of control over their death rates through the improvement in the level of living of the masses of the people and through the application of science to health problems, belong in the first group. During the decades prior to 1930 most of these Western peoples had also come to exercise an increasing measure of control over their birth rates. In a word, all these peoples had relatively low death rates and birth rates. The dominant factor affecting their rates of increase from year to year *was no longer the death rate,* assuming no great and uncontrollable catastrophes. The *birth rate had become the dominant variable* in determining the rate of population growth among these peoples. As we have seen, the birth rate may and often does vary considerably over a relatively short period of time when its voluntary control is widespread (see Chapter 9).

On the whole, it appeared probable that these Group I peoples would have relatively low rates of natural increase in the future. Their death rates were so low that any further improvement in health would have a smaller effect on their rates of growth than in the recent past. In fact, in many of them the crude death rates were more likely to rise slowly because of the increasing proportion of older people, whose death rates were proving difficult to reduce (see Chapters 12 and 13). If for any reason these peoples were to decide to raise larger families, they could do so very quickly, because there is no evidence yet of any significant change in their physiological capacity to reproduce. But it did not seem probable that they would jeopardize their good levels of living and their low death rates by any large increase in the average size of their families. To summarize, the Group I peoples had low birth rates and low death rates, both under a large measure of voluntary control, and they seemed likely to have relatively small rates of increase or no increase at all if it became more difficult to acquire and maintain a good level of living. The following countries could be reasonably assigned to Group I: The United States, the United Kingdom, France, Denmark, Norway, Sweden, The Netherlands, Germany, Austria, Czechoslovakia, Hungary, the Baltic countries (Estonia, Latvia, and Lithuania—now part of the Soviet Union), Belgium, Finland, Switzerland, Italy, Canada (although French-Canadian Quebec still has a large increase), Australia, and New Zealand. They then contained approximately one-fifth of the world's people. The changes in these groupings since 1930 will be considered in some detail in the following chapter.

Group II. Most of the countries in the second group were characterized by a death rate which was coming under control to a limited extent but which, for most of them, was still at the level which prevailed in Group I countries 50 to 70 years earlier. The birth rates of Group II countries were under even less control than their death rates, although in some of them there could be no reasonable doubt that the birth rate had begun to decline. As a consequence of these changes in death rates with but little change in birth rates, their rates of increase were of much the same order as those of the Group I countries about the latter part of the nineteenth century or the beginning of this century, varying from 10 to 15 per 1,000 or more per year. In some cases the rates were higher. There is, of course, no sharp line of demarcation between Group I and Group II countries. A country in Group II in 1930 might pass into Group I any time that control over death rates and birth rates became more assured. Furthermore, there would be no general agreement among students of population on a list of countries to be included in these groups at any given moment. The decision on this point would rest in part upon one's own judgment as to the security of control over the death rate and the extent of control over the birth rate, if any, in the particular country. These Group II countries, sometimes called *areas of demographic transition*, appeared likely to have relatively high rates of natural increase for several decades to come. As a group, therefore, they would probably grow at a considerably faster rate than the Group I peoples and would contain an increasing proportion of the world's population for some time to come. The following countries appeared eligible for Group II: Spain, Portugal, Greece, Yugoslavia, Bulgaria, Romania, Poland, South Africa (white), Japan, and the Soviet Union; possibly also Egypt, French North Africa (Algeria, Tunis, and Morocco), Brazil, Argentina, and Uruguay. With all these countries included, the population of this group around 1930 amounted to a little over one-fifth of the world's total, perhaps 21 to 22 percent.

Group III. The third group consisted of the remaining peoples of the world and contained perhaps 58 to 59 per cent of its total population. These peoples were characterized by high death rates which were under only a small measure of control as compared with that of Group I and were also substantially higher than those of the Group II countries. In addition, such control as was then exercised over death rates was highly precarious. In these countries the death rate was still the decisive factor in determining the rate of increase at any given moment because the birth rates of all of them were high (probably over 40 per 1,000) and varied much less from year to year than their death rates (see Chapters 9 and 12). Among them there was as yet no evidence of any voluntary control over the birth rate. India was perhaps the best example of such a country for which we could get a fairly reliable picture of what was happening as regards natural increase, although the registration of births and deaths was woefully inadequate. Since India had begun taking censuses (1872) there were two decades out of the five before 1921 when the decennial increase was less than 1 percent, i.e., less than 1 per 1,000 per year. There was also one in which the 10-year increase was only 1.4 percent, or slightly over 1 per 1,000 per year. In the decade 1921–1931 the rate of increase was 11 percent, or a little over 10 per 1,000 per year. This evidence of a decline in the death rate might seem to place India in

Group II, but this classification did not seem justified because the measure of control over the death rate manifested during the five decades preceding 1921 was so precarious that one felt no assurance it could be maintained.

The important point to notice is that these Group III countries (the term "underdeveloped" had not come into vogue in 1930) varied in rate of growth from year to year as the death rate rose or declined, while the birth rates remained almost static. These countries could be said to have great growth possibilities because of their high birth rates, but they were likely to have highly variable rates of growth for some time. Some of the countries in Group III probably were not growing at all because their high birth rates were matched by their high death rates; others might at times even decline because of famines and/or epidemics which would raise their death rates above their birth rates. The level of the death rate would continue to be the chief determinant of the growth of the Group III countries during the next few decades just as it had been throughout human history. The modifications in this general statement as of 1930 will be discussed in some detail in the following chapter, but before passing to this discussion it will be well to note how World Wars I and II affected the growth of population in Europe.

WAR LOSSES IN WORLD WAR I

The effects of recent wars on population growth have probably been quite different from those of wars between preagricultural peoples and even from those between agricultural peoples before about the last quarter of the nineteenth century.

We shall consider here primarily the rather immediate and direct effects on population growth that are quite generally recognized as intimately associated with the war years, viz., the changes in birth rates and death rates during the war. Basically, these changes were of two kinds in World War I: (1) losses due to the excess of deaths over those to be expected if there had been no war, and (2) losses due to the deficit in number of births during the war years. The situation was somewhat different in World War II, as we shall note in due course. (See Table 15-1.) The excesses in deaths occurred both in the armed forces and in the civilian population. The deficit of births was due primarily to the mobilization of large military forces, which had the effect of separating great numbers of husbands and wives for relatively long periods and also of preventing many marriages which would normally have taken place during the war period. Secondarily, some of the birth deficit was probably due to the unwillingness of married persons not directly affected by war mobilization to give additional hostages to fortune at a time of such great uncertainty.

Military losses were very large in World War I, chiefly because of the vast

TABLE 15-1.   BIRTH RATES AS AFFECTED BY WAR

Country	World War II*			World War I†		
	Postwar, 1947–1949	War, 1940–1944	Prewar, 1937–1939	Postwar, 1920–1924	War, 1915–1919	Prewar, 1910–1914
England and Wales....	18.3	15.5	14.9	21.4	19.4	24.2
France..............	21.1	14.9	14.9	19.8	11.3	18.8
Belgium............	17.5	13.9	15.6	20.9	13.6	22.2
Germany............	16.9‡	17.3‡	19.6	23.1	16.8	28.2
Austria............	17.4	19.1	15.8	22.6	15.8	29.6
Hungary............	19.8‡	19.3‡	19.8	30.0	20.2	35.0
Italy..............	21.2	20.8	23.4	30.0	22.7	32.0
Bulgaria...........	24.0	22.1	22.8	39.6	26.6	39.2
Romania...........	—	23.2	29.6	36.8	31.9‡	41.8
Japan..............	33.6	30.1	28.2	34.8	32.4	33.6
United States§.......	25.8	23.1	18.9	26.8	28.4	29.8
Netherlands.........	25.6	21.8	20.3	26.5	25.5	28.2
Sweden.............	18.2	17.7	14.9	20.3	20.7	23.7
Norway.............	20.5	17.7	15.4	23.4	24.2	25.6
Denmark...........	20.4	20.3	18.0	23.1	23.8	26.4
Spain..............	21.9	22.0	19.8	30.3	29.0	31.3
Australia..........	23.3	19.4	17.5	24.4	25.7	27.7
New Zealand........	25.6	21.4	18.0	23.0	24.4	26.2
Switzerland.........	19.0	17.9	15.1	19.9	18.6	23.8

* United Nations, *Demographic Yearbook, 1951,* table 7, New York, 1952.

† France, Bureau de la Statistique Générale, *Annuaire statistique de la France, 1913,* p. 168*, 1929, p. 214*, Imprimerie Nationale, Paris; Institut International de Statistique, *Annuaire international de statistique,* vol. 5, pp. 47, 119, W. P. Van Stockum & Fils, the Hague, 1921; and New Zealand, Census and Statistics Office, *New Zealand Official Yearbook, 1926,* p. 109, Government Printer, Wellington, 1926.

‡ Federal Republic, 1947–1949, Germany, 1940–1943; Hungary, 1947–1948, 1940–1943; Bulgaria, 1947; Romania, 1915, 1918, and 1919.

§ U.S. Federal Security Agency, National Office of Vital Statistics, "Births and Birth Rates in the Entire United States, 1909–1948," *Vital Statistics: Special Reports, Selected Studies,* vol. 33, no. 8, 1948, p. 141.

size of the armed forces involved but also, in part, because the kind of weapons used led to trench warfare and great numbers of wounded, many of whom died from infected wounds. But even though excess civilian death rates were high in World War I, they were probably lower than in the days when armies lived off the land and when invading armies as well as resisting armies carried with them all manner of infectious diseases which they transmitted to the civilian populations along the lines of march.

On the eve of World War I, Europe west of Russia had a population of approximately 319 million.[12] Direct military losses in this area were reckoned at about 6.6 million and the excess of civilian deaths at about 5 million, while the deficit of births, after allowing for a smaller number of infant deaths because of fewer births, amounted to about 10.5 million (see Table 15-1 for declines in live birth rates). The deficit in births, therefore, constituted the largest component of war losses. The total war losses in this area amounted to about 22.4 million.[13] (See Figure 15-1 for approximate losses in several countries.)

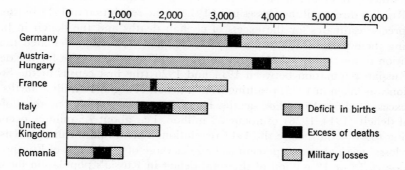

FIGURE 15-1. **Population deficits in selected countries as a result of World War I (in thousands).** (Frank W. Notestein et al., *The Future Population of Europe and the Soviet Union,* **League of Nations, Geneva, 1944, p. 75.**)

Hence it seems reasonable to assume that this part of Europe would have had a natural increase (excess of births over deaths) of 33 to 35 million if there had been no war. The war losses as calculated amounted to about two-thirds or a little more of the normal natural increase that would have been expected during the decade 1910–1920.

The *actual increase* of population in this part of Europe had for several decades been well below the *natural increase* because of a rather large net emigration; hence, the actual increase of population from 1910 to 1920 would probably have been several million less than the expected natural increase of 33 to 35 million,

[12] The brief discussion here of war losses in World War I will follow that in Frank W. Notestein et al., *The Future Population of Europe and the Soviet Union,* chap. 3, League of Nations, Geneva, 1944.

[13] No effort will be made to take account of the reduction in number of births in the 20 to 25 years following the war due to the fact that millions of marriages were broken permanently by the war deaths of husbands and other millions never occurred because of the vast numbers of young men killed before marriage.

perhaps 6 or 7 million less, as was the case in the preceding decade (1900–1910). Allowing for this net emigration, the expected increase would have been 26 or 27 million. The actual increase in population of this part of Europe during the war decade, however, was only about 8 million, 17 to 18 million less than the expected 26 or 27 million. It is clear that World War I was a severe check to population growth in this part of Europe, which then contained about one-fifth of the world's population.

The largest war losses suffered by any belligerent in World War I were undoubtedly those of Russia. Lorimer[14] accepts 2 million as a reasonable figure for Russia's direct military losses from 1914 to the revolution in 1917 but makes no precise estimates for the excess of civilian deaths and the deficit in births during these prerevolutionary war years. He has, however, calculated that in addition to the military deaths just noted (2 million) there was a further deficit in Russian population between 1914 and 1926 (the first census in the Soviet Union was taken in 1926) resulting from a deficit of about 10 million births and an excess of about 16 million deaths. He suggests that possibly one-third of this total deficit (1914–1926) of about 28 million, i.e., about 9.5 million, occurred during the war but before the 1917 revolution. This would mean that Russia's war losses were about 40 percent as large as those of all the rest of Europe. On this basis, 18 or 19 million of the total deficit in Russia's population incurred between 1914 and 1926 would be charged to civil war following the revolution of 1917, to the famine of 1918–1922, and to the pestilence accompanying the famine. The slow growth of population in the U.S.S.R. from 1914–1926 illustrates clearly how war may be instrumental in touching off and/or abetting a series of reactions, political, economic, and social, that may have great influence on population growth. World War I certainly did not cause the drought of 1918–1922, nor did the revolution, but the revolution added heavily to war losses between 1917 and 1926, while both the war and the revolution did limit very greatly the ability of the U.S.S.R. to relieve the famine conditions that ensued and to control the epidemics which accompanied the famine. The net effect of these calamities—World War I, civil war (revolution), famine, and disease—on population growth (1914–1926) was that the U.S.S.R. grew only from about 140.4 million in 1914 (Russian Empire) to about 147 million in 1926 (U.S.S.R.). A reasonable expectation of population in 1926, assuming no great calamity, was about 175 million. Instead of increasing by 35 million, the U.S.S.R. increased by only 7 million, a deficit of 28 million, or practically four-fifths of the expected increase. World War I and its aftermath in Russia may very well have reduced normal population growth *in the whole of Europe* by about 50 million between 1900 and 1930.

Although there were substantial military losses outside of Europe in World

[14] Frank Lorimer, *The Population of the Soviet Union, History and Prospects*, chap. 3, The League of Nations, Geneva, 1946. (See also Roof and Selegen in Supplementary Readings to this chapter.)

War I, they were relatively small and had comparatively little effect on population growth in Canada, Australia, New Zealand, and South Africa, and still less on growth in the United States. In all these countries, however, the deficits in births due to the mobilization of large armed forces were moderately large. These losses were made up rather quickly by the higher birth rates in the three or four years following the close of the war (see Table 15-1). (For approximate war losses by source see Figure 15-1.)

WAR LOSSES IN WORLD WAR II

It seems best to describe war losses in World War II at this point although they did not occur until after 1930. Although war losses in World War II were certainly affected significantly by the changes in control over the infectious diseases which was the outstanding characteristic of the period 1930–1960, from the standpoint of population growth (see following chapter) they were not affected to any such degree as were the civilian death rates in those countries which still had moderately high to high death rates in 1930.

Two types of civilian deaths in World War II had previously had no counterpart in modern war. The aerial bombing of civilian populations was begun by the Germans early in the war. The United Kingdom suffered heavily from such bombing both early in the war and again near its close. Germany also suffered heavy civilian losses from aerial bombing after the Allied Powers gained ascendancy in the air. France also suffered considerable losses from bombing during its reconquest by the Allies. The second and by far the greatest civilian losses were due to the deliberate efforts of the Nazis to exterminate the Jews, to wipe out anti-Nazis, and to terrorize by wholesale slaughter all the conquered peoples engaged in resistance movements. The extent of these civilian losses can only be guessed at. Some of these guesses will be mentioned below.

In Europe *west of Germany*, war losses were, on the whole, less than in World War I. In France strictly military losses (about 200,000) were about one-tenth of those in World War I. However, deaths of war prisoners and of men deported to Germany for forced labor and civilian deaths due directly to war action, chiefly to aerial bombing, must be added, making a total of perhaps 600,000 deaths in France due rather directly to the war. Altogether, these losses were nearly one-third as large as similar losses in World War I. However, the birth rate in France did not decline during World War II as much as it did during World War I (see Table 15-1).[15] As a result of these differences, from the standpoint of population growth, France suffered far less from World War II than from World War I. Although this was also true of the United Kingdom, in part,

[15] Paul Vincent, "Conséquences de six années de guerre sur la population française," *Population*, vol. 1, no. 3, pp. 429–440, 1946.

because, as in France, the birth rate did not decline to the same extent as in World War I, nevertheless, direct British war losses were far heavier than those of France.

On the other hand, The Netherlands, Norway, and Denmark, all of which were neutral in World War I, were occupied by the Germans during World War II, and they, together with Belgium, suffered substantial war losses. But in practically all the Western European countries the birth rate did not decline nearly so much during World War II as it had during World War I, and hence their war losses from this source were relatively smaller.

But if population growth in the countries of Western Europe as a whole was much less affected by direct war losses in World War II than in World War I, this was not the case in Eastern and Southern Europe and in Germany.

Total German losses (territory of 1937) were probably little different in the two wars. Direct military deaths are estimated at more than 3 million, about one-half greater than such losses in World War I (territory of 1914). Sauvy and Ledermann[16] have estimated that in the neighborhood of 400,000 persons may have been killed in the aerial bombing of Germany and that the excess of deaths in the civilian population from other *military causes* was of about the same magnitude,[17] while the deficit of births amounted to only about 1 million (see Table 15-1). According to these calculations, the total direct war losses of Germany (area of 1937) would have been somewhat over 4.8 million, possibly a little over 5 million. Admittedly, these figures involve considerable estimating and make use of assumptions as to what normal vital rates would have been. But it appears reasonable to compare the figure of about 5 million war losses in World War II with the figure of about 5.4 million in World War I (see Figure 15-1), if excess civilian deaths due to murders in concentration camps and for terrorizing purposes are not included in World War II losses.

However, when the combined population of West Germany and East Germany in 1946—about 62 million—is compared with that of Germany in 1941 in the territory of 1937—approximately 70 million—there is a net loss of about 8 million. Unfortunately, this is not exactly the same territory in 1946 as in 1937 and there were still great numbers of German prisoners of war in the U.S.S.R. in 1946, so that the following calculations should be considered as merely suggestive rather than even approximate. This deficit of 8 million is about 3 million more than the war losses just noted, viz., about 5 million. Moreover, the 70 million people in Germany in 1941 would normally have had about 6.8 million births between 1941 and 1946 (5 years) and they would normally have had about 4.2 million deaths. This leaves a natural increase of 2.6 million which

[16] Alfred Sauvy and Sully Ledermann, "La guerre biologique (1933–1945); population de l'Allemagne et des pays voisins," *Population*, vol. 1, no. 3, pp. 471–488, 1946.
[17] Clearly this figure does not include the Jews and others murdered in German concentration camps nor the civilians killed for terrorizing purposes.

would add up to an expected population in 1946 of about 72.6 million if there had been no war. The war losses as calculated above amounted to about 5 million as compared with the 10 million which represents the difference between the expected population and the actual population of Germany in 1946. Is this difference, amounting to about 5 million, a realistic measure of the excess of civilian deaths of Germans during the war? This question cannot be answered with any confidence, for it must be recognized that there are so many uncertainties in the figures regarding the number of war prisoners never returned, the refugees in camps in different countries, the emigration of German citizens before, during, and immediately after the war, and the size of the populations within changed boundaries, that we shall never know exactly how many German people were murdered in Hitler's concentration camps and how many were summarily disposed of as anti-Nazis.

But if the Western countries of Europe (not including Germany) escaped with lighter losses in World War II than in World War I, and even if Germany, not including civilian murders, had about the same war losses in World War II as in World War I, this was not true for most of the countries in Central and Eastern Europe. Poland is supposed to have had a loss of population amounting to 5 or 6 million, perhaps 20 percent of its prewar population, a considerable part of which came from concentration camp murders, the bombardment of civilians within cities, and other reprisals against civilians.[18] Because of the changes in boundaries and migration this figure must always remain uncertain. The possible deficit of births is not included.

Yugoslavia probably experienced war losses of over 10 percent of her prewar population through the excess of military and civilian deaths (about 1.6 million); Greece lost about ½ million, or about 7 percent of her total population, without taking account of the deficit of births in either case.

In a number of countries outside of Europe there were substantial war losses during World War II. The United States, Canada, Australia, New Zealand, Japan, the Philippines, Burma, China, and several others suffered heavily. These losses must have totaled some millions.

As in World War I, the war losses of the Soviet Union during World War II were apparently the greatest of all. However, there are no reasonably satisfactory data on which to base an estimate in which one can feel any degree of confidence. (See articles by Galina V. Selegen and Michael K. Roof in Supplementary Readings.) Nevertheless, there can be little doubt that the war losses of the U.S.S.R. in World War II were very great. A few figures will make this clear, even though they may be in error by several millions.

In the judgment of the authors, about 256 million people could reasonably have been expected to live in the U.S.S.R. in 1959 (including the annexed

[18] Grzegorz Frumkin, "Pologne: dix années d'histoire démographique," *Population*, vol. 4, no. 4, p. 706, 1949.

territory) if there had been no war. However, the census of 1959 reported a population of 208.8 million. This is somewhere in the neighborhood of 48 million fewer than the expected population. Although there was great hardship in the U.S.S.R. during the war and immediately following it, there was no devastating famine or pestilence similar to that of the years 1918–1922. It would seem reasonable, therefore, to assume that a great part of this deficit was incurred by the civilian population during the 5 years following June, 1941, when Germany attacked the U.S.S.R. One estimate of the population of the Soviet Union in mid-1946 that has been much used and seems as reasonable to the authors as any other is that the population then numbered approximately 181 million.[19] In arriving at this estimate, Timasheff took into account annexations to the territory of the U.S.S.R. and total war losses of 37.5 million. He allocated these war losses as follows: (1) military deaths, 7 million; (2) emigration, 1.3 million; (3) birth deficit, 10.9 million; (4) civilian deaths, 18.5 million.

About all one can be certain of is that war losses in the U.S.S.R. during World War II were very large but cannot be calculated with any precision and that civilian losses were probably much larger than would have been anticipated. The scanty information available regarding the sex ratio in the 1959 census shows a deficit of males amounting to 20.8 million as compared with deficits of males amounting to 7.8 million in the census of 1939 and 5.1 million in the census of 1926.[20] If true, this deficit of males (unfortunately ages are not given) indicates a terrific loss of civilian males as well as of military personnel during World War II. With such an enormous loss of males, one would expect a large decline in birth rates in the U.S.S.R. during the war and for several postwar years, since a very large proportion of the *unmarried* men killed during the war both in the armed forces and in the civilian population were of the ages when they would have founded families either during the war years or soon after it, and a great number of the married men killed would have added to their families if they had survived.

All told, it seems probable to the authors that the war losses, military and civilian combined, during World War II in Europe and in the countries settled from Europe, were at least as large as in World War I, which, as we have seen, may have amounted to 50 million or more. (This takes no account of the losses in Japan, in the Philippines, and in other Asian lands; nor does it include any estimate of the longer-time effects on the birth rate during the 20 to 25 years following the war.) In countries like the U.S.S.R., Poland, and Yugoslavia a

[19] N. S. Timasheff, "The Postwar Population of the Soviet Union," *American Journal of Sociology*, vol. 54, no. 2, pp. 149, 153, and 155, 1948.
[20] Galina V. Selegen, "The First Report on the Recent Population Census in the Soviet Union," *Population Studies*, vol. 14, no. 1, pp. 17–27, July, 1960.

very large deficit of males has probably continued to affect the birth rate up to about the time of writing (1963).

SUMMARY

Until quite recently, man's natural propensity to reproduce has kept actual reproduction (fertility) rather close to the limit fixed by nature (fecundity) in most societies. With rather insignificant exceptions, this was true until about a century ago, in spite of the fact that the cultural values of practically all societies as expressed in their customs and practices affecting reproduction have had some influence in restraining fertility. Even in those societies in which abundant fertility was much exalted, it is almost certain that fertility never equaled fecundity. The period of population growth prior to 1650 has been discussed in Chapter 14. It appeared in the discussion that from the standpoint of population growth, the determinative demographic factor during this period was the death rate, since even with a *long-continued but very small regular* excess of births over deaths there would have been many times the number of people in the world in 1650 than there actually was.

In this chapter it has been shown that as more reliable data became available and as we have learned more about population growth in different parts of the world, we may conclude that the death rate continued to be the dominant active (dynamic) factor in determining a possible excess or deficit of births or deaths and the size of this difference, always being mindful of the fact that the birth rate (fertility) was definitely limited by fecundity and to some extent by custom in all societies. Our discussion here has been confined, therefore, largely to trying to find out how it happened that the death rate declined slowly in the West, especially after about 1700.

The answer to this question was found to be chiefly in two important and rather specific changes which took place in the West but were not found operative as continuously or as progressively in other parts of the world. These two changes were: (1) an increase in the productivity of man's labor, at first chiefly in agriculture but soon in nonagricultural production also; and (2) a slow growth of control over the infectious diseases which from time immemorial had taken a heavy toll of life. Attention was called to the probability that both of these changes were in turn the consequence of the increase of knowledge and the practical application of this knowledge to the alleviation of man's suffering from hunger and disease which had previously been so potent in keeping the death rate at a high level most of the time and occasionally raising it well above the birth rate.

We have further shown that after about 1850 the death rate came more rapidly under control in Western countries and that by 1930 in the more-developed countries it had fallen to somewhere in the vicinity of one-third what it had been in 1850. Moreover, in the latter half of the nineteenth century, a noticeable decline took place in the birth rate in many Western countries. We know now that in France and in certain regions of the United States, this decline in the birth rate became significant somewhat earlier, about 1800. Obviously any significant decline in the birth rate unaccompanied by a change in the death rate would reduce the rate of natural increase just as any decline in the death rate unaccompanied by any change in the birth rate would raise the natural increase.

By 1930 these changes in death rates and birth rates had wrought highly significant changes in natural increase in many Western countries. Furthermore, it was clear that much of the decline in the birth rates of these countries resulted from the voluntary control over the size of the family. Thus population growth in such countries and/or regions had become increasingly controllable because of this voluntary action of married couples just as the death rate had been more and more reduced by efficient health services. By 1930 some of the benefits of a more productive economy and of more efficient health services had spread somewhat beyond the bounds of the West, and death rates in a few other countries were gradually coming under control. This control was still rather precarious in most of the underdeveloped countries. Nevertheless, the world stage was being set for momentous changes in population growth in the near future—"the population explosion."

SUGGESTIONS FOR SUPPLEMENTARY READING

Bennett, Merrill K.: *The World's Food: A Study of the Interrelations of World Populations, National Diets, and Food Potentials,* Harper & Row, Publishers, Incorporated, New York, 1954.

de Castro, Josué (ed.): *Hunger and Food,* World Federation of Scientific Workers (London), 1958. Special edition of *Science and Mankind* (no. 1, 1958).

Eason, Warren W.: "The Soviet Population Today: An Analysis of the First Results of the 1959 Census," *Foreign Affairs,* vol. 37, no. 4, pp. 598–606, July, 1959. (Notes on the population size and structure indicated by the statistics released May 10, 1959; special reference to imputed war losses and recent vital trends.)

"Essays in the Quantitative Study of Economic Growth," *Economic Development and Cultural Change,* vol. 9, no. 3, pp. 225–560, 1961.

"Food Supplies and Population Growth," *Journal of the Royal Statistical Society,* ser. A, vol. 125, no. 3, pp. 373–450, 1962.

Roof, Michael K.: "The Russian Population Enigma Reconsidered," *Population Studies,* vol. 14, no. 1, pp. 3–16, 1960. (A review of estimates of the total population of the U.S.S.R. between 1939 and 1959, notably by Prokopovitch, Kulisher, Timasheff, and Eason, and their comparison with primary results of the 1959 census.)

Roos, Charles F.: *Dynamics of Economic Growth: The American Economy, 1957–1975*, The Economic Institute, New York, 1958. (In the present edition the Institute has chosen to make its own forecast of population.)

Selegen, Galina V.: "The First Report of the Recent Census in the Soviet Union," *Population Studies*, vol. 14, no. 1, pp. 17–27, 1960.

U.S.S.R., Preliminary data on 1959 census translated in *Population Bulletin*, Population Reference Bureau, vol. 15, no. 4, August, 1959, pp. 65–78.

CHAPTER SIXTEEN *Population Growth since 1930*

The term "population explosion" is widely used today to denote the changes in the rates of population growth since World War II. The authors believe that the term "explosion" describes fairly accurately only one feature of this change in the rate of population growth, viz., the change that has taken place rather suddenly in the underdeveloped countries. Moreover, even this speeding up of the rate of population growth in these countries is largely the natural consequence of scientific developments which have been in preparation for several decades. Students of world population have for some time expected these developments to lead to a much more rapid growth of population in those parts of the world where death rates are still high. However, the rate of growth in these regions and countries has exceeded their expectations, at least the expectations of the authors. The increased rates of population growth in the United States, Canada, and several other Western countries after 1945 arose primarily from what now looks like a temporary increase in their birth rates with only a modest assist from the decline in the death rates, whereas it was entirely the decline in the death rate that brought about the increased rate of growth in the underdeveloped countries.

BASIS OF THE RECENT RAPID POPULATION GROWTH

As we have shown in the preceding chapter, by about 1930 there were a number of indications that very significant changes in the pattern of world population growth were in the offing. The control of most of the infectious diseases could be expected to take place in much less time in the countries of the world still having high death rates than it had in Europe and in most European settlements. Thus, although only very modest health services, public and private combined, were yet available in most countries outside of Europe and North America in 1930, enough progress in health services had been made in several countries still having relatively high death rates to indicate clearly that their populations would grow at a much more rapid rate as soon as their health work was more effectively organized and better staffed (see Chapter 15). However, at that time there was no reason for the layman to expect that medical-chemical research would so soon make available the "miracle" drugs to combat the infectious diseases nor that another world war would provide opportunity to try out these new discoveries on a very large scale and to demonstrate within a few years that a new era in the control of the death rate had opened that would especially benefit the underdeveloped countries. We have already noted that by 1930 Japan's population was growing at a rate that could not possibly have prevailed for any considerable time in the past, and this was also the situation in Japan's colonies—Korea and Formosa. The Philippine censuses of 1903 and 1918 showed a rapid growth, averaging almost 2 percent per year. India likewise had rates of growth in 1901–1911 and 1921–1931 that were higher than any since census taking began in that country in 1872. The great loss of life in India during the influenza epidemic of 1918 showed, however, that she was still unable to take effective measures to protect herself against such a calamity.

By 1930 the U.S.S.R. was making very rapid strides in the improvement of the health of the people, especially in teaching mothers how to reduce infant mortality and to guard against local epidemics of the infectious diseases likely to attack young children. Moreover, even then in the U.S.S.R. the prevention of smallpox had become general, and malaria was being greatly reduced in many communities. In a word, although it may truly be said that by about 1930 health services in some of the underdeveloped countries were becoming more effective, it was in the more industrialized countries that they were improving in efficiency most rapidly. The chief reason for this differential development was probably the lack of funds to support, and of experienced personnel to operate, health services in the less-developed countries. Besides, modern private medical services for individuals were available to only a tiny fraction of their people.

About the middle of the 1930s the sulfa drugs became available to all countries in which the health services, both private and public, were so organized that they could make use of these drugs very quickly. The less-developed countries, which were also very poor, had almost no public or private medical service reaching the mass of their peoples and hence had limited contacts with the better-developed health services abroad. They were not in position to make much use of the sulfa drugs until during or after World War II. As an example of the value of the sulfa drugs in reducing the death rate in the United States, it may be mentioned that the death rate from pneumonia had been substantially reduced by their use by the end of the 1930s as had also the death rate from peritonitis following rupture of the appendix. In fact, all laparotomy operations had become increasingly safe, and some internal infections had come under a large measure of control. A similar decline in the death rates from such infections occurred in most other highly industrialized countries having fair to good health services. In World War II the use of the sulfa drugs is credited with having reduced the death rates of soldiers from infected wounds to about one-half or less of what it was in World War I.

In the 1940s, during the war, another new type of drugs came into use even faster than had sulfa—the antibiotics. These both supplemented and often replaced the sulfa drugs in the treatment of many infections. As a consequence, the death rates from a number of infectious diseases quickly declined to a new low point even in the more industrialized countries (see Chapter 12).

However, from the standpoint of the growth of population these "miracle" drugs had soon shown that it was no longer necessary to await the widespread adoption of sanitary or preventive cleanliness, both private and public, to reduce greatly the deaths from many infectious diseases. All any underdeveloped country needed to do to reduce its death rate very substantially was to organize health services capable of reaching the people who needed these drugs to cure themselves of infections already contracted. Besides, this same health service could readily undertake the immunization of vast numbers of people against many diseases by the mere injection of the proper shots. It was further quickly apparent that it was much easier to get the mass of the people in a poor, underdeveloped area to submit to *curative* and even *preventive* shots than to get them to adopt the practices required to ensure sanitary or preventive cleanliness.

It should also be noted here that the increased prevention of malaria during World War II constituted a striking advance in the control of one of man's greatest curses. Great numbers of military personnel from areas in which there was practically no malaria were moved into areas where this disease was almost universal. The urgency of the need to keep the disability rate of the armed forces low in these malaria-infested areas helped to hasten the development and the use of a new insecticide, DDT, far superior to any hitherto in use. It was easier to apply over large areas and was more effective in the destruction of the mosquitoes that carried the disease from person to person than the insecticides used previously. Thus malaria could be prevented in large measure without either the consent of the individual to, or his active participation in, a program of malaria control which benefited everyone in his community. This insecticide has been widely used in many countries since 1945, especially in tropical and subtropical areas. (See comments on Ceylon below.)

One other development of very great value in reducing the death rate, although already mentioned, deserves a little more attention, viz., the immunization of the individual against the attack of a particular disease. Such immunization began with Jenner's discovery (1798) of an effective inoculation against smallpox. However, the use of vaccination made comparatively little headway even in Europe until between 1825 and 1850, while the immunization against most other diseases made little progress until after 1900. But by 1930 immunization against several very destructive diseases was possible and was quite generally made use of by travelers and sojourners in areas of high death rates. By the time of World War II most countries required all their military personnel to take several inoculations ensuring immunity against typhoid, yellow fever, cholera and the plague, and, of course, smallpox, and in some countries an inoculation against tuberculosis had become standard practice. The inoculation of children against the diseases to which they were particularly prone had also become widespread in the more industrialized countries about 1930, thereby reducing the death rates from scarlet fever, diphtheria, whooping cough, and other diseases, and the list kept on increasing.

Although the stage was set for a rapid spread of the control of many of the infectious diseases in underdeveloped countries even before World War II, the new drugs and sprays then acquired and the experience in their use gained under the emergency conditions of war greatly expedited the decline of the death rate in the less-developed countries of the world.

It is of great interest to note that while the more industrialized countries benefited greatly from the use of the new drugs and the increasing use of immunization shots, it was the underdeveloped countries, in which the infectious diseases had hitherto run rampant, whose death rates were proportionally most reduced by these scientific achievements. The more-developed countries had slowly over a number of decades achieved a good level of sanitary cleanliness and at the same time made use of their scientific health knowledge as it increased, so that even before sulfa and the antibiotics, their death rates from the infectious diseases had already declined to the point where their almost complete elimination had comparatively little effect on their death rates.

To make clear why it was possible to extend the control of the infectious diseases in the less-developed countries so rapidly, we should say a word about the general character of these new drugs and the methods needed to ensure their use by the individual and/or the community. The sulfa drugs and the antibiotics are essentially curative in character. They are administered, for the most part, when the individual has definite symptoms indicating an infection for the control of which these drugs have been found effective. The individual is usually suffering aches and pains and running a high fever. He is already convinced that he is seriously ill when he asks for help. Under such circumstances, many persons who had never had any contact with modern medicine were willing to submit to an injection which they were assured by the health authorities would bring about their recovery within a few days.

Moreover, if some friend or neighbor manifesting the same symptoms had already taken an injection and had recovered rapidly, as was usually the case, little persuasion was needed. In general, these cures required only one, or at most, only two or three injections, and no skilled nursing or hospital treatment

was necessary, although such care might hasten recovery. Moreover, the traditional medical practitioners in most societies made use of medicines of various
kinds. Thus the use of these new curative drugs did not encounter much cultural
resistance among the illiterate peoples in the less-developed countries. Besides,
the reward was generally readily apparent in a short time. Since, in any case,
hospitalization was utterly out of the question for all but a very small fraction of
the population in any of these countries and since the people in the upper economic classes were often already making use of these drugs, it is not surprising
that the masses of the people were willing to be treated with them almost as fast
as the economic situation made it possible to provide the drugs and to establish
local medical centers where treatment could be given. Inadequate communications systems no doubt obstructed the still more rapid spread of their use, as did
the lack of well-trained physicians and nurses. Nevertheless, their use did spread
rapidly, and the *high death rates began to drop almost immediately and precipitously*.

Much the same conditions that led to the rapid spread of the use of the new
curative drugs also made it practicable to extend preventive treatment by the
immunization of individuals against specific diseases. Once an epidemic had
broken out and the people understood that an injection or two would render
them immune to smallpox, or typhoid, or cholera, or some other dread disease,
there was generally little or no difficulty in persuading as many of the people in
a community as could possibly be provided with dosages to take the proper
injections. The cultural problem of preparing the minds of the mass of the people
to accept these health innovations was relatively easy of solution.

The prevention of malaria or yellow fever by spraying to kill the mosquitoes
carrying the disease likewise encountered comparatively little cultural resistance
because most of the work could be performed by skilled crews spraying areas
(the swampy breeding places of the mosquitoes) which were generally of little
value for agriculture and therefore did not require either the consent or cooperation of the "man in the street."

There were, of course, some countries and some communities in nearly all
fairly large countries in which cultural barriers interfered seriously with the use
of these new curative and preventive medicines and sprays. But these were
exceptional rather than usual. Thus the very nature of the new medicines and
sprays, their amazing effects so readily observed, and the methods of use being
so simple that one trained health worker could inoculate whole villages against
smallpox or cholera or could administer curative drugs for many other infections
in a relatively short time, made the acceptance of these new medicines quite
easy. The most seriously limiting factors almost everywhere were the lack of
means to set up enough health centers to reach the people in the villages, to
train personnel to staff them adequately, and to buy the essential medicines and
sprays.

SOME EXAMPLES OF RAPID DECLINES IN DEATH RATES

At this point it will be well to note briefly the cumulative effect of the health services described above in reducing the death rates in several underdeveloped countries since World War II.

India is the most populous underdeveloped country for which we have quite reliable census data showing population growth for the past several decades (since 1872). The great fluctuations in India's rate of growth up to 1931 have been described in the preceding chapter.

It was shown that in the decade 1921–1931 the rate of growth rose to the high point of approximately 11 percent, or to about 10 per 1,000 per year. In the decades 1931–1941 and 1941–1951 the rate of increase rose to over 13 percent, or about 13 per 1,000 per year. These rates of growth since 1921 are comparable to those in a number of European countries from about 1850 to 1910. A birth rate about 44 and a death rate about 31 would yield the growth rates that actually took place during these two decades. This rate of increase would lead to a doubling of the population in about 55 years.

The health services of many underdeveloped countries, India among them, became much better organized within a few years following World War II to make use of the accumulated scientific medical knowledge and experience of the world. The effects of these improved health services in India are best shown in her increase in population between 1951 and 1961. In that decade India's population grew by a little over 20 percent, or at a rate almost one-half above that in the two preceding decades (1931–1951).

This is all the more remarkable because the health services of India passed completely into the hands of the Indians themselves only in 1947, and it took several years to get them in good working order. India is a very poor country, which cannot yet spend much on its health services. In view of the poverty of the country, the necessity of using many people with but little experience in staffing her health services, the ignorance of the mass of the people, and their strong adherence to tradition, the reduction of the death rate by 6 or 7 points per 1,000, probably from about 30 in the decade 1941–1951 to a range of perhaps 21 to 24 in the decade 1951–1961, must be regarded as an achievement of a high order. It took most Western countries from 50 to 100 years to effect a similar decline in death rates.

The assumption that virtually all this increase in the rate of growth was due to the decline in the death rate appears to be justified in view of the fact that there is as yet no reliable evidence of any significant decline in the birth rate. But in spite of this large reduction in the crude death rate, India's rate must still be not far from twice as high as that of many Western countries and as that of Japan, Ceylon, and Formosa in the Far East. There is much still to be done to reduce deaths from infectious diseases in India. It is, therefore, quite reasonable to assume that the death rate probably will continue to decline during the ensuing two or three decades but probably more slowly than since 1951. Such further declines could certainly take place even though there might be no improvement in the present low level of living. On the other hand, any decline in the present low level of living is almost certain to retard the achievement of lower death rates. If the level of living should decline significantly, a rise in the death rate is likely. There is as yet no sound economic advance in India and in most other densely populated underdeveloped countries sufficient to guarantee the steady decline of their death rates to the low level prevailing in most Western countries and in others where fairly good economic conditions exist.

In several of the smaller Eastern countries where the registration of deaths was fairly good before World War II, almost incredible reductions in death rates have been achieved since the war. A few data bearing on the decline of their crude death rates will be of interest.

Ceylon's death rate in 1939 was 21.7 (a low death rate for that time); in 1945 it was almost the same, but by 1959 it had fallen to 9.1 (provisional). Formosa's death rate in 1939 was 20.1 and by 1945, while the Japanese were still in control, had fallen slightly, to 19. By 1960 it had dropped to 6.9. Japan's crude death rate in 1939 was 17.8, about the same as that of the United States in 1900. (Japan, of course, is not underdeveloped.) Because of war conditions, the death rate in Japan leaped to about 29 in 1945. It then fell precipitously to 10 in 1950, i.e., by about 19 points in five years. It dropped still lower until it stood at only 7.6 (provisional) in 1960. Since these are all crude death rates, they do not take account of the age composition of these populations. The fact that they all had a favorable age composition will explain in part their low death rates; but improved health services are the chief factor.

It is obvious that where the death rates have fallen as rapidly as in the countries just mentioned, the rates of natural increase must have risen in like measure unless there had been a substantial decline in the birth rate. There may possibly have been some slight decline in the birth rates of Ceylon (37 in 1959) and Formosa (39.5 in 1960), but the evidence is not conclusive, and in any event they were small as compared with the declines in the death rates. However, assuming that the crude death rates and birth rates of Ceylon and Formosa give a true measure of their rates of growth in 1960, Ceylon's rate of growth would be 27.9 per 1,000, or 2.8 percent per year, and Formosa's rate would be 32.6 per 1,000, or 3.26 percent per year. At these rates, their populations would double in about 25 and 21 years, respectively. In Japan the decline in the birth rate is fully established. It fell from about 33 in 1948 and 1949 to 17 (provisional) in 1960. Hence, Japan's rate of increase is now only about 9 per 1,000 per year. In spite of this decline in the birth rate, Japan's population is still growing by about 900,000 per year.

Although the extremely rapid reduction of the death rates in Ceylon and Formosa probably has not been equaled in any of the larger underdeveloped countries since 1945, several of them now have annual rates of increase of about 2 percent or more. Some of the Latin American countries and the Philippines have even higher rates of increase because they have even higher birth rates than Ceylon and Formosa.

In spite of the very unsatisfactory data on population in Mainland China, there can be no doubt whatever that the death rate has fallen substantially since 1949, possibly even faster than in India. Hundreds of millions of preventive inoculations have been made: typhoid, cholera, dysentery, smallpox, and others. In addition, the curative drugs have been widely used, and malaria control has been undertaken on a large scale. Clinics to promote mother-and-child health have also been established on a large scale. Hence we cannot ignore, though we may not fully accept, the claims of many high officials in Communist China that their population is growing at rates of 2 to 2.5 percent per year. If we take the lower figure of a 2 percent annual increase of population and accept the official figure of 583 million as the 1953 population of Communist China, the 1963 population would amount to approximately 710 million. If this rate were to continue until 1988, i.e., for 25 years from 1963, when the student reader of this book would just be reaching middle age, this population would have grown to 1,166 million.

The general situation, then, as regards population growth in practically all the underdeveloped countries is that since World War II the crude death rates have been greatly reduced within a few years and that in a few of them the present death rates are now only one-half, or even less than one-half, of their prewar rates. On the other hand, there has been little or no reduction in their birth rates. (This latter point will be discussed more fully in Chapters 20 and 21.) At present, therefore, many of these countries have rates of growth ranging from 2 to 3 percent per year, which if continued, would double their numbers in from 35 to 24 years.

GROWTH OF WORLD POPULATION, 1950–1960

Probably no group of experienced demographers in the world is more fully aware of the shortcomings of demographic data in many of the economically underdeveloped countries of the world than is the United Nations' staff that prepares its Demographic Yearbook. Nevertheless, this staff feels justified in publishing the most reliable data available in the belief that they give a substantially true view of what is happening demographically in the several continents and their chief regions. These data are given in Table 16-1.

For our purposes, the rates of population growth for 1950–1956 and for the

TABLE 16-1.   POPULATION, BIRTH RATES, DEATH RATES, AND RATES OF INCREASE, FOR THE WORLD, FOR CONTINENTS, AND REGIONS, 1950–1960

Continent and region	Midyear estimates (in millions)		Vital statistics, 1956–1960		Annual rate of increase, percent	
	1960	1950	Birth rate (per 1,000)	Death rate (per 1,000)	1950–1960	1950–1956
World total	2,995	2,510	36	18	1.8	1.6
Africa...................	254	206	47	25	2.2	1.7
North Africa...........	88	71	45	23	2.2	1.7
Tropical and Southern Africa..............	166	135	48	27	2.1	1.8
America.................	405	329	34	13	2.1	2.1
Northern America.......	199	167	25*	9*	1.8	1.7
Middle America.........	66	51	42	15	2.7	2.7
South America.........	140	111	42	19	2.3	2.4
Asia....................	1,679	1,386	41	22	1.9	1.6
Southwest Asia.........	77	60	48	22	2.6	2.5
South Central Asia......	559	472	41	24	1.7	1.4
Southeast Asia.........	214	175	41	21	2.0	1.8
East Asia..............	829	679	40	20	2.0	1.6
Europe.................	427	395	19*	11*	0.8	0.8
Northern and Western Europe..............	142	133	18*	11*	0.7	0.6
Central Europe.........	139	128	19*	11*	0.8	0.9
Southern Europe........	146	134	21*	10*	0.9	0.9
Oceania.................	16.5	13.0	24*	9*	2.4	2.3
U.S.S.R.................	214	181	25*	8*	1.7	——

* Weighted averages.
Source: United Nations, *Demographic Yearbooks, 1957*, p. 125, and *1961*, p. 120.

entire decade 1950–1960 and the birth rates and death rates for the years 1956–1960 are the most important (see Table 16-1). The rate of growth in the world rose from 1.6 percent (1950–1956) to 1.8 percent for the entire decade, 1950–1960. This indicates that there must have been a very considerable rise in the rate of growth during the last four years of the decade ending in 1960. When continents and their subdivisions are considered, Europe and Northern America (United States and Canada) had the lowest birth rates and death rates and the lowest rates of population growth except for South Central Asia, where the rate of growth was about the same as in Northern America but well above that in Europe. The rates of change in population growth between 1950 and 1956 and between 1956 and 1960 were decidedly upward in Africa and Asia and were extremely high in Middle and South America throughout this decade. Clearly, the rates of population growth in the underdeveloped countries were everywhere *above* those of the more developed countries and were *rising* in most of the former.

The crude birth rates in the underdeveloped areas (1956–1960) were generally well above 40 per 1,000, while in Europe they were well below 20 per 1,000 and in Northern America, Oceania, and the U.S.S.R. they were 24 to 25 per 1,000. The death rates in most of the underdeveloped countries were still high according to present Western standards, but the highest were probably no higher than the average rates in most Western countries in the period 1850–1900, while in most of Latin America they are already near the level of the Western countries in 1900. The decline in the death rate, which took many Western countries 100 years to achieve, has already been achieved in many of the underdeveloped countries since World War II and bids fair to be reached by the rest of them in another decade or two. Furthermore, these lower death rates have been unaccompanied by any perceptible declines in their birth rates or any perceptible improvement in the economic status of the mass of the people.

From the standpoint of the scientific control of the infectious diseases, there is no good reason to suppose that in the next two decades most of the underdeveloped areas cannot practically eliminate them as causes of death, *provided* their economies can be made more productive with sufficient speed to care for their rapidly growing numbers even at a very *slowly rising level of living*. (This judgment assumes, of course, that there will be no man-made holocaust.) This proviso—a slowly rising level of living—has been made because the authors believe it is doubtful that a declining death rate based chiefly on the elimination of the infectious diseases can be reduced to a *very low* death rate such as now prevails in the more advanced Western countries and can be maintained at this low level unless the *level of living* rises somewhat above that now prevailing among the mass of these peoples. (This point will be elaborated somewhat in Chapter 19.)

MODERN DECLINE IN THE BIRTH RATE

In modern times no society has succeeded in reducing its birth rate significantly until substantial numbers of its people have attained a level of living well above subsistence. Moreover, these people must also have come to desire a still higher level of living for themselves and for their children. In addition, they must have come to realize that it is very difficult to achieve and maintain such standards if the number of children born to a couple remains near to the physiological maximum while the death rate declines lower and lower. How long will it take the peoples in the underdeveloped countries to realize that they must reduce their birth rates if they are to enjoy the higher levels of living they so greatly desire and are also to prepare their children to live in a modern industrialized society? Unfortunately this question cannot be answered with any assurance. In France, it appears that the voluntary control of the birth rate was commencing to have an appreciable influence on the rate of population growth by the end of the eighteenth century, although France was less industrialized than England. England and Wales were probably the most industrialized countries at that time, and yet there was no significant decline in the birth rate until about the last quarter of the nineteenth century. In the United States and especially in the Northeastern states, which were the most urbanized and industrialized, the birth rate had begun to fall early in the nineteenth century and possibly some-what earlier. Much of this change may have been due to later marriage in the more urbanized states. In other of the more developed countries today the birth rate began to decline at different dates, but in most of them the decline of the crude birth rate did not exceed that of the crude death rate in magnitude until several decades after there was clear evidence that the birth rate was falling. On the other hand, in Japan the decline of the birth rate proceeded very rapidly after 1949, falling from an average of about 30 in the five years 1945–1949 to about 18 in 1955–1959, or by about 40 percent in a decade. But it should be noted that by 1930 Japan had become quite highly industrialized, and a goodly proportion of its people lived in cities.

Because the authors regard this very rapid reduction in the birth rate of Japan as the consequence of special features of Japan's historical and cultural development, abetted by the distinctive conditions existing in Japan after her defeat in World War II, they do not believe that a similar reduction of the birth rate in so short a time is at all likely to occur in more than a few, if any, of even the smaller underdeveloped countries.

Stated briefly and quite dogmatically, the conditions preparing the way for a rapid reduction of the birth rate in Japan were: (1) Abortion, which had been used rather extensively in feudal Japan to stabilize the size of the family, had never been regarded with the same repugnance there as in the cultures of the West. Hence, when it was legalized after the war, and when social and economic reasons for its practice as well as therapeutic reasons were considered sufficient to justify it, and when abortions were performed openly by physicians in good hospitals, this method of birth control became quickly available. (2) The Japanese people had become one of the most literate peoples in the world as early as 1920. Hence they were able to follow closely the very widespread post-war discussion of the economic plight of the country and its relation to the high birth rate. They were also well aware that their death rate had fallen with such rapidity that from 1946 to 1949 Japan had a much higher rate of growth than at any time in her past. (3) Because their industry and commerce had been practically destroyed by the war and because many of their leaders were telling them almost daily through newspapers and by radio that the birth rate should be reduced if they wanted to live as well as they did before the war, to say nothing of improving this level and providing better opportunities for their children, it was not surprising that birth-control practices spread rapidly. However, speaking only for themselves, the authors were surprised that it became so highly effective in so short a time.

Since conditions encouraging the spread of voluntary control over the size of the family even remotely similar to those in Japan do not exist in any of the underdeveloped countries, it does not seem likely that the decline in their birth rates will be nearly so precipitous. Strongly traditional cultures prevail in most underdeveloped countries, so that social and economic institutions have long been almost static; many of them have governments that are quite oblivious of the relation between the rate of population growth and the rate of economic development; and most of them have traditional patterns of reproductive behavior encouraging a high birth rate because it has long been considered essential to survival. It takes time to educate the mass of the people so that they will appreciate the need of modifying their reproductive practices if they are going to control their death rates and hold them at a low level.

Only a word will be said here about the probable slow spread of contraceptive practices in underdeveloped countries, since they will be discussed in more detail in Chapters 20 and 21. The government of India, from the time it became independent (1947), has believed in the need for contraception and has encouraged family planning, but there is not yet any clear evidence that the birth rate has begun to decline. The same may be said of the intermittent and poorly planned efforts to introduce widespread contraception in Communist China. Again, there is no evidence that the birth rate is declining.

It seems to the authors, therefore, that with the facts now available we have no sound basis for expecting that the birth rates of the peoples living in the underdeveloped areas of the world will begin to decline faster than their death rates within the next two or three decades. They think it is more probable that among these peoples as a group the death rates will decline faster than the birth rates for two or three decades and that then, for several years, both death rates and birth rates will decline in about the same amount, with the rate of population growth remaining at a high level. After this, perhaps in three or four decades from now, the rate of population growth will begin to decline. *Always the proviso must be made that there is no per capita decline in their food supplies, a point about which there can be no certainty today.*

PROBLEMS ARISING OUT OF A HIGH RATE OF POPULATION GROWTH

The authors think that in the world as a whole there is likely to be about a 2 percent increase in population per year for a few decades, assuming the above proviso is realized. They therefore wish to mention here the most urgent problems posed by such a rate of increase and the alternative if this proviso as regards per capita food supplies is not realized. These problems will be treated at more length later in Chapter 19.

A world population of approximately 3,000 million in 1960 and growing by 2 percent per year will number approximately 6,600 million, that is, will increase by 120 percent by the end of this century. Assuming that the per capita consumption of the necessities of life does not rise above its present low level in most of the underdeveloped countries and that world population grows by 2 percent per year, there must be a like rate of growth of the necessities of life. The vast majority of the people of the world would still have an inadequate diet and would probably be unable to achieve really low death rates similar to those prevailing in most European populations. It would be foolish to say that the volume of these necessities could not be increased by 120 percent in the 40-year period 1960–2000. But attention should be called to two points. The first of these is that we need to distinguish carefully between the *possible* increase in the necessities of life during a given period and the *probable* increase.

The authors are fully convinced that such an increase in the necessities of life in the world as a whole is *possible*, but they are by no means convinced that it is *probable* within 40 years, or that it will proceed regularly from year to year at the same rate as that at which population will grow even if the death rates in the underdeveloped countries remain at their present levels. In the second place, assuming that such an increase in the necessities of life does take place in the world as a whole, would this fact ensure the people in any particular country the share needed to support its own growing population? The real problem of caring for the rapid increase of population in any underdeveloped country today remains basically a *national* problem, not a *world* problem. The world is not so organized, politically or economically, that the surpluses of the countries producing more than is needed for domestic consumption can be transferred to countries needing more than they can produce; nor can aid to underdeveloped countries be counted on to fill the gap (see Chapter 19). These urgent problems will almost certainly remain national problems so long as nationalism remains highly predominant in our political thinking and so long as there are large groups of people in the different regions of the world adhering to fundamentally antagonistic political and economic ideologies.

Because of these facts, any meaningful question regarding the support of a rapidly growing population in any country must be rephrased in more concrete terms. It must take some such form as this: Is it reasonable to expect that India or Mainland China or Mexico or Ceylon or Nigeria or any other of several scores of political entities in the underdeveloped portions of the world can increase its own food supply and the other necessities of life through its own production or through trade as fast as its population is likely to grow, i.e., by 2 percent or more each year? This is what would be necessary just to maintain the same level of living in its population. Like Alice in Wonderland, its economy would have to run much faster than in the past just to stand still.

It must be recognized, of course, that even in this more definite and more realistic form, this question regarding the availability of a rapidly increasing quantity of the necessities of life to the people in any underdeveloped country cannot be answered categorically. The data are not available to permit of such an answer; nor can anyone surely foresee future political and economic developments. The opinion of the authors regarding the probability of supplying a rapidly growing world population with necessities adequate to ensure low and declining death rates during the next few decades, and of arousing effective motives for reducing the number of births per family during the ensuing three or four decades, will be found in more detail in Chapters 19, 20, and 21.

It should be pointed out here, however, that the social, economic, and political conditions which enabled the Western peoples, except possibly those in most parts of Latin America,[1] to grow relatively fast in numbers for about two centuries and yet to improve their levels of living rather steadily were quite different from those which prevail today in the underdeveloped countries. As a consequence, it is a wide-open question whether the peoples living in the less-developed countries can reasonably hope to attain these Western levels of living in the near future.

During the relatively long period when the social and economic revolutions in the area of European settlement were in process, these peoples were never confronted with the problem of providing even the customary necessities of life for a *large* increase in population year after year. This was fortunate, because their economies were already expanding at a slow rate but just a little faster than the rate of population growth. Almost certainly this slow increase in productivity could not have been accelerated by a more rapid population growth. Indeed, their rate of economic development would probably have been retarded by it.

It is clear that the peoples in the area of European settlement (excluding Latin America) never had to provide for an increase of population rising above 11 per 1,000 per year (see Chapter 15) as compared with many of the peoples in underdeveloped countries today in which the population is growing by 20, 25, or even 30 per 1,000 per year. Unfortunately, an increase in the per capita intake of food has played a very minor role, if any, as a cause of the decline in the death rates of the present underdeveloped countries. In the West the increase in the per capita consumption of food, of other necessities, and of goods making life a little easier was long the dominant factor in reducing the death rate and thus provided a sound economic base for the increase in population at a slow rate over a period of many

---

[1] Latin America is excepted here because the social and economic revolutions which took place in the other parts of the area of European settlement after about 1750 have never been carried through in most of the countries in this region. Most Latin American peoples must still be regarded as living in economically underdeveloped areas and under semifeudal political conditions.

years. Indigenous economic improvement preceded and was the chief cause of the slow decline in death rates until after about 1850, when science became of increasing importance.

On the other hand, today in the underdeveloped countries the control of the infectious diseases is based very largely on scientific discoveries which have no direct relation to the increase in production of food or of the other necessities of life. Hence there is no sound economic basis for this very rapid growth of population in the underdeveloped countries such as there was for the much slower growth of population in the area of European settlement after about 1750. In North America, however, for about two centuries under unusually favorable geographic, political, and economic conditions, the rate of population growth was even higher than at present in most underdeveloped countries.

The authors have already expressed the opinion that whether or not an appreciable decline in the birth rate occurs within the next two or three decades within the underdeveloped countries will depend above all upon a rapidly growing realization of the fact that a large decline in the death rate with little or no decline in the birth rate will quickly raise the actual number of children that must be cared for in the average family to about twice as many as survived to adulthood in the past. This understanding will have to be expressed in a rapid change in the cultural patterns of reproductive behavior, such as raising the age at marriage, increasing the intervals between births, and preventing further conceptions once the desired size of family has been attained. The choice is a rather simple one, and the stakes are high. The alternatives are a large increase in the welfare of at least two-thirds of the population of the world, or the continuance of and possible increase in the great hardships they now suffer. For the first time in man's history he can make a choice. What will it be?

The authors believe that a change in the reproductive patterns of behavior will take place in the course of time among the people in the underdeveloped countries, but they are less sanguine than many people that it will occur within two or three decades. If the people in these underdeveloped areas can increase their food supplies only fast enough to maintain their *present per capita consumption* their numbers will probably grow at a somewhat faster rate than at present for the next two or three decades. In such a situation there is almost certain to be a great increase in the feeling of population pressure among these peoples (see Chapter 19). It took two centuries or more for European peoples to develop a new economic order which would ensure a good level of living to every one, and then this was only accomplished after their rates of reproduction had been greatly reduced, chiefly since about 1875 to 1900. Yet many Westerners as well as the leaders in many of the underdeveloped countries seem to expect that the people in these areas can develop this new economic order accompanied by a slower rate of population growth within a few years.

The implications of this new phase of world population growth will be discussed more fully in Chapters 19, 20, and 21.

SUGGESTIONS FOR SUPPLEMENTARY READING

Agarwala, S. N. (ed.): *India's Population: Some Problems in Perspective Planning*, Asia Publishing House, Bombay, 1960. (A group of useful and interesting essays.)

Borrie, W. D.: *The World's Population: Perspective and Prospect*, Canadian Institute of International Affairs, Contemporary Affairs, no. 29, Toronto, 1961.

Duesenberry, James S.: *Business Cycles and Economic Growth*, Economics Handbook Series, McGraw-Hill Book Company, New York, 1958.

Easterlin, R. S.: "The American Baby Boom in Historical Perspective," *American Economic Review*, vol. 60, no. 5, pp. 869–911, 1961.

Hauser, Philip M.: *Population Perspectives*, Rutgers University Press, New Brunswick, N.J., 1960.

Kuznets, Simon: "Long Swings in the Growth of Population and in Related Economic Variables," *Proceedings of the American Philosophical Society*, vol. 102, no. 1, February 17, 1958, pp. 25–52.

Mujumdar, N. A.: "Agriculture in India's Economic Development," *Farm Economist*, vol. 10, no. 1, pp. 29–39, 1962.

Sax, Karl: *Standing Room Only: The World's Exploding Population*, Beacon Press, Boston, 1960. (A botanist's statement of the world prospects of population growth in relation to resources and a plea for contraceptive measures.)

Sukhatme, V.: "The World's Hunger and Future Needs in Food Supplies," *Journal of the Royal Statistical Society*, vol. 124, part 4, pp. 463–508, 1961.

Taeuber, Irene B.: "Asia's Increasing Population," *Annals of the American Academy of Political and Social Science*, vol. 318, pp. 1–7, July, 1958.

Thompson, Warren S.: "The Population 'Explosion,'" *Teachers College Record*, vol. 63, no. 6, pp. 407–417, March, 1962.

United Nations, Population Division: *The Determinants and Consequences of Population Trends*, ST/SOA/ser. A/17, sales no.: 1953, XIII.3, New York, 1953.

Woytinsky, W. S., and E. S. Woytinsky: *World Population and Production: Trends and Outlook*, The Twentieth Century Fund, New York, 1953.

CHAPTER SEVENTEEN *Some Consequences of Future Population Growth in the United States*

The probable growth of population in any nation is of interest to its people for many reasons. Obviously, any long-time plans for national development will be more useful if they are based on estimates of future changes in the size of the population made in the light of the best information available rather than if they are based on mere guesses. This also holds within the nation for different communities which must plan their own public works. The ability to foresee with reasonable accuracy certain important characteristics of the population is also of considerable value for many practical purposes.

SOME GENERAL CONSIDERATIONS

The need for population estimates can be seen most clearly when concrete problems arise for consideration; e.g., in planning to meet the transportation and communication needs in the nation, in the several states, and in local communities, there *must* be some estimate of the number of persons in different areas likely to make use of the different means of transportation and communication as well as estimates of the changing per capita needs for these services. We are not saying that accurate estimates of population for any considerable future period can be made for any or all of these different areas needing them; but estimates that take into account the best information available regarding the aspects of population change which are of importance to the community are more helpful in planning for future needs than are mere guesses or the simple extension of past trends.

One cannot mention any type of planning for the future development of a nation or a community that does not involve, either directly or implicitly, some assumptions regarding the size of the future population similar to those needed in planning future transportation and communication developments. Many plans also depend upon estimates of the population having concrete characteristics, e.g., age and sex (see Chapter 5). Local communities must plan how the essential services and utilities in daily use can be kept adequate to the needs of the community, how industrial and residential areas are to be developed, how many schools will be needed during the next few years, and where these schools should be located. In a hundred other ways communities must try to foresee the problems which will arise as population grows (or declines) in numbers, the changes in character (composition), the changes in structure and in residential and service requirements, if they are to avoid unnecessary waste and are to provide themselves with more effective means for improving everyday living. Without the best estimates possible regarding the number and kind of people who will be affected by these many different services, some very serious and costly mistakes are sure to be made which might have been avoided, at least in part, by the more careful study of the factors affecting population changes in the area concerned. It should be realized, however, that, in general, the errors in estimates of future population are likely to increase as the size of the population decreases, as the estimates are extended in time, and as they are made more specific in describing the characteristics of the group being considered. For example, projections for the United States as a whole will probably be more accurate than for a region, for a region than for an individual state, for a state than for particular communities in a state. The chief reason for the probable decreasing accuracy of estimates of future population in smaller areas is that the net amount and the regularity of migration into or out of any particular community or area becomes increasingly unpredictable as the size of the population decreases.

Changes in the size of the population in any specified area arise from two sources: (1) from differences between birth rates and death rates in the resident population and (2) from variations in the net amounts of in- and out-migration. Birth rates, death rates, and migration are all closely related causally to social and economic changes, and these changes, in turn, are the causes of changes in size as well as of many changes in the characteristics of the population. Even when there is little change in the population of the nation as a whole or in a state, either in size or in composition, rather wide fluctuations in growth and rather rapid changes in the composition of local populations may occur because of migration.

The greater variations in the growth of one part of the United States than in the nation as a whole may be illustrated by noting how the Pacific states have grown in comparison with the United States. Table 17-1 shows the rate of growth by decades (1900–1960) of the United States and the Pacific states (columns 2 and 3); it also shows (column 4) the ratio of the rate of growth of the Pacific states to that of the United States considered as unity. The growth of population in the United States from 1900–1910 was 21 percent, while in the

Pacific states it was 73.5 percent. In the decade 1910–1920, the United States' rate was 14.9 percent, that of the Pacific states 32.8 percent. In the other decades there were also large differences in rates of growth in the United States and in the Pacific states. This difference in rate of growth in each decade is measured precisely by the ratios in column 4. In the Pacific states these rates have varied from 3.5 times as high as those of the United States to only 2.2 times as high; in other words, the fluctuations from decade to decade (up to 1960) were much larger in the Pacific states. Thus it would appear that while the same conditions

TABLE 17-1.   THE RATE OF INCREASE IN THE POPULATION FOR THE UNITED STATES COMPARED WITH THAT FOR THE PACIFIC STATES, 1900–1960

Decade	Rates of increase in population		Ratio of national rate of increase to rate for Pacific states
	United States*	Pacific states*	
(1)	(2)	(3)	(4)
1950–1960	18.4	40.4	1:2.20
1940–1950	14.5	48.8	1:3.37
1930–1940	7.2	18.8	1:2.61
1920–1930	16.1	47.2	1:2.93
1910–1920	14.9	32.8	1:2.20
1900–1910	21.0	73.5	1:3.50

* Does not include Alaska and Hawaii.

Source: U.S. Bureau of the Census, *U.S. Census of Population, 1960, Number of Inhabitants, United States Summary*, pp. 1-4 and 1-16.

which led to substantial changes in the rate of population growth in the United States were also operative in the Pacific states, there were, in addition, other factors, which must have been quite powerful and peculiar to this region to produce such violent fluctuations as are shown here. Such differences in rates of growth in different regions of the United States were to be expected in the early days of settlement and had actually occurred over and over again in the states and regions between the Appalachian and the Rocky Mountains. But it might have been expected that by 1900 high ratios of growth even in the Far West would have declined to a more moderate level.

As a consequence of this very rapid growth, this region has had to meet many problems, in particular those problems involved in absorbing a very large increase into its urban areas. Probably the fact that California, more than any other state, has recognized the need to plan for an extremely large growth in its cities will go far to explain its success in absorbing so many migrants with less difficulty than might have been expected.

The very rapid growth of the *standard metropolitan statistical areas* (SMSAs in census parlance; see Chapter 6) of the United States also forced many communities to meet unusual problems of increase in numbers rather suddenly; failure to plan for them has frequently had distressing consequences. There were 212 SMSAs in 1960; their population had grown from 89.3 million in 1950 to 112.9 million in 1960, or by 26.4 percent compared with 18.4 percent in the United States. These SMSAs have proved very attractive since World War II, especially in the areas outside the central cities. The central cities of these SMSAs grew by only 10.7 percent during the decade 1950–1960, while the rings around these cities grew by 48.6 percent, and the total population of these rings is now approaching that of the central cities. It should be noted, however, that a number of these SMSAs either grew very slowly or even lost population. Some SMSAs which grew very rapidly and some which grew slowly often found themselves confronted with serious problems which they were not prepared to handle satisfactorily, in part at least, because they knew too little about probable growth prospects and the composition of the population that would be crowding (or leaving) their communities. Some SMSAs, especially those growing very rapidly, either took a special census or devised other methods of gathering social and economic data which enabled them to cope more effectively with their growth problems. Of course a knowledge of probable population changes, even if exact, would not inevitably enable a community to deal satisfactorily with all the consequences of such changes; but the best possible knowledge of probable growth will be of great aid to a community in meeting the many problems arising in connection with too much and too rapid population growth and/or of little or no growth. Often population changes cannot be foreseen very clearly, and even when foreseen with reasonable clarity the local community can do little about them. California, on the whole, has done a very good job in meeting the needs of its rapidly increasing population. Its success must be attributed, in part, to the fact that it is better organized than most states to know what is happening to its population and is actually using this knowledge more effectively than many. We should state clearly that although we believe it is important to know as much as possible about probable population changes, we are not implying that population changes are the primary causes of social and economic changes. Population changes in amount and rate of growth are more probably caused chiefly by changes in economic and social factors. Hence these factors are of more basic significance. Nevertheless, probable population changes both as evidence of more basic factors at work and as dynamic factors in their own right remain important and should be taken into account by private and public enterprises when planning at all levels—national, regional, state, and local.

THE FUTURE POPULATION OF THE UNITED STATES

During the past two centuries a number of Americans have made estimates of probable future growth of population in the colonies and later in the United States. It did not appear at all unreasonable to many people in the latter half of the eighteenth century and the first half of the nineteenth century to expect that our population would double every 25 years. In fact, our population at the first census (1790) was approximately 4 million and there could be little doubt it had been doubling about every 25 years since 1660. If this 1790 population continued to double every 25 years, it would number 32 million in 1865, i.e., 75 years later. As a matter of fact, it exceeded this rate of increase and amounted to 31.4 million in 1860. Had the rate of growth that prevailed from 1660 to 1860 continued until 1960 our population would now be in excess of 500 million. This rather simple extrapolation of past rates worked out well for the two centuries from 1660 to 1860. As the rate of growth declined after 1860, it became clear that the simple extrapolation of past rates was inadequate, and estimates of future population were largely based on guesses of what the rate of increase would be in the future.

As our vital statistics improved and as we learned more about the composition of our immigrants, it seemed better to use these data as a basis for projecting birth rates and death rates and amounts of net in-migration into the future. This method has been called *empirical* because it used actual data and trends in the past as a basis for assuming future trends. It is also called the *component* method because it assumed separate trends for each of the three components determining all changes in the size of any population—births, deaths, and net migration. Such estimates of future population are generally spoken of as *projections* because they are actual calculations based on clearly stated assumptions regarding future changes in birth rates, death rates, and net amounts of in- or out-migration. Recently, almost all projections have been made on two or three separate sets of assumptions—high, medium, and low. All these represent the judgment of the person or group making the projection regarding probable changes in each of the three components: (1) The high projection usually results from a judgment regarding the maximum probable birth rates (age-specific), the minimum probable death rates (age-specific), and the maximum probable net in-migration; (2) the low projection embodies a judgment of the minimum probable birth rates, the maximum probable death rates, and the minimum net in-migration; (3) the medium projection, as the name indicates, falls between the high and low limits assumed for each component but is not necessarily the midpoint between each of these limits.

Lest the term *projection* be misunderstood, it should be said again that the assumptions used in the component method, even when they are based on thorough familiarity with all the relevant information, remain personal or group judgments. They are not facts showing future changes. Since any set of projected age-specific birth rates and death rates and of amounts of net in- or out-migration by age and sex is applied to a particular population having a known age and sex composition at a specified date, it is possible to calculate not only the changes in the size of the total population at some future date on the assumption stated but also the changes over time in the age and sex composition of this projected population. At the beginning of any projection period, any large population has certain numbers and proportions of males and females from birth to about 100 years. Projecting the survivors of these actual groups into the future is much less likely to involve significant error than is the projection of the number of births in the same population. (The reasons for expecting a relatively high degree of accuracy in projecting age-specific death rates for two or three decades into the future have been explained in Chapter 12, The Trend in Mortality.) Thus in Table 17-2, all persons in the sex and age groups 15 years of age and over in 1975 were alive in 1960, and the vast majority were also living in the United States at that time. (An error of a few hundreds of thousands in the net number of in-migrants between 1960 and 1975 would make little difference in the total population, nor should it make much difference in any of the sex and age groups in 1975.)

On the other hand, we know from recent experience that age-specific birth rates can change significantly within a few years (see Chapters 9 and 10). Hence the most important element in any projection of this character, because it is also likely to be the most variable, is the projection of the age-specific birth rates. By 1975 (Table 17-3) close to one-third of our total population (practically all persons under 15 years of age) will have been born into our population after 1960, and by 1990 about one-half of the total population will consist of people born into it since 1960. Any departure of actual birth rates from projected birth rates in one direction (upward or downward) during the projection period becomes cumulative in due course. That departures from projected rates might offset one another is rather unlikely within a period of 30 years.

A great deal of thought and work has been given to the study of fertility in the United States in recent years. Much of this study has been devoted to finding a more reliable basis for the projection of age-specific birth rates. Professor Whelpton, who has probably given more attention to the making of population projections than any other American and who has also been intimately associated with both the 1955[1] and 1960[2] studies of the Growth of American Families (GAF), believes that these studies will help materially in determining more reliable age-specific birth rates to use in future projections than has heretofore been possible. This opinion rests chiefly on the fact that the average number of

[1] Ronald Freedman, Pascal K. Whelpton, and Arthur A. Campbell, *Family Planning, Sterility, and Population Growth*, McGraw-Hill Book Company, New York, 1959.
[2] This report has not yet been published. Whelpton and Campbell will be the principal authors.

TABLE 17-2. **PROJECTED POPULATION OF THE UNITED STATES BY AGE AND SEX, 1960–1990, MEDIUM SERIES (In thousands)**

Age	1960	1975	1990
	Total		
Total...............	184,582	222,533	273,265
Under 6............	24,232	26,934	32,430
6–13...............	29,193	30,139	41,292
14–17..............	11,904	15,923	18,886
18–21..............	9,972	16,125	17,113
22–29..............	18,036	28,737	30,149
30–44..............	37,089	37,127	57,114
45–64..............	37,417	44,815	46,185
65–69..............	6,348	8,071	9,985
70 and over........	10,391	14,662	20,111
	Males		
Total...............	91,602	109,833	135,196
Under 6............	12,382	13,777	16,596
6–13...............	14,909	15,402	21,117
14–17..............	6,072	8,122	9,645
18–21..............	5,043	8,189	8,703
22–29..............	9,055	14,497	15,231
30–44..............	18,476	18,569	28,700
45–64..............	18,185	21,718	22,531
65–69..............	2,914	3,616	4,533
70 and over........	4,566	5,943	8,140
	Females		
Total...............	92,980	112,700	138,069
Under 6............	11,850	13,157	15,834
6–13...............	14,284	14,737	20,175
14–17..............	5,832	7,801	9,241
18–21..............	4,929	7,936	8,410
22–29..............	8,981	14,240	14,918
30–44..............	18,613	18,558	28,414
45–64..............	19,232	23,097	23,654
65–69..............	3,434	4,455	5,452
70 and over........	5,825	8,719	11,971

Source: Ronald Freedman, Pascal K. Whelpton, and Arthur A. Campbell, *Family Planning, Sterility, and Population Growth,* McGraw-Hill Book Company, New York, 1959, p. 390.

TABLE 17-3. PERCENT DISTRIBUTION AND PERCENT INCREASE OF THE PROJECTED POPULATION OF THE UNITED STATES, BY AGE AND SEX, 1960–1990, MEDIUM SERIES

Age	Percent distribution			Percent increase		
	1960	1975	1990	1960–1975	1975–1990	1960–1990
	Total					
Total..............	100.0	100.0	100.0	20.6	22.8	48.0
Under 6.............	13.1	12.1	11.9	11.2	20.4	33.8
6–13................	15.8	13.5	15.1	3.2	37.0	41.4
14–17...............	6.5	7.2	6.9	33.8	18.6	58.7
18–21...............	5.4	7.2	6.3	61.7	6.1	71.6
22–29...............	9.8	12.9	11.0	59.3	4.9	67.2
30–44...............	20.1	16.7	20.9	0.1	53.8	54.0
45–64...............	20.3	20.1	16.9	19.8	3.1	23.4
65–69...............	3.4	3.6	3.7	27.1	23.7	57.7
70 and over.........	5.6	6.6	7.4	41.1	37.2	93.5
	Males					
Total..............	100.0	100.0	100.0	19.9	23.1	47.6
Under 6.............	13.5	12.5	12.3	11.3	20.5	34.0
6–13................	16.3	14.0	15.6	3.3	37.1	41.6
14–17...............	6.6	7.4	7.1	33.8	18.8	58.8
18–21...............	5.5	7.5	6.4	62.4	6.3	72.6
22–29...............	9.9	13.2	11.3	60.1	5.1	68.2
30–44...............	20.2	16.9	21.2	0.5	54.6	55.3
45–64...............	19.9	19.8	16.7	19.4	3.7	23.9
65–69...............	3.2	3.3	3.4	24.1	25.4	55.6
70 and over.........	5.0	5.4	6.0	30.2	37.0	78.3
	Females					
Total..............	100.0	100.0	100.0	21.2	22.5	48.5
Under 6.............	12.7	11.7	11.5	11.0	20.3	33.6
6–13................	15.4	13.1	14.6	3.2	36.9	41.2
14–17...............	6.3	6.9	6.7	33.8	18.5	58.5
18–21...............	5.3	7.0	6.1	61.0	6.0	70.6
22–29...............	9.7	12.6	10.8	58.6	4.8	66.1
30–44...............	20.0	16.5	20.6	−0.3	53.1	52.7
45–64...............	20.7	20.5	17.1	20.1	2.4	23.0
65–69...............	3.7	4.0	3.9	29.7	22.4	58.8
70 and over.........	6.3	7.7	8.7	49.7	37.3	105.5

Source: Table 17-2.

children expected by wives 18–39 years of age in the five years following the GAF interview of 1955 was very closely approximated by women belonging to the same cohorts but five years older at the GAF interview of 1960 (not the same women). There were, of course, significant departures from this average by particular wives, but in the aggregate, the actual birth performance (1955–1960) was predicted quite accurately by the 1955 expected-birth performance. If these findings are confirmed by later studies made at fairly regular intervals and if it appears that the size of family expected by married women in their twenties, let us say, is highly correlated with their completed reproductive experience, the projection of a set of age-specific birth rates yielding a total number of births for any cohort of women from their early expectations would be more reliable than those used heretofore. But we should remember that substantial changes in social and economic conditions may also lead to substantial changes in expectations of births within a relatively short period.

Unfortunately from our standpoint, a projection of the population of the United States making use of this latest knowledge is not yet available. Table 17-2, which we use here, is adapted from the first (1955) GAF study. The fact that the 1960 data in this table are in part calculated does not in any way impair its usefulness for illustrative purposes.

PROBABLE CHANGES IN THE AGE STRUCTURE IN OUR FUTURE POPULATION

The discussion of mortality in Chapters 12 and 13 has shown that in countries where the expectation of life at birth is now about 70 years, the death rates at ages under about 45 are quite low as compared with those of even two or three decades ago. Moreover, in the last decade or two the declines have been quite small at ages over 45. There is good reason to believe that death rates at all ages will fall still lower, but further declines will be relatively slow, especially at ages under 35. In the United States and several other countries, the death rates are already so low from 1 to about 35 years of age that further reductions are almost certain to be small and to take place slowly. Even the gradual elimination of as much as one-half of the deaths in these age groups during the next 30 years would have comparatively little effect on the size of the population or on the age composition of the total population.

At older ages, on the other hand, the elimination of two clusters of diseases which the layman thinks of as heart disease and cancer would have a great effect on survival at all ages of 40 and over but especially at ages of over 50.

On the assumption that future declines in the death rates in the United States will be rather slow, the projection of the size of future age groups for persons already alive at any given time, e.g., in 1960, can be made for two or three decades ahead with a considerable degree of assurance. As we have already noted, the same cannot be said regarding the projection of age-specific birth rates. Although these projections may be improved somewhat in the near future, they are likely, for some time to come, to remain much more uncertain than the projections of death rates. Even if future economic cycles (prosperity and depression) should be far less pronounced than in the past, it seems reasonable to expect that they will continue to cause significant changes in the birth rate in any population in which there is a high degree of voluntary birth control. Although the decline in the birth rate since about 1959 is almost certainly associated in some degree with demographic changes which can be and are to some extent allowed for in these projections, we cannot be sure that the increasing volume of unemployment in the last several years is not already becoming a contributory cause of considerable significance in reducing the birth rate, which may become even more important before long, although it cannot be predicted with precision.

In spite of these uncertainties in projecting future population, the authors are so fully convinced of their usefulness that they wish to discuss some of the principal implications of the projections given in Table 17-2 as illustrative of their uses.

Space will not permit us to describe in detail how the 1960 population in Table 17-2 was arrived at. It must suffice to say (1) that the proportions in certain age groups differ slightly from the census age groups because they are corrected for well-known misstatements of age commonly reported to the census; and (2) that the excess of total population (1960) in Table 17-2 over the census count of 1960 also includes an allowance for underenumeration. The age-specific birth rates and death rates used represent the best judgment of men well acquainted with all the pertinent information on these matters. The assumptions of the trend in these rates are the *medium* assumptions, i.e., they are based on assumptions standing between the *low* and the *high* assumptions which are believed to represent the lower and upper limits within which the growth of population in the United States might range during the next three decades. These medium assumptions, in the judgment of the authors, may be regarded as the most probable.[3]

Table 17-2 was chosen for use here not only because it represents a very careful projection of population trends in the United States in the light of all the knowledge pertinent to the making of such projections, but also because the age groups

---

[3] For more details regarding the construction of this table, see Freedman, Whelpton, and Campbell, *op. cit.*, Chap. 11 (first GAF study). Special reports of the census occasionally include projections, and the National Vital Statistics Division, Public Health Service, also issues reports from time to time that contain much information of importance in making projections. By the time this book is published or within a short time afterwards, it is probable that the second GAF study will be published. This will contain later projections making use of the new knowledge mentioned above and will explain them fully.

used represent certain very important stages in the lives of all citizens. The use of the data for 1960, 1975, and 1990 was decided on by the authors because they believed that the points of greatest significance in projections of this character could be more readily understood if only a few points in time were involved. In addition, the intervals 1960–1975 and 1975–1990 show most clearly the demographic effects, after an interval of 30 years, of the two very important changes in birth rates since about 1930, *viz.*, the relatively low birth rates during the period 1930–1945 and the recovery to higher birth rates in the period 1945–1960.

On the basis of the component projections used here and the adjusted 1960 population as noted above, the total population of the United States would increase from approximately 184.6 million in 1960 to 222.5 million by 1975 and to 273.3 million by 1990. Thus the numerical increase is approximately 38 million in the first 15-year period and 51 million in the second 15-year period. The percentage increases are 20.6 and 22.8, respectively (see Table 17-3). By the beginning of the next century (A.D. 2000) our population would amount to approximately 312 million. These are large absolute increases. No one will question the statement that even if the actual numbers should happen to be somewhat above or below these projections, such a prospect is of very great importance in all planning, public and private, which is concerned with providing goods and services to our future population. This statement is not intended to imply that the mere knowledge of the probable increase in numbers is sufficient to enable the planners for goods and services even on a national scale to do their jobs in a satisfactory manner.

Here the component method of making projections offers some very important aids to planners since, as already noted, it enables one to calculate the probable numerical changes in the several age groups by sex. Hence one can also obtain the changes in the proportions each of these age and sex groups constitute in the total population (see Figure 17-1). Moreover, when a total population increases at a specified rate, e.g., 20 percent in 15 years, it is almost certain that each age group (1, 2, 3, 4, 5, etc., or 0–4, 5–9, etc.) will increase at a different rate. Any significant variation in the age-specific birth rate at any time will affect the number of births and if continued for even a few years, the number of children will be larger or smaller than at the time this change began. Their proportion in the total population will also probably change, and this change in the proportion of children will, of course, affect the proportions in all or most other age groups, since there can be only 100 percent in the total population. Likewise, a significant change in the age-specific death rates will almost certainly affect the number of persons in some age groups more than in others. This holds for numbers added to specified age groups due to net in-migration. Furthermore, as we have just noted with regard to young children, any change in the number of persons in any age group is almost certain not only to change the proportion it constitutes in the total population, but also the proportions in all other age classes. However, changes in age-specific birth rates are likely to be of greatest significance in this respect.

Let us now consider the probable changes in the numbers and in the proportions to be found in the several age groups shown here and some of the more significant social and economic implications of these changes. Again, we should urge the reader to remember that although we believe the population changes

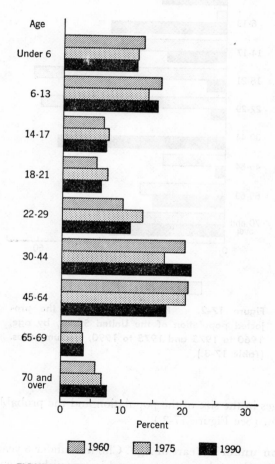

FIGURE 17-1.   Percent distribution of the projected population of the United States, by age, 1960, 1975, and 1990, medium series. (Table 17-3.)

considered here have important social and economic implications, we do not regard them as the *causes* of the social and economic problems noted. But we do believe that many of the social and economic problems we shall have to face in the not distant future can be much better understood if we are aware of the

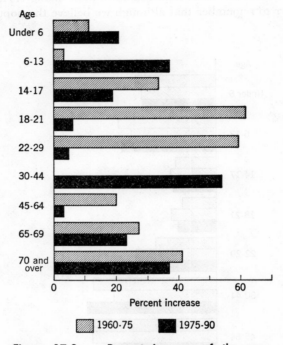

Figure 17-2. Percent increase of the projected population of the United States, by age, 1960 to 1975 and 1975 to 1990, medium series. (Table 17-3.)

probable changes in the size of the population and the probable changes in its age composition. (See Figure 17-2.)

The Population under 6 Years of Age. Children under 6 years of age are the very young dependents whose greatest need is a good home environment with good health services. On the basis of the assumptions and data used here, this 0–5 age group, which numbered 24.2 million in 1960 and constituted 13.1 percent of the total population (see Tables 17-2 and 17-3), will grow to 26.9

million in 1975 but will then constitute only 12.1 percent of the population. By 1990, it will increase to 32.4 million but will fall to 11.9 percent of the total. Thus, though there will be a large absolute increase in this age class between 1960 and 1990, most of this will come between 1975 and 1990. Its growth during the 30 years, 1960–1990, will be proportionally much less than that of the total population—33.8 percent as compared with 48.0 percent. Such a change in this 0–5 age group would not appear to create any *new* or more *urgent* social and economic problems than we are now encountering, if we are satisfied with the present conditions of living in the lower-income groups. Actually, however, every one is aware that there is great need of better housing and of improved health and recreation services in most communities and of better preparation of parents for the care of young children. These are all matters of improving the quality of living, and the point here is that the probable change in numbers and in the proportion of the total population constituted by the children aged 0–5 should render the improvement in their quality of living, in so far as it depends on the economic circumstances of the family, easier rather than more difficult. The importance of an adequate economic environment at home for these young children can scarcely be exaggerated.

The Population 6–13 Years of Age. The absolute increase in this age group will be from 29.2 million in 1960 to 30.1 million in 1975 and then to 41.3 million in 1990. Proportionally, this group will decline from 15.8 percent of the total population in 1960 to 13.5 percent in 1975 and then rise to 15.1 percent in 1990. Thus we are now (1964) in a period during which this 6–13 age group is declining proportionally, and it should be easier to provide its members with more adequate educational facilities than they have had for about a decade or a little more. This group, like the younger (under 6) group, is in great need of improved living conditions at home and in even greater need of expanded recreational facilities near home if the children are to get a good start in life. These recreational facilities, like the educational facilities, should also be easier to provide because of the declining proportion of these children in the total population during the next decade. After 1975, however, the number in this 6–13 group will begin to rise rather rapidly, and it will increase by approximately 11.2 million by 1990. The proportion this group constitutes of the total population will also rise rapidly after 1975 and by 1990 will be only a little lower than it was in 1960. Hence, the country seems very likely to face another elementary school crisis between 1975 and 1990 quite similar to that of the 1950s and early 1960s.

The Population 14–17 Years of Age. The future changes in the numbers and proportions of children aged 14–17 will be quite different from those of the 6–13 group. In 1960 there were 11.9 million children aged 14–17, and they constituted 6.5 percent of the total population. In 1975 they will number about

15.9 million and will constitute 7.2 percent of the population. Thus their growth in 1960–1975 will be very rapid (33.8 percent). Their number will increase only about 3 million between 1975 and 1990, and in the latter year they will constitute a somewhat smaller proportion of the total population (6.9 percent) than in 1975. Thus, as the pressure for the expansion of elementary schools relaxes in the period 1960–1975, the need for the expansion of secondary education facilities will increase. Moreover, in the period 1975–1990 when, as we have seen, there will again be need of a very large increase in the facilities for elementary education, there will be some relaxation in the need for secondary school facilities. But even so, the children aged 14–17 will increase in numbers (18.6 percent) in the period 1975–1990 almost as fast as the total population (22.8 percent). (See Chapter 7.)

Moreover, we should not forget that although the proportion of the children 14–17 years of age attending school has been increasing steadily in recent years, many in this age group are still not in school. In 1960 only 78.5 percent of the children 15 years of age, only 80.5 percent of those 16 years of age, and only 70.9 percent of those 17 years of age were enrolled in high schools.[4] It is quite widely believed that many of the unemployed persons in the labor force today cannot find jobs not only because they dropped out of school without preparation for any particular kind of work (see Chapter 8) but also because they are without the basic training in mathematics and science needed in many jobs today. Some years ago, to be young, strong, and willing would ensure most men a job, since there was much unskilled work to be done which did not require much school training. This is no longer true. The young people entering the labor force today need more and better training in science and mathematics, which must be supplied by our educational system. Many young people do not profit much from formal education of the kind now available to them. These people should have the opportunity to attend schools primarily technical in character after they have completed, let us say, a junior high school course. If such technical training for an increasing proportion of the children of high school age were available there can be little doubt that the proportion of children 14–17 years of age attending school would increase quite rapidly. In addition, the per capita cost of expanding technical education will probably be greater than that of expanding the conventional type of high school work. Very large additional educational expenditures, therefore, will be needed for our youth at ages 14–17 or 18.

This teen-aged group of high school age is also in very great need of public recreational facilities. The great majority of homes are even less able to care for the recreational needs of these high school children than of the children in the later years of elementary school. There is urgent need to tackle this problem

---

[4] U.S. Bureau of the Census, *United States Census of Population, 1960, Detailed Characteristics, United States Summary*, table 167, p. 374. (See Table 7–21.)

now while this age group is a smaller proportion of our population than it will be at any time in the next three decades.

The Population 18–21 Years of Age. The 18–21 age group includes most of the regular college students, but by far the greater portion of persons in this age group are already in the labor force—either working or seeking work. A great many of the college students are definitely training for the professions and other jobs in which advanced education is becoming more and more essential. In 1960 this 18–21-year group numbered approximately 10 million and constituted 5.4 percent of our total population. It will increase *very rapidly* between 1960 and 1975—by approximately 6 million, or by 61.7 percent. Hence it will rise to 7.2 percent of the total population by that date. Between 1975 and 1990 this group will increase in numbers by only about 1 million, and the rate of increase will be only 6.1 percent. As a result, persons 18–21 years of age will decline to only 6.3 percent of the total population.

These data show that the need for a very large expansion of the facilities for higher education is now urgent, and this urgency will increase within the next few years as a larger proportion of this rapidly increasing age group decides to go to college. This is almost certain to happen because the demand is growing steadily for people who have well-developed and flexible minds, trained to respond objectively to new situations.

It should be said in passing that since comparatively few persons aged 18–21 (18.9 percent) were attending college in 1960, an increase to 23 percent in the proportion of this age group in college would mean an actual increase of over one-fifth in college attendance, whereas an increase of 4 percent of persons of high school age actually attending high school would add only about one-twentieth to the enrollment of our high schools. Thus any significant increase in the proportion of persons aged 18–21 attending college will increase very greatly the need of facilities for higher education with greater emphasis on science and mathematics.

In addition, under present conditions it would not be surprising to find that adequate schooling will tend to occupy another year or two for those who are preparing for many of the more exacting professional and semiprofessional jobs in our increasingly complex society. Our institutions of higher education are going to be very hard pressed to meet both the quantitative and qualitative demands that will be made upon them in the near future.

The Population 22–29 Years of Age. The group aged 22–29 in 1960 numbered about 18 million and can be expected to increase by about 10.7 million by 1975. Hence it will increase from 9.8 percent of the total population in 1960 to 12.9 percent in 1975. We should expect such an increase to have a favorable effect on the economy, assuming, of course, that the members of the group are employed to good advantage. However, this large increase might raise some very serious employment problems. In the second period—1975–1990—the number in this age group will increase by only about 1.4 million, and it will decline to only 11.0 percent of the total population. In the first period, its growth will be 59.3 percent and in the second period, only 4.9 percent. This decline in proportion might have a depressing effect on the economy. However, this small growth in numbers of persons aged 22–29 is likely to result in some decline in the crude birth rate even if there is no decline in the age-specific birth rates, since these are highly fertile ages for most couples.

The Population 30–44 Years of Age. The age group 30–44, like the preceding, may be regarded as at the height of its productive power. Its numbers will be practically the same in 1975 as in 1960 (37.1 million). Consequently, it will become a substantially smaller proportion of the total, falling from 20.1 percent in 1960 to 16.7 percent in 1975. In the second period (1975–1990) the number in this age group will increase rapidly—from about 37.1 million to 57.5 million, or by 53.8 percent. Its proportion in the total population will also increase rapidly and will be much higher in 1990 (20.9 percent) than in 1975 (16.7 percent). This very large increase, both numerically and proportionally, in this age group 30–44 in the period 1975–1990 will probably raise some serious problems of unemployment similar to those likely to be encountered in the period 1960–1975 by the preceding age group (22–29). The wide fluctuations in the growth of this 30–44 age group in these two periods, like those of the other age groups born before 1960, are due primarily to the large fluctuations in births between the two periods 1930–1945 and 1946–1960.

Since this age group (30–44) will be almost stationary in numbers between 1960 and 1975 and since the youth of high school age, most of whose parents will be in this age group, will increase in numbers quite rapidly (Table 17-3) it would appear that these people aged 30–44 are likely to encounter some very difficult problems in providing a good secondary and college education for their children.

Up to this point the educational implications of the projections of population by age groups have been emphasized. The chief reason for this is that education certainly should be, assuming the progressive attainment of good living conditions by all classes of the population, one of the most important personal concerns of all people from the time they start to attend school themselves until their own children have completed their formal schooling. Of course, a great interest in and dependence on education should not and, in fact, does not cease with the completion of school attendance by one's children. However, it tends to diminish after this event. As a consequence, many people lose much of the direct interest they had in adequate education while they were in school or were sending their children to school.

One would not expect much active interest in good education on the part of most elementary school pupils, but unfortunately, a great many high school pupils also have little appreciation of the importance of the training they should be acquiring at this time. This is especially true where the parents have had no schooling beyond that required by law. They often have little interest in, or understanding of, the increasing need of better education. The community for its own protection should not only provide good education for all its members but should also stimulate children to use the educational facilities it provides. More and more, even the families in comfortable circumstances are dependent on the community for the educational opportunities which will enable them to earn the better and more certain incomes on which better family life, better public services, and better citizenship must be founded.

It seems abundantly clear to most thoughtful people that we live in a time when truly revolutionary changes in technology and in social organization are going forward and when most young people need not only more education but broader education to enable them to make satisfactory adjustments to these rapidly changing demands of the social order on individuals and on groups. However, though in the opinion of the authors the educational needs of the next few decades should stand near the top of any list of "musts" for our society, our task here is merely to illustrate some of the advantages for planning purposes that inhere in population projections based on the best data available.

The Population 45–64 Years of Age. Leaving the probable changes in the age groups which are most directly concerned with training in the home and with education, we find there are very likely to be significant changes in the older groups. The more important problems these changes will raise will be quite different in many respects from those of most concern to people under 45 years of age.

There will be a rather large numerical gain in the middle-aged group (45–64) between 1960 and 1975—about 7.4 million. In proportion of the total, however, there will be almost no change—from 20.3 percent in 1960 to 20.1 percent in 1975. In the second period (1975–1990) there will be only a very small change in numbers (1.4 million) but a rather large decline in the proportion of the total—from 20.1 percent to 16.9 percent. The large numerical increase in the period 1960–1975 may raise serious problems of employment. Many of the unskilled, semiskilled, and even of the skilled jobs held by these middle-aged workers are disappearing, and there are as yet no adequate retraining facilities for the new types of jobs that are opening up. Moreover, many of the older of these middle-aged workers never had the basic education and the type of job training that would be of aid in keeping them adaptable. Thus the quite sudden advent and spread of automation is going to hit workers over 50 years of age especially hard.

To offset this hardship in part, the widespread improvements in health that have taken place in the past 30 years should enable many of these middle-aged people to continue at work longer than people of the same ages in the past few decades if this seems advisable. Also at these ages family responsibilities begin to lessen, and with social security and the variety of pension plans in operation, a considerable proportion of these middle-aged people should be relieved of many of the economic cares to which they were subject earlier. Furthermore, some of the technological changes that have been taking place have relieved many older workers from heavy manual labor, so that men 55–64 years of age, who have been able to make satisfactory adjustments to new jobs, should be able to carry on with less strain than in the past.

However, up to the present, neither management nor labor nor government have squarely faced the problems raised by automation. They have not yet come up with any acceptable plan that will make it possible for the middle-aged man thrown out of employment through no fault of his own to find a new job that will enable him to retain his self-respect by performing a useful function in society. No age group appears to be free from the threat of technological unemployment, but his age group (45–64) would appear to be particularly vulnerable. Drastic solutions are required because mild reforms will not suffice to meet the situation that confronts middle-aged workers in trying to retain their jobs.

It is also important to note that in this age group consumption needs begin to change rather rapidly. After children leave home, housing needs decrease in so far as the particular couple is concerned. Likewise, food and clothing needs take less of their income. Since this group constitutes from one-sixth to one-fifth of the total population and since it almost certainly draws a considerably larger proportion of the total national expendable income, its changes in the allocation of its expenditures cannot fail to be of considerable importance to the economy as a whole.

The Population Aged 65 and Over. At ages 65 and over there will certainly be substantial increases both in numbers and in proportion in both periods, 1960 –1975 and 1975–1990. These old people, who numbered 16.7 million in 1960, will increase to 22.7 million in 1975 and to 30 million in 1990. They constituted 9 percent of the total population in 1960. Their proportion will rise to 10.2 percent in 1975, and to 11.1 percent in 1990. This is an important change both absolutely and relatively, and it will necessitate many changes in American life— personal, social, economic, and political (see Chapters 5 to 8). Attention should again be called to the possibility that health research within a few years might reduce considerably deaths from the diseases of the circulatory system and cancer. It is somewhat more probable, however, that some progress will be made in retarding the onset of the general organic deterioration that accompanies advancing age. If either of these changes took place, the proportion of old people in our population would rise more rapidly than this projection shows. Instead of almost doubling in numbers between 1960 and 1990, they might triple in numbers. These are such big *ifs* at the present time that they need not be considered any further here.

How this increase in people aged 65 and over will affect national productivity it is impossible to say. The same health considerations which may help to make more effective workers out of persons in later middle age (55–64 years of age) may also extend in some degree to old people, so that the amount of assistance needed by old people from the community may not increase as fast as their numbers. There is a growing feeling on the part of many old people and of many others as well that retirement should not be determined by age alone but that ability and desire to do useful work should be taken into account. In addition, there is increasing discussion of part-time work and adjustment of jobs to the capacities of older people which, if put into effect in a large way, might very well enable many of them to remain in part-time employment for a few years beyond 65. This would not only redound to their own benefit both physically and psychologically, but also to that of the nation. However, we should not overlook the fact that with actual unemployment growing and the threat of technological unemployment on a large scale hovering ever closer, many younger workers are increasingly anxious to see the older workers retire even before they are 65.

It is, of course, impossible to say whether an increasing proportion of persons aged 65 and over will remain employed or whether the pressure of younger workers for jobs will force their earlier retirement, say at 62 or 63 years of age, thus shortening the working life of several million people. But even if we assume that several million additional persons in the age class 65 and over will remain employed for a few years, there is no reasonable doubt that persons of these ages will need much more, both absolutely and proportionally, of the goods and services produced annually in the nation than they have consumed in the past. Between 1960 and 1990, by far the largest proportional increase of old people will be in the age class 70 and over (93.5 percent) as compared with the increase of persons aged 65–69 (57.7 percent). (See Table 17-3.) There is no serious consideration as yet for providing regular employment for persons 70 years of age and over. Moreover, it should not be forgotten that the death rates at 70 years of age and over are very high and that there has been comparatively little reduction in these rates during this century even in the more developed countries.

The needs of older people are quite different in many respects from those of any other group. This holds even for the customary essentials of life, for food, for housing and for clothing, which are less than even for middle-aged persons, to say nothing of the needs of younger adults with growing families. On the other hand, per capita expenditures for health services and for personal services which many older people can no longer perform for themselves are quite certain to be far larger than in the past. This fact is inevitably going to raise the question: At what point in the aging process must even an affluent society cease to provide services which will keep the physical organism functioning a little longer? Whether we like it or not, this is a moral problem as well as an economic problem, and we shall soon be compelled to face it.

In two other respects, the increasing proportion of old people in our population is also likely to be highly significant: (1) On the basis of the projections used here, the persons 65 years of age and over in 1960 constituted approximately 15 percent of all those 21 years of age and over, that is, about 15 percent of all persons of voting age;[5] by 1965 they will constitute 16.5 percent of all persons aged 21 and over and by 1990 they will constitute almost 18 percent of this same age group. It would seem highly probable, therefore, that old people will gain in political power during the next few decades. (2) It is quite generally recognized that the control of property is increasingly passing into the hands of older people and especially into the hands of widows, who are interested chiefly in security of income. The estates and trusts which are of appreciable size are managed by trust companies and banks whose managers are highly conservative investors and who dare not, under supervision of the courts, take chances on investments which are not generally recognized as "sound" or of "blue-chip" quality. Thus an increasing proportion of investment funds may for all practical purposes be barred from participating in the risk ventures which have been so important in the development of our economy in the past and will probably be needed even more in the future to keep our economy expanding.

FUTURE CHANGES IN SEX RATIOS

At this point a word should be said about probable sex changes in our future population during the period being considered here. Table 17-2 shows, as would be expected from the sex ratio at birth (approximately 105), that there are and will continue to be more males than females in our population at ages under 30 or 35. In the 30–44 age group as a whole the sex ratio is approximately 100. At ages 45 and over the sex ratio increasingly falls below 100, reaching the low level of 80.8 in the 65-and-over age group in 1960, and then declines further to about 72.6 in 1975 and in 1990. Between 1960 and 1990, males 70 years of age and over will increase by 78.3 percent, while females will increase by 105.5 percent. This shows very clearly the increasing predominance of females in the older age groups. Even in the later middle-aged group (55–64) women are significantly more numerous than men. One possible economic consequence of this preponderance of women in the older age groups has already been suggested. (See preceding paragraph.) At the same time, the predominance of older women, who

[5] Some states already allow persons under 21 to vote. Hence, these percentages are even now slightly too high and will decline as more persons under 21 become voters.

usually have less interest in political matters than men, may, to a considerable extent, weaken any political influence older people as a group might exercise in determining social and economic policies. But it seems rather more probable to the authors that both the political and economic influence of old people will continue to increase.

POPULATION GROWTH AND ECONOMIC GROWTH

Changes in the rate of population growth. At any given level of living, a slower rate of population growth means a slower increase in the demand for the goods *customarily* consumed. When our population increased at only about 0.7 percent per year (1930–1940) the rate of increase in the amount of goods needed to support the increase of population at the 1930 level of living was obviously only about one-half as much as was needed to support the population growth of 1940–1950, when the rate of population growth was about 1.4 percent per year, assuming the continuance of the 1930 level of living. It was less than one-half that needed during the decade 1950–1960, when the rate of population growth rose to about 1.8 percent per year. Whether or not the physical fact of a relatively slow growth in numbers between 1930 and 1940 played a causal role in reducing economic activity during that decade, and if it did, how important a cause it was, can never be known with any assurance. However, it is a fact that the slow growth of population figured prominently in the numerous discussions of a "saturated" economy, of a "lack of economic opportunity," and of a "stagnation of enterprise," touched off by the Depression of the 1930s. The slower population growth after about 1926 without doubt reacted on the willingness of businessmen to expand their activities, and this in due course depressed the marriage rate and the birth rate and thus reduced still more the rate of population increase.

We are not suggesting that a relatively slow rate of population growth necessarily leads to economic stagnation, but in a free economy it may be an important factor in the minds of businessmen in determining the volume of investment and the creation of new and better-paying jobs. When they see the number of new customers increasing more slowly than has been customary and are powerless, through their individual actions or even by concerted action, to improve the purchasing power of the average customer, they are quite likely to curtail investment and hence employment. Thus, although there is no proof of an inevitable causal connection of an economic character between these two phenomena, there may well be an important psychological connection closely related to the rate of economic growth and the maintenance of full employment. The authors consider it a serious mistake to assume that the rate of population growth acts directly as an economic cause in stimulating or depressing economic growth.

In a free economy it is the judgment of businessmen regarding the profitability of investment in definite enterprises and their willingness or ability to share the anticipated larger profits with the public that determines the rate of economic growth. The growth of population is only one factor, and probably quite a minor causal factor, in arriving at a decision to invest or not to invest.

Even with a stationary or a slowly growing population, there might very well be a thriving and expanding economy if a rapid increase in the efficiency of production were accompanied by a continuing change in the distribution of the national product sufficiently fundamental to make possible a rising level of living in population as a whole, but especially in the one-half, let us say, receiving the lower incomes. Witness the expansion of the economies in the nations of Western Europe since 1947 in spite of slow population increase (about 0.9 percent per year).

If it seemed highly probable to the business leaders in a free economy that each 1 million of their present customers would have a purchasing power 20 percent larger within 5 or 10 years, i.e., would be able to purchase as much goods and services as 1.2 million present customers, the effect on the growth of the economy would probably be much the same as though a 20 percent increase in population were assured. Indeed, such an increase in per capita purchasing power might be even more stimulating to the economy because this additional 20 percent would certainly not be spent securing larger amounts of the same goods and services; rather it would be spent on a greater variety of goods and services and would be quite likely to stimulate many businessmen to establish new enterprises and to increase the efficiency of those already in operation.

Although the subject has no direct connection with the changes in the rate of population growth and their relation to economic growth in advanced industrial societies, it may be of interest at this point to mention one very important relation between population growth and economic growth in underdeveloped countries.

All underdeveloped countries are relatively poor. They are also predominantly agricultural, producing their crops by relatively inefficient techniques, from the standpoint of the more advanced countries. Many of these underdeveloped countries possess little new land that can be tilled without expensive and time-consuming reclamation works. Their industries are largely hand-operated in very small units and are about as inefficient in their use of labor as is their agriculture. In large measure because of these inefficiencies in production and because of the relative scarcity of new land of fair to good quality in most such countries, the agricultural workers produce very little beyond the necessities of life for their own families. Rapid growth of population under such conditions is likely to be a first-class calamity to many of these countries. At the very best, in most of the large and densely settled underdeveloped countries, getting the information to the farmers that is essential to the improvement of agriculture and stimulating them to the use of this information is a slow and tedious task. Moreover, uninformed farmers are very reluctant to change their traditional farming habits and practices at the request of government officials whom they often regard as spies of the government and/or as exploiters employed by the landlords.

As we shall note in somewhat more detail below (Chapter 21), the leaders in most of these newly developed countries do not regard the increase of population as a matter of concern to be dealt with rationally in connection with their plans of national economic development. Population increase is rather considered in the same category as rain and drought, day and night, or a pestilence. It is regarded as beyond man's ability to control. Moreover, many of these leaders, even when they do understand the significance of population growth for the national economy, are afraid to speak out for fear of attack on ideological, or political, or religious grounds. They ask themselves, "Would not speaking out on this matter be an admission of our own incompetence as leaders?" This attitude will certainly delay any positive efforts in many underdeveloped countries to adjust the rate of population growth to the rate of actual economic development.

SUGGESTIONS FOR SUPPLEMENTARY READING

Bancroft, Gertrude: "Older Persons in the Labor Force," *Annals of the American Academy of Political and Social Science*, vol. 279, pp. 52–61, January, 1952. Present status and future prospects in the United States.

Bogue, Donald J., and Wilson H. Grabill: *The Population of the United States*, The Free Press of Glencoe, New York, 1959.

Borrie, W. D.: *Population Trends and Policies: A Study in Australian and World Demography*, chap. 11, Australian Publishing Company, Sydney, 1948.

Bowley, A. L.: *Estimates of the Working Population of Certain Countries in 1931 and 1941*, submitted to the preparatory committee for the International Economic Conference, League of Nations, Geneva, 1926.

Federal Security Agency: *Man and His Years: An Account of the First National Conference on Aging*, Health Publications Institute, Raleigh, N.C., 1951.

Francis, Roy G.: *The Population Ahead*, The University of Minnesota Press, Minneapolis, 1958.

Freedman, Ronald F., Pascal K. Whelpton, and Arthur A. Campbell: *Family Planning, Sterility, and Population Growth*, McGraw-Hill Book Company, New York, 1959.

Hagood, Margaret J., and Jacob S. Siegel: "Projections of the Regional Distribution of the Population of the United States to 1975," *Agricultural Economics Research*, vol. 3, no. 2, pp. 41–52, 1951.

Hansen, A. H.: *Economic Policy and Full Employment*, McGraw-Hill Book Company, New York, 1947.

————: "Extensive Expansion and Population Growth," *Journal of Political Economy*, vol. 48, no. 4, pp. 583–585, 1940.

Hauser, Philip M.: *Population Perspectives*, Rutgers University Press, New Brunswick, N.J., 1960.

Kuznets, Simon: *National Income and Capital Formation*, National Bureau of Economic Research, Inc., New York, 1937.

Myrdal, Gunnar: *Population: A Problem for Democracy*, Harvard University Press, Cambridge, Mass., 1940.

Pearl, Raymond, and Lowell J. Reed: "On the Rate of Growth of the Population of the United States since 1790 and Its Mathematical Representation," *Proceedings of the National Academy of Science*, vol. 6, pp. 275–288, 1920.

Reddaway, W. B.: *The Economics of a Declining Population*, George Allen & Unwin, Ltd., London, 1939.

Reed, Lowell J.: "Population Growth and Forecasts," *Annals of the American Academy of Political Social Science*, vol. 188, pp. 159–166, 1936.

Taeuber, Irene B.: "Literature on Future Populations, 1943–1948," *Population Index*, vol. 15, no. 1, pp. 2–30, 1949.

Terborgh, George: *The Bogey of Economic Maturity*, Machinery and Allied Products Institute, Chicago, 1945.

Thompson, Warren S.: "The Economic Consequences of Slow Population Growth in the United States," *Proceedings*, 1939 Ohio Conference of Statisticians on Business Research, Ohio State University, Columbus, Ohio, pp. 3–11, 1940.

————: "Future Population Growth and Real Estate Values," *Journal of Real Estate Appraisers*, vol. 3, pp. 34–41, 1934.

————, and P. Whelpton: "Counting Tomorrow's Customers: How Will America's Growth Affect Your Business?" *Nation's Business*, vol. 17, pp. 41–42, 154–155, February, 1929.

Whelpton, P. K.: *Forecasts of the Population of the United States, 1945–1975*, U.S. Bureau of the Census, 1947.

PART FIVE

Some Important
Implications of World
Population Changes

CHAPTER EIGHTEEN

Distribution of World Population

We know very little about the prehistoric migratory movements of man. We do know that they must have been very extensive and must have gone on for ages, because as information about the world and its inhabitants accumulated in increasing volume after about A.D. 1500, it became clear that man had already learned how to live in almost every type of physical environment. In most environments, however, his numbers were few, and settlement was sparse. The earliest knowledge available also showed that there were very substantial differences between regions both in the size of their populations and their density, even when the environments were physically quite similar and would seem to us equally favorable to the support of human life. Three factors probably determined in large measure the prehistoric distribution of population in the world: (1) the nature of the physical environment; (2) the techniques and the tools the group had developed to make use of the resources found in its particular environment; and (3) the social organization of the group. In a broad sense, these latter two compose the culture of the group.

PREHISTORIC MIGRATION

It is well known that population is very sparse in the Arctic and sub-Arctic regions, in deserts and semideserts, and in the more mountainous regions. On the other hand, coastal plains and river valleys in the tropical and temperate zones have generally had larger and denser populations than the less hospitable regions of the earth. The climate, the topography, the fertility of the soil, and the flora and fauna of the environment must always have played a very prominent part in determining man's distribution over the earth, a much more prominent part than they now do in many regions.

Man's cultural achievements in developing techniques to make use of the resources existing in any environment must generally have been most important in determining his growth and distribution over the world in prehistoric times. An example will aid in the appreciation of the role of culture in this respect. There is probably no region in the world of equal size better endowed with agricultural resources than the Mississippi Valley of the United States, stretching from the Appalachian Mountains to a line running through western Kansas, Nebraska, and the Dakotas. Yet up to the time of the settlement of Europeans in this region, it probably never supported a population of half a million, and it almost certainly was much less populated in 1790. "General Henry Knox, Secretary of War under President Washington, . . . placed the total Indian population in 1789 at 76,000."[1] His estimate referred to the Indian population east of the Mississippi River and did not include the Plains Indians nor those in the West and Southwest areas which later became part of the United States. On the other hand, many centuries ago, some of the great river valleys of China and India were supporting millions of people who lived as well or better than the Indians of the Mississippi Valley. The difference in the density and size of these populations was due chiefly to the differences in their techniques for making a living and in their political and social organization, i.e., in their cultures.

Space will not permit us to state a theory that might explain the differences in cultural forms and techniques which would enable some peoples to support much larger populations than others when their geographic environments would appear to offer them quite comparable resources. Moreover, we have no evidence to prove that differences in native intelligence will explain these cultural differences. Anthropologists tend to stress the importance of intercultural contacts among different peoples; i.e., they believe that major cultural developments took place at intercultural "crossroads." The character and the frequency of such crossroads contacts will probably explain the backwardness or the greater efficiency of the techniques of different peoples.

In general terms, it may be said that the peoples who depended for their living very largely on hunting and fishing and gathering natural vegetable products, and the pastoral peoples who depended chiefly on their flocks, always lived in rather small clan or tribal groups scattered over a considerable area. Because they were very little, if at all, dependent on agriculture, they could move about easily. Most hunters had few possessions to move, while pastoral peoples could drive their animals before them, a few of which were laden with their tents and the scanty household necessities they customarily used. For ages such peoples must have played an important role in taking possession of neighboring lands, either by war, or merely by moving into nearby areas which were not yet inhabited or at best were sparsely settled.

The development of agriculture tends both to tie a group to a given area and

[1] U.S. Bureau of the Census, *A Century of Population Growth from the First Census of the United States to the Twelfth*, 1909, pp. 39–40.

at the same time to make possible improvements in food production which will support a much denser population than can be supported by hunting and/or by gathering wild edibles. River valleys in mild climates with reasonably certain rainfall have generally encouraged agriculture, and most of the early well-known civilizations developed in such areas. But good resources were not sufficient to ensure increasingly efficient techniques. However, when agriculture developed in such areas, it was so efficient as compared with hunting and grazing and gathering edibles that the farmers in these valleys could generally produce somewhat more of the necessities of life than were needed for their own families.

As a consequence of these developments, new choices became available, a range of alternatives beyond the activities necessary to survival. Which of these would be selected would depend, among other things, upon the cultural values and the social organization of the people in question. This surplus could be used in both nonagricultural and agricultural enterprises, e.g., to build monuments like the pyramids of Egypt or to build irrigation systems as in Mesopotamia. The surplus could also be used to support a military establishment or to employ artisans in making luxury goods or to maintain scholars and artists or to build temples served by a strong priestly class. Some of the uses chosen would be directly *productive* and would encourage increased efficiency in the use of man's labor; some would be largely *ceremonial* and *ostentatious* expenditures. The results of these choices would lead to cumulative differences in productivity and to the development of varying patterns of culture.

When any area suitable for agricultural development was first being settled, the population must have been relatively small, so that there was good untilled land nearby on which the children of farmers could settle. Thus the population of these valleys could expand merely by slow dispersion into these neighboring untilled areas where the agricultural techniques already developed could be readily applied. Such populations grew in size as the tilled area was expanded, and in density if and when their agricultural techniques became more efficient. A political organization capable of keeping the peace and of driving off would-be invaders was probably also essential to the increase of the density of population in such areas. Settled life, in turn, encouraged further improvement in agricultural practices.

EARLY MIGRATION

Although most parts of the world must at first have been settled by the slow and age-long penetration of small tribal groups of hunters, gatherers, and fishers into adjacent areas as a natural response to the need for more of the goods essential to life, we now know that there must have been quite different types of migration at different times and in different regions before the dawn of history, as there have been since that time.

The peoples living in river valleys, on islands, or on the shores of lakes and seas generally developed means of water transportation which affected their distribution in many ways. Sometimes their boats were adequate to move enough people from one location to another at some distance to establish a new settlement, which in turn became a new center for the distribution of this particular people; e.g., the Polynesians in the course of centuries spread over much of the Central Pacific. For the most part, however, such movements by water, although probably averaging longer than those by land, were relatively short by present-day standards. Moreover, all group movements having any chance of becoming permanent settlements were necessarily largely restricted to areas where the techniques of the migrants for making a living could be applied with comparatively little change. Thus in early historical times the establishment of the Greeks in Asia Minor involved only relatively short voyages on which the voyagers were seldom, if ever, out of sight of land. Such transport, in the course of time, also played a very important role, perhaps a decisive role, in the distribution and in the cultural development of the populations that settled early in the valleys of the Ganges, of the Nile, and in Mesopotamia. In such valleys the relatively heavy and bulky grains, rice, wheat, barley, the sorghums, and other food grains, could be moved from areas of production to the centers of government and trade along the river and its tributaries with less labor than was required for land transport. Thus considerable concentrations of population (cities) became possible, and these concentrations of population in turn encouraged the arts and sciences and more efficient practices in the production of the necessities of life.

WAR AND MIGRATION BEFORE MODERN TIMES

War has also played a very significant role in determining the distribution of population. As we have suggested above, tribal and local wars, about which little is known, were probably highly influential in determining the direction of population dispersion. Moreover, there is little doubt that whereas they have at times accelerated the speed with which dispersion took place, at other times, by killing large numbers of potential migrants, they have probably retarded the settlement of new areas. Today we know that there have been numerous organized migrations of a military character which probably affected the distribution of population in particular regions, although we cannot be certain just how they did so. An example or two will aid in understanding the possible significance of these military or semimilitary incursions in determining the distribution of the population and the cultural development of a people.

An incursion of Aryan peoples from central Asia (whole nations or large groups of tribes well organized for conquest) into India probably began about 1500 B.C. and continued intermittently for several centuries, perhaps for 1,000 years. Such a movement probably had a significant influence on the distribution of population not only in India but throughout all Asia. It may also have been instrumental in destroying a great civilization which flourished, perhaps 4,000 to 5,000 years ago in the valley of the Indus River. But even if such an incursion by force into an already well-peopled land led to the immediate reduction in the size of the indigenous population, in the longer run—a century, or two, or three —it may have led to a more substantial increase in India's population than would otherwise have taken place, by reason of importing new and better techniques for agriculture and by keeping the peace over a larger part of the country once the conquest was completed. Hence, in the course of several generations, they may have changed substantially the proportion of the population of the world living in the conquered area. Such conquests have probably had much less effect in extending the area of human habitation.

The incursions of Attila into Central Europe about the middle of the fifth century A.D. and of Genghis Khan into Europe in the early thirteenth century probably destroyed considerable numbers of both the invading and the invaded peoples by spreading disease and reducing the amount of food available as well as by battle deaths, and hence were detrimental to population growth for some decades. In the longer run, they probably had little effect on either the size or the distribution of population unless they hastened the spread and/or the development of better techniques of production. This appears unlikely.

The rather extensive but comparatively peaceful settlement of disbanded Roman soldiers in some of the areas they had conquered is more likely to have had significant demographic effects than did the better-known military incursions just mentioned. These ex-soldiers often married the widows of the men they had killed in battle. They were also familiar with agricultural techniques more efficient than those of the peoples they had vanquished. In many other respects also the Roman culture of these settlers introduced more efficient techniques than had been used by the indigenous populations among whom they settled, while their political organization, in particular, enabled them to undertake valuable public enterprises, e.g., more effective measures for defense and for the building of public improvements. All such more advanced political, cultural, and technical achievements were favorable to population growth and expansion. Whether Roman settlement directly affected the wider distribution of population in Europe is not known. However, it seems more likely to have increased the density of population in the areas of settlement than to have led soon to the settlement of new areas.

In the preceding discussion, the authors have attempted to depict briefly the character of some of the chief factors determining the dispersion of man over the globe. In general, it may be said that in the early days of his dispersion man moved as a member of a small kinship group (clan, tribe, or a confederation of tribes) to establish himself in all parts of the world before the dawn of history. Later even the larger warlike incursions referred to above partook of the character of the migration of a people held together more by ties of kinship than by ties of adherence to a political entity living in a specified area. Moreover, there is little evidence of any significant amount of migration by individuals and/or nonkinship groups such as we know today until relatively recent times. Occasionally, of course, individuals and small kinship groups rebelled against the restrictions of the dominant kinship group imposed upon them and tried to live outside this group. But such persons and splinter groups soon found everyman's hand against them and probably counted for little in the settlement of new lands. Only gradually, as a greater degree of uniformity of culture developed over relatively large and contiguous areas, was it possible for any considerable amount of individual and/or *small* family migration to take place. (By *small* family we mean father, mother, and children, in contrast to the clan or tribe.)

The international aspects of this newer type of migration are of considerable interest because this movement of individuals and families overseas and between political entities (nations) has played a very important role in determining both the growth and distribution of population in the world during the past three or four centuries, particularly in the Western world, and therefore aids us in understanding the distribution of population as found in the world today.

Before discussing modern migration as affecting the growth and distribution of population, we shall note briefly the chief motives which have led man to move from place to place.

MOTIVES FOR MIGRATION

The motives leading to migration have probably varied but little in general character from age to age. The economic motive has probably been dominant at all times, although not of equal importance in all particular movements. Clans, tribes, nomadic shepherds, and other regularly migratory groups have always moved as seemed best to them in order to make a living, although the force exerted on weaker by more powerful kinship groups and by military groups in search of better living has very frequently made necessary the migration of a weaker group in order to escape annihilation. In the period of European expansion during the past three or four centuries, the motives for migration have, no doubt, been somewhat more varied, since individual and family and political circumstances entered more and more into consideration. But even so, the desire to better one's position economically—the search for better opportunities —has been the dominant motive in modern international migration. Comparatively few groups of people or individuals who are reasonably well satisfied with their economic position in their native land move to new homes in new countries, although there are many particular cases both of groups and individuals in which other motives have been more powerful than economic motives in determining migration, such as religious and political persecution and personal and family maladjustments of many kinds.

The more recent forced types of migration are motivated chiefly by the desire to escape persecution. In the recent authoritarian states people are forced to migrate abroad or are forbidden to migrate, according to the needs and purposes of the dictators.

To assert that until these modern *forced migrations* came into the picture the dominant motive of individual and family migration was, for some centuries, economic is not to deny that a great many individuals and some small groups migrated for noneconomic reasons. It is merely a recognition of the fact that far and away the most important cause of migration during the great emigration from Europe was the desire to improve economic status.

CHARACTERISTICS OF MODERN MIGRATION

The migration of large numbers of people as organized groups and in the direct interest of the migrating group, the sending group, or the receiving group, did not play a very important part in the modern expansion of Europe until the rise of the totalitarian governments in the twentieth century. Prior to World War I, we, in the West, had become accustomed to think of migrants as individuals or families moving rather freely from country to country in search of more satisfactory living conditions. As we said above, the motivation was largely economic and personal. The migrants were not often aided in their decision by any public authority, nor were they, as a rule, assisted financially in making the move, although at times public policies operated to a significant extent. By and large, it was more often the attraction of the new country than the noneconomic expulsive forces of the sending country which exerted the decisive influence. Even the knowledge of the attractiveness of the new land was conveyed chiefly from relative to relative or from friend to friend by word of mouth or by letter, although occasionally both private organizations and public agencies in the receiving country made definite efforts to acquaint prospective migrants with the advantages open to them. The governments of the sending countries interested in establishing colonies abroad, e.g., the British colonies in North America, also often encouraged emigration by giving various forms of aid, chiefly large grants of land, to individuals or groups that would undertake the settlement of these grants either as entrepreneurs or as actual emigrants. The United Kingdom also deported many criminals to its settlements.

The natural result of this relatively free play of forces on individuals and families was that there was a large movement of people from the areas of relatively dense population and low economic opportunity to areas of less density and greater opportunity, provided that the same general pattern of culture prevailed in the receiving area, and provided that climatic conditions were also sufficiently similar to permit the growing of familiar crops. In much of the modern international migration, poor peasants and farm workers with little or no land tend to predominate, both because they were numerous in the European populations of their day and because, although poor, they had the personal qualities and the essential techniques to enable them to become successful pioneers on undeveloped land. Since there was comparatively little advantage to these modern migrants in rigorously maintaining the cultural patterns of their home areas and since the countries sending out migrants expended little effort in encouraging their native sons to remain loyal, these migrants who came as individuals and families soon ceased to feel any great loyalty to their homelands. Furthermore, to remain culturally isolated from their neighbors in the community in which they settled generally entailed definite economic and social disadvantages. These disadvantages were even more strongly felt by their children. The absence of pressure, or at most the rather light and intermittent pressure, of the native group did not drive the newcomers to seek safety and comfort in their own community to the same extent as often happened among international migrants in Europe. On the whole, modern international migration tended to encourage the migrant to adapt himself to life in the new community, and if the migrants themselves failed to do this because of preference for old and accustomed ways of living and because of difficulties in acquiring a new language, their children tried all the harder. If the migrants themselves failed to achieve full integration in their new homes, they failed not primarily because they wanted to remain Poles, or Germans, or Swedes, or Englishmen, but because they did not know how to make the transition from old to new cultural values and practices. This was almost as true for those who settled in farming communities as for those who settled in cities, although the former had fewer disturbing contacts with strange groups and were necessarily somewhat slower in making the transition, i.e., in acquiring assimilation.

Even the increasing ease of transportation and speed of communication did little to maintain the bonds between the migrant and the homeland, except for those who planned to return at some future time. Although there were many who so intended, they were generally a rather small minority. It is not misrepresenting the nature of modern international migration to say that never in the history of the world had a great migratory movement carried with it so little of adherence to traditions and customs; never had the individual found so easy a way to break the bonds binding him to family and community by moving to a new land, leaving behind his past and embarking on a new career. The individual and family character of modern international migration, prior to the rise of the recent authoritarian governments, is its most distinguishing feature. It is also the feature most determinative of the migrant's development and of the character of the culture developed in lands where immigrants were many and of somewhat similar backgrounds.

THE EXTENT OF MODERN EUROPEAN MIGRATION

Modern migratory movements of the character described above have involved very large numbers and have had a profound influence on the distribution and growth of population in the world in the past three centuries. There is comparatively little accurate information, however, regarding either the number of persons emigrating from European countries or the number of immigrants into America or into other non-European areas, before the nineteenth century. Spain sent the first permanent immigrants to America, but the total number sent out during the sixteenth, seventeenth, and eighteenth centuries could not have exceeded a few hundred thousand. However, they have determined the general cultural development of Central and South America.

If one judges from the scanty information available regarding the inflow of colonists into North America during the seventeenth and eighteenth centuries, there were probably relatively large annual variations in the volume of such migration. There can be little doubt, however, that during the seventeenth and eighteenth centuries the outflow from the British Isles was by far the largest of these migratory movements and that most of these migrants settled in North America. Even so, the annual average must be thought of in terms of thousands rather than in tens of thousands. Only about 8,000 immigrants a year entered the United States between 1790 and 1819.[2] Since 1819 the United States has had reasonably good data on immigrants entering the country. The total number entering the United States between 1820 and 1961 (inclusive) was approximately 42 million. Of course, not all of these remained permanently, but probably not far from 34 to 35 million, or over 80 percent, remained here and were incorporated into our national life. This is the largest free movement of immigrants into any country known to history, and considering the national political controls over international migration now prevailing in the world (see below), it is not likely to be surpassed in the foreseeable future.[3]

If we add to the immigrants into the United States the voluntary immigrants

---

[2] U.S. Bureau of the Census, *Population of the United States in 1860; Compiled from the Original Returns of the Eighth Census*, 1864, p. xviii; Marcus Lee Hansen, *The Atlantic Migration, 1607–1860*, Harvard University Press, Cambridge, Mass., 1940.

[3] For a more detailed discussion of immigration into the United States, see Donald J. Bogue, *The Population of the United States*, chap. 14.

into the other parts of America, there has probably been a total immigration of 62 to 64 million people, nearly all from Europe, into the Western Hemisphere since about 1800. The proportion of immigrants into Latin America returning to Europe is generally believed to have been considerably larger than among the immigrants into North America. The total emigration from Europe since early in the nineteenth century was probably 4 to 6 million larger than that to America because of the movement to Australia and South Africa as well as the emigration of small numbers to many other parts of the world where European control had been established. But the United States and Canada furnished by far the chief outlet to Europeans seeking larger opportunities. Probably about 68 to 70 million people migrated from Europe since about 1800 and 75 percent of them remained abroad permanently. The descendants of the permanent emigrants from Europe to North America since 1800 plus the descendants of those who came before 1800 are now probably only a little less than one-half as numerous as the peoples now living in the European countries lying west of the U.S.S.R. It is impossible to make even a rough guess regarding the proportion of the population of Latin America that can be classed as of European origin, but a substantial proportion of the 200 million or more Latin Americans belong in this category. If the European migrants and their descendants living in other parts of the world were added to the European-American groups, it would not be far wrong to say that almost as many people of European descent now live in other continents as in Europe west of the U.S.S.R. This constitutes a tremendous expansion of the people coming chiefly from the rather small group of people, estimated at about 80 million by the authors, living in Europe west of the U.S.S.R. in 1650. Since the really great migration from Europe occurred after 1800, it raises the very interesting question whether such a movement as this did not greatly reduce the rate of population growth in the area from which these migrants came. This question will be discussed rather briefly below, although it cannot be answered positively.

During the three centuries while Europe, west of Russia, was expanding chiefly westward, Russia was expanding eastward into Siberia, especially after serfdom was abolished in 1861. From 1800 to the outbreak of World War I, probably about 7 million Russians had moved eastward across the Ural Mountains. This movement was considerably accelerated after the revolution of 1917, i.e., between World War I and World War II. But from 1800 to World War II, the migration affecting the growth and distribution of the Russian peoples was very largely an internal movement, i.e., took place within the long-recognized boundaries of Russia.[4]

There have also been other substantial migratory movements between nations during the past 150 years, but they have had comparatively little effect in

---

[4] See article on Migration, Eugene N. Kulischer, *Encyclopaedia Britannica*, 1957 edition, vol. 15, p. 446.

changing either the growth or the distribution of world population although some of them have affected the growth of population in certain small areas.

China. Considerable numbers of Chinese have moved to the Philippines, Indonesia, the Malay Peninsula, Cambodia, Thailand, and other countries of Southeast Asia, as well as smaller movements into other areas; for example, into the United States, Peru, and Formosa. The total of these movements from China proper will probably never be known with accuracy.[5]

As of 1922, Ta Chen estimated that there were about 8,179,000 Chinese living abroad.[6] The large movement from China proper into Manchuria after about 1900 was really an internal movement similar to westward migration in the United States and was probably larger than all the other movements out of China proper. It appears that preceding World War II, about four-fifths of the Chinese who went abroad later returned to China. Moreover, during the Depression years of the 1930s the movement of Chinese to foreign lands decreased in volume, while the return movement increased.[7] During World War II, it is doubtful whether there was any net outward movement. After the war, however, as the Communists gained control of a larger proportion of the mainland, the outward movement increased sharply. Hong Kong has received the lion's share of these refugees although Formosa and Singapore have also received considerable numbers. A few have also filtered into the Philippines, Indonesia, and other countries in Southeast Asia. This movement may have been large enough to justify the 1953 figure given by the Communist census for Chinese living abroad (11,743,320), but this cannot be stated as a fact.

India. The migration from India before World War II was much smaller than that from China. About 2,130,000 Indians lived abroad in 1924.[8] All but about 100,000 of these lived in other parts of the British Empire—chiefly in Ceylon, Malaya, the Straits Settlements, South Africa, Fiji, and Mauritius.

[5] Persia Crawford Campbell, *Chinese Coolie Emigration in the Countries within the British Empire*, P. S. King & Staples, Ltd., London, 1923; Ta Chen, *Chinese Migrations, with Special Reference to Labor Conditions*, U.S. Bureau of Labor Statistics, *Bulletin 340*, miscellaneous ser., 1923, p. 161.
[6] The census of Communist China in 1953 gave the number of Chinese living overseas as 11,743,320, all of whom were regarded as citizens of Communist China. Since the census gave no indication of how this figure was arrived at, it should not be given too much credence. If true, this would mean a gain of over 40 percent in the number of Chinese living overseas between the time of Ta Chen's estimate and 1953. See also Ta Chen, *Population in Modern China*, chap. 6, Migration, The University of Chicago Press, 1946.
[7] T. E. Smith, *Population Growth in Malaya*, Royal Institute of International Affairs, London, 1952, p. 63. The growth of population in Singapore was undoubtedly hastened by the relatively large migration of Chinese to Malaya.
[8] Walter F. Willcox (ed.), *International Migration*, vol. 1, no. 14, Publications of the National Bureau of Economic Research, New York, 1929, p. 148.

With the coming of the Depression in 1930, there was an even stronger return movement among the Indians than among the Chinese.

The above statements apply to prepartition India, i.e., to India as politically organized before 1947. There is no way of apportioning these emigrants between the Indian Union and Pakistan (the successor states) with even approximate accuracy. However, there can be little doubt that the large majority came from the territory now incorporated into the Indian Union. The really important modern migratory movements from and into the present Indian Union and Pakistan occurred at the time of the partition (1947) and shortly thereafter. These movements probably had comparatively little effect on the *size* of population in either of these countries although they did have substantial effect on the *distribution* of Hindus and Muslims in the Indian subcontinent.

In theory, the areas of prepartition India which were predominantly Hindu in religion were to be allotted to the new Indian Union and those which were predominantly Muslim were to be allotted to Pakistan. However, in practice, there were major exceptions to this rule; e.g., the large state of Hyderabad located near the center of the peninsular area and entirely surrounded by Hindu states was assigned to the Indian Union although its inhabitants were predominantly Muslim in religion. Practically all small communities of both Hindus and Muslims, when surrounded by large majorities of the opposite faith, were included with these majorities in establishing their nationality status. However, in order to eliminate as far as possible disturbances which might arise from religious differences after partition, both Hindus and Muslims who preferred citizenship in the state other than the one to which the territory where they were then living was assigned were permitted to migrate to the territory of the state in which they preferred to maintain citizenship.

The result was a migration of tremendous size. The 1951 census of Pakistan[9] gives the total number of displaced persons enumerated as 7,227,000. The second Five-Year Plan of India[10] refers to the 8,550,000 displaced persons for whom rehabilitation was undertaken. These were former residents in territory allotted to Pakistan in 1947. This 15.77 million probably understates by a substantial amount the actual migration resulting from partition, because not all the migrants would fall into the above categories and a number of very young and of old migrants would have died before these counts were made.

There is some reason to think that this migration had only a slightly adverse effect on population growth between 1941 and 1951 in the Indian Union but a somewhat more significant effect on the growth of population in Pakistan. The census of India (Indian Union) in the postpartition area showed a slightly

[9] Pakistan, Office of the Census Commissioner, *First Census of Pakistan, 1951*, vol. 1, Report and Tables, Manager of Publications, Karachi, 1952, p. 31.
[10] India, Planning Commission, *Second Five-Year Plan*, Government of India Press, New Delhi, 1956, p. 610. (A draft outline.)

larger increase in population between 1941 and 1951 (14.1 percent) than between 1931 and 1941 (13.5 percent). The 1951 census of Pakistan showed less
than one-half as large a percentage increase between 1941 and 1951 (7.9 percent)
in the postpartition area as between 1931 and 1941 (18.8 percent) in the same
area. The 1951 census of Pakistan may very well have been somewhat less complete than that of India because of less efficient administrative services. Although
considerable but unknown numbers of both Hindu and Muslim migrants died in
transit, it is highly probable that many more died prematurely because of the
hardships encountered in transit after arrival in camps for displaced persons and
before the official counts were made (see above). Neither country was prepared
to care for such vast numbers of displaced persons, but India was somewhat
better prepared to do so than Pakistan. As a consequence, although both suffered
heavy death losses as a consequence of partition, Pakistan's growth (1941–1951)
was probably more adversely affected by the hardships resulting from partition
than was that of the Indian Union.

Japan. The movement of emigrants from Japan is of quite recent date. Until
about the last third of the nineteenth century it was a capital offense to leave the
country. Once the Japanese restrictions on emigration were relaxed and the
people began to learn of economic opportunities elsewhere, they started to
emigrate. The first emigration of any appreciable size was to the United States
(Hawaii). About 65,000 Japanese immigrants entered the United States between
1885 and 1899, most of them in the decade 1890–1899, since there were only
about 14,600 living in the United States in 1890. The early Japanese immigrants
to Hawaii received some assistance, chiefly from planters wanting laborers, but
this did not continue for long, because the knowledge of the opportunities open
in the United States to Japanese immigrants spread fairly rapidly in the communities from which the first laborers came and soon there was no further need
of assistance. Although most of the earlier immigrants went to Hawaii, they soon
began to move on to the mainland (West Coast). In 1890 almost 85 percent of
the 14,600 Japanese (immigrants and their children) living in the United States
were found in Hawaii. By 1900, only 71 percent of the 85,400 Japanese living in
the United States lived in Hawaii. The total number of Japanese entering the
United States from 1901 to 1930 was slightly over 247,000, and of the 278,000
Japanese living in the United States in 1930, almost one-half lived on the mainland. Because there has been very little Japanese immigration into the United
States since 1930, the increase in their numbers from 278,000 in 1930 to 464,000
in 1960, about 66 percent, arises almost entirely from their natural increase. In
1960 the Japanese constituted only about 0.25 percent of the total population of
the United States.

Japan obtained her first colonies (Korea and Formosa) as the result of her
victory over China in the Sino-Japanese War (1895). Although the data are not

wholly satisfactory, it appears that there were about 275,000 to 300,000 Japanese in these colonies by 1910. After her victory in the Russo-Japanese War (1905) Japan began to send a considerable number of colonists to Manchuria, and by 1914 it was claimed that there were somewhat more than 100,000 Japanese in this area. By 1940 there were probably somewhat more than 1.2 million Japanese in Korea, Formosa, and Manchuria. In the meantime, the number of Japanese in the United States had risen to about 285,000. All the above figures include the descendants of the emigrants as well as the surviving emigrants.

There were, of course, some Japanese settlers in other countries in 1940. Brazil had about 190,000, and a few thousand lived on some of the islands in the Western Pacific. The actual Japanese settlers outside Japan in 1940, therefore, numbered somewhere around 1.7 to 1.8 million. Practically all of these, except those in the United States and Brazil amounting to about 500,000, were repatriated after the war.

The total number of Japanese civilians repatriated after the war amounted to a little over 3 million. Approximately 1.2 to 1.3 million of these are accounted for as living abroad in 1940 but not in the United States or Brazil. The 1.2 to 1.3 million civilians just mentioned may have had a fairly substantial natural increase during the war, but even if this amounted to as much as 150,000 to 200,000, there would still remain about 1.5 million civilians repatriated who must have gone abroad during the years 1937–1944 to establish the coprosperity sphere. (Japan attacked China in 1937).[11]

Japanese emigration, either as a means of relieving population pressure in Japan or as a measure for enlarging the Japanese Empire, must be regarded as a complete failure. As providing better economic opportunities for the 300,000 to 400,000 permanent emigrants settling in the Americas and for their descendants it was a success. However, the Japanese living in the United States and Brazil constitute such a tiny proportion of the populations of these countries (about 0.25 percent) that they have added but little to the increase of their populations. Because of these small numbers, they have had comparatively little cultural influence, except in a few localities where they constitute a significant proportion of the population, e.g., in Hawaii and a portion of one state (São Paulo) in Brazil.

Korea. Korea had sent considerable numbers of migrants to Manchuria, Russia, and Japan before World War II. Possibly 2.5 million Koreans lived abroad in 1940. Most of these have since been repatriated. There had been very little international migration from other Asian countries, i.e., across national bound-

---

[11] "Coprosperity sphere" is the name the Japanese gave to the territory they occupied by military force in East Asia and the Western Pacific, and which they hoped to control after the war as an integral part of an enlarged Japanese Empire.

aries before World War II. Since then there have been very few migrants from or to any Asian country, except from Communist China as noted above.

RECENT FORCED MIGRATIONS

The great migratory movement in Europe associated with Hitler's attempt to establish "a great German Empire" that would "endure one thousand years" and the loss of World War II by the Germans must be noted here, but they can only be briefly recapitulated. Hitler hoped to concentrate all the people of German stock living in Europe in one solid bloc. The area this empire was to occupy initially may be roughly defined as follows: the Rhine River on the west, the Balkans, the Black Sea, and the Caucasus Mountains on the south, the Volga River on the east; and on the north the boundary was even less definite but probably coincided rather closely with an east-west line at about the latitude of Moscow. The people of German stock living outside of Hitler's Germany as of the time of his attack on Poland (September, 1939) were to be moved into the region he expected to conquer. These peoples altogether numbered several million (perhaps 5 to 7 million), and they lived in some dozen or more states, some in Czechoslovakia, some in northern Italy, some in practically all of the Balkan states, and some even in Poland and the U.S.S.R. Altogether, Hitler hoped to establish a bloc of German-speaking people numbering perhaps 75 to 80 million in 1940. There would be but few and rather small minority groups within this enlarged German Empire because the non-Germans would be forced either to emigrate or would be killed off.

By his agreement with Stalin after the conquest of Poland (1939), Hitler gained a substantial portion of western Poland and began to move some of the Balts—people of German stock in the Baltic states—into this area. After the attack on the U.S.S.R. in 1941, and as the victorious German armies marched eastward, a few people from the German minorities in other countries were moved into Poland and the Ukraine (southern U.S.S.R.). The migrants into the latter were very few.

Following the reverses suffered by the German armies in the Caucasus and at Stalingrad and after their retreat westward began, any German migrants into U.S.S.R. territory and in due course those peoples already settled in former Polish territory were swept back and became part of the much larger stream of Germans from East Prussia and other parts of eastern Germany forced to move westward.

The number of expellees into the shrunken area of postwar Germany in 1946 was about 9.7 million, and by 1957 the number in West Germany alone had grown to about 12.2 million.[12]

[12] International Labour Office, *International Migration, 1945–1957*, new ser. no. 54, table 1, Geneva, 1959, pp. 8–9.

Clearly, the vast amount of international migration arising from World War II was essentially of a political character and war accomplished by the direct use of force and/or by the creation of such a fear for their lives that vast numbers migrated wherever they would be received.

From the standpoint of the receiving countries, postwar West Germany had no choice in accepting immediately large numbers of Germans from areas overrun by the troops of the U.S.S.R. and Poland. In addition, West Germany has voluntarily accepted 5 million immigrants since 1946, chiefly from East Germany. The acceptance of expellees from Central Europe by France, Belgium, Sweden, and Switzerland in Europe and by Canada, the United States, Australia, and the South American countries has been voluntary, and the number has been large; net immigration into these countries is believed to amount to from 7 to 9 million.

At the present time, it seems highly unlikely that there will be any return to the large relatively free migration in the area of European settlement such as prevailed before World War I. The Communist countries as a rule forbid all emigration and accept only negligible numbers of immigrants. The "Free World" countries, almost without exception, severely limit the number of immigrants they will accept, and there is no indication of any substantial relaxation of the present restrictions.

MIGRATION AND THE GROWTH OF POPULATION

We have seen above that in the entire area of Western and Central Europe the *rate* of population growth rose slowly from the latter part of the eighteenth century until about the time of World War I (1914). This rise in the rate of growth began at different times in different countries and also attained different levels in different countries (see Chapter 15). The level of the rate of natural increase—birth rate minus death rate—for this region as a whole was over 15 percent higher in the second half of the nineteenth century than in the first half. Moreover, in the first decade of the twentieth century (1900–1910), it was over one-half higher than in the period 1800 to 1850. As the volume of emigration from Western and Central Europe increased during the nineteenth century, the rate of natural increase in this region also rose. It would be a serious mistake, however, to assume that emigration was the cause of this more rapid natural increase (*post hoc, ergo propter hoc*). But it would be an equally great mistake to assume that the 1910 population of Western and Central Europe would have been significantly larger than it actually was if there had been no substantial emigration from this region between 1800 and 1910. It is fatuous to argue the question of *what might have been* if the dynamic social and economic factors affecting population growth had been different from what they actually were. This can never be known. But it is a significant fact that the great emigration from Europe between 1800 and 1910 did not prevent a long-sustained and slowly increasing rate of growth of the populations from which it came. Moreover, the population growth in this region of emigration was also more rapid than in most other parts of the world at that time, except in the receiving countries. Besides, it cannot be known with any assurance just how much of the growth of the countries (or regions) receiving large numbers of immigrants was to be attributed to immigration once settlement had been well established.

About 70 years ago General Walker championed the theory that immigration into a country such as that into the United States during the nineteenth century did not constitute a net addition to its population but rather was a substitution of the immigrant and his children for the children of people already there.[13] He pointed out that the birth rate of the native population was declining most rapidly in those parts of the United States where immigrants were proportionally most numerous, and he held that there was a causal connection between the volume of immigration and the decline in the native birth rate. He believed that the unwillingness of the natives to have their children compete economically with the immigrants and their children was the chief reason for this decline in the native birth rate. If this was the case, then allowing immigrants to enter at will merely meant that large numbers of children of native parents would remain unborn. Since there is always some antagonism between natives and newcomers (immigrants) where the latter are numerous and where there are differences in language and even minor variations in cultural backgrounds, this view was very naturally seized upon by those natives opposed to immigration for whatever reasons. They used Walker's argument as an effective weapon in their campaign to reduce the volume of immigration and to select the immigrants more carefully. We are concerned here only with the truth involved in General Walker's position.

It is quite impossible, of course, to prove conclusively the truth of a proposition such as Walker's. It is true that native birth rates (if we use ratios of children to women as indicative of these rates in the days before birth registration in the United States became adequate) have long been lower in the Northeastern states, where immigrants were proportionally most numerous, than in most other parts of the country. It is also true that when much of the rough heavy labor in construction work and in mines and factories passed into the hands of the immigrants, many natives did not want their children to take such jobs. But it does not follow that immigration is the sole factor, or even the chief one, in producing the lower birth rate among the natives who lived alongside the immigrants.

In the discussion of the decline of the birth rate (see Chapter 11), the authors have pointed out that the profound changes in the manner of life involved in the urbanization and industrialization of an increasing proportion of the population

[13] Francis A. Walker, "Immigration and Degradation," *Forum*, vol. 11, pp. 638, 642, 1891.

have probably been the factors most closely associated in Western countries with the decline in their birth rates. In this connection, the fact that a substantial decline in the birth rate has taken place in Western countries and in Japan, where industrialization and urbanization were proceeding rapidly but into which there was little or no immigration, also seems to them highly significant. If it is the changes in the manner of living and the creation of a strong desire to live better and to rise in the social scale created by industrialization and urbanization that led to the reduction of the size of the family, then the question to which we are really interested in finding an answer is whether immigration has any effect upon the speed of the changes in our rate of reproduction by hastening our industrialization and urbanization. This is quite a different question from the one as to whether the direct economic competition of immigrants and natives causes the latter to reduce their birth rates.

Even this question regarding the effect of a large amount of immigration upon the speed of industrialization and urbanization cannot be answered definitely. However, it seems likely that the presence of large numbers of unorganized and poorly paid but industrious immigrants did somewhat hasten the industrialization and the urbanization of our population. Even while there was still a frontier with good land and while many immigrants were still going directly to this land, our Eastern cities and states and the industrial cities of the Great Lakes were retaining large numbers of these immigrants and employing them in construction work, in mines, in mills and factories. The existence of this abundant supply of cheap and willing labor probably did hasten our industrial development. It made capital accumulation easier by making investment in industry and trade more profitable than it would have been if only higher-priced native labor had been available. It also gave impetus to social mobility, to the effort of parents to prepare their children for better jobs than their fathers had and than those the immigrants were so willing to take. Naturally it was the natives who were in the best position to foresee and to take advantage of the rapidly expanding openings in business, in commerce, and in the professions which meant upgrading the family in the social scale and at the expense of a lower rate of reproduction. Hence, although the causal relation between more rapid industrialization and a large volume of immigration cannot be stated with any degree of precision, it seems to the authors quite probable that the coming of large numbers of immigrants had a substantial influence in intensifying the social mobility of the native population. It increased the rapidity with which the natives were able to secure better-paid urban jobs, and the people moving up into such jobs were among the first to adopt the voluntary limitation of the size of their families. Although it is probable that the immigrants and their children did not constitute a net gain in numbers at any given date over what we would have had if the amount of immigration had been substantially less, it certainly cannot be proved that we should have had just as many people in this country today as we now have if there had been no immigration after the adoption of the Constitution.[14] We were certain to develop cities and industry and the new modes of living they induced. The birth rate would almost certainly have fallen in our cities much as it did in European cities, but the rate of decline in the birth rate of our native population might very well have been somewhat slower than it actually was.

The effects of emigration upon the population growth in the sending country have also attracted much attention. Malthus's views regarding the effects of migration are well worthy of our attention at this point. Over and over he cited the growth of population in the United States as showing how rapidly population would grow from a small amount of immigration when the necessities of life were relatively easy to obtain. He had not the least doubt that a comparatively few tens of thousands of immigrants into an area where they could readily provide themselves with the necessities of life and where war took comparatively few lives would multiply at a very rapid rate—doubling their numbers in about 25 years. Regarding the effect of emigration on population growth in the sending country the following quotations are of interest:

> The population of the United States of America, according to the fourth census, in 1820, was 7,861,710. We have no reason to believe that Great Britain is less populous at present for the emigration of the small parent stock which produced these numbers. On the contrary, a certain degree of emigration is known to be favorable to the population of the mother country. It has been particularly remarked that the two Spanish provinces from which the greatest number of people emigrated to America became in consequence more populous.[15]

> It is clear, therefore, that with any view of making room for an unrestricted increase of population, emigration is perfectly inadequate; but as a partial and temporary expedient, and with a view to the more general cultivation of the earth, it seems to be both useful and proper. . . . There are no fears so totally ill-grounded as the fears of depopulation from emigration. The vis inertiae of the great body of the people, and their attachment to their homes, are qualities so strong and general that we may rest assured they will not emigrate unless, from political discontent or extreme poverty, they are in such a state as will make it as much for the advantage of their country as of themselves that they should go out of it.[16]

Although it must be recognized that no precise statement can be made regarding the effect of emigration on the growth of population in the sending country, it will be of some interest to examine briefly the case of Ireland, which is quite

[14] Warren S. Thompson and P. K. Whelpton, *Population Trends in the United States*, McGraw-Hill Book Company, New York, 1933, pp. 304–311.
[15] Thomas Robert Malthus, *An Essay on Population*, vol. 1, J. M. Dent & Sons, Ltd., London, E. P. Dutton & Co., Inc., New York, n.d., p. 306. This same statement, using 1800 census figures instead of those for 1820, occurs on p. 56 in the first American edition of the Essay, printed from the third London edition in 1809.
[16] *Ibid.*, vol. 2, p. 36.

widely believed to be a good example of a poor country whose rate of growth was much reduced by emigration and whose population pressure was much relieved thereby.

It was quite generally recognized by those who had occasion to familiarize themselves with Irish living conditions in the early nineteenth century that Ireland was a poverty-stricken country on the verge of famine. Many of the Irish people even then knew about the possibility of migrating to the United States. As early as 1820 they had begun to emigrate to the United States in appreciable numbers (4,000 in the years 1819 and 1820). In 1821, the population was approximately 6.8 million. During the next two decades (1821–1841) almost 260,000, or a little less than 4 percent of its 1821 population, emigrated to the United States. If we assume that one-half (390,500) of the Irish migrants to the United States in the decade 1841–1851 (781,000) left before severe famine struck in the fall of 1846, the total number of migrants to the United States in the period 1821–1846 was approximately 650,000; this is equal to 10 percent of the 1821 population. In spite of this very large number of migrants to the United States and also of a large migration to England, the population of Ireland rose from 6.8 million in 1821 to approximately 8.5 million in 1846, or by 25 percent, and the danger of famine was visibly increasing. Emigration, even on this scale, as a remedy for dire poverty had seriously failed. Famine struck in the autumn of 1846 because of the failure of the potato crop, and about 850,000 persons died between then and the last of March, 1851, from starvation and the diseases accompanying the famine, in addition to the normally expected deaths, and in spite of the emigration of approximately 970,000 persons during this same period (1846–1851).

Emigration from Ireland continued at a high rate, and almost 40 percent as many Irish came to the United States alone between 1851 and 1910 (2.87 million) as there were people in Ireland in 1851 (6.55 million).[17]

There can be little doubt that this very large (relatively) emigration both during and after the famine was an important factor in the decline of Ireland's population after 1846. By 1851, the population had fallen to 6.55 million and was then somewhat smaller than in 1821 (6.8 million). This decline continued, and it was only about 4.24 million in 1961, of which 2.8 million lived in Eire.

The improvement in economic conditions which began after the famine was no doubt hastened by the very large emigration during the 40 years after 1851 (over 2.4 million) but it should also be noted that although emigration fell off after 1890, it remained quite high until 1910. Before this latter date the birth rate had also begun to decline. At first the decline in the birth rate was probably due in a significant degree to the relative scarcity of marriageable men arising from large emigration. Gradually a substantial rise in the age of women at

[17] Most of these figures were taken from S. H. Couzens, "Regional Death Rates in Ireland during the Great Famine from 1846 to 1851," *Population Studies*, vol. XIV, no. 1, pp. 55–74.

marriage has taken place in Eire, which will account for a large part of the decline in the birth rate in the last several decades. It is generally believed that contraception is not widely practiced in Eire.[18]

The following data show clearly that the age of brides at marriage is substantially higher in Eire than in England and Wales.[19] Only 45.5 percent of the Eire brides were married at under 25 years of age as compared with 71.1 percent of those in England and Wales, while in Eire 41.6 percent of the brides were married at 25 to 34 years of age as compared with 17.2 percent of those in England and Wales.

Age at marriage	15–19	20–24	25–29	30–34
Percentage of brides of specified ages:				
England and Wales (1959)..........	22.7	48.4	12.1	5.1
Erie (1960).....................	7.2	38.3	28.2	13.4

If lasting relief from severe population pressure has come to Ireland in recent decades, as appears probable, it is more because the birth rate has declined substantially and economic productivity has improved quite rapidly than because of emigration, for emigration has also been declining rather rapidly while this improvement has been taking place. Moreover, it is reasonably certain that if Eire had continued to have a high rate of natural increase so that it continued to need large emigration it would have encountered increasing difficulties in finding areas to which to send these emigrants. It is also important to remember that in absolute numbers Ireland's population has always been small and that the number of emigrants sufficient to afford substantial relief was almost negligible as compared with the numbers needed to afford any relief to the poverty-stricken countries today (see following chapter).

There cannot be the least doubt that immigration lay at the base of rapid population growth in the Americas, Australia, and a few other areas, but it cannot be shown just how important additional immigration was numerically to any country or region once it had achieved a number of well-established settlements with several tens of thousands of people having a normal sex and age distribution. If the early settlers already possessed the techniques with which they could obtain a reasonably good living from their natural resources and also

---

[18] The data for emigrants from Ireland to the United States include both those from Eire and from Northern Ireland. See Taeuber and Taeuber, *The Changing Population of the United States*, chap. 3, passim.

[19] United Nations, *Demographic Yearbook, 1961*, table 28, pp. 692 and 694.

had a social organization that was relatively *dynamic* as opposed to *traditional*, and if natural resources were relatively abundant, there was good reason to expect a high rate of reproduction. How long this rate would continue in the descendants of the early settlers would depend largely on the speed with which social and cultural developments demanding a different mode of living took place. The faster the Industrial Revolution developed and the faster city populations grew, the faster the birth rate of the urban portion of the native population was likely to decline. The native population on farms in contrast to the growing city population maintained a high birth rate much longer. Moreover, their birth rate was much the same as that of the new immigrants, who to a large extent came from farms in the sending countries where birth rates were also relatively high. For both native farmers and peasant immigrants, traditional patterns of uncontrolled birth rates endured until they, too, were faced with the problems of making adjustments in modes of living which became highly incompatible with large families. Thus, as suggested above, the effect of immigration on population growth was quite likely to be different at different times because of changes in the social structure.

When the population of any country having considerable numbers of immigrants was highly homogeneous in its methods of making a living (agricultural) and land was easy to come by, later immigrants no doubt added as rapidly to the total population in relation to their numbers as had the original immigrants. However, when more and more of the natives descended from immigrants began to enter nonagricultural occupations and to move to the cities where they needed more education and specialized training, they began to marry later and to exercise some deliberate control over the size of their families, and the newer immigrants with large families began to contribute a larger number of children per thousand than the natives to the next generation. But it is our belief that this was only an incidental effect of immigration, that the decline in the native birth rate was due chiefly to the changing character of our social and economic organization, one aspect of which was a very rapid development of social mobility, i.e., of the upward movement from class to class.

In a word, the effect of migration on the growth of population both in the sending and receiving countries depends so much on a number of variables that it can be assessed in any particular case only in general terms of probability because we do not know the relative importance of the different variables in different situations. The same must be said about the effects of migration upon the distribution of population. We do know, however, that in some cases international migration has had profound effects on man's growth in numbers and on the distribution of these numbers between countries. It has also had much influence on the cultural development of vast masses of people. Whether it will continue to have similar effects no one can tell, but we venture the opinion that with the filling up of the earth and with more and more efficient means of communication, the actual movement of people from country to country, except as visitors, will become less important than it has been in the past three or four centuries.

CAN INTERNATIONAL MIGRATION EASE POPULATION PRESSURES TODAY?

This question has been much mooted in recent years and deserves much more extended consideration than is possible here. Perhaps about 65 to 70 percent of the people in the world today live in underdeveloped countries. In these countries the birth rates are high—averaging about 40 per 1,000 or higher—and in most of them death rates have already fallen substantially below what they were 15 to 20 years ago. As a consequence, most of these people are now increasing rapidly, from 1.5 to 3 percent per year, averaging in the neighborhood of 2 percent per year, a rate which will double their numbers in about 35 years. Of this approximate 2 billion of people living in underdeveloped countries, about 1,200 to 1,300 million live in Asian countries where population is already dense and where there is little new land that can be tilled without costly reclamation. This is about eight times the population of Europe in 1800 (not including the U.S.S.R.). This 1,200 million to 1,300 million does not include the populations of Burma, Indonesia, the Philippines, Thailand, and other countries of Southeast Asia—total population a little over 200 million—because these countries still have considerable amounts of unused but tillable lands. Indonesia is especially favored in this respect. It will be assumed that these peoples are not yet much interested in emigration, and it will also be assumed that the same holds for the peoples of Africa and Latin America at the present time.

The question in which we are most interested here may be phrased thus: Is it reasonable to expect that the population pressures[20] building up in these densely settled but underdeveloped lands can be substantially relieved by emigration? This is another of those questions regarding the effects of migration to which no very satisfactory answer can be given. However, several aspects of this question can be usefully explored a little further.

1. In the first place, it is obvious that the unsettled tillable lands in the world today bear an entirely different ratio to the population that might want to emigrate to them than was the case in 1800 when European migration to the New World was already well established. The combined population of the Americas in 1800 is estimated at about 25 million. They now have a population about 16 times as large—400 million or more. Africa had an estimated population of 90 million in 1800 and now has over 250 million. Most of the countries of

[20] For a fuller discussion of population pressure see Chap. 19.

East, South, and Southeast Asia now have far larger populations than in 1800, and the population of Oceania, though not yet large, has grown to many times its size in 1800. Clearly, in 1960 there are vastly more people needing outlets and far fewer outlets open to them than in 1800.

2. From 1800 to about 1914 there was little restraint on European emigration by either the sending or receiving countries. But when Asiatics began to enter any of the predominantly European settlements in significant numbers, barriers were soon raised. Today, restrictions on international migration are in effect in most countries. None of the countries of Southeast Asia, including Indonesia, want Chinese immigrants, and it is reasonably certain that if Indians and Pakistanis started to migrate into them in appreciable numbers, they also would be barred. The days of relatively free immigration into all countries are past. Moreover, practically all authoritarian states permit little if any emigration or immigration.

3. Under the strong political nationalism prevailing in the world at present, any substantial migration from the densely settled countries of Asia would almost certainly depend upon the prior conquest of new territory by the country desiring to send out emigrants. Indonesia, which of all Asian countries has the largest area of thinly settled lands, will oppose to the limit of its ability any immigration of Chinese, Japanese, or Indians. The political obstacles to substantial international migration probably cannot be changed in the next few decades except by conquest.

4. In order to give somewhat more precision to our thinking about the feasibility of international migration as a means of relieving population pressures today, we may well ask some specific questions: (a) How many Chinese, or Indians, or Japanese, or Pakistanis would need to migrate each year in order to ease the pressures on the necessities of life for the populations remaining in these countries? (b) How could the lands needed by these emigrants be acquired? (c) How could this migration be financed and managed?

Although none of these questions can be answered with assurance, attention may be directed to a few pertinent facts. If we accept the figure of 583 million given by the Communist census of 1953 as the population of Mainland China and if the rate of growth is 2 percent per year (the minimum figure claimed by China's leaders), by the middle of 1963 the population of Communist China would already have increased to about 710 million. If 10 million had emigrated each year since 1953 and if this had reduced the calculated 1963 figure for the mainland by the full amount of 100 million, it would still have left China a net gain of about 28 million in this 10-year period.

Moreover, the living conditions within Communist China are still so rigorous that any substantial improvement in the per capita consumption of the necessities of life would almost certainly have decreased the death rate at an even faster pace than has yet been attained. Hence the rate of natural increase might very well have risen from the minimum figure used by the leaders of China—2 percent per year—to 2.5 percent, for there is as yet no evidence of any significant decline in the birth rate. Such a rate (2.5 percent) is frequently used by the Communist leaders in recent years.

Assuming that improvements in living conditions resulted from this large emigration and that better health services raised the rate of natural increase to 2.5 percent annually during the last 5 years of the 10-year period 1953 to 1963, we can estimate that the total increase within the boundaries of Mainland China during these 10 years, assuming a net emigration of 100 million, would be about 45 million. Certainly this smaller average annual increase, about 4.5 million per year, as compared with an average annual increase of 12 to 13 million with no emigration, should be favorable to a somewhat faster improvement in living conditions. But, of course, what would actually take place depends upon simultaneous and complementary changes in so many other factors affecting production and its distribution that one cannot assert with any confidence that an improvement would take place. Nevertheless, it seems reasonable to assume that such a vast emigration from Mainland China might at least be of substantial assistance in getting a more efficient economy started and thereby making possible some slight improvement in the living conditions of the mass of the people, if the cost of supporting such an emigration did not seriously interfere with the accumulation of capital for development at home.

But we should not forget that the other densely settled countries in Asia mentioned above have a combined population almost as large as China and need any relief that might result from large-scale emigration just as badly as China. Elsewhere,[21] the senior author has discussed briefly some of the most outstanding problems, political, economic, and logistic, involved in the migration of 10 million people annually from all of these densely settled Asian countries as a group. He arrived at the conclusion from the political standpoint that "no country in South and East Asia can start large-scale emigration without acquiring actual political control of the area to be colonized, and such control can be achieved only by conquest."

In the second place, assuming that political control has been established over an area of sufficient size to make possible large-scale emigration for some years, we think it highly improbable that China (or any other country or group of underdeveloped countries) would have the economic means to undertake large-scale emigration at once. It is much more likely that it would take a decade or even two decades to establish a steady outflow large enough to assure the migration of even 3 or 4 million annually. Meanwhile, population would be accumulating at home about as at present, and the areas receiving such emigrants would be filling up at a surprising rate if the experience in European coloniza-

[21] Warren S. Thompson, *Population and Progress in the Far East*, The University of Chicago Press, Chicago, 1959, pp. 391–397.

tion during the eighteenth and nineteenth centuries is any guide as to what would happen in the Far East.

In the third place, the mere logistic problems involved in transferring 10 million persons any considerable distance overseas and supplying them with the necessities of life until they could become self-supporting are tremendous but probably would not be insuperable if the economic capacity of the home country were increasing at a very rapid rate—a far more rapid rate than any Western country ever achieved during its early decades of economic modernization.

By way of illustrating the magnitude of this logistics operation, we may give a few hypothetical figures. If this were an overseas operation, as it must be, and if each ship could carry 2,000 emigrants and their necessary household goods and agricultural equipment on each trip, and if this ship could make 12 round trips per year, it would require the services of about 425 ships making a total of over 5,000 round trips to do this job. This would mean the loading and unloading of approximately 14 ships every day of the year. In addition, vast quantities of materials would have to be transported each year for several years to establish temporary quarters for the arriving immigrants, to carry the machinery needed to build roads and prepare land for cultivation, and to build the villages needed by the new immigrants arriving daily—somewhat over 27,000 every day.

The organization required at each end of such an operation to carry it out successfully staggers the imagination both by its intricacy and its cost. Moreover, if only 10 million emigrants were moved annually from all of these densely settled Asian countries combined, this would constitute considerably less than one-half of their present annual increase. Quite aside from the practical impossibility of achieving such a large migration for a decade or two, the increase within these countries would thus still be such as to require a steady and very rapid economic development at home merely to keep up with population growth, to say nothing of making possible a modest improvement in food and other goods essential to decent living and in the services such as education and health. The broad conclusion regarding the effectiveness of migration in relieving the pressure of population in the more densely settled countries of Asia based on the best information now available can be summed up in the simple statement: *Emigration can do very little within the next three or four decades to relieve population pressure in these Asian countries, which now contain about 40 percent of the population of the world and over 60 percent of the population in all the underdeveloped countries.*

SUGGESTIONS FOR SUPPLEMENTARY READING

Cook, Robert C. (ed.): "World Migration, 1946–1955," *Population Bulletin*, vol. 13, no. 5, August, 1957, pp. 77–95. (The third in a series of three, summarizing demographic change in the postwar decade.)

Duke University School of Law: "Immigration" (a series of articles), *Law and Contemporary Problems*, vol. 21, no. 2, pp. 212–426, 1956.

George Washington University: *A Report on World Population Migrations as Related to the U.S. of America*, Washington, D.C., 1956. An exploratory survey of past studies and researches on world-population migration, with the view to evaluating areas already covered and outlining areas which warrant development.

Hutchinson, E. F.: *Immigrants and Their Children*, John Wiley & Sons, Inc., New York, 1956.

Kirk, Dudley, and Earl Huyck: "Overseas Migration from Europe since World War II," *American Sociological Review*, vol. 19, no. 4, pp. 447–456, 1954.

Kulischer, Eugene M.: "Displaced Persons in the Modern World," *Annals of the American Academy of Political and Social Science*, vol. 262, pp. 166–177, March, 1949.

Lee, Everett S., et al.: *Population Redistribution and Economic Growth, United States, 1870–1950, I, Methodological Considerations and Reference Tables*, American Philosophical Societies, Philadelphia, 1957; Simon Kuznets et al., *II, Analyses of Economic Change*, 1960.

McKelvey, V. E.: "Resources, Population Growth, and Levels of Living," *Science*, vol. 129, no. 3,353, pp. 875–881, April 3, 1959. (A society's wealth depends on the use it makes of raw materials, energy, and especially ingenuity.)

Milbank Memorial Fund: "Selected Studies of Migration since World War II," *Proceedings of the 34th annual conference of the Milbank Memorial Fund*, New York, 1958.

Rubin, Ernest: "Immigration and the Economic Growth of the United States: 1790–1914," *R.E.M.P. Bulletin* (The Hague), vol. 7, October–December, 1959, pp. 87–95.

Ta Chen: *Population in Modern China*, The University of Chicago Press, Chicago, 1946.

Taeuber, Irene B.: "Hong Kong: Migrants and Metropolis," *Population Index*, vol. 29, no. 1, pp. 3–25, 1963.

United Nations: *Economic Characteristics of International Migrations: Statistics for Selected Countries, 1918–1954*, Population Studies, no. 12 ST/SOA, ser. A/no. 12, New York, 1949.

Vernant, Jacques; *The Refugee in the Postwar World*, George Allen & Unwin, Ltd., London, 1953. (Results from a request of U.S. High Commission.)

CHAPTER NINETEEN

Population Pressure
and Its
Political Implications

The term "population pressure" has been used several times in preceding chapters. Before undertaking the discussion of the political implications of population pressure, we should define the term more carefully as it is used here.

WHAT IS POPULATION PRESSURE?

In very general terms, population pressure may be thought of as the difficulties people encounter in trying to make a living. Throughout most of man's experience, as we have seen, these difficulties have been so great that comparatively few of the persons born have been able to live long enough to reproduce, and only a few have exceeded the "ripe old age" of 45 or 50 years. In general, these difficulties in making a living arise from two factors: (1) the nature of the particular environment, such as deserts, high altitudes, high latitudes, the abundance or scarcity of natural resources, and finally, but now becoming increasingly important, the limited quantities of natural resources; and (2) the state of development of man's technology by means of which he can utilize natural resources. The forms of social organization man has developed should be included in this second category because they in large measure determine his technological achievements and the use he makes of them. For example, India possesses by far the largest number of cattle of any country in the world, but because of the distinctive social organization of Indian society, these cattle contribute far less to India's food supply and to her animal power than they would in a society where the people ate meat and had less reluctance to control the breeding of better cattle. We do not need to proceed further with this general statement of the nature of population pressure. We are concerned here chiefly with its political implications in the world today.

For our purposes it will be well to distinguish two types of population pressure

—*absolute* and *relative*—and to discuss how they are related to the political development of the world in which we live.

Absolute population pressure can best be described as the actual need of physical goods—chiefly food and shelter—to ensure survival and, at present, also a few of the amenities or comforts of life. Such population pressure can be measured by the per capita amounts of the necessities of life consumed; the lower this amount, the greater the absolute pressure. Since food is essential to life, a very low intake of food both from the standpoint of calories consumed and of the adequacy of its other nutritional elements can be considered a fairly satisfactory measure of absolute population pressure. Although it is quite possible that in earlier times the dire need of more food by the great majority of the population was an important factor in instigating and perpetuating tribal conflicts which often endured for generations, the authors doubt that absolute pressure has been of much significance in leading to dangerous political tensions between nations during the past two or three centuries. In the modern world severe absolute pressure has been so generally accompanied by the lack of the material means for carrying on an aggressive war and by such feeble national political organization for concerted action that these nations have not dared to undertake the conquest of neighbors, although these neighbors were also militarily weak. China, for more than a century before the Communists gained control, is a good example of a nation with great absolute population pressure among the masses while the country was too weak politically and militarily to be dangerously aggressive. However, the military weakness of a country which has a very high absolute pressure of population has not infrequently encouraged other peoples with much lower absolute pressures but with strong military power to seek political and/or economic control over these weaker peoples; we may illustrate by noting Japan's gains from China and Britain's occupation of India. The wars so engendered during the past two or three centuries have not been "big" wars and have probably had little influence on population growth as compared with the destruction of life wrought by hunger and disease. In general, the wars through which the European and Japanese colonial systems were established were "small" wars and in all probability were favorable to population growth in such areas to the extent that they maintained better internal order in these colonies than had prevailed previously.

In contrast to absolute population pressure, the relative pressure of population will be defined as the degree of deprivation *felt* by a people as it comes to know of the meagerness of its manner of living as compared with that enjoyed by other peoples or by other classes in the same country. Today, this is a factor of much greater significance as a cause of increasing political tensions between nations than is absolute pressure. Once the people of any country begin to know of these differences and also begin to make some progress toward better living through a more efficient economy, the *feeling of pressure or deprivation* is almost certain to be intensified. This is the case not only, and perhaps not chiefly, because some achievement in better living begets increased desire for the further easing of life's hardships, but rather because this feeling of deprivation can rather easily be encouraged and directed into channels of aggressive action by shrewd and unscrupulous leaders.

The importance of *feeling* is shown clearly in the means used by Mussolini, Hitler, and the expansionist leaders of Japan to gain the support of their peoples when they decided to expand the political and economic power of their empires. These leaders found it comparatively easy to convince their peoples that they needed more land and larger industrial resources, more "lebensraum." Without the exploitation by ambitious leaders of this trumped-up feeling of deprivation, it is highly doubtful whether any of these peoples would have felt their deprivations strongly enough to demand that their governments adopt the aggressive measures actually employed in the enlargement of their territories. But the strong nationalistic feelings abroad today, the spreading knowledge of the differences in the natural resources available to different peoples, and the very real difficulties a number of countries are encountering in providing even subsistence for their rapidly expanding populations furnish a fertile soil in which to plant the seeds of aggression. This is doubly true when the ideologies and the ambitions of the political leaders also drive them to do everything in their power to enhance the feeling of deprivation.

The distinction between absolute and relative population pressure has been dwelt upon at some length because the writers believe that even if there should be a moderate but fairly steady relaxation of the rigor of absolute population pressures in the countries where this type of pressure has been and still is greatest, there is almost certain to be an intensification of the feeling of population pressure, which will tend to increase international tensions for some years to come.

POPULATION PRESSURE IN UNDERDEVELOPED COUNTRIES

Many of the largest of the underdeveloped countries were, before World War II, colonies or semicolonies like China, over which foreign powers exercised varying measures of political and economic control. The leaders of their independence movements and/or of their revolutionary activities never ceased to remind the people of their hardships and to attribute these hardships largely to the rapacity of their colonial masters and/or to the restrictions, both political and economic, imposed upon them by treaties made at gun's point even when they were not colonies in the political sense. Increasing numbers of people in all these poverty-stricken and dependent countries came to feel that breaking the control of their foreign masters would almost immediately lead to substantial improvements in their living conditions. Most of these leaders were, without doubt, entirely honest in their conviction that such improvements in living conditions would be greatly hastened by the acquirement of independence, and they may have been right, but they certainly were largely instrumental in creating expectations of improvement among their followers far beyond any reasonable hope of attainment in the near future. In addition, the Communist revolutionary leaders were ready to make almost unlimited promises of economic improvement in the course of a few years if communism were adopted as the national policy in these underdeveloped areas.

All the peoples who have a high degree of absolute population pressure are now struggling with extremely difficult and complex problems of economic development which the mass of their populations did not even dream would confront them after independence was gained or a revolution had been effected. Moreover, practically all of these leaders, especially if they were Communists, probably had no realization that their own country would almost immediately face new and extremely complex problems arising out of a far more rapid increase in its population than had ever occurred in the past. Nehru in India was probably the only important exception; he was aware that the rapid growth of population would create serious economic difficulties, and even he underestimated their seriousness. (See Chapter 21 for a discussion of India's population policy.) It should be noted here, in passing, that orthodox Marxist doctrine denies that economic hardship can ever exist in a Communist state, except as a temporary hangover from capitalist exploitation of the workers. In spite of this orthodox Communist doctrine, the Chinese Communists from 1954 to 1958 undertook to reduce the birth rate quickly by intensive propaganda urging contraceptive practices, not because China was *overpopulated* but because the population was growing too fast, a distinction without a difference to anyone but an orthodox Marxist. This campaign was accompanied by the usual claims that previous capitalistic abuses were responsible for the fact that population was, for the moment, growing faster than the economy could be expanded. But apparently, misled by their own claims that the "great leap forward," which became the magic phrase late in 1957 and in 1958, was resulting in a marvelous economic advance, this campaign for smaller families was completely abandoned for several years and has only recently (1962) been resumed. (For further discussion of China's population policies see Chapter 21.)

So far as can be judged from any information now available, there is very little, if any, relaxation of absolute population pressure in China, although it appears that a somewhat better distribution of the necessities of life may have mitigated somewhat the suffering caused by local food shortages. Severe absolute pressure also prevails in most of the other underdeveloped countries. In a few of them, however, considerable amounts of good tillable land are still available for settlement. In these countries it should be easier to effect substantial improvements in living conditions than in the more densely populated countries like China and India and Pakistan, and in a number of smaller countries having little unused land.

Although the authors are fully convinced that the increase in the feeling of population pressure in many countries is an important factor in intensifying international tensions and that the rapid growth of population in many underdeveloped countries will continue to act in this manner for several decades, they do not believe that this is the only or even the most important factor in many situations where these tensions are becoming acute; they do believe, however, that the more rapid growth of population among some of the peoples living in the underdeveloped countries is certain to become of increasing international importance.[1] This feeling of population pressure will rise not only because of the more rapid increase of population in the less-developed countries but also because economic changes such as those which took place in Japan after about 1880 are certain to increase their need for resources of many kinds. These economic and social changes are also leading to the establishment of more effective governments, thus increasing their ability to mobilize their national resources for military purposes if they so desire. Witness the large military forces now maintained by Communist China and the necessity India is under to enlarge and strengthen her military forces to meet the threat of the Chinese army nibbling at her northern borders. This nibbling process consists of taking possession of relatively small parcels of land chiefly in areas where boundaries are in dispute and in repeating this process as often as it seems unlikely to provoke serious retaliatory measures.

Today, there is no longer any need to discuss "colonialism" (in its pre-World War II form) as a factor in the increase of the feeling of population pressure among the peoples living in underdeveloped countries. Such colonialism no longer plays a significant part in preventing the access of growing peoples to their own resources. However, as has been shown in discussing the population explosion (Chapter 16), in most underdeveloped countries there is now a more urgent and more widely felt need for more food, for more and better manufactured goods, and for many more types of services than has ever existed in the past. In addition, better food, new goods, and services which were recently regarded as luxuries or semiluxuries are rapidly coming to be regarded as necessities by an increasing proportion of the people. At the same time, the strong nationalistic feelings which played such a decisive role in overthrowing colonialism keep on growing. Most of these new states (nations), even those that have relatively large

[1] Warren S. Thompson, *Danger Spots in World Population*, Alfred A. Knopf, Inc., New York, 1929, pp. 10–17; *idem*, "Recent Trends in World Population," *American Journal of Sociology*, vol. 34, no. 6, pp. 959–975, 1929; *idem*, *Population and Progress in the Far East*, The University of Chicago Press, Chicago, 1959.

areas of tillable land still unused, are more adamant in refusing to accept immigrants from densely settled Asian countries than the European colonial powers ever were. They are also more opposed to the establishment of industrial and commercial enterprises by capitalists from other countries than were the prewar colonial powers because they fear that such enterprises will be used as an entering wedge to reestablish the economic control of the colonial powers from which they have just been freed.

The consequences of these attitudes, from the standpoint of the alleviation of the population pressures now building up so rapidly in many of the underdeveloped countries, are probably even more threatening to the maintenance of peace than those arising from the policies followed by European and Japanese colonialism of the past. These underdeveloped countries, for the reasons already mentioned, feel that they must depend more largely on their own *natural, capital*, and *personnel resources* for their economic development than they did when they were colonies. In making this statement we do not overlook the aid given these countries from outside; but the fact is that governmental aid from the outside can never be expected to supply more than a small fraction of those goods and services and amounts of capital that are indispensable if even a modestly rapid economic growth is to be achieved in the near future. It is now clear that economic growth must be far more rapid than ever in the past if it is to march apace with the increasing rate of population growth in most of these countries. *An even faster rate of economic growth would be necessary to raise the level of living substantially.*

In Chapter 18 (pp. 496–499) we pointed out that emigration can probably afford no significant amount of relief to the increasing population pressures in those countries which, like China, India, and Pakistan, now have large and dense populations and also have comparatively small amounts of good tillable land that is at present unused. Since this is true, we should comment briefly on other possible sources of relieving the population pressures of these countries, viz., international trade and industrialization. This discussion will assume that a more rapid growth in the populations of most of the underdeveloped countries than before World War II is now, and will continue to be for some time, a very important factor in increasing *felt population pressure* in these countries.

TRADE AND INDUSTRY AND POPULATION PRESSURE

Great Britain has for a long time derived a highly significant share of its income from international trade; since World War I, Japan has also become increasingly dependent on such trade. The trade consisted to a considerable extent in the exchange of manufactured goods and certain services for the raw materials and the food stuffs of other countries, including, of course, their colonial possessions. This arrangement worked very well for the rather long period during which Great Britain, by reason of her early start in the use of power (steam) to operate increasingly complex and efficient machines, had a near-monopoly of world trade in manufactured goods. But in the late nineteenth and early twentieth centuries, Germany and Japan began to compete with Britain in the export of more and more types of manufactured goods.

World War I showed clearly that a high degree of dependence on such trade as had developed in Great Britain placed any country in a very precarious position in time of war even when it possessed great naval power. (See the discussion of national rural-urban balance in Chapter 6.) In turn, Japan found that her increasing dependence on foreign trade rendered her economy more and more vulnerable to fluctuations in the economic conditions of the world at large, e.g., on the measures being taken by other countries to maintain and/or to increase their foreign trade by imposing restrictions of many kinds on imports not only into the metropolitan centers but also into the colonial areas controlled from these centers. The precariousness of Japan's foreign trade and, as a consequence, the fluctuations in her industrial activity were undoubtedly important factors in the decision of her leaders during the 1930s to undertake the expansion of her empire. They were greatly impressed by the economic benefits which they believed Great Britain derived from her colonial possessions, whose foreign trade she largely controlled.

There cannot be the least doubt that industry and trade have been very important factors in achieving a higher level of living in most parts of the area of European settlement than in most other parts of the world and in Japan than in other Eastern countries. At the same time it has also become clear that a high degree of dependence on such economic activities without commensurate national production of food and fiber sooner or later renders this higher level of living precarious and leads to serious political tensions between nations.

We might note here in general terms a few of the difficulties arising from a high degree of dependence on industry and foreign trade as bases for the support of growing populations, before we consider these sectors of economic development as means of alleviating population pressures in the more densely peopled and little-developed (economically) countries.

The competition for foreign markets for manufactured products is now so keen that even Britain and Japan are finding it increasingly difficult to maintain a volume of trade sufficient to pay for the raw materials they need to import if they are to keep their people employed at what they consider acceptable wages. Moreover, even though the first aim of industrialization in most underdeveloped countries is to supply their own needs for manufactured goods that have heretofore been imported, some of them are already beginning to compete with European, Japanese, and American exporters in certain fields. They are desperately in need of the foreign exchange they hope to secure from such trade. It is urgently needed for many purposes, e.g., to buy the tools and machinery and the construction materials they cannot yet produce but must have in order to undertake new industrial enterprises; also to hire the experienced foreign personnel that is absolutely essential to construct and operate many types of modern enterprises, until such time as they can develop their own training and research facilities and can train their own technicians. The leaders of these underdeveloped countries are now coming to realize that foreign trade cannot be created in a few years.

The process of establishing new industrial enterprises and likewise of creating and staffing commercial and financial organizations adequate to get economic growth soundly started takes considerable time. Many of the underdeveloped countries did not seem to realize this and have tried to force industrialization and foreign trade in manufactured goods at an impossible pace, and many, if not all, have been disappointed in obtaining quickly a sufficiency of industrial products for home consumption and for foreign trade which would contribute significantly to the improvement of their living conditions. Moreover, very few of them had taken into account the strong probability that even the very modest health services they had introduced would lead to a rapid increase in population.

What has just been said is not meant to imply that there will be no increase in the ability of underdeveloped countries to supply their own needs for many types of manufactured goods, nor that the volume of their foreign trade will not increase; but it does mean that when their populations are increasing very rapidly, the volume of capital that can be accumulated and the ability to train personnel competent to manage an increasingly complex economy are seriously retarded, perhaps even critically so. Experience is showing that in spite of all political and economic barriers erected by many well-developed countries both to protect home industries and to retain foreign trade, such trade is subject to large and rapid fluctuations both as to volume and as to types of goods. Because of this, it is increasingly necessary that the countries expecting to increase their foreign trade rapidly be so organized economically, financially, and commercially that they can make very rapid and often highly significant shifts in the types of products they offer for sale, in the terms on which they will finance their exports, and in their political policies affecting trade. Most underdeveloped countries will hardly be able to develop these characteristics in a short time. As a consequence, it does not seem likely that foreign trade in manufactured goods will, in the near future, bring any large amount of foreign exchange in addition to that which they are already acquiring through the export of their raw materials and food specialties. Neither emigration (see pp. 496–499, preceding chapter) nor foreign trade in manufactured goods can, in all probability, offer much hope for the relief of population pressure in the underdeveloped countries during the next two or three decades. This is especially to be expected in the densely settled countries in which population is also growing rapidly.

The authors wish to make it clear that they do not mean that no substantial development of industry will take place in underdeveloped countries in the next few decades; but they do believe this development will be relatively slow even with the utmost foreign aid that can be provided. They believe that some other types of development appear likely to be of more immediate benefit in relieving the growing population pressures in these countries. These should be explored briefly.

AGRICULTURAL DEVELOPMENT AND POPULATION PRESSURE

The most urgent need of economic development for all underdeveloped countries is the improvement of their agriculture. At present all but a relatively small proportion of the people in these countries are living very close to a mere subsistence level chiefly because agriculture is far and away the most important of their productive activities and at the same time is very inefficiently managed. Three-quarters or more of all the people in most of these countries are directly dependent on agriculture (chiefly the production of food and fibers), and they produce so little beyond their own necessities that there is comparatively little left over to be used as capital for the improvement of agriculture or as wages and capital for the development of nonagricultural industries and services. *It does not seem to be widely realized that improved agricultural practice is so fundamental to the development of a more efficient economy that if it lags the whole economy lags.* Moreover, it *must not, even for a moment, be forgotten* that the underdeveloped countries of today have a great burden to carry in their rapidly increasing populations which the Western and Central European countries did not have when they began to industrialize. These countries did not have this burden in 1800 because almost no one even dreamed of reducing the death rate rapidly. Indeed, only an occasional utopian had the vision of attaining a reasonably comfortable level of living for the masses of the people. In the authors' opinion, the improvement of agriculture has been much neglected by the leaders both in the underdeveloped countries and in the foreign-aid programs operating them. We shall therefore devote some space to the discussion of agriculture as a necessity for the easing of the population pressures accumulating in many of the underdeveloped countries by reason of their rapid population growth in advance of a revolution in their agricultural practices.

Many discussions of economic development in underdeveloped countries leave one with the impression that the dynamic factors inducing greater national productivity are to be found primarily, if not exclusively, in the development of manufacturing, transportation, and trade. A study of national plans for economic development will show that many of the native planners treat the agriculture of their countries as a poor stepchild of industry and commerce, and hence as deserving of comparatively little investment or effort to improve it. The fact is that agriculture is of such overwhelming importance in these countries that if it is neglected and expands slowly the entire economy will be sluggish and will progress slowly if at all. Moreover, since by far the greater part of the funds for economic development in any country must always come from internal taxation, if agriculture is not able to provide some taxable surplus (above subsistence), there is likely to be an extremely slow accumulation of capital for all other purposes as well. Foreign aid, either as outright grants or as loans, can supply only a small proportion of the capital needed for even slow economic development.

There can be little doubt that the level of living of China's and India's populations is not improving much, if any. The fact that their populations are growing at rates of about 2 percent per year and that these rates seem likely to increase in the near future, even though the present low level of per capita consumption is not improved, is one very important factor in this situation. The good tillable land in these countries is already in use, and the expensive reclamation works which have been completed and which are said to have added some millions of acres of new irrigated land in both countries either are not yet in production or are yielding far less than was expected.

Furthermore, although it is true that the years 1958 to 1961 were *disaster years* in China, this country has always in some areas known frequent years when crops were short and hunger and even starvation were present. As far as is now known, no provision has yet been made to store food against such recurring contingencies; probably there has been little or no surplus even in the "better years." It would appear probable that the claims of great agricultural improvement made year after year by Chinese leaders, claims which were often quite fantastic, have in many cases been deliberately falsified. Their great gains in agricultural production must be regarded as fantasy rather than fact.

Everywhere in the world crop yields in any given year are dependent on the weather. In monsoon areas such as China and India, the variations in rainfall from year to year over the better agricultural lands are considerably larger than in our Mississippi Valley. Consequently, larger annual variations in crop yields are to be expected in these climates. Likewise, the well-known subregional variations in rainfall within any large region like the valleys of the Yangtze, the Ganges, or the Mississippi are wide and are the chief determinants of the regular differentials in crop yields expected in the subregions of these great valleys. These subregional differences in rainfall also determine in large measure the varieties of crops that can be depended upon.

No scientific formula will transform poor land into good land without long-continued and careful management. Improved practices based on scientific knowledge will, however, produce higher average annual yields in most of the underdeveloped countries. Poor and ignorant farmers cannot get the most out of either good or poor land; nor can most poor and ignorant farmers of 30 years of age or over be made into good farmers in a few years. This is our central theme here. Expressed in different terms, a poor and ignorant farmer will also generally be a traditional farmer, who gets much less return for his labor than a knowledgeable farmer who also has some capital to finance improvements. Tradition always has been and no doubt will continue to be for perhaps a generation (25 years) the chief obstacle to change when farmers are too ignorant to understand why the change in question is desirable. If they are to learn acceptance of improved agricultural practices, the mass of the farmers in the underdeveloped countries must be educated, i.e., given the information that will enable them to understand how the agricultural changes being advocated will benefit them and their families. *Better farming, i.e., larger returns for a given amount of labor on a specified land area, depends in large measure upon the education of the farmers.* The training and the personality of the village workers being sent out to agricultural villages are also of great importance. These workers must be able to understand the social values of the farmers with whom they are working. Some actual examples may help to make this point clear.

The village workers, to be successful, must know why farmer X refuses to plant, or discontinues the planting of, a particular variety of rice or wheat or potato that gives a higher yield than the one he is now using. He may have a number of reasons, and the village worker must know the real explanation of the farmer's reluctance if he is to be of real service. For example, the farmer's wife may find that the new variety of wheat is too hard to grind properly with the household utensils she now has and hence makes inferior bread or perhaps a bread that is of different texture because the meal from which it is baked is coarser. She may never think about finding some way to grind the wheat finer. The farmer may object to the taste of the new variety of rice and therefore refuse to plant it again; or he may fear that his neighbors will downgrade him as a farmer if he buys seed instead of using his own, because the neighbors do not understand the problems involved in producing better seeds, especially hybrid seeds; or he may refuse to adopt a new method of planting and cultivating rice just because it has never been done in his community; or he may so distrust all strangers that he has no confidence in anything they tell him, and he may continue to feel this way because he cannot read about the experiments with these crops and cannot understand the semitechnical explanations of the village workers.

Many other *reasons* why the farmers refuse to change their practices or take a long time to do so which appear *unreasonable* to you and me are entirely satisfactory to the tradition-minded farmer. At times the experts may make quite impracticable suggestions which leave the farmers suspicious of their advice, and occasionally they make really serious mistakes which tend to discredit all advisers. One type of serious mistake made in a number of countries may be cited. Naturally most lands that are irrigated are arid or semiarid. Because of inadequate soil surveys on some irrigation projects, the surveyors have not known until too late that the soil is so impregnated with alkali salts that after a few years of cropping the alkali rises to the surface because of the high rate of surface evaporation and kills off all useful vegetation; in some other irrigated areas the land lying below the larger canals becomes waterlogged by seepage from these high-level canals, and the drainage needed to make this waterlogged land again usable may be more costly than the original irrigation works. To be more specific, India and Pakistan are both losing the use of many thousands of acres of irrigated land each year because of such difficulties. The farmers are aware of these errors and often become suspicious of "expert" advice.

The authors are convinced that China and India and quite possibly all other underdeveloped countries can much improve the yields of their staple food and fiber crops on the land already in use. Much has been learned in the past several decades regarding the proper fertilization of crops to increase yields. Increased yields may also be expected from the use of new varieties of the staple crops that have been developed by scientific plant breeding. Increasing yields of animal products of all kinds through animal breeding and the more scientific feeding of animals are also entirely feasible. It is abundantly clear that improved methods of planting and caring for crops will likewise lead to higher yields. No one will doubt that in time all this knowledge will be put to good use in the underdeveloped countries, nor that the harvests per unit of labor and of land will rise as will also the quality of the food products from the standpoint of their nutritional value. All this is possible, but here we should distinguish carefully between the *possible* and *probable* improvements in agriculture in the near future in these underdeveloped countries. We must also give thought to the *timing* of these improvements.

The really important question is not: Can these improvements in agricultural production be achieved in the underdeveloped countries? but, How long will it take the Chinese, or the Indian, or the Filipino, or the Ecuadorian farmer to change over from his long-established, traditional type of agriculture to this new scientific type? Can this changeover to a scientific agriculture be speeded up to attain a rate of increase equal to, or higher than, the rate of population growth now prevailing and likely to prevail in most of these countries during the next few decades? The essence of the immediate problem arising out of the present rate of population growth is *how long* it will take to improve the agriculture of a particular country by 20 percent or 25 percent or 30 percent, not whether such an improvement is possible in some indefinite future.

Furthermore, as has been shown at several points in our discussion of recent population growth in the world, there is a strong probability that in many of these underdeveloped countries the rate of population growth will increase for some time yet even though there should be no increase in the per capita supply of the necessities of life. On the other hand, if the per capita supply of necessities should decrease in any appreciable degree, the death rate will almost certainly increase in most of them in spite of better health services.

This changeover to scientific agriculture is by no means a simple matter which can be accomplished by telling tradition-minded farmers that a new variety of rice or wheat or maize will yield one-tenth more per acre than the variety they have been using, and that an additional 10 percent can be expected if a small amount of fertilizer is used, and that still another 10 percent or more is to be obtained if the crop is planted in a different way and is cared for in a specified manner. Practically everything the farmer is told he must do to obtain larger yields involves a departure from the practices that have been used by his forebears for generations. For a variety of reasons the tradition-minded farmer can scarcely be censured for not immediately adopting these new ideas. At the risk of some repetition, we shall summarize here a few of the more important reasons for his reluctance to try out new crops and new methods of planting and cultivation.

1. For time out of mind, all agents of the government or the landlord or those coming from the temple or from any other institution looking for financial support from the public have come to the farmer when they wanted money or produce or labor from him, e.g., to collect taxes, to require personal service, or to squeeze a little more out of him by all manner of sharp practices and by playing on his fear of the authorities. Is it any wonder that the government agents who come professing to be interested only in the farmers' welfare are often, if not generally, regarded with suspicion? It will take time to overcome this traditional suspicion of authority and of strangers.

2. Very many of the new agricultural practices the farmer is asked to adopt require some expenditure on his part for seed or fertilizer, for new implements or new irrigation facilities, or to buy thoroughbred cattle. Though this may be only a token payment, many of the farmers cannot afford even a small sum. In most of these countries the governments cannot afford to give these goods freely because they are too poor to do so, and besides, if something is given freely the farmer is likely to regard it as useless or as involving him in some new obligation; otherwise it would not be free.

3. Even when a farmer has visited a local demonstration farm and has seen the better crop produced by a new variety of seed and the addition of fertilizer and can afford to pay for these goods, he may yet be unwilling to change his ways because his neighbors will say that Mr. X is not as good a farmer as they thought he was or he would not need to *buy* his seed and *buy* magic dust (fertilizer) to put on his land to make his crops grow better. Besides, this dust will probably only poison his soil; or the new crop may require a change in work habits, e.g., weeding winter wheat by hand during the winter months. This is regarded as

unnecessary because it has never been done in this community, and besides, "it will probably do no good."

4. All too frequently the young men and women sent into the farm villages to help the people improve both their agriculture and the sanitation of the village and the household have never before come in close contact with life in a farm village and know almost as little about it as does the foreign agricultural expert. They are city boys and girls who have had opportunity to acquire the equivalent of a high school education. At least this much education is necessary if they are to profit from the special training for village workers who are expected to live in the villages and teach the farmers and their wives how to grow better crops and clean up the villages. But since so many of these workers are accustomed to better standards of living and do not know village life, it is not surprising that many of them make unforgivable mistakes by adopting a condescending attitude toward the ignorant villagers and by refusing to live in the villages with the people they are expected to win over to the use of more efficient agricultural methods and to more sanitary household practices.

5. In most underdeveloped countries very few of the village people over 15 or 20 years of age can read. They must get all their information by the spoken word or by visual demonstration. Hence the problem of communicating adequately with the villagers depends quite largely on the personality of the worker who has been sent to help them. It is very difficult to tell in advance whether the personality of the would-be village worker is such as to make reasonably certain that he or she will be able to communicate readily with the farmers and their wives. Besides, the many local dialects in a number of the underdeveloped countries greatly increase the difficulties of communication; not infrequently they cannot yet be fully surmounted.

6. In very general terms, the farming population in practically all underdeveloped countries possesses a culture which has long since become strongly traditional as regards the kind of crops raised, their care, and their desirability for food. Breaking away from these traditional patterns of thought regarding proper agricultural practices and the most desirable types of food is quite generally condemned by the more influential elders. These elders are influential not only because of their age, which makes them the repositories of village traditions, but also because they are generally "well-to-do" according to village standards.

In contrast to the slowness in the adoption of new agricultural practices which generally require the disregard of tradition, many health-improving services do not require people to adopt new practices or even to participate actively in sanitary reforms in order to profit from them. For example, malaria may be almost wiped out in a group of villages in a few weeks by spraying the breeding places of the mosquitoes that carry the malaria bacteria. In most villages even inoculations, both preventive and curative, are not objected to so much as are the new practices in farming and changes in reproductive behavior, e.g., later marriage. Hence the death rate can be and is being changed without any compensating cultural changes leading to the improvement of agricultural practices or in the traditional reproductive behavior leading to the maintenance of a high birth rate (see also Chapter 21). The population dilemma in the underdeveloped countries today arises chiefly because it is easier to gain acceptance of new services which *quickly* reduce the death rate but require little or no cooperation on the part of the individual than to secure his acceptance of the new ideas and practices which will improve his crops or will require him to discard all the traditional ideas regarding the necessity of a high birth rate and take positive measures to reduce the number of children per couple.

7. Finally, it should be emphasized that in most underdeveloped countries nearly all the farmers live in small villages and seldom associate with people living in other types of communities—market towns and cities. In the village the mode of daily living changes little when health services are brought into it. The pattern of household work also remains fixed, and the pattern of farm work is determined largely by tradition and by the type of farm implements the people already have. Few villagers can afford an outlay of even $25 or $50 for seed or fertilizer or new implements, and if new implements requiring occasional servicing were given them, the implements would soon become unusable because no one would know how to keep them in repair. In a word, village life discourages initiative because it presents few problems so unfamiliar that they cannot be met in a socially approved manner by following the traditional practices of the community. On the other hand, departure from custom is anathema. It lays one open not only to being regarded as "odd" but as "evil." In contrast, a young farmer going to a city is compelled to make many adjustments to his new living conditions and is regarded as foolish if he does not break with village tradition and conform to the new pattern of behavior customary in his new environment. The villager as the conservator of tradition moves slowly in adopting new agricultural practices and new modes of family life.

Because no way has yet been found to ensure that as the death rate declines agricultural production will increase and/or the birth rate will decline, there will probably be some increase in absolute population pressure because of lower per capita consumption in many underdeveloped countries in the near future. There will almost certainly be a large increase in the relative (felt) pressure of population, which will be especially severe in those countries where population is already dense and new land is scarce and where most of the people already live close to the subsistence level. In the world as it is today, this may very well mean, to be more specific, that the leaders of Communist China or of Pakistan or of even some of the smaller underdeveloped countries will decide to exploit this increasing feeling of population pressure in their own countries to gain support for aggressive action against some of their neighbors.

It is, of course, impossible for any outsider to know the relative importance of the Communist ideology, on the one hand, and of the very real absolute population pressure existing in China, on the other hand, in determining the present aggressive attitude of China's leaders toward her neighbors and toward the "free" world, but there can be no doubt that these leaders will, like Hitler, make all possible use of the *feeling* of population pressure to secure popular support for aggressive action when for any reason they deem it desirable.

NEED FOR BALANCE IN ECONOMIC DEVELOPMENT AND POPULATION GROWTH

Capital and technical personnel are generally recognized as of outstanding importance in the economic development of underdeveloped countries.[2] Since both are always scarce in underdeveloped countries and are likely to remain scarce for some years, there is often much bitter competition between the men or groups interested in the development of different sectors of the economy to secure as large allocations as possible of both capital and expert personnel for their own particular projects.

In this struggle it is perhaps inevitable that the different types of manufacturing and transportation projects, the building of power plants, and many other types of industrial projects will be allocated *more* or *less* of the available capital and personnel than they can use to the best advantage of the nation. The result is that the economy may easily get rather badly out of balance; i.e., not every new project will be able to contribute effectively to the smooth operation of the economy as a whole. This has very serious effects upon the productiveness of the entire economy. For example, a tractor factory may be planned and built capable of turning out 10,000 tractors of a certain type each year for which only a fraction of the steel needed will be available during the next several years. Elaborate machinery may be bought and installed for which no qualified operators and maintenance workers can be found, with the result that one-half or more of the machines may stand idle for years. A good quality of cloth may be woven in an up-to-date mill for which there is no market because the people are too poor to buy it and there is no adequate export outlet. A big railroad junction and marshaling yards may be built which cannot be operated effectively except by well-trained and experienced men who cannot be found, with the result that many perishable goods do not reach their destination in usable condition. All such blunders lead to much waste of precious capital and personnel and seriously delay the increase in the national product and hence add to the growth of population pressure.

[2] The term "technical personnel," as used here, includes also experienced managerial personnel of all kinds as well as men with engineering experience and competent machine operators.

THE DEMAND FOR UP-TO-DATE EQUIPMENT AND ITS EFFECT ON EMPLOYMENT

Practically all the underdeveloped countries insist that their new industrial construction, their steel mills, their transportation equipment, their textile factories, their roads, their dams, etc., etc., be the very *best;* and in this case *best* means not only of good quality but of such a nature that the equipment will use a minimum amount of labor and will demand workers who have a degree of technical skill which is relatively scarce even in semi-industrialized countries. Hence, the use of the *best* machinery and the *most efficient* methods of production and construction creates very serious employment problems in most of the underdeveloped countries. Almost every improvement in agricultural techniques increases the area which one man can cultivate efficiently. The very nature of agricultural progress is to reduce the proportion of workers engaged in agriculture. But *common* labor is the most important surplus commodity in most underdeveloped countries even before improvements in agriculture begin to release any considerable body of young men from farming. It had been expected by the leaders that this abundant supply of common labor would be absorbed quickly into the nonagricultural sectors of their developing economies. But this is not proving to be so. Already many of the youths of an age to enter the labor force are unable to find work and are remaining on the farms as underemployed family workers or are on relief. Furthermore, after about the middle of the 1960s, in practically all these countries a greatly enlarged number of teen-agers will reach working age because of the decline of the death rates of infants and young children which has been taking place so rapidly since about 1950. Can there be any doubt that these unemployed and underemployed young people will be attracted to ideologies which take great pains to promise them steady employment and a rising level of living?

It has already been noted in Chapter 17 that the United States will also have a flood of young people coming into the labor force after about 1965, many of whom may have difficulty in finding steady work. We are much better equipped to meet and to deal with this problem of unemployment and underemployment than are any of the underdeveloped countries, and yet we already have a backlog of unemployment which is giving all thoughtful people much uneasiness. We foresee the problem, and yet we are taking very inadequate measures to ensure the employability of young people. Can we wonder that the underdeveloped countries which are unexpectedly encountering such difficulties at the very outset of their efforts to industrialize are not making much headway in creating jobs as fast as they are needed?

We do not intend to imply that economic development is useless in relieving the population pressures now building up in many of the underdeveloped countries which possess *little unused land suitable for agriculture.* (They now contain about one-half, or more, of the population of the world.) But we do imply, indeed assert, that economic development in most of them is encountering such great difficulties that it cannot be expected to effect a *rapid* decrease in population pressures with their peoples multiplying as they now are. Furthermore, every appreciable improvement in the control of the infectious diseases, although it contributes somewhat to the increase of the efficiency of labor, also tends to raise the rate of population growth at the stage of demographic development prevailing among these peoples, because while it reduces their death rates a little, as yet it has no ascertainable effect on their birth rates.

The only underdeveloped countries in which it seems probable that a rather rapid increase in agricultural products, both per capita and total, is likely to take place are those which still have *considerable amounts of unused tillable land*. If these countries adopt land policies which will encourage the rapid settlement of the new lands by young people through making ownership easy, even a very rapid growth of population should not prevent substantial improvement in the level of living in these areas until these new lands are tilled. By that time their new industries and their new services might be able to absorb an increasing proportion of all workers year after year. Moreover, it would be reasonable to expect that an increasing proportion of the people would by then have developed an effective interest in smaller families. Only about 15 to 20 percent of the world's people now live in underdeveloped countries still having considerable amounts of good untilled agricultural land. Several of these countries are in Southeast Asia, but most of them are in Africa and Latin America.

THE WORLD'S FOOD SUPPLY

Of much importance in preventing the development of critical population pressures in the underdeveloped countries is what is often spoken of as the *world food supply*. Since World War II severe famines have been avoided in several countries by drawing on the food surpluses in other countries. This resource, coupled with the more just and more efficient organization for food distribution in these countries having severe shortages, has staved off actual famine. The success achieved in famine relief and in reducing malnutrition in children by the free distribution of milk and a few other foods of high nutritional value (UNICEF) has led some people to think that the *world food supply* is sufficient to eliminate hunger and malnutrition as well as famine until such time as the more needy underdeveloped countries have expanded their own agricultural production to the point where it will be sufficient to meet their growing needs even if present rates of growth are maintained.

The authors believe, however, that it is one thing for a country to meet its *emergency needs* for food at a particular time from surpluses already accumulated in other countries but quite another matter for poor countries with inefficient agriculture to meet regularly the nutritional needs of large and rapidly growing populations by imports of food from a few other countries able to produce more grain than they need at present.

In a time of famine it is relatively easy to arouse the sympathy of large numbers of people in the countries with food surpluses and to secure very considerable donations of money and in kind. In addition, public sentiment in countries with surpluses will generally support their governments in the purchase of large amounts of surplus foods to be donated or sold cheaply to people in distress. This experience is commonplace and needs no further comment here.

On the other hand, the annual making up of large nutritional deficits which have long existed in many populations would require great political and economic modifications in the institutions of the surplus countries before they could undertake such a continuing obligation. Today, there is no reason to believe that an effective *world food supply* can become a reality in any foreseeable future. Nationalism is too strong a political force to permit of any rational hope that an effective international organization capable of feeding the hungry millions of the world and their rapidly increasing progeny can be established for many years to come.

Moreover, there is no assurance that the total of all food production in the world today, if pooled and doled out on a per capita basis, would be sufficient to supply an adequate diet to all the people in the world. Much less is it probable that with an average of about 50 to 60 million people being added to the population of the world each year, the surpluses in countries having surpluses in 1965 would increase fast enough to maintain an *adequate* diet for themselves and for the people in the needy countries for even one decade. Some concrete data may help us to realize the magnitude of the problem of feeding the world's population increase. In those countries living principally on the food grains (as is true in practically all underdeveloped countries) it will take about the equivalent of 5 to 6 bushels of wheat or rice, or other highly nutritious food grains (60 pounds to the bushel), per person per year to meet their needs at standards very little, if any, above their present inadequate standards. At 5 bushels per person, this allows a little less than 1 pound per person per day, or about 1,800 calories. An *average* person would need 2,200 to 2,500 carloies to ensure a reasonably adequate energy-producing diet. In addition, some vitamins, animal proteins, amino acids, and other food ingredients are needed.

If we assume that about three-fourths of a 60 million annual increase in the world's population takes place in the underdeveloped countries (probably a too conservative guess), the increase in food grains alone needed by these countries would rise by about five times 45 million or by 225 million bushels per year. In 10 years these peoples would need *an increase* in the food grains alone amounting to about twice the annual production of wheat in the United States in a *good wheat year*.

Although a part of the imports needed to supplement domestic production in the underdeveloped countries would consist of rice, corn, oats, rye, barley, or other minor food grains, all but the rice imports would have to be found in the more developed countries, in which the level of living of the farmers is relatively high. In consequence, the prices of these food grains would be relatively high. The exports from most underdeveloped countries needing more food consist chiefly of agricultural exports used as raw materials in industry, e.g., jute and rubber, or of food specialties—coffee, tea, cocoa, oils pressed from nuts or seeds. The prices of such exports are notoriously unstable and cannot be depended upon to pay for needed food imports. Hence it is difficult to see how these underdeveloped countries can import any considerable amounts of the food grains they would need so badly year after year unless these imports are subsidized by the governments of the exporting countries or by some new type of international organization which can guarantee prices to the growers of these food grains that are high enough to meet the living standards of the wheat and corn farmers in the United States, Canada, and Australia. These are the farmers who are best equipped to increase food grain exports quickly and to store surpluses sufficient for famine demands.

In effect, no such entity as a *world food supply* exists at the present time and there is no prospect that it will exist in the foreseeable future. The sum of *national* food supplies does not automatically become a *world supply*. There is little point in speculating as to what size of population the world can support in the next few decades. The real problem that must be faced in preventing or alleviating population pressure on food supplies during these decades arises because of the difficulties pointed out above in raising their agricultural and industrial production and in improving the services needed to assure better living in particular countries (nations). With regard to the underdeveloped countries, the realistic questions we must face, phrased in concrete terms, take somewhat the following forms: Can a particular underdeveloped country increase its agricultural production by 3 or 4 percent a year? Can it stabilize its food supply by arranging for the storage of carry-overs from *good* years to meet deficits in *bad* years? Already the population in most of these countries is growing by somewhat more than 2 percent per year, and at least another 1 or 2 percent of food is needed to assure even a slightly more adequate diet for all the people all the time. Besides, most of the capital needed for the rapid development of both industry and agriculture must come from agricultural surpluses for some years to come. About 50 to 60 percent of the world's people live in countries facing these difficulties in trying to relieve their absolute pressures of population on the necessities of life. The point of greatest importance here is that the actual problems to be overcome in relieving population pressures are largely national, about which comparatively little can be done by the more-developed nations, either individually or collectively even with the best of intentions.

After careful consideration of all the means discussed above for avoiding or for alleviating both *absolute and relative* population pressures of a critical character being built up because of the recent precipitous reduction in the death rates of the peoples living in underdeveloped countries, the authors find themselves in doubt that any or all of these means will be adequate to prevent really dangerous population pressures from developing during the next few decades. There is, however, one other possible avenue of escape, viz., the reduction of the birth rate. This needs very thoughtful consideration.

REDUCTION OF THE BIRTH RATE IN THE UNDERDEVELOPED COUNTRIES

The prospect of soon reducing the birth rates in underdeveloped countries at an equal pace with the reduction of their death rates, or better, at a more rapid pace, merits much closer attention than can be given in this book. It has been noted above that there is as yet no convincing evidence of any decline in the birth rate in any underdeveloped country with a population of more than a few million. In the first place, let us note the implications of the present growth rates in the underdeveloped countries if they remain at about 2 percent per year. Almost two-thirds (about 2 billion, or 2,000 million) of the people in the world live in the underdeveloped countries.[3] Any population growing at a rate of 2 percent per year will double in numbers in approximately 35 years. Thus by the year 2100, the people living in the underdeveloped countries in 1962 would increase to about 32 billion (32,000 million) if they maintained their present rate of growth. This is very unlikely to happen, for by no stretch of the imagination can we expect the present volume of subsistence produced by the descendants of the present population of the underdeveloped countries to be increased sixteenfold in 135 to 140 years. Moreover, even such an increase would not provide any per capita increase in the intake of food or in the use of other agricultural products. An increase in agricultural production sufficient to ensure ade-

[3] United Nations, *Demographic Yearbook, 1961,* p. 120, gives the average crude death rates and birth rates for the years 1956 to 1960 for several continents as follows (birth rate in parentheses): Africa, 25 (47); North America, 9 (25); Middle America, 15 (42); South America, 19 (42); Asia 22 (41); East Asia, 20 (40); Europe, 11 (19); Oceania, 9 (24); and the U.S.S.R., 8 (25). The rates for much of South America, Asia, and Africa must be regarded as only approximate but probably are not substantially in error as to the differences between birth rates and death rates. Hence it does not seem unreasonable to estimate a death rate of 20 to 25 and a birth rate of 40 to 42 per 1,000 for the underdeveloped countries as a group in the period specified.

quate nutrition and clothing for such a population would have to be nearer 25 times as large as at present instead of 16 times as large.

If it is regarded as fantastic even to suggest the continuation of a rate of population growth of 2 percent per year for 140 years in the underdeveloped countries of today, it may be pointed out that in the United States between 1750 and 1890 the average annual *natural increase* exceeded 2 percent by close to one-half. We are not suggesting that the present rate in the underdeveloped countries will continue. In fact we are fully convinced that the death rate *will* begin to rise in many, probably in most, of the underdeveloped countries of the world within two or three decades *if* in the meantime the birth rate has not begun to decline significantly. (By *significantly* we mean that the birth rate will have begun to decline faster than the death rate so that the rate of natural increase will also be declining.)

How soon is it reasonable to expect this significant decline in the birth rate among these peoples, let us say a decline from 40 or a little more to 32 to 35 while the death rate declines from about 20 or 21 to about 16 to 18? Obviously, this question cannot be answered with any degree of satisfaction. But it may be pointed out that only in Japan of all the countries in the world now having low birth rates (see Chapters 16 and 20) has the birth rate declined so much within a few years that the rate of natural increase has fallen to a relatively low level (about 10 per 1,000 per year for the period 1953 to 1960). The decline in the birth rate was from 33.7 per 1,000 per year in 1948 to 18.5 per 1,000 in 1956, and between 1956 and 1961 there was a further decline in the birth rate to 16.8. This is a much larger decline proportionally than took place in the United States and in most European countries even during the Depression of the 1930s. Furthermore, up to the present time, there is no indication of any rise in Japan's birth rate in spite of the great improvement in her economic conditions since about 1953.

Since the writers believe that this very rapid decline in the birth rate in Japan was due in large part to the very unusual circumstances existing in that country for several years following the war, coupled with cultural values peculiar to Japan, they do not believe that a decline in the birth rate even approximating the rapidity of Japan's rate is to be expected in any of the present underdeveloped countries. (See Chapter 20, section on Japan for the reasons on which this opinion is based.)

The efforts of India to reduce the birth rate since 1947 seem to throw much more light on the probable reduction of the birth rate in most underdeveloped countries during the next few decades than do those of Japan. Premier Nehru, even before independence, had definitely expressed his belief that there was an urgent need to reduce India's birth rate so that her rate of population growth would be relatively slow. Some funds to promote family planning were included in the budget of the first Five-Year Plan, and considerably larger funds were allotted to the promotion of voluntary family limitation in the second Five-Year Plan. (See section on India, Chapter 21.) Moreover, India has had an active private Family Planning Association for some years. The few Indian studies set up to find out whether there has yet been any change in the birth rate surveyed only a few small communities. Although they show some significant differences in birth rates between communities, they do not justify the positive assertion that the birth rate has yet begun to decline in any of them. There can be little doubt that in certain groups in Indian society, particularly in the well-to-do and educated classes, birth control is being practiced effectively, but the persons in these groups constitute such a small proportion of the total population that a significant decline in the birth rate of these classes would have no appreciable effect on the birth rate of the entire population. Moreover, since the tabu on the remarriage of widows is being broken down and since there is a considerable excess of males at ages 20 to 35 in the population, the remarriage of any considerable proportion of the several million widows of those ages might very well counteract any effect on the national birth rate brought by a substantial increase in the voluntary control of the size of the family in the upper social and economic classes. Finally, although the legal age for marriage is now higher than in the past, it is extremely doubtful that for the mass of the people any increase of the age of women at marriage has as yet had any appreciable effect on the birth rate.

In very general terms, the peoples living in practically all the underdeveloped countries possess cultural patterns of reproductive behavior which serve to ensure that a large proportion of the physiological reproductive capacity of all females in the population is realized. This is true even when due allowance is made for the fact, noted above at several points, that practically all cultures require compliance with certain traditional practices affecting reproduction that in varying degrees reduce the average number of births per woman somewhat below the potential physiological maximum.

CONCLUSION

It was probably the terrific loss of life due to the continuous operation of very severe positive checks—hunger, disease, war—that led most societies in the past to consider it highly desirable for each female to bear as large a number of children as possible, subject to the few cultural restrictions that had become traditional. *High birth rates were necessary for sheer survival.* This situation is now somewhat modified among most of the peoples living in underdeveloped lands. Up to the present, however, there seems to be very little realization in most such countries that the decline in their death rates makes any significant change in the desirability of maintaining high fertility. In fact, among all the people living in underdeveloped countries only a very small proportion, viz., those in the better-educated classes, as yet realize that most couples are or soon will be raising a larger number of children to maturity than their parents. The traditional cultural patterns of behavior that are closely associated with high fertility may be expected to hold out strongly against significant modification until the mass of the people come to feel that they can improve their living condition, can make "progress," can enjoy some of the amenities of life they desire, only if they reduce the number of births per family. Such control of family size heretofore has come fairly rapidly in the present low-birth-rate countries only after industrialization and urbanization have been well under way. However, the people in the underdeveloped countries today do not need to wait until their countries are well industrialized before they can enjoy the benefits to be derived from having rather small families. Education, health services, and other social services will have to become much more influential than they now are in moulding the thoughts and the behavior of the people, especially the rural people, before they will abandon traditional practices which tend to keep productivity low and reproductivity high.

The great difficulty encountered in breaking down traditional practices in agriculture and in modifying the equally persistent traditions leading to high fertility, coupled with the proved effectiveness of the health services now spreading so rapidly among people in the underdeveloped countries, lead us to believe in a very strong probability that even *absolute* population pressures may mount quite rapidly in some of the underdeveloped countries. Moreover, for three or four decades at least, probably every slight improvement in living conditions in these countries, every increase in the effectiveness of health services, every increase in the spread of knowledge of how people in the more-developed countries live, will tend to enhance *relative* population pressure, i.e., will increase the feeling of deprivation, even in those underdeveloped countries in which the greatest progress in raising the level of living is being made. This sense of deprivation will be at work even if family planning catches on faster than the authors expect, for there can be no doubt that once the people in an underdeveloped country begin to enjoy the benefits of a more efficient economy and of the social services that go with it, their desires for more goods and services will for some time grow more rapidly than the means for satisfying these desires.

It needs no argument here to convince any one who has given some attention to the rise of Hitler and Mussolini in Europe and to the attainment of power by the expansionist leaders of Japan that a strong feeling of deprivation can be rather easily aroused in peoples already enjoying a fair to good level of living as compared with most of the peoples in the underdeveloped countries. In the light of these recent experiences with authoritarian governments and dictators, it seems rather unrealistic to assume that somewhat similar attempts to whip-up popular support for the conquest of other countries, for more lebensraum, will not be made in the not-distant future.

Furthermore, today, under the stimulus of social and economic ideologies held with religious intensity by even a small proportion of the people, we find the leaders of both the U.S.S.R. and China (Communist) eager to force the acceptance of their ideologies on all other peoples and confident that their own people will support them in their efforts. Thus even though absolute population pressures may be easing for some peoples, we cannot afford to ignore the likelihood that the need for larger resources, both agricultural and industrial, will continue to be used by ambitious and/or fanatical leaders to increase the *feeling* of deprivation among their peoples.

This being the case, the slow and disappointing improvement in the living conditions of the great mass of the people in most of the present underdeveloped countries will add intensity to the feeling of deprivation already growing in many of them. Besides, today under ruthless authoritarian control, even a poverty-stricken country like China can build up great military power in a comparatively short time. Since there can also be no doubt of the great need of China for more land to till, for greater forestry resources, and for larger resources of various kinds, e.g., oil and iron, it would be surprising if the Chinese leaders did not exploit these needs to the limit to further their personal and ideological ambitions. The population pressure in China may very well be even now an important factor encouraging the nibbling process by which the leaders hope to increase China's power in Southeast Asia. But even if the spread of Communist ideology as understood by the Chinese leaders were the underlying motive for China's expansion, the leaders will certainly not fail to dwell upon the need for more resources as justifying expansion by force, seeking the oil of Burma and Indonesia, acquiring new rice lands, which can be found in substantial amounts in Burma, Thailand, and elsewhere in Southeast Asia, especially in Indonesia.

In the long run there is only one sure way out of the population dilemma we have been describing, i.e., to relieve the population pressures which at the very *least* aggravate the tensions between nations and at the *most* may be the prime motivating cause of particular wars. This one sure way of relieving population pressure is for man to adjust his birth rate to his ability to make a decent living with the resources at his disposal. We do not want to appear unduly pessimistic of man's chances to extricate himself from this population dilemma, but neither do we want to leave the impression that the sure way out will come quickly and will be easy. It will require the best efforts of all men of goodwill continued over a long period. During this time we can hope that a growing proportion of the people in the world will realize the nature of this dilemma and will understand that escape from it involves cooperation with all other people everywhere.

SUGGESTIONS FOR SUPPLEMENTARY READING

Ackerman, Edward A.: *Japan's Natural Resources and Their Relation to Japan's Economic Future*, The University of Chicago Press, Chicago, 1953.

Brown, Harrison: *The Challenge of Man's Future; An Inquiry Concerning the Condition of Man during the Years That Lie Ahead*, The Viking Press, Inc., New York, 1954.

Clark, Colin: *The Conditions of Economic Progress*, 3d ed., St Martin's Press, Inc., New York, 1957.

Coale, Ansley J., and Edgar M. Hoover: *Population Growth and Economic Development in Low-income Countries*, Princeton University Press, Princeton, N.J., 1958. (See also *Milbank Memorial Fund Quarterly*, vol. 39, no. 4, pp. 631–646, October, 1961 [Hutterites]).

Dorn, Harold F.: "World Population Growth: An International Dilemma," *Science*, vol. 135, no. 3,500, pp. 283–290, 1962.

Jarrett, Henry (ed.): *Perspective on Conservation: Essays on America's Resources*, The Johns Hopkins Press, Baltimore, 1958.

Kuznets, Simon, et al. (eds.): *Economic Growth: Brazil, India, Japan*, The Duke University Press, Durham, N.C., 1955.

McCormack, Arthur: *People, Space, Food*, Sheed & Ward, Inc., New York, 1960.

McDougall, Frank J.: *Food and Population*, Carnegie Endowment for International Peace, International Conciliation, no. 486, 1953, pp. 537–584.

Osborn, Fairfield (ed.): *Our Crowded Planet: Essays on the Pressures of Population*, Doubleday & Company, Inc., Garden City, N.Y., 1962.

Political and Economic Planning: *World Population and Resources*, London, 1955.

Sauvy, Alfred: *Fertility and Survival: Population Problems from Malthus to Mao Tse-tung*, Criterion Books, New York, 1961.

Schurr, Sam H., et al.: *Energy in the American Economy, 1850–1975: An Economic Study of Its History and Prospects, A Resource for the Future Study*, The Johns Hopkins Press, Baltimore, 1960.

Steiner, H. Arthur (ed.): "Report on China," *Annals of the American Academy of Political and Social Science*, vol. 277, September, 1951. (Series of papers covering economic, social, and political aspects of China today.)

Thompson, Warren S.: *Population and Progress in the Far East*, The University of Chicago Press, Chicago, 1959.

Williamson, Harold F., and John A. Buttrick: *Economic Development: Principles and Patterns*, Prentice-Hall, Inc., Englewood Cliffs, N.J., 1954. (Miami University library has this.)

CHAPTER TWENTY

Population Policies

The primary urge of all living beings has always been survival. But we should not think of this urge as a policy but rather as the source of policies. Natural selection merely means that the organisms best equipped with instincts or characteristics that are the most useful for survival are those that have survived. Successful biological adaptations leading to survival even in man are not to be considered population policies. They do not involve deliberate and purposeful efforts. Population policies are the distinctive prerogative of man's intelligence and his ability to organize his life, not merely to survive, but also to live better. We cannot be certain, of course, that even man's intelligent efforts to survive and to live better have always been the consequence of *deliberate intent*, which seems to the authors the essence of a population policy. Many of man's efforts to survive and to live better may very well have been the result of accidents, of having to meet crises demanding new types of personal and group behavior which were later rationalized as deliberate policies. But man alone could create and/or adopt traditions and customs which were transmitted to his offspring by learning rather than by heredity and hence can be called policies.

SOME GENERAL REFLECTIONS REGARDING POPULATION POLICY

If we make the deliberate intent of a group to control its size and/or its characteristics the criterion for judging whether that group has had or now has a population policy, we shall have to confine our remarks largely to the current situation. We know very little about population policies in the past, and besides, even when we do know something about the *social* policies of a group which may have had a profound effect on its size and demographic characteristics, we do not know how important a role the control of the demographic aspects of group growth and change played in the adoption of this policy. This point should be borne in mind in reading the following section.

SOME EXAMPLES OF PROBABLE POPULATION POLICIES IN THE PAST

Among so-called "primitive people," such practices as the prolonged breast feeding of children (sometimes for as long as four to seven years) may have reduced substantially the rate of conception and may very well have contributed, at some time, more to the survival of the clan or tribe than the birth of the additional children that would otherwise have taken place. Likewise, the exposure to certain death of crippled and weak babies and of old people who could no longer care for themselves or travel from one hunting ground to another probably had real survival value from the standpoint of the group. Polyandry (one woman having two or more husbands), whatever its cause, probably indicates a shortage of females in the population. This, too, may have had high survival value under certain conditions. Whether these group policies were ever population policies in the sense in which this term is used here is not known. However, they were social policies which certainly had important demographic effects on the groups in which these practices had become traditional.

The enumeration and description of similar traditional practices that can very properly be called social policies could be continued at some length. However, it is doubtful that they were thought of as population policies by their practitioners, and we know them only as traditional practices having to do chiefly with the survival and growth of the groups in which they prevailed. Some of these social policies, possibly more than we know about, were also concerned with the genetic characteristics of the people. But we do not know in any particular case whether the exposure of deformed babies was motivated chiefly by eugenic considerations, or by fear of the unusual, or in the interest of group survival; nor do we know whether such a policy was ever a deliberate population policy or arose as an unconscious adaptation to particular circumstances.

Although Sparta is often credited with a population policy deliberately intended to develop a tough and hardy people, we cannot be certain of this. The exposure of crippled and weak babies was a general practice, and the upbringing of the surviving babies was very rigorous and carefully planned to make them *good* citizens, as well as *strong* citizens. To this day the term "Spartan" carries with it the connotation of austere living, rigorous training, a capability and willingness to undergo hardships in the service of the community, and the possession of other characteristics which were highly valued in a society which had to struggle constantly to maintain itself in competition with its neighbors. How far this was a deliberate population policy must remain uncertain, but there can be no doubt that it affected the growth and the characteristics of Sparta's population.

Much the same policy of training and toughening the youth prevailed in many tribes of American Indians, and those selected as likely to become war leaders and counselors were given especially rigorous training to ensure that future warriors and chieftains would be not only physically fit but also well indoctrinated with the social attitudes considered *good* in the Indian community. No doubt numerous social policies in many societies played an active role not only in the survival of these societies but also in the growth and the composition of their populations.

All societies surviving today have had effective traditional patterns of behavior consisting of many and varied practices considered good. *Be fruitful and multiply and replenish the earth* was the essence of one social policy attributed by the Jews to Jehovah. In China, the teachings of Confucius regarding the reverence due to ancestors made it a prime sin to leave them without descendants. In India, the gods were greatly concerned over the fertility of the people, and their priests quite regularly made it their business to see that the people were reminded of their duty to multiply abundantly.

In many times and places, rulers have directly encouraged the people to reproduce abundantly because they believed their own power and the greatness of their kingdoms and empires would be enhanced by this growth in numbers. In fact, the identification of the size of the population with the greatness of the empire or the nation and its rulers has endured for several millennia and is still so common that several recent dictators in authoritarian societies have encouraged high fertility—Mussolini, Hitler, and Stalin. In the United States we have also been inclined to boast of our national and local growth in numbers and to feel that some special virtue is attached to large families. Income tax laws also place a monetary value on children. Such general social attitudes regarding population growth, although not population policies in the sense in which this term is used here, have often had great influence on population growth and the demographic characteristics of the people.

HIGH BIRTH RATES VERSUS RAPID POPULATION GROWTH

It should be noted that the general and continuing social policies mentioned above were directed chiefly at encouraging a high birth rate. Apparently, it was widely assumed by the enunciators and supporters of these policies that a high birth rate assured not only survival but also a high rate of population growth. There is much reason, however, to doubt whether these general social policies had any considerable effect on the birth rates prevailing even when they were first adopted unless they were accompanied by the removal of restrictions on marital relations then in effect. For example, we need to know whether the long periods of purification after childbirth were shortened, whether a prohibition of remarriage by widows was removed, whether the duration of breast feeding was reduced, whether the practice of abortion was effectively restrained, or whether earlier marriage was encouraged by economic and social conditions. When such changes in practices affecting the birth rate took place, fertility was probably raised. But man's natural reproductive drives have always been so powerful that a high birth rate has generally prevailed in most societies, although many different customs and traditions have at times interfered to some extent with conception and have also led to considerable amounts of abortion in different societies.

However, we must be careful not to assume that a social policy encouraging a higher birth rate, even when effective, necessarily leads to a more rapid rate of population growth. A high birth rate may have some measure of success in assuring the continuance of a particular family or clan or other small group, but it may under conditions of intense population pressure contribute more to a high death rate than to a higher rate of population growth. With only rare exceptions in the past has any civil society had a *medium* to *low* birth rate, let us say a crude birth rate as low as 25 to 30 per 1,000. It is clear that it avails nothing from the standpoint of population growth to encourage a society having a birth rate of 35 to 40 to raise that rate to 40 to 45 if a death rate of 35 to 40 will also rise to about 40 to 45.

The fact that for many thousands of years the numbers in practically all societies grew very, very slowly, grew not at all, or even decreased to the point of extinction was not due primarily to low birth rates but to the following facts: (1) that man's techniques for providing mere subsistence were traditional and were generally so inefficient in all societies that the food supply could be increased very slowly if at all; (2) that his protection against the infectious diseases was almost nil; and (3) that he always wasted so much of his energy, so much of his goods, and so much of his manpower in war, and in supporting a few members of his community at a level of ostentatious living, that little remained to feed additional mouths.

As we have seen in earlier chapters (see Chapters 14 to 16), in spite of the many policies, or statement of policies, which have prevailed among different peoples encouraging fertility, i.e., a high birth rate, it is only since yesterday in human history, about 300 years ago, that there has been any substantial and fairly prolonged growth in man's numbers either in the world as a whole or in particular societies. Although a number of men, even before Malthus (see Chapter 2), had called attention to the fact that a large proportion of all the babies born did not survive to reproduce, it does not seem to have been widely realized that the death rate rather than the birth rate had throughout human history played much the predominant role in determining population growth. If some few people realized the importance of the death rate, until quite recently almost no information was available anywhere to suggest, even to the inquiring mind, that anything could be done to reduce the death rate.

In spite of the lack of any significant organized effort to reduce man's death rate until recently, however, and in spite of the failure to realize that reducing the death rate would be the most effective method of assuring a more rapid growth in any society, man has made, in the course of time, a number of important advances that have had pronounced effects on his numbers. These advances have consisted largely in increasing agricultural production, in improving his protection against the elements, and in using his mineral resources more efficiently. For example, there was no doubt a time when the ancestors of the present Chinese and Indian peoples gathered wild rice but did not yet cultivate it. This period, of indefinite length, was followed by a period, also of indefinite length, when they began to cultivate rice in a very primitive manner and thus increased the yield per acre and extended the acreage devoted to its culture. This in turn was followed by further improvements in agriculture, such as the selection of better-yielding varieties of rice and wheat and other food grains and the invention of more efficient practices of planting and tending the crops. At some point in this centuries-long development process, irrigation was invented, and its use slowly spread. This development not only increased annual yields but also acted in some measure as insurance against crop failure, although all agricultural peoples and even all pastoral peoples have always suffered from frequent crop failures. Such improvements were almost certainly not regarded by the people who made them as practices in the furtherance of population policies, but they did more to make population growth certain than all the exhortations of sages, priests, and kings to have more babies. These improvements in techniques, both agricultural and nonagricultural, gradually supplied the increasing amounts of subsistence which reduced death rates for a time and thus led to some increase in numbers, which probably then remained almost stationary until new agricultural improvements were discovered. The interest of a Chinese emperor, or a great mogul in India, in improving rice yields and in maintaining peace within his country did more to increase the population than all the social encouragements to be fruitful.

In the same way, the slow and occasional improvements in housing and clothing and in the use of minerals contributed little by little to the support of larger populations, but as we have seen, it was not until quite recently that a relatively rapid increase in the production of the physical necessities made possible the support of a fairly rapid increase in man's numbers over large areas of the earth.

THE GROWING NEED FOR EFFECTIVE POPULATION POLICIES

Only two or three centuries ago did any appreciable number of people anywhere begin to give much thought to the factors controlling population growth and the characteristics of the population. The desirability of having an explicit policy regarding the adjustment of man's numbers to the production of the goods necessary to maintain a decent level of living developed even more recently. In Western Europe and in the areas settled by Western Europeans during the seventeenth, eighteenth, and nineteenth centuries, such ideas did not really catch hold among the people until about the middle or latter part of the nineteenth century. However, in the more "progressive" countries, where the advances both in agricultural and industrial techniques were greatest, there were a few people who, like Malthus, believed it would be wise to control reproduction in the interest of human welfare. But many of the people who most clearly realized that man's productivity was increasing rapidly and who were most certain that a new era in man's welfare was possible believed also that a laissez-faire policy as regards reproduction would be quite satisfactory because this same hands-off policy, applied to industry and agriculture, was increasing the goods available for consumption so fast that population would never again press heavily on subsistence. Many people today still have much the same unwarranted faith in the ability of science or of some other cure-all to overcome man's economic ills without tampering with his *natural* reproduction.

During most of the nineteenth century, there was much excuse for the ready acceptance of the view that uninhibited population growth could be more than matched by increased productivity. The unprecedented growth of population was being accompanied in the West by real improvement in living conditions arising out of the agricultural and industrial revolutions. Moreover, a point often overlooked, until about 1900 Western European farmers could and did migrate in great numbers to farms in many different parts of the world. These three highly dynamic factors: (1) the improvement in all manner of mechanical techniques; (2) the equally great improvements in agriculture leading to much greater productivity; and (3) the increasingly easy access to new land, seemed to promise increasing welfare even to an unlimited growth of man's numbers. The fact that the benefits of these great changes in man's productive capacity had not yet been made available to more than one-fifth to one-fourth of mankind appears to have been forgotten. Moreover, during most of this century, the decline in the death rate was slow even in the West.

Another factor of quite a different character also came into operation in parts of the West to obscure the need of giving careful public consideration to the relation of population growth to man's productivity. This was the personal control of the size of the family—the birth rate—in considerable segments of the populations in an increasing number of Western countries in which industry and urban living were developing. Malthus had urged the control of population growth by the use of *preventive* checks, chiefly later marriages, and had shown that in several countries in Western Europe such checks did reduce the size of the family in certain classes of the population. It is now reasonably certain that as early as 1750 the practice of contraception began to contribute to an increase in the number of families in France in which only a few children were born. This personal and voluntary control of the size of the family began to manifest itself perceptibly in other Western countries during the latter part of the nineteenth century and spread rather rapidly after about 1875 or 1880 in most of the areas of European settlement except Latin America. The resulting decline in the birth rate contributed to the persistence of the widely prevailing attitude that there was no need for any public policy aimed at providing a better adjustment of the size and rate of growth of the population to the rate of the growth of the goods upon which man was dependent.

During the 1920s and the 1930s, those people who were studying the growth of population in the world were coming to realize more clearly than ever before how unusual the growth of the Western European peoples had been since about 1700, and especially after 1800. It was also becoming clear that in the near future we could expect a much more rapid growth of population in many areas which had hitherto been believed to be almost static in numbers (see Chapter 15). Japan's first modern census (1920) left no doubt that a slow but more steady growth of population was taking place in that country and that by about 1880 the *rate* of growth was rising although rather slowly. Agriculture had been improving, and health services were becoming more effective by 1900. Little was known about population growth in China, but there seemed to be good reason to think that after the Manchu conquest (about 1650), peace had been quite well maintained for about 150 years, agriculture had been much improved, and there had been a large expansion of the cultivated land in the southern parts of the country. Thus although China had throughout her history suffered from frequent famines and great plagues, her population had probably been growing in numbers at what was then a fairly rapid rate, perhaps about 4 or 5 per 1,000 per year, from about 1650 to 1825. It seems doubtful, however, that even this low rate had been maintained after about 1825 (see Chapter 15).

In 1923 the senior author visited China and had his Malthusian leanings confirmed by what he saw and learned on that trip. Limited subsistence, disease, and war (civil disturbances) were the great checks to population growth. In regard to disease he had his eyes further opened by a visit to the headquarters of a health demonstration in one section of Peking. This demonstration was supported by Rockefeller funds. The doctor in charge was enthusiastic regarding the progress that had been made in a short time in reducing the death rate in the demonstration area and was fully convinced that it could soon be cut to

50 percent of what it had been when the demonstration began. This was before most of the toxin-antitoxin preventives had been developed, before the sulfa drugs were yet in use; the antibiotics had not been heard of, and the insecticides, which have done so much to control malaria since World War II, had not yet been developed. But in spite of the lack of these remedies, this demonstration of what could be done even then to reduce the death rate from infectious diseases in a crowded city in a poverty-stricken country convinced the author that an increase of 2 percent or more a year was even then feasible in China, if only the means of carrying modest health services to all the people could be provided, if the war lords could be controlled, and if the production of food could be increased as rapidly.

He suggested to the doctor in charge of this demonstration that it would be a great calamity not only to China but to the whole world to reduce China's death rate by one-half within a few years if the people were not also shown how to reduce their birth rate in about the same measure. The doctor replied that this was none of the doctor's business and appeared to be offended that anyone should make such a suggestion to a medical man. His business was merely to save lives. This view has prevailed widely in the medical profession in the United States up to the present time, and only now does a definite change in attitude appear to be taking place.

It took another 25 years and the further development of the sulfa drugs, the antibiotics, and more efficient insecticides to do *quickly* and *cheaply* and on a *wide scale* what was being undertaken in this Peking demonstration in 1923, viz., to control the infectious diseases in the less-developed countries. This reduction in death rates from infectious diseases is now taking place all over the world at an even faster pace than most of us who were studying such matters anticipated. The almost incredible achievements of public health services since World War II are very widely known and acclaimed (see Chapter 16). As a result, a great many people have rather suddenly come to realize that there is need to give careful consideration to the deliberate control of population growth if even the present death rates of the poorer peoples in the world, which are still very much higher than need be (perhaps in the low twenties or high teens as compared with 9 or 10 in many of the more highly developed countries), are to be maintained for more than a few decades (Chapter 16). As a consequence of these conditions there is increasing interest in and talk about a world-population policy.

A WORLD-POPULATION POLICY

In view of the almost universal desire among the people in all countries to improve their health services and thus reduce their death rates as fast as possible, it will be in order to note briefly the more important implications involved in the establishment of health services aimed at reducing these rates to new and still lower levels in the underdeveloped countries which now contain about two-thirds of the world's population. The first fruits of even modest health services are already clearly evident. As has been shown in Chapter 16, practically all national and international programs of health improvement have already attained an astounding success. Health programs meet with comparatively little resistance from even the most tradition-minded peoples—even the ones who generally oppose all change. Scotching an epidemic of smallpox by vaccination, saving a pneumonia victim or a victim of a dozen other diseases from death by the use of penicillin, teaching a mother how to protect her baby from diarrhea and enteritis are such obvious benefits that almost all people are glad to avail themselves of these services almost as soon as they know about them. The immediate effect of the services is so much to be desired by individuals that the more distant social and economic effects of reducing the death rates rapidly in perhaps two-thirds of mankind are quite generally overlooked.

We do not intend to imply that these health services should not be established and made effective whenever possible, but we do urge that the more distant social and economic effects of these health services should be anticipated and deliberately controlled as far as this is possible. Indeed, under certain circumstances, we should be prepared to defend the thesis that an efficient public health service in the underdeveloped areas of the world is an essential prerequisite if rapid headway is to be made in the establishment of a world-population policy, the purpose of which would be to bring about a better adjustment of the rate of population growth to the rate of increase of the goods and services man needs to assure himself of a decent level of living.

Stated briefly, the circumstances under which we should feel justified in urging better and better health services are: (1) that the health services' staffs, from the top to the bottom, are made fully cognizant of the effects of their work in reducing death rates on the growth of the population, including the fact that as matters now stand, the more efficient the health services become the more rapid the growth of the population will be; (2) that the health services of a country and its physicians, where private practice prevails, are ready and willing to inform the mothers who bring young children to them for advice regarding their care, that they can control the size of their families and are also willing to show them how this can be done if the mothers are interested and want to know. At present, in underdeveloped countries, few mothers know that the voluntary control of the size of the family is possible and even fewer know how to exercise such control.

This conception of the obligation of health services, both public and private, goes well beyond the generally recognized function of health services prevailing in the United States today. But there is more and more evidence that it is gaining acceptance. People are rapidly recognizing that the health worker not only has a right to give information on family planning but has also a duty to do so when he is asked for it.

Perhaps the greatest obstacle to the establishment of a *world-population policy* is the fact that very few nations are ready today to adopt national policies, and in the underdeveloped countries whose governments have openly espoused population policies they cannot implement them quickly. Until the mass of the people in any country are able to control the size of their families and are willing to do so, no government can guarantee cooperation with other nations in a world-population policy aimed at adjusting man's numbers to his ability to support them well. But there are also other serious obstacles to the formulation and implementation of a world-population policy—nationalism, racism, ideologies, and, perhaps most of all, the sheer inertia of traditionalism in most underdeveloped countries. The importance of these several obstacles will vary from country to country, and it will be impossible here to discuss all these obstacles as they operate in different countries and among different peoples. Nationalism as an obstacle to the effectuating of a world-population policy perhaps needs little discussion as it is quite widely realized today that the citizens of every country are generally much more concerned with the welfare of their fellow countrymen than with that of the people in the other countries. Racism is of importance because now for the first time the colored peoples of the world see a chance to attain equality of living conditions with the whites. Indeed, by reason of their present numbers and their more rapid growth, some of their leaders are hoping not only to become equal with the whites economically but also to become dominant politically. It is not surprising that some of the leaders of these peoples are reluctant to adopt a population policy which would equate the growth of the colored peoples with that of the white peoples.

As regards the conflicting ideologies of different peoples, it must be recognized that orthodox communism denies that the growth of population poses any threat to the welfare of man and that this doctrine appeals to many of the leaders in underdeveloped countries. Moreover, these leaders are often conditioned by past experience to accept the view of the Communists that imperialism, colonialism, and capitalism are the root causes of their poverty and its accompanying hardships. The point here is that several very potent forces make a *world-population policy* very unlikely to become an effective agency in reducing the rate of population growth in the foreseeable future.

Furthermore, it should be realized that the control of population growth is much less urgent in some regions and countries than in others; i.e., in some countries the population is not growing so fast and/or the natural resources are so abundant that there is little danger of a significant deterioration in the living conditions of the people during the lifetime of the present leaders if their resources are exploited intelligently. In others the need for slower growth is already urgent. Can *any* government in *any* country set up "a most desirable size of family" for its people and enforce the adoption of this standard within a few years? The answer must be No for those countries which still have good unused land and large natural resources. This being the case, can these countries be expected to cooperate in encouraging slower population growth even though it might hasten considerably the attainment of a higher level of living for their people through more rapid economic development?

Most of the people in any country, even when they know how to control the size of their families, may be expected to conform more or less closely to some standard size of family only if they are convinced that their community approves of such control and that it is to the advantage of their own family to do so. There can be no doubt that the governments of most countries, through education and propaganda, can in the course of time influence the judgment of their people in the determination of what family size is best and can also hasten the adoption of the small-family pattern if that seems desirable. But the range of family size within which governmental efforts of this character can operate even in the more developed countries appears to be quite small at the present time. As a matter of fact, when the leaders of the authoritarian governments in Germany and Italy tried to influence their peoples to have more children, they did not succeed because the people as a whole did not regard the alleged need of lebensraum as a sufficient reason for increasing the size of their own families although they could be manipulated into fighting for it.

The simple fact is that at the present time only a few countries have birth rates and death rates which appear sufficiently low to give some assurance that their natural increase can also be expected to remain at a fairly low level consistent with their ability to provide a decent living for all citizens. The leaders of these few countries might feel sufficiently confident of the direction and the amount of their population growth for several years in the future to feel justified in subscribing in good faith to a world-population policy for the control of population growth. The leaders of most of the nations of the world, however, could not do so even with a small degree of confidence in the ability or the willingness of their people to conform to some world standard, chiefly because they do not know how long it will take their people to adopt effective control over the birth rate and how fast the death rate will decline in the next few decades. (This assumes that any world-population policy must have as its first and primary objective for the next few decades the reduction of the rate of population increase in those countries which now have high birth rates and in which death rates are falling rapidly.) Moreover, as we have already noted, there is no unanimity of opinion among leaders of the high-birth-rate peoples as to the desirability of a policy to reduce the rate of population growth.

In spite of the fact that no effective world policy calculated to reduce the rate of population growth can be achieved in the near future, the authors regard it as highly desirable to get a statement of world policy regarding population growth from as many nations as possible and even from private organizations in nations unready to declare any official attitude toward population growth. Such declarations of the desirability of population control or even in opposition to a policy of population control would help to get the whole matter before the people and would almost certainly hasten the thoughtful decision of an increasing proportion of couples regarding the desirable size of their own families. In the long run this decision must be personal, but any expression of opinion, official or private, which stimulates the consideration of voluntary population control is preferable to ignoring the problem which faces the world when a large majority of the more than 3,000 million people in the world suddenly begin to increase at a rapid rate—2 percent or more per year—before these people have the know-how and the physical means to increase their goods and services fast enough to assure for themselves even the same low per capita consumption they now have, to say nothing of providing themselves with goods and services increasing faster than their numbers.

This point regarding the value of an expression of opinion, public or private, on any phase of population control may be illustrated by a recent statement from the United States Department of State outlining the policy of the United States in the granting of aid to countries desiring it for the purpose of reducing their rates of population growth. This comes near to a statement of the United States's view of what the most-needed world population policy should be, although it is only implied. However, there is no suggestion whatever that the United States might adopt a national policy encouraging smaller families in conformity with any world population policy, as the reader can see by reading the statement made by Deputy Assistant Secretary Gardner before the United Nations Committee II on December 10, 1962:

1. The United States is concerned about the social consequences of its own population trends and is devoting attention to them.

2. The United States wants to know more, and help others to know more, about population trends in less developed countries where present levels of population growth may constitute a major obstacle to the realization of goals of human economic and social development.

3. The United States would oppose any effort to dictate to any country the means to be employed in dealing with its population problem. The population policy of any country must be determined by that country and that country alone.

4. While the United States will not suggest to any other government what its attitudes or policies should be as they relate to population, or the adoption of specific measures in its implementation, the United States believes that obstacles should not be placed in the way of other governments which, in the light of their own economic needs and cultural and religious values, seek solutions to their population problems. While we will not advocate any specific policy regarding population growth to another country, we can help other countries, upon request, to find

potential sources of information and assistance on ways and means of dealing with population problems.

5. The United States believes that there is a great need for additional knowledge on population matters. There is need for more information about the actual size and composition of existing populations and about future population trends—and both private organizations and governments as well as international organizations can help provide it. There is a need for more facts about alternative methods of family planning that are consistent with different economic, social, cultural and religious circumstances. There is a need for more facts about the impact of economic and social development on population trends and of population trends on economic and social development.[1]

This statement evidently goes as far as any country should or can go in making effective the population policies of other countries without interfering obnoxiously in their internal affairs. Under these circumstances, it is difficult to see how there can be any world-population policy in the near future. The situation is much like that we discussed in connection with a *world food supply* (Chapter 19). Some other aspects of national population policy versus world-population policy will be discussed in the following section of this chapter and in the following chapter.

SOME NATIONAL POPULATION POLICIES

At this point it will be in order to note very briefly a few of the avowed policies adopted by different countries in order to illustrate the trend of thought regarding national population policies today. It is neither possible nor necessary to give detailed descriptions of these policies here.

Sweden. About 30 years ago Sweden undertook to examine with care the relation of her population growth to the welfare of her people. Since Sweden already possessed highly efficient health services, a good educational system, an efficient economy, a low birth rate and a *very* low death rate, the question of most interest to the country was: Does Sweden need a population policy to enhance further the welfare of its people? If it does, what form should it take? In the first place, there appears to have been comparatively little difference of opinion between thoughtful people as regards what was desirable in the way of population growth. The population was already growing but slowly, and a continuance of this slow growth did not seem likely to have any harmful effect on the welfare of the people. Sweden did not have to face the problem of a probable growth of population at a faster rate than could be provided for by the

[1] Department of State, "United States' Policy *re* Population Growth," *AIDTO Circular* A-173, 12/4/62-M.O. 1018.2 (*Unclassified AIDTO Circular* A-187, 12/27/62).

expansion of her economy that could reasonably be expected. Indeed, there was good reason to believe that the steadily increasing efficiency of the national economy could provide a substantially better level of living for the poorer portion of her population if the distribution of the national income were improved while the volume of the output was being expanded.

In Sweden as in most other Western countries, but probably to a lesser extent than in most of them, the poorer families were frequently above average size and could not provide for themselves under existing conditions all the essentials of what was generally regarded in Sweden as a decent living. It would, therefore, be necessary for the state to come to their aid to a limited extent if they were to attain a desirable standard of living and if their children were to be given good opportunities to prepare themselves to contribute more efficiently to the national life.

Many of these larger families had more children than the parents desired. It seemed reasonable therefore, as a matter of public policy, to make certain that every couple had easy access to the information and to the means necessary to control the size of the family. It was believed that if control were thus facilitated and if the general level of living were reasonably good, the government would not need to place much emphasis upon the restriction of the size of the family, that most couples would, of their own accord, decide to have relatively small families. For mentally normal families having more children than could be provided with a good home environment and good opportunities to secure more education where desired, some aid would be provided. In addition, measures were taken to discourage or even to prevent the subnormal couples (mentally) from having children when it appeared reasonably certain that these children would be a life-time burden to the community.

Actually, as far as the direct control of population growth was concerned, only two measures were then activated in the Swedish program: (1) making contraceptive information more readily available to all couples; and (2) discouraging the reproduction of the mentally subnormal. The other measures were only indirectly related to population growth. The assistance given to normal families unable to provide for their children in a satisfactory manner may be classed as a welfare measure, a redistribution of the national product undertaken by the community in its own interest rather than as a measure intended to have any significant effect on the growth of population. Altogether, then, the Swedish population policy seems to be aimed chiefly at improving the quality of the population by improving the living conditions and the opportunities of the poorer classes and by reducing the size of the genetically subnormal population. The expectation was that when good living conditions for all the people were reasonably well assured, the average normal couple would so adjust its number of children to its economic status that there would be no need to campaign actively for either larger or smaller families.

France. France was the first country in the world in modern times in which a significant proportion of the people undertook the voluntary control over the size of their families. The decline in the birth rate became so large that after the Franco-Prussian War (1870–1871) many people in France were much concerned over the slow growth of their population as compared with neighboring countries. Indeed, after 1900, during a few years there was no natural increase. In World War I France lost about 2 million men. This gave a further great setback to population growth and was an important factor in the development of a policy of family assistance which, it was hoped, would lead more families to raise three or four children and thus induce a steady, if slow, growth of population.

Since this policy was adopted only shortly before World War II, it was not possible to judge whether it was effective until several years after the war ended in 1945. Since that time France has had a natural increase of about 6 per 1,000 per year. Although a part of this increase must be attributed to further reduction in the death rate, it would appear that the policy of encouraging a modest increase in population by providing fairly substantial family assistance graduated to the number of children in the family is beginning to have some effect.

France, like Sweden, should experience comparatively little economic difficulty in providing well for this relatively slow increase in population for some time to come. The chief reasons for such a judgment are: (1) France's economy has recovered in a remarkable manner since World War II; (2) the demographic effects of the great loss of males aged from about 18 to 35 in World War I were largely over by the end of World War II, in which France's military losses were much smaller than in World War I. France's population now has a more normal age and sex composition than at any time since the close of World War I (1918). This may explain in part the rather steady birth rate of about 18 per 1,000 per year in recent years. However, French students of population seem inclined to give considerable credit for the steady but low natural increase to the family-assistance program. Besides, a public opinion favorable to a small increase in average family size appears to be developing.

When the French population policies are compared with those of Sweden, the chief differences appear to be: There is (1) more emphasis on increasing numbers in the French policy and (2) less on improving the quality of the population through the extension of social services (health, education, recreation facilities, etc.) and through the discouragement of the reproduction of the mentally subnormal.

Other European Countries. A number of other countries in Western Europe have population policies somewhat similar to those of Sweden and France. Probably the chief reason for the mildness of the encouragement to increase population (if any) in most of these countries is that the present rates of population growth, though low, are felt to be quite satisfactory from the standpoint of maintaining a favorable ratio between population growth and economic growth. This feeling appears to prevail rather widely in Western, Central, and Southern Europe.

European Settlements Abroad. In most of the areas settled by Europeans since about 1650, except in Latin America as will be noted (Chapter 21), the birth rates, although somewhat higher than in Europe, are now quite low compared with what they were before the Depression of the 1930s, and in the United States and Canada their higher postwar birth rates have now begun to decline. These countries are all relatively thinly settled in comparison with the European countries and in general have birth rates that show a strong sensitivity to fluctuations in economic conditions. They also have quite efficient industrialized economies, and as yet their agricultural and other resources are relatively abundant, so that they should have little difficulty in providing a decent living to such increases in population as appear probable in the foreseeable future. None of these countries has formulated a public population policy intended to influence directly the natural increase of its population, although Canada's family subsidies may have some tendency to do so. Several of them, however, have long had definite public policies which did influence population growth, though neither the man in the street nor the politicians thought of them as population policies since they were not adopted with the intent of influencing couples in determining the size of their families. For example, the land policy prevailing in North American colonies through the seventeenth and eighteenth centuries and later in the United States and Canada was perhaps the most effective ever devised for encouraging the rapid growth of population. Moreover, this land policy was coupled with an immigration policy placing only mild restrictions on the free movement of Europeans into this area until after World War I. It is not surprising, therefore, that population grew very rapidly for a long time— until the better land was occupied and industrialization and urbanization were well under way.

At present, however, in all areas settled by Europeans, again excepting Latin America, the natural increase of population is slow as compared with what it was until about 1900, and immigration is now being restricted quite drastically. There is little immediate likelihood that the rate of population growth in these countries will exceed the rate of expansion in their economies if they are ready and able to make some rather substantial readjustments in the distribution of their national incomes. It should be noted, however, that the *new industrial revolution—automation*—may lead to considerable temporary unemployment even in these rather thinly settled countries with moderately low rates of population increase. This would probably tend to reduce the level of living for the unemployed, but it seems reasonable to expect that under these conditions further declines in the birth rates will take place in the near future without any organized public efforts in this direction.

Japan. The leaders of Japan for some years before World War II had taken the same attitude toward population growth that Hitler and Mussolini had taken. They wanted a rapidly growing population because they believed that such growth would give stronger support to their efforts to enlarge the Japanese Empire and would also provide enough settlers in the conquered territories to bind them firmly to Japan. During this period when the expansionists were in control, propaganda for birth control was forbidden, and not a few people were imprisoned for propagandizing for it. There is no evidence that this expansionist population policy had any effect in raising the birth rate. At the most it may possibly have retarded its decline to a slight extent.

Japan had been highly successful in acquiring new territory and larger resources in her wars with China and Russia, which for all practical purposes had brought Korea, Formosa, and Manchuria within her empire. Moreover, these wars were won at comparatively little cost in lives or money. Assuming that the co-prosperity sphere of East and Southeast Asia would be established with proportionally light costs, Japan would then have the land and other resources needed to support a rapidly growing population and could soon have become the dominant power in all of Asia and one of the three or four great powers in the world. This was the vision of the future that led the imperialists to prepare for World War II.

The loss of World War II shattered these dreams of empire and completely discredited the expansionists in the eyes of the growing middle classes in Japan. These people began to question the effectiveness of war in securing needed resources and to discuss more realistically what could be done to enable the Japanese people to live even as well as they had before the war. The repatriation to Japan of over 6 million Japanese nationals from the co-prosperity sphere within a little over a year after the close of the war added greatly to Japan's economic difficulties. About 3 million of these repatriates were military personnel, mostly young men who rejoined their families or were married soon after their return. The others were people who had settled in the colonies or had followed the armies into the co-prosperity-sphere countries. A large proportion of these were young adults. As a consequence of repatriation and speedy demobilization, the birth rate of Japan from 1946 to 1950 was the highest ever recorded. Moreover, at the same time, with the effective cooperation of the United States Occupation Administration, the death rate in Japan almost immediately began to decline in a very remarkable manner. It had been about 17 per 1,000 per year before the war but had risen to about 29 in the last year of the war and remained quite high during the first year and a half of the Occupation. Since 1948 the death rate has averaged only about one-half of what it was before the war, i.e., about 8.5 to 9 per 1,000 per year. The sudden increase in birth rates and sudden drop in death rates resulted in much the largest total annual increases in population, as well as in the largest rates of increase, Japan had ever had. Since Japan had lost her colonies, since her foreign trade was completely wiped out, and since the Occupation authorities permitted practically free discussion of all matters of public interest, it is not surprising that Japan's population dilemma began to receive a truly vast amount of attention. How to support themselves was a pressing question in millions of families, and the reduction of the size of the family came to be widely recognized as the most reasonable and practical solution of their difficulty. There were several very important conditions peculiar to Japan, as compared with other Asian countries, which favored this solution.

The Japanese people were one of the most literate populations in the world. Even the farmers were able to follow closely much of the discussion of Japan's population problem day by day in the press and indeed could hardly avoid doing so because of the large amount of space allotted to this topic in the papers and the time allotted it over the radio. Besides, for about 200 to 250 years before the opening of Japan to the West, which occurred about the middle of the nineteenth century, the people of Japan had actually exercised sufficient control over their growth in numbers to keep the total population within a relatively narrow range. They had learned how to adjust their numbers to the production of the tillable land. The most potent operative factor during that period in keeping numbers relatively stationary was no doubt the same as in most other populations in the world at that time, viz., the high death rate, especially among infants and young children. However, infanticide was by no means rare, and abortion was widely practiced and socially approved where the family was unable to support more children at the near-subsistence standards then prevailing. Japanese culture sanctioned these practices, which aided materially in maintaining a balance between population growth and agricultural production.

Still other factors uniquely conducive to the rapid decline of the birth rate in Japan after World War II that should be mentioned here are: (1) The Emperor, for whom the Japanese people have great reverence, let it be known that the control of the size of the family met with his approval. (2) Practically all the Japanese people speak one language. This is in strong contrast to China and India, where many languages and dialects are still in use and where there are far greater cultural differences between the people living in different parts of the country than in Japan. (3) Japan was already rather highly industrialized, and a large proportion of the people (63.5 percent) lived in cities and worked at nonagricultural tasks. (4) Japan was the one country in Asia having a large number of well-trained physicians and surgeons fully competent to perform abortions and sterilizations safely and to instruct their patients in the techniques of contraception once the legal restrictions against such practices were removed.

(5) The Japanese people had long been accustomed to the acceptance of the leadership of the central government, and when the loss of the war manifestly called for new policies, they were ready to follow new leaders and new policies which seemed to promise some amelioration of the hardships of the war and its aftermath. (6) Whether the United States can be said to have played any role in the adoption of the new population policy in Japan must remain open to question. But it can be said that the United States Occupation Administration officially took great care to let the Japanese know that the United States had no intention of taking a hand in the formation of a Japanese population policy. The United States officially would neither support nor oppose any policy since this was regarded as a matter the Japanese must decide for themselves and face the consequences of their own decision.

It would be rather premature at this time to assert that Japan has finally solved her population problem for she still has an annual increase of about 900,000 a year. This absolute increase will probably be reduced somewhat as the crude death rate rises, for it soon must begin to rise from the present low level of 8.5 to 9 per 1,000 per year as the median age of the population begins to rise, i.e., as her population becomes older. (A permanent death rate of 9 per 1,000 in a stationary population would mean an average expectation of life at birth of 111 years.) (See Chapter 12.)

The speed with which Japan reduced her birth rate has led many people to believe that some of the underdeveloped countries having urgent need for slower population growth might follow quickly in Japan's footsteps and achieve a like reduction of 40 to 50 percent in the birth rate within a few years. Since, as just indicated, the authors feel that in many respects Japan was uniquely prepared to adopt and to put into effect a policy of reducing the birth rate faster than the death rate, they believe that Japan's experience will be of only indirect aid to the governments of India or China or Pakistan in their efforts to hasten the adoption of family limitation in those countries and that it will be of even less help to the peoples of Africa and Latin America when, and if, their governments should decide that the voluntary control of the size of the family is urgently needed in their countries.

U.S.S.R. The attitude of the U.S.S.R. toward the need for control over population growth was mentioned in Chapter 3. It was pointed out there that any policy deliberately calculated to reduce the rate of population growth was inconsistent with the basic claim of communism, viz., that it had discovered the cure-all, the panacea, for all man's economic ills.

In spite of the fact that at times the leaders of the U.S.S.R. have bestowed large economic bonuses on mothers of unusually large families and that other forms of family assistance graduated according to the size of the family are in operation, they do not seem to have supported any one population policy consistently. Rather they have pursued a laissez-faire, a hands-off, policy. The policy makers in the U.S.S.R. have been so concerned with economic development that the policies they adopted, although they may have had significant effects on population growth, were not supported for this reason but rather because they were intended to aid directly in rapid economic development. Until quite recently they have encouraged women to take regular jobs in industry, in the professions, and in offices, although the experience of all industrialized countries has shown that women in the labor force have relatively small families. Likewise, they have at times made abortion very easy to secure, safe, and very cheap and at other times have discouraged it. For economic reasons also, they have recently encouraged contraception in place of abortion as the most desirable means of controlling the size of the family. Besides, the means for the successful practice of contraception have been readily available and in adequate supply at all times in the state stores.

On the other hand, the U.S.S.R. has adopted certain policies in addition to the family assistance noted above which could be interpreted as favoring large families. It has provided nurseries for the daytime care of children of women working in factories and offices and in the professions in order to encourage them to have families while remaining at work. It has provided rather long vacation periods with full pay and certain other perquisites to women preceding and following the birth of a baby, and free medical services are available to all families. Free education beyond the compulsory school age for children showing promise might appear as an encouragement to larger families. It seems more probable, however, that these practices are intended chiefly to secure a greater amount of productive work from women than a larger number of children.

In addition, the leaders of the U.S.S.R. do not seem to have been much disturbed by the rather rapid decline in the birth rate of the country in the past two or three decades. The birth rate for the ten years 1952 to 1961 as given in the United Nations Demographic Yearbook, but not vouched for by its statistical officials, is about 25 per 1,000, only slightly higher than our own during the same period. Some more recent newspaper reports indicate that it may have fallen by an additional two or three points since 1960. This would mean a decline from a birth rate of about 40 or more at the time of the revolution (1917) and probably until after the census of 1926, to 25 or even to 22 or 23 in a period of about 30 years. Since at present this decline cannot be attributed chiefly to abortion as in Japan, we must conclude that contraception is widely practiced, at least in the urbanized and industrialized portions of the population of the U.S.S.R. The economic development of the country has led to a rapid increase in urban population which now constitutes nearly one-half of the total, to the increasing employment of women, and to the urgent demand for more education for more young people, especially in science and technology. It would not be in the least surprising if these changes have led to the increasing postponement of marriage for a few years in significantly large groups and to the increasing desire for small families among a larger proportion of all city dwellers. The constant housing shortage in the cities ever since the revolution (1917) has no doubt also contributed to the voluntary reduction of the average size of the family.

Nevertheless, about one-half of the population of the U.S.S.R. still lives on farms and in little-developed regions where the birth rate is almost certainly well above that of the urban population. There can be little doubt that if the crude birth rate of the total population is 22 to 25 per 1,000, the birth rate of the urban population is highly unlikely to be over 20 per 1,000 and may be even lower. This is a very large decline in the face of the fact that of all countries in the world the U.S.S.R. is probably the most fortunately situated as regards an abundance of resources both for agriculture and for industry.

Under the existing circumstances, it seems reasonable to attribute this marked decline in the birth rate in recent years chiefly to the reaction of the people themselves to the changes in modes of living inevitably occurring among every people when they pass from a primarily agricultural economy to a more highly industrialized economy. Where this transition has been quite rapid, as in the U.S.S.R., one might expect a rapid response in the adjustment of the size of the family to the new living conditions being encountered by the increasing urbanization of the population. This would appear especially probable where a large and rapid decline in the death rate had taken place simultaneously as it did in the U.S.S.R. Under these circumstances the *average* number of children reared to maturity even in urban families might not decline as rapidly as the birth rate.

The rate of natural increase in the U.S.S.R. at present would appear to be in the neighborhood of 16 to 18 per 1,000 per year. However, we cannot feel very certain on many points of Soviet demography until better and more regular data are provided (see Chapter 15). A rate of natural increase of 18 per 1,000 per year doubles any population in about 40 years. A population of 30 million in the present territory of the U.S.S.R. in 1800 would now amount to about 480 million if such a rate had prevailed uninterruptedly. This is well over twice the present population (officially 208.8 million in 1959). Thus it would appear that the population of the U.S.S.R., in spite of the fairly rapid decline in the birth rate in recent years, is even now growing at a considerably more rapid rate than that which prevailed, *on the average*, for the past century and a half.

Since the U.S.S.R. has had no consistent and avowed population policy, it seems reasonable to believe that much the same conditions which led to a rather rapid decline in the birth rate among many of the Western peoples during the period 1850 to 1914, i.e., in the six decades before World War I, are now exerting a similar influence on the population of the U.S.S.R. and that the decline in the birth rate has taken place in a somewhat shorter period, largely since about 1926. In addition, within this period the U.S.S.R. has reduced its age-specific death rates to the point that further reductions at most ages will be about as slow as is to be expected in Western Europe. Hence, its crude death rate, like that of most industrialized countries, will almost certainly begin to rise within two or three decades as the age composition of its population becomes more normal by reason of large increases in the population 50 years of age or over.

That both the death rate and the birth rate in the U.S.S.R. should have declined more rapidly than in the West is not surprising because: (1) As has been noted, the tempo of industrialization in the U.S.S.R. has been rapid; (2) the efficient use of the means of contraception had increased greatly in the three or four decades preceding 1930;[2] (3) also, by about this date (1930) the health services had attained a fair degree of efficiency, and the mortality of infants and young children was being rapidly reduced, while local epidemics of the infectious diseases were rapidly coming under control and thus prevented from becoming widespread epidemics. This relatively rapid decline in the death rates of babies and young children caught the attention of many mothers in the cities and may well have served to stimulate their interest in contraception.

In the U.S.S.R., as in the United States, no question has ever been seriously raised regarding the adequacy of the natural resources of the nation to support any probable natural increase of population within the next few decades. The failure of U.S.S.R. agriculture to produce the abundance and variety of food-stuffs desired is not due to the inadequacy of agricultural resources but to the failure of the Soviet system of collective and state farms to supply adequate motives to encourage the people who remain on the land to produce more efficiently. Besides, private initiative in the settlement of new lands has been absolutely forbidden.

As we have shown in Chapter 3, the theory of Malthus that population tended to outrun the capacity of man to produce subsistence was very bitterly repudiated by Marx without any effort to disprove it. Moreover, the reference at the close of that chapter to the statement in the Great Soviet Encyclopaedia to the effect that "there cannot be any surplus population under a socialist regime, in spite of rapid demographic growth" seems to indicate acceptance of this view as official. The policies which have actually most affected population growth in the U.S.S.R. have not been deliberately planned as population policies. They appear rather to have been motivated chiefly by the desire to increase the speed of industrialization without regard to their effects on population growth. This is the reason why we believe the U.S.S.R. can truly be said to have adopted no deliberate policy as regards population growth, although it subscribes to orthodox Marxian theory in respect to the relation between population growth and economic welfare. There are rumors that some change in this Marxian attitude may now (1963) be taking place.

---

[2] This date is used here because by 1930 the industrialization of the U.S.S.R. was well started, and in consequence, the number of people in the cities was growing rapidly. Also there was a growing interest in contraception as a method of reducing the size of the family as opposed to the increasingly frequent use of abortion, which had been taking place since the legal restrictions against it had been removed several years earlier.

CHAPTER TWENTY-ONE

Population Policies (Continued)

We have seen in the preceding chapter that about one-third of the people in the world now have birth rates that are so well under voluntary control that they can reasonably be expected to keep their numbers within the limits of their capacity to maintain a rising level of living for some time to come; also, except in Japan, this status has been achieved under a hands-off policy, i.e., without any considerable governmental encouragement or assistance in family planning. In most of these countries the reduction in the size of families has taken place in spite of more or less governmental and/or religious opposition. Why then are most students of world population movements so greatly concerned over the burgeoning population in those countries and regions containing the other two-thirds of mankind? Why not leave the reduction of the birth rate to the voluntary action of the people themselves?

The facts showing the recent population growth in the underdeveloped countries have been set forth at some length in Chapter 16, and the more important factors likely to determine the intensity of population pressures in the near future have been discussed in Chapter 19. Here we shall discuss the population policies being undertaken in a few of the underdeveloped countries and their probable role in the control of population growth in the near future; also some general social changes which are likely to play an important role in determining the rate of decline in the birth rate in those countries still having high birth rates.

POPULATION POLICIES IN UNDERDEVELOPED COUNTRIES

Approximately two-thirds of the people in the world live in the underdeveloped countries. Here the social and economic conditions which led to the gradual reduction of the birth rate in the West over varying periods of about six to ten decades since about 1850 do not yet prevail. The people in these countries are still in large measure preindustrial, i.e., agricultural. The great majority perhaps 70 to 80 percent, live in agricultural villages, and only about one-half of the remainder live in large towns and small cities with perhaps one-eighth to one-tenth of their total populations in cities of less than 20,000. Thus the pattern of daily living of the great mass of these peoples has as yet scarcely been touched by the new and very powerful social and economic forces accompanying industrialization and urbanization. Outside of the West the two most industrialized countries are Japan and the U.S.S.R. Already in both of them a rather rapidly growing proportion of the people have found it advisable to control the size of their families if they are to raise their levels of living and are to give their children adequate training for living in a modern industrial society. Perhaps the fertility of the approximate two-thirds of mankind living in the underdeveloped countries can best be described in connection with the discussion of the population policies that have recently been adopted in several of them.

THE POPULATION POLICY OF INDIA

The modern censuses of India from the beginning in 1872 have been carefully planned and executed with a view to securing a true picture of Indian population growth and of the composition of the population. They are generally regarded as reasonably reliable, much more reliable than the registration of births and deaths, for measuring the growth of population, and they are the only satisfactory source of data showing the composition of the population for the entire country. Recently, some sample surveys have supplemented these census materials.[1]

There could not be clearer statistical support for Malthus's view that, under the conditions prevailing in his day (which had much in common with those of India today), when the positive checks are severe, population grows little or not at all, while it grows substantially when these hardships diminish. From India's first census (1872) and including that of 1921, the growth of India's population shows a very close relation between the intensity of food shortages and the violence of epidemics, on the one hand, and the growth of population on the other hand. When the weather records show weak monsoons (inadequate rainfall) and when there have been unusual visitations of disease, the censuses show little or no population increase. The census of 1881 (the second) showed a growth (India and Pakistan were then one colony) of only 0.8 percent or *8 per 1,000 in the 9-year period of 1872 to 1881;* the census of 1901 again showed a very low

---

[1] For more details of India's population policy to about 1957 and China's first birth-control campaign, see Warren S. Thompson, *Population and Progress in the Far East*, chaps. 8 and 11, The University of Chicago Press, Chicago, 1959.

rate of growth, only 1.1 percent (11 per 1,000) in the decade 1891–1901, and that of 1921 showed an increase of only 0.9 percent in the decade 1911–1921. (The annual average would be nearly one-tenth of the rate during a decade.) The two intervening censuses, that of 1891 with a growth of 9.6 percent between 1881 and 1891 and that of 1911 with a growth of 6.2 percent between 1901 and 1911, both had fairly large increases for that time in an underdeveloped country with a relatively dense population. These were very definitely periods of better-than-average rainfall and of rather mild epidemics.

Beginning with the decade of 1921–1931, the operation of the positive checks in India has been substantially and increasingly moderated. The ravages of famine have been largely eliminated by the improvements in transport and by better political and economic organization for famine relief. Rather large reclamation projects and some modest improvements in agricultural practices have also contributed to a larger and more certain food supply. Epidemics of infectious diseases have been somewhat checked, at first by better quarantine regulations in the port cities and by a growing appreciation of the value of public and household sanitation. Since World War II the health services have been greatly improved, and the miracle drugs and the new and more effective insecticides have played a major role. As a result, the population in the territory of the present *Indian Union* increased from about 275.5 million in 1931 to 434.8 million in 1961. The rate of growth in the decade 1951 to 1961 was approximately 2 percent per year, or a little over 21 percent for the decade.

For some years a number of Indian scholars had been greatly concerned with their population growth. Even before World War II, most of them had come to feel that India was facing the Malthusian dilemma, that her population was growing so fast that it endangered any substantial improvement in the welfare of the great mass of the people.

Nehru, who became premier of the Indian Union with independence (1947), had long held the view that India was suffering from overpopulation and that birth control was badly needed if her death rate was to be reduced and then kept low, and if a better level of living was to be assured to all the people. It was not surprising, therefore, that the government of the Indian Union decided to promote family planning as an integral part of its plan for modernizing the economy. This view must have been widely accepted by well-informed Indians for there was practically no organized opposition to the adoption of the policy to encourage by all possible means the voluntary control of the size of the family by the practice of contraception. In the first Five-Year Plan, a small amount of money (about $1.3 million) was earmarked for the encouragement of family planning. This was obviously only a token amount to begin work among about 360 million people, only a few of whom had ever heard of the voluntary control of conception. In the second Five-Year Plan, this allotment was raised to $8 million. This again was a mere pittance, for even if all the projects that could possibly be supported by these funds were made fully operative by 1961 (the end of the second Five-Year Plan), they would at most have reached only about 40,000 villages out of a total of perhaps 550,000, less than one-tenth of the agricultural population.

For a number of reasons, only the most important of which can even be enumerated here, many people, both Indians and foreign observers, seemed to expect a rather rapid decline in India's birth rate. The chief reasons are as follows: (1) Definite governmental support of birth control through family planning was widely approved by the educated class. (2) A law was passed forbidding marriage of women under 15 years of age. (3) Great advances in education leading to the rapid reduction of illiteracy and wide use of the radio were expected to assist materially in spreading the knowledge that family size could be controlled by contraception, and in directing the people to the agencies both public and private that were equipped to give information about, and instruction in, the methods of contraception. (4) Many mother-and-child health centers, which were first established solely as health centers, were soon found to be of great assistance in spreading the knowledge that family planning was both possible and desirable and also in giving precise instruction in the best methods of contraception. In these clinics it could be pointed out easily and convincingly to mothers that as many children would be raised to maturity under improving health conditions from three or four children born as their mothers had raised to maturity from six or more births. (5) A number of surveys in communities in various parts of India showed that the women would quite readily attend meetings to discuss family planning, indeed that they seemed rather eager to discuss how they might reduce the number of births.

Taking into account these and other seemingly favorable conditions, it is not surprising that many people believed that family planning with fewer births per family was likely to spread quite rapidly in India. However, it soon became clear that in spite of the fact that there was no organized opposition, religious or other, to the practice of contraception, the campaign for smaller families was making little headway. On the other hand, the decline in the death rate was proceeding more rapidly than had been expected by even the most knowledgeable people, chiefly because of the increasing efficiency of the public health services using the miracle drugs and insecticides, the better distribution of the food available, some increase in agricultural production arising from slowly improving agricultural practices and, finally, easier access by the government to surplus food supplies in Western countries in times of crisis. As a result, the census of 1961, as just noted, showed a more rapid increase in the rate of population growth than ever before—*considerably larger than that contemplated by the government when the first and second Five-Year Plans were drawn up.*

The basic reason for the slow adoption of family planning in India, described in the most general terms, is that traditional culture values still determine the

behavior of the vast majority of India's people. This is true of behavior determining reproduction as well as most other aspects of personal and social behavior.
It is not to be expected that reproductive practices will change quickly where
practically all traditional cultural values remain almost intact; the actual living
conditions of the great majority of the people have not changed sufficiently to
provide motives for the adoption of new patterns of reproductive behavior.
Conservatism characterizes India's agricultural population, which constitutes
about three-fourths of the total and (in 1961) numbers perhaps 325 million.
Only a small proportion of India's people have as yet been uprooted from the
agricultural villages and moved to the cities, where they necessarily have to make
many new and mentally painful adjustments—personal, familial, occupational,
social, and economic. In fact, the village environment still strongly encourages
conformity to traditional patterns of behavior. Few if any motives for acting or
thinking differently from the traditional patterns are operating on the children
and young people growing up in the villages. This situation will no doubt change
more rapidly as illiteracy diminishes, but it is not reasonable to expect a rapid
increase of openmindedness in the village population for some years to come.
The traditional pattern of daily behavior still works fairly well in the villages
where the farmers live. Therefore, it should not occasion surprise that the need
for control of their population growth has not yet been realized by more than a
very small proportion of India's people, nor that the Indian leaders are themselves bewildered as to how they can rapidly influence more people to realize
what it means to them personally, to their families, and to the nation as a whole,
to maintain a practically uncontrolled birth rate while rapid strides in reducing
the death rate are being made year by year.

In what has just been said we do not mean to imply that a substantial reduction in the size of the family in India or in any other economically underdeveloped country must follow either the same pattern of change or the same rate of
change as in the West. But we do believe that encountering the crises in daily
living that are inevitable in making the transition from a simple, traditional
agricultural society to a complex industrial society has played a large role in
bringing about the planned reduction in the size of families in all the societies
that have actually reduced their birth rates substantially during the past century. Consequently, it appears reasonable to assume that the people of India and
of other underdeveloped countries must be confronted with the necessity of
adjustment to somewhat similar conditions or to other circumstances which will
be *compelling* to them, before the masses will adopt the voluntary control of the
size of the family. There can be no solid assurance that similar conditions or
what will appear to Western people as "compelling circumstances" will inevitably arise in India or in any other underdeveloped country. Hence, waiting for
the conditions to develop which led to smaller families in Western lands may
mean waiting for something of doubtful achievement in many underdeveloped

countries in the foreseeable future because their rates of population growth may of themselves delay economic growth and development indefinitely. This possibility of long-delayed economic improvement suggests that what is urgently needed to bring about a rapid decline in the birth rate in these underdeveloped countries is an effective approach to the problem of supplying strong motives for fewer births per family among those peoples who may have to wait a relatively long time for industrialization and urbanization to change their uncontrolled reproduction into controlled reproduction. If this should be true, the really important question to be faced is: *How can the great mass of the people of India (or any other underdeveloped country) be made to realize the necessity of controlling the size of the family as long as they live in small villages where traditional patterns of behavior are so firmly entrenched?*

No one yet has found a satisfactory answer to this question. The senior author has been greatly interested in this question ever since he has been convinced that substantial declines in death rates were likely to take place faster among the peoples in underdeveloped countries today than they had in the Western countries. (See the description of his visit to a health demonstration in Peking in 1923 in the preceding chapter.) On a recent trip to India (1955–1956), he was much impressed by the difficulties the people working in *family planning organizations* encountered in persuading women to come to clinics to learn the methods of contraception. Some of the birth-control clinics visited could have cared for two or three times as many women as applied for instruction. On the other hand, he was also much impressed by the fact that some of the *health centers* established for the care of mothers and young children were overcrowded and that where these health centers were staffed by doctors, nurses, and helpers interested in family planning they frequently found more demand for family-planning services than they could supply. The mothers who came to these health centers apparently could be quite easily convinced that their own health and that of their babies could be more certainly assured if they did not have another baby until after a longer interval than was customary. Indeed, the word soon passed from mother to mother, and many mothers of their own accord began to inquire how the intervals between births might be prolonged. In several centers at first devoted entirely to health services, the writer was told that inquiries regarding family planning became so numerous they could not be met satisfactorily because of insufficient supplies and/or inadequate personnel. This situation very naturally suggests combining both services in all health centers so that every mother-and-child health clinic becomes also a center not only for spreading knowledge that family planning is possible but also for giving instruction in safe and effective methods for the control of conception. It is of much interest that with regard to the combining of health and family-planning services, only very recently have some of the leaders in health work in the United States come to recognize that health services are so closely related to family planning that the latter should be made an integral part of health services to mothers when it is desired by them. Many doctors, however, still consider this heresy.

It is reasonably certain that in practically all the countries now having a large measure of voluntary control over the size of the family, this control began among the more educated and more prosperous people living in cities and then spread rather slowly to the less fortunate urban groups and finally with considerable further lag to their farming populations. However, there is no good reason to believe that this Western pattern of the adoption of family planning is the best and quickest way to hasten family planning among the people living in the underdeveloped countries. On the other hand, if the public health services of these countries, and especially those services for mothers and children, also undertake to provide family-planning service, there is much reason to believe that the masses of the people in these countries will more quickly adopt family planning than was the case in the West.

Although the situation in India has been emphasized here, it should be made clear that India's problem of equating the growth of population with the expansion of its economy is not essentially different from that of most other underdeveloped countries. Every improvement in health services will reduce the death rate, provided even the present low per capita consumption of the necessities of life can be maintained. But if every improvement in health services to mothers and their children can also be made to contribute to the wider spacing of children, the birth rate might decline substantially before urbanization and industrialization can be relied on to assume an important role in keeping the birth rate at a desirable level.

Perhaps the most hopeful sign that conception control will spread fairly rapidly in the future in many underdeveloped countries is that more and more parents are beginning to complain of growing economic difficulties in raising their families. It may seem odd to call this a hopeful sign, but it does indicate that parents are beginning to wonder what can be done to improve the living conditions of their families. Consequently, here is another opportunity for health agencies to explain the relation between these hardships and the growing size of their families as more and more of the babies born survive to adulthood. It can be pointed out, when these complaints are made, that the quickest and best way for the parents to ease their economic burdens as well as to care for their children better, is to space the births at wider intervals and to cease having children when the desired size of family has been attained. It would appear that this better understanding of family economic difficulties would supply a new and increasingly powerful motive for keeping families relatively small. But it must be remembered that most of the parents are still illiterate, and that great hardships have so long been the lot of the mass of the people, that they are quite commonly accepted as inevitable. Improvement and progress are concepts which as yet have little meaning to most of the people in the underdeveloped countries.

THE POPULATION POLICY OF COMMUNIST CHINA

Communist China took its first census as of June 30, 1953. This is the first census of China, at least in modern times, which could lay claim to fair accuracy. By 1953 the Communists had been in control of all China (Mainland) for about four years and had accomplished a complete redistribution of agricultural holdings. In order to carry through this land reform, they must have had an administrative apparatus actively at work in every political subdivision which could reach the people in every agricultural village in that subdivision. This organization should have been able to count noses everywhere, except possibly in some isolated mountain communities. Hence it would seem that they possessed an administrative setup quite capable of taking a fairly accurate census. Furthermore, the higher officials badly needed accurate census data for purposes of planning not only national social and economic development but also for planning community developments of all kinds. The higher officials undoubtedly did what they could to ensure accurate returns, and they accepted the returns as a basis for much of their planning.

The 1953 census showed a total of about 583 million persons in Mainland China, of whom 574 million were "counted directly and registered," while between 8 and 9 million were "surveyed indirectly." When the overseas Chinese and the population of Formosa were included, the total Chinese population came to 602 million. Considering only the mainland (583 million), we see that the population was close to 100 million more than might have been expected in view of the best information previously available.

The vast excess of population above the figures the Communist leaders had been using and might reasonably have been expecting probably will help to explain the fact that in 1954, not long after the census results were released, a campaign for birth control got under way and was pressed quite vigorously for nearly four years.[2] The chief reasons given for urging a reduction in the birth rate were the need to improve the health of mothers and children, to enable the state to provide better educational facilities for children and youth, and to make more female labor available for economic development. Two measures in particular were recommended to the people to accomplish these ends: (1) the postponement of marriage by all couples for several years beyond the lower legal age, which was 21 for males and 18 for females, and (2) the use of contraception both for preventing large families and for the spacing of births at longer intervals. For the most part, great care was taken to deny that the population was too large, although it was frequently said that its growth was too rapid. If occasionally the population appeared to be too large, it was only because of the evil effects of capitalism and colonialism, which could not be sloughed off at once. The views of Marx, Engels, and Lenin were quite generally cited as suffi-

[2] *Ibid.*, chap. 11.

cient *proof* that a Communist society never need be concerned over having so many people that it could not ensure them a satisfactory level of living once this society was well established. However, it might happen that a population would grow too fast at a particular time to permit of as substantial an improvement in the level of living and of as rapid economic development as was desirable. This was not because the population was too large. Apparently the contradiction between these views was not perceived or, at least, it was not acknowledged.

A brief but typical propaganda statement will illustrate the strange line of reasoning used to justify their encouragement of birth control:

> In order to lessen the difficulties currently facing us, to protect the health of maternity womanhood [sic] and finally to ensure that the next generation may be brought up better, we are not opposed at all to birth control. At the same time publicity given by certain newspapers and magazines to the methods of birth control is also necessary as well as proper. *This has no point in common with Malthus' theory at all.*[3]

It is of considerable interest that the position taken in the first sentence of this quotation is stated very clearly in Malthus's writings in several places (see Chapter 2). Malthus did not oppose "preventive checks"; he advocated them. He strongly supported the postponement of marriage and continence within marriage although he did not think the latter would be of much use as a preventive check. Malthus also definitely recognized that there could never be too many people for the subsistence available, except at times of actual starvation, for no matter what the size of the population, its mere existence proved it was being supported even though not at a desirable level. But if one meant by "too many people" that there were more than could be supported at a *fairly good level of living*, Malthus held that there had generally been too many because population tended to increase faster than man could, in most circumstances, increase his means of subsistence. The reasoning resorted to by the Chinese in justifying their campaign for birth control while holding every word of Malthus anathema is weird and wonderful and shows either complete ignorance of Malthus's views, or a mere blind adherence to the *infallible* pronouncements of Marx,[4] or a conscious rationalization developed for popular consumption by ideologists who knew what they were doing and why they were doing it.

But this first campaign for birth control was not destined to endure for long. About the middle of 1958 it was suddenly abandoned. The reasons for this rather sudden abandonment at about the time the "forward leap" of 1958 began to be

---

[3] *Ibid.*, p. 223, from Hsueh Hsi (Study), Oct. 2, 1955, pp. 1–6. (Chief ideological magazine of the Chinese Communist party, published in Peking.) *Italics are the authors'.*

[4] John S. Aird, "Population Policy in Mainland China," *Population Studies*, vol. 16, no. 1, pp. 38–57, 1962.

hailed as the sure means of China's economic salvation are obscure. The much heralded *vast increase* in food production in 1957 (almost double that of the preceding year), which was later shown to be nonexistent, may have led the leaders to believe that their economy could support any possible increase in population in the years ahead and that hence there was no need to involve themselves in such contradictions as noted above; population *could not* grow too fast or be too large for a Communist economy to make good its guarantee of better living. Moreover, this forward leap was to become perpetual by organizing the entire Chinese population within a few years into 20,000 or 30,000 communes, each having 25,000 to 40,000 members. Each of these communes was to be made practically a self-sufficing economic and social unit. The workers, both male and female, would be organized into militarylike units which could be thrown into specific economic projects in much the same manner as military units can be maneuvered in battle. Moreover, these communes were to perform many services for their members that had previously been the functions of the family and would do so at a greatly reduced cost in labor, thus freeing a vast amount of female labor for projects of national and community economic development.

In these communes there would be common dining rooms and recreation rooms, and dormitory quarters would be provided for all. Care of children would be furnished when mothers were at work on community projects or at school or attending indoctrination meetings. All health facilities, all educational facilities, and all else needed to ensure better and better living would be provided at a much lower cost than when families lived separately in their own quarters and looked after themselves. If the leaders really believed they had already overcome any possible shortage of the amenities of better living and that the establishment of communes would once and for all break up the traditional Chinese family, thus saving a vast amount of household labor that might be used elsewhere to good advantage, the abandonment of the birth-control campaign in 1958 might have seemed highly desirable. The inconsistencies involved in arguing that a slower growth of population was essential to substantial and fairly rapid economic improvement in China, while maintaining in their propaganda aimed at other Asian countries that communism alone provided a sure road to plenty without regard to the size of the population, may also have become so apparent that it was embarrassing.

Some of the discussions of the advantages to be derived from organizing the people in militarylike communes suggested that the perfect commune would necessarily involve a large measure of segregation of the sexes, so large that one cannot help wondering whether this was also a reason (unavowed) for so vigorously pushing the organization of communes at this time. Did the leaders hope that this militarylike organization might lead quickly to a reduction in the birth rate by a skillfully managed segregation of the sexes? In any event, the sudden abandonment of the birth-control campaign, with the advent of an even more vigorous campaign to organize communes, suggests the possibility that the latter might be considered, to some extent, a substitute for the former. Might it be that communal living as envisaged by the Communist leaders would lead rather quickly to a postponement of marriage by many couples for several years? Might it also be that the projects undertaken by the communes could be so adroitly managed that rather long periods of segregation of husbands and wives would ensue, similar to that of military mobilization during a war?

The years 1959, 1960, and 1961 following the abandonment of the birth-control campaign saw real agricultural disaster strike Communist China. The building of communes was almost stopped, and many migrants (perhaps millions) to the cities were sent back to their families in the villages to be supported and/or to work on the farms as underemployed family workers. Hardships due to the shortage of food increased rapidly. Economic development almost ceased, and in certain industrial sectors of the economy production actually diminished. This economic disaster must have frightened the leaders. In any event, a new campaign for birth control was launched in 1962. It seems to have regained rather quickly much of the vigor the first campaign showed when it was at its height. The differences between the new campaign for birth control and the first campaign are not yet entirely clear (1964). It appears, however, that in the new campaign somewhat more emphasis is now being placed on postponement of marriage. The most desirable age for marriage is often specified precisely as 23 to 25 for women and 25 to 29 for men. Furthermore, people who marry early and have large families are now being called *unpatriotic* because their concern to produce the necessities of life for their growing families diminishes their contribution to the production of goods the leaders consider most desirable for furthering the nation's economic development and increase in military power. More attention is apparently given to specifying the most desirable size of family in this new campaign, with considerable emphasis being placed on the two-child family with an interval of three to five years between the children. There are definite statements in some of the propaganda articles to the effect that service to the state, meaning work directly furthering the state program of economic development and increased military power, is more important than the raising of children. The suggestion that voluntary sterilization, especially of males, should be practiced on a large scale after two or three children are born is also coming to the fore as compared with the previous campaign.[5]

This second birth-control campaign is also producing even more fantastic statements by scientists, chiefly physicians, regarding the relation between good

[5] Frederick Nossal, "How Many Chinese?" *Far Eastern Review*, pp. 353 and 355, Feb. 2, 1963.

health and small families than were issued in the first campaign. Many of these statements remind one of the shibboleths of the sorcerers of the Middle Ages regarding causes of human ailments; "the life juices" and the "spirits" of the air are being conjured into frightful forces of destruction for those who begin to reproduce too young and continue to reproduce too long. Such propaganda would seem to be a deliberate attempt to frighten ignorant people into reducing the number of births per couple.

Shortly after this new birth-control campaign got under way, the plan to organize all the people into communes was also revived. Again one wonders if the leaders believe that the reduction of the birth rate will be greatly hastened through communal living. At this time no facts are available to justify an expression of opinion on this point. But in so far as communization of living affects the size of the family much as urbanization and industrialization did in Western countries, it might prove quite effective in reducing the birth rate rather rapidly.

It should again be noted that if there were 583 million people in China in 1953 and if the population has been growing at the rate of 2 to 2.5 percent per year as has been claimed over and over again, by mid-1963 China's population would number somewhere around 710 to 725 million. Such a growth in a decade, in view of the great uncertainty either that any substantial increase in tilled land has been achieved or that the yield of food grains per acre has risen, would certainly seem to justify the renewal of the birth-control campaign.[6] In addition, it should be remembered that the second birth-control campaign was started after three bad crop years. Under these circumstances it is not surprising that irrational arguments should be resorted to in order to impress upon the mass of the Chinese people the urgency of reducing the number of births per family; nor is it surprising that this urgency should at times become hysteria. One example of irrationality in this campaign is worth noting.

It is obvious (see pages 270 and 271) that an average of two children per couple, now being much urged in Communist China as highly desirable, is not sufficient to maintain the population. Therefore, either it is irrational to advocate strongly families of two children, or the true object of the campaign must be to reduce the size of the population. Urging that the first duty of the *good* Chinese citizen is to devote his efforts to the realization of the aims of the state and to sacrifice even his desire for children to this end may, of course, be only another attempt to destroy the traditional Chinese family. However, it may also indicate a great fear on the part of the leaders that communism cannot succeed in China if population does not decline in size at least for some years to come.

[6] The nibbling of the Chinese at their borders with India, Burma, and Thailand, and through their satellite—Communist North Viet Nam—at the borders of Laos and South Viet Nam may also be motivated in part by the great need for more land to raise more food as well as by their desire to spread Communist ideology in Southeast Asia.

It should be noted in this connection that by 1963 a great many of the youth reaching marriageable age during the next few years (the Communists gained complete control in 1949) will have probably been strongly influenced by Communist propaganda against the family since they are not old enough to remember, or to have a decided bias for, the "old" family type. If this is the case, the greater emphasis in this second birth-control campaign on the prior claim of the state to the time and effort of the *good* citizen may prove more effective in the near future than it would have been even in the late 1950s. But assuming that this is true, we still believe that China will encounter many cultural difficulties quite similar to those being encountered in India in establishing widespread family planning. The great mass of China's people still live in agricultural villages and small towns where traditional patterns of reproduction will give way much more slowly than in the cities and larger towns, which probably do not yet contain more than one-fourth of all the people.

It is true that China is much better organized than India to propagandize for birth control and against the continuation of the traditional patterns of family life, but it is by no means certain that these traditional patterns can be destroyed even by communism in a few years. Resistance to change will be especially stubborn in the areas where rice is the dominant crop, as it is in a large part of China, because good rice farming does not lend itself so well to mechanization as does the raising of most other food grains. Good rice farming is based to a large extent on adequate family labor at planting and at harvest and employs a distinctive form of irrigation on small plots of land. Hence, for some years it is not likely that the mechanization of the most important part of China's agriculture will be of much aid to the government in breaking down the traditional patterns of family life in the agricultural villages. The mechanization of rice farming in Japan began only in the mid-1950s, and has not yet made much headway.

Several other underdeveloped countries have already adopted national population policies intended to reduce their rates of population growth through family planning. These policies have not yet been in operation long enough to have had any appreciable effect on their birth rates. But the very fact that a number of countries are trying to implement such policies and are making careful studies to enable them to find out how their policies may be made effective in the shortest time possible is very encouraging. However, the authors believe that it is going to be some years yet before effective methods of family planning can be adopted widely in most of these countries. Any listing of the countries that have already adopted family-planning policies and of the studies being made in these and other countries to assist in implementing these policies would be out of date before this book reaches the reader.[7]

[7] It is suggested that anyone particularly interested in keeping abreast of developments in this field of population policies and their implementation write to the Population Council, 230 Park Avenue, New York, and ask for its "Studies in Family Planning."

A BRIEF RECAPITULATION

Up to this point in the discussion of population policy, we have found that almost one-third of the world's people already have a large measure of voluntary control over their birth rates. Whether or not the countries in which the people now have relatively low controlled birth rates can be said to have definite population policies is not important. But it is important to know that if the difficulty of maintaining a reasonably good level of living in any of these countries increases, i.e., if felt population pressure grows, these peoples are able to reduce the size of their families still more within a short time in order to avoid the hardships associated with a general decline in their levels of living. (The U.S.S.R., Japan, and the more-developed Western countries constitute this one-third.)

Of the remaining two-thirds of the world's population, somewhat more than one-half lives in countries now having avowed (governmental) policies aimed at reducing the number of births per family. In these there is as yet no satisfactory evidence that their policies are even mildly effective, except among their small well-to-do and educated classes. For reasons noted above, there can be no assurance that Mainland China's policy will not again change suddenly to a hands-off policy. Since China contains between one-fifth and one-fourth of the world's people, it is necessary to make a very significant reservation as to the proportion of the population in the underdeveloped countries of the world that will be consistently assisted by their governments, first to realize the urgency of preventing the more rapid growth of their numbers than of their production of necessities and, second, to provide the instruction and the means essential for the successful planning of their families.

In underdeveloped countries, containing perhaps somewhat less than one-third of the world's population, there are as yet no official population policies. Moreover, only a few of them as yet have private family-planning organizations doing effective work. As was said in the preceding chapter, in some of these countries the leaders have already put themselves on record as favoring a rapid population growth, while the remainder appear to be satisfied with "letting nature take its course," although practically all of them are doing everything possible under their impoverished conditions to prevent nature taking its course in determining the death rate.

In view of the great difficulties being encountered in implementing restrictionist population policies among agriculturalists even in those underdeveloped countries where the governments are wholeheartedly supporting such policies and in view of the almost universal success of all underdeveloped countries in reducing death rates quite rapidly, the authors are less sanguine than many that there will be a substantial decline in the number of births per family in the underdeveloped countries as a whole during the next three or four decades. Let us not forget that to reduce the present rates of population growth in these countries the birth rate must decline considerably faster than the death rate during this time.

In this connection it is important to realize that more and more the people in the underdeveloped countries are coming to feel that they have a right to demand aid from the more-developed countries not only to make up their food deficits in bad years but also to make up the deficits of capital and personnel essential to hasten all types of economic development. This growing attitude of claiming by right a share in the production of the more-developed nations is practically certain to become a new and potent factor in enhancing the *feeling* of population pressures (deprivation) in the underdeveloped countries even though there may actually be some little easing of their *absolute* pressures.

As has already been noted in Chapter 19, several underdeveloped countries do not *at present* have much need of restrictionist population policies if they can rapidly put into effect resettlement projects which will ensure the efficient cultivation of their tillable but as yet unused lands. Unfortunately, in only a few countries is there a relative abundance of good land not already being tilled. Outstanding examples of such countries are Brazil and Indonesia. But several smaller countries in Southeast Asia, in Latin America, and in Africa also have considerable amounts of good unused land readily tillable. At present these countries are much more likely to be interested in undertaking to raise their levels of living by putting this land into use than by reducing their birth rates. They will feel much as we did in the United States so long as we were primarily an agricultural country and there was an abundance of good land readily available. They will want larger and rapidly growing populations. The rapid growth of population where good new land is relatively abundant should not prevent a substantial improvement in levels of living taking place at the same time.

However, most of these countries already have fairly large populations, some of which are also dense according to United States standards. Indonesia's population in 1961 was probably in excess of 95 million, and Brazil's was in excess of 70 million. Both were growing at high rates, which will almost certainly become somewhat higher during the next two or three decades if the settlement of large numbers of farmers on the land is made easy by land reform and by the establishment of improved transportation facilities. The expansion of the tilled area in all these countries to absorb their growing numbers is highly desirable and should be encouraged in every possible way. However, good land readily tillable will soon become scarce at present rates of population growth even in Brazil and Indonesia.

Again, we wish to remind the reader (see Chapter 19) that in most of these underdeveloped countries that have a relative abundance of unused lands nationalistic feelings are so strong that immigrants from other nations greatly in need of more land are excluded altogether or are admitted in such small numbers that their emigration affords no significant relief to their homelands. This situation does not appear likely to alter in the foreseeable future. No country in Southeast Asia with any considerable amount of unused tillable land will admit the Chinese. Most African countries do not want Indians, nor do the South American countries want Chinese or Japanese. All these countries want to pre-serve their unused lands for their "own kind of people."

AID TO UNDERDEVELOPED COUNTRIES
FOR POPULATION CONTROL

The statement of the policy of the United States regarding direct aid to countries desiring to control their population growth quoted in the preceding chapter would seem to cover this matter quite adequately. No nation should attempt unilaterally to determine the population policy of another nation. But any nation that believes the very rapid growth of population in the underdeveloped countries endangers not only the attainment of a desirable measure of social welfare in those countries but also the maintenance of peace in the world (see Chapter 19) should be willing to respond, to the extent of its ability, to the request of any country desiring aid in reducing its rate of population growth. The authors believe that the policy outlined in the statement referred to is quite adequate. It does not and should not specify the details of any aid program in the field of population control. It will be well therefore to examine the chief implications of this policy as regards the granting of aid for the purpose of reduc-ing the birth rate in those countries desiring such assistance.

We have stated at several points in our discussion that the level of fertility in every people, below its maximum physiological capacity to reproduce, is largely determined by its culture, i.e., is the consequence of its social values and of its socially sanctioned patterns of behavior as they affect reproduction. The authors believe that practically all types of aid to the underdeveloped countries will con-tribute sooner or later to the better adjustment of human fertility in these coun-tries to the new social order arising out of their industrialization. What this policy does, in the authors' judgment, therefore, is only to make it clear that direct financial aid from the United States is now available, upon request, and, of course, within the limits of congressional appropriations, for projects whose avowed purpose is the control of population growth, as well as for the types of projects already being given aid. This extension of the field within which United States funds may be used in aiding development in the underdeveloped coun-tries is all to the good.

However, it should be realized that direct aid to official programs for reducing the birth rate may not always be the quickest way to bring about this decline. We Americans are perhaps inclined to overvalue the importance of this policy of direct governmental assistance to birth-control projects because it represents a definite release from past legal and religious restrictions in our country limiting the advocacy and the practice of birth control. Most of the more-developed countries had long ago ridded themselves of such handicaps to family planning, and most of the underdeveloped countries never have regarded controlling the birth rate as a sin. Hence, although this broader aid policy is highly desirable and is a step forward in United States foreign aid, it is not at all certain that direct aid in enlarging national programs of family planning will be highly effective in hastening the reduction of the size of the family in these countries in the near future. At least we should not overlook the probability that aid to certain other sectors of national programs for social and economic improvement may also contribute substantially to the goal of voluntary population control.

For example, foreign aid in spreading elementary education meets ready approval in practically every country able and willing to give aid, and such aid is greatly desired by most, if not all, the leaders in the underdeveloped countries. One could make a very strong case for reading, writing, and arithmetic as the most important of the prerequisites for rapid development, socially, economically and politically, in all underdeveloped countries. Elementary education is essential not only as a tool in aid of economic and political development in underdeveloped countries but also as a tool for making a decisive breach in the wall of tradition which at present is seriously delaying the development of a new pattern of reduced fertility. Education is not only desirable as a personal accomplishment but perhaps is even more necessary as a preparation for meeting all of life's problems a little more rationally in every dynamic (progressive) society.

It is quite widely recognized that elementary education will hasten the adoption of better agricultural practices because young people will be able to learn more quickly about what is being done elsewhere and will be better prepared to understand the reasons for making abrupt changes in their customary farm practices. Why will not the same line of reasoning also apply to the adoption of a new pattern of reproduction which will aid in the achievement of a better adjustment between population and economic activity? Without elementary education, we may add, it will be impossible or at least very difficult for most people in underdeveloped countries to understand the simple arithmetic involved in appreciating how their own families will increase in size if their death rates are plummeting downward while their birth rates remain almost unchanged. Very decidedly, elementary education should be considered a highly important, although indirect aid in hastening the spread of family planning. As such, it is deserving of all possible support in any program of aid to underdeveloped countries.

We have indicated above (Chapter 20) that the mother-and-child health clinics might well become the most effective agency in acquainting mothers with need for family planning to ensure not only their own better health but the health of the children they already have and of those they may have in the future. On these grounds a rapid increase in the number of the clinics for mothers and children would be highly desirable. However, one cannot but wonder whether a large increase in the number and effectiveness of such health clinics is to be desired unless it is reasonably certain that they will also be made centers for the dissemination of information regarding the need for family planning and instruction in the methods of contraception.

Still another aspect of family planning should be mentioned here. It is quite generally recognized that the methods of contraception heretofore used by most of the peoples now having low birth rates are not practicable for use by most of the peoples living in underdeveloped countries. To make feasible the widespread practice of contraception in the shortest time possible there must be new or at least improved methods having the following characteristics: (1) They must be *very cheap;* (2) they must be *highly effective;* (3) they must be *very easy to use;* (4) they must not have any *side effects that are dangerous or disagreeable;* (5) they must be *usable under the relatively primitive living conditions* which prevail among 90 to 95 percent of the people in most underdeveloped countries; (6) finally, they must *conflict as little as possible with traditional reproductive beliefs and practices;* or, expressed positively, they must be *easy to reconcile with the prevailing pattern fo determining reproductive behavior in many different groups.*

Since for some time it has been widely realized that even where the birth rates were already being kept low through the use of contraceptives, the development of new contraceptive methods meeting the requirements just stated would be highly desirable, a considerable amount of research in the physiology of reproduction and in the improvement of contraceptive devices has been carried out during the past several years. These studies have resulted in some new and important achievements in the control of conception. Two of these new developments are particularly worthy of brief mention.

One of these products is quite commonly given the generic name of "the pill." This pill is for females. It prevents pregnancy by keeping the ovum from becoming mature; hence it cannot be impregnated. The pill has proved highly effective when taken for 20 days consecutively, starting a few days after menstruation and continuing until a few days preceding the next menstruation. It is said to be entirely free from undesirable side effects, although some physiologists still question this. At present the pill must be taken regularly as just noted, and its cost is entirely beyond the means of almost all the people living in the underdeveloped countries. It would seem probable that its cost can be greatly reduced if produced on a large scale. It also appears rather probable that the number of pills needed every month may be substantially reduced.

In addition, there is also considerable expectation among the experts in this field that a pill for males can be developed, which if taken once a month will render the spermatozoa incapable of fertilizing the ovum. This male pill is not yet on the market (1964) because it has not yet been thoroughly tested, but rumor has it that it may be available within two or three years. Such a pill might before long meet most of the requirements mentioned above. It should be realized, however, that even the ideal pill would not eliminate the necessity of convincing the mass of the people in the underdeveloped countries of the desirability of fewer births per family nor would it automatically and easily replace the traditional patterns of reproductive behavior. The second development particularly worthy of note here is the improvement of the intrauterine coil spring as a contraceptive device. This spring can now be made of plastic material which takes the desired shape after introduction into the uterus. This new development meets most of the *musts* specified above but unlike the pill it costs very little. Moreover, it is proving much more acceptable to women than the use of pills, although its proper placement requires some skill. (The spring may be left in place, however, for several months.) Like the pill its use requires the discarding of traditional reproductive patterns and hence is certain to encounter some of the same cultural obstacles which retard the adoption of all modern contraceptive devices.

The rhythm method of contraception (safe period) has heretofore been found rather unreliable because the period during which the matured ovum can be fertilized cannot yet be predicted accurately for many women. It is believed by some investigators, however, that further research may provide a simple method of determining the exact time of the maturation of the ovum and the exact period when it can be impregnated. If this were to become possible, the use of the safe period might, to some extent, replace some of the present methods of contraception fairly rapidly in the countries already having relatively low birth rates, especially in European and North American countries that have large Roman Catholic populations, since this is the only method of controlling conception now officially approved by this church. But whether any substantial improvement in the reliability of the rhythm method would quickly lead to any reduction in the average number of births per family in Latin America with its 200 million or more Roman Catholics or in other underdeveloped countries where Roman Catholics are numerous is open to doubt, since its use involves more deliberate calculation of the social and economic consequences of large families than can be expected of ignorant and poverty-stricken people wherever they may live or whatever religion they may profess.

It is highly probable that a few decades ago the condemnation of *all methods* of controlling conception as "unnatural" by the Roman Catholic Church retarded the spread of voluntary control of the size of the family in some countries, particularly in the predominantly agricultural societies like Poland and some of the other countries of central Europe which were also primarily agricultural in their economy and Roman Catholic in religion. It may also have retarded the practice of contraception in Italy and Spain for some time. But after the discovery of the *safe-period* method, it was not long until the Roman Catholic Church found this method natural and under certain conditions approved it.

Since the discovery of the pill method of contraception, some scientists who are themselves members of the Roman Catholic Church are arguing that the action of the pill in preventing the maturation of the ovum is a natural method for controlling the onset and the duration of the safe period and is therefore morally acceptable. Because this interpretation of the action of the pill does not appear to be meeting with much active opposition from the Catholic hierarchy it seems likely that it may before long be accepted as natural. Moreover, the rather passive acceptance by the Roman Catholic hierarchy of the declaration of policy by our Department of State, referred to above, also seems to indicate that the opposition of this church to contraception is becoming milder. More and more members of the Roman Catholic Church, both clerical and lay, are recognizing that the rapid increase in population in the world today is creating many problems which must be faced squarely.[8] They see that many of the people living in underdeveloped countries have not yet acquired the knowledge, the techniques, nor the political and economic organization that are prerequisite to a rapid increase in the goods and services now widely considered essential to decent living and to good family life. They also recognize that the acquirement of these better modes of living in the near future is being seriously jeopardized by the rapid growth in numbers of many populations. In view of these facts, the authors believe that the Roman Catholic Church will, in the not distant future, offer comparatively little opposition to the voluntary control of the size of the family by accepting several effective means of contraception as *natural* although it may continue for some time to designate certain other methods as *unnatural* and therefore *immoral*. But it should not be forgotten that of the peoples living in underdeveloped countries only about one-tenth are likely to be influenced to a significant degree by the attitude of this church in opposing certain methods of contraception.

On the whole, the outlook for the adoption of population policies aimed at adjusting the growth in man's numbers to his ability to provide the physical goods essential to *decent* living is mildly encouraging. More and more of the poverty-stricken countries in which the levels of living are close to subsistence are embarking on family-planning policies. In addition, more of the peoples in countries already having low birth rates and good levels of living are manifesting a willingness to aid the peoples in the poorer countries in their family-planning efforts as well as in their economic development. At this point the reader is requested to turn back to the quotation from Malthus beginning on page 33 and to read again the last paragraph in which Malthus expresses this view regarding the outlook for the control of man's numbers in the hope of thus assuring all men a better life than all but a few of them have had in the past.

[8] "The World Population Problem," a symposium of original articles first published in *Marriage Magazine.* Seven articles that have received the imprimatur of the Roman Catholic Archbishop of Indianapolis.

It is now more than fifty years since I first became deeply interested in the changes in man's numbers as an important factor in determining his welfare. I was then (1912) a graduate student at Columbia University. In canvassing the opportunities for a doctoral dissertation with Professor Giddings, he suggested that there was need for a reexamination of Malthus's doctrine. For me this turned out to be a very happy suggestion. I found in Malthus a strong motivation for studying the facts showing changes in the size and composition of populations as related to man's welfare. This, I came to believe, was the prime motive leading Malthus to write his *First Essay* and to continue to give what attention he could spare from his other duties to this subject throughout the second half of his life.

In studying Malthus's work, I also became convinced that he manifested a high degree of the scientific spirit in his use of such data as were available to him. By this I do not mean that Malthus was always right in his use of population data and in assessing their significance for human welfare. But he did have a deep-seated respect for facts relating to all aspects of population change and believed that they could and should be put to use in discussing how man's welfare could be increased. This view of Malthus has always been a stimulus to me in my efforts to add a little to our understanding of the human significance of population changes, in particular, changes in the growth of population as they affect man's welfare.

I could not feel easy in sending this book to press after a lifetime of study of population changes without saying again, as I have so often said in the past, that I believe one of the most urgent problems facing the world today is still the adjustment of man's numbers to the production of the goods and services essential to a *decent living*. If we interpret *decent living:* (1) to mean a sufficient per capita consumption of all those goods and services essential to support a considerable personal development of man's inherited potentialities, there can be no doubt that the number of people the world can support will be relatively small as compared with the size of the population it can support if we interpret *decent living* (2) to mean only a moderately adequate diet, enough protection from the elements to prevent unnecessary deaths from exposure, plus a health service sufficient to enable nearly all of the babies born to live out a span of about 70 years or a little more. Today this latter concept of decent living is still of prime importance for much the greater portion of mankind—about two-thirds of the total. The other one-third is becoming increasingly interested in *decent living* as defined in the more comprehensive first concept. But leaving concept 1 aside for the moment, I must say that after reflecting at length upon the facts that seem to me germane, I still have very serious doubts that we shall be able to assure all the people born into the world in the next generation a *decent living* even as defined in concept 2.

Many of the reasons for this judgment have been set forth with more or less factual support in the body of this book; but many others represent my own syntheses of conditions and facts and observations arrived at after many years of study and reflection. They cannot be put in the form of a syllogism or stated in any other form that can properly be considered proof as contrasted with opinion. But I hold this opinion because I believe I have good reason to do so. I believe we must learn rather quickly to control population growth to a greater degree than now seems probable, or we shall not be able to ensure a decent living to all men even at the level envisaged in concept 2, to say nothing of making perceptible progress toward the realization of concept 1. Furthermore, I believe the failure to achieve the decent living of concept 2 will increase the probability that some of the leaders of the peoples who are coming to *feel* population pressures more and more severely will undertake to relieve these pressures by war. Today, and even more tomorrow, any attempt to secure larger resources (lebensraum) on the scale undertaken by Hitler, Mussolini, and the Japanese imperialists will almost certainly lead to a holocaust, compared with which World Wars I and II will appear mere skirmishes.

One other opinion, and I shall conclude this epilogue. I have never been convinced that there was any good reason to consider the attainment of a large and dense population as more desirable for man's welfare than a population of moderate size and density. For example, I cannot see how the doubling of the present population of the world will supply a better human base for the more complete development of man's personality than our present population. Indeed, if space permitted, I would argue that any increase in the density of population beyond a very modest level interposes many serious obstacles to the satisfactory development of man's inherited qualities. I cannot concede that merely because man has a large innate capacity to reproduce he has an obligation to use this capacity to any greater extent than he decides is to his advantage. It seems to me more human for man to use the reasoning powers he possesses to attain what he judges to be a good life than to limit his achievement of such a life by the uncontrolled use of his ability to reproduce.

SUGGESTIONS FOR SUPPLEMENTARY READING

Aird, John S.: "Population Policy in Mainland China," *Population Studies*, vol. 16, no. 1, pp. 38–57, 1962.

————: *The Size, Composition, and Growth of Population of Mainland China*, International Population Statistics Reports, ser. P-90, no. 15, Government Printing Office, Washington, D.C., 1961.

Brackett, James W.: "Population Dynamics in the USSR," *American Statistician*, vol. 13, no. 1, pp. 16–19, February, 1959. (An attempt to evaluate recent data on fertility, morality, and natural increase.)

Eldridge, Hope T.: *Population Policies: A Survey of Recent Developments*. Prepared under the auspices of the Committee on Investigation of Population Policies. The International Union for the Scientific Study of Population, Washington, D.C., 1954.

Enke, Stephen: "Government Bonuses for Smaller Families," *Population Review* (Madras), vol. 4, pp. 47–54, July, 1960.

France: Institut Nationale d'Études Demographiques, "Family Subsidies in France during 1951," *Population*, vol. 8, no. 1, pp. 142–147, January–March, 1953.

Galbraith, John K.: *The Affluent Society*, Houghton Mifflin Company, Boston, 1956.

Gille, Halvor: "Family Welfare Measures in Denmark," *Population Problems*, vol. 6, no. 2, pp. 172–210, November, 1962.

Milbank Memorial Fund: *The Interrelations of Demographic, Economic, and Social Problems of Selected Underdeveloped Areas*, New York, 1954. (1953 Annual Conference Round Table.)

————: *Population Trends in Eastern Europe, the USSR, and Mainland China*, New York, 1960. (1959 Annual Conference.)

Mukherjee, P. K.: *Economic Surveys in Under-developed Countries: A Study in Methodology*, 2d ed., Asia Publishing House, London, 1960.

Myrdal, Gunnar: *An International Economy: Problems and Prospects*, Harper & Row, Publishers, Incorporated, New York, 1956.

National Bureau of Economic Research: *Demographic and Economic Change in Developed Countries*, Princeton University Press, Princeton, N.J., 1960. (A conference of the Universities–National Bureau Committee for Economic Research.)

Ogburn, William F., and Francis R. Allen: "Technological Development and Per Capita Income," *American Journal of Sociology*, vol. 65, no. 2, pp. 127–131, September, 1959. (Different states and countries investigated to see whether the peoples with greatest technological developments have the highest standard of living.)

Organski, Katherine, and A. F. K. Organski: *Population and World Power*, Alfred A. Knopf, New York, 1961. (Chapter 7 is on National Population Policies.)

Petersen, William; "Family Subsidies in the Netherlands," *Marriage and Family Living*, vol. 17, no. 3, pp. 260–266, August, 1955.

Putnam, Palmer C.: *Energy in the Future,* D. Van Nostrand Company, Inc., New York, 1953.

Spengler, Joseph J., and Otis Dudley Duncan (eds.): *Population Theory and Policy: Selected Readings,* The Free Press of Glencoe, New York, 1956.

Taeuber, Irene B.: Population Policies in Communist China," *Population Index,* vol. 22, no. 4, pp. 261–274, 1956.

Thompson, Warren S.: "Some Implications of Population Changes for National Policies," *Statistical Reporter* (Manila), vol. 5, no. 3, pp. 12–17, 1961.

Vadakin, James C.: *Family Allowances: An Analysis of Their Development and Implications,* University of Miami Publications in Economics, no. 3 (Coral Gables), University of Miami Press, 1958.

Villanova, Giorgio: "Family Allowances in Common Market Countries," *Migration News* (Geneva), vol. 11, no. 4, pp. 14–17, 1962.

Watson, Cicely: "Population Policy in France: Family Allowances and Other Benefits, I," *Population Studies,* vol. 7, no. 3, pp. 263–286, March, 1954.

———: "A Survey of Recent Belgian Population Policy," *Population Studies,* vol. 8, no. 2, pp. 152–187, November, 1954. (A history of family allowances and recommendations for revision.)

INDEX

References to tables and figures are indicated by **boldface** numbers.